MOTOR
LEARNING AND
HUMAN
PERFORMANCE

MOTOR LEARNING AND HUMAN PERFORMANCE

AN APPLICATION TO PHYSICAL EDUCATION SKILLS

SECOND EDITION

ROBERT N. SINGER
FLORIDA STATE UNIVERSITY

MACMILLAN PUBLISHING CO., INC.
NEW YORK

COLLIER MACMILLAN PUBLISHERS
LONDON

MACMILLAN PUBLISHING CO., INC.
866 THIRD AVENUE, NEW YORK,
NEW YORK 10022

COLLIER-MACMILLAN CANADA, LTD.

LIBRARY OF CONGRESS CATALOGING
IN PUBLICATION DATA

Singer, Robert N
  Motor learning and human performance.

  Includes bibliographies and indexes.
  1. Physical education and training. 2. Motor
learning. I. Title.
GV436.S55 1975   152.3   74-10456
ISBN 0-02-410740-9

Printing: 1 2 3 4 5 6 7 8
Year: 5 6 7 8 9 0

TO THE MANY STUDENTS I
HAVE COME TO KNOW AND LOVE.

PREFACE

The second edition of this book has undergone a complete "facelifting." It may, in fact, not be recognized when compared to the first book. Not only has the material been updated, but its organization reveals contemporary approaches to view behaviors and events systematically.

In 1968, when the first edition of *Motor Learning and Human Performance* was published, motor learning as a body of knowledge in physical education was in its infantile stage. Courses were being initiated at this time in a number of universities, with dedicated professors attempting to organize contents and learning matter. Many disturbing questions were raised. What is motor learning? What should be taught in a motor-learning class? What kinds of experiences? For what level student? Naturally, the preparation of a book —its contents and organization in particular—under these conditions was especially frustrating and challenging.

Since 1968 physical education has witnessed an extreme amount of scholarly activity on the part of teachers and researchers concerned with motor learning. As old questions were satisfactorily resolved, new ones were raised. A body of information, broadly or narrowly identified, has been developed in motor learning. Its significance in the educational process in terms of applications to teaching and coaching situations is beyond doubt. Its worthiness of study in research and theory is likewise essential and is recognized accordingly.

Although we were satisfied with the contribution made at the time by the first edition of this book to physical education and education in general (for example, it was selected as one of the top twenty-one books in education published in 1968), room for improvement was evident and has become more apparent each year. Of all the vulnerable points, one of the most prominent was the organization of the book's contents. In the first edition, the contents were arranged "logically" by traditional scholarly areas. For example, a chapter was especially prepared on the nervous system and its relationship to learning and performance. Another was devoted to personality and motor activity. Another was on practice considerations, such as learning, motivation, knowledge of results, and retention. The order of the first edition is no longer appropriate.

With current emphasis on systems and models, orderly ways of examining the relationship of processes have been suggested. Behaviors are examined in more logical and meaningful ways. The dynamic interplay of man and his environment, of systems within man, is being incorporated in models to account for human behavior. They are in the preliminary and formative stages. The ultimate hope is (1) to present relevant information in an orderly and systematic fashion; (2) to interpret information more reasonably and practically for the teacher; and (3) to propose a model or system that will serve as a framework for past and future research and theoretical directions. Accordingly, a model has been prepared for the second edition of this book that reflects the interplay of subsystems as they interact to explain human behavior in the area of motor learning and performance.

Everywhere we turn we see examples of systems. The nervous system, the coach's system, and the educational systems are commonly used references. A system identifies the parts and demonstrates the functioning relationship of these parts in producing some form of output. There are smaller and larger systems. There are mechanical, biological, educational, and industrial systems. There are systems within systems, sometimes referred to as minisystems or subsystems. A system dealing with such complex human behaviors as serving a tennis ball, hitting a golf ball, kicking a soccer ball, playing the piano, or typing must recognize the many integrated subsystems that help produce desired results.

These subsystems relate to one's ability to initiate and terminate behaviors appropriately, demonstrated in such a fashion as to represent coordinated or skilled performance. What are those factors that must be included in the system? How are they interdependent? How can learning occur most effectively and efficiently so that performance yields are superior? These are some of the many questions dealt with in this book. The ultimate aim of the book is systematically to present information pertinent to the understanding of motor learning and performance. The scope of the contents is great, because motor behaviors can be quite complex. Research support is offered for statements made and none are knowingly presented that contradict the majority of related research findings. If anything, the approach may be considered a cautious one. The attempt is to stay away from speculation but to remain true to the research and theory that form the underpinnings of our knowledge of behavior.

Yet this is not merely a book geared for would-be or active researchers interested in studying motor behaviors. Many practical examples of human movement activity are interjected throughout the pages, in the hope that research and practice can come together. There are also many implications for teaching and coaching situations. After all, how can one instruct adequately without a knowledge of how the student learns, why he learns, and how the learning process can be enhanced for more productive outcomes?

I wish to take this opportunity to express my appreciation to students and colleagues, in my own working environment and throughout the world, for accepting and generously endorsing the first edition of this book. Many have taken the time to make constructive suggestions on its contents. More specifically, special appreciation is offered to Dr. Richard Schmidt of the University of Southern California for his critical and constructive review of the original manuscript. Personal thanks are also extended to Dr. John Drowatsky of the University of Toledo, Dr. Marjorie A. Souder of the University of Illinois, and Dr. Richard Magill, a former doctoral student of mine and presently at Texas A. & M., for their assistance and advice. Because of their efforts, this edition should be that much more effective in covering and communicating the vast amount of material associated with motor skills.

R. N. S.

CONTENTS

CHAPTER **3**

FROM GENERAL LEARNING THEORIES TO MODELS OF SKILL ACQUISITION 53

DESIGN AND MEASUREMENT

DEVELOPMENTAL FACTORS AND INFLUENCE ON BEHAVIOR

CHAPTER **10**

ENVIRONMENTAL CONDITIONS AND SOCIAL FACTORS **480**

MOTOR
LEARNING AND
HUMAN
PERFORMANCE

1

BACKGROUND

The term *learning* is common to everyone's vocabulary. It is a frequently used term, and one that may apply to numerous situations. During our lifetimes we learn many things, including observable acts, as required in motor and verbal performances, and nonobservable acts, which include values, emotions, and attitudes. Habits, bad as well as good, are learned. Learning does not even have to be intentional. It is demonstrated under such diverse conditions as performing athletic skills, remembering past situations, disliking opponents in a game, and believing in the team.

Interestingly enough, as one penetrates deeper into the concepts related to the study of learning, he finds that more and more questions are raised than are answered. How can one tell if learning has taken place? Is there actually more than one type of learning? What is the difference between learning and performance, if any?

These questions are but few of many raised by persons bewildered with the learning situation. Learning is the concern of almost every individual regardless of profession or primary occupation: from educators to mothers raising infants, from professionals to blue-collar workers, from scientists to coaches. Children in mathematics classes or physical education classes are involved in the process of learning. With so many and varied types of people concerned with the way one makes adaptations in his behavior to achieve standards presumably indicative of learning, it should surprise no one that many and various types of researchers, theorists, and educators have been actively involved in discovering the intricacies of the learning process. The learner, the task, and the learning situation interact to produce behavioral changes. These three components, as they operate dynamically, comprise the essence of research in learning.

THE STUDY OF LEARNING
AND LEARNING PROCESSES

Learning phenomena were not studied through a formalized, scientific process until the end of the nineteenth century. When psychology became a distinct discipline and broke away from philosophy, behavioral scientists began examining the learning process and learning phenomena in controlled situations. Data were collected. Research laboratories were initiated and developed. Research was also conducted in the classroom and other real-life situations. Concepts related to the mind and casual observations of behaviors gave way to a science of learning.

From then until the present time, research efforts have intensified with regard to the study of all kinds of learning. The main goals, of course, are to improve instruction and to gain a better understanding of how people learn. A synthesis of research findings reveals a body of knowledge indicating generalizations in the learning expectancies of students under specified conditions. Contrarily, equivocal data suggest our inability neatly to compartmentalize statements. Learning is a complex, dynamic process. Many exceptions exist to the rule. At present we have both reasonable, clear-cut directional statements as well as conflicting opinions in certain aspects of learning.

The understanding of learning is drawn from the efforts of educators, psychologists, neurophysiologists, biochemists, and the like, and the field of learning is indeed broad. With so many factors to consider, it becomes apparent that to understand the nature of human behavior is at the very best a challenging task.

The study of learning entails the grasping of knowledge of the myriad of factors that contribute to changes in behavior. It means understanding the learning process and the acquisition of skill as regards this development. It includes an examination of environmental changes (e.g., situational, instructional) and how they might facilitate or impede learning. Furthermore, it involves an appreciation of individual differences in abilities, characteristics, development, aspirations, and the like—and how they affect learning rates and outcomes.

Through the years different schools of psychological and educational thought have reflected the contributions made in attempting to understand, explain, and predict behavior with a reasonable degree of certainty. One of the first and the most influential schools of thought affecting research on behavior was behaviorism. S–R psychology, as it was also to be known, yielded many formal expressions of learning. Formalized, systematic measurements were taken on subjects in controlled situations by S–R psychologists who wanted to study behavior precisely. The research and theory were highly mechanistic as contrasted with humanistic approaches to studying human behavior. Learning generalizations were made from group-collected data. They were nonindividual-centered. That is, it was felt that particular events in a situation would cause certain responses to occur, and that all persons would be generally affected in the same manner:

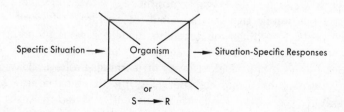

Specific Situation → Organism → Situation-Specific Responses

or

S ——→ R

A number of other scholars responded against this simplistic viewpoint of explaining and understanding human behavior. Emphasis was placed on cognition and perception, as well as on attitudes and feelings. What soon became apparent was that there are great differences in the way individuals respond, behave, and learn, but also many commonalities. The real task in interpreting learning research and theory is to incorporate what we know generally to be true about human behavior along with possible exceptions (in the form of individual differences).

Generally and Specifically

The average person is interested in general "principles" of behavior. He wants information that is broadly applicable to a variety of people and circumstances. As we attempt to become knowledgeable and scholarly in an area of interest, it becomes readily apparent that the assimilation of highly technical information is a time-consuming and laborious process. In other words, there are many specifics that we have to attend to. Therefore the individual who transmits information can be a superficial disscussant or a probing, penetrating analyst.

Likewise, some research efforts are attuned to answering more general problems; others are highly specific. Research on a specifically designed curriculum or course of learning experiences provides general guidelines for instruction. The analysis and comparison of premotor and motor reaction times is a highly refined process leading to understanding and theory building in a very specific area. Research reported by educational psychologists, for example, is usually applied and general. Experimental psychologists, on the other hand, are usually involved in laboratory research that zeros in on a highly specific problem.

Different Breeds of Scholars

During this century, educators and psychologists have made the most impact on instruction and contributions to a body of knowledge on learning. More recent breakthroughs by biochemists and neurophysiologists have contributed to a more complete understanding of the learning process. Thus, when we pool the concepts produced by Swiss psychologist Jean Piaget on the intellectual development of children, Harvard emeritus psychologist B. F. Skinner on teaching models dependent on reinforcement and shaping behaviors, Canadian Donald Hebb and Russia's Alexander Luria on neurological bases of learning, Professor David Krech of the University of California, Berkeley, on the biochemical bases of learning, A. T. Welford of England and presently located in Australia, and the late Paul Fitts, last of the University of Michigan, on the nature of skill acquisition, we see representatives of different lines of research who all contribute in important and fundamental ways to a body of knowledge dealing with human behavior and behavioral modifications.

Because of the accumulation of research on a wide range of learning matter employing assorted conditions and procedures, an attempt must be made to relate the findings to a major concern of the physical educator: the learning of motor skills. Besides learning how to teach, educators must understand how learners learn. Physical educators have, in recent years, demonstrated an increasing interest in this area, as evidenced by the number of investigations and writings in the physical education literature. Fortunately, the combined efforts of all the researchers interested in the area of learning and its facilitation, from the experimental psychologist to the industrial psychologist, from the physical educator to the engineer, from the educator to the neurophysiologist, have produced a substantial body of scientifically verified statements that together form the known aspects of learning. This book will present that information, with necessary qualifications, as it applies to physical education, and specifically to the learning of any motor skills.

Laboratory and Field Situations

The fact remains that educators in general and psychologists in particular are the ones most concerned with advancing knowledge in the area of learning. Educational research undertaken directly in the classroom in order to work with the materials actually taught has been criticized as being too broadly defined and lacking in necessary research controls to be meaningful. Difficulty in controlling classroom investigations in the same manner as laboratory research, however, certainly does not negate the worth of educational research. Experimental psychologists have primarily used such lower forms of organisms as rats, dogs, chimpanzees, and chickens in their research. They have also been concerned with human learning, but in highly artificial situations and with such unusual learning material as nonsense syllables, mazes, pursuit rotors, and novel fine motor skills, in order to provide more scientific control. Applications from such studies have been advanced to help explain and predict aspects of human learning.

These psychologists have been able to control effectively many extraneous variables in their research; however, the application of their findings to typical human learning situations leads to still further questions. Are nonsense syllables learned in a controlled situation mastered in the same manner as is prose studied by children in the classroom? Are the conditions prevailing in pursuit rotor tasks (maintaining a stylus on a moving target) comparable to those found related to other educational materials, or physical education skills?

Although there are objections to both educational and psychological techniques, there has emerged from them both an adequate amount of scientifically verifiable information.

A laboratory can be almost anything. In the traditional sense, it implies an area away from the mainstream of traffic where situations can be controlled fairly effectively. Freedom to control and dictate circumstances that will occur from the initiation of testing to its completion is associated with laboratory conditions. Although control is optimal in the research laboratory, usually the realism of learning situations is lost. We give artificial learning tasks, we test students under artificial conditions. Behavior observed may or may not be the same as the real-life circumstance.

On the other hand, the field situation can include the classroom, gym, swimming pool, or athletic fields. There is less artificiality here, but also a loss of experimental control over the subjects and conditions. Not that there is no concern for control. However, the situation does not usually permit the same amount of control over circumstances as in the laboratory. Somehow the control and artificiality of the laboratory along with the meaningfulness and realism with a loss of control in the field situation must be resolved.

Both laboratory and field kinds of research are necessary for our understanding of human behavior. They should be complementary, not antithetical. It should not be laboratory versus field research. Some problems can be studied more effectively in one situation rather than in another. Findings in one area give rise to possible studies in the other area, with the hope that they will be somewhat verifiable even though different kinds of subjects, tasks, and conditions may be present.

HOW MANY KINDS OF LEARNING?

In the early stages of learning theory development, it was widely believed that one theory could adequately explain any kind of learning. Although this is a desirable approach and because the law of parsimony should prevail, efforts were generated toward this ideal goal. Indeed, depending on one's interpretation of processes underlying the different manifestations of human behavior, one theory might be acceptable.

Yet with a refinement of investigations and the identification of unique considerations in various behaviors, many scholars became disenchanted with the profitability of following this line of thought. From the early development of all-encompassing learning theories, most notably represented by behaviorism and Gestaltism, in recent years we have witnessed the emergence of a variety of models. Each is advanced to describe specific kinds of learning or behaviors.

Indeed, experimental psychologist Arthur Melton (1964) proposed a taxonomy of human learning to order more systematically the vast amount of information produced on the topic. Seven categories, or kinds, of learning were identified:

1. Classical and operant conditioning.
2. Rote verbal learning.
3. Probability learning.
4. Short-term memory and incidental learning.
5. Concept learning.
6. Problem solving.
7. Perceptual–motor-skill learning.

Strong similarities can be demonstrated among these categories of learning. But Melton feels that the identification of these seven types of learning is a necessity for theoretical integration and a more precise understanding of each. Interestingly enough, he concludes that any conclusion on the taxonomy of human learning is sure to be inconclusive! In any event, this procedure encourages a recognition of ways of ordering knowledge of human learning.

Educational psychologists like Benjamin Bloom have attempted a different approach. He and his co-workers categorized human behaviors into three domains: the cognitive, the affective, and the psychomotor. The first major publication on this topic (Bloom et al., 1956) produced eventful changes in educational practices and ways of looking at school learning situations. After this book in the cognitive domain was published, one in the affective domain followed eight years later (Krathwohl et al., 1964). The least amount of work has been done in the psychomotor domain. A recent attempt is offered by Anita Harrow (1971).

The convenience in categorizing behaviors according to the main type of behavioral component (to know, to feel, or to do) should not preclude the fact that most behaviors involve an interaction of all three components. Thus high levels of tennis skill reflect effective integrated movements (psychomotor), the application of strategies, tactics, and knowledge of rules (cognitive), and appropriate attitudes, competitive feelings, and motivation (affective). Nevertheless, these taxonomic ventures include the identification of hierarchical behaviors in each category, encouraging a more thorough analysis of teaching approaches, expected outcomes, and appraisal.

From another point of view, educational psychologist Robert Gagné (1970) proposed eight types of learning, each somewhat dependent on the other in a hierarchical sense. He expresses the hope that the types of learning described will have particular relevance toward improved instruction. Gagné identifies two basic forms of learning: signal learning and stimulus response learning. He then describes verbal and motor chaining (types 3 and 4). Continuing on, he refers to discrimination learning (5) and concept learning (6), rule learning (7), and problem solving (8).

The preceding material developed by Gagné encompasses a hierarchical arrangement of specified types of learning to the domain of intellectual skills. The execution of simple motor acts (Gagné's type 3: motor chaining) obviously does not reflect higher-order behavioral activity. Yet we are primarily concerned with complex movement-oriented behaviors, and the attainment of high levels of skilled performance. In this context, perhaps it is more rewarding to examine another classification approach of Gagné, that of identifying reasonably distinct domains of learning (Gagné, 1973).

The formulation of separate domains is intended to support the notion that all learning is not the same. Although a few similarities and general conditions may underlie a part or all of the domains, generalizations are presumably most powerful as they are found to be unique from domain to domain. Consequently, Gagné offers these five domains of learning:

1. Motor skills: Movement-oriented, represented by coordination of responses to situational cues.
2. Verbal information: exemplified by facts, principles, and generalizations, referred to as knowledge.
3. Intellectual skills: represented by discriminations, rules, and concepts (the application of knowledge).
4. Cognitive strategies: internally organized skills that govern one's learning, remembering, and thinking.
5. Attitudes: affective behaviors, such as feelings.

The establishment of five domains of learning (or any other number) presumes their logically and empirically determined distinctiveness. When research findings are more closely allied to a particular domain, information can be more precise and instructional guidelines more adequate. Certainly it makes more sense to talk of learning domains in terms of processes rather than content. Content domains would include mathematics learning, science learning, and foreign language learning. Common sense indicates the utility in treating these areas in a common way, for conditions of learning could generalize across them. Similarly, there are many examples of motor skills. Does each need separate consideration? No doubt there are certain basic similar factors operating when we learn to hit a baseball, to shoot a basketball, to operate machinery, to type, and to achieve in other behaviors that are primarily movement-oriented.

Instead of focusing on behavioral appearances and outcomes, Bruce Joyce and Marsha Weil (1972) have developed a unique approach. They describe four different families of approaches to teaching. Each method obviously is geared to produce different kinds of outcomes. They are identified as

1. The social-interaction approach.
2. The information-processing approach.
3. The personal approach.
4. The behavioral-modification approach.

Social interaction emphasizes improved social relations as a result of learning experiences. Information processing deals with the capabilities of the learner and improving ways of sensing, processing, organizing, and retrieving data. The personal approach is directed toward personal development, internal organization, personality, and self-image. Behavior modification involves structuring of learning experiences and shaping behavior toward desired specified outcomes. These approaches are not independent of each other, but their identification serves to indicate that different instructional emphases, regardless of learning matter, can work toward reaching different objectives.

As yet there is no agreement on how many kinds of learning or instructional processes exist. But the preceding descriptions of point of view suggest ways of looking at the problem. Some theorists still state that their laws and postulates can encompass all aspects of the learning process with all sorts of tasks. Others have deliberately tried to deal with specific types of learning and approaches toward behavioral changes. These assorted and somewhat unique interpretations of the nature of human behavior should provide intellectual stimulation and some interesting discussions for students of the learning process.

LEARNING

As we have seen in the preceding discussion, there is a lack of agreement on (1) whether there is more than one type of learning, and (2) if so, how many types there are. Part of the problem lies with an acceptable interpretation of the word *learning*. What are the constituents and parameters of learning? While referring to the strong possibility of the existence of different kinds of learning, is it possible to present a definition of learning compatible to any situation and task?

Interpretation

Meditate for a second. How would you define learning? Consider the process, the nature of the task, and expected results. If you are frustrated, discouraged, and disappointed, you have joined the ranks of established scholars in psychology, education, and elsewhere who have attempted to sponsor a satisfactory definition, for one has yet to be proposed.

A variety of circumstances contribute to the problem. Part of the difficulty rests in the confusion and failure to differentiate between the terms *learning* and *performance*. Another problem is the lack of separation between what occurs in learning in the early stages versus what occurs at the terminal stages. What of considerations for the process of learning and the final product; that is, the act of learning and the performance test that presumably reflects the level of learning? Should distinctions be made among tasks and behaviors as we attempt to define learning?

The process of learning will incorporate the features unique to the given circumstance. Learning motor skills, attitudes, cognitive behaviors, and the like, requires some degree of exposure to certain conditions that will result in changes in behavior or dispositions to act. No matter what the task or behavioral expression, learning obviously refers to some change that occurs within the person and is reflected by his observable behavior. This change becomes relatively permanent. In other words, temporary performance states do not truly represent learning. Variable factors such as fatigue, influence of drugs, boredom, and such really affect performance, not learning. Growth and development factors are also variables considered to influence performance rather than to be true indexes of learning. With increased maturation, greater capabilities to learn can be demonstrated. All the variables mentioned reflect temporary states in the organism and as such are associated with learning per se only indirectly or not at all.

It should be emphasized that behavior is not really permanent, in a technical sense. It varies on different occasions as a function of the status of organism and the nature of environment. Learning is associated with changes in the internal state of the person, and this process can be handled through the acknowledgment of biochemical and neurological modifications. Or, psychological properties, such as habit strength or abilities may be changed which in turn affect performance. Allan Buss (1973) makes an excellent argument for considering the relationship of learning with ability factors. According to him, relatively permanent changes in ability factors should be used as indices of learning rather than behavioral changes. More specifically, Buss concludes that "relatively permanent properties of an organism brought about by changes in ability factors (as a consequence of experience or practice) [is] that which is meant by learning" (p. 277).

For the purposes of this book, *increased learning is reflected or inferred by a relatively permanent change in performance or behavioral potential resulting from practice or past experience in the situation.*

A relatively permanent change implies that performance will not be represented by momentary fluctuations and inconsistencies. Also, well-learned acts usually persist for some time.

Performance, behavioral potential, habit strength, and associated abilities are convenient and practical ways of talking about learning. In order to ascribe some relative value to a person's activity, in order to determine what amount of learning is taking place, an evaluation of behavior is necessary. Behavior is changed when learning occurs. No change in behavior is associated with no change in learning.

Practice and past experience underlie the learning process. Because increased capacity to perform may be due merely to developmental factors, or for that matter, an act may be performed by chance without experience, it is wise to disassociate changes in behavior resulting from maturation and chance and relate these changes more to practice and experience.

One of the distinct features in learning complex motor skills is the need for practice. Attitudes can be changed with one dramatic experience. Concepts, definitions, and facts can be acquired slowly or quickly. But high proficiency in motor performance can only be shown after repeated experiences, the necessary number and quality of each dependent upon task complexity and skill level desired. The better learned the act, the more impervious it is to possible performance fluctuations. Therefore a well-learned motor skill has most likely required a great number of experiences and is fairly consistently and predictably performed upon request.

Learning and Performance

E. C. Tolman through his pioneer research and writings contributed much to the differentiation between learning and performance. His concept of latent learning indicates that learning may be taking place all the time during practice trials but is not demonstrated until reinforcement brings it out. Latent learning has been verified in many experiments in which

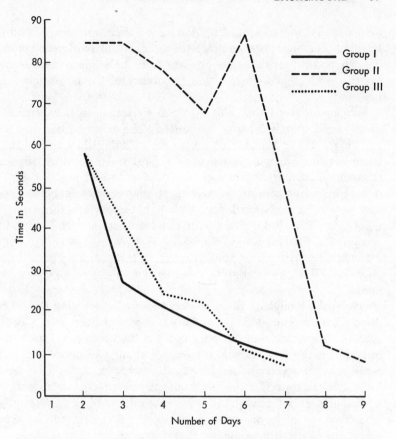

Figure 1-1.   Time curves for rats learning a maze under different reward conditions. (From Hugh C. Blodgett, "The Effect of the Introduction of Reward Upon the Maze Performance of Rats," *University of California Publications in Psychology,* 4:113–134, 1929.)

rats were employed as subjects. A representative study is one completed by Blodgett, and his data are illustrated in the form of learning and performance curves in Figure 1-1. Rats were timed in their speed to traverse a maze, and three groups of these animals were tested under different conditions: Group 1 was rewarded with food each day of the investigation; Group II was not rewarded until the seventh day; and Group III experienced reward on the fourth day. The role of reinforcement in the learning process has been extremely controversial in psychology, and the reader will obtain a better understanding of this issue when he understands the potential differences between learning and performance.

The distinction between learning and performance is sharpened when considering the factor of reinforcement, for there appears to be much evidence that the amount of reinforcement affects performance rather than learning. Some theorists indicate the necessity of reinforcement for learning whereas others minimize or even omit it. Reinforcement is by definition an event that increases the probability of the occurrence of certain behavior.

Tolman observed that differences in performance between the groups disappeared as reward was introduced. The nonrewarded rats were developing a latent learning of the maze, meaning they were learning the maze but this was not evident until reward was offered. At present, there is much conflicting evidence on the theoretical and practical implications of latent learning, even as there is in the distinction between learning and performance. Nevertheless, although the reward form of reinforcement may have little to do with the learning process, it certainly will account for differences in performance. *Performance may be thought of as a temporary occurrence, fluctuating from time to time because of many potentially operating variables, whereas learning is relatively more permanent.*

Obviously, though, in order to determine what learning has taken place, some measure is needed. We usually use performance as representing the amount of learning that has occurred, for the process of learning must be inferred on the basis of observations of change in performance. We can measure what a person does directly, but what he learns is subject to only indirect estimates. The limited value of this practice is reflected by the results of such studies as the one reported by Blodgett. Nevertheless, a truer measure of learning has yet to be devised, and performance scores reflect the best means available at the present time.

MOTOR LEARNING

Although a certain number of similarities may be found in all "types" of learning, in this book we are interested in examining processes and factors related to the acquisition and performance of motor skills. As contrasted with other types of behavior the primary characteristic of motor behavior is movement. As can be readily sensed, the categorization of a form of behavior permits greater examination and understanding. Yet conflicts over terminologies and semantics can even plague this domain of behavior.

Descriptions and Terminologies

Scholars representing diverse professional backgrounds and personal research and theoretical interests have contributed to the growing body of knowledge surrounding motor learning and performance. It should be quite understandable that "pet" terms and expressions would be developed by these people. Often similar tasks and learning phenomena are referred to in different ways. Although this situation is understandable it is often confusing and frustrating for both student and scholar alike.

For instance, we have decided to use the term *motor learning* when relating the organismic and situational factors to the acquisition and performance of behaviors that are generally reflected by movement. Generalized patterns and highly specific skills are included in the study of motor learning. Athletic, secretarial, agricultural, dance, musical, and industrial activities include many motoric activities. Some activities seemingly involve many of the large muscles of the bodies; others require the coordinated precision of fine muscles.

Yet *motor learning* and *motor behaviors* appear to be terms favored by scholars in physical education, whereas psychologists, educators, and others have on many occasions used such descriptions as *psychomotor, perceptualmotor,* and *sensorimotor* instead of *motor*. Aileene Lockhart (1964) has effectively addressed this persisting issue of semantics. Recognition of terms that can often be used interchangeably will assist you in reading literature of relevance to the topics covered in this book. The obvious advantage in using *perceptual* or *psycho* in front of *motor* is that they more adequately suggest the true nature of the behaviors. *Motor* by itself implies muscular movement, as if reflexive or with little cognitive and perceptual involvement. But the truth is that the real-life skills that we learn are usually somewhat complex and involve a high degree of cue detection, evaluation, and decision making. The actual response is only one feature of the entire act.

The wisdom in using the word *motor* by itself instead of *perceptualmotor* or *psychomotor* cannot be easily defended. Perhaps it can be, though, on these grounds: (1) it is commonly used in the physical education literature; (2) *psychomotor* and *perceptual-motor* are terms used to describe almost any kind of movement behavior, with educators and psychologists usually concerned with discussing (a) a child's developmental activities, (b) cognitive behaviors expressed with movement (e.g., talking and writing), and (c) laboratory tasks demanding precision; and (3) the focus of this book is on motor-skill acquisition, with direct or implied applications to physical education and recreational activities as well as sport.

Gross and Fine Motor Tasks

Motor skills are often categorized as being fine or gross, and a distinction should be made between the two. The word *fine* denotes a delicate or sensitive quality.

Certain segments of the body move within a limited area in order to yield an accurate response. The neuromuscular coordinations involved in fine motor skills are usually precision oriented and often refer to eye–hand coordination. Typing, tracking with pursuit rotors, and piano playing have been described as fine motor skills by psychologists in their investigations.

The term *gross* refers to a quality opposed to fine: large, whole, entire, or obvious. A gross motor skill involves contractions and usage of the large muscles of the body. The whole body is usually in movement. Sport skills of all kinds may be considered as gross motor skills, and though reference is usually made to these skills without the term *gross,* it is implied.

From a theoretical point of view, we might successfully argue that there are certain fine elements to every sport skill. Acts must be placed on a continuum, for nothing is purely black or white, and certainly sport skills would be concentrated toward the gross-motor-skill end. Such factors as strength, precision, and timing underlie gross and fine motor skills, with extreme emphasis on any of these factors distinguishing gross from fine skills.

Self-paced, Mixed-paced, and Externally Paced Tasks

Motor tasks can be classified in three categories according to their nature and the demands placed on the learner. Learning strategies will differ according to task category.

A *self-paced task* is represented by the student being able to initiate the activity when ready. Typically this brief behavior is associated with a student preparing to respond to a fixed object or static environment in a situation that permits him to move at his own rate of speed. Self-paced strategies underlie playing a note on the piano, typing a letter, writing, starting a plane, and rolling a bowling ball. Because the environment and objects are stable, the learner needs to be primarily concerned with consistency of response.

A *mixed-paced task* occurs where the situation is partially dynamic: (1) the student is in motion but the object or situation is fixed (still), or (2) the student is fixed (set) and the object is in motion. Dancing a sequence of steps in predesignated tempo represents a performance in motion on a stable (fixed) platform. The baseball batter, on the other hand, is in a state of preparation while the baseball (object) is pitched. Sequential patterns of activity are observed. Many industrial skills, recreational endeavors, and military assignments require a mixed-paced strategy.

An *externally paced task* occurs when both the student and the object are in motion during the performance of the activity. This highly complex and dynamic type of behavior is often witnessed in competitive sport, such as in rallying in tennis and handball. Another illustration would be a marksman on a boat being rocked by the waves aiming at a moving target in the form of a bird. The complexity of this task is apparent when one imagines how much easier it would be if it were mixed-paced, that is, if either the target were still or the boat were motionless.

The self-paced strategy suggests that the student be less concerned about quickness in perceptual adjustments toward the activity and more about the appropriate sequence of responses. Because the stimulus or object is stable and the student has time to be alerted prior to performance, "pressured intellectualization" of the task is at a minimum. When there are many variations of stimulus input, especially unexpected in nature, response demands are great. This is not the case here. The self-paced strategy permits a sensitivity to individual differences and instructions can be developed accordingly. The student has time to study the situation and to respond when he is ready (within reason). He paces himself during the activity rather than being paced by external stimuli. To the extent that the student may find himself in various situations that require the modification of responses, he should practice accordingly.

As an example, learning to hit a golf ball is easiest from the tee, where the ground is level and the grass is low. However, in order to become a good golfer, one must practice with all the irons and woods, at different distances from the green, with various lies, confronted with assorted hazards, and under various environmental (heat, humidity, cold wind) conditions. The response made in any given situation should have been so well practiced that it is habitual. Thus there is heavy emphasis on the demonstrated movement. If the student will be required to perform the act in a variety of real-world situations, he should have the opportunity to practice under several of these different conditions.

Because the self-paced strategy can be applied to discrete or continuous tasks (see discussion on p. 19), there are certain unique as well as common practice considerations for both. In either task, sufficient practice time should be allotted to the students to reach the goal level. Practice conditions are easiest to control and manipulate for the self-paced strategy. Because the student and the situation are in fixed and self-dependent states, main emphasis in practice should be directed toward response consistency. The student has time to be prepared for the activity, the act itself is brief, and the main response requirements are conditioned.

In the mixed-paced strategy, the more complex movement in either the performer or the object along with uncertainties in the situation dictate more possible alternative practice possibilities. Practice should initially occur under a standard, most probable situation. After an adequate amount of competence is shown, practice situations should be varied. In the mixed-paced strategy the student should experience the variety of ways he might find himself in motion or in which the object would be in motion.

An accomplished baseball batter has trained with pitching machines or ball players as pitchers, where balls are thrown in a predesignated and specified manner (fastball, curve, toward the middle of the strike zone, on the outside corner) or in the concealed way pitchers throw in the game. Experience with a variety of pitches, pitchers, and situations contributes to the batter's realization of his potential. When learning to drive a car, changing situational demands, either expected or unexpected, prepare the student to be better able to fulfill his driving responsibilities.

In the mixed-paced strategy, appropriate responses may be dictated by unexpected situational demands upon the student. In other cases, a series of movements will be acceptable only if each was correctly executed in serial order, the response in one part of the activity acting as the succeeding stimulus for the next response, and so on. Because either the student or the object will be in motion, practice conditions become more complicated than for the self-paced strategy. Whereas the self-paced strategy is applicable to many sitting eye–hand coordination tasks, the mixed-paced strategy suggests (1) more space needs, (2) more gross bodily movement and involvement, and (3) more instructional difficulties with large groups of learners.

The student has usually learned more simple tasks leading up to those requiring the externally paced strategy. He should therefore be ready to pursue his present task with a model that attempts to simplify the complex components and yet is detailed enough (perhaps through verbal explanation) so as adequately to direct the learner. The ability to undertake a task requiring the externally paced strategy presupposes the maturation of the organism and the demonstrated mastery of enabling tasks that might have been self-paced or mixed-paced.

Because both the student and the object are in motion, a multitude of possible situations exist in which the student might have to perform in real life. Suggestions expressed for the self-paced and mixed-paced strategies apply here.

Successful behaviors can only be demonstrated after much practice under favorable practice conditions. Because specified timing techniques are designated between student and object as the criterion for mastery, the externally paced strategy is primarily applied to acts requiring skilled performance. Precision in response(s) to appropriate stimuli occur in any skilled act. Thus the ability to catch a ball while on the run, to operate running machinery while in motion, to perform tricks on water skis while being pulled by a boat, or to shoot at a moving target while running, reveals high-level, sophisticated psychomotor behaviors. These skills do not come easily. Practice considerations lie in specific modeling procedures, precise cuing, simulation where appropriate, an emphasis on lead-up skills, and so on.

The concept of categories of self-paced, mixed-paced, and externally paced tasks probably has its origin in the work of E. C. Poulton (1957). Although his model is geared for predictions in industrial work, it is certainly applicable to the learning of physical education skills. He distinguishes skills as being either closed or open. A *closed skill* depends on internal feedback, that is, the kinesthetic feedback from the execution of the skill. There are no external requirements; no reference to the environment is needed for the performance of a closed skill. Requirements of the act are therefore predictable, for the concern is for the body's operation in a fixed environment. Such skills can be performed with the eyes closed. Closed skills are probably similar to the self-paced skills discussed previously.

Poulton describes an *open skill* as one performed either in an unpredictable series of environmental requirements or in an exacting series, predictable or not. However, these skills usually occur in unstable environments. Feedback comes from external and internal sources when open skills are performed, and these skills may be likened to the externally paced skills discussed in the context of self-paced skills. Most team and dual activities transpire in environments that are changing unpredictably.

Poulton would probably include advanced gymnastic and diving skills, which require extremely exacting movements, in the category of open skills. Usually associated with closed skills are repetitive, monotonous tasks that demand little, if any, perceptability. Obviously, different requirements are placed on the performer with closed skills than with open skills. These two categories of skills may be divided even further, encouraging more specific consideration for the requirements imposed by different types of tasks.

There are greater barriers to success in skills performed in unpredictable situations and/or skills composed of precision movements. According to Poulton, smooth movements in open skills can be made if (1) the requirements are not too exacting; (2) the requirements are presented to the individual before he is ready for them; and (3) the requirements are not separated by inactivity. These considerations are basic to not only industrial work, but athletic performance as well. A. M. Gentile (1972) has recently elaborated on the nature of open and closed skills, providing special practical considerations for the learning of physical education activities. Robert N. Singer (1972a) has offered similar suggestions for athletes.

Barbara Knapp (1964) pointed out that skills might be classified as predominantly perceptual or predominantly habitual. Such sports as tennis, basketball, and fencing would be *perceptually oriented*, whereas diving, putting of the shot, and trampolining would be habitually oriented. In other words, in some sports and activities the prime concern of the performer is the potential changing environment. His reaction cannot be fixed but, rather, depends on the circumstance. Other skills require repetitious practice until the act can be performed as a habit; perceptual need is minimized and the ability to reproduce the same act continuously and consistently is emphasized.

Habitual skills, those requiring a fixed response to a given situation, appear to be associated with stimulus–response theory. The stimulus environment is relatively stable. Desired response can only be achieved through constant practice, and the performer's attention is to the act itself. With successful practice, skill sets in, and the individual may execute the skill as if automatically without any direct concern over the intricacies of the act. Self-paced skills, closed skills, and habitual skills possess many similar characteristics.

The diver's environment consists of a diving board and a pool, with the board a certain height over the pool. This condition is constant, wherever he goes to compete. True, things are never quite the same day to day or place to place, but then, no skill is purely habitual or purely perceptual. Elements of both are necessary for successful skill execution, but emphasis on each is dependent on the nature of the skill. Differences in diving-board structure, pool temperature, and spectators present, among many other factors, will contribute to an altered stimulus environment. In some cases, the diver must perform the same regardless of this change, for example, not paying attention to the crowd of people. In other situations, such as the board having more or less spring than the diver is accustomed to, he must use his perceptual mechanisms and adjust his dive accordingly.

But basically, the dive is an example of an habitual skill. The act is to be repeatedly performed under the condition in which it must ultimately be demonstrated for success to be probable. Any sport where the participant initiates the action rather than having to respond to thrown objects or moving players can be identified as primarily habitual.

Stimulus–response theory appears to have limited value in team sports as well as in many individual and dual sports where perceiving a changing environment is necessary (perceptual skills). Gestalt theory appears to be more appropriate for this situation. However, the initial learning of the basic skills underlying a sport might very well be conditioned, using the S–R approach. Common sense would dictate that a skill must be learned well under stable conditions before the individual will be able to execute it regardless of unpredictable circumstances.

But a fixed response is of no use to the performer reacting under varying conditions. The emphasis later would be on the environment, understanding relationships and patterns, utilizing Gestalt methodology. A tennis player might have beautiful form and execution when hitting against a ball-throwing machine. A game situation, however, requires much flexibility in response, for the ball now comes to the stroker at varying speeds, with curves and slices, and with indiscriminate bounces. Now he needs to demonstrate his awareness of spatial relationships and an ability to perceive and react according to changing stimuli. In team sports, the same condition exists. The basketball player must consider not only his own developed skill, but also his position on the court with regard to fellow and opposing players. It is not enough merely to assume a definite response pattern each time a specific situation is present. The player who mistakenly fixates an offensive or defensive move, who reacts in an inflexible manner to given stimuli will certainly be discovered shortly and advantage will be taken of these conditioned patterns. It is much more desirable to have skills developed to be called into play at any time, regardless of the situation. Externally paced skills, open skills, and perceptual skills contain many similar characteristics.

Most motor acts require more than a conditioned reaction. Their complexity requires an understanding of many facets of the learning process on the part of the teacher and performer for the skill to be most effectively demonstrated. Therefore the physical educator should be aware of the nature of both habitual and perceptual learning, and know how an emphasis on one or the other might better facilitate the desired outcome.

Continuous and Discrete Tasks

Psychomotor tasks may be designated as discrete or continuous. Discrete and continuous tasks can assume varied forms for any of the strategies just described. A discrete task may contain one unit or a series of separate units, with a fixed beginning or end, whereas a continuous task involves a series of adjustments of flowing movements, usually without an acknowledged termination point in time or specified movement. Feedback is often available during the performance of continuous tasks, and the attempt is to remedy errors during performance. A notable exception is in extremely rapid performance, such as piano playing, where knowledge of performance occurs too late to be of practical value except to assist in the execution of future movements. Performance decisions are more integrated in the action than in discrete tasks, where decisions are made in a more distinctive fashion to each unit. In either type of task, movements may be repetitive or sequentially varied. Feedback may be controlled or open loop in discrete tasks, depending on the duration of the movement.

Discrete tasks in their most elementary form are binary-key presses, or the simple reaction-time test. The student is required to respond in a situation with a clearly defined beginning and end in an all-or-none manner. Some discrete tasks are repetitive and performed in a specified rhythmic tempo. Other discrete tasks call for sequential steps without concern for tempo. The event may contain a predictable stimulus, in which case the response demand is not too taxing but fixed and stable. Where there are unpredictable stimuli, the response set must be more flexible. A discrete task associated with the self-paced strategy would be pressing a key or series of keys on the typewriter. Turning a light switch on or off is another example.

In the mixed-paced strategy, discrete as well as continuous responses are used in landing a plane. The plane is in motion and the pilot makes a series of discrete movements to achieve his goal. He also uses an error-nulling procedure in his efforts, a process associated with continuous tasks. Another example is the little boy playing the game "pinning the tail on the donkey" (the boy is in locomotion and blindfolded as he attempts to pin a tail on a picture of a donkey hanging on a wall). Error and/or performance time are important variables in discrete tasks. To identify a task for the externally paced strategy would also require a broad interpretation of the word *discrete*. Perhaps an illustration might be the volleyball player attempting to spike the ball over the net (both the object and the student are in motion in this brief act).

Continuous tasks are often more lengthy than discrete tasks and involve tracking and error nulling, where the attempt is to modify performance by constantly adjusting to errors. The initiation of this activity may be self-paced, or situationally paced, and terminated unexpectedly or after a defined series of behaviors is demonstrated. The self-paced strategy is deployed in the continuous task of striking a golf ball. Sequential patterns of motion are made in an organized form to deliver the club or iron to the resting ball and hopefully direct it in the desired direction and to the desired distance. Writing one's name in cursive form and painting a picture are other examples.

The mixed-paced strategy is utilized in driving a car. The car is guided within the confines of the road and the steering wheel is rotated according to the demands of the situation. This is a good example of a tracking task, where the student hopes to make continual appropriate adjustments as the car proceeds, in other words, keeping the car on the road at the specified speed. In sport, the youngster swimming the crawl stroke and attempting to propel himself vertically within the lane is involved in a continuous event. As contrasted with the car example, swimming contains a sequential and reasonably predictable situation.

An attempt at integrating the concepts of degree of continuity, type of pacing, and availability and type of feedback has been developed by· John Kreifeldt (1972). The scheme is presented in Figure 1–2. As we have suggested, the categorization of tasks helps to suggest instructional strategies and understandings.

Generally speaking, an open-loop task is one in which information generated about the performance comes at its termination. Was the performance accurate? Off target? When playing a composition on the piano, which requires rapid finger movements, performance results are obtained on the outcome of the performance, but there is no time to use feedback to correct and adjust the finger movements. On the contrary, in a closed-loop task we have the advantage of being able to utilize knowledge about

Figure 1–2. Some possible psychomotor tasks categorized by extreme condition of pacing, knowledge of results, and continuity. (From John G. Kreifeldt, "A Dynamic Model of Behaviors in a Discrete Open-Loop Self-paced Motor Skill," *IEEE Transactions on Systems, Man, and Cybernetics,* SCM-2:262–273, 1972.)

performance, to make continual adjustments through constant monitoring so as to match responses to input cues. Continual feedback during the driving of a car encourages proper adjustments for effective performance. Of course, in one sense both piano playing and car driving reflect the usage of feedback in that previously made erroneous movements are corrected in later performance. Self-paced and externally (forced) paced tasks, as well as continuous and discrete tasks, have been discussed previously.

We will continually refer back to this section of the book as we discuss learning phenomena and practice conditions later. Obviously, unique considerations must be made according to activity classification. Effective performance in continuous tasks, for instance, will depend heavily on the type and appropriateness of the feedback present *during* performance. Self-paced tasks, where no time criterion is present, suggest the possibility of emphasizing fixed-pattern responses, with little concern for swift cue perception and reaction. Perhaps these examples suffice for now to indicate the importance of recognizing activity distinctions in the application of practice conditions and instructional techniques.

History of the Study of Motor Skills

The first *Research Quarterly,* the research organ of the American Association for Health, Physical Education, and Recreation, was not published until 1930. Nevertheless the psychological research literature includes studies dealing with motor learning and performance in the early 1900's. True, there were not many at that time. But they did consider very practical concerns, such as optimal practice conditions for archery shooting and the long-term retention of juggling skills.

Workers in the field of physical education examined the concepts of motor ability, capacity, and educability in the 1930's and 1940's. Many years later this area was to become highly controversial. Psychologists were refining laboratory studies, and analyzed such behaviors as reaction time in great detail. But it was not really until after World War II, at the time of the Korean War and the space movement in the early 1960's, that a number of psychologists interested in learning and ability made their contributions. Military and space operations called for information on the way people could best learn to perform tasks, many of which involved keen attention, performance under trying conditions, and high degrees of skill. Predictive test batteries were developed to determine possible success in such tasks. Industrial psychologists also devoted their energies to determining the most effective means for encouraging worker output in manual and operational tasks. Arthur Irion's (1969) background material traces the research movements in a precise fashion in the area of psychology.

But besides the efforts of a few eminent physical educators, like Franklin Henry, A. T. Slater-Hammel, John Lawther, and Alfred Hubbard, little serious work could be found in physical education literature until the middle 1960's. With impetus from the extremely productive pen of Bryant Cratty, applied psychologists such as A. T. Welford, F. C. Bartlett, E. A. and Ina Bilodeau, Clyde Noble, and Ed Fleishman, and experimental psychologists such as the late Paul Fitts, Jack Adams, Robert and Carol Ammons, Michael Posner, and others, more and more scholars in physical education realized that the area of motor learning and skill acquisition was virtually untapped and that they could make major contributions to a body of knowledge. Serious research has been increasing at a fantastic rate. Many of the concepts developed in a preliminary sense by the scholars mentioned before are being analyzed and developed further.

The directions of this work run essentially in two identifiable but not necessarily exclusive tracks: the formulation of theory and advancement of pure research, and the application to instructional techniques.

THE PSYCHOMOTOR DOMAIN

A wide variety of movement behaviors is encompassed in the psychomotor domain. Previously in this chapter a classification scheme was presented that categorized behaviors as being *cognitive* ("knowing"), *affective* ("feeling"), or *psychomotor* ("doing"). These distinctions are by no means pure. Considerable overlap often is exhibited among behaviors. As has been pointed out elsewhere (Singer, 1972b), it is primarily for the sake of convenience that such distinctions are made. Activities that are primarily movement oriented and that emphasize overt physical responses bear the label *psychomotor*. The psychomotor domain is concerned with bodily movement and/or control. Such behaviors when performed in a general way represent a movement pattern or patterns, and when highly specific and task refined indicate a skill or sequence of skills. They include the following kinds of behaviors, all of which could be interrelated or any of which could be independent.

- Contacting, manipulating, and/or moving an object.
- Controlling the body of objects, as in balancing.
- Moving and/or controlling the body or parts of the body in space with timing in a brief or long *act* or *sequence* under predictable and/or unpredictable situations.

Assuming the basis and validity of laws or principles of learning, the logical step is to use them in the psychomotor domain where applicable. Even research findings, not of sufficient quality and quantity to form the basis of a "principle" but strong enough to indicate a trend, constitute available support for action. Unfortunately, this "logical step" is not as easy as it sounds.

In the first place, acceptable principles of learning are usually so broad and generalizable as to constitute nothing more than the obvious. Secondly, there is some question as to the practical application of more specific learning principles, formulated on a conceptual basis from laboratory work in artificial situations. Gagné (1962) for one has raised serious doubts as to the usefulness of learning principles for the learning of military skills. Thirdly, and of most frustration, is the diverse nature present research takes in the various areas concerned with the acquisition of motor skills.

On the last point, miniature models, nomenclature, and research projects in each area reflect the uniqueness of the matter dealt with. Can one tie together various approaches to the solution of how effective motor learning occurs? In the early portion of the century, behaviorists and Gestaltists demonstrated distinct approaches to learning, formed unique terms, and emphasized various aspects of learning. Problem solving, the nature of the stimulus, perception, response, and the nature and effect of intervening variables were some of these sources of emphasis. What with the advent of mathematical models, neuropsychological models, information theory, cybernetics, and man–machine dynamics, the problem has been magnified (Singer, 1966).

Military and industrial psychologists talk in terms of training factors. Knowledge of results, guidance and instructional techniques, cues in the display, task operations, and job analysis are basic concerns. Experimental psychologists still cling to concepts of conditioning. They are procedure and man centered, studying such things as instructional methods, practice variations, habit formations, and hypothetical constructs called intervening variables. Those interested in operant conditioning and the Skinnerian approach emphasize reinforcement and the shaping of behavior. Information or communication theorists research the processing and transmitting of information. The standard reference is "bits," which refers to information the organism receives in a situation. Engineering psychologists stress task variables and closed-loop servosystems, where the main interest is the difference between input and output and the nature of the transmission system. Cyberneticians compare man to a machine and provide a conceptual framework of control where feedback is of the utmost import. Social psychologists analyze man's behaviors in terms of attitudes, values, social systems, and family and peer influences. Physical educators, home economists, vocational educators, and special educators glean odds and ends from all these approaches but generally adhere to guidelines suggested by educational psychologists. Thorndike-type laws, terms, and research associated with the period before the 1940's and the explosion of sophisticated learning models and designs generally make this group of educators "comfortable."

Each of the previously mentioned groups is interested in skill development and modification in the psychomotor domain. The accumulation, consolidation, and syntheses of behavioral "facts" from so many diverse approaches may be beyond reconciliation. Nevertheless, anyone concerned with behavior in the psychomotor domain in general should at least attempt to confront and resolve all these conceptual and experimental approaches. Certainly Berelson and Steiner (1964) must be praised for their valiant effort to construct an inventory of scientific findings with regard to human behavior. Categories of behaviors were described succinctly and descriptive statements made within each as representative of research findings.

On the other hand, it can be legitimately argued that because of the unique complexities of each learning task area, research and theory should be developed and applied to the specific situation. The present trend toward the formulation of miniature models of learning, applicable to unique problems associated within the area of interest, contrasts with the original goals of psychologists to describe all of learning in one theory. An attempt at formulating a new taxonomy of human learning, with discussions on the problems relevant to the seven categories representing the various types of research, is presented by Melton (1964). In the psychomotor domain it may be necessary for the physical educator, the vocational specialist, and the military psychologist each to attend to his own unique problems. Much depends on the degree to which we believe in task specificity. For that matter, the nature of the task (e.g., discrete, continuous, serial) might serve as a special consideration.

Signal detection, or vigilance, theory was developed by military psychologists for situations pertinent to the military. In Swets' (1964) detection theory, human behavior in a variety of perceptual tasks is analyzed. Welford (1960) forwards the single-channel hypothesis as an explanation for the information processing of motor skills. Smith (1962) terms his cybernetic approach to the evaluation of man's behavior a neurogeometric theory. Poulton's (1954) model is geared for predictions in industrial work. Fitts (1964) favors an approach to studying motor learning that contains a framework of three types of models: communication, control system, and adaptive. Henry (1960), a physical educator, has proposed a memory drum theory of neuromotor reaction, that deals with various aspects of motor performance. These represent but a sampling of diverse theoretical advancements to be applied to the learning and performing of motor skills.

Thus the problem of task-specific or area-specific research and theory versus a general-domain approach is a real one. Evidently, those concerned with instructional settings must consider situational-specific evidence and task-related information, as well as general behavioral knowledge.

Adams (1971) very insightfully describes the current status of research and theory in the motor skills area. By way of contrasting efforts in verbal behavior with those in motor behavior, we can more easily identify the major problem for those who are concerned with the history and direction of scholarly work with motor skills. Adams writes (p. 112):

> The research on skills today is as many-sided as the definition of skills, about as McGeoch found it fifty years ago, with research being done on such diverse topics as sports, music, the factory, and military jobs. In their totality these fields can embrace a full span of human performance from lifting a finger to flying an airplane or delivering a speech. In experimental psychology, topics like conditioning, for example, started out with a well-defined subject matter and paradigm, and pursued a systematic search for variables, laws, and theory. Research on skills, by contrast, has studied anything that looks skillful to the common-sense eye. If the study of verbal behavior had gone the same way, we would have journals filled with studies on how to learn and remember novels, billboards, and theater marquees. Compared to the study of skills, the history of verbal behavior and conditioning over the same period is a scientific story to be envied.

Going further, Adams calls for more basic research efforts. The focus should be on common elements and mechanisms in what is usually considered to be skilled behavior. He writes (pp. 112–113):

> The villain that has robbed "skills" of its precision is applied research that investigates an activity to solve a particular problem, like kicking a football, flying an airplane, or operating a lathe. This accusation sounds more damaging than intended, because applied research is necessary when basic science lacks the answers. Nevertheless, the overall outcome of applied research is a collection of answers on specific problems, practically important to someone at a particular moment, but not the steady building of scientific knowledge that can some day have power to answer all the problems. Instead of starting with ideas about the laws and theory of movements and then finding the best situations in which to test them, investigators of skills have often started with

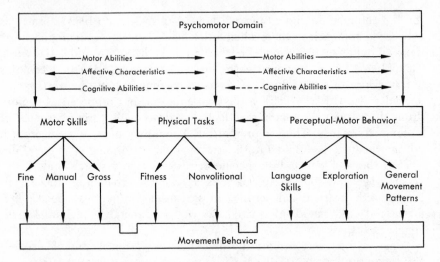

Figure 1–3.   A schematic plan of the factors included in the psychomotor domain. [From Robert N. Singer, "The Psychomotor Domain: General Considerations," in National Special Media Institutes (ed.), *The Psychomotor Domain* (Washington, D.C.: Gryphon House, 1972).]

tasks that looked skillful and, by studying them, hope to arrive at laws and theory. This approach is backwards for scientific productivity because it results in disconnected pockets of data that lack the unifying ideas that are general scientific principles. The task-centered approach is justified when practical reasons require us to know about tasks and efficiency in them, but it is a limited way of achieving the larger scientific goals of laws and theory.

The boundaries of the psychomotor domain are difficult to ascertain. It is a challenge to identify and distinguish tasks that are incorporated in this domain. Figure 1–3 depicts the possible scope of the psychomotor domain and the kinds of abilities leading to various acts that constitute movement behavior (no continuum of activities is intended). It can be seen that motor abilities and affective characteristics (attitudes, motivation) contribute to success in a variety of skills, tasks, and behaviors. Cognitive abilities (note dotted line) are probably least involved in physical tasks.

1. A motor skill refers to muscular movement or motion of the body required for the successful execution of a desired act (same as perceptual-motor skill). Specific criteria are set for the acceptability or performance.
   a. *Fine motor skills* encompass the neuromuscular coordinations involved in precision-oriented tasks, such as typing, piano playing, watchmaking, needle threading, and tracking with pursuit rotors.

They are highly refined and distinguished from other tasks because of the high degree of eye–hand precision required in their execution. Furthermore, they are usually sitting-down tasks.

b. *Manual skills* are typically midway between fine and gross skills. They are usually eye–arm–hard manipulative tasks that are fairly repetitive. Examples are found in factory work and industrial technology areas. Equipment, apparatus, or objects are usually the source of manipulation.

c. *Gross motor skills* involve the large muscles and the movement of most of the body. Sports skills of all kinds may be considered as gross motor skills, although there is no clear-cut distinction between fine, manual, and gross motor skills.

2. Physical tasks are characterized by a minimal, if any, involvement of the higher cortical centers of the nervous system.

a. *Physical fitness tests* require minimal coordination of body parts and cognitive activity. Strength, endurance, speed, and flexibility describe factors in this category. Following an understanding of the act, the execution of it becomes quite repetitive; skills, as alluded to before, include activities demanding cue discrimination of changing and unpredictable stimuli and the temporal patterning of adaptive responses, e.g., sports skills. Physical fitness tests accent the "physical," that is, a push-up test demands gross, continuous, predescribed movements of the body until the onset of fatigue. Motor skills are more complex and involve more motor coordination of the body itself, as well as more coordination of cognitive and motor abilities.

b. *Nonvolitional* behavior is primarily reflexive. The knee jerk, autonomic processes, and extremely well-learned acts are probably performed at a subcortical level.

3. Perceptual-motor behavior includes those tasks that have a high degree of the perceptual component present. It is popularly used to connote the special training programs for youngsters classified as mentally retarded, emotionally disturbed, or slow learners, in the hope of improving their learning capacity. The perception and recognition of spatial relationships and patterns, the estimation of distance, speed, and accuracy, and the ability to temporally pattern responses could easily describe motor skill as well as perceptual-motor behaviors. But to distinguish between these terms, motor skills refer to *specific* acts and sequences of responses whereas perceptual-motor behaviors are more *general* movements. In comparing motor skills with perceptual-motor behaviors, there is a greater emphasis on response development in the former case. A greater degree of the perceptual component is present in the latter case, as is allowance for varied behavioral expression.

a. *Exploration* of space and body awareness activities represent perceptual-motor movement patterns. Moving and controlling appropriate parts of the body in space to reach objectives demonstrate body awareness and space exploration activities. In perceptual-motor training programs, these are general, appropriate, relatively nondifficult movement responses to specific directions, involving the interpretation of directions and the activation of acceptable responses.

b. *Language skills* are heavily perceptually oriented and reflect perceptual-motor behavior. The conception of words, the formation of mouth movements and facial expressions, and the production of words describe activity in this area.

c. General movement patterns, as contrasted with skills, have been discussed earlier. Patterns connote the ability to achieve objectives, in a variety of ways, without a high degree of precision or refinement.

No reference is made to psychomotor tasks per se, for almost any kind of movement-oriented task could probably be considered a psychomotor task. For the most part in the literature, psychomotor tasks are indicated by laboratory-created situations. Reaction time, coordination-apparatus tests, positioning tests, speed tests, and the like, have often been referred to as psychomotor tests. The term is so vague as to have little real practical meaning.

Contrarily, Noble (1968, p. 204) argues that "the label 'motor' skills is less satisfactory than 'perceptual-motor' or 'psychomotor' skills." Motor skills are defined as "merely . . . any cued striate-muscular action that is modified by learning variables." Psychomotor tasks (or perceptual-motor) are elaborately interpreted to be "those situations that require the identification and combination of stimulus-organism-response elements into coordinated spatiotemporal patterns of receptor-effector activity as a joint function of practice repetitions and reinforcing feedback so as to optimize probability, amplitude, and time scores (or their derivatives) in acquisition, retention, and transfer." Nonetheless, simplicity in interpretation may be more desirable than complex and wordy descriptions.

A general framework has been suggested as to the types of tasks representing the psychomotor domain. Research on motor skills will in this book be primarily considered with regard to learner and environmental variables. Proficiency in skills is dependent on many factors and an attempt will be made to mention most of them in this book. No depth treatments of these considerations can be made. Research will be examined mostly from the motor skills area in order that applications can be made without the usual fear of the possible lack of relationship between the learning of nonsense syllables, prose, and other verbal material and the learning of motor tasks. Although research findings are argued to be task and situation specific, hopefully evidence on the learning of certain types of tasks in the psychomotor domain may legitimately be applicable to other tasks in this domain.

THE IMPORTANCE
OF STUDYING LEARNING

At the onset of this chapter it was pointed out that many people, with diverse backgrounds and interests, were concerned with learning. Questions they pose range from those reflecting a personal need to understanding how to learn and master material quicker and better, to those making a major contribution to research and theory. From your (the reader's) point of view, the study of learning dynamics may contribute to your (1) own knowledge and ability to learn tasks, (2) helping skills (as a teacher or parent), (3) ability and interest in undertaking research, and (4) role as a designer of training and instructional programs.

The objectives in reading this text or any references that encompass topics in learning can be quite diverse but not necessarily mutually exclusive. Most of us would like to know more about learning phenomena, simply because we spend a lifetime attempting minimally or maximally to master a great variety of materials, tasks, and activities. Any personal insights can be advantageous and rewarding. For potential or present parents, responsibilities rest in their influencing and changing the behavior of the young.

A number of occupational roles require knowledge of human behavior and ways of constructively changing them. For motor skills, we may identify specialists in industry, military, aerospace programs, recreation, physical education, special education, elementary education, dance, and many more areas. Whether for personal or occupational purposes, the study of the nature of learning is a fascinating and rewarding journey.

REFERENCES

ADAMS, JACK A. "A Closed-Loop Theory of Motor Behavior," *Journal of Motor Behavior,* 3:111–149, 1971.

BERELSON, BERNARD, and GARY A. STEINER. *Human Behavior: An Inventory of Scientific Findings.* New York: Harcourt Brace Jovanovich, Inc., 1964.

BLODGETT, HUGH C. "The Effect of the Introduction of Reward Upon the Maze Performance of Rats," *University of California Publications in Psychology,* 4:113–134, 1929.

BLOOM, BENJAMIN S., MAX D. ENGELHART, EDWARD J. FURST, WALTER H. HILL, and DAVID R. KRATHWOHL. *Taxonomy of Educational Objectives, Handbook I: Cognitive Domain.* New York: David McKay Company, Inc., 1956.

BUSS, ALLAN R. "A Conceptual Framework for Learning Effecting the Development of Ability Factors," *Human Development,* 16:273–292, 1973.

FITTS, PAUL M. "Perceptual-Motor Skill Learning," in Arthur W. Melton (ed.), *Categories of Human Learning.* New York: Academic Press, Inc., 1964.

GAGNÉ, ROBERT M. "The Domains of Learning," *Interchange,* 3:1–8, 1973.

————. "Military Training and Principles of Learning," *American Psychologist,* 17:83–91, 1962.

————. *The Conditions of Learning.* New York: Holt, Rinehart and Winston, Inc., 1970.

GENTILE, A. M. "A Working Model of Skill Acquisition with Application to Teaching," *Quest,* Monograph XVII, 1972, pp. 3–23.

HARROW, ANITA J. *A Taxonomy of the Psychomotor Domain.* New York: David McKay Company, Inc., 1971.

HENRY, FRANKLIN M. "Increased Response Latency for Complicated Movement and a 'Memory Drum' Theory of Neuromotor Reaction," *Research Quarterly,* 31:448–458, 1960.

IRION, ARTHUR L. "Historical Introduction," in E. A. Bilodeau and Ina McD. Bilodeau (eds.), *Principles of Skill Acquisition.* New York: Academic Press, Inc., 1969.

JOYCE, BRUCE, and MARSHA WEIL. *Models of Teaching.* Englewood Cliffs, N.J.: Prentice-Hall, Inc., 1972.

KNAPP, BARBARA. *Skill in Sport: The Attainment of Proficiency,* London: Routledge & Kegan Paul, 1964.

KRATHWOHL, DAVID R., BENJAMIN S. BLOOM, and BERTRAM B. MASIA. *Taxonomy of Educational Objectives, Handbook II: Affective Domain.* New York: David McKay Company, Inc., 1964.

KREIFELDT, JOHN G. "A Dynamic Model of Behaviors in a Discrete Open-Loop Self-Paced Motor Skill," *IEEE Transactions on Systems, Man, and Cybernetics,* SMC–2:262–273, 1972.

LOCKHART, AILEENE. "What's in a Name?" *Quest,* Monograph II, 1964, pp. 9–13.

MELTON, ARTHUR W. (ed.). *Categories of Human Learning.* New York: Academic Press, Inc., 1964.

NOBLE, CLYDE E. "The Learning of Psychomotor Skills," *Annual Review of Psychology,* 19:203–250, 1968.

POULTON, E. C. "On Prediction in Skilled Movements," *Psychological Bulletin,* 54:467–478, 1957.

SINGER, ROBERT N. *Coaching, Athletics, and Psychology.* New York: McGraw-Hill Book Company, 1972a.

————. "Learning Theory as Applied to Physical Education," *Proceed-*

ings of the National College Physical Education Association for Men, 69:59–66, 1966.

———— (ed.). *The Psychomotor Domain: Movement Behavior.* Philadelphia: Lea & Febiger, 1972b.

SMITH, KARL U. *Delayed Sensory Feedback and Behavior.* Philadelphia: W. B. Saunders Company, 1962.

SWETS, JOHN A. (ed.). *Signal Detection and Recognition by Human Observers.* New York: John Wiley & Sons, Inc., 1964.

WELFORD, A. T. "The Measurement of Sensory Motor Performance: Survey and Reappraisal of Twelve Years' Progress," *Ergonomics,* 3:189–230, 1960.

2

SKILLED PERFORMANCE

Although there may exist a number of objectives in the learning situation, one of the immediate or ultimate goals is the mastery of the task and the attainment of skill. Different standards of achievement are established, but essentially the most efficient and effective ways of reaching goals should be sought. This implies a need to understand the nature of the task, the learner, the learning process, and learning conditions.

Many factors apparently contribute to the skilled performance of any task. Genetics, childhood experiences, personal goals, environmental influences, and other interactions lead to the state of "excellence." Ideally, in order to determine potentials for developing proficiency in any task, genetic factors, familial tendencies, past experiences, and the individual's personality should be reasonably understood prior to the training of a given task in a particular situation. General learning principles and specific considerations, with appropriate environmental modifications and instructional techniques, should then be utilized.

WHAT IS SKILL?

The term *skill*, like the word *learning*, is difficult to measure and interpret. It may have various connotations, depending on what is to be defined and who is defining it. The Winston dictionary states that "skill is knowledge of any art together with expert ability to put that knowledge to use."

Skill can refer to a particular act performed or to the manner in which it is executed. All physical education activities may be considered as skills or as being comprised of skills, and the degree of proficiency attained by the individual reflects his *skill level.*

Skill is a relative quality, not to be defined in absolute terms. Performance displayed by an individual may be so outstanding as to warrant his being considered skilled, by comparison with a group of his peers on the neighborhood football field. The same person when placed with members of the varsity team may appear relatively unskilled. Skill as demonstrated by performance is an indication of that which has been learned. Skill and performance can be greatly influenced by a host of factors that may have psychological or emotional origins. However, it is usually thought that the highly skilled individual will be able to perform fairly consistently regardless of the factors present that might cause the "average" person's performance to fluctuate.

Requirements of various activities necessitate a complex development of both perceptual and motor facilities, with degree of emphasis dependent on the situation. In sports, physical processes must be developed before skill can be demonstrated. For example, gymnasts, wrestlers, and soccer players find their performances hindered if they have not shown concern for such underlying physical elements as strength, endurance, and flexibility.

Whereas the diver or gymnast primarily can concentrate on the act itself and display skill through a consistent performance, the team sport player must have mastered not only the basic skills but also an ability to react to changing, less predictable situations. Many people can shoot a basketball with a high degree of accuracy when called on to play 21, Horse, or other games not influenced by defensive players or players on the same team in a competitive situation. Their skills are limited to the given circumstance. Success may not be nearly as pronounced when these people have to demonstrate their skill in a game that requires a mastery of techniques, response flexibility, perception, and emotional stability.

High degrees of skill coincide with high degrees of spatial precision and timing. If certain actions are performed at the wrong time they can be disruptive. During skilled performance responses to stimuli are set in an appropriate sequential order. Another aspect of skill is that the act is executed within a certain time limitation. The tennis player must stroke the ball at the proper moment and in a productive manner. He does not have time to ponder the situation; his response must be appropriate and quick. Generally, in a given situation a person who is skilled anticipates quickly and has more time to react.

The highly skilled individual demonstrates less variability in performance because he does not respond to every potential cue in the environment. He receives maximum information from a minimum number of identified cues. Skill is developed through constantly well-guided and informative practice, resulting in selective perception and reactions to appropriate stimuli.

It appears that in order for skill to be present, for most motor acts at least four variables must be considered. These aspects of skill must be developed to a sufficient degree if the performer is to be called skilled. Johnson (1961) relates a colorful tale involving woodchoppers in a contest involving skill. Through the story, he describes how each of the following factors plays a role in determining skill:

$$\text{Skill} = \text{speed} \times \text{accuracy} \times \text{form} \times \text{adaptability}$$

Most skills have to be performed within a time limitation, hence the importance of speed. Accuracy is also involved in acts of skill, for accurate movements will determine how successfully these acts are performed. Form refers to economy of effort, and certainly, skilled acts should be executed with a minimal amount of energy expenditure. Finally, a skilled individual is adaptive; he can perform proficiently under varying and even unpredictable conditions.

Therefore it can be seen that the development of skill is highly complex. Consistency in excellent performance infers the activation and formation of good habits. But habits if they are bad can weaken skill. Perhaps an acceptable interpretation of *skill* as referred to in these pages is *the degree of success in achieving an objective with efficiency and effectiveness*. The ease with which an act is performed is also part of the skill of the act. The object in a baseball game for the outfielder is to catch a fly ball. Certainly there would be a great deal of difference in the method employed by Pete Rose to achieve this goal as compared with the writer of this book, even though both might succeed (the former with ease and grace, the latter with reckless abandon and a prayer).

Skills, Patterns, and Abilities

At this point, it is wise to examine similarities and differences between the terms *ability* and *skill*. An *ability* is thought to be something that is general and enduring. It is a trait affected by both learning and heredity. A *skill*, on the other hand, is specific to given tasks and is attained with experience. Because it is task oriented, skill usually refers to a highly developed specific sequence of responses. As an example, balance is an ability, and a person may demonstrate skill in trampolining, a sport that requires balancing ability. Balance is necessary for success in other sports as well. However, although each sport may call for expressions of balancing ability, the skill demonstrated is specific to the situation in which it is practiced. Researchers have tried and currently are attempting to describe skills in terms of more basic abilities with varying degrees of success. Edwin Fleishman has spent almost twenty years investigating the relationship of abilities to skilled performance and has provided meaningful distinctions and relationships for discussing skills and abilities (e.g., Fleishman, 1972).

Motor patterns and motor skills can be differentiated as well. This is especially appropriate for scholars studying the developmental process. Barbara Godfrey and Newell Kephart (1969, p. 8) write that:

> Motor skill is a motor activity limited in extent and involving a single movement or a limited group of movements which are performed with high degrees of precision and accuracy. A motor pattern, on the other hand, is a much more extensive group or series of motor acts which are performed with lesser degrees of skill, but which are directed toward accomplishment of some external purpose. On the motor *skill*, movement is limited but accuracy is stressed. On the motor *pattern*, movement is stressed but accuracy is limited.

An example offered of a motor pattern is locomotion. The child is free to select from alternatives to go from one place to another. He may run, jump, crawl, or use some other pattern to achieve the goal. Walking, however, is a specific skill. The child must learn the specific placements of the feet, how to shift weight, and how to function on various terrains and surfaces.

Skills are apparently refined from basic movement patterns, which in turn are related to the degree of presence of relevant abilities. Skills and patterns are acquired through learning. Some abilities depend more on genetic than learning factors, but it appears that all depend on both to some degree. Whenever the learner attempts to master a task, he brings these abilities to the situation. The intricate relationship of abilities with successful task performance at various stages of development will be discussed later in the book.

Motor Skill

The word *skill* by itself might imply an art in writing, memorizing, acting, painting, talking, or playing. To delineate the confusion, muscular movement or motion of the body required for the successful execution of a desired act is termed motor skill. It is difficult to isolate skill completely as being perceptual, motor, or verbal but primarily the emphasis of each process on the skill will decide its nature.

Motor does imply movement. Various processes interact (e.g., cognitive, perceptual, affective, and motor) in order that the act may be integrated, meaningful, and successful. It is important to realize that the presence of these factors is necessary to almost any skilled performance.

THREE MAIN CONSIDERATIONS

Most of us find it hard to believe that so many factors can conceivably contribute to highly skilled performance. Two major categories of variables may generally be thought of as affecting the status of the learner: (1) personal or organismic, and (2) environmental and instructional influences.[1] These vary with each learner and each instructional program. Because learners can differ in so many ways, it is desirable to prepare practice conditions that are sensitive to these differences. Yet there are certain generalities, certain similarities, in the way we acquire skills, and this variable should be recognized along with the other two. The process of learning, of skill acquisition, reveals a number of consistencies among learners. Figure 2–1 indicates that consideration should be given to the three categories of variables that affect performance and help to explain performance: the learner, the learning process, and situational factors.

In the following chapter and in various sections of this book attempts to explain the learning process and skill acquisition will be introduced. Disregard is shown for individual difference factors. No attempt is made to show different training regimens, and techniques may alter expected outcomes. It is important to understand how people in general learn. A model or framework is thereby created that provides guidelines for improved practice situations.

Yet learning-process explanations are incomplete by themselves for the serious student of motor learning. Knowledge of those personal factors that lead to successful performance, how they differ from individual to

Figure 2–1. Three major considerations in skilled performance.

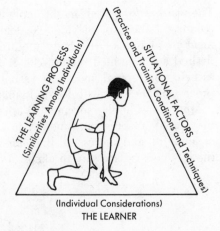

(Individual Considerations)
THE LEARNER

---

[1] Much of the material in the sections dealing with personal factors and instructional conditions has been taken and abridged from Singer (1972).

individual, and how and why they should be considered also leads to better instructional and learning environments. Furthermore, ways in which the learner himself or a teacher or coach can modify learning situations for others in order that most productive results be realized in the time allotted is a necessity. Identified in the remainder of this chapter will be the more pertinent personal and situational factors. These and others will be elaborated upon in other chapters.

PERSONAL FACTORS
LEADING TO PROFICIENCY

When we consider the learner, irrespective of practice conditions and settings, it becomes apparent that a number of factors emerge that might affect the learning of most motor tasks. These are graphically illustrated in Figure 2–2. Because individuals differ considerably in many of these characteristics, we can expect dissimilar outcomes when the same instructional strategies are used for all.

In most learning situations, it is virtually impossible to make all these individual considerations. Yet one of the fallacies in any group-learning effort is to treat all individuals as if they possess the same characteristics,

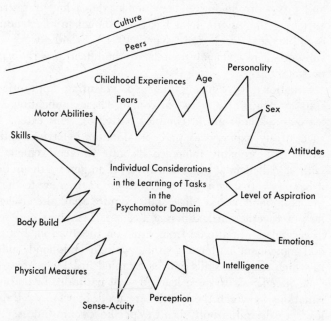

Figure 2–2.   The learner.

abilities, experiences, and motivation to achieve. For instance, it is suggested that approximately 80 per cent of the variance in intelligence may be attributed to hereditary factors; 20 per cent to environmental experiences. When all sorts of familial characteristics are considered (e.g., intelligence, height, weight, and body build), an average correlation of 0.50 is obtained between parents and children. To the extent that such personal qualities may be related to the probability of success in a given endeavor in the psychomotor domain, they must be acknowledged.

1. In athletics, a given *body build* has been found to be related to excellence in particular athletic endeavors. The average athlete representing one sport has been somatotyped (a method of determining body build) and is usually distinguished in this dimension from athletes representing other sports (Carter, 1968, 1969), or, for that matter, from so-called nonathletes. Although a given body type is not a necessity for excellence in athletic endeavors, its presence may increase the probability of success. The relationship may hold true for all types of motor skills. Inherited and developed personal qualities may increase the likelihood of one accomplishing certain activities associated with industry, business, the military, and the arts. Physical characteristics, of little concern in the cognitive domain, are very much associated with the mastery of varied motor skills.

2. Enriched and varied *early childhood experiences* is a second factor leading to the probability of success in a wide range of undertakings. In work with lower forms of young organisms—chimpanzees, chickens, dogs, and rats—introducing an experience, depriving or restricting a sense, or enriching the environment has been shown to affect adult behavior. (For example, see Beach and Jaynes, 1954.) Freud's work and the efforts of subsequent psychoanalysts indicate the effect of early experiences on adult personalities.

Situations for figuring out and executing appropriate movement responses begin at a very early age. These foundational blocks serve the learning of later-in-life complex activities. The extent to which a child successfully experiences perceptual-motor behaviors and develops motorically will probably influence his rate of achievement when confronted with so-called new tasks. However, it might be theoretically argued, and it has been, that very few activities are really new to the learner following the childhood years. Most skills require that already-learned movements be put together in a different fashion. Temporal and sequential patterns of responses are altered from situation to situation. But essential and general movement patterns, learned well in childhood, influence the degree to which complex skills will be attained in later years.

3. *Specific skills,* once learned, will naturally favorably transfer over to situations in which these skills are used. Specialized training in childhood leads to desirable outcomes in specific circumstances. There exists much evidence on the specificity nature of motor skills; that in order for one to

reach a high degree of proficiency in any skill, practice must be specific to that skill.

4. Aspects of *personality* relate to task achievement in some ways, although clear-cut patterns are often difficult to establish. On more complex tasks, studies generally show highly anxious individuals do more poorly than those low in anxiety. Also, those who score low on anxiety tests perform more effectively under stress than under normal conditions. This is not the case with high-anxiety people, who are less effective performers under stress (Wiener, 1959).

Insight and sensitivity on the part of the teacher, supervisor, or other forms of leadership to the personality characteristics of the learner-performer may help to detect possible behavioral choices, patterns, and achievement. In the area of choices, vocational researchers and theoreticians point to level and direction of vocational aspiration, self-esteem, need to achieve, and other personality characteristics. Self-esteem is a strong moderator variable in one's vocational decisions (Korman, 1966). Individuals are more apt to favor social roles, positions, and occupations that are consistent with their image of personal abilities and talents.

Athletes representing different sport groups have been shown on occasion to possess unique personality profiles. Superior athletes, average athletes, and nonathletes are also uniquely characterized. (A brief summary of the research is reported by Cooper, 1969.) A few psychologists, notably Ogilvie (1968), are quite enthusiastic about the identification of unique personality dimensions of champion athletes. However, agreement on these matters is still lacking. When traits can be ascribed with a reasonable degree of confidence to athletes representing a sport, or workers involved in certain occupations, statistical analysis will help to predict the probability of an individual's achievement on a team, in an event, or at a position.

5. *General motor abilities,* as influenced by hereditary and environmental variables, will certainly have a bearing on the learner's potential for successful achievement in any endeavor. In predicting proficiency, a young child is more apt to have more "generalizable" abilities than high school or older-aged individuals. With age comes a maturation and differentiation process. Complex and specialized tasks must be continuously and conscientiously practiced for one to attain relatively high degrees of skill as he develops to maturity. Less time can be devoted to other pursuits. The endeavors of youngsters demand more gross movements and they are fairly similar from activity to activity. This is not the case as the individual begins the adolescent years. The maturing organism is capable of undertaking and completing more highly refined tasks. Interests, too, change, and become more specialized.

Obviously, then, *a test that presumably measures general motor ability is almost meaningless* in differentiating among the reasonably or highly skilled. Because none has been developed that is truly general, each is almost meaningless for instructional design. In the case of sports, gross bodily activity along with intricate and refined movements are involved. One test, or even a battery of tests, cannot conceivably produce discriminating judgments among athletic individuals and between specific sports participants. Specialized skills tests, related to the sport at hand, will do a more acceptable job. The same is true in the vocational area. Instead of speaking about one manual ability, recognition should be given to the probability that there exists a number of manual abilities. And specific manual tests, related to the task at hand, will yield better distinctions among individuals than will a test of general manual ability.

Even so, successful job completion or athletic participation are related to so many variables that the practice of isolating particular skills to test for classification and prediction purposes is of questionable value. Simpler motor skills can be handled more easily with tests when such is the intent. But complex tasks, involving not only a number of human abilities, but specified skills, personality variables, and physical and physiological characteristics as well, defy the implication that an ability test or abilities test alone can satisfactorily account for enough of the achievement variance to be of practical value.

6. Physical measures needed for task success (e.g., adequate strength, flexibility, and endurance) must be present. Practice can then be sustained which will in turn result in performance improvement. The condition of the body with respect to those and other underlying personal attributes relevant to the skill(s) at hand will greatly determine the effectiveness of the practice conditions arranged for learning to occur. Even in such acts as typing, piano playing, and card sorting, finger, wrist, and arm endurance is a prerequisite to skill acquisition.

7. *Sense acuity* is important prior to, during, and following an act. Kinesthetic, visual, and verbal cues provide important knowledge to the learner about his performance. Various kinds of sensory receptors, each specific to one stimulus form only, convert the input into electrical energy capable of going to various parts of the nervous system. Some impulses activate the perceptual mechanism, so that meaning can be made of that which was sensed. Others activate subcortical centers.

In order for information to be accurately processed, as a first step the input devices (sense organs and receptors) must be in good functioning order. Poor depth perception or peripheral vision, inferior audition, or ineffective proprioceptive activity will provide error-filled information.

8. Following the reception of information through the senses, *perceptual* operations typically precede motor activity. Interpretation of the situation must be made before correct responses can transpire. Selective attention to cues and disregard for irrelevant ones constitute the preliminary portion of effective movement behavior. How and what one perceives in a given situation depends on many factors. In turn, behavior reflects perception and the means to execute spatially and temporally appropriate movements.

9. *Intelligence,* which is usually measured by academic achievement or

IQ in the research, is positively but lowly related to physical characteristics and motor skills in the normal population of students. Within the normal intelligence range, we would generally not expect those who are more outstanding in motor skill accomplishments to be meaningfully more or less intelligent than others. Mental retardates, however, usually demonstrate poorer motor development and skills than similarly aged "normals."

With regard to training techniques, there is a possibility that brighter students may learn motor skills more effectively than less intelligent ones (1) under whole rather than part-learning methods, and (2) with problem-solving methods rather than traditional methods. Low academic achievers (slow learners, mental retardates) require simple explanations and step-by-step progressions in motor tasks.

10. *Emotions* are a part of most motor activity. Researchers have considered anxiety, stress, tension, and the effect of various motivational procedures on the learning and performance of motor skills.

With regard to emotions in general, an optimal level exists for the learning of any task. Stress, in the form of social presence, high incentives, and the like, is usually a hindrance to the learning of new complex skills. At later stages, it is no bother or may even facilitate performance.

11. The level of *aspiration,* or goals, established by an individual when he undertakes a motor task will greatly determine his achievement. Previous failures and successes determine the level one sets for himself. It is usually found that high, realistically attainable goals produce the most favorable results for the learner. The implication here is that general group standard performance expectancies, as set by the teacher, for example, are not conducive to a favorable learning climate. Individual status and individually set goals should be considered.

Early successes are important to motivation, in turn for continuing performance, and ultimately in learning. Performance expectancies should be contingent on prior personal accomplishments and potential achievement. Satisfaction achieved elevates the level of aspiration, which in turn increases the probability of better performance output.

12. A person's expectancy *attitudes* are related to task performance. When an individual has high expectancies, his performance is positively affected. Attitudes may also be viewed in another way. Interest in the task, a desire to achieve well, effort, and motivation lead to more meaningful practice sessions. The learner must have intentions of improving his performance. Merely going through routines in a haphazard and mechanical manner, disregarding important cues, and demonstrating purposeless activity is a good example of how not to master a task. One's attitude toward the task at hand is reflected in his attempt to improve himself and the ultimate consequences.

13. It should be added, of course, that the task itself may be *fear*-inducing because of its very nature. Gymnastics, trampolining, diving, swimming, and other athletic skills contain fear situations and require

safety precautions. Military, vocational, and driving skills have similar elements. Fear, causing anxiety, is a deterrent to the learning process in such activities. Although not considered in other areas, the psychological fear of success has been of great concern to psychiatrists, psychologists, and coaches dealing with athletes. Some athletes have been diagnosed as being afraid to stand success, or at least failing to wholeheartedly attempt to achieve. They deliberately injure themselves to gain sympathy or even a hero's recognition. They complain of pains that do not really exist. It is interesting to speculate how many confronted with any kind of task fear success. The added responsibility associated with achievement may be looked upon as a cause of increased anxiety by the person.

14. With regard to occupational choices, athletic endeavors, and task performances in general, *male and female* comparisons lead to interesting observations. Because of certain physiological, anatomical, and personality differences, performances on certain tasks are favored for one sex over the other. However, an often underplayed variable in task choice and accomplishments are sociocultural influences. Although physical-fitness testing, reaction time data, and sports' records indicate the general superiority of males, females are demonstrating feats that surprise most people. For example, some of the women's records in track and field and swimming at the 1952 Olympic Games were better than the men's records fifty-two years earlier!

With greater social acceptance and encouragement, women demonstrate skills fairly comparable with those exhibited by males. Naturally, there are those motor tasks typically associated with females at which they excel when compared to males. Nevertheless, present research indicates that sex differences in performance in varied motor tasks become more apparent with increasing age (Singer, 1969), in favor of the boys. Into adolescence and early adulthood, the separation between the sexes widens.

15. Various kinds of motor skills are affected in dissimilar fashion by the *aging process*. There are some vocational occupations and sports events that can be participated in successfully for a great duration of a person's life. Others, of course, cannot. Although the process of learning may be little affected by age, performance variables are, and they play an important role in output.

An older person needs more time to react; to perceive quickly and respond. When he can work at his own speed, and the task is self-paced (the response is initiated by the performer to a fixed stimulus rather than to some unpredictable stimulus), the individual is not handicapped. The increased inability to receive and transmit information is a symptom of older age. Also, tasks requiring large amounts of strength, endurance, speed, and flexibility work to his disadvantage. Complex motor tasks, with too much information in the display, may result in a tendency to pay attention to irrelevant information. All these considerations indicate the need to match the appropriate task with the aging person for best results.

These individual learner considerations by no means exhaust the list of possible variables, but they certainly should serve as warnings as to the complexity of the learning situation in the psychomotor domain. The task is now to interpret and identify the ways the learning process may be enhanced through the manipulation of environmental variables.

INSTRUCTIONAL CONDITIONS
LEADING TO PROFICIENCY

In any learning situation, there are a host of external conditions that can be manipulated. Of first concern is the nature of the display.

Display

The specific learning situation, or task, the individual is faced with is his display. In an experimental psychology laboratory experiment, the display is the equipment, cues, and task confronting the subject. In piloting a plane, it is represented by the flight conditions and response panel. The external information in a given situation, pertinent or nonpertinent to the task, represents the stimuli to which the organism will probably attend. The challenge in facilitating learning is to modify the display in such a way that desired outcomes are best met. The teacher or instructor is external to the subject's display, but serves as a potential display moderator or manipulator. Cues offered by the instructor can make the display easier to master for the learner.

1. Merely changing the atmosphere from the previous practice can induce improvement. The Hawthorne experiment, performed in the 1930s, is a classic example of this. Several secretaries were placed in rooms to work under various different working conditions. Light illumination was changed, and the girls were given free lunches, rest periods, and even allowed to go home early at times. Every time a change was made, for the better or worse, production improved. For example, when the rest periods were taken away, production still increased. Evidently, motivation was elevated with each situational change as the girls were reminded that someone was concerned with what they were doing. A variety of experiences and environmental modifications can remove boredom and induce attention and motivation.

The previous discussion indicates the social aspects of changes in the display. The physical layout, in terms of the placement and nature of cues, the means to obtain feedback, and the actual involvement of the learner (active or passive, guided or nonguided) is more fully documented in the literature as to effect on performance.

2. With regard to cues, the *visual* aspects of the task display can be modified in numerous ways. At initial levels of motor learning, the visual modality is apparently of prime importance in contributing to success. When visual, verbal, and kinesthetic modalities are compared for early importance in skill acquisition, the visual sense is usually found to be most relevant. Therefore anything the learner can contribute to the situation in already developed visual abilities (e.g., spatial orientation, depth perception, along with desirable specific modifications in the display) will be reflected in learning progress rates and achievement.

One of the problems a learner usually has when he confronts a new reasonably complex, learning task is that he attends to too many cues or aspects of the situation. He does not *selectively attend* to the most relevant ones without experience and/or guidance. A variety of cues can be distracting. Also, many tasks require a continual selective cue discrimination process. A basketball player in the midst of a fast break is bombarded with countless, ever-changing, potentially-influencing stimuli. The dribbling of the basketball, direction, awareness of the relative placement of opponents and teammates, the backboard, the rim, the spectators and noise, and the coach's screams constitute some major sources of input. Simultaneous attention to all these cues would obviously cause a breakdown in performance. High-level performance is demonstrated in part by concentration on the important cues of the moment, disregard for irrelevant ones, and perceptual awareness of possible immediate changes in the situation.

How does one reach that point in skill attainment? A good starting point is to examine the scope of the complex activity and to identify parts (mini-displays) of it that can be acquired separately. Returning to the athlete, he must go through stages of mastering the skills that contribute to overall success. Consequently he learns to dribble the ball so well that he can execute this act at a level not requiring conscious awareness. Shooting skills are perfected so that they are not disturbed by defensive maneuvers, off-balance positioning, crowd noise, and so on. Proficiency in mini-displays and combined display experience lead to overall competency.

A mini-display can be left as it is in the "real" situation or modified according to emphasized desirable cues.

Often certain visual cues are emphasized or artificial ones introduced to promote the learning of various skills. Sport examples of the artificial visual cues are found in (1) basketball, where spots or marks on the backboard provide specific points at which to aim for backboard shots; (2) archery, where sometimes the point-of-aim method is employed (a marker placed before the target is sighted upon); and (3) bowling, where the spot method of aiming is often used (a spot placed on the alley is aimed at instead of the pins).

Artificial visual cues are used either as an initial learning technique, to be disregarded later, or as a continual performance aid. Although research is scattered and inconclusive on the value of these techniques, it does appear that many of them are of value in fulfilling certain objectives. Theoretically analyzing the problem, *specific and precise* visual cues are easier to attend to than general vague ones. Furthermore, *nearer* cues should be easier to aim for than those more removed. However, not all learners will benefit equally from the identical cues in the same task.

Most of the work in the arrangement of displays can be found in the industrial and aviational psychology literature. Simplifying displays and rearranging them so that the perceptual information is more obvious and easier to attend to naturally results in greater insight into the task. In a study by Belbin, Belbin and Hill (1957), workers on complicated cloth weaves were subjected to special techniques of training. Essentially it was discovered that an inadequate number of visual cues were present in the task. By reconstructing the task so that the weaves were enlarged, the cues were made more visible. With improvement in performance, the display was once again placed into its original dimensions. The efficiency of this technique was demonstrated in the study as well as some subsequent research.

3. Besides the importance of cue arrangement in the display for understanding the task, *visual feedback* functions to motivate, reinforce, and direct behavior. In most tasks, a person can see how he has done. In other ones, visual feedback is withheld or distorted. As is the case with all forms of feedback, immediate and accurate returns are desirable. Visual task cues, when compared to verbal and kinesthetic ones under systems of withholding or emphasizing, have often been found to be the most beneficial to skill acquisition. Therefore, motor tasks should contain visual information on performance returns (seeing the results of one's operations) as well as clear and specific visual cues for information processing.

4. Finally, displays have been adapted from real situations to artificial ones. In many industrial, military, and vehicle operations tasks equipment is expensive and an element of danger may be present. Simulated equipment permits the training of large numbers of individuals who otherwise might not have the opportunity to learn. Devices are thus made specially to simulate to a certain extent the actual performance conditions or, perhaps, to prepare the individual for the actual task via emphasized audiovisual or tactile and kinesthetic cues.

These devices have been categorized according to their primary functions. A *trainer* is usually used as an aid in prompting cues necessary for the learning of a skill. Films or specially designed equipment help the learner to gain greater insight into the nature of the real task, although they generally do not simulate it. The purpose of a *simulator* is to provide simulated practice on the skill in the way it is to be generally performed. For instance, in many parts of the country it is impossible to play golf all year. However, it is possible to simulate realistic golfing conditions. Regulation woods, irons, and balls are used with this computerized apparatus, which simulates a golf course and true playing conditions. Golfers can improve their strokes, have the opportunity to play when outdoor weather does not permit it, and enjoy the competitiveness and reality of the golfing situation. Fake plane cockpits, automobile controls, and machinery displays may serve as simulators or trainers.

Practice Considerations

Not only can the display be manipulated to the benefit of the learner, but practice conditions may be specified as well. There are so many variables that a mere brief description is all that is possible in this chapter. Most of these considerations are "old-hat" to psychologists. That is, they have been investigated in different ways throughout the century, theories have arisen, and still disagreement exists on many crucial issues. Generally, research indicates the following:

1. A skill may be practiced continuously (*massed conditions*) or with rest pauses or interpolated skill learnings (*distributed practice*). For most skills, distributed practice exerts a more positive influence on performance than massed practice. This is evident, for although immediate skill acquisition is favored under distributed practice, tests of retention demonstrate little difference in performance between initially massed and distributed practice groups.
2. *Practice* alone is not sufficient for improvement. Without *knowledge of results, interest and attention, meaningfulness* of the task to the learner, *understanding of goals, intent* to learn, *readiness* to learn, and some degree of *relationship* of practice conditions to real conditions, practice for all practical purposes is wasted.
3. *Overlearning*, or practicing past a criterion, results in better retention of that which has been learned.
4. *Better learned skills* are less prone to be disrupted by manipulated environmental conditions. Experiences in varying instructional or stressful conditions will contribute to high levels of skill.
5. Reinforcement increases the probability that the desired act will occur. Random reinforcement is a more effective continual form of motivation than constant reinforcement.
6. Very high *motivation* impedes progress in complex tasks. Highest performance is attained by individuals with intermediate motivation or drive, and as tasks increase in complexity, individuals with moderate motivation do better. Evidently, there is an optimal motivational level for each task.
7. Reasonably *hard, specific, but attainable goals* produce better performance than easy goals or a general goal to do one's best.

8. Behavior is influenced by previous experiences. Greater resemblance between task elements, between their respective stimuli and responses, results in a greater amount of *positive transfer*. Transfer is influenced by such factors as amount of practice on the prior task, motivation to transfer skill, method of training, and intent of transfer.

Practice Conditions

The general practice considerations just mentioned, although based on research in the motor skills area, can also easily be applied to the learning of any matter. The list, of course, could be extended considerably. Let us examine at more depth some of the unique conditions associated with motor skills.

1. First of all, motor skills are usually *retained* better and longer than is other matter. It could be because there are less competing responses for them, they are overpracticed, and they are more important and meaningful to the learner. When the motor skills to be learned become more abstract and nonmeaningful, the retention curve resembles that of verbal or written matter.

2. In the area of *knowledge of results* (or feedback), various kinds have been identified. Information provided to the performer during and after his execution of an act, from internal and/or external sources, constitutes knowledge of results. Generally speaking, knowledge of one's performance outcomes may take two directions: as *action* feedback or *learning* feedback (Miller, 1953). Action feedback provides information on the adequacy of the individual's responses in the given situation but learning feedback goes a step further. It presumably enables the person to cope with the task more effectively. He actually learns how to adjust his responses in future similar situations.

The categories of knowledge of results (KR) enumerated by Holding (1965) are most useful in understanding the various dimensions of KR. In realistic situations, the learner is provided with some form of *intrinsic KR* with regard to his performance. Proprioceptive activity and the tactile senses inform him as to "feel" of the response. Visual feedback indicates accuracy in accomplishment. *Artificial KR*, also referred to as *augmented KR*, is incorporated into the learning situation when special cues are added. Comments by an outsider or supplementary artificial visual and kinesthetic cues may facilitate the early acquisition of a skill. There is danger, however, in the learner relying too heavily on augmented KR. In the real task, once artificial KR is removed, the effects may be quite detrimental. Therefore artificial information must be applied with caution, if it is to be used at all.

Verbal and nonverbal KR have been shown to improve skill acquisition. It was mentioned previously under the topic of display that a comparison of kinesthetic, visual, and verbal cues usually leads one to place least importance on verbal cues of the three avenues of information feedback. Nevertheless, verbal comments serve to motivate, direct, and reinforce actions. The nature of verbal KR must be viewed in relation to the learning level of the individual and the complexity of the task.

3. Various *guidance, demonstration,* and *instructional* techniques have been used in combination or alone in an attempt to improve the conditions under which one acquires motor skills. Verbal guidance is important for direction, although an early study and practical experience enables us to realize that too much talk or complex instructions will handicap learning in the initial stages. Manual guidance, or external manipulation of the passive learner on the part of the teacher, may prove beneficial. This procedure familiarizes the learner with appropriate responses. It activates the proprioceptors involved in the activity and provides the learner with a "feel" of the appropriate movement.

Demonstrations by experts, in person or on film, direct the learner to the desired objectives of the task. Seeing what is ultimately expected of the learner helps to yield mental images associated with motor performance. When objectives are clarified and specified, consequent attempts at attaining them become more purposeful and effective.

Instructional techniques encompass so many possibilities that it would be unreasonable to expect to do justice to them here. Nevertheless, the following include some of the variables of consequence in human performance.

Motion pictures, loopfilms, pictured representation of the task, video tape, tachistoscopes, and other visual aids have been employed in research with varying degrees of success. Musical accompaniment to the learning and performance of industrial tasks and athletic skills have also yielded inconclusive effects on relaxation, motivation, stimulation, rhythm development, or other specially designed purposes.

Whole and part techniques of instruction (practicing the task in its entirety or fractionating it for practice purposes) have reflected outcomes depending on the nature of the task. Efforts by Naylor and Briggs (1963) have helped to clarify the issue. They identify task complexity and task organization (interrelationship of parts) as dimensional considerations. One of the important conclusions is that tasks high in complexity and low in organization will be best favored under part-practice conditions and vice versa.

Mental rehearsal (conceptualization, self-verbalization, mental practice, covert practice, mental imagery) of a motor skill has been verified through substantial research findings as an aid in learning.

The teaching of mechanical or other principles prior to task learning in the hope of generalizable transfer to situations where they are applicable has sometimes proven to be an aid, and other times not. Consideration must be given to the learner's understanding and ability to apply these principles, among other factors.

In the area of bilateral transfer or cross-education, studies indicate the generalization effect of responses. For example, a limb trained in a task for learning or strength affects the performance of the "nonpracticed" corresponding limb. The sequence or order in which tasks are learned may effect total performance outcomes, as is the case with verbal material. Also on the topic of transfer, intratask difficulty has been investigated with conflicting results reported. Should individuals be taught a series of tasks leading from the simple to the most difficult or vice versa?

Because most motor skills require speed and accuracy, these variables are of special concern when training students. It would appear that the often employed process of slowing down responses in order to concentrate on initial accuracy is a questionable procedure if both speed and accuracy are equally contributing factors to proficiency. Practice should simulate actual conditions. Exceptions are made when the learner demonstrates a special need for a particular emphasis on one variable or the other.

One of the major broad issues is whether or not practice should proceed in a trial-and-error method or with errors minimized. Some believe the individual learns from his mistakes and that all possible responses, correct or incorrect, should be encouraged in a situation. Others uphold the Skinnerian approach in "shaping" behavior. Based on techniques employed in teaching machines or programmed texts, simple material is acquired first before the learner can go on to more complex endeavors. The learner cannot proceed until each step is mastered. Errors are omitted or at least minimized.

Researchers have compared traditional and programmed instructional differences in classroom settings where "academic" matter is learned. Usually, no performance distinctions are noted or else students subjected to programmed techniques fare better on written tests purported to measure content mastery. A much greater obstacle exists in attempting to design similar experiments in the psychomotor domain. How to program the learning of motor skills is a challenge to educators, trainers, and researchers. An attempt was made by Neuman and Singer (1968), who found little performance differences in beginning tennis players taught by traditional and programmed procedures. However, it was speculated that with a longer duration of the experimental period, the programmed method might have proved to be more effective.

Theoretically, the issue is whether errors or inappropriate responses will be beneficial in the learning process, or detrimental, as they may be perpetuated and stabilized. Logical retorts could be offered in favor of either stand. Although one might not believe in too rigid an approach in trying to omit errors, Skinner's (1968) suggestion to teach the learner to discriminate between good and bad form before embarking on the task sounds reasonable. What follows is automatic self-reinforcement when desired responses occur. Furthermore, he states that reinforcement should be made immediately contingent upon successful responses. With the current enthusiasm for programmed techniques for written matter and numerous books on operant conditioning (following Skinner) presently being published, such implications for motor learning should be seriously analyzed.

THE OBJECTIVE: PROFICIENCY

Although there may exist a number of objectives in the learning situation, one of the immediate or ultimate goals is the mastery of the task and the attainment of skill. Different standards of achievement are established, but essentially the most efficient and effective ways of reaching goals are sought. This implies a need to understand the nature of the task, the learner, the learning process, and learning conditions.

In the area of athletic proficiency, a number of factors contribute. They may generally be described as in Figure 2–3. Genetics, childhood experiences, personal goals, environmental influences, and other interactions lead to the state of "excellence." Ideally, to determine potentials for developing proficiency in any task, genetic factors, familial tendencies, past experiences, and the individual's personality would be reasonably understood

Figure 2–3. Foundational blocks toward achieving excellence in athletics.

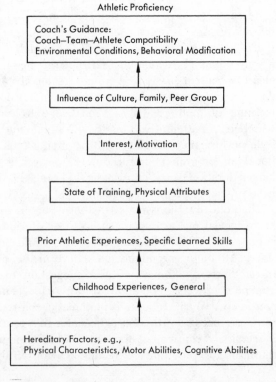

Figure   2–4.   Foundational   blocks   toward
achievement   in   any   psychomotor task.

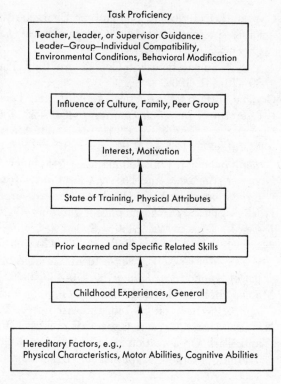

Task Proficiency

Teacher, Leader, or Supervisor Guidance:
Leader–Group–Individual Compatibility,
Environmental Conditions, Behavioral Modification

Influence of Culture, Family, Peer Group

Interest, Motivation

State of Training, Physical Attributes

Prior Learned and Specific Related Skills

Childhood Experiences, General

Hereditary Factors, e.g.,
Physical Characteristics, Motor Abilities, Cognitive Abilities

prior to training on a given task in a particular situation. General learning principles and specific considerations, with appropriate environmental modifications and instructional techniques, would then be utilized. The coach is thus the ultimate determiner of the athlete's productivity. Personal factors of the athletes are incorporated in the coach's plan in directing practice sessions. Figure 2–4 has been drawn to show parallels between the characteristics considered in Figure 2–3 for athletic proficiency and those underlying achievement in any vocational task. In this case, it is the teacher, leader, or supervisor who has the final responsibility in shaping the environment for best productivity.

REFERENCES

BEACH, FRANK A., and JULIAN JAYNES. "Effects of Early Experiences Upon the Behavior of Animals," *Psychological Bulletin,* 51:239–263, 1954.

BELBIN, E., R. M. BELBIN, and F. HILL. "A Comparison Between the Results of Three Different Methods of Operator Training," *Ergonomics,* 1:39–50, 1957.

CARTER, J. E. LINDSAY. "Somatotype Characteristics of Champion Athletes," Paper presented at the Anthropological Congress, Praha-Humpolec, Czechoslovakia, 1969.

_____. "Somatotypes of College Football Players," *Research Quarterly,* 39:476–481, 1968.

COOPER, LOWELL. "Athletics, Activity, and Personality: A Review of the Literature," *Research Quarterly,* 40:17–22, 1969.

FLEISHMAN, EDWIN A. "Structure and Measurement of Psychomotor Abilities," in Robert N. Singer (ed.), *The Psychomotor Domain: Movement Behavior.* Philadelphia: Lea & Febiger, 1972.

GODFREY, BARBARA, and NEWELL KEPHART. *Movement Patterns and Motor Education.* New York: Appleton-Century-Crofts, Inc., 1969.

HOLDING, DENNIS H. *Principles of Training.* Oxford: Pergamon Press, 1965.

JOHNSON, HARRY W. "Skill = Speed × Accuracy × Form × Adaptability," *Perceptual and Motor Skills,* 13:163–170, 1961.

KORMAN, ABRAHAM K. "Self-esteem Variable in Vocational Choice," *Journal of Applied Psychology,* 50:479–486, 1966.

MILLER, ROBERT B. *Handbook on Training and Training Equipment Design,* AFWADCTR 53–136, U.S. Air Force, Dayton, Ohio, 1953.

NAYLOR, JAMES C., and GEORGE E. BRIGGS. "Effects of Task Complexity and Task Organization on the Relative Efficiency of Part and Whole Training Methods," *Journal of Experimental Psychology,* 65:217–224, 1963.

NEUMAN, MILTON C., and ROBERT N. SINGER. "A Comparison of Traditional Versus Programed Methods of Learning Skills," *Research Quarterly,* 39:1044–1048, 1968.

OGILVIE, BRUCE C. "Psychological Consistencies of Competitors," *Journal of the American Medical Association,* 205:780–787, 1968.

SINGER, ROBERT N. "Physical Characteristic, Perceptual-Motor, and Intelligence Differences Between Third-Grade and Sixth-Grade Children," *Research Quarterly,* 40:803–811, 1969.

_____. "The Psychomotor Domain: General Considerations," in National Special Media Institutes, *The Psychomotor Domain: A Resource Book for Media Specialists.* Washington, D.C.: Gryphon House, 1972.

SKINNER, B. F. *The Technology of Teaching.* New York: Appleton-Century-Crofts, Inc., 1968.

WIENER, GERALD. "The Interaction Among Anxiety, Stress Instructions, and Difficulty," *Journal of Consulting Psychology,* 23:324–328, 1959.

3

FROM GENERAL
LEARNING THEORIES
TO MODELS OF
SKILL ACQUISITION

Psychologists during this entire century have been formulating and modifying theories of learning. Extensive research has been the basis for these theories as well as a means for questioning them. Although learning theories are far from fully developed and clearly defined, they, just as philosophies, can offer much to the physical educator. Familiarity with learning theories should encourage intellectual stimulation and thought, provide better understanding of learning phenomena and the laws regulating them, as well as promote a method of teaching consistent with scientific evidence. A theory provides the guidelines within which one may work. It suggests a frame of reference, a means of obtaining objectives. Basically, a theory deals with a particular area of knowledge in which large collections of facts and information are explained and interpreted in a limited number of words. It is an ordered and formal presentation of data. The theory explains relationships within the body of knowledge and permits deduction of new relationships or new facts.

Scientists interpret data, whereas theorists use these facts to formulate theories. Facts alone do not satisfy many individuals; hence, the need for a theory to organize the data into meaningful and unifying systems. Systems of laws explain the regularity of events surrounding us, and a theory integrates these laws. A few facts do not constitute a theory in themselves, for the quality and acceptability of a theory is determined by the scope of the scientific facts it represents.

Scientific inquiry, based on the search for the truth, serves as the foundation for theory formulation. With the accumulation of facts, laws are con-

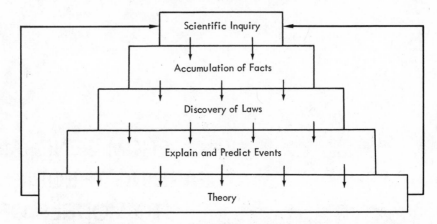

Figure 3–1.   Scientific inquiry leads to the development and formulation of a theory and in turn generates further inquiry and research.

structed that pertain to and govern isolated events. The explanation of many events allows us to interpret and predict behavior in given situations and the final result is a system of laws or theory. This state of transition in theory construction is depicted in Figure 3–1.

There are two levels in science: the observable, or empirical relationships, which contain most psychological research; and the theoretical, or inferred relationships. The implicit assumption in theory construction is that it is formed as a basis of scientific activity and stimulates further activity. The fruitfulness of theory is that it enables a person to deduce a large number of empirical relationships. Facts should support theory, which in turn should generate research and new hypotheses, resulting in a reformulation of theory.

VALUES AND CRITICISMS

Actually, theories should arise after the relevant variables have been studied extensively. Because it is debatable whether psychologists have met this responsibility, the noted psychologist B. F. Skinner (1965) questions whether we are ready for learning theory yet. He states that we may best understand learning from research not designated to test learning theories.

One of the major criticisms of earlier learning theories is that they attempted to explain all learning on the basis of fragmentary facts. Another problem arose and still persists that is associated with the conflicting results obtained with different learning materials when investigating certain learning phenomena. Theories have also presented problems in communication.

Some theories have been written in clear language whereas others are represented by sign language. Actually, theorists may talk about the same thing in different ways, a practice that serves to confuse the issue. Mathematical models and cybernetics are examples of sign language theories. Other variables have led some individuals to probe into the meaningfulness and practical application of theories.

Learning theories exhibit many questionable features, and these must be clarified before they will meet with more acceptance in education. The problem areas in the leading theories are as follows: (1) generalizations beyond actual scientific evidence; (2) selective use of facts, interpretation for convenience; (3) social problems not usually considered; (4) impractical and unrealistic application to everyday life; (5) too broad in scope; (6) disregard for developmental factors; and (7) too much concern for mass behavior rather than individual behavior.

Beyond their limitations, theories, if based on the scientific approach, serve a number of purposes. A scientific system meets the following criteria:

1. Material is presented in a systematic and orderly fashion. It is not a haphazard collection of statements or facts.
2. Material is essentially based on the most accurate scientific information present at the time. There is evidence or proof for existence of statements.
3. Material is such that it allows us to understand behavior better. It explains and predicts behavior in all its forms in relatively few principles.
4. Material is offered in a conceptual form. It allows a person to generalize over a series of related events as to expected occurrences.
5. Material is pertinent to given situations; it allows for predictions in these situations.
6. Material is of such a nature that it encourages further research.
7. Material is applicable to practical situations.

The last criterion, practical application, holds the greatest meaning for the average person. Unfortunately, as of the present time, it must be frankly stated that the present stage of theory development does not permit an easy transition from theory to practice. Theories disagree on certain points, although many theories are actually reconcilable on the larger issues. Theory can be helpful in governing teaching practices, but a number of problems still cannot be handled because of the lack of many well-established principles. Nevertheless, some theories appear to apply to certain situations better than others, and this chapter contains the highlights of particular theories as well as examples of potential applications to physical education. Unfortunately, because of the difficulties and dangers in applying psychological learning theory to physical education, very few articles on the topic exist in the literature (see, for example, Singer, 1966).

Modern theory no longer explains performance solely through simple conditioning. There is a tendency to go to miniature or mathematical systems in place of the broad theories, and thus to a more fine-grained analysis of particular areas of interest. Besides this, clinical and social psychologists, tired of seeing rats representing human behavior, have formulated their own theories to explain learning and behavior.

THEORIES

Of the many theories attempting to explain and predict learning and behavior, some have unique differences but have still managed to remain in existence in spite of the scrutiny of .researchers. Although earlier theories have usually been modified in later years because of certain contradictions from more controlled and extensive research, they should be studied for a number of reasons: (1) for their contribution toward bettering general teaching methods; (2) for the impetus to research that would at a later date uphold or refute these theories; (3) for an understanding of how theories have developed through the years and the direction in which they are going; and (4) for any possible direct application the educator might be able to make to his specific teaching situation.

At the beginning of this century, the behaviorists, led by Watson, battled against the idea that behavior was caused by preformed connections called instincts. Behavior, according to this group, was accounted for by stimulus-response conditioning. No other factors, including reinforcement, were thought to be important except that the S–R occur together (contiguity).

From this start the reinforcement theorists exerted great influence on education and psychology behind the leadership of Thorndike. The necessity of some form of reinforcement occurring to secure learning after the response was thus recognized. Many theories were formed in the 1930's and 1940's, from Gestalt (cognitive and field) theory, to Tolman's sign-learning theory, to Hull's drive-reduction theory, to Skinner's operant-conditioning theory. The earliest theories did not account for mentalistic actions (intervening variables) as they were based on the S–R conditioning made so famous by Pavlov and Watson. With more research and greater consideration for human as well as environmental conditions, theorists tended to become more aware of factors besides an S–R occurrence.

For convenience, the traditional theories have been classified as being *associative* (S–R) or cognitive (Gestalt). Some theorists believe in intervening variables occurring between the S–R, others do not. Still other theorists have combined elements from both types of theories. There is agreement that S–R theories are more exacting and lead to greater research, whereas cognitive theories are more general and elusive, emphasizing the perceptual and intellectual processes. Whereas the traditional behavioristic-type theories emphasize response, contiguity of stimulus-response, and reinforcement, other approaches to examining behavior are currently being intensively investigated. New language has been introduced; humans are compared to machines. Behavior is ascribed with sensory input channels as mechanisms for processing stimuli that are interacting with feedback from past experiences to affect responses. Some theory development stresses the temporal-expectancy mechanisms governing the timing of responses. There is a completely different vocabulary from the one we might be accustomed to. Let us briefly examine major theoretical approaches in studying behavior.

ASSOCIATION THEORIES

Thorndike's Laws

For many years Edward L. Thorndike (1931) was the leader in the formulation of learning theory. He was the forerunner in stimulus–response, or S–R, psychology of learning, and his theory has been termed *association theory, bond theory,* or *connectionism.*

These terms simply imply that there are no intervening ideas between the stimulus and response, that the connections are strengthened automatically when they occur. Thorndike gave much impetus to knowledge in the area of problem solving and contributed his famous laws of readiness, exercise, and effect. Even though many of his laws had to be revised in later years because of research findings that contradicted his theory, his laws are still acknowledged for their impact on education.

For example, his original *law of exercise* stated that during repetition the S–R connections were strengthened and the probability of the desired response was increased. However, studies have shown many instances where mere repetitions of an act were not enough to demonstrate learning. Thorndike modified his position and stated that for more effective learning the desired connection should be rewarded by praise, knowledge of right or wrong, food, or some other means.

The *law of effect* is another example of a famous Thorndike postulate, modified in his later years. Generally speaking, this law is concerned with what happens after an act. If the response is followed by a satisfier, i.e., it is pleasant and rewarding, the tendency is for that response to be strengthened. When an annoyer such as punishment occurs, the response is weakened. At first Thorndike felt that both conditions had an equal effect on the individual, but later he adjusted this law to give greater importance to satisfiers than annoyers. He was among the first to emphasize the value of reinforcement, for this is what the law of effect is concerned with.

Of interest to educators is Thorndike's belief that learning takes place through trial and error. In other words, the learner when faced with a problem does not suddenly perceive the solution, but rather gradually, through random behavior, learns the correct response. Motivation is extremely important, and the laws of readiness, exercise, and effect were utilized by Thorndike to explain how learning was promoted. With repeated responses, a problem is solved because of a diminishing of incorrect responses and a fixation of the correct response.

Instructors might consider the importance of reinforcement as well as acknowledge that practice alone does not make perfect; and, in addition, consider the readiness of the individual to learn. They might also observe whether their classes contain situations that are trial and error by nature. Are the learners being taught? Are there too many trials and too many errors before success is achieved? It will be interesting for the reader to note Skinner's thinking on this matter of learning and how he would "shape" behavior.

In some situations, behavior does seem to be random and thus of a trial-and-error nature. Instead of selecting this type of learning, it would seem wiser to replace chance success with directed strivings and an understanding of relations.

Another part of Thorndike's learning theory dealt with transfer, and it is referred to as the *identical-elements theory of transfer*. Basically, he states that all learning is specific and may appear to be general only because the new situations or acts contain elements similar to elements of old situations or acts. It is in this area of transfer that Thorndike made one of his most significant contributions to education. He attacked the then popular belief in the generalized theory of transfer (logic, memorization, reasoning, and the like transferred from specific school subjects to everyday life's experiences) and emphasized specific training and education for desired behavior.

It is important to remember that in trial-and-error theory the emphasis is on the learner and his motives, readiness, and needs. Also considered are the rewards and effects that "stamp in" or imprint the portions of a random activity that bring chance success. All parts are regarded singularly and as isolated. This emphasis is in contrast to Gestalt theory, as will be seen later. Finally, the theory stresses the importance of the need or intention to learn. To learn well, the learner must participate actively; to do that, he must have drive.

Hull's Drive Theory

Clark L. Hull (1943) developed many postulates and definitively described the effect of intervening variables on behavior. For example, Hull's theory of a performed act would be described by the symbols $S^{\dot{E}}R = (S^{H}R \times D \times K \times V) - ('R + S \; 'R) - S \; ^{\circ}R - S \; ^{L}R$. Interpreted in an over simplified manner, this means that the momentary affective reaction potential is equal to the number of reinforced trials × drive × incentive × intensity of stimulus − (reactive inhibition + conditioned inhibition) − the fluctuation of the individual from moment to moment − reaction threshold.

Hull's theory was one of the most formal, precise, and elaborate of all behaviorist theories to be propsed. He mathematically arrived at figures which were used as constants and helped to quantify his postulates. Hull talks mainly in terms of needs and drives, and his theory has been often referred to as a drive-reduction theory. His efforts encouraged much research and his most famous disciple, Spence, continued his work.

An important consideration of Hull's theory for skill instructors is the effect of mere practice on performance. Hull demonstrated that repetitious practice led to what he termed *inhibition,* a sort of depressant variable that is built up during nonreinforced trials and that offsets the strength of the performance. Reactive inhibition dissipates with rest. This would explain why a basketball player who attempts 100 consecutive foul shots would most likely perform best in the middle trials and worst near the termination of the trials. Yet the following day he is able to begin again at a greater skill level than he had at the end of the previous practice session. This is a perfect example of the effect of practice on performance, rather than on learning. Obviously the performance level of the participant can be raised or hindered, depending on the manner in which skills are practiced. However, the true extent of learning may be disguised.

Gagné's Motor Chaining Hypothesis

Many of the ideas of William James expressed in 1890 are incorporated in Robert Gagné's (1970) motor chaining model, one of the eight different types of learning he proposes. The model represents behavioristic, or S–R, thinking (or an open-loop approach as contrasted with Adam's closed-loop model). Central in any response chaining model is the concept of proprioceptive information as stimuli, functioning as any stimuli. Responses are, of course, made to stimuli. Perhaps the basic difference between closed-loop and open-loop theory is, in the words of Adams (1968, p. 499), that the latter holds that "proprioception is stimuli which can be the cues to which relatively long sequences of motor responses can be learned, and be secondary reinforcers. Closed-loop theory would say proprioceptive stimuli can guide well-learned responses because current proprioceptive stimuli from our movements are compared against their reference levels from past learning and are recognized as correct."

For Gagńe, chaining is the sequencing of a set of individual S–R's. Chainlike skills would include buttoning, tying, using scissors, throwing and catching balls, and countless other examples. In order for the complete act to be successful, each individual link (S–R) in the chain must be mastered. An example of chained behavior would be unlocking a door with a key. Each S–R or link, when completed, serves as the cue or stimulus for the next one until the act is terminated. For instance,

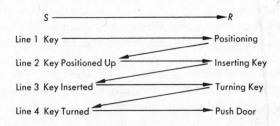

Verbal cues assist learner in the appropriate chaining of events. These cues can be provided by the person learning, for most likely the learner "talks to himself" as he initially learns the routine. Nonspoken, internally thought cues direct behavior for a while, but well-learned acts probably flow without any need for additional control. In order for chaining to be effectively demonstrated, certain conditions must be present. They are that

1. Each link should be fully learned. Because each line is related to the preceding one, any breakdown in one would probably hamper the entire activity.
2. Each link should be demonstrated in the proper order. This can be encouraged with proper cuing techniques, or else a backward chaining technique (starting from the last link and working backward) can be practiced.
3. Individual links should occur appropriately in time. The principle of contiguity is relevant here, for responses should be made upon receipt of the right stimuli. Delays in the performance of certain links might ruin the goal of the activity, for timing and association often lead to successful executions.
4. Sufficient repetitious practice should occur if the chain is to be well learned.
5. Reinforcement, in the form of successful completion of the act or terminal satisfaction, is necessary, otherwise chaining behavior is extinguished.

It should be emphasized that Gagné's motor chaining model is not really a theory for motor learning. Rather, it is one of the steps or tasks he proposes in the hierarchical development of cognitive behaviors. Nevertheless, there are a number of people who would view behavior as a series of discrete and related acts. Gagné's model serves to represent this viewpoint and to offer an alternative mode of looking at behavior.

Skinner's Operant Conditioning

Of all the psychologists prominent in the field of learning in this century, B. F. Skinner has had the most impact on our culture. He is interested not only in predicting behavior but also in controlling it—an idea objected to by many people.

Among other contributions, Skinner is the author of *Walden Two,* a novel on the development of a Utopian society made possible by controlling human behavior. He invented the Skinner Box, where animal behavior could be observed and data produced visually and made readily comprehensible. He developed the "baby box," an enclosed compartment in which the baby lives and the temperature is maintained. Skinner's promotion of the teaching machine has caused the method of programmed instruction to gain wide theoretical and practical acceptance and has had an enormous impact on industry and education.

Skinner's theory of operant conditioning contrasts with respondent conditioning (S–R standard theory, e.g., Pavlov's works). In respondent behavior, the subject has to respond in a certain way to a given stimulus. Standard laboratory experiments demonstrate such specific S–R connections, which are also called reflexes. Operant learning is reflected by behavior emitted by the organism instead of by external stimuli. Most human behavior is of the operant kind (for example, playing in sports), and Skinner is mainly concerned with responses instead of stimuli.

Perhaps Skinner's theory can best be represented by the widely used *shaping concept.* If there is a response desired and the possibility of occurrence is quite remote, the chance for success would increase if the act were reinforced in some way whenever it occurs. However, there is an alternate possibility. The desired response should be thought of as in the larger domain of behavior. Therefore reinforcement should be made for a general response in the direction of the desired response. This is the procedure followed by animal trainers.

For example, the desired response might be for a novice bowler to execute a four-step approach and roll a hook ball into the 1–3 pocket. He should be reinforced (verbal reward) increasingly as he approaches the ultimate goal. According to Skinner, the effect of reinforcement is extremely important. The bowler, instead of achieving the desired movement by chance in trial-and-error performance, is channeled into the correct groove through constant verbal encouragement. Concern would first be focused on the skill in the approach and ball release, later on accuracy and score.

The teaching machine apparently is an extension of this shaping concept and perhaps has great implications for educators. The teaching machine discourages any wrong response throughout the learning of a subject. It shapes learning from the simple to the complex. If a child is learning to read he must first know about forms. Matter becomes more complicated as the child learns about forms, letters, simple words, more complex words, and finally sentences. He is not permitted to continue until he has mastered all the information presented up to that point. He never has to go back because he was not permitted to learn errors along the way, as incorrect responses were rejected, requiring these responses to be repeated. Academic courses might be taught this way satisfactorily. The machines allow students to move at their own speed while the teacher assists those students having difficulties.

Then again, perhaps the entire concept of the teaching machine can be applied to the teaching of skills (Neuman and Singer, 1968). When learning a skill (hitting a tennis ball with a forehand stroke, for example), each element of the movement is taught and correctly executed before advancing to additional or more complex movements. The student learns the correct stance, the correct movement, and, in a stationary position, strikes a ball thrown from a machine. He does not begin hitting balls on the run until this act is performed successfully.

The tennis student learns to hit balls accurately when running sideward, then forward, then backward. It is important to remember that complex movements are building on simpler ones. No advancement is allowed until mastery is shown at a particular level of skill. No errors are accepted. Later on in the course there will be no competing responses (wrong and right) for only the right ones have been learned.

How many of us as youngsters learned a sport skill incorrectly? Trying to execute that skill in good form later in life presents a difficulty. The situation is a consequence of the effect of competing responses. Is it not easier to learn a skill correctly for the first time than to undo past error-filled experiences?

Skinner is a firm believer in the power of reinforcement in promoting learning, advocating the principle that a response followed by reinforcement increases the probability of the occurrence of that response. His classification of reinforcement manipulations, or the schedule of reinforcements—concerning *ratio* and *interval, fixed* or *variable*—has permitted a better understanding of reinforcement and the relative values of the different kinds. Skinner states that behavior is determined by law, not chance. Behavior is related to environmental manipulation, and as teachers we can manipulate the movement patterns of students. How much behavior and performance can and should be controlled is a matter of conjecture. Perhaps time, knowledge, and experience will tell.

EARLY COGNITIVE THEORY

The Gestalt movement had its greatest impact on American learning theories in the 1930's and is usually associated with the names of Max Wertheimer, Wolfgang Kohler, Kurt Koffka, and Kurt Lewin, all of whom fled to America from Hitler's Germany. The German word *gestalt* means "form" or "shape." Gestalt theory indicates that the learner perceives meaningful relationships in his environment and gains insight into the understanding and solving of problems.

Gestaltism was perhaps the earliest form of cognitive theory and developed as an alternative to behaviorism theory. Gestalt psychology came into prominence as educators, primarily because of the Dewey influence, were more concerned with the individual and his own ability to determine outcomes in a situation. To these educators, Thorndike was too mechanistic and his theory too laboratory oriented. Gestaltists believe that learning is not random and accidental, but instead, a result of organized, meaningful, and perceived experiences. The learner perceives the environment as a whole; he constantly reorganizes his experiences, and eventual insight is inevitable. The theory goes beyond the simple S–R explanation of learning. Whereas S–R theorists are concerned with overt behavior, the Gestalt theorist is more interested in the cognitive process, in what the learner understands. A greater understanding of Gestalt psychology may be obtained by reading *The Principles of Gestalt Psychology* by Koffka (1935).

Perhaps one of the greatest contributions of Gestalt theory to education is the concept of emphasizing the holistic manner of teaching material as contrasted to an atomistic relationship of parts. Putting it another way, the whole method of teaching would be advocated by Gestaltists over the part method.

Many instructors introduce a skill in its entirety first and then break it down into its components. The learner understands what he is attempting to achieve and constantly re-evaluates his experiences until finally he is able to put into action that which he perceives as being the desired act. He strives to make sense of each task, to search for significant relationships between tasks, until progressive change occurs through the discovery of insightful wholes. The learner, once he gains insight in shooting a basketball from 10 feet in front of the basket will be able to transpose this experience so that it leads to skill in shooting from 15 or 20 feet away from the basket. Basically, it is important to comprehend the Gestaltist belief that during practice changes go on within repetition, not as a result of repetition. Also, transfer from one skill to another takes place not because of identical elements, but because of similar patterns.

There are a number of cognitive theorists having a great impact today in education and society. With Gestalt theory in the past and a number of scholars distressed with behavioristic approaches, cognitive psychology and resulting theories are the "in thing" in many quarters. People such as Ausubel, Bruner, Estes, Mandler, and Atkinson, among others, are associated with the cognitive school of thought.

ASSOCIATION AND COGNITIVE THEORIES APPLIED TO SKILL LEARNING

A simple S–R explanation might be enough to describe the learning of motor skills. True, the stimulus, whether it be an isolated object or a particular situation, must be understood and controlled to a certain extent if the desired response is to be made. The relative complexity or simplicity of the stimulus and the type of response to be made are important considerations in the learning situation. Maintaining a constant uncomplicated stimulus is most necessary, especially during the early trials of learning a new skill.

The tennis instructor might avoid having beginning tennis players hit the ball back and forth in every manner and position conceivable hoping that they would learn the correct movements. Instead, each player would stand constantly in the same position on the court, the ball being tossed to him at the same rate of speed and distance from the body, and he would hit forehands over and over until he had mastered the technique somewhat. The stimulus situation is stable and relatively simple. It becomes more complex as player improvement necessitates the progressive change.

This method of teaching might not be the best nor the most practical. Perhaps, when a student learns a new skill, he should initially be allowed to explore, to feel his way about, to be permitted to practice the skill in a trial-and-error method. The student should have observed the ultimate desired skill via film or demonstration so as to have an idea what is expected of him. After some exploratory trials, a more controlled learning situation might be followed in which desired responses are shaped whenever possible. The learner who is in danger of fixating an error that is giving trouble must be interrupted and the significant parts isolated and related to the whole. By means of appropriately timed guidance and emphasis, the teacher can direct the conditioning process so that the proper cues are reacted to and the conditions reinforce the desired response.

These two opposing learning methods are concerned mainly with the stimulus environment. But the learning of one skill or all skills in tennis or any sport probably is determined by factors in addition to the isolated stimulus and response. The roles of perception, motivation, stress, and other variables relevant to learning must also be considered.

In order for the student to perceive, to structure his environment, past experiences relevant to the new skill to be learned are necessary to promote this process. Insight is best achieved when understanding is present. A foreign soccer player, unfamiliar with squash, may have great difficulty in learning this sport. The tennis player would probably have much greater success with squash because of similarities between these two sports. The tennis player perceives the object of the game, its movement, style, and manner. The soccer player questions the value of a sport enclosed by four walls, utilizing a racket and a small hard ball. He cannot conceive of this being a sport; he has trouble visualizing its goals, purposes, techniques, and strategy.

This does not mean that insight will not occur eventually. The point made here is that the teacher must consider the background of his students, their familiarity and past participation in various sports, in order to determine the success they will have learning a particular sport. The growth of skill is affected by the learner's perceptions of the relationship between cues. It is not enough to have the cues and their relations present. They must be interpreted and activate responses.

Gestalt and S–R theories have a basic difference in educational purpose and application. Whereas Gestaltists have demonstrated interest in the individual, his personality and cognitive processes, S–R theorists have attempted to develop learning principles after studying group behavior. In reality, the lack of ideal teacher–learner situations in education has encouraged many teachers to follow behaviorist practices. However, the revolt against mechanistic theory has been strong in education, and physical educators should be aware that both theories contain elements of merit. Drill and problem-solving approaches may both be employed effectively when teaching motor skills.

NEUROPHYSIOLOGICAL THEORY

Other theory encompasses neurophysiological mechanisms. For instance, D. O. Hebb has constructed a neurological model, consistent with neurological and psychological evidence. Hebb (1949) received great acclaim for his contributions, first enunciated in his book *Organization of*

Behavior. He blends associative and cognitive theories into a developmental model.

Hebb emphasized the role of neural action in learning and described changes resulting from maturational development and learning experience. It is no wonder that his theory has been widely accepted by developmental psychologists. Hebb suggests that as a result of experience, such structural changes as a closer physical contact of the neurons occur. Although not verifiable, he hypothesizes the growth of end bulbs on the dendrites as a result of learning which allow them to fire (eject impulses) more easily and more quickly. The closer proximity of the neurons at the synapse causes an act to be performed skillfully, for when something is well learned, the same neural pathways are constantly invoked (aroused and stirred up).

According to Hebb, maturation, or the result of aging, causes changes in the nerve cells and cell assemblies. A *cell assembly* is a series of neurons that provides a circular type of circuit for the nerve impulse. An effective response can only appear if all the assembly units are at a state of maturity. An elaboration of many cell assemblies has been termed a *phase sequence* by Hebb.

In comparing different species, he describes why (1) more complex tasks can be learned in higher species at maturity, (2) simple relationships are learned equally well in high and low species, and (3) the first things to be learned in the higher species are learned more slowly than in the lower species. The ratio of association (A) fibers to sensory (S) projection fibers in the brain determines the primary learning period. A longer learning period occurs when there are more A's than S's. A larger number of A's yield a larger number of alternate pathways, and a human organism demonstrates a tremendous variability in response and takes so long to learn (compared with lower animals) because of the many alternate pathways for different responses.

Hebb, in describing learning and synapse changes, calls his theory *a recruitment theory.* Neurons are recruited for a particular circuit and usually are not used in a competing circuit. This primary law of first come, first served, is used by Hebb in conjunction with the maturation and readiness of cell assemblies concept to explain what occurs during critical learning periods. Once past a critical period, the particular cell assemblies have to be re-recruited, a difficult task for the body. As was pointed out earlier in the book, it is important to determine the state of readiness to learn various skills. Practice prior to the optimal period is wasted, and later practice has to be concentrated in order to be effective. Indeed, it may never result in the same learning as practice that occurs during the critical learning period.

Hebb also handles the problem of injury to the nervous system in a plausible manner. With repeated stimulation, cells in the cell assemblies increase and overlay in function. Damage to a portion of the critical sensory area later in life has little effect because alternate routes, previously built up, can work to do the desired acts. Early brain damage is thus worse than later-in-life brain damage.

One weakness in Hebb's theory is that much of it is not experimentally verifiable. However, it does provide promise in handling that area of learning theory so often neglected by other theorists: growth and development. In particular, stages of readiness and effects of maturity and experience are confronted in Hebb's work. His approach to learning is unique and refreshing.

MATHEMATICAL STATISTICAL MODELS

It is probably evident in reviewing the theories of learning presented thus far that a great deal of precision is lacking in their formulation. The interest of mathematically oriented people in theory construction produced a new wave of statistical models about 1950. This emergence of more specific, restricted theories has solved many problems but created others.

The use of mathematical equations actually dates back to an earlier portion of this century with Thurstone as one of the primary contributors. There were attempts to deduce curves of learning mathematically, to fit the best curve to data already available. The learning function via the learning curve was analytically defined on the basis of simple probability theory and differential equations. How a measure of performance improved with practice was mathematically described.

Hull was the first proponent of formal theory, and he pioneered in mathematically translating certain learning phenomena. However, his primary concern was with mean performances, not other details of learning data. The efforts of Estes, Bush and Mosteller, and Miller and Frick have resulted in models successful in demonstrating the great impact of mathematics on psychology and learning. Models are not as complete as theories; they do not attempt to deal with all aspects of learning.

The present models predict the shape of learning curves, but have limited value because they cannot describe all learning situations. However, they do treat all that can be known from the data recorded. Most present efforts encompass the process of acquisition, of how something is learned in a choice situation. They try to answer the question of why a certain response is made in a given situation and how long it takes before the response is stabilized. Probability theory is important here and is applied to the stimulus population in a given situation. The number and nature of stimuli associated with an act is of central importance to model formulators such as Estes. The present mathematically inclined theorists are mainly disciples of such famous behaviorist theoreticians as Guthrie and Hull and have tended to fit their loosely stated postulates in precise statistical form. For instance, Frank Restle (1964), building on Guthrie's concept of one-trial learning, contends that learning is a single all-or-none event. Performance supposedly stabilizes that which has been learned. Equations are based on probabilities and the supposition is supported through mathematical deductions.

W. K. Estes (1959) has probably formulated the most widely accepted statistical model. He has constructed a probabilistic response model, and his approach is better understood when one realizes that his definition of learning is a systematic change in response probability. Unfortunately, most statistical models appear to describe the acquisition of verbal material better than motor-skill learning; and, indeed, the concern of most psychologists has been in the former area. Because of this, other models and theories have been developed, especially by those interested in industrial and military performance. Although the resultant works, information theory and feedback theory, are constructed on certain mathematical bases, their differences from statistical models entitle them to be analyzed as separate categories.

PERFORMANCE THEORIES

The dissatisfaction of industrial engineers and psychologists as well as military psychologists with the traditional theories of learning has been evidenced by the new approaches taken to theorize about the learning of motor skills. World War II brought about a great involvement of psychologists in assisting the armed forces to develop better training devices and techniques. The revolution in industry, advancing the most sophisticated of computer models, has promoted an interest in comparing machine methods of operation with human operational techniques. Industry as well as the military encourages the maximum efficiency on motor tasks.

These operational and theoretical factors have caused departure from theories geared mainly to describe verbal learning or rat performance to others intended to explain and predict human performance in the motor-skill area. It should be realized that the motor skills considered in these newer theories are of positioning or tracking type, not the athletic skills so familiar to physical educators. However, it does appear that physical education activities might have more in common with the military and industrial tasks than with verbal learning or rat performances.

The concept of *signal detection* or *vigilance*, which is involved with perceiving above threshold events during a period of time, is of interest to military personnel. After all, rare events are important to detect during war. A vigilance situation is very boring, because of infrequent signals and silence, and psychologists disagree as to why performance decrements occur during vigilance.

The practice of athletic skills to a high level of proficiency can often be repetitious and monotonous. Vigilance is the attentiveness of a subject and his capability of detecting changes in stimulus events during a lengthy period of observation. Although vigilance does not apply directly to the performance of most athletic skills, the concern for maintaining motivation and perceptibility is certainly there. Evidently, motivation and vigilance are decreased very little if (1) the task is complex, (2) knowledge of results is provided, (3) many cues are present, (4) the period of involvement contains some break or recess, and (5) the stimuli are of greater intensity and longer duration.

Theories have been developed to explain vigilance. Broadbent's (1958) filter theory, which is actually an attention theory, attempts to explain more than just performance decrements. He states that there is a *filter* at the entrance of the nervous system that permits some classes of stimuli to pass but not others. The priority of selection is given to stimuli that are physically intense, that are of greater biological importance, and that are novel. Decrements in performance are attributed to competition of the stimuli.

According to Broadbent, the person is selective in what he takes in from the environment. He absorbs some stimuli and leaves out others, and the selection varies from time to time. The uniqueness of signals or cues will result in attention; but after a long time period attention is lost with the absence of a unique signal. With practice on a task fewer cues are needed and the capacity required for performance is reduced, freeing neural mechanisms for other tasks.

Broadbent's theory in its entirety is actually a communication or information theory. The S–R approach of simply considering the presence or absence of particular stimuli is not satisfactory to information theorists. They feel that the whole ensemble of stimuli has to be considered as well as the coding of input into output. Patterns, situations, and temporal sequences of stimuli rather than simultaneous patterns are central to information theory. The evolvement of information theory and its characteristics are described somewhat later.

The *detection theory* (Swets, 1964) provides a framework for human behavior in a variety of perceptual tasks. Statistical decision theory has been translated into signal detection theory. The detection or perceptual process is based upon the observer's detection of the goal and the information he has about probabilities and values concerning it. He does not merely passively reflect environmental events, but makes a substantial contribution to what he perceives. A decision or detection process depends on the stimulus condition as well as the instructions to the observer.

The concept that a human samples stimuli from his environment in a predictable manner is, of course, relevant to military warfare and possibly to athletic competition. Theoretically, if you have sufficient data on an enemy or opponent, you can know his cut-off point for making a decision or executing an act. Thus far, though, the theory has had limited application for all types of behavior and has been restricted mainly to visual experiences.

This theory, which is concerned with the decision-making process, contradicts previous theories that advocated that stimuli were only detected where a certain threshold level was present. Perceptual decisions, which usually preclude motor acts, are based on rewards and expectancies according to the signal detection theory. In other words, a person makes a decision after considering his pay-offs from the possible outcomes of his responses as well as estimating the actual stimulus. Perhaps an example in sport will serve to demonstrate the theory in actual practice.

Consider the batter in a baseball game. He can perceive any pitch to be a strike or a ball, and in fact, the pitch may be a strike or a ball. There are two kinds of possible mistakes in this situation: (1) if the pitch is a strike and the batter does not swing, or (2) if the batter swings when a pitch is not a strike. The batter is actually faced with several alternatives. See Table 3–1:

TABLE 3–1.   THE DECISION-MAKING PROCESS AS FACED BY THE BASEBALL BATTER, SHOWING THE OUTCOME OF RESPONSES

Event	Swing	No-Swing
Strike	Possible hit	Possible strike out
Ball	Possible strike out or badly hit ball	Possible walk

The respondent has to weigh the possible pay-offs of his response in terms of rewards and penalties. Past experiences and the present situation will influence expectations and pay-offs. Although the precise methodology for predicting signal detection will not be discussed here, the signal detection theory does permit specific predictions on stimuli detection and behavioral responses.

CONTEMPORARY THEORIES AND MODELS

It perhaps does an injustice to those theories already presented and those to be discussed arbitrarily to classify them as "older" and "newer." There is no doubt that the older theories are in existence today, only modified to be more consistent with our latest knowledge. Many of the newer theories have their roots in traditionally accepted psychological laws and principles.

However, the theories described in this section have used different approaches to describe and predict behavior than the standard S–R and perceptually oriented theories. Their prominence and impact on education and skill learning may be traced back to the last twenty or so years, and therefore may be categorized as recent. One can readily perceive unique terminology, methodology, and intent of application, as well as some resemblance to the standard and well-known theories.

In recent years we have witnessed the development of models that are specific to motor-skill acquisition. Models, unlike theories, do not attempt to explain all kinds of behavior. Many models have sprung up from the concepts and theories already described. These developments are extremely exciting to those interested in motor skills, for they indicate that serious scholarly thought is being given to the skills area. Some are highly theoretical. Others appear to be quite practical and applied. The ones described here are not necessarily unique from each other or independent of previous efforts in theory and model construction. They do, however, reflect the latest thinking in regard to skill acquisition.

For convenience, these models are characterized in the following manner:

1. Associative—emphasis on stimulus-response relationships.
2. Cybernetic—emphasis on self-control and self-regulating mechanisms.
3. Information-processing—emphasis on perception, decision-making, and retrieval capabilities.
4. Adaptive—emphasis on higher-order and lower-order routines and man–computer analogies.
5. General descriptive—emphasis on general characteristics of skilled performance, usually for practical consideration.

Paul Fitts (1964) favors an approach to studying motor-skill learning that contains a framework of three types of theoretical models. These models have been termed by Fitts as *communication, control system,* and *adaptive system* models. Communication models deal mainly with information processing and coding; control system models, or servo-mechanisms, with feedback and the transfer function of input to output; and adaptive system models with memory, or information storage, and hierarchical processes, which handle different levels (higher-order, lower-order) of programs. Within the general framework of the composite of these three models it is easier to deal with more concepts and events associated with skill learning. For most of this century behaviorist theories tended to dominate the way scholars and laymen viewed learning and learning phenomena. During the 1940's, with the increased reliance on technological products, new approaches to study and behavior were introduced. Terminologies tended to represent these technological advancements. Many concepts applied in the area of technology were applied to human behavior. Cybernetic models were advanced to explain the way a person exhibits behavior and behavioral changes. Also advanced were information-processing models, which tended to describe the capabilities and limitations of man's perceptual, decision-making, and retrieval abilities. Both of these kinds of models, along with adaptive ones, are extremely popular today, especially in the skills area, where they appear to be more relevant in describing movement-oriented behaviors than do association and cognitive theories.

CYBERNETIC (CONTROL) MODELS

Association theory infers stimulus–response connections, fixed responses, and the formation of habits. According to this theoretical approach, repetition results in habits or preferred reactions. The interpretation of behavior is rather rigid. Through this theoretical approach it is difficult to explain adaptation and new or changed responses. Cybernetics explains human behavior as a flexible internal model and actions are dependent on flexibility and adaptability. The type of environmental feedback influences the adaptability of the response. Consequently, responses will vary.

The idea that man and machine might be compared on the basis of their activities and means of functioning is by no means new. However, it took the work of Norbert Wiener in 1948 to crystallize the relationship and formulate a new science: *cybernetics*. Cybernetics, formally defined, is the study of control processes and mechanisms in machines and human organisms. Human beings are thought of as complex machines. The theory in its original presentation as well as developments in this area is presented by Wiener (1961).

The cybernetic viewpoint considers biological evidence in terms of mathematical precision; it cuts across many disciplines, namely, biology, psychology, communication, engineering, mathematics, and physiology. Actually, the origin of the word *cybernetics* is Greek: it is based on *kybernetes*, meaning "steersman; one who operates a ship and has to keep it on course." The human brain and machine computer are both types of control systems, hence the descriptive term to describe and compare them. Cybernetics deals with control and communication, an analogy to which is the human and his behavior and the electronic transmission system and transmitted events. The digital computer contains an input and output system, a control, and a storage system. The human organism receives stimuli, responds, has a brain as a controlling process, and a storage system in the form of memory.

F. H. George's cybernetic theory (1962) provides a conceptual framework for experimental psychology. His easy-to-follow analysis of cybernetics as well as his proposed theory will well reward the interested reader. Cybernetic theory operates under the principle of feedback. *Feedback* occurs when some of the output is isolated and fed back into the machine as input. The principle of feedback is characteristic of all organisms and closed-loop control systems.

Another name for the feedback mechanism is *servomechanism*. A servosystem is a closed-loop control system operating on the principle of feedback. Information, in the form of errors, is sent back to the device controlling the output, the input is then modified, and the output is corrected. Every human organism must know or see his results; otherwise, he will not improve. In a skilled act, responses cause sensations from the proprioceptors, eyes, and other sense organs, and this feedback or knowledge of results tells the person how he is doing. When errors in movement are made, feedback informs us as to the nature and extent of the correction needed. Motor skills with which the physical educator are concerned may be thought of as continuous closed-loop system interactions between performance and the sensory effects of each performance. Activity is controlled and regulated by means of this sensory input.

Adaptive behavior is modified through experience. George (1965) suggests that feedback brings about simple adaptation whereas complete adaptation is the outcome of learning. The typical example of a device that operates on the principle of feedback is the thermostat. This is a self-controlling, self-regulating device, for temperature itself controls the change of temperature. When the temperature is low, the thermostat turns on the heating unit, causing the temperature to rise. When the temperature reaches the desired level, the thermostat turns off the unit, the temperature will eventually fall, and the process will be reversed. Room temperature is the input, furnace activity the output, and the difference between the thermostat and the room temperature is fed back into the system as input.

Theoretical approaches in cybernetics emphasize different areas of interest, but there is no doubt that these theorists display dissatisfaction with traditional learning theory. Namely, they question whether learning is a sequential process, conditioned by reinforced ideal responses to given stimuli. Of great concern to these theorists are the spatial and temporal factors in behavior, and more specifically, the feedback mechanism that affects temporal and spatial behavior.

The study of delayed sensory feedback and organized motion in man has led to what K. U. Smith (1962) terms a *neurogeometric theory*. This theory is formulated on the premise that all significant behavior is space-structured and based on the sensory feedback process. The main human factors in the learning and training of motions in man accordingly are not those of stimulus or reward reinforcement but of the dimensions and conditions of relative space displacement of the dynamic efferent–afferent interactions between sensory and motor system. The justification for studying sensory feedback lies in the fact that man, in most of his behavior, reacts to stimulus changes that are caused by his own actions. Sense receptors feed back information on his movements and provide a check on their precision.

Smith distinguishes sensory feedback which involves intrinsic body mechanisms, from reinforcement which is a part of external stimulus relationships. Learning situations, writes that author, are dependent on space-time patterns of motions. Basic bodily movements are space-structured, and learning is a process of establishing new spatial relationships in patterns of motion. The human organism is not a "victim" of his environment responding passively to environmental stimuli, but rather dynamically with the resultant activity processed in the form of feedback for control and guidance. Smith, with his interest in realistic learning problems and a concern for motor patterns and skills learned outside the laboratory, has demonstrated but another of the recent attempts to move away from an S–R viewpoint of learning, which he calls artificial and restricting to our acquisition of knowledge on the learning process.

Perhaps cybernetic theory in general has done more for promoting interest and providing information in motor-skill learning than any other type of theory. Some researchers are critical of research utilizing computer simulations of perceptual processes because it has been sensory as opposed to a sensorimotor or active process. They feel that the tasks are artificial. Although the point is a valid one, the relative contributions of this mode of research to other types in creating a new approach to analyzing the learning process certainly cannot be denied. In cybernetics, the descriptive phrase often referred to is closed-loop systems. That is, certain types of apparatus and apparently many kinds of human behaviors appear to be self-regulating. Adjustments are made according to the detection of discrepancies within the system. The primary mechanism is feedback, which encourages and permits detection and correction. Feedback, in this type of theory, refers to the sensory aftereffects of responding, when referring to humans. This information is then used by the learner to make adjustments in his behavior until the goal and behavior are matched.

By contrast, an open-loop system does not make adjustments, as no error regulator or feedback mechanism is postulated. Typically, association (S–R) theories might be thought of as open-loop systems. The control belief is in the external control over the learner, that adjustments made in the environment can influence the learner's actions. Such researchers as K. U. Smith at the University of Wisconsin and Jack Adams at the University of Illinois have attacked association theories as not appropriately describing motor behaviors as well as closed-loop models. Smith has written extensively for many years in this area and has undertaken much research to support his notions about cybernetic theory (e.g., see Smith, 1972). A theory that has produced a considerable amount of attention recently is Jack Adams's closed-loop theory of motor learning.

Adams's Closed-Loop Theory

The beginnings of the closed-loop theory were first presented in an article in the *Psychological Bulletin* (1968) and in the *Journal of Motor Behavior* in 1971.

Adams proposes a reference mechanism, a *perceptual trace*, as central to closed-loop theory. Previously executed movements leave a trace, or image, and are used by the learner to modify his next actions. Knowledge of results (KR) of the movement is compared to the trace. The sense of the movement (proprioception) is a major contributor to knowledge of results, and in turn to the perceptual trace. Other types of sense receptors, such as tactile and visual, are sources also. According to Adams, the perceptual trace is based upon response-produced feedback stimuli.

Early in learning, knowledge of results provided from someone else is extremely important, as the learner continually must adjust the trace accordingly. This stage has been termed the *verbal–motor stage*. The final stage, where skill is demonstrated at the highest levels, is referred to as the *motor stage*. When appropriate responses are continually made, knowledge of results reveals very little discrepancy with the perceptual trace. Essentially knowledge of results is ignored and the perceptual trace is strong. In principle, the description is likened to volitional or willed behavior that ultimately becomes automatic.

Whereas a perceptual trace serves as the comparison base for knowledge of results, especially in early learning, a *memory trace* is posited as the selector and initiator of a response. Although both fast and slow movements are initiated by a memory trace, the perceptual trace and KR are used in different ways. In a fast movement, the response is over before KR can be used effectively during its execution. The KR match with the perceptual trace occurs after the movement and is valuable for the adjustment in the next response, if an adjustment is appropriate. During slow continuous movements and in the verbal–motor stage, trace matches occur frequently and assist in correcting performance for its duration.

Many aspects of knowledge of results, e.g., delays and removals, are discussed by Adams. Presumably, without KR in the beginning stages of skill acquisition, the perceptual trace, which is weak, undergoes forgetting. As was mentioned previously, with high task proficiency additional learning occurs without KR and is based on internal information. To summarize, the most unique concepts in the closed-loop theory would be

1. The identification of two traces in motor learning: the memory trace and the perceptual trace.
2. The heavy reliance on peripheral rather than central feedback mechanisms, where a person's performance output is compared against a reference model for the detection of errors.
3. The association of error correction with the selection of a new memory trace that yields a response to match the perceptual trace.

Keele's Motor Program

The belief in a motor program that governs a sequence of movements, allowing this sequence to be executed without any peripheral feedback, is in conflict with closed-loop theory. Remember that within closed-loop theory no central mechanism of control was hypothesized. Yet it is always of interest to speculate how skilled motor performance occurs, especially when it is rapidly and accurately demonstrated in a short time period. Steven Keele (1968) believes that motor programs exist for predictable and well-learned events. Such a program would act to control the direction, extent, and speed of the movements.

Movements may be controlled with the use of visual feedback and/or kinesthetic feedback if these movements are slow enough. Keele indicates that movements may be preprogrammed in that the particular muscle fibers to be activated, the timing of their innervation, are determined prior to the actual movement. A motor program would exert control until a certain period of time has elapsed, at which point peripheral feedback could influence a change in the movements. Control in a series of well-established and predictable movements most likely shifts from visual and kinesthetic feedback to preprogrammed conditions. Preprogramming would suggest

1. Reduced necessity to attend to cues.
2. Increased anticipation of successive stimuli.
3. Faster possible movements.

Keele feels that the research evidence demonstrates that movement control may become internalized, and free from visual influence for briefly timed tasks. But can good performance be shown without kinesthetic feedback? Adams speculated that movement generated a trace and that timing is based on kinesthesis. Keele raises the question of "whether the individual movements within the series are initiated by feedback from the previous movement or whether kinesthesis is used only intermittently in correcting a motor program" (p. 398). He concludes that the ability to perform movements probably depends on a motor program, as well as other cues. To Keele, Adams's memory trace is a small-scale motor or movement program.

It only helps to select and initiate responses, not to monitor a long sequence of learned responses that might be executed in continuous activity.

Further elaborating upon these thoughts, Keele (1973) reports experiments that might support the notion that kinesthetic feedback functions in certain ways in skilled performance and yet not necessarily in directly controlling the patterning of movements. Insisting against a closed-loop theory (e.g., Adams) as well as the S–R chaining concept (e.g., Gagné's motor chaining hypothesis), Keele feels that the skilled performer constructs a motor program. In a sense, then, the activity that contains a series of predictable and perhaps rapidly executed movements is open-loop in nature. That is, feedback in this case does not and cannot monitor, control, or regulate such movements. It would appear, though, that feedback helps the learner to formulate motor programs. It also might initiate programs and help in the adjustment of movements in certain ways until the movements are well learned. In those movements where it is necessary continually to make adaptations and modifications to cues, learner attention is necessary for their correction. In predictable situations where corrections will not be necessary, attention and feedback need not operate for the governance of a sequence of movements.

A comparison of Keele's and Adams's models might lead us to accept the possibility that both types can indeed explain motor performance, especially if we categorize tasks as involving (1) extremely fast movements without time for the performer to benefit immediately from feedback, or (2) movement slow enough that feedback can assist the individual during task performance. Thus the availability of feedback during performance becomes the central issue between the two models.

Although it is true that Adams proposes the memory trace as an open-loop motor program, operating without feedback, it is not presented and developed to the extent that Keele considers movement control to occur. Adams suggests a motor program that only selects and stimulates a response. Keele would stress its function in controlling longer sequences of behavior as well. The position taken by the present author throughout this text is that the execution of different categories of tasks will contain commonalities for explanation purposes as well as distinctions. In the Keele–Adams issue, preprogrammed plans could conceivably operate in case (1) and closed-loop control in case (2). This point has been elaborated upon, with an extensive review of pertinent research, by Ronald Marteniuk and Eric Roy (1973).

Bernstein's Model

From a perspective different from many of those reported in the literature, N. Bernstein, the late renowned Russian physiologist, contributed many cybernetic and biomechanical notions about coordinated and skilled activ-

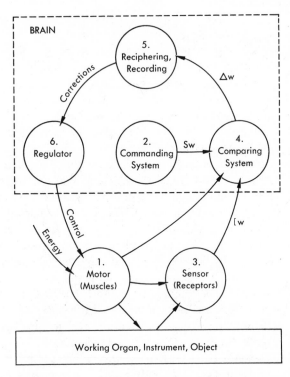

Figure 3–2. The simplest possible block diagram of an apparatus for the control of movements.

(1) *effector* (motor) activity, which is to be regulated along the given parameter;

(2) *a control element,* which conveys to the system in one way or another the *required value* of the parameter which is to be regulated;

(3) *a receptor* which perceives the *factual* course of the *value* of the parameter and signals it by some means to

(4) *a comparator device,* which perceives the discrepancy between the *factual* and *required* values with its magnitude and sign;

(5) *an apparatus* which encodes the data provided by the comparator device into correctional impulses which are transmitted by feedback linkages to

(6) *a regulator* which controls the function of the *effector* along the given parameter.

[From N. Bernstein, *The Coordination and Regulation of Movements* (Elmsford, N.Y.: Pergamon Press, 1967).]

ity. A number of his prominent papers have been translated in English (1967), although of special consideration here is the one entitled "Some Emergent Problems of the Regulation of Motor Acts." As in any cybernetic model, the emphasis in this one is on the role of feedback for control and self-regulation. Differences are apparent as well, however, for Bernstein incorporates a heavy emphasis of physiology. A main point of Bernstein's is that the performer's changing and adaptive movements cannot be described only by efferent impulses. The prominent role of afferent feedback (stimuli produced from responses) was recognized by Bernstein for controlled movement.

Those of us who deal with skilled movements are obviously concerned with the coordination of the appropriate parts. Man has an enormous number of "degrees of freedom" (Bernstein's term) that he can attain in successfully completing activities. There is great internal flexibility and elasticity. The more degrees of freedom one has in an activity, the more complicated the system and difficult to control it. Thus, to Bernstein, coordination in movement "is the process of mastering redundant degrees of freedom of the moving organ, in other words its conversion to a controllable system" (p. 127). It is the organization of control. Which mechanisms are involved and how in this process? Let us examine Figure 3–2.

This diagram is typical in cybernetic theory in that it reveals a closed-loop interaction among the mechanisms to describe coordinated movement. It is unusual in some respects in regard to terminology and the conceptual relationship and the framework presented. The acquisition of skill suggests the stabilization of movements. Bernstein uses the term *motor structure of movements* to mean style in the execution of sports skills. According to him,

the process of practice towards the achievement of new motor habits essentially consists in the gradual success of a search for optimal motor solutions to the appropriate problems. Because of this, practice, when properly undertaken, does not consist in repeating the *means of solution* of a motor problem time after time, but in the *process of solving* this problem again and again by techniques which we changed and perfected from repetition to repetition. It is already apparent here that, in many cases, practice is a particular type of repetition without repetition and that motor repetition, if this position is ignored, is merely mechanical repetition by rote, a method which has been discredited in pedagogy for some time [p. 134].

Interesting comments for sure! Through practice we learn how to solve problems. Bernstein emphasizes the intellectual involvement of the individual achieving skill, not only the response itself. These and other explanations of movements are to be found in his writings.

INFORMATION-PROCESSING
(COMMUNICATION) MODELS

Whereas the focus in cybernetic models is on the organization and control of behavior, on closed-loop feedback-controlled processes, on response-generated sensory cues and self-regulation stimulation through dynamic movement (see, for example, Smith, 1968), information-processing models tend to provide the framework for examining limitations of attention, perceptions, memory, and decision making in the performance of skills (for instance, Posner, 1966). The proficient execution of simple or complex movement behaviors is greatly dependent upon the organism's capacity for discriminating effectively among a variety of cues. The capacity of the learner to handle a number of cues, to transmit information at a fast rate, to retrieve derived information from memory stores is of interest to information processing theorists.

An understanding of man's capacity to attend to a number of stimuli simultaneously leads to applications that might be made for useful instructional techniques. This is also the case when we learn about limitations in one's ability to register and code information in storage as well as to retrieve it at the right time. The ability to anticipate events is an outstanding feature of the skilled performer. The skilled performer responds to the fewest possible cues and can think ahead and anticipate circumstances while executing acts as if in a programmed state. Attempts made by information-processing theorists have been most fruitful in describing variables of influence on skilled performances, and in more recent years, in suggesting the internal operations that occur during performance. Actually, many information-processing models are cybernetic as well, because self-control and regulation systems are considered. Often there is great difficulty in describing a model as strictly cybernetic or information processing, for the approaches to understanding and explaining skill learning overlap considerably.

Information theory, also called *communication theory*, is another example of probability theory serving as a basis for a model. Shannon and Weaver are given credit for its development in 1948 and their publication (1962) describes the formulation of the theory and contributions to it. This descriptive and quantitative theory has been used mainly for verbal learning, with visual displays, and tracking, but it is inviting to speculate on its application to gross motor skills, as Harry Kay did in 1957.

The capacity to transmit information is determined by assigning numbers to various magnitudes of stimuli. Uncertainty and information are terms used interchangeably, for the more uncertainty in a situation, the greater information can be of assistance. In other words, information removes or reduces uncertainty. George Miller (1956) compares variance

Figure 3–3.   The relationship of output to input.

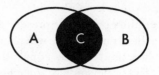

A–Input, Stimuli
B–Output, Response
C–Overlap, Transmitted Information

to amount of information, because greater variance indicates more uncertainty. In any communication system, man or machine, there is a great deal of variability of what goes in and what comes out. Naturally, a good system will show some relation between input and output. The amount of overlap between input and output, whether expressed as variance or amount of information, is illustrated in Figure 3–3. In this case, the relationship between input and output would not be great. Performance output would not be of a high caliber.

The binary digit (two possibilities—yes or no), a bit, is the unit used in the measurement of information and uncertainty. The object, then, is to determine the number of bits (the power to which 2 must be raised to equal the number of alternatives) needed to solve a particular problem. Fred Attneave (1959) presents the simple illustrative case where, of sixty-four square cells in a large square, the learner must guess the predesignated cell. With the formula $M = 2^H$, where M = number of alternatives and H = binary possibilities, we substitute $64 = 2^6$ for the example. Six questions, or six bits, are needed to find the cell in question. The first question might be if the cell is in the right thirty-two cells. (1) Yes. Is it in the upper half? (2) No. Is it in the right lower half? (3) Yes. In this line of questioning, the correct cell could be discovered in six statements. One bit of information is needed to make a decision between two alternatives, two between four alternatives, four between sixteen alternatives, and six bits for sixty-four alternatives.

We often talk about the uncertainty in stimuli and responses. How much can we remember in a given situation; how many objects or words can be recalled after a short exposure to them? Information transmission is another way of talking about accuracy, and Figure 3–4 serves to represent the information-processing system. The sensory processes encode the stimuli; they are then transmitted in the organism and decoded and translated

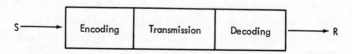

Figure 3–4.   Information processing.

into muscle movements. No mechanism is perfect; *noise* (amount of uncertainty) may be present anywhere—in the encoder, in the decoder, or in the transmission where processing takes place. Therefore it is a rarity when the response equals the stimuli.

Every person has a *channel capacity* above which information cannot be transmitted. This capacity can be determined by increasing the input and measuring it with the responses, for if the material can be handled accurately, there will be few errors. With too much of an increase, more errors are expected. Greater input results in increased output, to a point, as there is an asymptotic value for every channel. For example, it is not difficult to distinguish among a few tones. When more tones are presented to the observer, he will be able to recognize and distinguish a limited number of them.

It has been found that 2.5 bits is the average channel capacity of the typical listener making judgments in pitch. This number of bits is equal to about six alternatives. In other words, if an infinite number of alternate pitches are presented, the average listener can only distinguish about six of them. Other studies indicate that unidimensional judgments, for individual sensory attributes, 6.5 bits is average. More dimensions increase the total channel capacity but decrease accuracy for any particular variable. In this case the person makes rough judgments.

Studies have shown that an individual can increase the amount of information he can store. When the object is to memorize a series of numbers, more can be remembered if these numbers are recoded. If the channel capacity of the learner of motor activities could be determined, the appropriate amount of material would be taught to him at one time. Too much material would be wasted and not monitored, too little would not promote maximum use of the time allotted. The search for the number of bits that could be transferred in a motor-learning situation certainly is worthwhile.

One of the most valuable contributions of information theory has been the demonstration and analysis of stimulus selection, perception, and decision making in skilled performance. Previously in theory and research most emphasis was on the observation of the response alone. It is recommended that the reader examine Kay's (1957) article for a better understanding of the relationship of information theory and skilled performance.

One of the more interesting phenomena called to our attention by information-processing theorists concerns encoding, decoding, and retrieval processes. When learning written material, knowing how to "chunk" information is extremely important. That is, if we had to learn a serial listing of fifteen different numbers, progress would be slow indeed if we took each number one at a time and attempted to "chunk" them. By chunking, that is, grouping them perhaps in groups of two or three, learning, memory, and retrieval are vastly improved. We can only process so much material at one time. But we can improve upon the efficiency of the system. Instead of fifteen separate numbers to learn, chunking (a coding system) in groups of three results in five "numbers" to be acquired. Let us say that the list was as follows:

1 8 2 9 0 4 6 3 8 7 1 9 5 9 2

Try to memorize the list with each number in correct order, one by one. Now try chunking:

182 904 638 719 592

Easier? It should be. The point is that we can improve upon our learning when we know how to organize stimuli in a meaningful and more simplified way. Chunking and making associations help.

Welford's Model

One of the most impressive scholars in the area of skilled performance for many years has been A. T. Welford. He and his British colleagues have researched the human mechanisms that operate between sensory input and motor output, primarily using relatively simple laboratory tasks involving reaction time or the tracking of moving targets. His concept of these mechanisms as composing a "communication channel of limited capacity" indicates a desire to determine which mechanisms function, how, and with what restrictions during human performance.

Motor performance for Welford is illustrated in Figure 3–5. Of major interest is how a stimulus is perceived and translated into action, with special reference to short- and long-term storage systems in response control. He advocates (1) quantifiable behavioral theories and improved

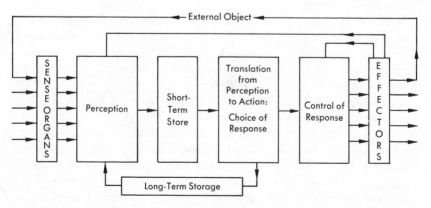

Figure 3–5.   Hypothetical block diagram of the human sensorimotor system. Only a few of the many feedback-loops which exist are shown. [From A. T. Welford, *Fundamentals of Skill* (London: Methuen & Co., 1968).]

metric techniques, (2) man–machine comparisons to study similar operations, (3) close ties between neurophysiology and psychology in the study of the sensorimotor chain of mechanism, and (4) the study of the components of complex behaviors within the appropriate broad and natural context.

Mathematical formula and logic, along with extensive data, have enabled Welford to propose "laws" about a person's channel capacities. One of the most famous of his proposals is the single-channel operation of the human organism. An examination of an individual's ability to process information presented simultaneously and to perform on dual tasks led Welford to postulate limitations in the channel capacity to attend to cues, process information, and respond effectively in a number of ongoing acts. Welford has also suggested a formula for predicting speed of arm movement as reflected by the nature and distance of the target and other variables. Space does not permit a summary of all of Welford's contributions to theory and research, but the reader might very well want to examine his last major and comprehensive book, *Fundamentals of Skill* (1968).

A person may not only recognize a stimulus but do something about it. For example, a subject makes one of several responses on a choice reaction time test. The single-channel hypothesis predicts that the central mechanisms can handle only one signal or set of signals at one time. If a second signal occurs right after a first signal, response to the second one takes longer, as it has to wait until the central mechanisms are free.

The three major mechanisms needed for information processing are the perceptual mechanism, which perceives and identifies information sent from the sense organs; translation mechanism, which decides the choice of action; and the effector mechanism, which coordinates and phases the action. Feedback from the central effector controls information in the perceptual–transmission process.

Welford theorizes that movement time is determined more by central processes controlling movement than by factors of muscular effort involved. Choice reaction time is primarily affected by the translation mechanism. Performance is limited by the phasing and coordinating movement of the central mechanism.

The writings of Welford and other scholars concerned with skill acquisition and motor performance tend to be in agreement on the fact that the learner responds to both external or situational demands, and internal (self-controlling and regulating) mechanisms that operate as response-produced stimuli. An understanding of how a person processes situational or response-induced information, with what capabilities and rapidity, suggests instructional techniques that would be favorable to the learner. Redundant information or too much information could be a waste of time or overtax the channel capacity. Too little information might result in inadequate cues and poor performance. It also might indicate that the channel capacity is not being used to its fullest advantage.

ADAPTIVE MODELS

Behavior can be viewed in terms of activities and subactivities. Certain enabling tasks must be mastered before higher-ordered ones can be displayed. The identification of all the activities, in sequential order, that must be performed if the goal is to be realized is an aspect of sound instructional procedures. Likewise, skilled behavior can be explored through the identification of higher- and lower-order operational processes. How these processes, or routines, exist in relation to each other and at different levels of skilled mastery is of interest to speculate about.

Assuming that man, like a computer, functions with higher-order (executive) programs or routines and subroutines or subprograms, it would appear logical that executive routines function with higher-order subroutines, at early levels of learning, but they "delegate" their authority to lower-order routines in later skill development, thus freeing the system to attend to other matters. As an example, the boy learning to play basketball for the first time concentrates very hard on dribbling the ball. There is little choice or chance for him to do anything else. Yet once the skill has been mastered, he apparently dribbles with very little conscious control over his activity and attends to such matters as previewing the game situation, thinking ahead about alternatives, and making decisions. The subroutines of control for dribbling have been freed, and other lower-order subroutines are activated for this role. Additional subroutines for other movements are operative. The executive program can be broadened, that is, contain a greater goal.

An executive program contains subroutines that often operate in sequential fashion. Many skills involve sequential activities that when properly timed, indicate optimal performance. In other words, the executive program, or master plan, contains the necessary subroutines when the act is well learned. In order for the executive program associated with serving the tennis ball with a twist to the opponent's backhand and rushing to the net to be operational, subroutines (parts of the executor) must already be mastered. Figure 3–6 presents a superficial and partial example of this discussion.

The subroutines can be observed as foundational building blocks, mastery at each level helping to insure goal realization. They can also be viewed in sequential format, with each one, from initial to terminal, contributing to the overall quality of the execution. The hierarchical concept of control over movement with increased skill helps to explain why certain acts, like walking, appear to occur as if automatic. There is little need for conscious control over routinized and well-learned responses. The executor program can be thought of as the plan, idea, or goal in a situation. The subroutines are the processes, e.g., movements, that enable the plan to be executed.

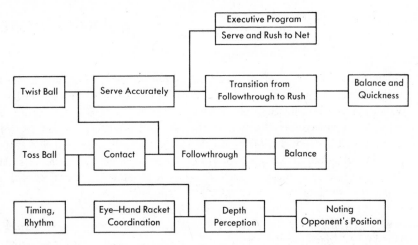

Figure 3–6.   The relationship of subroutines to the executive plan of serving the tennis ball with a twist and rushing to the net.

Some scholars have gone beyond the descriptive terminology of man–computer comparisons and have demonstrated the hierarchical functional organization of the nervous system. Jacques Paillard (1960), for instance, talks in terms of two levels of nervous systems structures as he analyzes skilled movements: the lower motor-neuron keyboard and the upper motor-neuron keyboard.

Skilled movement patterns depend upon the role of the corticomotor-neural tracts in conveying messages. The lower motor-neuron keyboard consist of the medulla and spinal cord, and directly controls peripherial activity. The upper motor-neuron keyboard is associated with critical involvement and represents highest-level control. The activities within and between these keyboards are integrated in a manner depending upon functional requirements. Less complex or better learned responses will be performed in a nonvolitional manner and be under control of the lower keyboard. Complex routines are under the control of the upper keyboard. The ability to perform highly skilled acts will depend upon the internal organization of the entire motor arrangement. The lower keyboard will respond accurately to the signals of the upper keyboard as a function of the upper keyboard as well as the close connection between the two boards. Using neurological terminology and concepts, Paillard's work attempts to identify executive programs and subroutines, discussing ways in which they work dependently and more or less independently.

Plans

The idea that a plan guides behavior is analogous to the notion of a program that guides a computer's operations. Dwelling heavily on cybernetic concepts, George Miller, Eugene Galanter, and Karl Pribram (1960) developed their notions about the hierarchical nature of the organization of behavior. The basis of human activity is what these authors term *plans*. A plan is conceived to be a hierarchy of instructions. More specifically, "A Plan is any hierarchial process in the organism that can control the order in which a sequence of operations is to be performed" (p. 16).

Instead of talking about reflex areas as the basic elements of behavior, Miller and his colleagues introduced the TOTE unit. A reflex is one of the many possibilities in a TOTE pattern, which is itself a feedback loop. TOTE refers to Test–Operate–Test–Exit. A simple TOTE unit would be as follows:

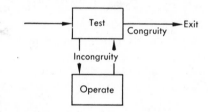

Where the person initiates an action and if his state and the one being tested for are congruous, it is satisfactorily completed. If they are incongruous the action would persist until incongruity vanishes. Feedback allows for comparison and testing, and it may be in the form of information or control. When a desirable state is achieved within the organism, the operations are satisfactorily performed and the test satisfied, the organism exits and moves on to the next activity or continues the activity with increased probability.

Complex plans of activities are hierarchies of TOTE units. The baseball batter will swing, make good contact with the ball, and run speedily to first base. The whole action appears like a simultaneous series of events, controlled by a single plan. It is composed of a number of distinct phases, each with its own plan, and in turn subplans and more subplans. The planning stage for any activity consists of constructing a number of alternative tests (plans for action), attempting to select one that appears to fulfill the desired outcome. The operational stage contains the execution of the plan, with both tests and operations (TOTE units).

When a learner attempts to master a skill, it is assumed he has some notion of what he is supposed to do and the proper strategies to follow. He has a plan. Complex tasks require integrated strategies which are developed through extensive practice. "The construction of these subplans enables a person to deal 'digitally' with an 'analogue' process" (p. 90). This comparison of human behavior to computers in the chapter entitled "Motor Skills and Habits" is most insightful. Digital operations are discrete—yes–no, on–off. Analogue devices produce qualitative data—variations, magnitudes, and so on. The skilled performer appears to make desirable operations to continuously varying input. The baseball pitch (speed, location) is responded to by a swing or no swing. The superb batter has learned how to translate this type of information like an analogue device because his plans are formulated symbolically and digitally. A hierarchy of learning–performance strategies occurs. In the words of Miller, Galanter, and Pribram, "planning at the higher levels looks like the sort of information processes we see in digital computers, whereas the execution of a Plan at the lowest levels looks like the sort of process we see in analogue computers" (p. 91). A motor vocabulary is established whereby well-learned skills are represented digitally. The authors feel that association and chaining theories inadequately describe this type of behavior. Skilled behavior is viewed as ongoing actions, directed toward specific situations that guide them. This behavior is organized hierarchically into units with varying levels of complexity.

GENERAL DESCRIPTIVE MODELS: NONSYSTEM

A number of models of skilled acquisition seem generally to describe involved processes, without leaning to cybernetic, associative, information-processing, or adaptive camps. Sometimes the approach is toward a specific aspect of performance, such as the ability to transfer previous experiences to present demands, or the quality of skills retention. An interesting model, leading to much research on the ability of subjects to perform generally well in a number of tasks versus specifically in task performance, was developed by Franklin Henry. The value of this model is the fruitfulness in encouraging research efforts in this area to support or challenge its basic tenants. It also contributes to the body of knowledge that should be known by the practitioner, with implications for understanding human performance probabilities and capabilities in a range of activities.

Cratty's model is a three-level approach at suggesting these categories of variables influencing learning and performance. He suggests a consideration for general human abilities and characteristics as well as task-specific factors as determiners of level of achievement. The Fitts–Posner model of skill acquisition indicates three stages of development in the learning process, going from learner helplessness and dependence on many sources of information to independence and self-controlling operations. It is particularly appealing as a general descriptive overview of the nature of the acquisition of skill, from initial performance level to the most proficient. Ann Gentile's flow model of the mechanisms involved in the early learning of skills is derived from research and theory with special direct applications to instruction. It is especially useful for teachers involved in instructing students how to learn skills.

In many respects, the models presented here and throughout this chapter are quite complementary to each other. In other words, similar operational mechanisms and processes are indicated within the models, although at times different terminologies are employed by the proposers. Emphasis differs at times. If research evidence in interpreted correctly, we should expect similarities among the models. On occasion, however, data may be interpreted in a variety of ways for the purpose of model construction, and incomplete data lead to alternative hypotheses.

Henry's Memory-Drum Theory

Under the memory-drum theory, an analysis of motor-skill performance is offered by Franklin Henry (1960). The method by which a human functions in motor performance is likened to a computer. That is, the computer contains stored programs, ready to function in a desired fashion upon the appropriate signal. Humans also store specific well-learned motor acts in the form of neural patterns in the higher centers of the nervous system. This *unconscious motor memory* is retained as programmed movements on a so-called *memory drum*. Particular stimuli cause the arousal of a neuro-motor center, resulting in the execution of an act.

A well-coordinated skill will be performed in an efficient manner because it has been stored on the drum. It can be initiated effortlessly at a point just above the unconscious level. A complicated less-learned or unlearned task is performed continuously at the conscious level in uncoordinated style. This is because of the lack of stored, organized information. An important concept of the theory is that *only* specific acts are stored, and even generally similar movement patterns will not correspond to the same program. Henry emphasizes this point through his research. One of his conclusions is, "Individual differences in speed of arm movement ability are predominantly specific to the type of movement that is made; there is only a relatively small amount of general ability to move the arm rapidly."

This statement summarizes an analysis of data obtained from subjects who performed three similar but distinct arm movements (Henry, 1960, p. 457). Low relationships from task to task were observed—individuals were not consistent on these tasks with regard to each other in their times to execute the prescribed movements. In other words, Henry did not find a general speed ability.

What these results indicate, in a practical situation, is that abilities to perform in the various sports are, perhaps, independent. Success in more than one skill is to be explained by means other than general abilities. Some plausible explanations are as follows. The person who is highly motivated to succeed, especially in sports, will put a greater effort into his undertakings. This general motivation may carry across many skill-learning situations. The athlete who has acquired skill and success in one sport may find himself struck with the urge to make a good showing of himself in other sports.

Secondly, past experiences are of tremendous import in determining present motor-performance status. When an individual performs a new skill well with little apparent practice, perhaps it is due to his previous experience in highly related movement patterns. Motor ability tests reflect the ability to achieve well in whatever items are included on these tests. Sports demand certain skills, and initial ease in demonstrating success in some sports is dependent on these developed skills. According to Henry, past experiences contributing to proficient acts are stored on the memory drum, ready to be unlocked and put into action when the situation demands. And, of course, the situation must be specifically related to the situation in which the skills were learned. Much research has been completed on the specificity–generality problems of motor performance, directly or indirectly by psychologists and physical educators. We will deal with this topic later in the text.

Cratty's Three-Level Theory

B. J. Cratty (1966) has incorporated in his theory three levels of factors that presumably influence learning and performance. Level 1 is represented by general factors in human performance, including level of aspiration, task persistence, and ability to analyze task mechanics. This level contains attributes associated with a wide range of motor tasks. Specific ability traits associated with success in motor performance are presented in level 2. Examples of these abilities are trunk strength, arm–leg speed, and extent flexibility. At the third and highest level are found factors specific to the given task, such as practice conditions, past experience, and the unique movement patterns required by the task. Figure 3–7 illustrates this theory.

Cratty calls for the teacher to be aware of all three levels and their interactional effects on skilled performance. General and specific factors operate in the learning of all tasks, according to Cratty's schematization. Although this is no doubt true, one might question why Cratty's second level, which he calls perceptual-motor ability traits, appears to include only abilities that are primarily physical in nature. In fact, the traits he lists have been proposed by E. A. Fleishman as representing physical proficiency.

There are other abilities that may account for performance levels, and

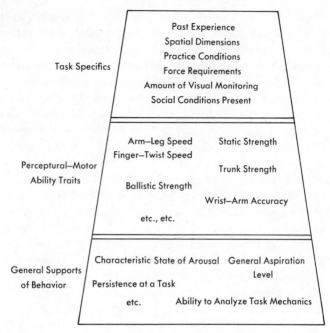

Figure 3–7. A theory of motor behavior. (From B. J. Cratty, "A Three-Factor Level Theory of Perceptual-Motor Behavior," *Quest,* 6:3–10, 1966.)

Fleishman has extensively researched these possibilities as well. From his experiments, he suggests eleven psychomotor factors (Fleishman, 1967) that seem to appear consistently in the tasks he utilizes. Their labels are manual dexterity, control precision, multilimb coordination, reaction time, arm–hand steadiness, wrist–finger speed, aiming, speed-of-arm movement, response orientation, finger dexterity, and rate control. Certainly psychomotor abilities should be considered along with physical proficiency measures as important to the attainment of skill.

The Fitts–Posner Model

Paul Fitts and Michael Posner (1967) have described skill learning as occurring in three phases. A recognition of these stages leads to more effective instructional techniques and an understanding of the learning process. The three phases are

Phase I. Early or Cognitive.

Phase II. Intermediate or Associative.

Phase III. Final or Autonomous.

In the earliest stages of skill learning, the cognitive, there is a heavy emphasis on the individual to understand directions, to attach verbal labels to movement responses. The thought processes are extremely active: What is the learner to do? How? The learner attends to the variety of cues that surround the situation and attempts to reduce the number that he must use. He has to use written directions, verbal instructions, and/or live models and translate this information into personally effective movements.

In the intermediate or associative stage, primary concern is for practice conditions and requirements. Which kind of training schedules should be followed? Should practice be continual or spaced with rests? Should the emphases be on speed, accuracy, or both in the execution of movements? Should the whole or part methods of practice be followed? The learner understands what he is supposed to do and now the concern is for these practice conditions that will most efficiently and effectively lead to proficiency.

The third and final stage according to Fitts and Posner would be the autonomous stage. The highest level of skill is demonstrated with a minimal amount of conscious involvement. Acts performed in this stage are almost impervious to distractions and stress. The basketball player dribbles the ball without attention to this activity; he is thinking ahead about the particular situation, where to go, whether and when to pass or shoot. The gymnast executes his routine with little attention to the specific details of the movements.

Thus the learner progresses from an extremely conscious role in the activity where verbalization and understanding is crucial and where, of course, the movements are quite crude and probably inappropriate on many occasions to an autonomous stage, where execution occurs with a minimal amount of conscious involvement. You might recognize these stages incorporated in the Jack Adams model.

Gentile's Model

In one of the few attempts to apply a skill acquisition model directly to teaching, A. M. Gentile (1972) has delicately balanced a concern for neurophysiological and psychological experimental data, behavioral concepts, and the relatively naive teacher of skills. This model is presented in Figure 3–8. It indicates the factors involved in the initial stage of skill acquisition, and the illustration is clear enough so that further discussion of it is probably not necessary.

Gentile differentiates closed and open skills (see Chapter 1) and suggests alternate teacher strategies for dealing with them. Two stages of skill development are suggested: (1) general ideas of the act and (2) fixation and diversification. Stage 1 would involve accomplishing a goal with a general movement pattern; stage 2 is associated with a particular level of skill. The demonstration of excellence in closed skills suggests a

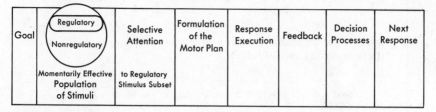

Goal	Regulatory / Nonregulatory	Selective Attention	Formulation of the Motor Plan	Response Execution	Feedback	Decision Processes	Next Response
	Momentarily Effective Population of Stimuli	to Regulatory Stimulus Subset					

Figure 3–8.   Initial stage of skill acquisition. (From A. M. Gentile, "A Working Model of Skill Acquisition with Application to Teaching," *Quest,* 17:3–23, 1972.)

fixation process; that is, the movement patterns become refined and stable. For open skills, a diversification of patterns must be mastered because situational cues vary easily and often unpredictably. In some respects, Gentile's model is an elaboration of the TOTE unit. The contrast of open and closed skills, in terms of their characteristics and appropriate learning strategies, represents a major contribution of Gentile's work.

GENERAL DESCRIPTIVE MODELS: SYSTEMS

Because we will be discussing systems and system models shortly, as well as formulating a particular model for the purpose of this book in examining motor learning, performance, and skilled behavior, there is little need to do the same here. Briefly, though, systems models for describing anything help to identify components and their functional relationships. A good systems model would include pertinent and major mechanisms that are involved in the acquisition of skill, if this is what we were interested in. The interdependence of these mechanisms would be illustrated in order that the entire flow of activity and the system could be appreciated. Systems models represent organized and scientific techniques for understanding how machines work, people function, and so on. Simplicity, clarity, and accuracy are characteristic of effective systems.

Whiting's Systems Model of Skilled Performance

One of the more popular models developed in recent years is attributed to H. T. A. Whiting (1969, 1972). His work is an excellent example of how a relatively simple systematic model can lead to greater perceptivity of the

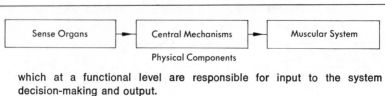

Physical Components

which at a functional level are responsible for input to the system decision-making and output.

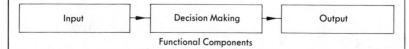

Functional Components

At a more complex level of analysis, the central mechanisms may be considered to carry out three major functions: perception, translation, and effector control.

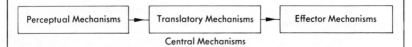

Central Mechanisms

These three subanalyses can be incorporated into a composite model:

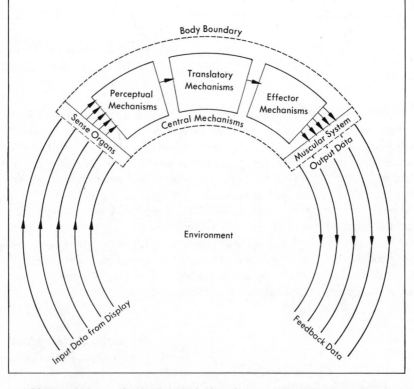

Figure 3–9. *Systems analysis of perceptual-motor perform-ance.* (From H. T. A. Whiting, "Overview of the Skill Learning Process," *Research Quarterly,* 43:266–294, 1972.)

relationships of subsystems associated with motor performance. Structural components, functional components, central mechanisms, and a composite are shown in Figure 3–9. The composite model reflects not only the general processes all persons use in performance, but the effects of individual differences in body capabilities and in environmental influences as well. As we have seen thus far, very few models have taken into account individual differences (such as those referred to in Chapter 2) and their effects on performance. The same is true for the effects of various practice conditions and environmental situations on learning and performance (also briefly alluded to in Chapter 2). Although Whiting is primarily interested in the similar mechanisms by which most individuals acquire skill, at least his model reflects factors influencing differential outcomes in human performance. But primarily, in the current British wave of thought, his model would fall into the information-processing category. The emphasis of Whiting's work has been directed to the neurophysiology and psychology of the central mechanisms involved in performance, on such factors as selective attention, arousal, and decision making.

Robb's Model

Although Margaret Robb describes her model as information processing, as we can see from Figure 3–10, her concepts for applying research and theory to instruction in the area of task analysis would fall into the learning systems category. Instructional systems suggest the heavy reliance on task analysis (see, for example, Singer and Dick, 1974). Given a particular

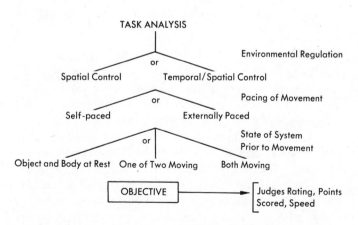

Figure 3–10. *Task classification approaches.* (From Margaret D. Robb, "Task Analysis: A Consideration for Teachers of Skills," *Research Quarterly*, 43:362–373, 1972.)

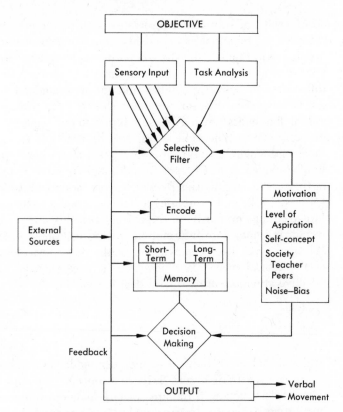

Figure 3–11. *A "working" model of information processing and skill acquisition.* (From Margaret D. Robb, "Task Analysis: A Consideration for Teachers of Skills," *Research Quarterly,* 43:362–373, 1972.)

task to be learned, the instructor (or the learner) should carefully analyze it to determine prerequisite and lower-level enabling learning activities (as suggested by Singer and Dick) and its characteristics. These characteristics suggest appropriate instructional learning strategies.

If we look at Figure 3–11, we note an attempt at task classification by Robb (1972), similar in a few respects to some notions advanced earlier in this book. The unique dimensions of a task, e.g., whether it is externally or self-paced, suggest specific considerations that should be made by and for the learner. In educational circles, systems approaches include the identification of relevant subsystems and interrelationships with regard to the tasks at hand, as well as task analysis that will help to identify the most appropriate and efficient learning techniques.

Therefore whether a task analysis consists of (1) the identification of hierarchical subtasks or (2) the composition of it, implications are great for improved instructional methodologies. Robb and Gentile have attempted, more than most model builders, to apply their materials directly to the teaching and learning of physical education skills. Furthermore, Robb's information-processing model is quite dynamic and descriptive of the skill-acquisition process. The subsystems identified by Robb, Whiting, and others will, along with other considerations, serve as the basis of this text.

AN OVERVIEW

As we have noticed, the trend in theory and model development has indicated less reliance on association (S–R) rules and more dependence on adaptive, communication, and control models to describe the nature of skill acquisition. Nevertheless each approach emphasizes factors that the other does not. Some are deeply embedded in behavioral science, highly dependent on experimental findings and intended to contribute to basic theory. Others are far more general and descriptive, with obvious ramifications for teachers and learners.

The purpose of this chapter was to discuss what theories and models of behavior are, how they contribute to our knowledge, and how they have been derived. With increased dissatisfaction with general learning approaches to explain processes involved in skilled acquisition, other ways of examining them were developed.

Although the distinction is often not clear, and the terms theory and model have been used interchangeably in the literature, theories have tended to be associated with more general attempts to explain more of behavior than have models. Models have usually been more restricted in scope and concentrated in effort. Conceptual trends in understanding behavior reveal that the popularity of general learning theories has given way to the much needed development of models that can more specifically deal with aspects or particular types of learning and performance.

Theories overlap or are distinguished by emphasis on unique features. For some scholars, it is the contiguity of the correct response to a given stimulus. Skinner, although nontheoretical in experimental procedures and admittedly against the notion of theories of learning, is associated with reinforcement, the Gestaltists with perception and cognition, and cybernetic theorists with feedback loops. Theories differ in vocabulary. Stimulus–response, input–output, reinforcement–feedback, and other terms serve to distinguish methods of analyzing the learning process.

Both generalized and specific theories have their respective values. The more general theories provide general laws of learning, consistent over a wide assortment of learning materials. Specific theories are concerned with particular situations and therefore apply to those unique problems associated within the area of interest more adequately. Learning theorists have been primarily interested in verbal learning and classroom methodology. More recent developments indicate trends in which dissatisfaction with traditional theories has resulted in the theories of communication and control. Although tracking studies are the basis for much in the formulation of these theories, at least tracking is a form of perceptual-motor behavior.

The efforts of the likes of K. U. Smith and Jack Adams in cybernetic and closed-loop approaches; A. T. Welford and Paul Fitts in mathematical, engineering, and information-processing concepts; Jacques Paillard and Miller, Galanter, and Pribram in adaptive models; Franklin Henry in performance abilities; and Ann Gentile, Margaret Robb, and H. T. A. Whiting in flow diagrams and systems models with special implications for teachers have represented recent trends in regard to understanding skilled behaviors. Optimism is higher than ever that scholarly activity will continue and increase during the next decade, providing more complete models dealing with skilled performance and learning processes.

The current emphasis on going beyond stimulus–response analysis, on identifying those intervening variables influencing performance, and on determining the relationships of mechanisms and processes is healthy and fruitful. Systematic approaches to model development clarify such considerations.

It needs to be reiterated, however, that the true value of theories and models lies in their ability to generate workable and testable hypotheses for research efforts. Naturally, the more data that are available to support a particular set of beliefs, the more acceptable the models or theories. They should stimulate and generate research. If not, much of their value is lost. Many of the theories and models presented in this chapter help us to understand behavior more adequately, but by the same token, a number of them are so vague and general that they cannot be proved wrong. They do not encourage specific testable research hypotheses. They contain much logic and interesting approaches to analyzing behavior but need to be laid out in a more specific and sophisticated fashion if they are truly to be meaningful for practical purposes and at the same time act as a stimulant for research efforts (e.g., to see if behavior can truly be predicted from them).

Adams's, Welford's, and Keele's models can be contrasted with Gentile's, Cratty's, and Robb's models, for instance, in the following way. The former three have been developed with scientific scrutiny and allow and encourage experimental work that might substantiate or refute their basic tenets. The latter three are more general and descriptive, and are geared primarily for the teacher of skills. In this perspective, each has an important role to play.

I have deliberately avoided taking a stand on evaluating the work of each approach described in this chapter. The purpose has been primarily to familiarize the reader with beginning and contemporary efforts in theory and model development. The brief overviews will hopefully accomplish this goal. The serious scholar will readily see that many of the conceptual approaches are quite elusive, evasive and general in their statements.

OTHER MODELS

To this point models have been described as prepared by various scholars that generally attempt to analyze skill acquisition and performance (1) similarly across all kinds of tasks, or (2) for a particular kind of task. In the latter case some models have been prepared to deal with continuous and fast adjustment movements. In the former case the same model is to describe mechanisms or processes involved in all motor performances.

It would seem logical that great similarities exist in the way we function in the learning and performing of a broad spectrum of learning tasks. The law of parsimony suggests that we look for commonalities and attempt to describe behaviors in their least common denominators. But inaccuracies occur in some cases and data are "forced" to fit the model. Why not different models for different task classifications? An attempt might lead to the systems models prepared for Figures 3–12 and 3–13. One model at-

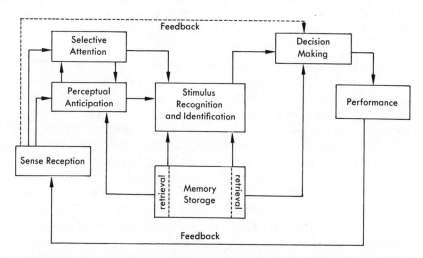

Figure 3–12. A closed-loop model for dynamic, continuous, and externally paced tasks. An indication of primary processes involved in performance. Feedback is used throughout task performances for control, regulation, and modification of movements upon situational demands.

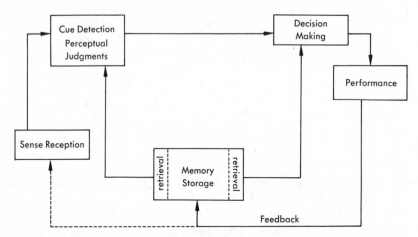

Figure 3–13.   An open-loop model for brief, self-paced tasks. Self-regulation through feedback does not occur at all, or can occur to a minimal extent.

tempts to describe the processes involved in performing a continuously performed, externally paced task. The other model describes a discrete, self-paced activity. It is conceivable that other models could be developed for other categories of tasks. However, these will suffice for the purposes of demonstrating similarities and dissimilarities among models that might be used to explain two different types of activities.

The externally paced continuous task requires constant selective attention to cues and perceptual anticipation of events. Perceptual anticipation includes the ideal intermix of arousal level and set for oncoming unpredictable cues. Selective attention and perceptual anticipation work together, leading to recognition and identification processes. Memory, the result of previous experiences in similar situations, influences the work all these processes do. Decision making must usually occur instantaneously. Based on situational analysis, previous experiences in similar situations (retrieved from the storage system), and the feedback of information as to the match of performance to the situation, movements are continuously adjusted for appropriate action. The memory storage contains stored movement programs, with executive and subordinate routines that correspond to them. The degree to which acts have been learned will be reflected by the ability to respond as instantaneously and accurately as the situation demands, with alternative plans ready and available for usage when necessary. The importance of feedback of ongoing performance as a performance regulator is underscored. Thus a closed-loop model seems quite appropriate here.

Yet success in self-paced, brief tasks appears to be governed by carefully made analyses of the situation, dependent upon similar factors as in the previously described task. There is much more time, however, to formulate the plan and to put it into action. Feedback in this case is in the form of knowledge of the results of performance rather than knowledge of on-going performance. As such, the act may be completed without any immediate function of feedback except as an additional source of stored matter to be called upon when the act is repeated. There are cases where feedback can be of some value in adjusting performance in these tasks. Think of the pitcher throwing the baseball or the tennis player hitting the serve. These are relatively discrete acts in which results of performance are of no value for those events but can be employed as useful information for subsequent events. But during these acts it is possible to respond to visual or proprioceptive cues that inform the performer to some extent whether movement adjustments are necessary. A particular plan for hitting the tennis ball may have to be modified upon recognition of a poorly tossed ball. While throwing the baseball, slight slippage should result in compensating movements so that the pitch is still effective. A more rapid and briefly timed movement is less apt to be regulated by feedback processes.

The emphasis on certain processes for excellence in performance in some activities and on other processes in other activities is useful information for the learner and the teacher. Practice situations should be geared to reflect these considerations.

REFERENCES

ADAMS, JACK A. "Response Feedback and Learning," *Psychological Bulletin*, 70:486–504, 1968.

————. "A Closed-Loop Theory of Motor Behavior," *Journal of Motor Behavior*, 3:111–149, 1971.

ATTNEAVE, FRED. *Applications of Information Theory to Psychology.* New York: Holt, Rinehart and Winston, Inc., 1959.

BERNSTEIN, N. *The Coordination and Regulation of Movements.* Elmsford, N.Y.: Pergamon Press, Inc., 1967.

BROADBENT, D. E. *Perception and Communication.* Elmsford, N.Y.: Pergamon Press, Inc., 1958.

CRATTY, BRYANT J. "A Three-Factor Level Theory of Perceptual-Motor Behavior," *Quest*, 6:3–10, 1966.

ESTES, W. K. "The Statistical Approach to Learning Theory," in Sigmund Koch (ed.), *Psychology: A Study of a Science*, Vol. II. New York: McGraw-Hill Book Company, 1959.

FITTS, PAUL M. "Perceptual-Motor Skill Learning," in Arthur W. Melton (ed.), *Categories of Human Learning.* New York: Academic Press, Inc., 1964.

————, and MICHAEL POSNER. *Human Performance*. Belmont, Calif.: Brooks/Cole Publishing Co., 1967.

FLEISHMAN, EDWIN A. "Development of a Behavior Taxonomy for Describing Human Tasks: A Correlational-Experimental Approach," *Journal of Applied Psychology*, 51:1–10, 1967.

GAGNÉ, ROBERT M. *The Conditions of Learning*. New York: Holt, Rinehart and Winston, Inc., 1970.

GENTILE, A. M. "A Working Model of Skill Acquisition with Application to Teaching," *Quest*, 17:3–23, 1972.

GEORGE, F. H. *The Brain as a Computer*. Elmsford, N.Y.: Pergamon Press, Inc., 1962.

————. *Cybernetics and Biology*. San Francisco: W. H. Freeman and Co., Publishers, 1965.

HEBB, D. O. *The Organization of Behavior*. New York: John Wiley & Sons, Inc., 1949.

HENRY, FRANKLIN M. "Increased Response Latency for Complicated Movements and a 'Memory Drum' Theory of Neuromotor Reaction," *Research Quarterly*, 31:448–458, 1960.

HULL, C. L. *Principles of Behavior*. New York: Appleton-Century-Crofts, Inc., 1943.

KAY, HARRY. "Information Theory in the Understanding of Skills," *Occupational Psychology*, 31:218–224, 1957.

KEELE, STEVEN W. "Movement Control in Skilled Motor Performance," *Psychological Bulletin*, 70:387–403, 1968.

————. *Attention and Human Performance*. Pacific Palisades, Calif.: Goodyear Publishing Co., 1973.

KOFFKA, K. *The Principles of Gestalt Psychology*. New York: Harcourt Brace Jovanovich, Inc., 1935.

MARTENIUK, RONALD G., and ERIC ROY. "Closed-Loop vs. Motor Programming Control in Motor Performance," paper presented at the Symposium of the North American Society for the Psychology of Sport and Physical Activity, Allerton Park, Ill., May 14–16, 1973.

MILLER, GEORGE A. "The Magical Number Seven, Plus or Minus Two: Some Limits on Our Capacity for Processing Information," *Psychological Review*, 63:81–97, 1956.

————, EUGENE GALANTER, and KARL H. PRIBRAM. *Plans and the Structure of Behavior*. New York: Holt, Rinehart and Winston, Inc., 1960.

NEUMAN, MILTON C., and ROBERT N. SINGER. "A Comparison of Traditional Versus Programed Methods of Learning Skills," *Research Quarterly*, 39:1044–1048, 1968.

PAILLARD, JACQUES. "The Patterning of Skilled Movement," in John Field (ed.), *Handbook of Physiology: Neurophysiology*, Vol. III. Baltimore: The Williams & Wilkins Co., 1960.

POSNER, MICHAEL I. "Components of Skilled Performance," *Science*, 152: 1712–1718, 1966.

RESTLE, FRANK. "The Relevance of Mathematical Models for Education," in Ernest R. Hilgard (ed.), *Theories of Learning and Instruction, Sixty-Third Yearbook of the National Society for the Study of Education.* Chicago: University of Chicago Press, 1964.

ROBB, MARGARET D. "Task Analysis: A Consideration for Teachers of Skills," *Research Quarterly,* 43:362–373, 1972.

SHANNON, CLAUDE E., and WARREN WEAVER. *The Mathematical Theory of Communication,* Urbana: University of Illinois Press, 1962.

SINGER, ROBERT N. "Learning Theory as Applied to Physical Education," *National College Physical Education Association for Men Proceedings,* 69:59–66, 1966.

————, and WALTER DICK. *Teaching Physical Education: A Systems Approach.* Boston: Houghton Mifflin Company, 1974.

SKINNER, B. F. "Are Theories of Learning Necessary?" in Henry Goldstein, David L. Krantz, and Jack D. Rains (eds.), *Controversial Issues in Learning.* New York: Appleton-Century-Crofts, Inc., 1965.

SMITH, K. U. "Cybernetic Foundations of Physical Behavioral Science," *Quest,* 8:26–82, 1968.

————. *Delayed Sensory Feedback and Behavior.* Philadelphia: W. B. Saunders Company, 1962.

————. "Cybernetic Psychology," in Robert N. Singer (ed.), *The Psychomotor Domain: Movement Behavior.* Philadelphia: Lea & Febiger, 1972.

SWETS, JOHN A. (ed.). *Signal Detection and Recognition by Human Observers.* New York: John Wiley & Sons, Inc., 1964.

THORNDIKE, E. L. *Human Learning.* New York: Appleton-Century-Crofts, Inc., 1931.

WELFORD, A. T. *Fundamentals of Skill.* London: Methuen & Co., Ltd., 1968.

WHITING, H. T. A. *Acquiring Ball Skill: A Psychological Interpretation.* London: G. Bell & Sons, Ltd., 1969.

————. "Overview of the Skill Learning Process," *Research Quarterly,* 43:266–294, 1972.

WIENER, NORBERT. *Cybernetics.* New York: The M.I.T. Press and John Wiley & Sons, Inc., 1961.

4

DESIGN AND
MEASUREMENT

In order to derive a scientific body of knowledge about behavior, data must be collected. This information should not be casually expressed but rather recorded with care and in detail. Research, conducted through a scientific method of analysis, provides a reasonably objective means of answering questions about animal and human behavior. Problems are studied and procedures designed for their solution. Inferences to large numbers (a specified population) are often made from the results of data collected on sample subjects.

Most of the research reported in this book will be experimental in nature. Investigations in the motor-learning area tend to be experimental, for researchers are attempting to determine antecedent and consequential relationships. What kinds of effects will a particular condition produce on behavior? If we were to help learners set reasonably high but attainable goals for themselves before and during the practice of a task, will performances be any more proficient than when learners practice without such assistance? Experimental projects would help to solve this issue. Motor-learning specialists often compare different treatments (situational modifications), as administered through practice, in their quest to ascertain best practice or training techniques.

They also look at relationships among variables. One example of a study of interest might be the relationship between the age of a person and his ability to learn a moderately difficult motor task. How about the association of personality traits, intelligence scores, and motor performance? Further study might be done on the learning process itself; e.g., the generality of rates of learning across a variety of learning tasks, the relationship of initial level of success with later task proficiency, or abilities underlying achievement in particular activities at different stages of practice.

Motor behaviors can be observed under artificial and manipulated conditions as well as in natural situations. The research laboratory or the gymnasium may provide the appropriate data for the problem of concern. Regardless of the task used, variables of interest, and the setting, the scores of the subjects are typically recorded and analyzed in some way so as to reach conclusions with regard to the stated problem. Thus scores—how they are obtained and how they are used—become the essence of the report. In learning experiments where the effects of some variable on learning are to be determined, a crucial decision must be made with regard to a score that constitutes learning. In other words, how is this score to be derived?

DECISIONS
IN THE MEASUREMENT
OF LEARNING

Although scientifically accepted methods for the study of motor learning can easily be decided upon on occasion, certain procedural aspects require careful deliberation, as the consequences of these decisions might be more dramatic than perceived at a superficial level. With this thought in mind, let us identify problems and decisions in the experimentation of motor behaviors. This discussion should help you to recognize and to be sensitive to these problems, aiding in the interpretation of research findings or the undertaking of research. Major decisions must be made in the following areas:

1. Selection of appropriate learning tasks.
2. Determination of number of practice trials.
3. Selection of dependent variable (what and how to measure).
4. Determination of a learning score or scores.

Selection of Appropriate
Learning Tasks

If the investigator wants to study the learning process or the effect of situational changes on the acquisition of skill, the typical concern is for subjects who are naive to the task that will be practiced and learned. Saying it another way, the task should be novel, or new, to the subjects. Because there is difficulty in finding real-life activities that are novel to a group of subjects, the usual recourse is to select an artificial laboratory task or a contrived athletic task for a study.

Once a nonfamiliar task has been selected (assuming this is desirable), the investigator must consider its degree of complexity. Complexity will be a function of input demands (the number of cues needed to be attended to and under what conditions), processing demands (speed to initiate response), and response demands (number of movements, refinement of movement, and so on). The nature of the learning phenomenon to be studied will suggest the type of task that might be used. As the reader will see, many of the tasks employed by motor-learning researchers are of the laboratory variety, and relatively simple to perform at that. That is, they are easy relative to the dimensions of athletic activities, like learning to fence, to play tennis, or to perform gymnastic routines. The laboratory tasks may be fairly well learned after ten or twenty trials, whereas it takes years to become a good tennis player. However, more simple tasks often permit the study of a learning variable(s) if taught in purer settings under good control, and in a brief time span.

If the task is learned too quickly, however, it is probable that learning variables of interest might be camouflaged. The effects of an imposed condition might go unnoticed. For instance, if one selected task is simple to learn well and we want to study the differential effects of reward and punishment on task proficiency, the two groups might not show any difference in performance, primarily because of the simplicity of the task. A related problem is that where a criterion of task mastery is predetermined and turns out to be unrealistically low, or easy to attain.

All things being equal, the more desirable learning task is one that can be measured with a minimal amount of interference and bias. Response measures are never pure. The challenge is to obtain measures that reveal "true" scores. Disturbing environmental cues, subjective experimenter observations, direct experimenter interactions with the subject, and noncalibrated and nonchecked-out equipment will produce artifacts contributing to nonvalid data. Finally, a task should be appropriate for the maturational level of the subjects. Inability to perform because of immaturity of the nervous system and the musculature would certainly be a factor contributing to confounded data.

Learning Tasks

The most commonly used laboratory tasks in motor-learning research, reported in one form or another, are pursuit rotors, star-tracing tasks, positioning tasks, and stabilometers. They are invariably novel to the subjects and yet can be acquired to a reasonable degree in a relatively short time. A wide range of learning phenomena can be studied with these tasks and implications are made about motor behavior activities. A pursuit rotor, illustrated in Figure 4–1, is composed of a moving turntable on which a small disc must be pursued by the subject with a stylus. Time on target is usually recorded to 0.01 of a second. The star-tracing task (Figure 4–2)

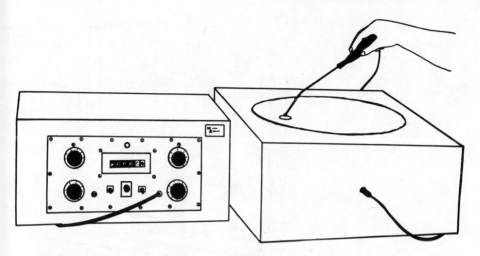

Figure 4–1. A pursuit rotor with a control unit with which test periods and rest periods can be preset.

requires a subject to trace the pattern with a stylus as quickly as possible but while making a minimum of errors (an error being determined by the stylus touching the side of the tract). Viewing the mirror instead of the actual pattern makes it a reversal task and increases difficulty.

Positioning tasks make demands on the subject to replicate predetermined movement speeds and distances. Judgment and timing are important. A stabilometer is a movable platform that the subject attempts to stabilize. During a prescribed testing period, he must keep the platform as horizontal as he can. This balancing task is shown in Figure 4–3, and balance within the designated range is usually timed to 0.01 second.

Creative investigators have devised other kinds of laboratory tasks as well as field tasks. Furthermore, far more complex tasks have also been reported in the literature. For instance, Figure 4–4 indicates the complex coordinator, an apparatus that demands the appropriate timing of leg and hand responses to specific cues. Task difficulty increases when investigators develop tasks that contain a variety of cues that require complex decision making and a variety of response possibilities from which the subject must select the correct ones.

Another type of task frequently found in the literature is one involving reaction time and/or speed of limb movement. Many situational variables can be manipulated to determine how an individual processes information and responds. Although the tasks are relatively simple, much of what we know about human behavior has been determined from data collected in reaction-time experiments. A choice reaction-time task and timer are illustrated in Figure 4–5.

An experiment must be of long enough duration, in terms of trials, experi-

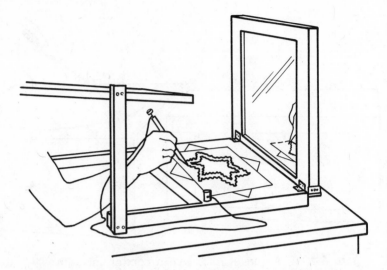

Figure 4–2.   Star-tracing task. The star is traced as accurately as possible with the subject viewing it in the mirror. (From R. Fulton, "Speed and Accuracy in Learning Movements," *Archives of Psychology*, No. 300, 1945.)

ences, or days, for behavior to be altered due to specially designed practice examining the effects of manipulated practice conditions. If too much practice is provided, it is equally possible that special treatment effects will not be revealed when a treatment group of subjects is compared to a control group of subjects. More practice does not necessarily result in better data. Careful consideration must be given to the purpose of the study, and along with a review of previous research completed in related areas, decisions can be arrived at in a meaningful and logical way.

Sometimes the question of warm-up trials is an issue. Should any warm-up, or task-familiarization, experience be given to the subjects? Once again, the answer is not simple. If the task is very unusual, there may be good reason for allowing a few task-familiarization trials. Sometimes warm-up trials can confound data, especially if the task is rather easy. Once again, the purpose of the study must be reviewed critically, the advantages and disadvantages of warm-up trials evaluated carefully, and decisions made accordingly.

Motor and Sensory Measurements

The instruments and tasks described in the preceding section, as well as many others, have been used for the experimental analysis of behavioral

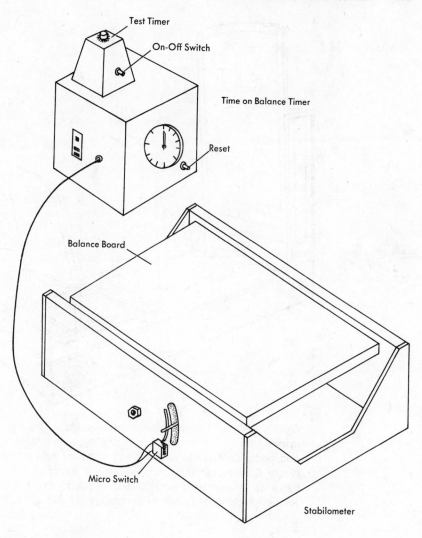

Test Timer

On-Off Switch

Time on Balance Timer

Reset

Balance Board

Micro Switch

Stabilometer

(Stabilometer and Timer Not to Scale)

Figure 4–3. A constructed stabilometer.

change, or learning. Yet there may be other purposes for conducting research in the motor-learning area. Specific motor behaviors may be of
interest, either for the establishment of norms or to determine the effects
of such factors as fatigue or drugs on them. Sensory measurements, on the
other hand, are primarily used to detect phenomena associated with perceiving physical stimuli (psychophysics). The level of functioning of sense
organs may be related to proficiency in various motor-skill endeavors.

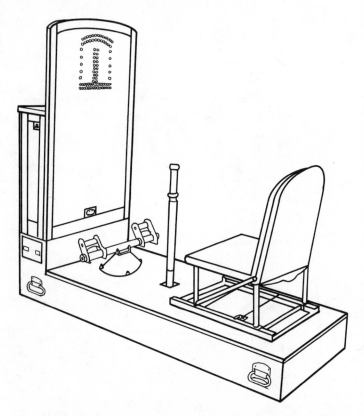

Figure 4–4.   Complex coordination test. The subject is required to make complex motor adjustments of stick and pedal controls in response to stimulus light patterns. (From E. A. Fleishman, "A Comparative Study of Aptitude Patterns in Unskilled and Skilled Psychomotor Performances," *Journal of Applied Psychology, 41:263–272,* 1957.)

Instruments to evaluate motor responses or performance of the sense organs are found in many motor-learning laboratories. A dynamometer measures exerted force, or static strength. There is equipment to measure hand steadiness or body sway. Pieces of equipment used in the testing of learning changes can also be used for measuring motor responses, e.g., pursuit rotors for hand–eye coordination and stabilometers for balance.

In regard to sensory measurements, there are apparatuses to analyze depth perception and field of vision. Visual perception is evaluated with a tachistoscope, in which presentation times in sequences of visual displays are varied. An audiometer measures hearing acuity, weighted cylinders help to detect the sensitivity of tactile sense receptors, and positioning tests require proprioceptive involvement. An excellent source book on biomedical instrumentation—an introduction to various apparatus, their

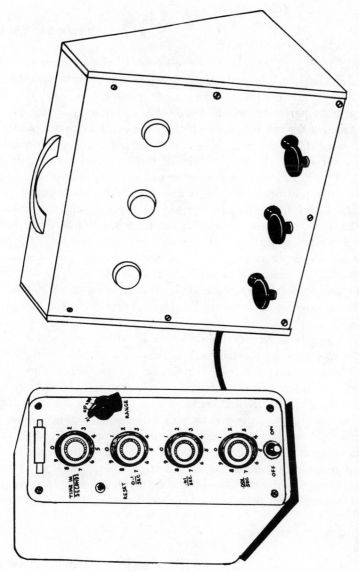

Figure 4–5. Choice reaction timer (Marietta Apparatus Co., Marietta, Ohio) and Hunter Klockounter, which measures to 0.001 second (Hunter Manufacturing Co., Iowa City, Iowa).

design and usage, and applications to the measurement of body functions—is *Biomedical Instrumentation and Measurements,* by Leslie Cromwell and his colleagues (1973).

Duration of Study

Most published research studies on learning reveal data collection that extends over a relatively brief time span. One reason is that the tasks used are not too difficult and the *ceiling effect* is noticeable before long. That is, potential maximum performance is attained easily and quickly. Performance scores with such tasks are insensitive to improvements as they approach the upper limits set for the task. Upper limits in performance are set by the experimenter or by the very nature of the task and the length of practice or test periods. Quick gains in performance are observed in about the first five trials and an asymptote is approximated after about ten or fifteen trials on such tasks as the pursuit rotor, stabilometer, and star-tracing apparatus. Thus, a study may be completed in from one to four days. Such constraints in laboratory settings bias the data although relatively "clean" data can be observed otherwise, as environmental and personal variables can be controlled in a reasonable manner. In contrast, a ceiling effect is nearly impossible to reach in athletic skills. The criterion of excellence is difficult if not impossible to ascertain. There is always room for improvement.

Of course if long-term retention is under study, an experiment may last a few months or a year. By the same token, long-term retention is not only studied with long retention intervals. If retention of information from long-term memory is of interest, it could be that a retention test is administered only five minutes from the original learning in some studies. An advantage to a short duration study is the general lack of subject mortality, a fancy term for the loss of subjects that is usually found to be proportional to the length of the project. The longer a study goes on, the better the chance subjects will miss testing occasions for one reason or another. Consequently, long-term experiments should include more subjects than might be included in short-term ones to compensate for expected subject mortality.

The Dependent Measure(s)

Experiments contain independent and dependent measures. The independent measure is the variable of interest, the dependent variable represents the recorded data. For instance, we might be concerned with the effects of motivation on performance. The independent variable, motivation, would be introduced in some form and compared to a control situation. An example might be one group of subjects experiencing the learning of a task where verbal encouragement is constantly offered. Another group of subjects, the control, would learn the task without any comments offered. The dependent measure would be the method of recording the behavior observed. If the task were a pursuit rotor, the dependent measure would probably be the time the subject maintained the stylus in contact with the moving disc during a particular timed trial. If the task involved archery shooting, the dependent measure would be the subject's score.

Although the dependent measure may be an obvious decision in a number of tasks, it is often controversial in others. When there exists a variety of possibilities for recording data, the experimenter dilemma is increased. The severity of the consequences in selecting an inappropriate or less desirable measure from the alternatives should never be understated. Conclusions based on the selected dependent measure may be more or less valid, depending on the experimenter's wisdom.

The classic article by Barick, Fitts, and Briggs (1957) demonstrates the effects of changing the response-sensitivity measures used for subjects performing a tracking task. The size of the target zone (various-sized scoring zones) resulted in varying shapes in the learning curves. The arbitrary selection of a cut-off point (what is considered on-target or off-target) can significantly affect the data and the conclusions derived from them. The magnitude of the errors in performance, for example, seems to be a more justifiable measure than a gross recording of time on or off target. The latter score has limited value in research. Any task that is scored with an all-or-none performance measure instead of considering a continuous and normal distribution of scores is subject to experimental artifacts.

With many tasks it might be wise to record and analyze more than one dependent measure. The acquisition of skill, especially on more complex tasks, usually encompasses the mastery of a number of task components. The analysis of more than one dependent variable may provide additional insight into learning progress. As an example, the oft-employed star-tracing task calls for the performer to trace a pattern as quickly as possible with a minimum of errors. What then should constitute the subject's score? A number of techniques have been suggested, and John Drowatzky (1969) compared five scoring techniques, arriving at interesting conclusions. The methods were

1. Time required for the completion of each trial.
2. Number of errors committed during each trial.
3. The product of task completion time and number of errors per trial.
4. The number 1,000 divided by the product of completion time and errors per trial.
5. The sum of completion time and number of errors per trial.

Drowatzky's conclusion was that "no one . . . performance measure appeared to fully meet all requirements of an optimal measure of skill, and . . . that evaluation of star-tracing performance should include the measures of completion time, errors/trial, and product of time and errors" (p. 229).

Sometimes the reporting of too many performance variables may be redundant and unnecessary. Obviously, if two measures are really measuring the same thing, there would be little gain in analyzing both of them. For instance, it is fairly common to see three dependent variables—(1) algebraic error, or constant error (CE); (2) absolute error (AE); and (3) within-subject variance, or variable error (VE)—presented in experiments dealing with positioning tasks. These tasks require the subjects to match movements against standards, with error or deviation scores the variable of interest. The less the deviation, the better the performance. Robert Schutz and Eric Roy (1973) have questioned the assumption of the independence of CE, AE, and VE scores and in turn the wisdom in using all of them in the same experiment. Using their definitions:

Error: The algebraic difference $(X_{ij} - Y)$
Constant Error (CE): The mean algebraic error

$$\frac{\Sigma(X - Y)}{k} = \frac{\Sigma(e)}{k}$$

Absolute Error (AE): The average error or mean deviation

$$\frac{\Sigma(X - Y)}{k} = \frac{\Sigma(e)}{k}$$

Variable Error (VE): Intravariance, intraindividual variance, and within-subject variance

$$\frac{1}{k} \Sigma \left[(X - Y) - \frac{\Sigma(X - Y)}{k} \right]^2 =$$
$$\frac{1}{k} \Sigma(e - CE)^2$$

Or because Y is a constant and therefore does not affect the variance:

$$\frac{1}{k} \Sigma[X - \overline{X}]^2$$

Reworking data published in other studies and applying mathematical theory, Schutz and Roy arrive at the conclusion that both AE and VE are quite interdependent and therefore it is unwarranted to report both variables. AE is determined to be completely dependent on CE and CE on VE. The authors call for the elimination of AE as a dependent measure in experiments, for CE and VE are statistically independent and can adequately describe most data.

The Learning Score

Another difficult decision is related to the measure or score that best represents learning, or the effects of practice. Returning to the hypothetical study on motivation, with two groups, one a control and one experimental, what should be used as the achievement measures with which the groups can be compared to determine if verbal encouragement indeed resulted in increased learning over no verbal encouragement in either the pursuit rotor task or in archery shooting? Perhaps twenty trials of thirty seconds duration each were interspersed with thirty-second rest periods in pursuit rotor performance. Shall we compare both groups on their scores attained on trial twenty? Would it be better to work with gain scores; that is, the difference scores between the last and first trials? How about the best score reached by each subject on any one trial? What about the average score for each subject across all twenty trials? Is there a particular formula that might be more sensitive and valid than any of the preceding measured?

As we become more familiar with the research literature dealing with motor learning, it will become apparent that a wide variety of approaches has been described in an attempt to make comparisons between learning situations. As is the case with any step in an experiment, more appropriate decisions will lead to more valid conclusions. Unfortunately there appears to be no easy answer to the question of how learning should be determined. Probably the most widely accepted techniques include some form of arriving at a (1) gain or difference score, (2) average score, or (3) final score(s). The use of the average, or mean, score across all trials administered to the subjects can be defended if no trend is present. Walter Kroll (1967) supports this notion with the use of reliability theory. If a trend appears, alternatives for a criterion measure might include (1) a search for a measurement schedule free of systematic measure error variance, or (2) the use of the high or low score for each subject, with necessary cautions.

The argument of whether to use the best score or average score of subjects on trials appears frequently in the literature. Although Kroll (1967) and Henry (1967) generally favor the use of the average score, Heatherington (1973) has taken issue with their statistical rationale used in support of their positions. He favors the best score obtained on any trial whenever the measurement error is believed to be small relative to within-subject variation. He raises the question of whether the between-trial variation is normally distributed about the "true" score, especially in cases where an estimation of maximum performance is derived. The relative advantages of the best or average score as "the score" are still being debated, and certainly a number of factors must be considered before a choice can be made for one or the other. Perhaps neither may be acceptable.

In certain kinds of experiments it might be advisable for the experimenter to establish a criterion performance measure that the subjects are expected to achieve. In many laboratory motor-learning studies data are usually analyzed in terms of three different measures:

1. The total time taken by the subject to reach a given criterion of performance.
2. The total number of errors made in reaching the criterion.
3. The total number of trials taken to reach the criterion.

These three measures of learning performance are confounded by several factors, notably:

1. The learning ability of the subject.
2. The subject's initial skill level.
3. The criterion of achievement established by the experimenter.

A satisfactory resolution of these factors that influence data deserves considerable attention.

There are various methods of analyzing changes within practice. Measurement of these changes usually associated with differences between initial and terminal performances indicates the degree of learning that has occurred. McCraw (1951, 1955) has compared many of the possible ways of measuring and scoring tests of motor learning. In each of his two studies, McCraw obtained data from subjects performing two novel motor skills. Learning that has occurred because of practice may be measured by considering such factors as initial status versus final score, difference between first and last scores, and percentage of improvement. Also, there is the problem of ascertaining the number of trials that should represent the first score as well as the final score. How many trials are necessary for warm-up and task familiarity are open to question, but most authorities agree that at least a few should be provided before an actual initial score is recorded.

In attempting to reconcile these problems, McCraw (1955) formulated eight methods, based on those found in other experiments, to score the practice effects on learning two tasks. Some of these procedures were

1. *Total Learning Score Method.* Consisted of cumulatively adding all the trial scores during practice.
2. *Difference in Raw Score Method No. I.* Required finding the difference between the final and initial trials.
3. *Three Per Cent Gain of Possible Gain Method.* Represented by the formula:

$$\frac{(\text{Sum of last } N \text{ trials}) \text{ minus } (\text{Sum of first } N \text{ trials})}{(\text{Highest possible score of } N \text{ trials}) \text{ minus } (\text{Sum of first } N \text{ trials})}$$

4. *Two Per Cent Gain of Initial Score Method.* Depicted by this formula:

$$\frac{(\text{Sum of last } N \text{ trials}) \text{ minus } (\text{Sum of first } N \text{ trials})}{(\text{Sum of first } N \text{ trials})}$$

McCraw reported considerable variability in the scores as yielded by the diverse means of measuring improvement. As to a comparison of methods, he states that the most acceptable appear to be those that relate gain to possible gain while the least desirable are those that interpret gain in relation to the initial score. The Total Learning Method and the Three Per Cent Gain of Possible Gain Method were the most valid measures in comparing individuals with dissimilar initial scores. The author generally found little relationship between the various scoring methods, i.e., each yielded different results.

Thus, it can be seen that varying the techniques for measuring improvement results in dissimilar outcomes and interpretations of the data. The nature of each study must be scrutinized before the procedure of data analysis is selected, although some methods are apparently more acceptable than others. One of the difficulties in determining laws of learning pertaining to any factor is the variation in design from investigation to investigation, including the selected method of data analysis.

In the typical case of measuring change that is the result of practice, the "raw" change score is computed, which consists of the difference between a pretest and a posttest on the variable of concern. The definition of this measure from variable A to variable B (e.g., pretest A and posttest B) is $B - A$. The usual contaminant in this methodology is that $B - A$ is negatively correlated with A. That is to say, the higher the pretest score, the smaller the gain score. If a person had had no experience with the task and was beginning at a zero level of proficiency, any achievement later would be a gain. This assumption is reasonable with very unusual tasks, such as learning nonsense syllables and mazes. In real situations, however, everyone comes to the "new" learning situation with some previously related experience. Consequently subjects start at different skill levels. If we measure progression in a task where thirty points is maximum, we cannot at all assume that the gain from zero to twelve is the same as from twelve to twenty-four points. As the potential ceiling (score limits) are closer to being reached, gains are much more difficult to demonstrate. The same gain score for any two people, in this case twelve, does not truly reveal enough information when starting points are dissimilar.

In particular situations it is of advantage to have a change score that is dependent of the pretest. An alternate to the raw change score is the *residual change* score, also known as a basefree measure, where final scores are uncorrelated with initial scores (see, for example, Tucker et al., 1966). The portion of the posttest that is linearly predictable from the pretest is eliminated. The residual gain procedure yields estimates of deviations from the expected scores of individuals (or groups). A zero residual gain means that the actual gain for the individual or group was identical with the gain that was predicted from a knowledge of the pretest score by linear regression techniques.

Franklin Henry (1956) used three motor learning experiments with the tasks in each involving (1) jumping, (2) speed of arm movement, or (3) balancing. As expected, he found raw learning scores to be unrelated to final skill accomplishments but negatively correlated with initial performance. He shows how the use of the residual method can alleviate this circumstance. It estimates the individual learning that would have occurred had all subjects begun at the same initial skill level.

Another model with a number of variations that has been supported in the literature is the *true change* approach. If the pretest and posttest were measured without error (experimental contamination), then a true change score is observed. Because this is rarely the case, some estimate must be made of the observed gain in performance attributable to measurement errors so that an estimate of true gain is possible. Regression equations have been proposed to handle this problem, and these models as well as other approaches are summarized by Chester Harris (1963).

An excellent summary of the many residual gain and true change models is offered by Lee Cronbach and Lita Furby (1970). Relative strengths and weaknesses are discussed. Interestingly enough, after laboriously representing the various measures of change, these writers argue against their usage. Assuming equality between groups of subjects at the start of the experiment as well as errors of measurement on the posttest that are randomly distributed, a simple posttest comparison would do. Other suggestions are made for specific situations.

Nevertheless, let us examine sample equations to estimate true change scores (Davis, 1964, Chapter 11). Data were collected in our laboratory with six subjects forming one group. They were pretested and posttested after ten trials on the pursuit rotor. In a typical study of change an initial measure (A) is obtained on each individual in a group, a "treatment" is given, and a final measure (B) is then obtained. If A and B are measured without error, then g ($B - A = g$) is the true change. But if A and B are fallible the conclusion is different. In the following, the true change, G, is estimated for each individual as distinct from the observed change, g.

If we let A stand for one's initial score, B for one's final score, and G for an estimate of one's true change in the period between the two measurements, equation (1) should be used to obtain a numerical value for G.

$$G = W_B B + W_A A + K \qquad (1)$$

Where:

$$W_A = \frac{s_B r_{AB}(1 - r_{BB'}) - s_A(r_{AA'} - r_{AB})}{s(1 - r)} \qquad (2)$$

$$W_B = \frac{s_B(r_{BB'} - r_{AB}) - s_A r_{AB}(1 - r_{AA'})}{s_B(1 - r_{AB})} \qquad (3)$$

Equation (4) involves W_A and W_B as well as the average score on initial trial (denoted A) and on final trial (denoted B).

$$K = B - \bar{A} - W_B\bar{B} - W_A\bar{A} \qquad (4)$$

The standard error of measurement of any estimate of true change found by equation (1) is defined the following equation (5).

$$s_{\text{meas } G} = \sqrt{W_A s^2_{\text{meas } A} + W_B s^2_{\text{meas } B}}$$

'meas G is multiplied by '$(\alpha, df = n - 1)$ to obtain the smallest change significant at the α level.

Data fitted to the formulas:

	M	SD	$r_{AA'}$ or $_{BB'}$	r_{AB}
Initial trial:	10.2650	5.1363	0.9353	0.8371
Final trial:	15.7010	1.7481	0.9053	

Computation:

$$W_A = \frac{(1.7481)(.8371)(1 - .9053) - 5.1363(.9353 - 0.7007)}{(5.1363)(1 - .7007)} = -0.6937$$

$$W_B = \frac{(1.7481)(.9053 - 0.7007) - (5.1363)(0.8371)(1 - 0.9353)}{(1.7481)(1 - .7007)} = -0.1519$$

$$K = 15.7017 - 10.2650 - (0.1519)(15.7017) - (-0.6937)(10.265)$$
$$= 10.1724$$

$$\therefore G = (0.1519)B + (-0.6937)A + 10.1724 \qquad \text{tabled } t = 2.3387$$

For each subject:

			Rank Order
(1) R. M.	$G = (0.1519)13.34 + (-0.6937)\ 5.37 + 10.1724 =$	8.4735	1
(2) S. I.	$G = (0.1519)17.76 + (-0.6937)13.64 + 10.1724 =$	3.4080	5
(3) K. I.	$G = (0.1519)17.26 + (-0.6937)18.90 + 10.1724 =$	−0.3167	6
(4) L. K.	$G = (0.1519)14.76 + (-0.6937)\ 6.20 + 10.1724 =$	8.1135	2
(5) M. L.	$G = (0.1519)16.57 + (-0.6937)\ 9.38 + 10.1724 =$	6.1825	3
(6) L. G.	$G = (0.1519)14.52 + (-0.6937)\ 8.10 + 10.1724 =$	6.7590	4

$$r_{AA'} = 1 - \frac{s^2_{\text{meas}A}}{s^-_A} \qquad r_{BB'} = 1 - \frac{s^2_{\text{meas}B}}{s^2_B}$$

$$s^2_{\text{meas } A} = (5.1363)^2(1 - 0.9353) = 1.7069$$
$$s^2_{\text{meas } B} = (1.7481)^2(1 - 0.9053) = 0.2894$$

$$s_{\text{meas } G} = \sqrt{(-0.6937)^2(1.7069) + (0.1519)^2(0.2894)}$$
$$= 0.91 \qquad\qquad 0.91 \qquad 2.57(t\,0.05, df = 5)$$

The smallest change significant at the 0.05 level is 2.3387.

Conclusion: It is concluded that R. M., S. I., L. K., M. L., and L. G. made real gains in pursuit rotor task during the practice period (ten trials), but not K.I.

Whereas the preceding model allowed us to determine individual significant gains in performance, Patricia Hale and Robert Hale (1972) have developed a technique to assess relative improvement scores more accu-

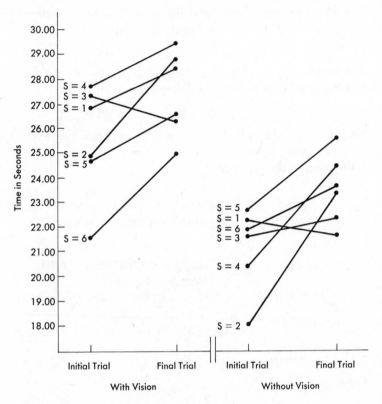

Figure 4–6.   Individual differences in initial and final trial scores.

rately when subjects begin an activity with varying levels of skill. Students could be ranked as to their relative true gains. Using an example in archery shooting and with special implications for grading purposes, the technique is especially sensitive to the large increases shown by beginners and the smaller increases revealed by the more advanced. As has been pointed out before, the higher the quality of performance, the more difficult it is to improve.

Using the Hale and Hale technique, let us see what happens when two groups are compared. The data are derived from six subjects performing a stabilometer task for ten trials with vision and ten trials without vision. The subjects were divided in half, each subgroup performing the sequence differently, one with vision, then no vision, the other without vision, then vision, to counterbalance treatment effects. Notice that under both conditions, the raw rank difference scores between the pretest and posttest are not the same. In other words, subjects ranked in different order under each condition.

Figure 4–6 illustrates the differences among and within subjects in initial and final time-on-balance stabilometer performances. Under each condition, with vision (V) and without vision (WV), all but one of the six subjects demonstrated an increase in time on balance. In Figure 4–6 these gains (and losses) are ranked by the numerical difference between trial 1 (initial) and trial 10 (final) scores. Ranking by the absolute gain scores ignored the evident differences between the initial ability of the subjects.

Application of the Hale and Hale equation to the data converted each score exponentially. Improvement gains from the differing initial scores were converted into comparable units. The converted scores took into consideration the initial position, the gain, and the difficulty of the gain from the initial position. The A per cent scores in Table 4–1 are the weighted improvement percentage scores representing, for each subject, the amount of progress in relation to the initial score.

The following calculations typify the application of the exponential equation to the initial and final scores of each subject. The coefficient $\propto$ (constant), appearing in both the numerator and denominator of the original equation, is determined by the formula

$$\propto = \frac{ln(S_{max} + 1)}{X}$$

where S_{max} is used to fix $\propto$, the coefficient which measures the difficulty of attainment for a given skill. In those activities with a top limit score occasionally attainable by a subject, Hale and Hale suggest that S_{max} be set

TABLE 4–1.   COMPARISON OF NUMERICAL AND ADJUSTED PERFORMANCE GAIN SCORES

			With Vision			
	Score		Numerical		Adjusted Score	
Subject	Initial	Final	Difference	Rank	A%	Rank
1	26.79	28.33	1.54	5	16.70	3
2	24.89	28.49	3.60	1	33.78	1
3	27.34	26.18	−1.16	6	−10.43	6
4	27.61	29.26	1.65	4	19.91	2
5	24.67	26.46	1.79	3	14.30	5
6	21.59	24.89	3.30	2	18.40	3
			Without Vision			
1	22.28	21.66	− .62	6	− 2.94	6
2	18.23	23.36	5.13	1	19.78	2
3	21.66	22.43	.77	5	3.56	5
4	20.37	24.50	3.84	2	20.51	1
5	22.80	25.60	2.80	3	17.97	3
6	21.85	23.74	1.89	4	9.69	4

equal to 100. Because it was possible for a subject to obtain the top score of 30 seconds on-balance, S_{max} was set equal to 100 for all calculations. The denominator X represents the maximum obtainable score for a given skill and was set equal to 30, the time limit for each of the ten stabilometer trials. Substituting the appropriate numerical values,

$$\propto = \frac{ln(100 + 1)}{30} = \frac{4.61512 \,{}^{*}}{30} = 0.1538$$

The denominator of the original equation can then be calculated:

$$e^{\propto X} - 1 = e^{0.1538(30)} - 1 = e^{4.615} - 1 = 100.887{\dagger} - 1 = 99.887 \approx 100$$

As can be seen, the denominator, $e^{\propto X} - 1$, is equal to the selected value of S_{max}. The numerator of the original equation requires x, the S's initial performance score; and Δx, the change in x from initial to final performance. Using the V performance scores of subject 4 (Table 4–1), the term becomes

$$(x + \Delta x) = 27.61 + (29.26 - 27.61) = 27.61 + 1.65 = 29.26$$

or the subject's final performance score.

Substituting the values calculated in other equations, the original equation for subject 4 is

$$A_{S-4} = \frac{e^{\propto (x + \Delta x)} - e^{\propto (x)}}{e^{\propto x} - 1}$$

and becomes

$$A_{S-4} = \frac{e^{0.1538(29.26)} - e^{0.1538(27.61)}}{100} \,(100) \,{\ddagger}$$
$$= e^{4.50} - e^{\,4.25}$$
$$= 90.02 - 70.11$$
$$= 19.91 \text{ per cent}$$

As can be seen in Table 4–1, ranking performance gains by the numerical differences between initial and final scores identified subject 4 as fourth with a gain in on-balance performance of 1.65 seconds. However, taking into account initial position, the amount of gain, and the difficulty of the gain from that initial position, the subject's adjusted gain score (A per cent) becomes 19.91 per cent. S-4 actually ranked second among the six subjects in performance gain under vision conditions.

Most learning-change measurement techniques are useful for describing individuals, as the preceding model indicates. However, when encompassing groups other procedures might be used, such as those suggested by

---

* The natural logarithm ($1n$) of $101 = 4.61512$
† The exponential function $e^{4.61512} = 101$
‡ To convert A into a percentage expression of improvement, the equation must be multiplied by 100.

Davis in his book (1964) and through personal correspondence. Note the following equations.

The standard deviation of $\bar{G}_1$ and $\bar{G}_2$ (where these denote the average raw-score gains in samples 1 and 2) are:

$$s_{G_1} = \frac{s^2_{G_1}}{N_1} \quad \text{and} \quad s_{G_2} = \frac{s^2_{G_2}}{N_2}$$

where

and
$$G = B - A \qquad G = \bar{B} - \bar{A}$$
$$s^2_{G_1} = s^2_{A_1} + s^2_{B_1} - 2s_{A_1}\, s_{B_1}\, r_{A_1 B_1}$$

and

$$s^2_{G_2} = s^2_{A_2} + s^2_{B_2} - 2s_{A_2}\, s_{B_2}\, r_{A_2\, B_2}$$

The two subscripts 1 and 2 indicate the two nonoverlapping samples drawn at random from the same population. The symbol s refers to an estimate of the population standard deviation.

To test the null hypothesis that $\bar{\bar{G}}_1 = \bar{\bar{G}}_2$, where the tildes denote that these are true means, the t ratio is given by equation:

$$t(\text{df} = N_1 + N_2 - 2) = \frac{\bar{G}_1 - \bar{G}_2}{s_{(\bar{G}_1 - \bar{G}_2)}}$$

where an estimate of the denominator is the conventional

$$s_{(G_1 - G_2)} = \frac{s^2_{G_1}}{N_1} + \frac{s^2_{G_2}}{N_2}$$

because the samples are nonoverlapping. This procedure is especially reliable in that it requires no reliability coefficient for the pre- or posttests.

When using raw gain scores, the assumption is made that the groups of subjects to be compared are equal at the start of the experiment on the parameters that might be influential on the performance outcomes. This may occur, at least theoretically, when large enough samples of subjects are randomly placed into groups and the groups in turn randomly assigned to specific treatments. But there are instances when it is known that the groups are in fact dissimilar prior to any administered treatments. For instance, it is conceivable that one group of subjects might show a lower pretest score than another group in the same experiment. Or one group might, for some reason, possess a greater prominence of an influential factor, say desirable body builds, for the learning of a particular activity. In many cases, an analysis of covariance will be the statistical tool that can adjust posttest scores according to pretest differences or differences on a variable(s) of influence. Yet the limitations of covariance should be recognized. If differences exist between the groups prior to the experiment other than in the covariate (e.g., pretest), confounded data will still occur.

LEARNING CURVES

One leading method of depicting skill acquisition is through the use of the learning curve. The curve is a graphic illustration of practice trials versus performance and an indicator of what one or more individuals accomplish from trial to trial. The abscissa line (horizontal) usually corresponds to trials or days of practice, and the ordinate line (vertical) represents the unit of measurement. Measurement might be in terms of points made, errors, or some other score. Typically, the vertical units are laid out to represent two thirds of the graphic dimension of the horizontal units. The appearance of the curves and their general interpretation can be influenced by the manner in which they are presented. Many factors, such as method of practice, administration of practice sessions, method of measurement, and nature and level of skill, and age of the subjects, will result in different curves for the same practiced skill. Some curves reflect factors facilitating or hindering performance, and as such are not truly representative learning curves.

Although it is extremely difficult to obtain a true learning curve, four distinct types probably exist. Practice conditions, the nature of the task, and the learner's abilities and organismic state will be reflected in the type of curve obtained from the data. It should be emphasized here that typical examples of learning curves that are found in real-life examples have been smoothed out in order to make it easier to follow any apparent trends in skill acquisition. Actually, great irregularities usually exist from trial to trial and performer to performer.

Figure 4–7 presents four typical smoothed curves for a limited practice session. Curve A has been termed a negatively accelerated curve. Greatest gains are made in the early practice trials, with decreasing improvements in later trials. A leveling-off point appears to be reached, but positive gains, ever so small, still are occurring. This type of curve usually denotes the learning of a skill that is relatively easy and where insight into the skill occurs quickly, as exemplified by the satisfactory performance on the early trials. As upper levels of skill are reached quickly, improvement diminishes, for little is left to be mastered.

Curve D is an example of a positively accelerated curve in which performance is poor in the early trials but increases from trial to trial. Although it appears to leave no upper limit, this curve would ultimately level off with practice. The example offered in Figure 4–7 represents relatively few practice trials, so the curve appears to be accelerating indefinitely. Curve B, the linear curve, is essentially a straight line. This curve has been obtained in a few cases where proportional increments are noted from trial to trial. It too would become asymptotic with increasing trials. Curve C, which is an S-shaped curve, indicates positive acceleration, approaching

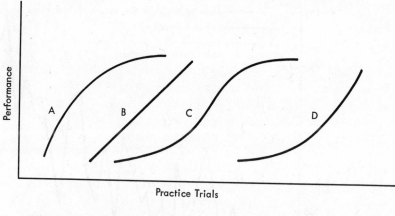

A-Negatively Accelerated Curve
B-Linear Curve

C-S-shaped Curve
D-Positively Accelerated Curve

Figure 4–7. Typical learning curves.

linearity, and finally negative acceleration. It contains many of the qualities of the other three curves.

It is important to note that no single curve of learning exists, that the nature of the skill or the learner will be reflected in the manner in which he acquires skill. Some psychologists, Thurstone (1930) and Estes (1950), for example, have attempted to form mathematical equations in order to predict and fit learning curves. Varying degrees of success have been achieved in this endeavor. Certain data might very well be described by one of the equations whereas this same operation would not be appropriate for other data. However, Culler (1928) and Culler and Girden (1951) present evidence which seems to indicate that complete learning curves are ogive (S-shaped). They employed a mathematical equation that is proportional to the product of the amount already learned and the amount remaining to be learned before the limit of learning is reached. As of the present time, there is no equation that would fit all types of data. Therefore one concludes that the nature of the learning task (e.g., motor skill, nonsense syllables, prose, or puzzle), and its degree of difficulty, as well as the nature of the learner, determine the method in which the task is learned.

The method of measurement will often determine the smoothness or irregularity of a curve. Although a typical learning curve is obtained from practice trials completed in one or a few meetings, Figure 4–8 presents data collected on one discus thrower in competition during his four years at college. No doubt growth and development factors influence the curve, but it is presented for two reasons: (1) the similarity between this curve and a typical learning curve and, more important, (2) a comparison of three methods of measuring performance and each one's effect on the curve.

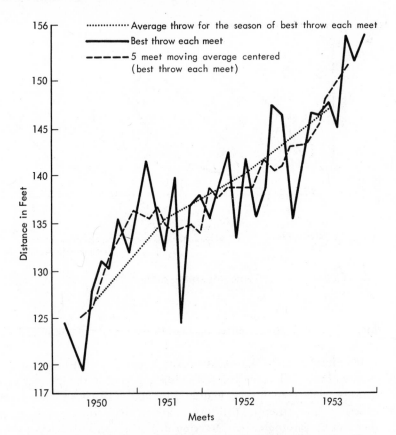

Figure 4–8.   Three methods of analyzing performance. Representative of one discus thrower's record for four years.

Coach Carl Heldt of the Illinois State University track and field team has collected typical data such as these on all his performers during his many years as a coach.

It can be observed that when more scores are averaged together, the lines become smoother. The most irregular line represents the best throw each meet, a smoother line is obtained by averaging five throws per meet, and the smoothest curve is derived from the average throw each season. The athlete's record indicates fairly consistent improvement from meet to meet and year to year, although irregularities in performance are clearly apparent.

Because it would be erroneous to believe that every athlete's record would be comparable with the preceding case and improve so consistently, three other athletes, all javelin throwers, have their performances recorded by the five-throw-per-meet-average method for comparison in Figure 4–9. Note the differences in the curves, many of which may be explained by

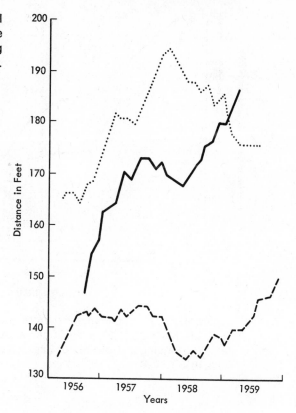

Figure 4–9. Individual performances of three javelin throwers during four years of competition.

such factors as a student getting married, loss or gain in motivation, proper or improper understanding of mechanics, poorer or better health, and, in general a host of psychological and physiological variables.

If these curves were smoothed by such a method as averaging the throws per season, they would more nearly approach those curves found in Figure 4–7. Poorer records, caused by backache, marriage, or lack of interest are really factors in performance and not truly indicative of learning as such. True curves of learning should reflect positive increments, event if they are so slight as to be outwardly unobservable. The plotting of individual trials results in more noticeable trial increments and decrements and can serve a definite purpose. Without any major detrimental factors operating, averaged practice trials should yield positive learning performances.

Figure 4–10 illustrates learning curves for two different groups of subjects receiving ten practice trials each in the same time period on the stabilometer (an apparatus used to measure balance ability). The time in each trial in which the board was not ideally balanced is recorded, and the curve decreases because performance was plotted against time off balance. If it were plotted against time on balance, the curve would go upward instead of downward, and it should be observable in either case that there is

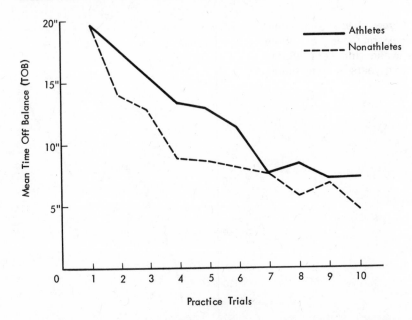

Figure 4–10.   Stabilometer performance as a result of practice. (From R. N. Singer, "Effects of Spectators on Athletes and Nonathletes Performing a Gross Motor Task," *Research Quarterly,* 36:473–482, 1965.)

improvement in performance, hence learning, within the trials allocated for the experiment. If the curves are smoothed further, they would approach the typical negatively accelerated curve.

The shape of the learning curve is greatly dependent upon the response measures utilized in the plotting of the data. The curve, as pointed out in the article by Bahrick, Fitts, and Briggs (1957), referred to earlier in this chapter, may be misinterpreted at various stages of practice, and effects deemed important are in reality confounded by the artifacts produced. These researchers used a tracking task to illustrate the effects of errors in the measurement of learning curves. However, they believe that their data have implications for a variety of tasks and conditions.

W. K. Estes (1956) supports the notion of group curves, data averaged across subjects for each trial. They are useful for summarizing information and for theoretical interpretation. However, he is also against transfering inferences made from group learning curves to individual learning curves. Although the form of the averaged curve does not determine the forms of the individual curves, it does provide a means for testing hypotheses about them. The risks in making generalizations from group to individual learning curves are powerful, and Estes discusses them especially as experimental and statistical violations might be involved. We should always remember that much information about individual learning rates is lost when data are averaged.

Another aspect of learning and performance curves concerns practice to an asymptote as a criterion used in certain learning studies. A task is usually thought of as being "learned" when stabilization of performance becomes apparent. In real-life skills, as in sports, years of practice contribute to proficiency and consistency. Yet, in a few practice sessions, it is not unusual for researchers to expect similar occurrences with relatively simple laboratory tasks. James Bradley's (1969) data, on one subject administered thousands of practice trials, led him to conclude that asymptotes are not truly reached. A subject could still be learning or showing upswings or downswings in behavior, depending on situational and personal variables. Bradley favors doing away with practice to an asymptote as a means of eliminating unwanted learning effects in an experiment. He feels that group means might mask individual scores. Although precautions might be taken against unwarranted overgeneralizations, there are many types of learning experiments in which the analysis of specified learning phenomena depends on the learners' attainment of a relative degree of stability in performance. A plateau in performance, to be examined next, is an excellent example of a potential temporary asymptote (perhaps even a nontrue asymptote).

PLATEAUS

Almost everyone in a lifetime experiences a frustrating point of no apparent improvement in performance though the task to be learned is practiced over and over—maybe the golf game, which consistently stays in the low 90's, or perhaps the bowling average, which always remains about 145. Specific skill acquisition or general sport performance appear to level off and may remain there seemingly forever or for a short period of time before an acceleration occurs in performance.

This phenomenon has been termed a *plateau in the learning curve. A plateau represents stationary performance preceded and sometimes followed by accelerated learning increments.* It is a condition that has not been found to occur in many experimental learning tasks, but the classic example of a plateau in the learning curve is the one obtained by Bryan and Harter (1897). The graphic illustration taken from their data and presented in Figure 4–11 refers to one's ability to learn to receive telegraphic signals in the American Morse Code.

A hypothesis set forth to explain the plateau in learning is that there is a hierarchy of habits to be mastered by the individual when he attempts to learn a complex task. After succeeding in the first order, he may be fixated at that level for some time before becoming able to integrate the patterns

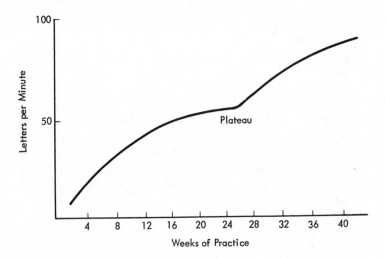

Figure 4–11. Learning curve with plateau representing telegraphic coding. (From W. Bryan and N. Harter, "Studies in the Physiology and Psychology of the Telegraphic Language," *Psychological Review,* 4:27–53, 1897.)

needed in the second-order habits. Information is consolidated and reorganized. An example of this situation is found in tennis. First-order habits might be the acquisition of basic strokes and skills underlying the sport, such as learning to stroke the ball when in a stationary position. Second-order habits could include hitting the ball while on the move, and a third-order category might include the integration of effective movement patterns in the game situation. Theoretically, depending on the manner in which the sport is taught and the performer involved, a plateau could occur at any one of these transitional periods.

After a period of time in which one attempts to transcend from one hierarchy of habits to another, insight manifests itself in the form of an integration of past learned responses and new ones to be utilized. The curve accelerates sharply until the next plateau. Because actual plateaus are rare in experimental evidence, possibly because of the difficulty in setting up investigations that might demonstrate this phenomenon, we must draw more from theoretical implications and everyday experience. The latter evidence appears to indicate the reality of such an effect in the acquisition of skill, at least in some of the more complex sports. But damage to the concept of plateaus is presented by F. S. Keller (1958). By the title of his article, "The Phantom Plateau," one can surmise the content.

Two questions naturally arise concerning the plateau in the learning curve and its theoretical explanation. (1) Will the manner in which the skill is taught affect the learning curve and any possible plateaus? In other words, a complex activity may be treated in parts and learning directed toward gaining insight into the parts in a progressive manner. Will this method of approach lessen the possibility of a plateau occurring during skill acquisition more than if the skill is taught as a whole? (2) Is there really such a thing as the plateau in the learning curve? One reason for the leveling of performance may be a loss of motivation. If the learner is continually motivated, a plateau in performance might not be observable.

Concerning the factor of motivation, disappointment and discouragement when not improving in performance make it even more difficult to advance the learning cause. Perhaps all these factors—task complexity, hierarchy of habits, interest, and frustration—contribute to the plateau, if indeed it does exist. Many other questions remain unanswered. No definite conclusions may be reached at this time until further experimental evidence is examined.

If, in fact, plateaus can occur in the learning of real-life activities (although not demonstrated with artificial laboratory tasks), several recommendations could be made to remediate the situation.

1. Attempt to maintain the ideal level of motivation throughout the learning experiences.
2. Attempt to maintain the learner's attention to the appropriate cues so that practice is not wasteful but instead meaningful.
3. Watch for fatiguing conditions that might be detrimental to learning, where inappropriate responses are released.
4. Analyze the final performance goal, breaking down the activity to smaller units so that transitions are smooth and logical from one performance level of the activity to a higher-level expectation. Pushing the learner fast in a complex activity places hardships on his ability to apply lower-order learned skills to higher-order ones that must eventually be mastered.
5. Analyze the learner's physical development. He might possess physical capacities to perform a task at a certain level of proficiency, but will need further development if higher-order skills are to be demonstrated.
6. Understand the learner's level of aspiration. Low goal levels result in lower performances, whereas higher but realistic goals will inevitably increase performance output.

MOTOR-LEARNING LABORATORIES AND EQUIPMENT

In order to investigate learning processes, the effects of training manipulations, learning and performance correlates, and other related considerations, decisions must be made about locations, subjects, and learning tasks. A laboratory in the formal sense of the word connotes an isolated area in which extremely controlled testing can occur. Motor-learning laboratories exist in many physical education departments, experimental and engineering psychology areas, and military and aerospace programs. Often they are equipped with a minimum amount of expensive equipment (much handmade apparatus) or, to the other extreme, computerized controlled operations. Depending on the sophistication of the experimenter, the equipment, the testing conditions, and the type of learning phenomenon investigated, the data will usually be handled in a technical manner, contributing to theory and knowledge, with implications for practical conditions.

If we expand our interpretation of the laboratory or consider field testing environments, subjects are tested under more real-life conditions and with more familiar motor tasks, often not involving equipment. These data are usually more directly applicable to programmatic or instructional concerns. As we will see, studies in the area of motor learning range considerably as to testing conditions, learning phenomena, and performance variables investigated.

With the assumption that you can readily comprehend how research might be conducted in gymnasiums, classrooms, and other familiar situations, let us discuss the nature and use of more formal established laboratories. Because one of the major thrusts in the motor-learning area is to determine how we learn skills and how we can learn them more effectively and efficiently, the identification of the "right" task is of paramount concern. As was mentioned earlier in this chapter, the need is for novel and unusual tasks, those with which the learner is unfamiliar so that processes and the effects of situational manipulations can be examined in a technical manner. These tasks can be purchased, but in many motor-learning laboratories they are constructed to fit the needs of the experimenter and the particular area he is investigating.

Such tasks so commonly used as pursuit rotors or star tracers can be purchased or made. Stabilometers and positioning tasks can be easily made. [See illustrations and discussion earlier in this chapter but especially the laboratory manual developed by Singer, Milne, Magill, Powell, and Vachon (1975) for a much more intensive description of a variety of purchased and constructed tasks.] Simple tasks can effectively provide answers to problems in the motor-learning area. Because the usual data are recorded in the form of speed of performance and/or accuracy, timers and counters are often hooked up to constructed or purchased equipment. It is quite usual to see motor-learning laboratories heavily armed with workshop tools and materials as well as electrical and electronic accessories. Learning experiments usually make innovative demands upon the researcher in a variety of forms, one of which is task development and utilization.

Besides those already illustrated, another versatile piece of equipment is the Automatic Performance Analyzer (Figure 4–12), which can be used to

Figure 4–12. The Automatic Perform- ance Analyzer (Dekan Timing Devices, P. O. Box 712, Glen Ellyn, Illinois).

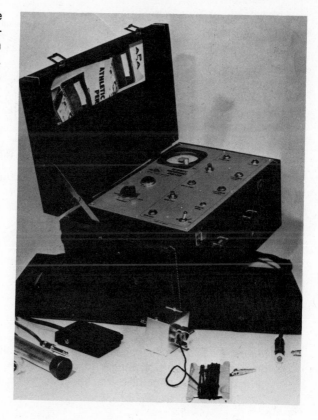

time a variety of events. Various stimuli and response modes can be adapted with the Analyzer. One possible application of the Analyzer is il- lustrated in Figure 4–13. As described elsewhere (Singer, Llewellyn, and Darden, 1973), the Analyzer was used with an interval timer, a 0.01-second performance timer, and a photoelectric relay system. The subject began the test (to determine reaction- and movement-time scores under specified con- ditions) seated in a ready position with the index finger of his dominant hand depressing a key. Upon illumination of a light on the interval timer (randomly timed following the preparation signal) the subject, as quickly as possible, removed his finger from the starting key and moved his hand through the ray of the photoelectric relay system in a prespecified direc- tion. The elapsed time from the illumination of the light stimulus to the release of the starting key was recorded as the subject's reaction time. Upon release from the key another timer was initiated. When the subject's hand passed through the ray the second timer was deactivated, providing a measure of movement time. Note in Figure 4–13 that the experimenter and subject were separated with the use of a divider so as to minimize any ex- perimenter and subject interaction effects.

Space is needed in any laboratory to store testing equipment and shop

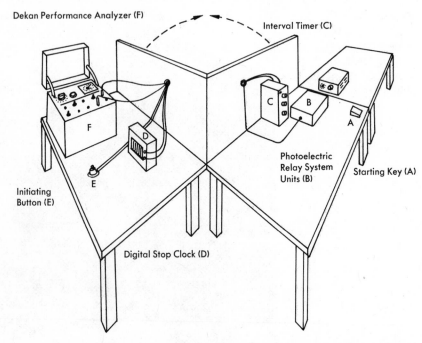

Figure 4–13.   Arrangement for testing reaction time and movement time. (From Robert N. Singer, Jack Llewellyn, and Ellington Darden, "Placebo and Competitive Placebo Effects on Motor Skill," *Research Quarterly*, 44:51–58, 1973.)

tools and materials. Space is also needed to construct equipment and to arrange various testing configurations. Another space consideration is testing privacy through the use of separate rooms or isolation booths. Distractions can contaminate data. An illustration of how pursuit rotor testing can occur without the noticeable presence of the experimenter appears in Figure 4–14. The subject operates the rotary pursuit apparatus in an isolation booth. The interval timer connected to the rotor provided the subject with a 5-second warning in the form of an illuminated light prior to the initiation of each trial. A series of trials, with tests and rests of 20-second duration, was administered. Performance was measured by time on target for each trial, using a 0.01-second timer located outside the isolation booth. The experimenter recorded the time on target for each trial and then reset the timer.

The apparatus and testing situations described thus far are relatively simple. Expense is small and testing arrangements are not difficult to formulate. With increasing sensitivity of the experimenter for control of extraneous sociopsychological variables as well as advances in technology and lowered prices of computers and solid-state systems, behavioral data are being collected more validly under improved testing conditions. Small-scale

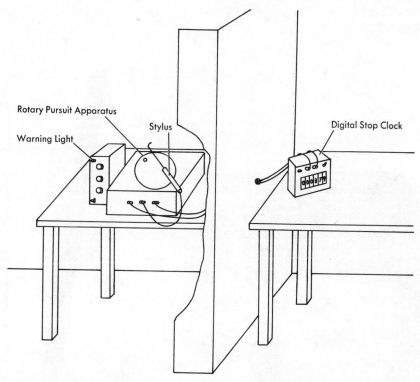

Figure 4–14. Arrangement for testing pursuit rotor performance. (From Robert N. Singer and Jack H. Llewellyn, "Effects of Experimenter's Gender on Subject Performance," *Research Quarterly,* 44:185–191, 1973.)

computers and solid-state programmers are becoming more widely used in behavioral laboratories, resulting in controlled cue presentations and response recordings.

For instance, the model presented in Figure 4–15 is very versatile and inexpensive. The experiment can be programmed on a plugboard, which is inserted in the console control panel with the appropriate stimuli input and response output accessories. The subject's performance data can be recorded with timers or counters. The user must be familiar with digital logic. Preprogrammed experiments free the experimenter's time and usually contain more precision and control than nonprogrammed experiments.

In an experiment done at Florida State University to determine relationships of factors associated with reaction time and movement time, Magill and Powell (1974) used the Foringer model. Two millisecond timers were used to record RT and MT latencies to a visual stimulus. The stimulus warning light, stimulus light, random presentation (1 to 4 seconds of the

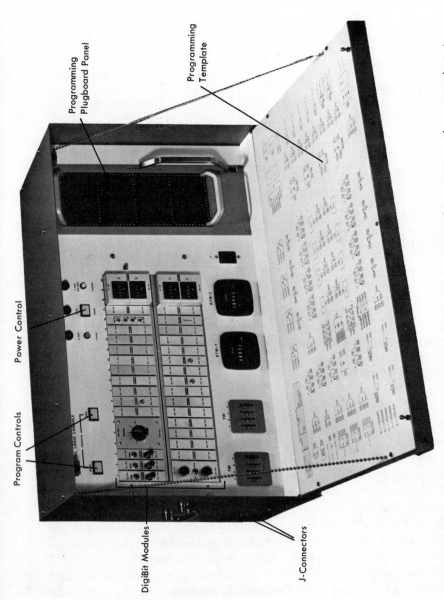

Programming
Plugboard Panel

Programming
Template

Power Control

Program Controls

DigiBit Modules

J-Connectors

Figure 4-15. The Digilab, a portable solid-state system for programming experiments. (From BRS Foringer, 5451 Holland Drive, Beltsville, Maryland.)

136

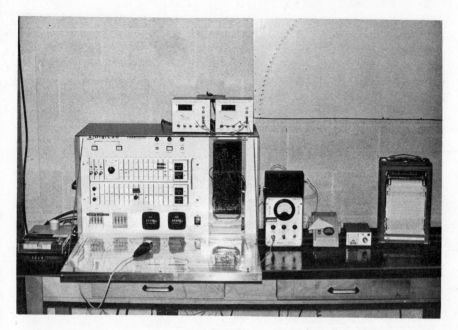

Figure 4–16. Experimenter's display, with the BRS programmer and appropriate accessory equipment, for reaction-time–movement-time experiment. [From Richard A. Magill and Frank M. Powell, "A Consideration of Equipment and Method as Experimental Variables in RT-MT Experiments". (unpublished study, 1974).]

stimulus light following the onset of the warning light), intertrial interval, total experimental time, number of stimulus presentations, and number of subject responses were controlled and recorded by a BRS Foringer DigiLab (DLC-002). The DLC is a portable solid-state digital logic system allowing great flexibility in programming. Because the experiment was controlled from a room adjacent to the testing area, the experimenter communicated with the subject by means of an intercom. A white-noise generator provided a masking noise to the subjects of 72 decibels intensity at ear level. During verbal interaction the ambient noise level was automatically attenuated to 66 decibels. Task instructions were prerecorded on magnetic tape and presented to each subject via the intercom. Displays are presented in Figures 4–16 and 4–17.

Regardless of the available financial and apparatus resources, the crux of any model experiment rests with the researcher's talents and abilities. Being aware of experimental control factors and understanding the nature of the learning phenomenon under investigation lead to a quality research project. We can all be envious of working in the most elaborate settings and with the finest and most expensive apparatus. But there are many examples

Figure 4–17.   Subject's display, in separate room from experimenter's display, for reaction-time–movement-time experiment. [From Richard A. Magill and Frank M. Powell, "A Consideration of Equipment and Method as Experimental Variables in RT-MT Experiments" (unpublished study, 1974).]

of experiments that have made outstanding contributions to learning theory and practice with a minimal amount of costly equipment.

RESEARCH METHODOLOGY AND EXPERIMENTAL DESIGN

The scientific study of learning and behavior is based upon research evidence. *Research* refers to a product completed in a systematic, controlled way, using a formalized type of process, and following a scientific method. By *systematic*, we mean that there is a definite arrangement of the processes used. They are not undertaken in a haphazard way. Certain generalized rules must be followed in order that confidence can be held in the results of the study. And the use of the word *formal* implies a similar interpretation. There are formal rules governing the conducting of research. The planning and execution of the study do not transpire solely out of logic, intuition, and reasoning. There is a set of concrete interrelated steps one follows.

The use of the word *control* means that the investigator has control over the situation. The study does not run him; he runs it. He is the one who selects the subjects and the content matter. If it is an experimental study, he chooses the task and the way the subjects will be manipulated and tested. Control is thus exhibited in numerous ways. He does not, of course, have total control as to how the subjects will perform in the experiment. Nevertheless, valid, or true, measurements are, one hopes, obtained. The researcher tries to exhibit control by successfully manipulating variables that will result in true results—not in chance, haphazard outcomes.

All of these procedures have to do with scientific methods of analyses. At one time, researchers spoke of *the scientific method* of analysis. Books on research methodology consistently inferred that there was only one scientific method. Well, that is simply not true. There are actually a number of acceptable ways in which one can conduct research, and a given scientific method may be applicable in a particular situation. Distinctions may be made in the nature of research projects (e.g., historical, descriptive, and experimental), although there is a certain amount of formalized routine that is followed from study to study. Thus the novice should be aware that there are distinctions within research and acceptable types of procedures and techniques, as well as overlapping.

Gaining Information

To know something, to gain information about the universe or behavior, or any aspect of life, research is not the only answer. Other techniques besides a scientific approach may be reasonably acceptable. Knowledge can be obtained through at least three approaches.

Intuition and reason are used by all of us every day. Perhaps some of us do not use them enough. Some involved in research, it is argued, should call upon reason more when designing experiments or interpreting results. Nevertheless, by only reacting according to rationale, we are in danger of being too subjective in the way we view things. Objectivity is tossed aside. One must consider this when appraising or evaluating anything. When you say you know something—how do you know it? Through belief, reason, feeling, thought? How accurate is this process? Is there a better way? At any rate, reason and rationale are approaches to understanding and gaining information.

A second technique employed fairly often is the acquisition of beliefs through *authority*, a person directing another's thoughts or actions. We listen to individuals who are in positions of power, and have a tendency to go along with everything that is said. Are their statements all truisms? It is true that authorities provide a way to learn. Is it the best arrangement? You have to decide for yourself if being told what is right and wrong is desirable. Naturally some knowledge can be assimilated through the authoritarian approach. However, the danger exists of being misinformed or misled. Furthermore, the discouragement of probing, questioning, and problem solving can also be detrimental to the learning process.

Finally, the third avenue to knowledge is *a scientific approach*, in which some sort of formalized system and more objective ways are used for obtaining answers to questions that disturb us. Who discovered the game of baseball? I can tell you who I think invented it. The answer can also come from a book. But perhaps you are not ready to accept these sources and the information offered. So you take a year and examine all possible resources in the archives and determine that Abner Doubleday probably did not invent the game of baseball after all, as is popularly thought. The circumstantial evidence would lead us to believe that he could not be responsible for its origin although, for some reason, scattered evidence has been passed on through the years suggesting that he did invent the sport.

Nonacceptance of "factual" material or the viewpoints of authorities can be countered by a personal undertaking of scientific processes to establish the "truth." In the case of baseball, you did not accept an established "fact." Much time and effort was spent in order to come closer to the truth. Of course, each of us would not care to utilize such a lengthy and precise process to ascertain the answers to our questions. But we can scrutinize the means by which others have arrived at their conclusions and determine their credence.

There is danger at times in accepting statements based on belief and intuition, or materials unquestioningly passed on through the years, as was the case with Doubleday and baseball. This point is quite apparent today, for the current generation of youthful scholars no longer accepts anything. Maybe the pendulum is swinging at too great an extreme today in this direction. But there is nothing wrong with probing, questioning, and searching. In other words, then, the product of a scientific method enables us to have greater objectivity and affirmation of the thoughts we hold on a given topic. To advocate scientific processes does not exclude other means that might yield solutions. Solutions may be found through logic and reasoning, or words written or spoken by authorities. But our greatest strength will come from answers that we actually have to find for ourselves, by using scientifically acceptable techniques in the search.

The Experiment

Experimentation is crucial in scientific research. Most of the research data reported in this book were collected in experimentally designed studies. In the classical sense, an *experiment* is a way of formulating and testing hypotheses. We begin with a hunch. These hunches provide direction for our thoughts on problems, and an experiment allows us, in a formal setting, to see if they are confirmed. With the experiment a planned attack is made on a particular problem. Typically, through well-constructed operations, changes are induced in natural events and results are observed, recorded, and analyzed. This is the outstanding feature of experimental research as constrasted with descriptive research; there must be some manipulation or change in at least one variable under study.

Historically speaking, concepts and implications of experimentation have been diverse and misunderstood. At one time people expected miraculous answers from experiments but were, instead, disappointed and disillusioned. It is now understood that experiments do not provide once-and-for-all answers. Facts are not necessarily permanent, and numerous experiments, constantly being refined in technique, provide tentative solutions to problems.

This is especially true of experiments dealing with human behavior. The degree of control and sophistication in an experiment in physics or chemistry is potentially far greater than in the human behavior experiments of psychology, sociology, physiology, or physical education.

The experimenter needs a spirit of curiosity, or *inquiry*. A search for the truth, a dissatisfaction with the present state of knowledge, a desire to resolve an issue in a scientifically acceptable manner are all involved. *Background* information is necessary before an experiment is attempted. Experience, reading, and communication contribute to the investigator's level of understanding of the problem, enabling him to raise legitimate questions, conceive of reasonable hypotheses, and formulate adequate experimental designs.

Because statistics and experiments often go hand in hand, an understanding of mathematics is most helpful. Statistics aid in various steps from the initial to the terminal stages of the experiment. Finally, good old-fashioned common sense is needed at all points throughout the experiment. The investigator must make numerous decisions as he proceeds, not all of which can be guided by directive statements. Evaluation of suggested procedures, analysis of the particular experimental conditions, and competencies to handle unpredictable and unexpected occurrences all require common sense. Through these and other personal qualities, the experimenter examines theories and statements, formulates workable hypotheses for a particular problem, and executes the investigation.

IMPORTANCE OF RESEARCH IN MOTOR LEARNING

As can be seen, research, and more specifically experimental research, is primarily associated with information gathered about the acquisition and performance of motor skills. Consequently, great care must be shown in the planning of studies, the collection of data, and the conclusions made from these data. It is a tremendous challenge to meticulously design an experiment that yields valid data, further advancing our state of knowledge.

REFERENCES

BAHRICK, HARRY P., PAUL M. FITTS, and GEORGE E. BRIGGS. "Learning Curves—Facts or Artifacts," *Psychological Bulletin,* 54:256–268, 1957.

BRADLEY, JAMES V. "Practice to an Asymptote?" *Journal of Motor Behavior,* 1:285–296, 1969.

BRYAN, W., and N. HARTER. "Studies in the Physiology and Psychology of Telegraphic Language," *Psychological Review,* 4:27–53, 1897.

CROMWELL, LESLIE, FRED J. WEIBELL, ERICH A. PFEIFFER, and LEO B. USSELMAN. *Biomedical Instrumentation and Measurements.* Englewood Cliffs, N.J.: Prentice-Hall, Inc., 1973.

CRONBACH, LEE J., and LITA FURBY. "How We Should Measure "Change" —Or Should We?" *Psychological Bulletin,* 74:68–80, 1970.

CULLER, E. "Nature of the Learning Curve," *Psychological Bulletin,* 34: 742–743, 1928.

———, and E. GIRDEN. "The Learning Curve in Relation to Other Psychometric Functions," *American Journal of Psychology,* 64:327–349, 1951.

DAVIS, FREDERICK B. *Educational Measurements and Their Interpretation.* Belmont, Calif.: Wadsworth, 1964.

DROWATZKY, JOHN. "Evaluation of Mirror-Tracing Performance Measures as Indicators of Learning," *Research Quarterly,* 40:228–230, 1969.

ESTES, W. K. "The Problem of Inference from Curves Based on Group Data," *Psychological Bulletin,* 53:134–140, 1956.

———. "Toward a Statistical Theory of Learning," *Psychological Review,* 57:94–107, 1950.

HALE, PATRICIA W., and ROBERT M. HALE. "Comparison of Student Improvement by Exponential Modification of Test-Retest Scores," *Research Quarterly,* 43:113–120, 1972.

HARRIS, CHESTER W. (ed.). *Problems in Measuring Change.* Madison: University of Wisconsin Press, 1963.

HEATHERINGTON, ROSS. "Within-Subject Variation, Measurement Error, and Selection of a Criterion Score," *Research Quarterly,* 44:113–117, 1973.

HENRY, FRANKLIN M. " 'Best' Versus 'Average' Individual Scores," *Research Quarterly,* 38:317–320, 1967.

KELLER, F. S. "The Phantom Plateau," *Journal of the Experimental Analysis of Behavior,* 1:1–13, 1958.

KROLL, WALTER. "Reliability Theory and Research Decision in Selection of a Criterion Score," *Research Quarterly,* 38:412–419, 1967.

MAGILL, RICHARD A., and FRANK M. POWELL. "A Consideration of Equipment and Method as Experimental Variables in RT-MT Experiments" (Unpublished Study, Florida State University, 1974).

McCRAW, L. W. "A Comparison of Methods of Measuring Improvement," *Research Quarterly*, 22:191–200, 1951.

———. "Comparative Analysis of Methods of Scoring Tests of Motor Learning," *Research Quarterly*, 26:440–453, 1955.

SCHUTZ, ROBERT W., and ERIC A. ROY. "Absolute Error: The Devil in Disguise," *Journal of Motor Behavior*, 5:141–153, 1973.

SINGER, ROBERT N., JACK LLEWELLYN, and ELLINGTON DARDEN. "Placebo and Competitive Placebo Effects on Motor Skill," *Research Quarterly*, 44:51–58, 1973.

SINGER, ROBERT N., and JACK K. LLEWELLYN. "Effects of Experimenter's Gender on Subject Performance," *Research Quarterly*, 44:185–191, 1973.

SINGER, ROBERT N., CONRAD MILNE, RICHARD MAGILL, FRANK POWELL, and LUCIEN VACHON. *Laboratory and Field Experiments in Motor Learning*, Springfield, Ill.: Charles C Thomas, Publisher, 1975.

THURSTONE, L. L. "The Learning Function," *Journal of General Psychology*, 3:469–493, 1930.

TUCKER, LEDYARD R., FRED DAMARIN, and SAMUEL MESSICK. "A Base-Free Measure of Change," *Psychometrika*, 31:457–473, 1966.

5

SYSTEMS ANALYSIS
AND HUMAN
BEHAVIOR

We introduced the term *systems models* in Chapter 3 and stated that such models describe components of a system and their functional interrelationships. The word *system* is used quite frequently. Physiologically oriented discussions will include reference to the digestive, nervous, and circulatory systems. Computer and machine systems include a network of mechanisms constructed for an expressed purpose. The teacher and the coach have formulated systems under which they and their students will work. Systems, whether the reference is to machinery, man–machine interactions, or human functioning and behavior, include purposes, systems parts, and relationships.

The system usually connotes a "wholeness." That is, the system is the entire functioning unit, complete with subsystems that work together to fulfill some objective. However, there are many examples of systems within systems; that is, a system may be complete when viewed one way and yet be part of a larger system. A person's behavior, as represented by a response made to a situation, could be examined systematically and referred to as a behavioral system, or it could be examined within the context of an organized sport activity. The system is thereby enlarged, more variables are viewed, and the arrangement becomes more complex and intricately woven. Look at the educational system, which contains an administrative system, a purchasing system, an instructional system, and many others. If the school system is to work, all of its comprising systems (subsystems) must operate interrelatedly at high levels of capability.

SYSTEMS ANALYSIS

Systems analysis helps to define the series of operations and the involvement of parts contributing to the objective. In this sense, such an analysis merely does the obvious. But it often happens that obvious procedures are not followed or are followed poorly. The systematic approach to studying human behavior requires the identification of contributing units and how they interact to influence learning and performance. Meaning is enhanced as scientific rigor is applied. Systems analysis provides a means for examining human behavior in an organized, dynamic manner, whereby links are identified and interdependently expressed, as research and theory permit. Decision making in practical situations, knowledge of behavior needs to be applied, and information description, based on scientific knowledge, are enhanced with systems analysis. The systems approach is a way (not the only one, but certainly one of the more popular today) of thinking of entire operations and component parts. Beyond description, it is an effective approach in instruction to examining alternatives and making decisions.

Systems design experts have been active in industry, the military, and, more recently, in education. Norman Heimstra and Vernon Ellingstad (1972) present a traditional introduction to psychology with a model of the human system. As they put it, there is little doubt of what material to cover, but the question is how to present it. Robert N. Singer and Walter Dick (1974) have proposed a systems model that can be used in instruction, and they have developed materials expressly for the teaching of physical education. Figure 5–1 contains the complete instructional systems model. It suggests a flow of activities that a teacher would conduct in order to produce effective instruction. There are many instructional models in use today; all have many similarities and differ primarily in certain components or in the sequence in which the components are diagramed.

Instructional analysis should proceed in a systematic way. A specific but partial analysis is made in Figure 5–2, where a hierarchy of skills is indicated for the learner to achieve the objective of effectively participating in a nine-inning baseball game. A task analysis must be made in order to determine the subordinate tasks prerequisite for the mastery of higher-level tasks. The process of specifying the tasks and indicating their relationships in order to achieve the goal suggests that instructional analysis, a component of the instructional systems model (see Figure 5–1), follows the principles of systems analysis also. These are examples of instructional systems. It is also possible to develop a system that describes human behavior.

As we saw in Chapter 3, a number of nonsystems and systems models have been proposed (e.g., cybernetic, information-processing, adaptive) to describe skill acquisition and motor performance. These were primarily

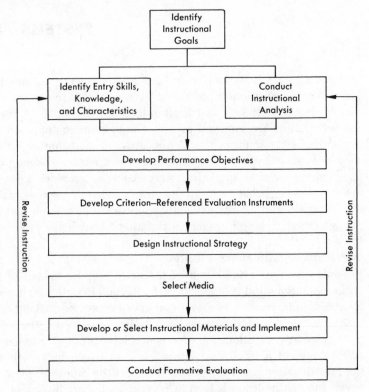

Figure 5–1. Systems approach model for instruction. [From Robert N. Singer and Walter Dick, *Teaching Physical Education: A Systems Approach* (Boston: Houghton Mifflin, 1974).]

developed by engineering and experimental psychologists. In all cases these systems demonstrated the organizational structures of the whole, with inter-relationships of components to each other and to the whole.

It might be argued, however, that certain models emphasized certain processes or components to the exclusion of others. Perhaps an insufficient number of variables were considered. If the objective is to determine how one performs at a particular time and how to improve upon this response, then a number of subsystems and potential processes must be examined. We cannot formulate plans and design operations that will affect learning until we understand (1) how learning occurs and (2) which factors influence the learning process. We must return to purpose. If our purpose was merely to describe skilled behavior, irrespective of task, environmental conditions, developmental factors, and the like, the system might appear one way. But it would be far more complex when our purposes included (1) describing the skill-acquisition process, from initial to highest levels,

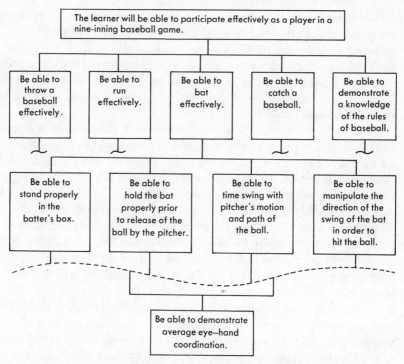

Figure 5–2.   Example of a partial learning hierarchy resulting from an instructional analysis. [From Robert N. Singer and Walter Dick, *Teaching Physical Education: A Systems Approach* (Boston: Houghton Mifflin, 1974).]

considering individual differences as well as those factors previously mentioned, and (2) suggesting instructional and training programs to facilitate the learning process. We will follow the latter course in this book.

The model proposed here describes the way individuals seem to acquire skill and to perform in certain situations. It is proposed as a visual aid for students of motor learning, not as a complete alternative to existing models. It attempts to combine many of the features of those models described in Chapter 3.

SYSTEMS MODEL OF HUMAN MOTOR BEHAVIOR

A behaving system, be it man or machine, contains certain prerequisite characteristics. In fact, a usual reference in the psychological literature is to man–machine systems, where several human and machine components are designed to work together to fulfill some goal. Transportation systems, such as flying a plane, require the harmonious interplay of man and machine. In such man–machine dynamics, there is present some form of sensing device that selectively allows some messages to continue on in the system. Noise or bias (confunding, distracting) cues can be coped with and should minimally affect output.

In these systems, operations can appear as if programmed (a set of internal instructions that assume the form of a master plan), thus the reliance on memory stores where programs can be built up and stored for usage at the appropriate signal. At the same time there is flexibility in the system— an ability to adapt to changing circumstances. There are times when a master plan must be altered, and the system should possess the desired arrangements with its components to allow for control and alteration. A well-designed system should be able to fulfill specified objectives. Effective output will be determined by internal and external control factors, the ability to process and handle a variety of stimuli by making correct responses.

A person can be considered as a system, selecting from available cues and responding in a purposeful manner following the activation of decision-making processes. If we were to consider various categories of tasks the human learns to perform, perhaps a variety of models, two of which were expressed in Figures 3–12 and 3–13, would be needed. Discounting the contrasting characteristics of tasks, a search for commonalities would probably lead to the model illustrated in Figure 5–3. This model highlights the basic human processes involved in motor learning and performance. The remainder of the material in this chapter provides an overview of the person as a behaving system, to be developed much more fully in Chapter 6. Influences on this system will be analyzed in detail in the remainder of the book.

Situational and Internal Cues

In any given circumstance, a host of cues external (situational) and internal can potentially impinge upon the system. The display is the immediate situation confronting the learner. From it as well as more removed or internalized cues, an excessive amount of sensory bombardment is possible. In any given situation, a magnificent array of relevant, redundant, and useless information may be present.

Sense Reception

The sensing subsystem is important in that it is the medium by which the system receives input. The capability to sense, to receive internal and ex-

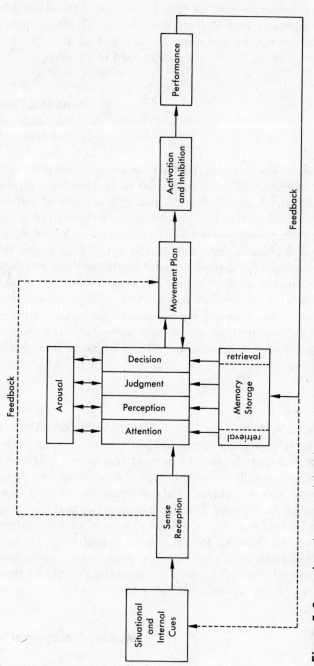

Figure 5–3. A systems model of human motor behavior.

ternal information, is prerequisite to the operation of the other subsystems. The human possesses several sensory modalities by which input can be received. The sensors, or receptors, are sensitive to a variety of stimuli, each sensor capable of handling a specific kind of stimulus.

Attention, Perception, Judgment, and Decision Making

Once information has been received by the sensory system it must be attended to, perceived, and judged in order to be effectively responded to. The ability to attend selectively to a minimum of relevant information is a process associated with skilled performance. The process of perception is synonymous with meaning. After knowledge of situational cues is gained, judgment and decision making follow. The speed with which this entire process must occur will depend on whether the activity is self-paced or externally paced. The amount of time necessary for processing information is directly related to the level of skill mastery, with processing time quickest for those activities in which we are most experienced. Task complexity will also be relative to time lags in this subsystem. The importance of cognitive aspects of task performance should never be minimized.

Arousal

The system's state of activation will reflect its ability attentively to select appropriate cues from a vast assortment of them, to perceive, evaluate, and make decisions accurately, and to respond effectively. It is one thing to arouse behavior generally, another for it to be activated and directed in a purposeful way. The desirable arousal conditions are different from task to task and learner to learner. Thus each processing and responding subsystem must be able to demonstrate the ideal level of arousal from movement to movement in order for meaningful output to occur. Behavior is energized when motivation is present. The person's own ability to generate an optimal arousal level, along with the arousal properties of the task, indicates the complexity of the workings of the subsystem.

Memory Storage and Retrieval

Two processes appear to comprise memory: primary and secondary. Information must pass through the primary, short-term store, to the secondary, long-term store, if meaningful retention is to occur. Experiences are stored, to be called upon when similar situations arise again. The system responds according to immediate circumstances and in the framework of previous experiences, both of which interact to direct performance. Retrieval abilities depend on the quality of the memory storage.

Movement Plan

Once the situation has been analyzed and the goal determined, an operational plan is put into effect. It may be a well-learned plan, which has been activated on many previous occasions, or a plan modified to meet sudden situational demands. The plan may be a "sure thing" or a trial-and-error operation. Plans must be available on short notice in some task performances, whereas in others plans can be formulated with more time and care. The plan is matched to the goal, and only knowledge of performance or the results of performance will reveal the plan's acceptability.

Activation and Inhibition

The movement plan will probably call for the innervation of certain muscle fiber units and the control of others. Although most people think of performance as the result of energized and activated tissue, in reality, coordinated activity is also greatly dependent upon the ability to control antagonistic tissues. Skilled performance is often referred to as controlled movement. Control, in the broadest interpretation of the word, refers to one's capability to activate and inhibit body tissues according to the spatial and temporal demands of the activity.

Performance

Any system must contain some output means in order to determine its capability of handling the assigned tasks. One's ability to cope with and act upon the internal and external environment is reflected by his behavior. To ascertain what has been learned and the capability to perform well, some measure of performance is necessary. Input in the form of sensory cues is transformed to output in the form of behavior. Thus a perfect match between output and input in the system indicates excellence in transmission and execution, in spite of the potential hampering factors that might operate anywhere in the system.

Feedback

To assess the performance output match with the sensory input, a comparison is made by using a feedback loop. The system has its own self-correcting device. For certain activities, correction and adjustment are ongoing and each performance reaction stimulates sense receptors to guide subsequent performance during these activities. And for other activities, when informational feedback is only present upon the completion of an act, it will be stored in the memory system to guide future acts. In all cases, whether knowledge is provided during or following performance, learning is potentially improved, for such information can be retrieved on subsequent occasions to guide the cognitive processes involved in motor performance. We saw two example tasks in Chapter 3, one being dynamic, continuous, and externally paced (Figure 3–13), and the other brief and self-paced (Figure 3–13). Feedback seemed to play different roles in each task. Depending on the task and one's theoretical framework, skilled performance is (1) directed by a central force, or movement program, or (2) guided by sensory feedback. Thus the model shows both possibilities: performance feedback loops can either go into central mechanisms or activate peripheral receptors and subsequent actions.

We have now briefly covered the basic components of the human system as they operate together to produce goal-oriented movement behaviors. These subsystems will be explained in more depth in following chapters.

It is important to realize that all systems are alike in certain ways and yet different in other ways. Genetic factors in the human species determine similarities among organisms. Genetics and experiences also contribute to differences among systems, differences in abilities and capabilities to perform and to achieve in specified tasks. Furthermore, there are systems with various degrees of sophistication. In human systems, the analogy would be the development and maturation process. Youthful systems possess less capability to perform complex and demanding activities than mature systems.

SYSTEMS DIFFERENCES

If all human systems were exactly alike, then we would expect all to respond exactly the same when in similar situations. Such is not the case. We can attempt to posit similarities in behavioral manifestations for the "average" person under certain conditions (laws of learning and behavioral modification). Countless research publications and theoretical notions provide us with some security in making general statements about behavior. In fact, most of the content of this book includes statements about how the average system works and how it is affected by external systems, such as peculiar environmental conditions.

Nonetheless, a recognition of individual differences suggests special considerations, for both general understanding and practical implications. Not only can individuals behave differently when present in the same circumstance, but it is conceivable that the same person might elicit varying behaviors in that same circumstance as well. In order to attain a better understanding of how systems function, then, we must be familiar with commonalities as well as distinctions.

Abilities and Capabilities

The design of many systems is such as to favor some to the disadvantage of others. Motor and intellectual abilities, physical characteristics, temperament, and personality traits vary from person to person, the product of hereditary and experiential factors. Extreme distinctions among human systems in any one or a combination of these characteristics may dissimilarly affect the learning of and performance in activities. Abilities are personal traits that underlie potential for success in specific skills. The ideal presence of abilities and capabilities suggests this system to be favored in skill acquisition and performance.

Developmental Factors

More elaborately structured systems have a greater probability of performing more complex tasks. Actually, with development and sophistication, each of the subsystems in the system can function at a higher level. Performance output is, among other things, a function of the complexity and performance capabilities of the system. The human system undergoes noticeable maturational changes, especially in the early and formative years. These changes affect the functioning possibilities of the sensoriperception process, memory and retrieval processes, cognitive processes, and motor mechanisms. At older age the system is also undergoing some change, usually influencing performance output in a negative manner.

THE HUMAN ORGANISM
AS A SUBSYSTEM

To this point we have observed the human behavioral system as it exists, irrespective for the most part of other systems. However, almost every system can fit into a larger system, and so cutoff points are established for convenience. The momentary behavioral potential of the system is not dictated solely by the operations of the subsystems themselves. Impinging upon the human system are external factors. Systems of instruction and

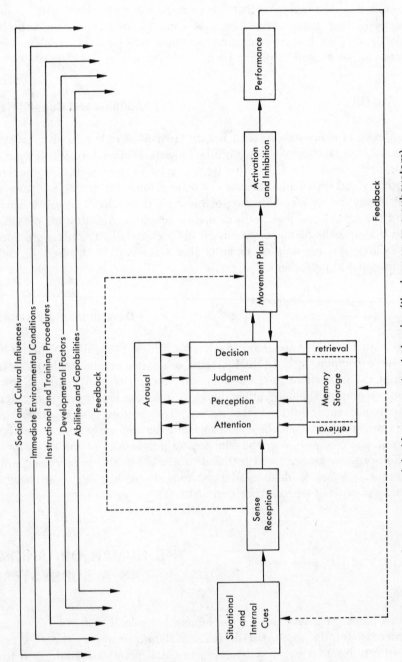

Figure 5–4. A systems model of human motor behavior (the human as a subsystem).

training affect performance output as well as the learning processes associated with every subsystem in the model along the way. So is the case with immediate environmental conditions: noise, temperature, lighting, and other variables. On the broadest scale, human behavior is shaped by the sociocultural system present in society. This system infiltrates the human behavioral system by manifesting itself in the form of interests in and attitudes toward activities, motivation and reinforcement, and outlet possibilities. The "complete picture" of the human system surrounded and influenced by other systems is illustrated in Figure 5–4.

Figure 5–5 depicts the learner or performer more formally as a system within a system. This much larger system describes the relationship of the human to other factors than internal ones that influence behaviorial output. As we can see, sociocultural variables influence the attitudes, interests, motivations, and general predispositions of the persons to want to participate in certain activities as well as to excel in them. Differential factors, such as developmental characteristics and abilities and capabilities, cause each human system to operate in different ways. Also, it is important to acknowledge the fact that there are broad-based abilities and capabilities that will influence the person to succeed in a wide variety of tasks as well as task-specific demands upon certain abilities and capabilities. The quality and extent of instruction and training the person has, with consideration of immediate environmental factors, will help to produce the human's behavior in specified situations. Viewed in this way, man is but one subsystem, along with others, having a role in influencing behavior. He influences, and is influenced by, the situation.

If we want to know how the *average* person will perform in a newly introduced task, a fairly good estimation can be obtained from an analysis of task characteristics (e.g., number of response alternatives, magnitude of response, timing, sequence, cue alternatives, cue predictability). But if we are after knowledge of an *individual's* performance with a newly introduced task, the task and the individual's unique characteristics must be known. Although practice techniques can be geared for the average or the individual, in general learning will occur to some degree through practice as

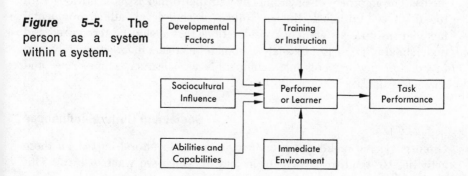

Figure 5–5. The person as a system within a system.

capabilities improve. Environmental characteristics (temperature, noise, illumination) as well as training techniques can affect learning and performance.

Instructional and Training Procedures

The complex human behavioral system can be modified through instruction and training, and must be if excellence in skilled performance is the goal. Specific practice regimens can influence one's ability to discriminate among and attend to relevant cues, to process information quickly and accurately, to formulate and enact appropriate movement plans, and to execute them effectively. Thus training systems can modify the human behavioral system. There are many practice considerations that will be dealt with later. Among them are speed–accuracy trade-offs, massed and distributed practice trade-offs, simulated versus real practice decisions, the availability of reinforcement, incentives, and knowledge of results, whole versus part task practice, and the use of principles of the transfer of training. An ample discussion on practice systems is presented later in this book, for it is believed that a teacher, coach, supervisor, or the learner himself can do much to modify the behavioral system with appropriate learning techniques. Man–machine designs are relevant here, for a person is usually involved with nonhuman elements (apparatus, projectiles, equipment) when called upon to demonstrate skilled motor performance.

Immediate Environmental Conditions

The surroundings in which the human performs will no doubt have some impact on behavior. The most influential environmental factors surrounding performance might be regarded as stressful. Audiences, noises, extreme temperatures, and the like, require adjustments on the part of the human system, although we usually think of the skilled performer as one who can accommodate himself to changed and even noxious-appearing environments. The interplay of environment with performer is most obvious with the relatively unskilled. But regardless of skill level, all environmental factors constitute a system of considerations that should be recognized and understood in order to (1) analyze human behaviors more adequately, and (2) design environments more compatible with learner competencies and characteristics.

Social and Cultural Influences

Often neglected or taken for granted is the sociocultural impact on those activities we tend to participate in and in which we want to excel. This influence is more obvious when we observe that in different societies and countries, relatively more craftsmen of one kind than another can be counted. Recreational pursuits differ. Forms of athletic competition, in variety and intensity, also vary from culture to culture. It is not within the scope of this book to analyze the philosophical ramifications of the effect of culture on behavior. But we would be remiss not to acknowledge the association, as B. F. Skinner has so powerfully done in his book *Beyond Freedom and Dignity* (1971).

AN OVERVIEW OF FACTORS IN PSYCHOMOTOR PERFORMANCE

To understand and explain movement-oriented behaviors requires the identification of a host of factors that contribute to successful performance. The learning process operates in similar ways for all tasks and yet there are unique considerations for different categories of tasks. Task dimensions, as to stimulus patterns and response patterns, dictate the appropriate learner operations for proficiency to be demonstrated. The sense modalities involved and their extent of involvement, the nature of the stimuli (predictability, number, sequence, and overall characteristics), as well as response possibilities, the number, type, precision, timing, speed, force, and the like, suggest operations the learner must follow.

Instructional and training procedures offer many trade-off possibilities. Instruction (how offered, to what degree) and practice (amount, use of reinforcement), knowledge of results, media, cuing, and motivational techniques) must be adjusted according to time, space, and equipment limitations and to learner capacities and task characteristics.

Finally, variables that contribute to individual differences in motor performance (physical and sensory characteristics, perceptual, cognitive, and motor abilities, genetics and previous experiences, and personality traits) suggest behavioral expectations as well as proper instructional and training techniques. The dynamic interplay of practice procedural variables, task dimensions, learning process constraints, and individual differences influences motor behaviors. The scientific study of motor behavior and skill acquisition encompasses all these categories of factors and more.

In the remaining pages, the heart of this book, we will examine the systems model of human motor behavior, with special recognition of the subsystems. Once completing this objective, special material will be presented in order to elaborate upon individual differences (abilities and capabilities as well as developmental factors). An abundance of literature will be reviewed that deals with instructional and training procedures. To a much lesser extent, immediate environmental and sociocultural influences on behavior will be treated.

REFERENCES

HEIMSTRA, NORMAN W., and VERNON S. ELLINGSTAD. *Human Behavior: A Systems Approach.* Monterey, Calif.: Brooks/Cole Publishing Co., 1972.
SINGER, ROBERT N., and WALTER DICK. *Teaching Physical Education: A Systems Approach.* Boston: Houghton Mifflin Company, 1974.
SKINNER, B. F. *Beyond Freedom and Dignity.* New York: Alfred A. Knopf, Inc., 1971.

6

THE HUMAN
BEHAVING SYSTEM

A brief description of the human behaving system was presented in the preceding chapter. We will elaborate upon the component parts and the way they interact in this chapter. Perhaps an introductory analogy between the human system and a computer system may best serve to provide an understanding of operations. Computers are quite elaborately designed today and can serve many purposes. These man-made machines can be programmed to problem-solve, sort and classify, handle mathematical problems, and even play checkers. Their potential appears to be limited only by man's conceptual framework. All that is required for the computer to function in desired form, stated rather simply, are an accurate blueprint, a large amount of money for its construction, and its own *machine language* or code.

The computer performs in a prescribed manner and yields appropriate data, the output of which depends on the input. It generates voltage patterns that result in a series of operations, which appear complex but nevertheless can be broken down into relatively simple steps. In essence, the typical computer contains an input system, a transmission system, a cental data processor with a permanent and temporary storage system, and an output system. With this brief description in mind, let us now examine the operational and mechanism similarities between the computer and the human nervous system. It has become quite fashionable today to compare the nervous system to an electronic digital computer. An excellent analogy is provided by Dean Wooldridge (1963). Both systems at a very general level obtain results by similar means. With a little stretch of the imagination, it is not too difficult to envision the similar operations each performs in order to produce desired outcomes.

Let us think of the computer as consisting of an orderly arrangement of wires that permits data to be processed accurately. The cabling organization is such as to interconnect certain wires with other wires and in turn certain mechanisms with other mechanisms. With the input of instructions or *coded words,* electronic operations begin, and appropriate wires and mechanisms are activated in order that the response, or output, be consistent with the input.

If the output is not consistent with the input, there then exists a state of incongruity. The machine is reprogrammed; the organism continues to respond until the desired response occurs. The theory proposed by Miller, Galanter, and Pribram (1960) and explained in Chapter 3 (p. 87) accounts for homeostatic mechanisms that operate via a feedback loop. Instead of dealing with reflex arcs, these authors have formulated a feedback loop, which they call TOTE (test–operate–test–exit), in order to describe all of human behavior.

Input–output comparisons are dependent upon energy, information, and control in the TOTE unit. Energy is represented by neural impulses, information related to that which is transmitted from one place to another, and control gives order to the way an act is executed. The notion of feedback helps to explain the relation between what is received and the resulting action. With appropriate feedback and motivation, the human system repeatedly performs until congruence is attained between input (the desired goal) and output (the actual performance).

All forms of life contain wiring arrangements of neural circuits with structures that permit particular behaviors to occur. The forms of behavior to be displayed by living organisms will depend on many factors, not the least of which will be the complexity of the arrangement of the neural pathways and associated structures. The computer accepts coded words and transforms them to electrical currents for processing; in the same way, the organism receives various types of environmental stimuli and may respond by immediately transforming them to electrical impulses, which will travel in the transmission system or neural network. In organisms, however, not all inputs are automatically transformed to impulses. The modulation of generator potential is affected by the nature of the input, in many cases not leading to an action potential.

The potential capabilities of the central data processor, or brain, will determine the resultant action. Specific and generalized areas of the nervous system are involved in every complex act, and without the appropriate structures, or at least these structures becoming activated at the proper time responses to given stimuli will not be appropriate. At the same time, the input must not exceed the amount of data to be processed at any one time. A live creature can sample and respond to just so many surrounding stimuli, a situation which has advantages and disadvantages, as will be seen.

From this introductory analogy, the reader may now be aware of the direction taken in this chapter. It becomes necessary to handle the nervous system of man in a more elaborate manner, to pay respect to the intricate mechanisms and processes that are apparently involved in human learning and movement. Let us now analyze in greater depth how coordinated activity occurs from input to central control to output.

ENERGIZING THE SYSTEM

Situational and Internal Cues

Any system lies dormant until it is activated. Except when we are sleeping, an infinite number of cues bombard our system. These may come from the immediate environment or from the internal state of affairs, and potentially serve as activating forces on and in the system. A ball thrown to us, words from another person, temperature, a stomach ache, an itch, and the like, are potential cues. Any cue must overcome a certain threshold in order to be attended to, and consequently the vast majority of them go unattended.

Sense Reception

An organism must have a means of receiving and transmitting a stimulus, hence allowing it to respond meaningfully to this stimulus. Actually, the entire nervous system, which permits this activity, is built up of independent units called *neurons*. These structures, though independent, are organized in how they function. The idea that the nervous system is composed of nerve cells was originated in the late 1800's, and the nerve cell was given the name neuron by Waldeyer in 1891. Neurons, or *nerve cells*, number over 10 billion in the typical individual, and there are basically only three types according to function. Before examining these cells by their specific roles, a note or two on the general structure and function of all neurons is in order. Besides a cell body, the typical neuron has extensions, or projections, termed *axons* and *dendrites*. The dendrites usually consist of a number of short fibers that always conduct the nerve impulses to the cell body. Axons, on the other hand, always transmit the impulses away from the cell body (although in certain cases, e.g., in excised nerve, may conduct in either direction) and are usually much longer than dendrites, sometimes measuring 3 feet in length and up to 20 microns in diameter. Only one axon projection may be noted with a given neuron. Axons may make functional connections (*synapses*) with other cell dendrites or bodies, or terminate in effector organs, such as muscles.

Axons, referred to also as *nerve fibers* or in a broader sense *tracts*, are usually surrounded by one or two protective sheaths; dendrites are not. The *myelin sheath* contains fatty substances which give these fibers a white appearance. *Nodes of Ranvier* are gaps between segments of this sheath, and it is believed that these permeable indentations allow ions to pass in and out of the axon more easily than through the sheath. The impulse goes from node to node, and a branching of nerve fibers may occur at these nodes. Myelinated nerves transmit impulses more rapidly than nonmyelinated nerves and therefore demonstrate improved signaling efficiency. Skeletal muscles, which respond quickly, are innervated by myelinated fibers, whereas the slow-moving muscles of the abdominal viscera are activated by nonmyelinated fibers. The *neurilemma sheath* surrounds the myelin sheath, and is a membrane responsible for transmitting electrical potentials as well as regenerating nerve fibers. It covers the fibers directly at the nodes of Ranvier, where the myelin sheath is interrupted. The structures may be observed in Figure 6–1.

Although all nerve cells are structurally similar, certain ones are responsible for the input of information, others function in the output, and yet others act as *connectors* between two nerve cells. *Sensory* or *receptor* neurons play the role of transducers; that is, they convert the information input into electrical signals capable of being transmitted to other parts of the nervous system. The amazing quality of these transducers is their ability to change a specific kind of stimulus (e.g., visual, tactile, or auditory) to the same common transmission: the impulse. Each receptor is specific to one stimulus form only. Not only do they transform various types of inputs,

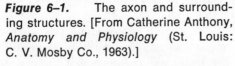

Figure 6–1.   The axon and surrounding structures. [From Catherine Anthony, *Anatomy and Physiology* (St. Louis: C. V. Mosby Co., 1963).]

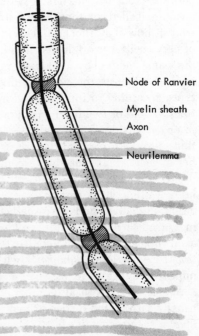

Node of Ranvier

Myelin sheath

Axon

Neurilemma

but sense receptors function to code information, too. The spatial and temporal patterns of nerve impulses, as well as their initiation point, trigger the appropriate subsequent activities in the human system.

The nervous system is so wired that when fibers from the neurons are in close proximity, they are grouped together to form a _nerve_. Imagine the wire hookup, with certain nerves designated to go to and come from specific structures in the nervous system. Information is transmitted from the sense receptors through the spinal cord and brought to the higher levels of the nervous system. In turn, instructions will be transmitted to the muscles and glands. The spinal cord is not a passive carrier of impulses, as it can handle simple kinds of reflex actions.

The first action necessary before an impulse can be transmitted requires the stimulation of an input device or receptor. Based on location, receptors may be classified into four categories: proprioceptors, exteroceptors, interoceptors, and distance receptors.

Proprioceptors are receptors found throughout the body in muscles, tendons, and joints. Different types of proprioceptors are located in these structures, for example, _neuromuscular spindles_ in the muscles, _Golgi tendon organs_ in the tendons, and _pacinian_ corpuscles and _Ruffini_ endings in tissues surrounding the joint. Neuromuscular spindles are stimulated when a muscle is stretched and cause the muscle to contract reflexly. Proprioceptors provide information to the body about changes in body position and movement; they also detect pressure. Along with the impulses from the inner ear, proprioceptors are responsible for the so-called _kinesthetic sense,_ the awareness of body and limb position in space. The _labyrinth_ of the inner ear contains proprioceptors that provide information about the movement of the head. It is a source of movement sensation.

Exteroceptors are receptors on the skin and provide information about the immediate external environment. These structures function in distinguishing light touch (tactile receptors), pressure (pressure receptors), warmth and coolness (thermal receptors), and pain (pain receptors). Specific types of receptors are associated with each of these sensations, many of which have proprioceptive functions as well. The Ruffini end organs respond to warmth, the Meissner corpuscles to light touch, the pacinian corpuscles to pressure, and Krause's end bulbs to cold. Figure 6–2 compares proprioceptive and exteroceptive sensation transmission.

Interoceptors are sense organs found in the viscera and are responsible for detecting information about the internal environment. Mainly they are free nerve endings found in such internal structures as in the walls of the heart and blood vessels, in the lungs, and mesentery. Such visceral sensations as pain, hunger, and thirst are initiated by the interoceptors.

Distance receptors include the eyes, ears, and nose, and they provide information on the remote environment. It is convenient to discuss the senses of sight, smell, equilibrium, hearing, and taste (called the _special senses_)

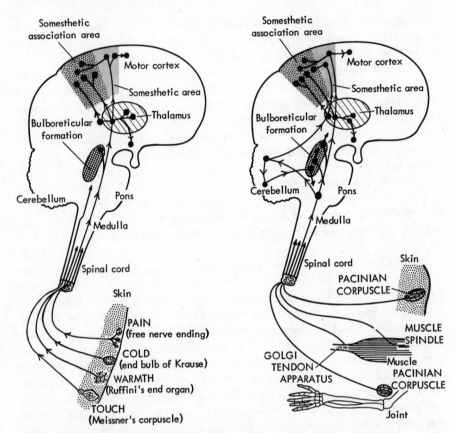

Figure 6–2. Transmission of exteroceptive sensations and proprioceptive sensations to the brain. (A) Exteroceptive transmission. [From Arthur C. Guyton, *Function of the Human Body* (Philadelphia: W. B. Saunders Co., 1963).] (B) Proprioceptive transmission. [From Arthur C. Guyton, *Textbook on Medical Physiology* (Philadelphia: W. B. Saunders Co., 1966).]

separately because of the more detailed information available on the mechanisms involved in these functions.

The senses serve as the interface between stimulation (from internal or external sources) and the transmission and interpreting systems. A phenomenon called *sensory adaptation* occurs under certain conditions. The sensitivity level of receptors to a given stimulus condition is lowered with continuous experience of that condition. For instance, when we first place a hat on our head, it is quite noticeable. We feel its placement and position. After a while and with sensory adaptation, we become unaware of its presence. Another example would be going into a dark room—a movie theater, for instance—which requires adaptation to the darkness.

Transmission

The modern concept of the nerve impulse began with the work of the great physiologist von Helmholtz, in 1850. Important strides have been made since that date in advancing knowledge related to the nature of the impulse and how it transmits information to and from the central transmitter, otherwise known as the brain. It appears that all *nerve impulses* are alike, regardless of their point of origin and termination. Although the impulse itself does not vary physiochemically, differences in sensations and responses can usually be attributed to the receptors and effectors stimulated. In a specific nerve fiber, impulses are of the same magnitude but travel at different rates of speed, depending on the strength of the stimulus. A variation in the stimulus will not affect the magnitude or the rate of the impulse but rather its frequency of discharge. The number of impulses a nerve fiber can potentially send in a second is influenced by the *refractory period* and the *size* of the fiber. For instance, the largest nerve fiber of 20 microns can transmit about 2,500 impulses per second, while a small fiber of 0.5 microns allows 250 impulses to pass through it.

During the resting stage, positively charged (*cation*) ions and negatively charged (*anion*) ions are found both inside and outside the neuron. However, there is a difference in relative concentrations of each; that is, the outside of the cell is positively charged as compared with the inside. This relationship of positively and negatively charged ions of electrical equilibrium is called *polarization*. Sodium (Na^+) ions are concentrated outside the neuron membrane and potassium (K^+) ions are abundantly found in the interior. When a fiber is stimulated, a portion of it undergoes reversal; that is, the ions exchange, thus giving rise to what can be recorded electrically as an impulse. Sodium ions diffuse in and potassium ions diffuse out of the permeable point. This *depolarization* occurs throughout the fiber, and once the impulse has gone through a section of the fiber, that area becomes polarized once again. The recently charged area is unable to conduct another impulse for approximately 0.001 to 0.005 second, and during this *refractory period* polarization is re-established. The refractory period may be broken down to absolute and relative refractory periods. No stimulus regardless of its strength, can excite the impulse during the *absolute refractory period*. A *relative refractory period* follows the absolute refractory period in which a greater stimulus than usual is needed for an effective stimulus. The absolute refractory period lasts from 0.5 to 3 milliseconds, whereas the relative refractory period extends up to 10 milliseconds. Figure 6–3 illustrates the passage of an impulse through an axon.

The speed with which an impulse is conducted depends upon the size of the nerve fiber; fibers with large diameters will have a greater rate of conduction than smaller fibers. In fact, Tasaki (1959) reports a correlation of 0.92 between fiber diameter and conduction velocity. Impulses in the

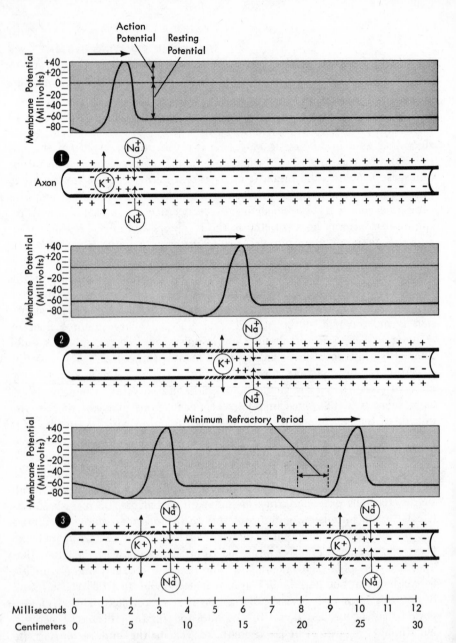

Figure 6–3. Propagation of nerve impulse coincides with changes in the permeability of the axon membrane. Normally the axon interior is rich in potassium ions and poor in sodium ions; the fluid outside has a reverse composition. When a nerve impulse arises, having been triggered in some fashion, a "gate" opens and lets sodium ions pour into the axon in advance of the impulse, making the axon interior locally positive. In the wake of the impulse the sodium gate closes and a potassium gate opens, allowing potassium ions to flow out, restoring the normal negative potential. As the nerve impulse moves along the axon (1 and 2) it leaves the axon in a refractory state briefly, after which a second impulse can follow (3). The impulse propagation speed is that of a squid axon. (From Bernard Katz, "How Cells Communicate," *Scientific American,* 205:209–220, 1961. Copyright © 1961 by Scientific American, Inc. All rights reserved.)

largest nerve fibers may travel at a rate of over 300 feet per second, whereas impulses in the smaller ones may conduct at a speed of three feet per second.

Each nerve fiber reacts under the *all-or-none principle* in a manner simi- lar to that of muscle cells. If a stimulus is powerful enough to influence neural activity, and every neuron has a specific threshold, the neuron will conduct. For the stimulus to excite nerve-fiber conduction of an impulse, two properties must be present: (1) *strength* of sufficient magnitude, and (2) ample *duration* of stimulus application.

Electrical activity of nerve impulses has been recorded with the use of a cathode-ray oscilloscope (see Figure 6–4). When nerve activity is studied, a phenomenon referred to as *action potential* is revealed. The nerve impulse involves electrochemical events, including depolarization and repolarization, and action potential is the accompanying voltage change. The *spike* takes up the shortest amount of time of the action potential and represents the actual passage of the impulse. The *negative after-potential* and *positive after-potential* components of the wave follow the spike in that order and apparently represent the passing of electrically charged particles across the neuron membrane.

For all practical purposes, assuming the nerve fiber obtains enough oxygen and nourishment it will not fatigue. Even isolated axons can conduct tens of thousands of impulses before they fail to work (Katz, 1961). General body fatigue, caused by other physiological factors, occurs before nerve fatigue. Muscles are still able to contract, nerve fibers conduct, and the myoneural junction can still function during the general body fatigue associated with typical exercise. Considering all parts of the neural transmission system, fatigue in the nervous system would occur first at a synapse.

The Greek word *synapse* means "to clasp," and within the nervous system it refers to the site where an impulse crosses from one neuron to the next neuron. Sherrington is given credit for the concept of a synapse. Certain electrical and chemical changes occur in this area that allow the impulse to pass from the axons of one neuron to the dendrites or cell body of another. There is evidence that the synapse actually represents a gap between two nerve cells.

Attention, Perception, Judgment, and Decisions

The central nervous system is the recipient of the electrical impulses and the transmitter of others. The brain acts as a control device and assorts and analyzes information, retains some, and sends forth "orders" for action. Through cranial and spinal nerves the peripheral system conducts impulses between the central nervous system and the peripheral effectors (muscles, organs, glands). It makes good sense to realize that there are

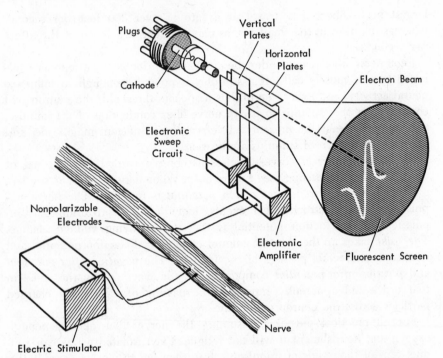

Figure 6–4.   The instrument of choice for recording potentials in nerves is the cathode ray oscilloscope, illustrated here. A cathode produces an electron beam, which is brought to a focus at some point on the fluorescent screen and may be viewed or photographed as a spot of light. A potential difference between the vertical plates causes the spot to shift horizontally from the left of the screen to the right at a certain velocity. Knowing the velocity, one can use this movement as a time measurement. A potential difference between the horizontal plates causes the spot to shift vertically. These plates are connected to an amplifier, which in turn is connected to the nerve by pickup electrodes. When the nerve impulse passes the proximal lead electrode, the electrical disturbance is amplified causing a potential difference in the upper horizontal plate, which causes an upward deflection of the spot, which rises to a maximum and then declines. The impulse reaching the distal lead electrode causes a charge on the lower horizontal plate, which causes a deflection of the spot downward. Thus the action potential which produces a diphasic wave when two electrodes are used, may be recorded. [From Sigmund Grollman, *The Human Body* (New York: Macmillan Publishing Co., Inc., 1964).]

simple and more complex operating computers. Likewise, lower and higher forms of organisms exhibit similar general neural characteristics, with the more advanced animals better able to demonstrate more complex behavior. On the evolutionary scale, the more advanced animals generally have a greater brain-weight to total-weight ratio, although brain weight to spinal-cord weight is probably a better measure of the organism's intelligence. Man has a much greater development of the terminal end of the nervous system than lower forms of living organisms. Also, complexity of the brain convolutions increases as one progresses along the phylogenetic scale. The large brain and complex convolutions are correlated with better developed mental processes and ability to perform the most complicated functions.

Selective attention occurs in the more highly skilled performer. That is, with experience and learning, situations place fewer demands on the attention process. One activity can be performed along with another or while anticipating subsequent actions. This is especially true if stimulus regularity and predictability are present. If not, greater demands are placed on the human behaving system, as can be observed in externally paced athletic tasks. The process of selective attention involves the selection of some information, the disregarding of other information, and the placement of yet other information in "hold."

Perceptual processes are responsible for making sense of information received into the system. *Perception* for purposeful activity involves the dynamic interplay of the sensory systems and appropriate cerebral areas. In fact, James J. Gibson (1966) considers the senses to be perceptual systems in enabling a person to cope with his environment and the tasks to be performed in it.

Although perception as a process is conveniently conceived of as an operation that occurs after sensation and before decision making and as located in one part of the human behaving system, it is more likely that it and selectivity occur from the beginning to the end of information processing (Erdelyi, 1974). In other words, there are many potential points in the system where selectivity occurs. It encompasses a sequence of events. For instance, selectivity occurs during sense reception, encoding from sensory storage to short-term storage, rehearsal for transfer of information from short- to long-term memory storage, retrieval of information for usage, and the like.

One of the major functions of the perceptual processes is to deal with information overload. Many skilled movements demand an efficient system, one that can quickly and expediently deal with a minimal amount of task-relevant cues. Therefore, effective perceptual processes may be thought of as containing a useful filtering mechanism.[1] It would appear that

1. Irrelevant and meaningless information is filtered out, leaving the person to attend to the bare necessities.

---

[1] Earlier and more established theory credits the filtering system as operating between sense reception and the activation of central processes. More recent theory questions this stance, and there is a suggestion that the filter system works later when the memory system is activated.

2. A priority is established with regard to incoming information and that to which the person will attend. A theoretical buffer zone is established.

Man possesses a limited channel capacity, and so it is imperative that he use his system intelligently. Capacity limitations suggest that one cue is handled a fraction of a second before a second cue can be attended to.

Detection is a function of a number of cue variables, namely, its type, a person's motivation, and the directions provided to him. The probability of detecting one signal over another is no doubt dependent upon the costs and payoffs associated with decision making. The personal equation in detection and decision making is influenced by experiences in similar situations and present expectations, and can be modified through external guidance.

Although there are many parts of the brain, for the sake of convenience, most of them will be left out of our discussion. Of apparent significance in learning and performance are such structures as the cerebrum, cerebellum, and medulla. These structures combined appear to have the dominant say on what and how much of the incoming data are processed.

The *cerebrum,* divided into two hemispheres and containing four lobes each, is the largest part of the brain. The outer surface of the cerebrum, called the cortex, contains many convolutions, grooves, and fissures, the most prominent of which are used to divide it systematically into areas. This surface is gray (*gray matter*) and contains nerve cell bodies. The interior is composed of white and some gray matter, with the *white matter* consisting of nerve fibers (axons) in bundles, called *tracts.* The fatty myelin sheath surrounding these fibers gives them their white appearance.

The four lobes found in the cerebral hemispheres and the general functions of each are (1) *frontal*—primary motor area, (2) *temporal*—auditory area, (3) *occipital*—visual area, (4) *parietal*—somesthetic or sensory area. The cerebrum is the *chief processor,* the master signal caller. Later we shall examine the structure and functions of the cerebral cortex closely, especially the motor and sensory areas.

The *cerebellum,* containing two hemispheres and an outer surface of gray matter and an inner surface of white and gray matter, appears to be quite similar in structure to the cerebrum. The cerebellum, which contains about 10 per cent of the brain's total mass, is second to the cerebrum in size.

There is an intricate relationship between the cerebellum and cerebrum in the coordination and refinement of motor activity to produce skilled movement patterns. Tactile, visual, and auditory areas are located here that correspond to the cortex centers. Proprioceptive information from all muscles concerning posture, equilibrium, and movement come to the cerebellum, which in turn exerts a certain amount of control over these factors. An intact cerebellum is necessary for the harmonious control of the various muscle groups in the body. Injury to this region in the brain may result in uncoordinated and poorly timed movements, a poor sense of balance, or tremors. The cerebellum is localized in the extreme front and rear surfaces, and these areas have specific controlling functions. It is necessary to remove large areas of the cerebellar cortex before severe loss of muscular coordination occurs.

The spinal cord is directly continuous with the *medulla oblongata*, which is the lowermost portion of the brain. Because of this fact, it is a connecting pathway for impulses exchanged between the spinal cord and brain and functions in many motor and sensory mechanisms. Approximately two thirds of the nerve fibers cross over (*decussate*) at the medulla, thus explaining why one side of the cerebral cortex controls the opposite side of the body. The medulla contains many of the vital reflex centers, for example, the respiratory center, which regulates the rate of inspirations and expirations; the cardiac center, controller of the heart beat; and the vasomotor center, which influences blood pressure.

Because of the many intercommunicating cables found in the brain, all parts are tuned in with each other. Tracts of white tissue serve as these cables. In the cable organization, there are subsystems responsible for computing and data processing which operate in orderly and computerlike fashion. It is not necessary for all mechanisms to be in active operation for all the functions of the body, an indication of the efficiency of the machinery. In fact, as a general rule, we may expect only the most complex behavior to be under the control of the higher nervous system, because most basic, unwilled movements are handled by the spinal cord.

Stimulation of the brain for a particular event leads to an activation of the perceptual, judgmental, and decision-making process. Depending on the nature of the task, information available, time constraints, and past experiences, these processes can be more or less effective. In continuous tasks of sufficient duration, concurrent monitoring and adjustments can occur. In discrete tasks, sufficient preplanning time is available. In any type of task the decision to deploy the appropriate plan of action is one of the major steps toward skilled performance.

Through scientific experimentation, areas of the brain have been designated as terminal points for the input signals from the various parts of the body. By removing (*extirpation*) or destroying specific cells or studying the action potentials of various cells in the cerebrum, it is possible to determine cerebral area functions. Also, stimulation of certain areas of the cortex results in movements in certain body parts.

Electrical Activity

Functions of the various areas in the cerebral cortex have been extensively studied through instrumentation. One of the forerunners in the study of

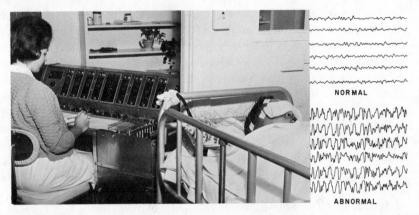

Figure 6–5.   Diagram illustrating the recording of electroencephalograms. Technician sits at the console of the electroencephalograph recording the electroencephalogram of a young patient. Both normal and abnormal tracings are shown. [From Sigmund Grollman, *The Human Body* (New York: Macmillan Publishing Co., 1964).]

brain electrical activity was Hans Berger, and his work led to the development of the *electroencephalograph* (see Figure 6–5). An electroencephalogram (*EEG*) is the recording of electrical waves of the brain obtained from electrodes attached to the scalp. These waves appear at different frequencies and amplitudes and, among other things, indicate changes in body activity. As the state of a person changes from relaxation to activity, the electric potentials (*wave patterns*) of the brain also change.

The shape of voltage waves in the brain determine the state of the organism. Although the operation of the brain is probably chemical, voltage changes are presently what we measure. Alpha, beta, and delta waves have been recognized and are designated according to the number of cycles occurring per second. The slowest waves, possibly less than one a second, are called *delta waves*. These are usually obtained during sleep. *Alpha waves* occur at a rate of about eight to thirteen times a second and are the most common, representing inattentive but waking states. During increased activity and tension, alpha waves give way to the small, irregular *beta waves*, and these fast waves may be timed at over fourteen cycles per second. The electroencephalogram has many clinical and diagnostic uses and usually indicates the nature of activity in specific sections of the cortex under varying degrees of behavior and movement.

An analysis of brain waves might indicate distinct patterns characteristic of specific abnormalities of the brain. One of the more typical problems is epilepsy. Other possible diagnoses are localized brain tumors or lesions of the brain.

Computer and Human Differences

At this point, it should be stressed that by no means is the computer–neural analogy perfect or near perfect. Similarities have been brought out, in simplified fashion, for the purpose of approaching the study of the nervous system consistent with the theme of the book. At the present time, the complex behavior of the human organism can in no way be completely accounted for by electronic principles in a mechanistic analogy.

How does one program emotions in a machine? Humans typically respond to a given situation in an emotional state that may vary from occasion to occasion. How does one learn to remember? A machine is programmed by a human to react in a particular way to a particular input. It does not, in a sense, have to learn anything. The machine must respond in a predictable manner, whereas the human organism appears not to be a deterministic model of behavior.

There are some things the machine can do better than man, and vice versa. Certainly, the machine can calculate more accurately and at a faster rate than any human. All aspects of the input must be in order if the machine is to relay the desired output, whereas human performance may attain objectives with parts of ideas or fragments of stimuli or even abstractions present. In other words, the data can be incomplete but still the brain can operate successfully; machines cannot.

The machine is limited in function by man's ability to construct; his knowledge and understanding of machine dynamics. Connections in the nervous system are vastly more complicated than the simple cabling arrangement of the computer. This, in essence, leads to the final point. The human brain is much more complicated, sophisticated, and versatile than any machines that have been built so far.

Arousal

As we saw before, the state of the voltage waves in the brain is associated with the level of activation within the individual. The optimal state of arousal is necessary for skilled performance, for obvious reasons. It is one thing to have the necessary paths and an orderly cabling arrangement as well as neural structures, but perhaps more should be said about attentiveness to certain situational cues and selection of appropriate responses. In other words, the action of certain parts of the nervous system determines consciousness, alertness, and preparation for activity, and has a bearing on the response. Appropriate arousal levels are responsible for activation, direction, and persistence in behavior.

These functions have been attributed to the *reticular formation* of the

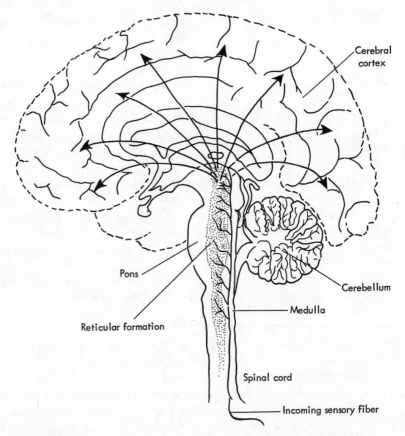

Figure 6–6. Section of brain showing the reticular formation. It is composed of interlacing fibers and nerve cells which form the central core of the brain stem. Incoming fibers from the spinal tracts send collaterals into the reticular formation. Arrows indicate the general arousal of higher brain centers which the reticular area controls. [From Diana Clifford Kimber, and others, *Anatomy and Physiology*, 15th ed. (New York: Macmillan Publishing Co., Inc., 1966).]

brain stem, also known as the *reticular activating system*. The reticular formation is a mesh of motor nerve cells, distributed from the top of the spinal cord to the thalamus and hypothalamus, that receives as well as distributes impulses to the lower as well as the highest centers of the central nervous system (see Figure 6–6). The main function of the formation appears to be that of alerting the individual, of placing him in a condition of arousal.

When an individual is in a sleeping state, little activity occurs in the reticular formation. However, stimulation of this center has an effect on the cortex and results in its awakening. Many of the afferent pathways feed into the reticular system, and if the impulses are strong enough they will pass on to the hypothalamus, thalamus, and, finally, cortex. Damage to the upper portion of the reticular system may result in extensive sleepiness or even pathological sleep.

Stimulation of the reticular formation facilitates or inhibits ongoing motor activity by increasing or decreasing activity in the *gamma efferent system*. Gamma motor neurons (efferents) are responsible for the control of sensitivity of the muscle spindles. When the gamma neurons are stimulated, reflex contractions and voluntary movements are encouraged.

Some scholars have attributed great significance to this formation. In fact, it has been termed a program-selection mechanism that determines the nature of a response. As a response selector, the reticular system assigns priorities to messages, determines which are important, and selects the appropriate responses in order of importance. Nearly all incoming and outgoing impulses of the brain pass through the reticular formation.

With the influence of the cerebrum, cerebellum, reticular formation, and other areas of the brain, the output of the nervous system, displayed in the form of complex coordinated movement, is made possible. Selective input is partly dependent upon attention processes, or an optimal level of activation of the system. Optimal arousal suggests the ability to discriminate and select from many available situational cues the most relevant one or ones to respond to.

Fatigue causes an overload of the system, and understimulation or underload results in boredom. There is a tendency not to respond to appropriate cues as practice time increases and there are fewer behavioral adaptions to the display. Attention is increased with greater stimulus intensity, less repetitious acts, personal motivation, and stimuli that contrast with other available stimuli. Warnings are likely to help performance, especially if the stimulus event is going to be weak or brief.

According to activation theory, the relationship between behavioral outputs and state of arousal assumes the form of an inverted U. Too little or too much arousal impedes the system; somewhere in the middle for most tasks, although the level varies for different tasks and different people, is most desirable. Some tasks require more inhibition and control over movements than others, and vice versa. Tasks requiring much information processing would be impeded by high arousal levels. The relation of exercise-induced changes to activation level and motor performance is analyzed by Bernard Gutin (1973).

The arousal state may be controlled by the system itself, a sign of a skilled performer. Nondesirable fluctuations in arousal in task performance indicate a relatively new experience for the learner. He has to learn how to optimize arousal levels for the task demands if effective cue selection and decision making are to occur. The energizing of the system to fit the task requires experience and familiarity with the situation and outcomes associated with various states of arousal. Activation is dependent upon emotional levels and motivational levels, such as level of aspiration. The goals we set for ourselves in task performance will be reflected in the way the system is geared for the activity and the manner in which it attempts to handle it.

DIRECTING THE SYSTEM

Memory Storage and Retrieval

Activation helps to provide direction to the system's output. So does the use of information stored in the memory banks. The speed with which we learn something and learning efficiency in general depend to a large extent on that which is remembered from previous similar experiences. Events are stored for future use. The location and nature of memory traces are difficult to ascertain, but they appear to be widely dispersed throughout the brain.

Breakthroughs in understanding memory and intelligence have been made from the findings of recent research concerned with these problems. Studies on rats, fish, and flatworms indicate an increase in ribonucleic acid (RNA), which is the genetic material in each brain cell's nucleus, in the cells, as learning takes place. Neurons produce RNA, with more cell activity resulting in more of this substance. RNA has even been termed the *memory molecule* by some scientists, even though research is still scanty in this area. Perhaps memory traces are stored permanently in the form of new protein molecules (Elio Maggio, 1971). Rats trained at problem solving, besides demonstrating an increase in their RNA and protein contents in the brain cells, also had heavier and larger brains. If RNA is the learning secret, there are great implications for improving learning abilities and performance in those individuals who previously were thought to be hopeless. Possibly, the administration of additional amounts of this substance to them would benefit their learning potential.

No one part of the brain can be called the central repository of stored information, and, as we have just seen, neuronal activity increases the RNA in all brain cells. However, as indicated by research evidence, the temporal lobes of the cortex are involved in the recall of many previous experiences. Penfield and Roberts (1959) write that in the mechanism of recall and comparison and interpretation the interpretive cortex of the temporal lobes plays its specialized role. Electrical stimulation of portions of these lobes sometimes results in the sudden remembrance of events that occurred many years earlier.

In contrast, Maggio (1971) summarizes the current thought on the matter by stating that

It seems that memory traces are made by entrance into the function of patterns of neuronal units which are widely represented throughout the cerebral cortex of both hemispheres. They are interconnected with each other and with some subcortical structures, especially those of the reticulo-limbic system, which also contribute to the emotional color with which the memory traces are reexperienced during the recall [p. 143].

E. Roy John (1967) has written a scholarly and well-documented book in which he refutes the idea that learning and memory are associated with neural pathways involving specific brain cells for receiving certain inputs and triggering certain outputs. He expresses the belief that "learned behaviors are motivated by systems which are anatomically extensive and involve many brain regions" (p. 418). John doubts that any one structure or set of neurons are responsible for storage of the memory of a particular experience. No specific set of cells must discharge for memory to operate. John proposes that stored information is associated with "spatiotemporal patterns of organization in enormous aggregates of neurons" (p. 417).

The later performance of once-learned skills is also dependent on the physical condition of the wiring. What happens when there is damage to a wire or two? Regeneration of nerve cells is believed to be possible only if at least the cell body (and its nucleus, which is the center of repair) is intact and a neurilemma sheath surrounds the fibers. Because neurons in the central nervous system lack a neurilemma, regeneration is only possible in the peripheral nervous system. Nerve cells that are completely destroyed cannot be replaced, but other neurons may be able to take over their function, to certain degrees. This ability will be dictated by the period in the individual's life when specific nerve cells are destroyed as well as the specific cells involved. Cells may die because of such factors as injury or disease, and if certain patterns of movement have been established before this occurs, there is a better chance neurons in surrounding areas will be able to compensate for their loss of function. A baby is handicapped to a greater extent than a more mature child or adult as he has not yet had the opportunity to develop skilled motor patterns. Greater experience and education result in more and varied learning patterns. Less behavioral deterioration thus might be expected to occur after brain damage in older and/or highly educated people.

Memory is theorized to be of two types: *long term* and *short term*. An elaboration of these processes is found in Chapter 9. Apparently, information is rapidly lost in short-term memory, for there is no sustained attention or rehearsal. With adequate rehearsal, information is sent on to long-term memory storage, ready to be called forth at a later date. Keele (1973) postulates the existence of a third store: short-term sensory. According to him, information remains in short-term sensory storage (approximately 1 to 20 seconds, depending upon the sensory store involved, e.g., visual or kinesthetic, and the conditions of stimulus presentation) and transformations and recoding occur when it is passed on to short-term and finally to long-term memory.

It is interesting to speculate why we remember so well certain things we did in childhood and yet have forgotten others. Also, why are motor skills often retained for a lengthier period of time than are once-learned literary passages? Are there different memory mechanisms involved in the operation of, say, long-term retention versus short-term retention? One fact remains sure at the present time: we cannot isolate or localize a memory trace, regardless of its nature. It does appear, though, that during the retention process of whatever is to be retained, a multiple representation in the cortex is established. That is to say, various portions of the cortex are capable of relaying previously gained information to the individual when he needs it.

Stored memory will affect judgments, for consideration of the costs and payoffs for certain decisions are based on previous experiences in similar situations. Previous successes, risk taking, and the ability to isolate and attend to certain cues reflect input from the memory system and the ability to retrieve effectively from it. Speed and accuracy of retrieval for the immediate task demands reflect learning and experience. All components discussed so far lead to the activation of an appropriate plan of action, which we call the movement plan.

Movement Plans

Plans may be under volitional or nonvolitional control, by or without intent. Although the concept of a movement plan was referred to in a theoretical framework in Chapter 3, we will interpret it in a much broader context here. The type and nature of output from the control system ranges in many directions, although in the motor-learning situation it is expected that coordinated, effective movement is that which is desired. The human organism is capable of demonstrating an assorted array of motor patterns from the most elemental motor acts to the most complicated stunts. As an example of the nervous system's efficiency, sensory information is usually rearranged in lower levels of the system. There is an interconnection and rearrangement in the interneurons of the spinal cord and brain stem before the data arrive at the cerebral cortex. Not all responses or movements need be mediated by past experiences and thought processes. Not all stimuli need be recorded in the cortex.

Some simple receptor–effector loops located outside and inside the brain free the cerebrum for other work. These circuits are associated with certain bodily activity, which transpires as if automatic. Consider, for example, the reflex, the most simple of motor movements. Reflexes do not usually require the attention of the higher levels of the nervous system, and reflect the most elementary movement plan.

Simple Movement Plans

Reflex arcs constitute the pathways involved in a simple reaction to a stimulus, usually not requiring the functioning of the higher centers of the nervous system. In the beginning of the twentieth century the outstanding physiologist Sherrington (1858–1952) experimented on reflex transmission and the reflex at the spinal level, and his efforts still have tremendous impact on present thinking about the nervous system. Reflex arcs may contain two, three, or more neurons. In any case these reflex arcs result in somewhat consistent responses, usually unconscious, to the same stimuli. Because a reflex is an unconscious response, it can be conditioned to be highly predictable.

The reflex arc, in its simplest form (two-neuron), contains five parts:

1. *Receptor:* specialized sensory nerve ending.
2. *Afferent neuron:* sensory transmitter of impulse from the receptor to the gray matter in the spinal cord.
3. *Synapse:* a gap in the anterior horn of the cord where an afferent and efferent neuron are in functional proximity.
4. *Efferent neuron:* motor neuron, passing the impulse from the cord to an effector.
5. *Effector:* organ responsible for response.

Examples of a two-neuron reflex arc are the *postural reflex* and *knee jerk reflex* (see Figure 6–7), both of which are classified as *stretch reflexes.* In the stretch reflex, or postural reflex, inhibiting impulses are sent to antagonist muscles while appropriate muscles contract in order to maintain body stability. When an extensor muscle contracts and the flexor relaxes, or vice versa, we have a condition known as *reciprocal innervation.* As to the actual stretch reflex, the process may be described in the following way: Stretch reflex: spindles stretched → afferent impulses to spinal cord → innervation of alpha neurons → reflex contraction of the appropriate muscle fibers.

The knee jerk reflex involves the stimulus of tapping the patellar tendon and response of leg extension. During stimulus application, the quadriceps muscle is stretched, causing the stimulation of receptors in the muscle and resulting in a reflex shortening of this muscle. Basic reflexes such as the knee jerk reflex can be used for diagnostic purposes; for if there is some disturbance in the reflex pathway, the reflex will not be reproduced normally. Some reflex acts can be facilitated intentionally. A clenching of the fists before the patellar tendon is struck would result in a greater response, hence the reason for an examining doctor to insist on complete relaxation of his patient before the test.

Certain reflexes are inborn, those needed for chewing and swallowing, simple defense reactions, defecation, micturation, and the like. Previous

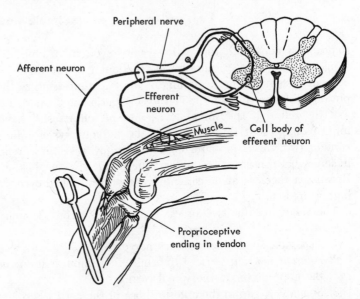

Figure 6–7.   Simple reflex arc (knee jerk). The four fundamental parts of a reflex arc are shown: (1) a receptor —proprioceptive ending in tendon; (2) a sensory transmitter—the afferent neuron; (3) a motor transmitter—the efferent neuron; (4) the effector—the muscle. [From Sigmund Grollman, *The Human Body* (New York: Macmillan Publishing Co., Inc., 1964).]

learning experience is not necessary for these responses, hence they are unconditioned. Others are *conditioned* or *acquired* (learned) reflexes. An example of the latter is best represented by the research of Pavlov, who contributed extensively in developing methods by which new responses mediated by the cerebral cortex could be studied. Salivation accompanies food as well as its anticipation in a hungry animal. Pavlov rang a bell each occasion he fed the dog involved in his experiment. After a number of trials in which the bell and food were presented together, the food was eliminated, but each time the bell rang, the animal salivated: thus, a conditioned reflex.

Other reflexes are concerned with body protection via withdrawal and are termed *flexor reflexes*. The quick withdrawal of the foot from contact with a sharp object is an example of a flexor reflex.

The complex reflex arc is exemplified by the withdrawal reflex. Figure 6–8 illustrates foot withdrawal from a painful stimulus. Although only a few localized receptors are involved, it is interesting to note the *spread of effect* (a generalized reflex response involving many effectors). Notice how many parts of the body actively respond to a stimulus that activates but a few skin receptors. This startle reflex appears to be a "stored-

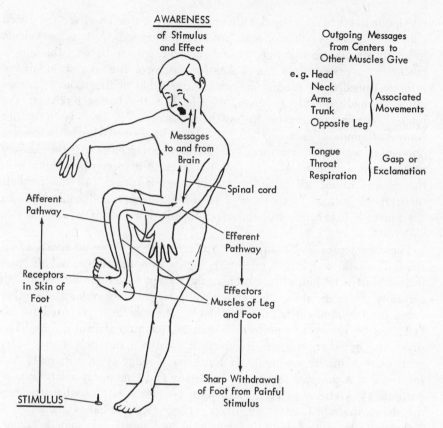

Figure 6–8.   Reflex action demonstrating many reflex arcs. [From A. McNaught and R. Callander, *Illustrated Physiology* (Baltimore: Williams and Wilkins Co., 1963).]

program" reflex, as an organized set of reactions occur without consciousness.

Incorrect withdrawal reflexes have been obtained in a series of experiments by R. W. Sperry (1959). After crossing sensory nerves of rats and frogs, extensive training still had no effect in re-educating their motor systems. During the rearrangement of nerve connections, rats would withdraw the right foot in response to an electric shock to the left foot. These results seem to indicate that although higher nervous system centers are capable of extensive learning, the anatomical arrangement of the lower ones are implastic. They cannot be modified much by use or training. Spinal reflexes do recover to some extent following disease or injury in the spinal cord. Damage to the spinal cord, however, will cause a total loss of sensory input and voluntary physical movement.

Simple reflexes are wired-in nerve circuits; the action is not premeditated, nor has it been learned. Other reflexes are learned and are associated with more complex behavior than heretofore discussed. Certain movements in sports situations, although termed reflexive, go far beyond the simple processes discussed thus far. Take, for instance, the almost automatic responses needed for success in sports. After slight deliberation, responses must be made quickly to given stimuli: (1) the batter interprets the pitch, its accuracy and type, in less than a second; (2) the wrestler under control attempts to escape when the referee blows his whistle, before his opponent can react to impede his sudden movement; (3) the hockey center must decide whether to pass the puck to a forward or shoot it at the goalie himself, all in a fraction of a second; and (4) the football quarterback decides, in the face of onrushing linemen and while he is on the move, if it is wiser to hand-off, run, fall down, or pass and pass to whom.

These responses and many more are required in dynamic sports situations. The total situation is ever-changing and unpredictable, but the performer must react almost instantaneously. Except under conditions of high certainty, there is always some temporal lag in performance. In other cases, the environment is relatively stable. The athlete is prepared for his task, and he attempts to perform a series of acts in a skillful fashion. The diver, the gymnast, and the trampolinist condition themselves to display routines that appear automatic. If we define a reflex as an automatic performance of a complex sequence of spatially and temporally related motor patterns (Wooldridge, 1963), then sports contain examples where reflexes are demonstrated. Then again, other writers [e.g., Miller, Galanter, and Pribram (1960)] find fault in explaining any form of human behavior, let alone reflex action, in reflex arc terms. Perhaps even reflex action is far more complex than we think. According to Miller et al., behavior is controlled in terms of the order in which a sequence of operations is to be performed. All action is guided by a "plan," which they liken to a computer program.

If we define reflex in traditional terms, as we did a few pages earlier, it is doubtful that the athlete's performance is usually based upon reflexive behavior. An athlete's reaction time or movement time should not be confused with reflex time, as these events might pertain to a particular task (see Chapter 7 for a discussion of these terms, how they are contrasted, and how they are measured in laboratory settings). As a point of interest, there are no data demonstrating that an athlete's reflex time is any faster than a non-athlete's reflex time.

Athletic situations are filled with examples of seemingly predetermined performances to predetermined stimuli. One might even go so far as to believe that there are stored programs (organized memory traces) in the brain. When sensory data are filtered into the nervous system, the appropriate program would be activated. Evidently, these programs become effective with repetition (practice). Most daily and athletic activity does not involve simple movements and responses, for frequently we have to select an appropriate response for a given stimulus. Because these actions go beyond the complex reflex stage, or what appears to be somewhat automatic responses, the highest levels of the nervous system become involved.

Complex Movement Plans

The development of the cerebral cortex is correlated with man's intellectual superiority over other animals. This structure of the highest order is necessary for refinement of movements, for precision and effectiveness. The cortex itself is not necessary in all motor activity, for gross bodily movements are but slightly interfered with by the loss of cortical function. However, we are referring here to the most gross of movements, such as walking, crawling, and moving a hand in prescribed directions, and obviously the learning and often the performance of athletic skills demands cortical involvement. We now address ourselves to the notion of complex movement plans.

The cerebrum contains motor, sensory, and association areas, which interact during most coordinated complex movement. Between various species, structural differences in the brain are related to differences in physical characteristics. For example, a bird has large-sized optic lobes but small olfactory lobes; vision, not smell, is important to the bird. There is a relationship between the number of cells in the motor area allocated to a particular portion of the body, the number of motor units in an effector, and the complexity of movements related to that area. Hence relatively fewer cells control feet and leg movements whereas a much greater motor area is related to finger and lip motions.

The upper part of the motor region stimulates the lower extremities, the middle sends impulses to the trunk, whereas the lower part is concerned with facial and head movements. Although the motor cortex exerts influence on the various parts of the body, integrated functioning will occur only if surrounding cerebral areas are in place. The nervous system is extremely complex and integrated, requiring coordination between the neural structures involved in a particular act.

The cerebral cortex plays an important role in voluntary movement as contrasted with reflex movement, which is usually regulated at lower levels of the nervous system. The function of the motor cortex in willed movements and the effects on the body if damage occurs has been confirmed.

One side of the motor area controls movement in the opposite side of the body. If, for example, there is damage to some cells in the left cerebral hemisphere's motor area, possible paralysis may be inflicted in the corresponding muscles on the right side of the body. The reason for this is that

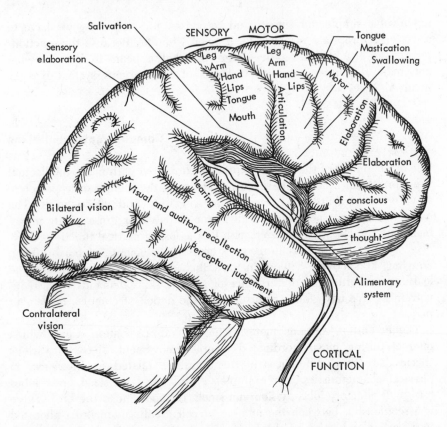

Figure 6–9.   Cortical function. This illustration serves as a summary restatement of conclusions, some hypothetical (e.g. the elaboration zones), others firmly established. The suggestion that the anterior portion of the occipital cortex is related to both fields of vision rather than to one alone is derived from the results of stimulation. [From W. Penfield and T. Rasmussen, *The Cerebral Cortex of Man* (New York: Macmillan Publishing Co., Inc., 1950).]

nerve pathways cross over at the medulla or spinal cord level on their way down to specific effectors. Although it is possible for some recovery to take place in the form of gross movements, finger skills very rarely if ever return.

The various sense areas of the cortex are just as important as the motor cortex in skilled movement. Sense impulses for vision are distinguished in the occipital lobe, whereas those for audition are distinguished in the temporal lobe. Muscle sensations are interpreted in the somesthetic or sensory area of the parietal lobe, located posterior to the motor area. Representation of the different parts of the body in the somesthetic area is similar to the representation of the motor area. The somesthetic region is concerned with such sensations as touch, pain, pressure, and body position. Although a habit abolished by the removal of certain areas in the cerebral cortex can be relearned, damage to the sensory areas of the brain cannot be compensated for by any amount of retraining. Figure 6–9 represents cortical functions in the sensory, motor, and association areas.

Association areas, which comprise the bulk of the cortex, are thought to be responsible for memory, speech, reasoning, intelligence, and thought and are not as localized as the other areas described. These functions are not usually designated to specific areas of the brain, as evidenced by the fact that such a process as discrimination learning is thought to be controlled in the posterior association areas, which include the parietal, occipital, and temporal sectors. There is a great interdependence when most acts are performed between motor, sensory, and association areas of the cerebrum.

The cerebellum offers an automatic control function, for it is responsible for smooth and coordinated movement. It receives information from muscles and the semicircular canals on body position and rate of movement, and produces a stabilizing effect on the body. The cerebellum and cerebrum work closely on all forms of coordinated motor acts.

After input, the impulse travels along a pre-established path to the appropriate part of the brain. Typical sensory pathways include a three-neuron relay: neuron I going to the spinal cord, neuron II extending from that point to the thalamus, and neuron III communicating with the sensory area of the cortex. One of the most important of the sensory tracts is the *spinothalamic tract,* responsible for feeling pain and temperature changes. Its path is as follows:

Neuron of the first order (I): skin receptors → posterior column of spinal cord →

Neuron of the second order (II): posterior column → decussates → thalamus →

Neuron of the third order (III): thalamus → sensory area of parietal lobe in cerebral cortex

Following sense activity, certain areas in the brain issue orders to the various parts of the body. Voluntary activity is initiated in the higher centers, although the site can only be conjectured. It has been found that stimulation of any part of the motor cortex does not result in skilled acts, leading Paillard (1960) to speculate on the presence of an intermediary system, capable of controlling the motor cortex but receiving its stimulation from some other area of the nervous system. Involuntary or reflex movements have their origin at lower levels of the central nervous system. A method of classifying motor pathways is based on the way their fibers enter the spinal cord. Two motor systems, pyramidal and extrapyramidal, are distinguished in this manner. These two systems are responsible for volitional movements.

The *extrapyramidal pathway* is extremely complicated, eventually affecting gross, coordinated movements of the body. These patterns require the contraction and relaxation of a number of muscles. The pathway involves motor and other areas of the cortex, basal ganglia, the cerebellum, other parts of the brain, and numerous tracts in the spinal cord. Damage to the cerebellum, for instance, results in difficulty in standing erect and performing simple movements. Disorders to the extrapyramidal system in general will be represented by jerky, uncoordinated movements.

The *pyramidal path* is simple and direct. It is responsible for fine, discrete movements involving such areas of the body as the fingers, toes, facial muscles, and lips. A specific area of the cerebral cortex contains unique cells called *Betz cells,* which connect to large, fast-conducting axons. The large axons enable the impulses to travel a great distance at rapid speed. The fibers from the cortex meet at the medulla and the crossing is pyramidal in shape and appearance, hence the name of this system, although it is also referred to as the *corticospinal pathway.*

The classical view is that the pyramidal system facilitates the maintenance of muscle tone, whereas the extrapyramidal system suppresses tone. However, as Jennifer Buchwald (1967) has reported, after analyzing recent evidence, the extrapyramidal mechanism is chiefly responsible for muscle tone. It can produce well-controlled volitional movements involving the trunk and limbs, even in the absence of the pyramidal system.

Assuming that well-learned acts do not require conscious control or at least much of it, perhaps something akin to these behaviors becoming almost like reflex acts is a plausible interpretation of the situation. Movement plans contain built-in mechanisms for the continuance of activities. For instance, the response from a just-performed act (part of the total activity) triggers the next act. Response feedback stimulates appropriate sense receptors to initiate subsequent movement. It has been suggested that "different anatomical structures or areas are involved in the acquisition of a motor skill and its final performance" (Isaacson, Douglas, Lubar, and Schmaltz, 1971, p. 180). These authors speculate further that, "A given area might be necessary for the trial-and-error process of mastering a given motor skill but no longer be involved once the skill has become automatic or reflex-like. If this were the case, it would account for the finding that very complex motor behaviors often remain intact after extensive damage to prime motor areas in the cortex" (p. 180).

A well-developed movement plan seems to be associated with highly skilled performance. In an act demanding instantaneous and extremely rapid and continuous movements, the plan must be well–constructed beforehand. Externally paced acts suggest the refinement of a number of plans, any one of which might be called into action with the appropriate cue. The ability to switch plans while action is occurring will be dependent upon the time available and adaptability of the performer to change channels. Task familiarity, repeated experiences, and the capabilities of the person will influence the refinement of movement plans and their effectiveness.

The learning of complex motor skills reveals a similar syndrome for both children and adults. Obviously, these skills are performed best when the person need not think about or plan for the sequence of actions. Yet, in the early stages of learning, the most elementary form of practice shows gross and often unnecessary movements. Precision occurs later. Successive experiences bring the learner closer to the goal of efficient and effective movement. With all learners, the transition is apparent from crude and uneconomical behaviors, as well as heavy reliance on external cues, to automatic, smooth behaviors. *Automatic* implies no need to attend deliberately to the various components of the whole movement or series of activities.

Our earlier discussion on reflex movements and the consideration of certain situations in sports as being reduced to reflexive-type behaviors deserves re-examination here.

There is some debate as to whether to favor a central or peripheral theory of learning when analyzing motor behaviors. The conflict persists over wherein lies the locus of control for complex coordinated motor movements: peripheral information, the sensory receptors using previous performance feedback to guide the next responses; or some central organization, where a behavioral sequence is viewed as not requiring sensory guidance. Evidence, primarily with lower forms of organisms, has been used to support both positions.

Research evidence using the technique of deafferentation (cutting nerve pathways) indicates that an organism can still function adequately under such adverse conditions. The belief in an internal feedback loop or a central programming organizer for movement patterns is supported primarily by these kinds of data. The heavy reliance on feedback systems, or peripheral information, has been confirmed in a great number of other studies. Furthermore, disputes exist over methodologies developed to study the problem (Hutton, 1972). The schemes developed in Figures 3–12 and 3–13, and Figures 5–3 and 5–4, reflect support for the centralist hypothesis, although acknowledging the functioning of peripheral feedback as well. (The dotted lines suggest the latter possibility.) Perhaps the nature of the task and the experimental paradigm strongly affect whether an experiment will support the central or peripheral control theories.

One of the leading exponents of the existence of motor programs is Steven Keele, as we saw in Chapter 3. He believes that there are a number of movement patterns for which neither visual nor kinesthetic feedback is needed. A program may be located in the brain or in the spinal cord: "As a motor program is executed, neural impulses are sent to the appropriate muscles in proper sequence, timing, and force, as predetermined by the program, and the neural impulses are largely reinfluenced by the resultant feedback" (Keele, 1973, p. 124).

Activation and Inhibition

An effective movement plan directs the activation and inhibition of various muscle fibers of the body. In a fast sequence of movements, it appears as though the activation and inhibition of responses are preplanned. In slower and continuous movements, control and adaptations can occur as a result of ongoing performance feedback. Skilled performance reflects the sensitive balance between activated and inhibited tissue. One of the most challenging tasks for a young child is to learn how to inhibit movements, to control them.

Coordinated movement encompasses the selection and stimulation of appropriate muscles (spatial control), their activation at the right time (temporal control), and gradual muscle inhibition (quantitative control).

With repetitious practice and mature enough neurophysiological structures, the organism begins to demonstrate structured movements, or complex movement plans. A sequence of bodily movements involved in a goal-oriented behavior is initiated with the onset of a particular cue. The nature of the task—discrete or continuous, self-paced or externally paced—will dictate the possibility of flexibility in the programming during the actual activity. Variability in performance decreases with practice, and the motor programs in the repertoire of programs yield the responses appropriate for the situations in which they are initiated. Practice helps to develop the programs essentially needed for the solution of problems. Learning how to solve motor problems, how to integrate effectively impulses that will innervate and deinnervate muscle tissues, is the key to successful performance. Movement in terms of direction, force, and velocity must be under conscious control or so well learned that subconscious volitional activity serves its intended purpose.

There are many cases where movement plans must be restructured during the course of activity, presuming time is available for an alternative. Plans are often disrupted because of an unpredictable change of events or the excitation of inappropriate muscle tissues. Feedback, which serves as a comparator, is useful in many activities as the source of performance information that will stimulate a modification of plans. A program established in advance of an act and in anticipation of cue occurrence may work effectively. Then again, adaptive restructuring of the program in progress is often called for as well, and the ability to modify is one aspect of skilled performance. The hierarchical system of behavior possessed by man indicates that many immediate changes in ongoing performance occur at subconscious levels of control.

Reflex activity can be seen as involving a feedback loop that operates within the skeletal muscle system. Alpha motor neurons, which are located between the ventral horn of the spinal cord and muscles, affect the quality of movements in the body. Sensory receptors in the skeletal muscles make smooth and coordinated movements possible. Extrafusal fibers form one type of muscle bundle and initiate movements when contracted by the alpha motor neurons. Intrafusal fibers are a second type, and are activated by gamma motor neurons, which, like the alpha neurons, have their origin in the ventral horn of the spinal cord. The gamma neurons also affect the contraction of extrafusal fibers because of the physiological and functional arrangement of the system.

The state of contraction and relaxation is monitored by the feedback loop. Central facilitation and inhibition is possible through this means. Muscle groups involved in the same body movements must cooperate. Synergist muscle groups work together and antagonist muscle groups produce opposite body movements. Two sets of muscle groups are involved in a motor response: one set contracts while the other set relaxes. When the spindle organs in a muscle are stimulated, increased activation occurs. The Golgi tendon organs have an inhibitory influence on muscle contraction when stimulated. The gamma motor neurons (efferents) are responsible for the control of sensitivity of muscle spindles and in turn control reflex muscle contractions. The highly skilled performer will probably demonstrate a greater ability to utilize the gamma system to his advantage, for many postural and movement adjustments require adequate functioning of the gamma neurons.

Alpha motor neurons mediate all reflex and voluntary movements in the body. Complete destruction of the pathway to a particular limb is reflected by a complete loss of movement in that limb. If the alpha motor system is intact but the afferent system is destroyed in a given area, no more reflex movements will occur there, but movement can still occur voluntarily.

With the upward progression of skill, changes occur in intramuscular and intermuscular mechanisms. The study of types of muscle fibers indicates that they respond differentially according to the nature of the task and the performer's level of skill. Electromyographical analysis permits a greater understanding of the pattern changes in motor units, and, in turn, the intramuscular changes, with the development of skill. Although it is true that the agonist (prime mover) musculature is important in coordinated movements, the antagonistic musculature plays a major role in motor control. Antagonistic musculature involvement needs to be conscientiously attended to in the early stages of learning. Gross motor activities involving speed, strength, and accuracy are refined and appear skilled when adequate control is present. Negative acceleration of a limb at the appropriate moment will make the difference in refined performance.

Highly skilled patterns of movement appear effortless and under subconscious control. Antagonist muscle spindles most likely contribute heavily to this feeling and the ability to perform proficiently. At the present time, it appears that the cerebellum coordinates alpha and gamma neurons and, in turn, excitory and inhibitory processes in selected muscle groups. Motor behavior is under the control of alpha and gamma neurons, which are linked to numerous descending pathways. The coactivation of these neurons and their involvement in movement is not clearly known as yet, although research by such scholars as J. L. Smith et al. (1972) has attempted to shed light on limb control when actions are slow and continuous as contrasted with extremely rapid movements. They concluded that linkage of the alpha and gamma neurons at supraspinal centers is fundamental for coordinated moderately rapid movements, and that the gamma loop contributes to precision in the temporal patterning of alpha neurons.

Motor units can be trained to respond in certain ways and therefore be under the control of a person with the proper training techniques. Efforts by J. V. Basmajian and others have led to breakthroughs in this area in recent years. Fine control over single motor units has been demonstrated. Even tonic motor unit activity normally not under voluntary control (the external sphincter is in a state of continuous contraction and is considered a tonic muscle) can be suppressed following motor unit training (E. R. Gray, 1971). In order for specific motor units to be activated, it appears that descending pathways are controlled in the spinal cord by proprioceptive input. With conscious efforts and appropriate feedback in the form of sensory information, motor units are activated. After training, volitional control is lessened.

The selective initiation of specified motor units and muscle fibers at a subcortical control level may help to explain complex movement patterns demonstrated by the highly skilled. Inhibition control, the timed role of antagonistic musculature in selected movements, influences the quality of performance. Excellent resource material on the topic of movement control from a neurophysiological frame of reference can be found in books by J. Maser (1973) and R. Granit (1970).

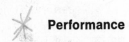

Performance

It is probable that specific receptor neurons are wired to specific terminals in the central nervous system, and it is equally probable that particular terminals are wired to particular effectors. *Motor or effector* neurons (see Figure 6–10) are responsible for the output of the system. Organs in which efferent nerve fibers terminate are called effectors. Of the different types of effectors, we are interested primarily in skeletal muscles and their role in following the orders of the nervous system.

The *myoneural junction* is the location where motor neuron axons supply muscle fibers with impulses. Each branch of the axon ends on one muscle fiber, and the axons themselves come directly from the spinal cord. Transmission of the impulse at the junction occurs in a manner similar to the synapse between two neurons. A *motor unit* refers to a motor neuron and the muscle fibers it activates. All muscle fibers responsible to a particular

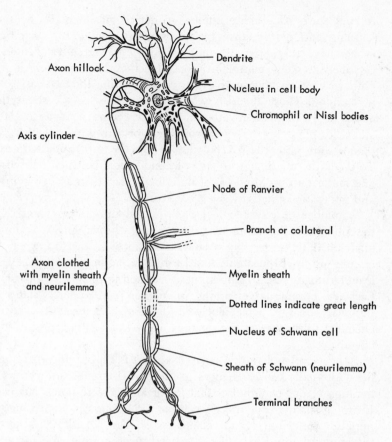

Axon hillock

Dendrite

Nucleus in cell body

Chromophil or Nissl bodies

Axis cylinder

Node of Ranvier

Branch or collateral

Axon clothed
with myelin sheath
and neurilemma

Myelin sheath

Dotted lines indicate great length

Nucleus of Schwann cell

Sheath of Schwann (neurilemma)

Terminal branches

Figure 6–10. Diagram of a motor neuron from the ventral gray area of the spinal cord. [From Diana Clifford Kimber and others, *Anatomy and Physiology,* 15th ed. (New York: Macmillan Publishing Co., Inc., 1966).]

neuron are innervated when an impulse is transmitted through this neuron.

The cabling arrangement, the specificity of the nervous system interconnections, is not yet adequately explained. Not only are sensory and motor neurons designated to and from certain points in the central points in the nervous system, but *internuncial* or *association* neurons are wired in the necessary places to send impulses from one neuron to another. Interestingly enough, of the billions of nerve cells in the organism, most of them are internuncial.

Skilled performance is associated with appropriate movements to cues in terms of pre-established goals. With the innervation and inhibition of the right receptors, coordinated movement patterns follow. An analysis of what actually happens internally, biochemically, and neurologically is still open to conjecture. Although a number of neurological theories do account for learning and performance by referring to changes in synaptic regions, others have presented different explanations. Actually, theories may be classified as being materialistic or subjective, because there is a dualistic point of view on how to go about understanding the nervous system's role in learning. Those theorists who are materialistic talk about the nature of the nerve impulse, reverberating nerve chains, changes at the synapse, and reflex physiology. These theorists are primarily physiologists. Subjective theorists are primarily psychologists who refer to the mind and experience. To them, the physiological basis of mind occurs between the sensory input and motor output. Mind is not described other than as being an organizer and integrator of activity.

A number of physiological theories fall into the general category of describing learning as a *change in the central synapses.* According to these anatomical theorists, the synaptic resistance is lowered when the same circuits are used repeatedly in a learning situation. Eccles believes that the axon terminals swell, Hebb argues that axon terminals multiply and synaptic knobs become larger during stimulation, and Konorski states that axon terminals enlarge. Some biochemical theorists believe that the release of chemical substances at the synapses allows nerve transmission to be more effective.

A theory related to this synaptic theory is that of *reverberation.* Learning supposedly causes changes in the neural circuits and results in reverberating chains of impulses that linger after the response has been made. Learning is a dynamic process causing a continuously circulating pattern of impulses in closed neural chains. A similar situation quickly activates the appropriate chain, which has been reverberating, and the appropriate response is made.

Russell (1959) believes in the development of paths, i.e., neuronal patterns, during learning. Repetition of the activity strengthens the pathway. Because the central nervous system constantly practices its skills and continually discharges impulses, even after years of no physical practice, one can still perform a motor skill. He feels that nerve cells show spontaneous activity, that they unconsciously strengthen simple patterns. Other learned skills only compete if closely related, because neuronal circuits are quite different—they will not disturb the pathway of the just-learned skill unless they are very similar.

Through the years, two schools of thought have been advanced to explain the manner in which the brain functions. As Alexander Luria (1966) writes, one group believes in the separateness in function of each part of the brain. He calls the people in this group localizationists, for they state that a function in a particular area of the brain can be localized. There is a second group which believes that the brain works as a whole, as a single entity.

Luria rejects both viewpoints in favor of the concept of the dynamic localization of functions. The following quotation exemplifies his position. "The motor act is not the 'function' of any one localized group of nerve cells situated in the cerebral cortex but is a complex functional system, whose working is controlled by many factors."

The brain, Luria believes, functions as a series of systems. Cerebral reflexes are the basic elements of behavior. He describes the reflex character of all processes, from the natural reflexes of the infant to the formation of complex systems of reflex connections. The formation of many functional systems occurs. The brain functions as a whole but at the same time is a "highly differentiated system whose parts are responsible for different aspects of the unified whole."

Luria emphasizes the influence of sensory information in motor activity, for the organism compares it to the intended output. Voluntary movement requires continuous sensory feedback information from the muscles and joints. Complex movement needs a flow of kinesthetic afferent impulses to direct motor impulses, which in turn give rise to appropriate movements. Besides kinesthetic impulses, the optic-spatial afferent system is also important in effective movement, Luria writes.

Karl Lashley (1964), like Luria, sees little value in considering the localization of function in the brain. However, contrary to Luria, Lashley feels the reflex theory is inadequate as the basis for the explanation of all behavior. He is very much against a concept that the integration of a motor act comes from a chain of reflexes. He also rejects the concept that the learning process is dependent upon definite anatomical paths specialized for particular neural integrations.

Rather, Lashley is of the opinion that higher-level activity is a function of some more general, dynamic organization of the brain. This highly respected physiological psychologist claimed that our interest should be in the dynamic relations of parts of the nervous system rather than in details of structural differentiation. There are no special cells for special functions, he writes. Patterns of energy, not localization, determine behavior. The unit of neural organization is not the reflex arc, to Lashley, but the mechanism by which reaction to ratios of excitation is produced. The brain cells react to patterns or combinations of excitation.

Lashley (1951) writes further that the cortex is a great network of continuously active reverberating circuits. Each new stimulus affects the system by changing the pattern of excitation throughout the entire system, not by exciting a new isolated reflex path. The brain is a dynamic, constantly active system, in fact, a composite of many interacting systems.

With regard to complex movement, Lashley believes that sensory control is not active, such as in the performance of a pianist. The pianist's movements are too quick for proprioceptive feedback or visual reaction time to the reading of notes of music. He postulates a central nervous mechanism that controls motor patterns and that "fires with predetermined intensity and duration or activates different muscles in predetermined order."

The effect of sensory activity on purposeful movement is noted by Arthur Guyton (1966). Sensory *engrams*, which are memory traces, result from willed movement. According to Guyton, the motor cortex does not control activities, for the patterns of activity are located in the sensory area. The motor area merely follows these patterns. If performance is bad, signals are sent to the motor cortex from the sensory area to change the movement.

Some skilled movements are performed very rapidly, with no time for sensory feedback. In these cases, Guyton states, the motor and premotor areas of the frontal lobe control quick movements. Research has indicated that ablation of these areas causes an inability to perform rapid, coordinated movements. The concept of memory traces, or engrams, is not new. However, the nature of a trace defies specific descriptors, although it is probable that it is not stored in a fixed place. E. Roy John (1967) questions the belief in anatomically localized engrams. An engram would appear to involve a more global process.

Many interpretations have been provided to explain the effect of learning on the nervous pathways, and theorists have tended to agree that when impulses continually travel the same pathways, there is less resistance at the synapse. Habits and memories are formed from repetitious impulses traveling the same routes, with the result that patterns become fixed. Whether learning should be thought of as a building up of a series of conditioned reflexes or the utilization of the appropriate neural pattern which was there all the time, is a question that can be perplexing to theorist and student alike. John (1967) questions the concept of the occurrence of decreased resistance in neural pathways and reduced synaptic resistance with repetitive experiences. He does not believe that new memory is acquired through repeated connections and established neural pathway routes.

Performance output, reflecting learning and memory capabilities, no doubt facilitated by global operations occurring in the brain, involves many and varied cells as well as biochemical changes within them.

Feedback

As has been mentioned throughout the text and will be discussed in greater detail in Chapter 9, feedback plays a major role in learning and performance. The learning of a skill encompasses the establishment of a series of successive behaviors. Each new practice trial is usually performed within a frame of stored past experiences and movement patterns and immediate objectives. Perhaps motor learning involves the following neural processes:

Performance → feedback of signals (visual, emotional, proprioceptive, and the like) → sensory input → strengthening or weakening of movement patterns.

Feedback refers to the information the individual gains from his performance which permits him to profit from the experience. Hopefully, the information will be accurate, although some researchers have suggested that the sensory pathways are subject to error. Although sensory pathways may be interfered with and thereby modify input patterns, fortunately, the interference is not usually detrimental to performance. Without feedback, without the organism's knowing how or what it is doing, progress, to say the least, would be impeded in many forms of activity. Knowledge about performance or the results of it is fed back into the memory system, to be stored as a comparator for use in similar future situations. Depending on the task, it may be used immediately to rectify ongoing inappropriate responses. Motor performance typically contains some form of feedback for the individual. Feedback is an essential and necessary component of the human behaving system for movement-oriented behaviors, at least in the beginning stages of learning. Its quality, availability, and effective use by the learner will help to determine optimal performance.

Feedback can help to monitor and regulate ongoing activity. Sensitive and fine adjustments are made when discrepancies are noticed between the performance output and the input signals. An especially heavy reliance on feedback, especially from external sources (sometimes referred to as knowledge of results) is observable in the early learning stages. More gross motor adjustments are made with feedback in the initial practice experiences, fine gross motor corrections at higher levels of proficiency.

Finally, feedback contains the property to initiate movements, or movement plans, as we saw earlier in the chapter. During activity, sensory feedback provides us with positioning cues relevant to the display demands. We continually activate new plans during prolonged activity, as can be witnessed in constantly changing fencing, wrestling, or badminton situations.

An attempt has been offered to describe the human behaving system in terms of its basic subsystems, especially as they are involved and interrelate in most coordinated and purposeful motor activities. A more brief but detailed description is offered by H. T. A. Whiting and other contributors to a recent special issue of *The Research Quarterly* (1972). Extensive treatments may be found in books by A. T. Welford (1968), N. Bernstein (1967), and Steven Keele (1973).

HANDICAPPING THE SYSTEM

A host of factors at any one given moment can contribute to variability in the output of a system. Restrictions in the design and functioning abilities of the system limit potential performance levels. The human system, like any other, depends upon the quality of the component parts and their ability to interact in appropriate coordinated fashion to fulfill reasonable objectives. Defects in any system can occur, however. Some can be remedied with functions restored to full usage. Others can never be restructured. In still other cases, compensation may overcome the dampening effect of an inferior component part of the system.

Because the functioning ability of a system is weighed against the criterion of input versus output match, it is useful to identify parts of the system that may trigger noise or bias, negatively influencing performance. A quick survey of the system would indicate that faulty working senses, perceptual distortions, learning disorders and damage to the nervous system, and physical handicaps can place a heavy toll on any expectations of quality performance.

An individual's chance at skilled behavior is greatly dependent upon being able to identify structural and functional handicaps, and remedying or compensating accordingly. In many situations, adjustments can be made so that reasonable performance is demonstrated. The seriousness of the system's limitation and its ability to compensate and adjust will obviously be reflected in the quality of its performance.

Physical Handicaps

The satisfactory functioning of the musculature involved in any motor task of concern depends on the extent of any temporary or permanent damage. Temporary damage needs to be repaired, permanent damage compensated for, and poor condition remediated. A structural defect leads to a functional problem. Yet functional problems may occur as well without structural defects. For instance, poor motor performance is noticed when appropriate muscles do not possess the needed tonus for strength, tissue elasticity is insufficient for flexibility, or cardiorespiratory functions are below par for the needed endurance to continue practicing a task.

The organic efficiency of the body can be improved upon in order that the person will possess the necessary physical properties to practice tasks and eventually demonstrate skilled performance. If the physical components involved in the tasks are carefully evaluated, practice can sufficiently improve them to provide the learner with the "tools" to proceed. On the other hand, temporary damage to body tissue may suggest nonparticipation in activity until healing occurs. Permanent damage to tissue requires the learner to seek out alternative methods of achieving goals. The performance may not appear smooth but nevertheless the task may be completed in a satisfactory manner.

Sensory Handicaps

Because what comes out of the system (behavior) is greatly dependent on what went into it (information), the senses should not be impaired in any way that might cause input to be distorted as it is transmitted throughout the system. Of interest in the research has been the effect of damage to the distance receptors (visual, auditory) on learning and performing a task.

In cognitively oriented tasks the deaf have often been found inferior to "normals." Yet recent researchers have pointed out that the deaf were restricted and penalized in the learning strategies they could employ under the design of the experiments. At present there is a strong belief that deaf people use different strategies than hearing people, and can consequently perform similarly in many tasks if they are (1) taught to use special strategies, or (2) allowed to, by removal of situational learning constraints.

Can individuals with a severe handicap in one sense modality compensate for it by developing a greater than average ability to use another sense modality? The question is one raised often. We will see some evidence to support the compensation notion for vision in Chapter 7 in the discussion of "The Senses." Larry Beutler (1970) offers data in the same line for deaf children. Deaf and hearing subjects learned three high-relief finger mazes of increasing complexity while blindfolded. The presumed verbal advantage of hearing subjects was not demonstrated in this study, in that they did not outperform the deaf on any of the tasks. In fact, the younger group of deaf children was superior to their hearing counterparts on the most difficult task. Perhaps with age these differences would not be noted, as language skill and verbal concepts are developed in the hearing children. These concepts are needed to achieve in verbal and motor tasks. At any rate, it appears as though deaf children use a different problem-solving approach on tasks when compared with hearing children.

Because individuals who possess a sense impairment are likely not to be active in vigorous activities in which that sense might have a major role, their overall physical fitness might be expected to be lower than average. Handicapped children need the opportunity to move and to stimulate physical development. In those educational programs where special planned physical activities are available to handicapped students, their development will be similar in general to the nonhandicapped. Balance ability stands out as a variable distinguishing the handicapped. As Samuel Case and his colleagues (1973) reported, 81 per cent of the deaf subjects failed to demonstrate a particular balance task, 50 per cent of the blind failed it, whereas only 15 per cent of the nonhandicapped subjects could not do it. Special balance training may help to compensate for a vestibular pathology associated with the deaf or the fear of the blind if they are to accomplish in those gross motor activities that require some degree of balance.

Perceptual Handicaps

As we will see in Chapter 8, which deals with developmental factors, the quality and nature of early and timely experiences in life for all living organisms may have some bearing on adult behavior. Enriched environments and experiences as contrasted with deprived ones stimulate the senses and in turn the perceptual processes. Coping behaviors are learned. So are problem-solving abilities. One learns to perceive relationships between objects, to determine functioning abilities of his body, and in general how to make sense of his environment. A number of theories related to cognitive achievements and dependence upon adequate perceptual-motor development of the child have been proposed, and the leading ones are presented and discussed in Chapter 8. As far as effective performance in motor skills is concerned, perception plays a major role in making sense of cues and helping to suggest those decisions leading to the right behavior. Insufficient previous experiences or neurological impairment will impede performance in the learning of complex motor skills.

Cognitive Handicaps

The human system that is retarded mentally will typically show an inferior level of performance in a variety of motor activities when compared to those systems in the normal intellectual range. The mentally retarded will also show a greater individual variability in scores than normals. This handicap suggests that special training procedures need to be considered, such as more time, simple explanations, and sufficient breakdown of the activity into subtasks.

The problem that the mentally retarded have with learning motor skills implies the degree cognition plays in skill mastery. Following verbal or written directions, applying verbal labels to motor acts (self-verbalization), using tactics and strategies, following rules, and problem solving are activities associated with the cognitive domain of behaviors. The ideal integration of cognitive, affective, and psychomotor behaviors can only occur if all subsystems are operational at an adequate level. Further discussion on cognition and the mentally retarded is found in Chapter 7.

Learning Disorders

Any inability to perform an activity typically performed by others within the same range of intelligence may be considered a *learning disability*. A *learning disorder*, by comparison, can be due to a host of problems (Edward Frierson and Walter Barbe, 1967, p. 4):

Learning disorder might best designate a known impairment in the nervous system. The impairment may be the result of genetic variation, biochemical irregularity, perinatal brain insult, or injury sustained by the nervous system as a result of disease, accident, sensory deprivation, nutritional deficit, or other direct influence.

Brain damage may only be one of several reasons why persons do not function properly. A number of alternatives have already been presented. We will concentrate here on any injury or damage to the central nervous system that can occur prior to, at the time of, or after birth. Injury, infection, and the like, can cause functional disturbances as manifested by perceptual, judgmental, emotional, and response impairment. The learning process is consequently impeded.

DAMPENING THE SYSTEM

The "normal" functioning system can be *temporarily* impaired, resulting in subpar performance. A system that is capable of functioning at a certain level will not when any one of the subsystems is disturbed. Some of those variables of possible negative influence on performance are examined here, notably, sense restriction, sleep deprivation, fatigue, and pain. Other variables are discussed elsewhere in this book, for example, warm-up. Presumably, warmup activity after a long period of no practice helps to reorient the individual to the task, and without it initial performance levels may be too low truly to represent that which has been learned. Also, such variables as injury to a body part or feelings of ill-health can temporarily dampen the system. They are not treated any further here, however, because their effects on performance are too obvious.

Many learning disorder syndromes and corresponding defects in the nervous system have been identified with the learning of cognitively oriented behaviors. Others are associated with the decomposition of movement, for example, dyssynergia. It is thought that this syndrome includes a loss of postural tone of the muscles and appearance of irregular movements, perhaps caused by the inability of the cerebellum to coordinate inhibiting and facilitating impulses. Tremor is another disease of the cerebellum, and can be detected with purposive movements. Tremor and other unnatural movements are no doubt reflective of problems in the motor cortex as well as the cerebellum.

Damage to the extrapyramidal system could result in Parkinson's disease. Muscle tone is disturbed and voluntary movement is characterized by rigidity. The rigidity paralysis in resisting movements may only be part of the syndrome, as tremor may be seen in the same muscle groups when the person is at rest.

Damage to the vestibular system impairs the maintenance of equilibrium. Vertigo gives one the feeling of rotation, a sense of movement of the person or the environment. Like many diseases, vertigo may involve disease of the cerebellum or the cerebrum, or, for that matter, the visual sense receptors, specifically, a nystagmus. A loss or impairment of proprioception may be reflected by a disease of the posterior spinal column, called ataxia. There is difficulty in gauging direction as well as loss of proprioception from the joints.

Motor impairment may be assessed from parent or teacher observations, clinical (neurological, electroencephalograph examinations), or motor performance tests especially designed to diagnosis disorders. Correct diagnosis is no easy matter. Obviously, though, the more accurate the diagnosis the easier it is to suggest remedial activities. Performance expectations are more realistic, and the learner will benefit most from the type of activites in which he is placed. Various tests of motor impairment are described by Morris and Whiting (1971) as are a variety of compensatory activities.

Sense Restriction

As the athlete desires to be physically fit and to maintain his motor-skill proficiency, his concern for sensory acuity is justified. A quick response to the starting command may determine the difference between winning and losing the 100-yard dash. To have the touch in bowling may produce a 200-plus game. To be visually alert may mean catching a ball thought to be uncatchable. And to feel the tennis serve can make the difference between an ace and just another serve.

In order to maintain the senses in a state of alertness (at least those involved in a particular motor activity), the individual must not restrict these senses preceding the time of performance. Sense restriction or deprivation study has been increasing, with evidence leading to the conviction that one needs varying sensory stimulation to function adaptively (William Neff, 1965). Although research is still not sufficient in this area, at least in practical situations, there is evidence to indicate the negative results of a non-variable sensory environment.

Bexton, Heron, and Scott (1956) studied twenty-two male subjects during a three-day isolation period. The subjects were confined to cubicles where they were restricted in their daily activities and therefore experienced decreased variations in their sensory environments. They were subjected at different periods to cognitive tests (e.g., multiplying, completing series of numbers, and making words from jumbled letters). The subjects were found to suffer from increasingly impaired intellectual ability and even suffered from visual hallucinations the longer they were under the experimental conditions.

This study emphasizes the need for varying stimuli to keep us aroused and mentally active. Although cognitive tasks were employed in the study described above, we might very well expect similar findings in motor tasks. When one is restricted to a bed for several days because of illness or injury, he commonly discovers acuity impairment in attempting skills he performed prior to the situation. This may be due to a nonpotent sensory environment. The bedridden state might influence actual structural changes, such as in muscle tissue (atrophy), which might also slightly impair motor performance, depending on the length of confinement and the complexity of the skill to be performed.

One of the few sense restriction studies dealing with perceptual and motor skills was undertaken by Jack Vernon and his associates (1959). Subjects in this study were isolated and deprived of sensory stimulation for twenty-four, forty-eight, or seventy-two hours. The five tests administered were color perception, depth perception, pursuit rotor, mirror drawing, and rail walking. The subjects were tested prior to isolation, upon release, and twenty-four hours afterward. Among the interesting findings, indicating the different but somewhat consistent effects of sense deprivation on the different tasks, were

1. Color perception was especially impaired when confinement was forty-eight and seventy-two hours.
2. Depth perception was not affected under the imposed conditions.
3. Pursuit rotor performance was only negatively affected when confinement lasted forty-eight hours.
4. Mirror tracing performance when speed to traverse was the dependent variable was similar to pursuit rotor performance.
5. Rail walking was especially negatively effected after seventy-two hours isolation.

In this study, and as has been found in others, the detrimental influence of sense deprivation was rather short-lived. Recovery in performance was reasonably good twenty-four hours after confinement was over.

The role of activity and exercise in counteracting perceptual loss has been studied by Zubek (1963). In comparing groups of subjects confined to a chamber for a period of one week, he determined that even a few exercise periods a day seemed to eliminate many of the impairments produced by perceptual deprivation. Other research findings on the effects of sense restriction on perceptual and motor activites have been conflicting because of varying methods of experimentation. As a point of interest, other studies since the pioneer one of Bexton, reported earlier, have not usually found such pronounced detrimental effects of sense restriction. Some results even indicate an improvement in certain functions as a result of sensory deprivation. However, it would appear that a variety of perceptual and motor functions are susceptible to impairment as a function of sensory restriction, but the range of effects does not seem to be as great as was first believed.

A good summary of the literature is offered by John Corso (1967, p. 574). He states that

> . . . sensory deprivation on perceptual motor performance will depend upon both the duration of the confinement and the nature of the specific task imposed. For most subjects, the maximal change in performance occurs at the end of a 48-hour confinement period. . . . The results indicate that difficulty is experienced in performing new perceptual motor tasks in a sensory-deprived environment, but the question of disruption of old motor responses (excluding handwriting) has not been posed and should be investigated. The evidence also indicates that the disruptive effects of sensory deprivation on perceptual motor behavior are of relatively short duration; additional studies are needed to determine the specific forms of the recovery functions.

The study of attention and alertness, called vigilance, has indicated that as a subject views the same stimuli, his attentiveness decreases. Vigilance studies have been performed under a wide range of experimental conditions, mainly in order to determine pilot and military effectiveness during those times when concentration is important for long periods in which a specific, unsuspecting stimulus may suddenly appear. The person must monitor and detect infrequent, random, and low-intensity events. Under such conditions it is desirable to provide an environment that will maintain the human behaving systems at a reasonable level of functioning. Even a novel stimulus will improve the subject's alertness. The baseball outfielder who rarely has a ball hit to him may be less alert than the third-baseman who has been frequently bombarded with shots directed toward him.

Situations similar to the baseball fielder having balls hit to him infrequently are piloting a plane under conditions of extended confinement, driving a car on a superhighway, or reading, studying, or listening to lectures for prolonged periods of time. Performance seems to decline with time as a person is subjected to too much monotony and repetition. Boredom and inattentiveness result. An important function of the instructor is to provide conditions that improve stimulation and motivation.

It is important to keep the senses in a state of alertness, for the information derived from sensory involvement in a given task is necessary for skilled movement patterns as well. The information, termed feedback, refers to the sensory information gained from a motor performance that helps to regulate present and future movements in terms of immediate and past experiences. Chase and others (1961) investigated delayed sensory feedback on two tapping tasks. One task involved simple regularity movements and the other required rhythmically patterned responses. Delayed sensory feedback did not appear to affect the regularity task negatively but there was a significantly impaired performance on the patterned task. Most motor skills are of the complex type, and it would seem that sensory involvement and feedback permit greater skill success.

Sleep Deprivation

The human behaving system needs to be properly energized and rested for productive outcomes. Personal physiological and psychological factors interplay with task characteristics and suggest the ideal amount of rest needed for each person to sustain himself according to task demands. We can easily think of military, industrial, agricultural, athletic, and other motor activities in which rest and sleep are sharply constrained because of situational factors. The obvious practical questions are the following: To what extent does sleep deprivation impair motor performance? How much sleep loss can the individual overcome? With which tasks?

A recent review of the literature was reported by Naitoh and Townsend (1970). As might be expected, performance becomes more variable and ultimately worsens if sleep deprivation continues long enough. Performance will be a function of such variables as

1. Task characteristics and demands (e.g., difficulty, duration, and the refined movements associated with a complex cue display).
2. The state of the organism (e.g., motivation, personality, and adjustment to the imposed sleep deprivation condition).
3. The duration of the sleep deprivation period.
4. The testing conditions.

Most of the research seems to cover the circumstance where subjects are deprived of sleep for a set period of time and are then tested in various performance measures. In this design the effects will probably run similar to those found in sense deprivation studies. George Holland (1968) used a similar design, except that he trained his subjects on the tasks of interest for four weeks. He examined the consequences of one night's sleep deprivation on the performance of a jump test (quickness and accuracy in moving through a pattern with a series of hops and steps), a manipulation test (a pattern similar to the jump test, scaled down, requiring the hand movement of a stylus), and a bicycle work performance test. The loss of sleep did not affect scores on the jump tests or the manipulation test. Work output on the bicycle showed a significant decrement. Holland conjectures that these tasks may have been too short term and brief to tax the attention span of sleep-deprived subjects.

Another approach is to re-examine performance work and rest ratios without sleep or to work continuously without sleep. Earl Alluisi (1969) recommends the synthetic-work technique to assess output during extended periods of work. A job or work situation is created in which a number of tasks are administered to subjects for continuous practice over days and weeks. Various work–rest schedules over time with different tasks reveal man's ability to sustain performance. Alluisi and his colleague are attempting to answer questions related to man's capability to sustain activity without sleep over extended time durations. One such approach is described by Ben Morgan, Bill Brown, and Earl Alluisi (1970). They report that (p. 22) "in evaluating men's endurance within the continuous-work situation, one is forced also to consider man's typical circadian rhythms [diurnal rhythms—physiological data such as pulse rates, axillary temperatures, etc., as related to time of day], his activities during the "rest" portions of the schedule, and the effects of his sleep-wakefulness cycles and habits on performance." The researchers conclude (p. iii) that

> Performance during the 48 hours of continuous work was greatly influenced by the circadian rhythm. The first performance decrements occurred after approximately 18 hours of work; during the early morning hours of the first night, average performance decreased to approximately 82% of baseline performance. During the first half of the second day of work, performance improved to about 90% of baseline, but decreased again during the night to approximately 67% of baseline. All measures of performance indicated that the recovery of performance was complete (to baseline levels) following the 24-hour period of rest and recovery.

Continuous work is more demanding than distributed work schedules and consequently will show more obvious impairments. Performance decrements are more pronounced with more complex or strenuous activities. Recovery of performance is usually found to be fairly complete following one night's sleep, thus suggesting the transient nature of the effects of sleep deprivation conditions. It might be speculated that people can be trained to perform without as much sleep as they think they need to be in a state of readiness. As Alluisi (1970) points out, men can follow a work–rest schedule of four hours of work and four hours off work for very long periods of time without noticeable deleterious effects on performance.

Fatigue

The previous discussion on sleep deprivation implied that performance decrements may be due to boredom, loss of motivation, and fatigue. Fatigue may be caused by excessive and strenuous work as well. The ability to resist fatigue, partly because of the physiological and fitness state of the person, will enable him to perform motor tasks continuously and effectively. As we review the human behaving system proposed in this chapter, it would appear that fatigue could influence the components from input to output.

A variety of interpretations, explanations, and definitions of the term *fatigue* have been offered by laymen and scholars. Physiologists usually offer one perspective, psychologists another. It is not unusual to associate the fatigue effects of muscular work with physiological processes. This is an oversimplistic interpretation, however. Writing for many years on the topic of fatigue, S. Howard Bartley prefers an extremely broad interpretation of the term: "Fatigue is an experienced state of discomfort, aversion, and inability to perform, otherwise known as tiredness or weariness. The term applies to the total individual (the organism-as-a-person) and not properly to an organ or tissue" (1968, p. 345).

When fatigue states are reached in the performance of most motor tasks, muscle discomfort is usually apparent. Extreme exertion or prolonged activity result in disrupted behavior. Performance becomes erratic and impaired. There is an interruption of control and a loss of efficiency. Irregularity in timing is observed. The person realizes that he can not proceed further with the task; the task demands are too great. In fact, we may view fatigue as the result of an *overload* on the system and *boredom* as the result of an *underload* on the system.

The solutions for overcoming fatigue depend on the task and the person. Rest may be the answer for many activities. Drugs such as amphetamines (pep pills) may work on occasion. Increased effort, motivation, and stimuli can help to overcome fatigue. Changing tasks (completely different), attitudes, or attention may assist in combating fatigue. Practice in fatiguing situations will aid the person in becoming adjusted to performing under such conditions; a state of performance resistance to fatigue will develop.

The human system behaves—that is, movements are enacted, after information is received, these signals are perceived, and decisions about them are made. Fatigue apparently affects primarily the central processes involved between information receipt and the initiation of movement. In tasks heavily laden with a perceptual component, less attention is paid to task-relevant signals. Externally paced tasks require immediate recognition of cues that might occur in an unpredictable fashion. Impaired attention and perception will negatively influence behavior. An inability to perform coordinated and well-timed movements will disrupt both self-paced and externally paced tasks.

One area of concern for skill instructors is the degree to which fatigue may be expected to inhibit learning and make performance erratic. Although there is an assumption on the part of many that fatigue disrupts learning and performance, this may not always be the case. The body may be stressed through continous local activity (an arm, for example) or through general activity involving many muscles in different sites. Tasks may primarily involve strength, endurance, speed, or accuracy. It may be expected, according to directions indicated in the research, that

1. General body activity and moderately high fatigue will impair performances requiring strength, endurance, and on occasion, rapid move-

ments, whereas accuracy or balance performance may not be affected (see Figure 6–11 for an illustration of the latter case).

2. Fatigue caused by one task does not necessarily influence the learning and performance of a subsequent task (e.g., Welch, 1969, showed that heavy fatigue caused by a step-up test did not impair performance on three coordination tests; Brzezinska, 1970, reports that there is no generalization of fatigue between unrelated tasks, fatigue caused by one task does not spread to other tasks except in cases where there are common factors).

3. General fatiguelike exercise may on occasion aid the learning of a motor task, perhaps serving as warm-up or causing an increased concentration on the learning task (e.g., Benson, 1968, noted that learning to juggle was enhanced when subjects practiced in a fatigued state).

4. For many tasks, moderately high fatiguing activities will impede performance rather than learning; that is, learning is occurring all the time but fatigue temporarily depresses performance, thereby producing lower levels of achievement (e.g., Schmidt, 1969, observed balance performed worse under fatigue but considerably improved without fatigue).

5. Severe exercise will be detrimental to both learning and performance (e.g., Carron, 1972, demonstrated the long-lasting effect of extremely fatiguing bicycle ergometer work in impairing balance on the ladder-climb task).

The influence of exhaustive exercise on learning can be proposed through consolidation theory, suggest Robert Hutton, James Stevens, and Faith Stevens (1972). It is thought that continued neural activity associated with an event goes on until a memory trace is established (consolidation). If the trace is vulnerable during the consolidation period, as thought, any sudden and strong stimuli can conceivably disrupt the trace. Vigorous exercise introduced immediately after a learning event may be one of many examples of stimuli providing an impedance to memory consolidation. Although Hutton and his co-workers embrace the theory, their data are quite preliminary and the theory itself represents primarily an extrapolation from research with variables other than fatigue. We will have to wait for more work in this line before any conclusions can be reached.

Instructors must determine the optimal period of time students should spend learning skills before fatigue effects would make this time wasteful. Common sense is perhaps one of the best indicators as to when a person is too tired mentally or physically to receive any value from continued practice. However, although there are times when performance may suffer slightly under minor conditions of fatigue, ultimate learning does not. Under excessive fatigue, it is quite difficult for the learner to be attentive to new cues and new material. The returns of the practice of pushing the

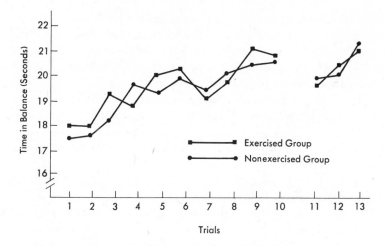

Figure 6–11. Performance on a stabilometer for groups exercised on a treadmill or nonexercised. No differences in performance were noted between the groups. (From Douglas W. Bartz and Leon E. Smith, "Effect of Moderate Exercise on the Performance and Learning of a Gross Motor Skill," *Perceptual and Motor Skills,* 31:187–190, 1970.)

learner when he is too tired are of little value and, consequently, this practice is regarded as undesirable. Furthermore, the learner may practice erroneous responses that will have to be unlearned at a later date. Consideration must also be given to safety factors and the danger involved in the execution of a particular task, especially if the performer is extremely weary.

Pain

Pain, or at least an individual's perception of it, will usually have some bearing on the performance of skills, especially in competitive situations. Physiologically, pain mechanisms are quite similar for all people. The ability to detect painful stimuli may operate in the same way we gain information related to vision, taste, and movement: specialized sense receptors have specific functions, and pain receptors are activated when painful experiences are present. Another point of view is that pain encompasses so many stimuli that it cannot be related to a single sense modality. Advocates of this concept suggest that intense stimulation activates nonspecific receptors and that pain patterns emerge instead.

Beyond the activation of pain receptors is the person's psychological attitude to the pain situation. Previous experiences influence the ability to cope with pain. Furthermore, pain thresholds may also be related to genetic factors. Experimental research and empirical observations suggest that some persons are able to withstand pain more than other persons. This situation may be related to an individual's pain threshold, conditioning factors related to previous experiences, and motivation to overcome the pain. Pain tolerance is related to a host of variables.

The ability to withstand pain is beneficial in demonstrating high levels of task proficiency under adverse conditions. Although physiological mechanisms and chemical substances can contribute to the curtailment of activity, conscious mental behavior operates to influence behavior as well.

For certain endeavors, namely those in the cognitive domain (i.e., verbal tasks or tasks involving exceptional amounts of attention, vigilance, and appropriate perceptions for accurate, fast responses), an ideal state of arousal seems to be desirable. However, when pain, fatigue, and physical endurance are occurring during practice and must be tolerated for achievement, it is possible that a mentally alert, sensitive state could be a disadvantage for the organism. The direction of thoughts, the conscious state, during such activity might enable an individual to be more or less tolerant of circumstances.

It is generally accepted that cerebral involvement and arousal level can affect autonomic functions. Adrenalin secretion and skin conductance as well as subjectively estimated arousal level can diminish with repeated trials on a perceptual-conflict test. This habituation response is commonly seen in cardiorespiratory responses to repeated administration of treadmill or ergometer work bouts. It has been suggested that in some cases control of arousal level can be accomplished by assigning subjects objective, cognitive tasks to be carried out during test administration (Brown, 1966; Collins et al., 1961). Similar procedures have been said to exert a regulatory influence on the reduction of blood oxygenation of well-trained athletes during breath holding (Yegerow, 1965). Whether this in fact occurs or whether differences in breath-holding time were a result of the subjects being predictably variable in their ability to withstand the discomfort of breath holding is a moot point; however, it is important that different conscious states may bring about different responses as a result of cerebral–autonomic interactions.

The ability to endure appears to reside in the willingness to withstand the pain experienced, a result of the accumulation of noxious metabolites in the working muscles (Dorpat and Holmes, 1955). Athletes often report that feelings of pain can be suppressed during endurance work by diverting their attention away from the exercise bout. However, this has not been supported by experimental evidence. Paradoxically, it has been shown that, generally, as pain appears, more effort is exerted (Evans and McGlashan, 1967). This increased effort would then bring about a greater production and accumulation of metabolites and, concomitantly, more pain, a cycle continuing until the quit point is reached. It would seem very difficult to maintain diversionary cognition during these latter stages of performance, but herein may be a key to enhanced task execution insofar as endurance is concerned.

The ability to endure pain and fatigue may not only be related to the subjects' training state and the nature of the task, but personality variables as well. For instance, the relationship of extraversion and the ability to withstand pain has been the topic of a few studies (Levine et al., 1966; Lynn and Eysenck, 1961). Eysenck hypothesizes that individuals who score high on an extraversion personality trait should have greater levels of pain tolerance than individuals who score low on extraversion.

Some researchers have examined the relationship of pain tolerance and participation in athletic activities. In one such study (Ryan and Kovacic, 1966) contact-sport athletes, noncontact-sport athletes, and nonathletes were compared and observed in their ability to tolerate induced pain. A definite relationship was found, with contact-sport athletes demonstrating a better ability to withstand pain. Perhaps they learn to tolerate pain as a result of their previous experiences. Willingness and ability to tolerate pain are associated with type and extent of athletic participation.

Perhaps there are persons who are pain reducers or pain augmenters. Individual perception in a situation would be related to these characteristics. The augmenter is one who amplifies the intensity of his perception of pain; the reducer is one who does the opposite. Internally based motivation and previous experiences are thought to be related to pain tolerance. Conjecturing, a contact-sport athlete might accept more pain because he is used to it and knows the consequences will be of no great significance. Noncontact athletes and especially nonathletes might not be familiar with absorbing extreme pain in an activity and therefore be apprehensive of the potential damaging effects.

Although athletes often perform better than nonathletes in contrived pain situations, pain threshold has by no means been determined as a generalized phenomenon to the variety of pain sources or parts of the body involved. Pain can evidently limit behavior in some human systems and not in others. Training to become used to pain and to perform in spite of it is useful in elevating performance, providing damage to body tissues is not an issue.

REFERENCES

Alluisi, Earl A. "Sustained Performance," in E. A. Bilodeau (ed.), *Principles of Skill Acquisition.* New York: Academic Press, Inc., 1969.

Bartley, S. Howard. "Fatigue," in *International Encyclopedia of the Social Sciences.* New York: Macmillan Publishing Co., Inc., 1968.

Bartz, Douglas W., and Leon E. Smith. "Effect of Moderate Exercise on the Performance and Learning of a Gross Motor Skill," *Perceptual and Motor Skills,* 31:187–190, 1970.

BENSON, DAVID W. "Influence of Imposed Fatigue on Learning a Jumping Task and a Juggling Task," *Research Quarterly*, 39:251–257, 1968.

BERNSTEIN, N. *The Co-ordination and Regulation of Movements*. Elmsford, N.Y.: Pergamon Press, Inc., 1969.

BEUTLER, LARRY E. "Hearing-Loss Effects on a Procedural Task Sequence," *Journal of Motor Behavior*, 2:207–215, 1970.

BEXTON, W. HAROLD, WOODBURN HERON, and THOMAS H. SCOTT. "Effects of Decreased Variation in the Sensory Environment," *Canadian Journal of Psychology*, 8:70–76, 1956.

BROWN, J. H. "Modification of Vestibular Nystogmus by Change of Task During Stimulation," *Perceptual and Motor Skills*, 22:603–611, 1966.

BRZEZINSKA, ZOFIA. "Generalization of Fatigue in Activity and Vigilance," *Polish Psychological Bulletin*, 1:32–38, 1970.

BUCHWALD, JENNIFER S. "A Functional Concept of Motor Control," *American Journal of Medicine*, 46:141–150, 1967.

CARRON, ALBERT V. "Motor Performance and Learning Under Physical Fatigue," *Medicine and Science in Sports*, 4:101–106, 1972.

CASE, SAMUEL, YVETTE DAWSON, JAMES SCHARTNER, and DALE DONAWAY. "Comparison of Levels of Fundamental Skill and Cardio-Respiratory Fitness of Blind, Deaf, and Non-handicapped High School Age Boys," *Perceptual and Motor Skills*, 36:1291–1294, 1973.

CHASE, RICHARD A., ISABELLE RAPIN, LLOYD GILDEN, SAMUEL SUTTON, and GEORGE GUILFOYLE. "Studies on Sensory Feedback: II. Sensory Feedback Influences on Keytapping Motor Tasks," *Quarterly Journal of Experimental Psychology*, 13:153–167, 1961.

COLLINS, W. E., G. H. CRAMPTON, and J. B. POSNER. "Effects of Mental Activity on Vestibular Nystogmus and the Electroencephalogram," *Nature*, 190:1964–1965, 1961.

CORSO, JOHN F. *The Experimental Psychology of Sensory Behavior*. New York: Holt, Rinehart and Winston, Inc., 1967.

DORPAT, T. L., and T. H. HOLMES. "Mechanisms of Skeletal Muscle Pain and Fatigue," *A.M.A. Archives of Neurology and Psychiatry*, 74:628–640, 1955.

ERDELYI, MATTHEW HUGH. "A New Look at the New Look: Perceptual Defense and Vigilance," *Psychological Review*, 81:1–25, 1974.

EVANS, F. J., and T. H. McGLASHAN. "Work and Effort During Pain," *Perceptual and Motor Skills*, 25:794, 1967.

FRIERSON, EDWARD C., and WALTER B. BARBE (eds.). *Educating Children with Learning Disabilities*. New York: Appleton-Century-Crofts, Inc., 1967.

GIBSON, JAMES J. *The Senses Considered as Perceptual Systems*. Boston: Houghton Mifflin Company, 1966.

GRANIT, R. *The Basis of Motor Control*. New York: Academic Press, Inc., 1970.

GRAY, EDWIN R. "Conscious Control of Motor Units in a Tonic Muscle," *American Journal of Physical Medicine,* 50:34–40, 1971.

GUTIN, BERNARD. "Exercise-Induced Activation and Human Performance: A Review," *Research Quarterly,* 44:256–268, 1973.

GUYTON, ARTHUR C. *Textbook of Medical Physiology.* Philadelphia: W. B. Saunders Company, 1966.

HOLLAND, GEORGE J. "Effects of Limited Sleep Deprivation on Performance of Selected Motor Tasks," *Research Quarterly,* 39:285–294, 1968.

HUTTON, ROBERT. "Neurosciences: Mechanisms of Motor Control," in Robert N. Singer (ed.), *The Psychomotor Domain: Movement Behavior.* Philadelphia: Lea & Febiger, 1972.

HUTTON, ROBERT S., JAMES L. STEVENS, and FAITH STEVENS. "The Effects of Strenuous and Exhaustive Exercise on Learning: A Theoretical Note and Preliminary Findings," *Journal of Motor Behavior,* 4:207–216, 1972.

ISAACSON, ROBERT L., ROBERT J. DOUGLAS, JOEL F. LUBAR, and LEONARD W. SCHMALTZ. *A Primer of Physiological Psychology.* New York: Harper & Row, Publishers, Inc., 1971.

KATZ, BERNHARD. "How Cells Communicate," *Scientific American,* 205:209–220, 1961.

KEELE, STEVEN W. *Attention and Human Performance.* Pacific Palisades, Calif.: Goodyear Publishing Co., 1973.

JOHN, E. ROY. *Mechanisms of Memory.* New York: Academic Press, Inc., 1967.

LASHLEY, KARL S. *Brain Mechanisms and Intelligence.* New York: Hafner Publishing Co., Inc., 1964.

————. "The Problems of Serial Order in Behavior," in Lloyd A. Jeffress (ed.), *Cerebral Mechanisms in Behavior.* New York: John Wiley & Sons, Inc., 1951.

LEVINE, F. M., B. TUSKY, and D. C. NICHOLS. "Tolerance for Pain, Extraversion, and Neuroticism: Failure to Replicate Results," *Perceptual and Motor Skills,* 23:847–850, 1966.

LURIA, ALEXANDER R. *Higher Cortical Functions in Man.* New York: Basic Books, Inc., Publishers, 1966.

LYNN, R., and H. F. EYSENCK. "Tolerance for Pain, Extraversion and Neuroticism," *Perceptual and Motor Skills,* 12:161–162, 1961.

MAGGIO, ELIO. *Psychophysiology of Learning and Memory.* Springfield, Ill.: Charles C Thomas, publisher, 1971.

MASER, JACK. *Efferent Organization and the Integration of Behavior,* New York: Academic Press, Inc., 1973.

MILLER, GEORGE A., EUGENE GALANTER, and KARL H. PRIBRAM. *Plans and the Structure of Behavior.* New York: Holt, Rinehart and Winston, Inc., 1960.

MORGAN, BEN B., BILL R. BROWN, and EARL A. ALLUISI. "Effects of 48 Hours of Continuous Work and Sleep Loss on Sustained Performance,"

Army THEMIS Contract, Interim Technical Report Number ITR–70–16, 1970.

MORRIS, P. R., and H. T. A. WHITING. *Motor Impairment and Compensatory Education.* Philadelphia: Lea & Febiger, 1971.

NAITOH, P., and R. E. TOWNSEND. "The Role of Sleep Deprivation Research in Human Factors," *Human Factors,* 12:575–585, 1970.

NEFF, WILLIAM D. *Contributions to Sensory Psychology.* New York: Academic Press, Inc., 1965.

PAILLARD, JACQUES. "The Patterning of Skilled Movement," in John Field (ed.), *Handbook of Physiology: Neurophysiology,* Vol. III. Baltimore: The Williams & Wilkins Co., 1960.

PENFIELD, WILDER, and LAMAR ROBERTS. *Speech and Brain-Mechanisms.* Princeton, N. J.: Princeton University Press, 1959.

RUSSELL, RITCHIE W. *Brain, Memory, Learning.* London: Oxford University Press, 1959.

RYAN, E. DEAN, and CHARLES KOVACIC. "Pain Tolerance and Athletic Participation," *Perceptual and Motor Skills,* 22:383–390, 1966.

SCHMIDT, RICHARD A. "Performance and Learning a Gross Motor Skill Under Conditions of Artificially Induced Fatigue," *Research Quarterly,* 40:185–190, 1969.

SMITH, J. L., E. M. ROBERTS, and E. ATKINS. "Fusimotor Neuron Block and Voluntary Arm Movement in Man," *American Journal of Physical Medicine,* 51:225–239, 1972.

SPERRY, R. W. "The Growth of Nerve Circuits," *Scientific American,* 201: 68–75, 1959.

TASAKI, ICHIJI. "Condition of the Nerve Impulse," in John Field (ed.), *Handbook of Physiology: Neurophysiology,* Vol. I. Baltimore: The Williams & Wilkins Co., 1959.

VERNON, JACK A., THOMAS E. McGILL, WALTER L. GULICK, and DOUGLAS K. CANDLAND. "Effect of Sensory Deprivation on Some Perceptual and Motor Skills," *Perceptual and Motor Skills,* 9:91–97, 1959.

WELCH, MARYA. "Specificity of Heavy Work Fatigue: Absence of Transfer from Heavy Leg Work to Coordination Tasks Using the Arms," *Research Quarterly,* 40:402–406, 1969.

WELFORD, A. T. *Fundamentals of Skill.* London: Methuen & Co., 1968.

WHITING, H. T. A. "Overview of the Skill Learning Process," *Research Quarterly,* 43:266–294, 1972.

WOOLDRIDGE, DEAN E. *The Machinery of the Brain.* New York: McGraw-Hill Book Company, 1963.

YEGEROW, A. S., cited by A. T. PUNI, "Problem of Voluntary Regulation of Motor Activity in Sports," in F. Antonelli (ed.), *Proceedings of the First International Congress of Sports Psychology,* Rome, Italy, 1965.

ZUBEK, J. P. "Counteracting Effects of Physical Exercises Performed During Prolonged Perceptual Deprivation," *Science,* 142:504–506, 1963.

7

ABILITIES AND
CAPABILITIES

Previously in the text we have examined the human behavioral system in order to determine the relationship of processes and mechanisms involved in motor acts without real concern for the way systems differ. Dissimilarities among systems become more obvious when more complex, higher-order behaviors are of interest. The ability to perform gross motor activities places few demands on any system. Highly skilled acts, however, reflect differential aspects of human systems, for although the learning process is similar for all people, capabilities to achieve are not. Some systems reveal more constraints than others. The status of the system, then, in terms of its distinguishing characteristics, marks its potential for achievement in assorted tasks.

In order to demonstrate higher-order learning in the form of successful motor performance, the presence of a wide variety of cognitive and perceptual abilities, motor abilities, physical and sensory characteristics, personality attributes, and control mechanisms for emotions is a necessity. Every skill reflects the need for varying degrees of physical, cognitive, motor, and emotional involvement. For example, although in some cases it may appear that certain activities are performed purely physically (running the dash) or cognitively (in the form of writing sentences), in reality there is always an interaction of some degree of both these processes. The human factors varying from individual to individual and yet underlying motor skill learning and performance in some way are presented in this chapter. Specific reference is made to the various physical and motor attributes, special senses, cognition, and perceptual mechanism, the effectiveness of which might very well be determined by the emotional climate surrounding the act. Therefore consideration is also provided for the emotional states that vary from individual to individual and their potential impact on learning and performance.

The performance of various skills may be handicapped for many reasons, such as inadequate physical qualities necessary for the skilled movement. All the appropriate teaching methods and understandings of the learning process will be of little use to the educator if the performer does not have, say, enough strength to undertake the task. Although specific acts require the exploitation and emphasis of unique qualities, certain general conditions operate consistently from task to task.

Summaries of research on individual differences in abilities and characteristics; behavioral manifestations; and age, sex, race, and the like, are offered in texts by Leona Tyler (1965) and Anne Anastasi (1958). An excellent scholarly source for individual considerations in learning has been edited by Robert Gagné (1967), whereas a more global and general approach is provided by Herbert Klausmeier and Richard E. Ripple (1971).

THE EXISTENCE OF
INDIVIDUAL DIFFERENCES

The easiest way to determine the fact that individuals do differ in a particular behavior or trait is randomly to select a number of subjects and administer a test. Test scores will be spread along a continuum. Yet there is something lawful the way these scores fall. For if indeed all subjects are chosen in a nonbiased way and there is an ample number of them, we

Figure 7–1. The distribution of scores in the normal probability curve.

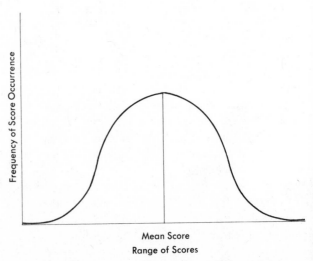

might predict with reasonable certainty how the scores will be arranged around the average score.

Look at Figure 7–1. Individuals will be expected to cluster around the mean, or average, score, with less scores in the extreme. We refer to this phenomenon as the normal curve. More people will attain a score surrounding the mean score than will attain a more removed score. Higher and lower scores are proportionally dispersed along the continuum.

But there are a number of occasions in which scores are disproportionately higher or lower. Symmetry does not always occur. Skewed curves are represented by an unusually large amount of scores at one or the other end of the continuum. The degree of peakedness of the curve is determined by the number of cases packed at the central point versus those that are more uniformly spread over a large portion of the range of scores.

Many factors contribute to the variation of scores in a particular sample of subjects. The way scores are obtained and the data-collecting instruments will certainly affect the nature and the appearance of the data. Still, variations among the scores of individuals are expected. How they vary in relation to each other will be a function of measurement, the particular sample tested, and the behavior of interest.

ABILITIES AND SKILLS

It is not unusual to hear the terms *ability* and *skill* used quite often, many times interchangeably. Yet, although related, they describe different behaviors. The similarities and differences between the terms *ability* and *skill* are subtle. Explanations of these terms were presented on p. 34, and therefore do not need to be repeated here. As might be expected, there is much more agreement among testing specialists regarding the way to measure a particular skill or knowledge about some subject matter than there is regarding how to evaluate cognitive or psychomotor abilities. Because abilities presumably underlie the potential of success in skills, and should theoretically be useful as predictors of task proficiency, an accurate assessment of abilities is quite desirable.

It should be expected therefore that there are many more skills than there are abilities. Skills are easy to observe and measure but the designation of abilities is more conceptual in nature. Abilities are derived by (1) general analysis and subjective appraisal or (2) statistical techniques, such as correlational and factor-analytic models. The former is a convenient but superficial approach. The latter includes the rigors of research and the application of statistics. Unfortunately, in spite of these efforts, an acceptable taxonomy of psychomotor abilities has yet to be created. A little later we will examine the current status of our knowledge on this topic.

When a number of different test scores correlate well together, the assumption is that there is something in common among them. This underlying characteristic is termed an ability. Thus the presence of an ability to a high degree increases an individual's probability to perform well in those tasks to which the ability contributes. If an accurate ability taxonomy were in existence today, prediction of task achievement from entering abilities could be a reality. However, such concerns are still in the development process. We must realize, though, that we do not know how to measure an ability in a "pure" way. That which is referred to in the literature as an ability score is invariably a score registered on a specific test, or skill.

TERMINOLOGY: MOTOR ABILITY, FITNESS, CAPACITY, AND EDUCABILITY

Terminology advanced primarily by physical educators interested in test construction in reality has confused the outsider and less sophisticated physical educator. Such terms as *motor fitness, motor ability, motor capacity,* and *motor educability,* though often used interchangeably in test titles, describe tests with different functions. Motor-ability, motor-fitness, motor-capacity, and motor-educability tests have numerous purposes and supposedly measure various aspects of human abilities and aptitudes. There are unique characteristics to tests of motor ability, motor fitness, motor capacity, and motor educability and in some instances a certain amount of overlap.

Motor ability indicates present athletic ability. It denotes the immediate state of the individual to perform in a wide range of motor skills. A number of motor-ability tests have been developed for application to both sexes at different stages in life. These tests have been proposed for classification and achievement expectancy, with the purpose of predicting an individual's possible competency in physical activities. Whether one general test can serve this broad function is debatable.

A term that has become confused with motor ability and physical fitness is *motor fitness.Physical fitness* implies the ability to perform a given task-in other words, having those physical qualities developed to the extent demanded by the task. *Motor fitness* refers to many of the qualities assumed to be included in physical fitness and motor ability. It is perhaps a more general term than physical fitness and at the same time, one aspect of general motor ability.

Physical educators do not necessarily agree with the elements included in each category. To many, there is very little difference, if any, between physical fitness tests and motor fitness tests. In fact, many authors of texts in measurement in physical education include the American Association of Health, Physical Education, and Recreation (AAHPER) Youth Physical Fitness Test in their motor fitness chapter. Motor fitness and physical fitness tests usually contain such items as a run, sit-ups, a jump, pull-ups, and the like. Motor-ability tests may include these items as well as measures of coordination.

Motor capacity depicts the maximum potential of an individual to succeed in motor-skill performance. It is presumably a person's innate ability, his motor aptitude. Whereas a motor-ability test purports to measure present ability or developed capacity, a capacity test is designed to predict ultimate motor potential, a sort of "intelligence test."

The last of the related terms, *motor educability*, refers to the ease with which one learns new athletic skills. Tests so classified must incorporate novel stunts, which have not been previously practiced or learned by the performers.

Nature of Tests

Very few tests designated as *motor-capacity* tests are found in the research literature. C. H. McCloy (1934), a pioneer leader in physical education for many years, reported a motor-capacity test in the early 1930's. Generally, the test contains weighted measures for size and maturity, the Sargeant Jump, the Brace Motor Ability Test, and squat thrusts; and it can be used for different age levels.

Motor educability tests are also conspicuous by their absence in the literature. Brace provided impetus to this area of testing with his work in the late 1920's. Although he considered his test one of motor ability, it has been classified as a motor-educability test by other researchers. McCloy revised this test, which included twenty stunts, and it was called the Iowa Brace Test. It contains the side kick, forward hand kick, one-knee balance, one foot–touch head, and stork stand, among others.

The nature of motor-fitness tests has already been briefly described. There are numerous fitness tests, but this type of test is not of primary concern in this book. A number of motor-ability tests have been constructed, those of Cozens (1936), Scott (1939), and Barrow (1954), for example. These few representative motor-ability tests will serve to familiarize you with the general nature of motor-ability tests elements:

1. *Cozens' athletic ability test:* dodging run, football and basketball throw for distance, dips, standing broad jump, quarter-mile run, and a bar-snap for distance.
2. *Scott's motor ability test (short-form):* obstacle race, standing broad jump, and basketball throw.

3. *Barrow's motor ability test* (*long-form*): standing broad jump, softball throw, zigzag run, wall pass, medicine ball put, and 60-yard dash.

Probably the most widely used test in psychology is the Sloan (1955) revision of the Oseretsky scale, entitled the Lincoln–Oseretsky Motor Development Scale. This test contains thirty-six items, mainly novel in nature, and is designed primarily for youngsters from six to fourteen years of age. It is a test that apparently has been disregarded by physical educators, in practice and in research.

Value of Tests

The worth of any test is determined by its validity, i.e., if the test measures what it purports to measure. Because of the dearth of motor capacity tests and investigations on this topic, we shall not attempt to discuss the value of those already in existence. This is not to deny the potential impact of developments in the area, but rather to wait for more elaborate research, which might provide more concrete answers.

Tests of motor educability received greatest recognition in the 1930's. An examination of investigations concerned with motor educability tests reveals that this is but another area not well researched. Validity coefficients obtained with the Brace Test were not exceptionally high and the criteria used have been questioned. Little work has been done with the Iowa Brace Test, and its stated function has also been attacked by numerous researchers. The Johnson Test evidently is restricted in predictive value in that studies have found high validity only through the use of tumbling stunts and track and field events as criterion measures. This might be expected owing to the nature of the educability test. It contains stunts requiring body movements best represented by these activities.

Motor-ability tests and related research have been of greater interest to physical educators than tests of and research on motor educability and motor capacity. This statement is confirmed by the greater number of publications associated with motor ability. Whether motor-ability tests measure immediate athletic ability can be verified only by an examination of research results. Motor-ability tests have not consistently achieved their stated purposes, that of determining present athletic ability. In general, most relationships between the motor-ability tests and test of athletic competencies have been rather low, often meaningless.

Implications of Research

What, then, does the research indicate as far as the educator is concerned? First, what about the research itself?

An interesting observation is that practically all the efforts in the respective areas of motor ability, motor educability, and motor capacity were put forth in the late 1920's, the 1930's, and the early 1940's. One may ask why this is so. Do physical educators feel that adequate tests for measuring skill have been constructed and well validated? Or is the trend away from viewing motor ability as something general, something that can be measured with one battery of tests? Through improved field research and intensive laboratory research as well as sound reasoning, the emerging concept is that motor-ability tests have limited value. Motor abilities in themselves are general measures, whereas task performance is specific to its peculiar nature and condition.

Many of these older studies employed research techniques that, although sound at that time, might be questioned in the light of present knowledge in research methodology. Appropriate experimental designs and statistics are of particular concern. Secondly, a number of the investigations lack clear and precise details on procedural operations. Finally, there have been consistent violations of terminology in the literature, with such terms as *capacity, ability, fitness,* and *educability* used interchangeably. The existence of these problems may account for many of the conflicting results obtained in the investigations. It certainly is difficult for one to arrive objectively at any definite conclusions with regard to the respective general motor tests.

Perhaps there is such a thing as general motor ability. If there is a general factor, certainly more research is needed before doubters and disbelievers will be convinced. Much progress has been made since 1914, when Whipple wrote that many people were of the opinion that speed in tapping was the best test–index of motor capacity. Other means used then to determine motor ability were hand, arm, and body steadiness tests, and precision (tracing) and accuracy (aiming) tasks. There is still a long way to go.

GENERAL ABILITY
vs. SPECIFIC ABILITIES

Do some individuals possess general abilities that allow them to succeed more easily in their undertakings when others are less favorably endowed? On the academic side, tests have been devised to predict success in college. According to Sanford (1962) mental abilities are highly generalized, that is, there are only a few and these are basic to expected general academic achievement. Verbal and mathematical tests are significant predictors of a student's average grades in college. As far as intellectual factors are concerned, though, we know that these include reasoning, abstract thinking, memorization, creativeness, and problem solving, to name a few. IQ tests do not measure all these qualities.

Even as there are many intellectual abilities, there are varied athletic abilities. A general mental ability test, such as an IQ test, will predict achievements in the various academic subjects fairly well. Specific tests, of course, will predict better. The general test will tend to correlate more highly with those subjects that have their matter better represented on the test. A motor-ability test that purports to measure general athletic ability resembles in nature the purpose and accomplishments of a general mental test. However, in recent years, as we have seen, the so-called motor-ability tests and the concept of a general motor ability have been questioned. For many years, researchers have attempted to discover general motor abilities, to isolate a few that would predict or measure general athletic achievement or ease in learning motor skills. Although their investigations have been valuable, the abundance of research attempting to find relationships between achievement in motor skills has tended to indicate the specificity of task performance. A person who performs well in one sport or in one skill will not necessarily do so in other sports or in other skills. There are many motor abilities, each applicable to certain situations. In highly refined research situations, the specificity of task performance has been well documented. Yet we do know that the essence of most if not all learning is the positive transfer that occurs from past experiences and familiar situations to new but related experiences. The pendulum has swung back and forth: from the concept of the general compatibility of behaviors to the belief in the specificity of performance. Perhaps a compromise position will best explain what really occurs.

Measurement

Statistically speaking, the degree of generality and specificity between task performances has been treated rather simply. The correlation between the two variables of interest has been squared. Thus r^2 indicates the degree of generality or specificity, and researchers have usually indicated the specificity between task performances if the value is lower than 50 per cent. As can readily be ascertained, a correlation of 0.7, which is reasonably high, yields a commonality percentage of only 49 when squared.

M. R. Hetherington and Thomas Maguire (1972) have questioned this approach as being desirable in all situations. It appears to be a conservative estimate of generality on occasion. Analysis of variance models may be appropriately used when several variables are measured over a number of trials. In ANOVA models, sources of error can be identified and indeed, higher estimates of generality obtained. As these researchers point out (p. 419), "A correlation of .50 would mean that only 25% of the variance in general using the squared correlation technique, whereas it is conceivable that about 50% of the variance might be attributed to generality, and considerably exceed the variance attributed to specificity, using ANOVA."

Research Favoring Task and Motor Specificity

It would appear as if much of the research indicates that excellence in one motor ability, sport, or skill provides no assurance of accomplishment in others. Positive but low intercorrelations obtained in many investigations between motor abilities as well as task accomplishments would support this statement. Most of the data have come from highly controlled laboratory settings.

Researchers have investigated relative success achieved when subjects perform in related movements as well as at dissimilar motor skills. The published research from the laboratory at the University of California at Berkeley under the direction of Franklin Henry (1961) indicates the uniqueness of apparently related tasks. For example, when comparing the reaction times and movement times of 120 subjects, he found a correlation of 0.02. Obviously, a person could not predict achievement in one movement very well from data on the other movement. Smith (1962) tested sixty male college subjects on speed of an adductive arm movement under resting muscle and pretensed muscle conditions. Timing stations were arranged at 15°, 53°, 90°, and 105°. Small and nonsignificant correlations were obtained between the conditions at each timing station.

Since that time until the present, most research efforts support the idea of specific achievements of parts of the body in specified speed tasks. Loockerman and Berger (1972), for instance, tested the reaction times and movement times of subjects informed to move in any one of four directions. They concluded that the ability to react and to move is specific to the direction of the response. Recorded times were not consistently fast or slow for the subjects when directional speeds were analyzed and when hand and total body times were compared in the same direction.

Speed is not conditioned uniformly in all activities by some unitary factor or set of factors. Research findings in general would tend to substantiate this proposition. For instance, Lotter (1961) timed his subjects on their ability to turn a two-handled arm crank versus the speed of the arms individually versus comparable movements of the legs. Low intercorrelations further supported a theory of motor specificity.

After administering seventeen manipulative tests, six printed tests, and twenty-three physical-performance tests, Hempel and Fleishman (1955) concluded that the factors that contributed to successful gross physical task performance were not the same as those in fine manipulated tasks. Fleishman (1958a) found a high degree of specificity among twenty-four position tasks. Singer (1966) attempted to determine the relationship of throwing and kicking skills. The subjects, thirty-eight college students enrolled in required physical education classes, threw a ball at a target and kicked a ball at a target, first using preferred limbs, then nonpreferred limbs. Correlations were obtained for all of the possible limb combinations. Five of the six correlations were low, positive, and significant. However, when statistically analyzed for generality and specificity factors, great specificity was noted in the limb relationships.

Some investigators have been interested in the effect of practice upon motor-skill relationships. Buxton and Humphreys (1935) using four motor skills found the intercorrelations to range from 0.08 to 0.4 in the beginning of the experiment. After practice, they were − 0.02 to 0.39. Achievement in motor performances was related only slightly in the initial stages and remained that way throughout the investigation. Tests of kinesthesis have also yielded low intercorrelations. Researchers have concluded that kinesthesis is composed of specific factors. Those subjects who performed well on one test did not necessarily do so on another test.

It can be observed, then, that the evidence from studies presented here (by no means exhausting all the available research) suggests a questioning of general motor ability. Task-to-task performance usually is related slightly, but not enough to justify predicting one's ability in many skills or sports from one test.

The ability to perform well in many motor activities is probably based on general factors, primarily a time element (speed), strength, and coordination. Many sports require abilities related to these variables. However, performance measures of each factor vary from activity to activity; hence speed in track is of a different nature from speed and quickness in a basketball game or on a tennis court. The balance demanded on gymnastic apparatus differs from body balance needed when striking a ball, shooting a jump-shot, or wrestling. In other words, an athlete may demonstrate a highly refined example of balance in one sport but not in another. Evidently, one can exhibit strength, coordination, speed, and other qualities in dissimilar ways, and the relationship of tasks within a factor will depend on their degree of overlap and similarity.

The All-round Athlete

Coaches and physical educators might be cautious in their interpretation and application of empirical evidence related to individual achievement in a number of sports. It is true that some people perform well in a variety of activities and have been termed *all-round athletes*. However, these motor prodigies are the exception, not the rule. Success in one sport does not imply that the same situation will occur in another sport, and only when

certain factors are operating will this probability increase. These underlying factors are as follows:

1. Experience and intensive practice in a wide range of motor skills will
   result in apparent ease in skill acquisition. The person who has benefited from a childhood enriched with experiences in basic movement
   patterns and an assortment of activities, will be more favored in
   motor-learning situations. These past experiences and the resultant
   skills serve as a foundation for the learning of new skills.
2. Genetics determine the limitations an individual faces in motor-skill
   attainment. Even as heredity determines potential intelligence levels,
   hair color, and body size, it creates the boundaries of motor development. It should be stressed here that research, especially on intelligence, points to the potential influence of the environment and
   life's experiences on an individual's achievements. As a further point,
   it should be realized that one has to go a long way before he reaches
   his maximum potential, whether in intellectual or motor pursuits.
   Thus it may be seen that although hereditary factors contribute to
   limit potential proficiency in motor acts, many of these factors can be
   overcome with the presence of the necessary drive and ambition.
3. Motivation is necessary for success. It is hypothesized that the athlete
   who has achieved success in one sport transfers his high motivation
   and perseverance to other motor-skill endeavors. The all-round athlete
   may very well be a highly motivated performer in general who possesses the necessary personality characteristics for varied motor accomplishments.
4. Related sports offer a greater probability of accomplishment for the
   athlete. Therefore if an athlete is proficient in a number of sports,
   there is a good chance that basic skills common to all of them have
   been mastered.

Other factors may also contribute to the relative ease a person shows in
attaining success in various sports. However, there are also many reasons
why an individual does not display proficiency in a number of activities.
Of major concern is the unrealistic approach the coach takes in a situation
involving a superior athlete in one sport attempting to progress in another
activity in which he is not nearly so talented. Achievement and satisfaction
may or may not come. Great success in one sport does not necessarily mean
corresponding achievements in other sports. The ability to be an outstanding performer in a number of sports, even in only two, indicates an ex-
traordinary human being, possessing remarkable talents and skills.

Although there has been an earlier attempt to determine an athletic
ability factor (Highmore and Taylor, 1954), the conclusions were very

limited because of the tests and subjects used. One hundred and ten eleven-year-old boys were administered eight tests:

1. Eighty-yard sprint.
2. Long jump.
3. Running.
4. High jump.
5. Standing upward jump.
6. Throw of a cricket ball for distance.
7. Football (soccer) throw-in.
8. Football (soccer) punt for distance.

A criterion of all-round performance in track and field events was obtained from a relative rating given to each boy by the physical education teacher. Because most of the tests were related to track and field performance and the boys were relatively young, it is not surprising that the correlations ranged from 0.4 to 0.63 for each test against the criterion ranking. The authors conclude that these tests indeed measure athletic ability, and especially three.tests—sprinting, high jump, and ball throw-in —give a good estimate of the entire battery. Factor analysis revealed that all the tests accounted for 42 per cent of the variance. Although this study reflects one of the few serious research investigations attempting to delineate the parameters of a general athletic ability and makes an interesting contribution to the literature, there are too many limitations to generalize that anything close to a general athletic ability has been defined. Perhaps it might be more accurate to state that, with eleven-year-olds, these tests measure achievement possibilities in track and field events fairly well.

Considerations for Task Specificity and Generality

So far it would appear as if we have made a pretty solid case in support of task specificity and the concept of many fairly independent abilities rather than a general motor ability. We can probably rule out, at least at the present time, the concept of one unifying motor ability that is associated with proficiency in a wider variety of activities. But this is not to say that a number of general motor abilities do not operate to contribute to task success. And, to the extent that tasks are related, similar abilities will serve as contributing factors for achievement in them. B. J. Cratty's model illustrated in Figure 3–7 approximates a happy medium between general supports and task-specific elements when describing what motor behavior is all about.

A serious review of all the published research on the topic would lead

Figure 7–2. Abilities primarily contribute to initial task success whereas specific task practice is required in addition to the ideal presence of these abilities for highly skilled behaviors.

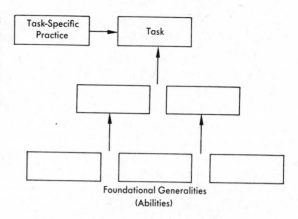

Foundational Generalities
(Abilities)

the searcher to be disappointed if his hypothesis was in favor of general factors operating to encourage some individuals to perform well in a wide range of motor tasks while others do poorly. Nevertheless, indirect implications of research findings and intuition suggest that general abilities as well as specific task practice contribute to excellence in the performance of complex skills. The presence of an ideal degree of certain task-related abilities will aid the learner in early stages of achievement. Other abilities will be more important for higher levels of proficiency. Although genetic factors and past experiences, contributing to the development of abilities, primarily assist the learner in the beginning stages of practice, superior skills can only be demonstrated with many hours of practice in the activity of concern. Figure 7–2 summarizes this concept.

Even the ability to acquire skills at a fast rate is probably unique to each particular task. That is to say, a general learning-rate ability probably does not exist in the "normal" population. It is specific of each task. The inconsistency of rate of learning scores among individuals across a variety of tasks has been reasonably well documented for over thirty years. Lee Cronbach (1967) feels that it is advisable to examine instructional conditions as they interact with learning rates. He assumes that a particular instructional technique in effect helps to define the nature of the task. So when different tasks are to be mastered under the same instructional conditions, the learner is required to demonstrate a general ability to learn those tasks under the imposed condition. Instructional method may very well dictate a person's learning rate.

MOTOR ABILITIES

Although other classifications of abilities no doubt are involved in skilled motor performance, the motor-abilities category is the one most usually associated with motor behaviors. Different approaches in the attempt to formulate basic abilities have demonstrated alternative ways of thinking about them, resulting in lively debates among scholars. The consequence for the practitioner has been one of confusion. Thus:

1. An ability could be looked at as a behavioral variable with parameters defined by the particular methods used in its measurement.
2. An ability could reflect individual differences in training conditions and experiences as well as the state of the organism as induced by the experimenter.
3. An ability could be viewed as a hypothetical construct, in which case a skill is defined as a behavioral variable, as in item 1.
4. An ability could be an artificial (observed) or constructed statistical variable, whereby a primary ability is derived from the hypothetical elements that are combined to form the ability.

Perhaps the most extensive work in the area of motor abilities completed thus far by any one scholar (and his colleagues) is attributed to E. A. Fleishman. In his many publications (e.g., Fleishman, 1964), he describes the statistical techniques (correlational, factor-analytic) he used to derive both motor-abilities and physical-proficiency factors. From the administration of over 200 different psychomotor tasks (most of them oriented to the laboratory and instrumentation) to thousands of subjects, Fleishman feels that he has been able to account for performance of these tasks in terms of a small number of abilities. They are identified as:

1. Control precision: primarily involves highly controlled large muscle movements.
2. Multilimb coordination: simultaneous coordination of the movements of a number of limbs.
3. Response orientation: selection of right response (visual discrimination), irrespective of precision and coordination.
4. Reaction time: speed of response to a stimulus.
5. Rate control: continuous anticipatory motor adjustments to changing situational cues (speed, direction).
6. Speed of arm movement: speed where accuracy is not important.
7. Manual dexterity: manipulation of large objects under speed conditions.
8. Finger dexterity: manipulation of tiny objects with precision and control.
9. Arm–hand steadiness: control of movements, while motionless or in motion.
10. Wrist–finger speed: tapping activity.
11. Aiming: printed tests requiring pencil accuracy and speed.

These eleven abilities, according to Fleishman, underlie achievement in many motor tasks. Yet it should be emphasized that most of the tasks from which these abilities have been derived have not been athletic or real-life in nature, a restriction in the interpretation and application of Fleishman's findings.

Fleishman also postulates nine physical-proficiency abilities that presumably are associated with athletic and gross physical performance. The factors identified are (1) static strength, (2) dynamic strength, (3) explosive strength, (4) trunk strength, (5) extent flexibility, (6) dynamic flexibility, (7) gross body coordination, (8) multi-limb coordination, and (9) stamina.

Over twenty years' work has led to the following interpretations of Fleishman's work:

1. A particular combination of abilities can be identified that contribute to motor-skill performance.
2. Changes in the combination of these abilities occur with continued practice and improvement.
3. Motor abilities become more important in task performance than nonmotor abilities with practice.
4. A task-specific factor emerges with practice.

Ability changes associated with practice and predictive possibilities will be discussed in more detail in a later chapter dealing with practice and training. It is sufficient here to indicate the high points of the research findings.

H. P. Bechtoldt (1970) has been extremely critical of Fleishman's work. An ability can refer to the power to perform an act, with or without training. Performances are clearly specified as to situations and responses. An ability is thereby defined by a specified test procedure and scoring method. Bechtoldt raises the issue that it is conceivable for every test to define a separate ability.

An ability can also be derived hypothetically rather than defined. It is assumed or inferred from the results of factor-analytic studies or from experiments when subjects with higher test scores are compared to subjects with lower test scores. Bechtoldt takes offense that Fleishman does not clearly define abilities but instead infers them. Other objections are made, including Fleishman's use of factor-analytic statistical techniques that Bechtoldt claims are inappropriate for the data measured. Nevertheless, at the present time, Fleishman's work remains the most prominent in the field of categorizing abilities and determining their relationship to motor-skill performance. Two useful recent summaries of his efforts and the conclusions are found in Fleishman (1972a, b).

The recognition of those abilities required for task proficiency assists in understanding task requirements more fully. A systems analysis would

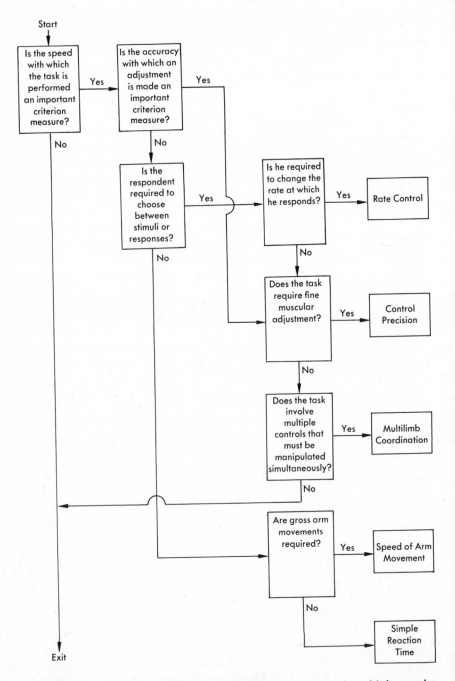

Figure 7–3. Tentative binary decision-flow diagrams which can be used to make decisions about the relevance of selected perceptual-motor abilities. [From Edwin A. Fleishman and Robert W. Stephenson, *Development of a Taxonomy of Human Performance: A Review of the Third Year's Progress* (Washington, D.C.: American Institutes for Research, 1970).]

require the identification of the hierarchical arrangement of abilities associated with achievement in a particular activity. Fleishman and Stephenson (1970), in reviewing the future plans of their taxonomy project, recommend the design and use of binary decision-flow diagrams in order to simplify decisions about ability requirements. The binary decision diagram (four tentatively described ones are illustrated in Figures 7-3 to 7-6), encourages go–no-go decisions at various steps in the task analysis. In order to be really meaningful, the flow diagrams presented here must be developed in much more detail, as admitted by Fleishman and Stephenson.

Dennis Roberts (1968–69) has provided a brief but comprehensive review of the research literature dealing with abilities and learning. The relationships between abilities, learning performance, and practice stage are complex, making it difficult to provide simple answers to trainers and teachers. He raises four major questions:

1. How do you assess a student's pattern of abilities? Strengths and weaknesses need to be assessed with one or several reliable and valid tests.
2. How do you identify, through task analysis, the abilities required to learn a task? The abilities necessary for a minimum level of performance should be specified as they relate to the task components.
3. Can deficiencies, or poorly developed abilities, be remediated? Abilities must be isolated, remedial activities identified and implemented, in order to contribute to task achievement.
4. Are abilities differentially related to practice stages? Initial task performance may be a poor indicator of later accomplishments, because certain abilities primarily contribute to early success, an indication that screening out procedures on the basis of early task performance may not be a good idea.

Although Fleishman and others have attempted to categorize motor abilities, there are at least four factors that seem to be of most interest to motor-learning researchers. They have been used to determine relationships to task proficiency. They have been used as identified by task requirements in order to study learning phenomena, with little particular concern for the actual abilities involved. Terminologies have not been consistent in different sources. But we will identify these factors as coordination, kinesthesis, balance, and speed of movement.

The four primary research purposes, then, of tasks that are associated with these factors, would be their usage

1. As learning tasks (novel, neutral).
2. For establishing ability norms.
3. For determining task specificity or generality.

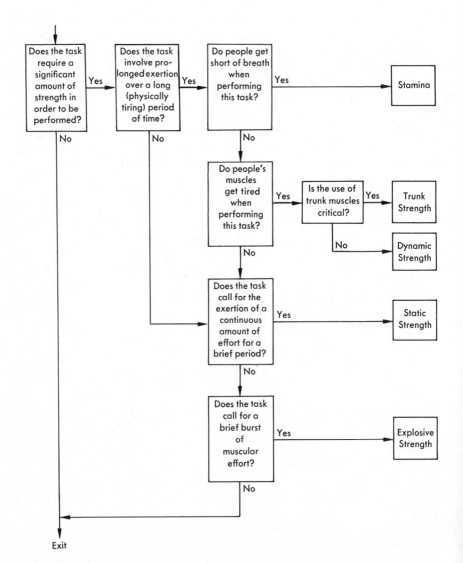

Figure 7–4. Tentative binary decision–flow diagrams which can be used to make decisions about the relevance of abilities of strength and stamina. [From Edwin A. Fleishman and Robert W. Stephenson, *Development of a Taxonomy of Human Performance: A Review of the Third Year's Progress* (Washington, D.C.: American Institutes for Research, 1970).]

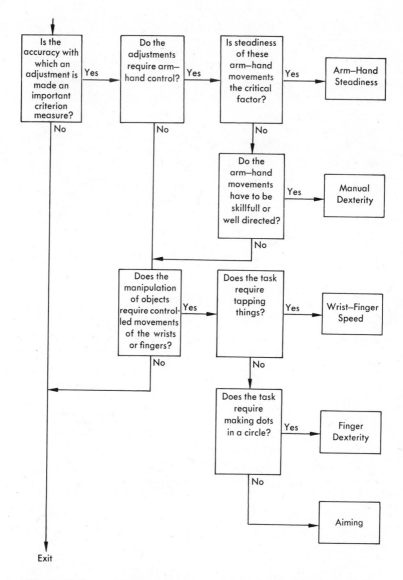

Figure 7–5. Tentative binary decision-flow diagrams which can be used to make decisions about the relevance of fine manipulative abilities. [From Edwin A. Fleishman and Robert W. Stephenson, *Development of a Taxonomy of Human Performance: A Review of the Third Year's Progress* (Washington, D.C.: American Institutes for Research, 1970).]

Figures 7–6. Tentative binary decision-flow diagrams which can be used to make decisions about the relevance of gross physical proficiencies. [From Edwin A. Fleishman and Robert W. Stephenson, *Development of a Taxonomy of Human Performance: A Review of the Third Year's Progress* (Washington, D.C.: American Institutes for Research, 1970).]

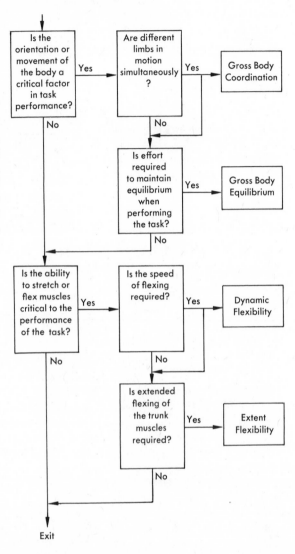

4. For predicting how well someone will learn and perform in a given activity.

Coordination

Coordination of various parts of the body implies an ability to perform a skilled movement pattern. The skill itself primarily may involve eye–foot coordination, an example of which is kicking a football or soccer ball; or eye–hand coordination, such as throwing an object at a target. Some sports require an overall coordination of the body: a gymnastic routine on the parallel bars requires perfect timing; a football halfback demonstrates agility and speed in movement; and swinging a golf club requires smoothness and rhythm.

Various types of body movements have been used as coordination tests. In answer to the question as to what coordination tests really do measure, the factor-analysis method has been applied by Cumbee (1954) to determine the factors present in tests that measure motor coordination. This statistical method was employed by Thurston in his classical study that attempted to discover the factors really being measured in the so-called intelligence tests. Two-hundred college women were tested in Cumbee's study, and from twenty-one variables of coordination eight were extracted. Although three of the factors were unnamed because they needed further classification, the other five distinguished were: balancing objects, body balance, two-handed agility, tempo, and speed of arm and hand change of direction.

Sometimes the word *coordination* is used interchangeably with *timing*, *skill*, or *general motor ability*. It has been determined from the research that coordination is important to potential athletic success as well as specific to the task achieved. Whether an individual is born with or develops body coordination, and to what extent, as reflected in certain motor-skill achievements, is a moot point elaborated on earlier in this chapter under "The All-round Athlete," as well as in the chapter dealing with developmental factors.

Many laboratory tasks have been developed to measure coordinated movements (primarily eye–hand), and to predetermine success in certain fields. In industrial jobs that require manual dexterity, for example, manipulative tasks help in predicting success. An example of a widely used task utilizing arm–hand coordination (manual dexterity) is the Minnesota Rate of Manipulation Test, whereas the Crawford Small Parts Dexterity Test requires finger dexterity (see Figure 7–7).

Other devices are used for testing potential pilot success or probable athletic achievement. Also, they serve as a medium for viewing the effects of environmental manipulations and understanding psychological phenomena associated with motor tasks. In physical education, coordinated movements may be demonstrated in target-accuracy skills and in the performance of various stunts. However, the laboratory environment is better for controlling the many extraneous variables apt to confound the field study. This is why various types of apparatus have been constructed by those interested in understanding and explaining the learning process, especially as it relates to motor skills. Unfortunately, there is a danger in assuming that the learning of practical skills, those performed in daily life, are governed by the same principles as skills learned and performed in the laboratory. Arguments have been presented for and against both laboratory research and classroom or gymnasium research; but both are

Minnesota Rate of Manipulation Test

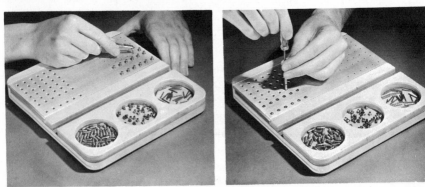

Crawford Small Parts Dexterity Test

Figure 7–7. The Minnesota Rate of Manipulation Test measures capacity for manipulative work. In the five tests that are administered with this equipment, the blocks are turned, moved, and placed in certain prescribed ways. This involves finger movement and hand-and-arm movement. It involves movements with the preferred hand and also with both hands simultaneously. As usage of this test has spread, it now appears that more than speed is involved in gross finger, hand, and arm movements. Also involved are gross body movements, intelligence, vision, and perseverance. (From American Guidance Service, Inc., Minneapolis, 1966.)

The Crawford Small Parts Dexterity Test measures fine eye–hand coordination. Part I measures dexterity in using tweezers to insert small pins in close-fitting holes in a plate and to place small collars over the protruding pins. Part II measures dexterity in placing small screws in threaded holes in a plate and screwing them down with a screwdriver until they drop through the plate into a metal dish below. (From the Psychological Corporation, New York, 1965.)

needed for a better understanding of the psychology of learning. Both research methods can and should complement each other and not provide fuel for debate.

Laboratory researchers concerned with coordination tasks have constructed ingenious devices for measuring coordination. One of the forerunners in attempting to uncover the factors underlying psychomotor-performance success was Fleishman (1957, 1958a, 1958b). Besides employing previously used tasks in other experiments, he devised other tasks to measure the many aspects of psychomotor skill. They are basically coordinating, positioning, and speed tasks. Figure 7–8 contains a number of these apparatuses that have been widely used in his investigations. These tasks include a response orientation task, a rotary pursuit task, a two-hand coordination task, and a single-dimensional pursuit task.

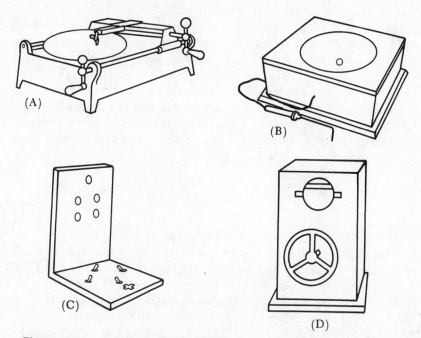

Figure 7–8.   (A) Two-Hand Coordination. Two handles must be controlled and manipulated in order to keep a target-follower on a target disk as the target moves unpredictably; (B) Rotary Pursuit. The stylus is kept in contact with a small metallic target which is set on a revolving phonograph-type disk; (C) Response Orientation. The subject manipulates one of four toggle switches as rapidly as possible in response to rapidly changing light patterns; (D) Single-Dimension Pursuit. The subject makes adjustments to the wheel in order to keep the line in the window centrally located as it moves unpredictably. (From E. A. Fleishman, "Dimensional Analysis of Movement Reactions," *Journal of Experimental Psychology,* 55:438–453, 1958.)

Although evidence is fragmentary, there has been an attempt to relate such tasks to success in industry, dentistry, and piloting a plane. The tests have demonstrated moderately predictive values in these cases. The Complex Coordination test, which requires stick and rudder movements in response to specific signal lights, has been reported to correlate 0.4 in predicting pilot success. The Hand-Tool Dexterity test correlated 0.46 with the actual performance of machinists, and the Metal Filling Work-sample correlated 0.53 with dentistry course grades. Obviously, the more related the task to the actual criterion, the higher the anticipated correlation. Relationships between movements required for the coordination tasks, often used by psychologists, and the coordinated movement patterns desired in sport should probably not be high because of the lack of similarity in the nature of the required responses.

A familiarity with the design and nature of coordination tasks, especially that of the pursuit rotor, will be most profitable for the person interested in reading and analyzing the literature concerning the learning of motor skills. Many deductions from the phenomena related to motor learning, transfer, retention, practice, and the like, have been derived from the utilization of these tasks under manipulated environmental conditions. Differences in terminology and applications exist among research specialists and educators. For instance, whereas physical educators may have regarded sports skills only as motor tasks, psychologists include in this category all previously discussed devices and the responses required for them as well as many others.

Balance

The ability to maintain body position, referred to as *balance,* is necessary for the successful performance of sports skills. It is essential in those dynamic sports requiring sudden changing movements, exemplified by the tennis player who has to pursue a ball, regain balance, and then strike the ball. The wrestler, whether standing or kneeling on the mat, has to retain his balance when moving toward or away from his opponent. Each sport demands a particular type of balance. In other words, an individual does not possess one general balancing ability that will enable him to balance himself well for all tasks and under all conditions.

Standing erect under trying or even normal conditions involves an interaction of a number of neurophysiological structures, senses, and pathways. Equilibrium is obtained through the combined efforts of simple reflexes, proprioceptive information relayed to the cerebrum and cerebellum, an activation of the reticular formation, the vestibular apparatus, visual information, and voluntary movements.

The *stretch reflex* works in sustaining body posture. *Proprioceptors* in various parts of the body contribute to equilibrium: the neck proprioceptors stimulate the reticular nuclei; the head receptors for movement activate the vestibular apparatus; and proprioceptors from other parts of the body stimulate the *reticular pathways cerebellum*, and *cerebral cortex*.

The *bony labyrinth*, which is a cavity in the temporal bone, contains the cochlear duct (concerned with hearing), the saccule, the semicircular canals, and the utricle (see Figure 7–9). The *semicircular canals* and *utricle* combined constitute the *vestibular apparatus*, and are sensitive to body movement and position. The canals respond to acceleration or deceleration changes in head velocity. Head movements stimulate proprioceptors and vestibular nerves, which in turn extend to the reticular nuclei and cerebellum, producing impulses that are sent to the appropriate muscles for body equilibrium.

Vision assists in providing information about the body's position with regard to its environment. Even with destruction of the vestibular apparatus, vision can compensate and allow the person to maintain a degree of equilibrium. *Voluntary movements*, directed from a cortical center, allow man to have a conscious awareness of his body's position and to do something about it. Man observes his environment and perceives the changing position of his body and, through conscious effort, can direct the necessary movement adjustments in order to maintain the desired posture.

Tests have been constructed to determine dynamic and static balancing ability. However, highly positive relationships between the two have not been obtained as is the case when comparing the results of tests measuring dynamic and static strength. Static equilibrium requires continuous, even muscle tension, which underlies standing perfectly still, without swaying. Dynamic balance demands body orientation in off-balance situations. Travis (1945) measured static balance with an ataxiameter (which records body sway while standing) and dynamic balance by means of a stabilometer. He

Figure 7–9. Bony labyrinth apparatus. The cochlea is concerned with audition. The semicircular canals, the utricle, and probably the sacule are essential for equilibration. [From L. L. Langley and E. Cheraskin, *Physiology of Man* (New York: Reinhold Publishing Co., 1965).]

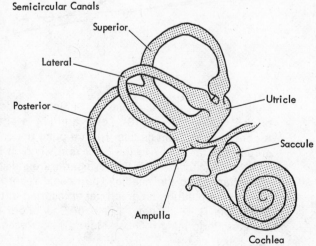

Semicircular Canals

Superior

Lateral

Posterior

Utricle

Saccule

Ampulla

Cochlea

found no relationship between static and dynamic balance. Additional interesting findings of this study indicated that weight, not height, was an important factor in dynamic performance. Subjects with greater weight balanced better. Also, there was a small, insignificant sex difference in balancing, favoring women. Finally, balancing scores were much greater with the eyes open than closed.

Balance required for each skill varies, and is evidently unique to the skill employed. However, it may be stated that there is inconclusive evidence on balance transference from task to task, task to sport, and sport to sport. The more similarity that exists between them, the more we can expect a positive influence.

An excellent example of this relationship is found in a study reported by Singer (1970). College athletes, fifteen in a group and representing basketball, baseball, football, gymnastics, and wrestling teams, water skiing ex-

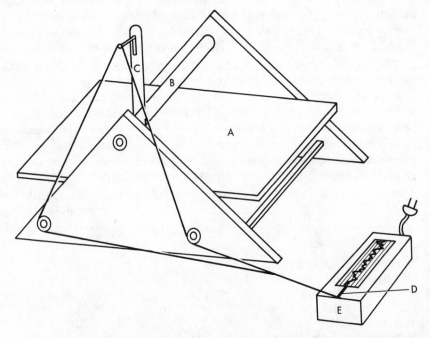

Figure 7–10.   Stabilometer A. Subject stands on platform (A) with his feet straddling axle (B). Lever arm (C) is attached to the platform. A cord extends from needle (D) to a point under the rear pulley to and around the far pulley to the lever arm where it is firmly attached. Another cord extends from the lever arm around the near pulley, and is also attached to the needle. The needle records the extent of movement of the platform on graph paper inserted in the electric kymograph (E). (From R. N. Singer, "Effect of Spectators on Athletes and Non-Athletes Performing a Gross Motor Task, *Research Quarterly,* 36:473–482, 1965.)

pertise, and nonathletes, were tested on a stabilometer apparatus, much the same as the one illustrated in Figure 4–3. Athletic groups were compared with each other and against the nonathletes in balance performance. The nonathletes scored lowest on the task, demonstrating some balance required in respective sports carried over to the stabilometer task. More interestingly, because the stabilometer requires skill similar to the balance required by the water skiers, it is not surprising that this group should attain the highest balancing performance, which it did. Gymnasts were second best, and in fact, these groups were significantly superior in achievement to most of the other groups. Evidently, although balance as an ability is demanded in a variety of athletic situations, those athletes who practice balance in skills similar to those tested on the stabilometer do better in this testing situation.

Balance tasks designed in varying degrees of complexity range from the simple balance beams to stabilometers. Basically, a stabilometer requires one to balance on an unstable platform. Investigators have constructed different types of stabilometers for determining balancing ability, and each apparatus has certain advantages and disadvantages not associated with another model. In one study, Singer (1965) graphically determined time on balance during a specific time period, and the diagram of this stabilometer apparatus appears in Figure 7–10 (Stabilometer A). A work-adder has been used in conjunction with a stabilometer in certain investigations. A picture and description of this apparatus appears in Figure 7–11 (Stabilometer B).

Other balance tasks found in the literature include rail-walking (walking a narrow beam without falling off), standing on one foot for a length of time, and the Bachman ladder climb (climbing as many rungs as possible before a free-standing ladder falls).

Kinesthesis

When a student is learning how to swing the golf club for the first time, it is not uncommon for the instructor to tell him to "feel the movement." Information about this awareness of what the muscles are doing and their position during a movement is extremely important to the learner of a new skill. It might also be successfully argued that this muscle sense, called *kinesthesis*, is equally necessary for the successful execution of well-learned skills. Kinesthesis is a consciousness of muscular movement and effort and a keenly developed sense required of beginners and experts alike for proficiency in many motor skills.

The terms *kinesthetic* and *proprioceptive* generally refer to the same sense —providing information concerning the body's position in space and the relationship of its parts. Experimental psychologists usually refer to this sense as kinesthetic, whereas physiologists prefer the term *proprioceptive,*

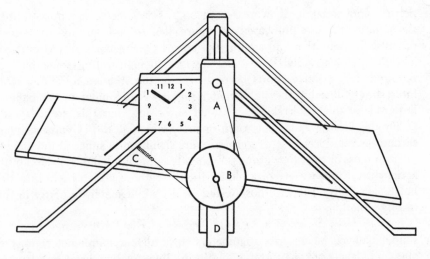

Figure 7–11.   Stabilometer B. A short cord drive lever is screwed into the protruding end of the main axle just above (A). The cord passes downward and bends over a large pulley on the back of the work-adder dial (B), terminating at a coil spring fastened to the frame just above (C). A pawl at (D) engages the milled periphery of the work-adder dial, restricting its turning to a single direction so that movement of the platform is cumulated on the dial. Various A-frame rods brace the platform and the vertical posts that rise from the base to carry the main axle. Motion of the board is measured by the work adder. (From John C. Bachman, "Specificity vs. Generality in Learning and Performing Two Large Muscle Motor Tasks," *Research Quarterly,* 32:3–11, 1961.)

this term having been introduced by the great physiologist, Sherrington. When the special sense receptors in the muscles, tendons, and joints (called *proprioceptors*) are stimulated, the impulses pass through the posterior column of the spinal cord to the thalamus and finally to the somatic area of the cerebral cortex. If the posterior column is destroyed, there results a loss of sensation in limb movement and position. Coordination of the visual, vestibular, and somatic sensory receptors contributes to the body's orientation in space.

Rose and Mountcastle (1959) present a convincing argument against the traditional belief that stretch receptors of muscles alone are responsible for kinesthesia. These receptors have not been found to provide information about joint position since they discharge over their full frequency range at any muscle length. They state that the joints contain the source of kinesthetic sensations and designate the following receptors located in articular tissue: the Ruffini receptors, which have spray-type endings and are the most common in connective tissue; the Golgi tendon organs, which are less numerous; and the pacinian corpuscles. Whether or not muscle spindles that react to muscle stretch also play an important role in kinesthesis is open to question. Rose and Mountcastle reject the traditional acceptance of their contribution in this sense.

Physical educators and athletes have realized the importance of the kinesthetic sense in skill learning for many years. Sir W. G. Stimpson in the year 1887 is quoted by Mrs. Stewart Hanley (1937, p. 366) on his advice for beginning golfers: "Let the beginner shake himself down naturally before the ball and hit. Till he has done this for a good many days, no advice has either use or meaning." She goes on to indicate a weakness in the imitative method of learning, that of ignoring muscle feel and muscle sense. She emphasizes the need for kinesthetic sensations during the swing and that the beginning golfer should think the swing, not merely imitate it.

Adams and Creamer (1962) have noted the importance of proprioceptor variables in contributing to proficiency in performance. Because movements give rise to proprioceptive stimuli, they provide feedback information that aids in similar future situations. These authors conclude that proprioception has not only its traditional role of information feedback but also a role in response timing, which is extremely important in skilled performance. The skill acquisition and performance models of Adams, Keele, and Fitts and Posner, among others, presented in Chapter 3, emphasize the necessity of kinesthetic feedback for immediate or later skill improvement. The works of Fleishman and others seem to show that kinesthetic ability is more important at more advanced stages of learning and performance than at early stages.

Prior to 1950, very few investigations concerning the role of kinesthesis in motor learning can be found in the literature. Research completed since that time, although not in total agreement, permits these overall conclusions:

1. There is no general kinesthetic sense. Intercorrelations between tests devised to measure this factor are extremely low unless the tests are similar in nature. Kinesthesis appears to be composed of specific factors and is specific to the test and the part of the body involved in the skill.
2. Skilled performers, athletes, musicians, and mechanics, for example, are better on kinesthetic tests than average or poorer performers.
3. Kinesthetic ability seems to be more related to higher levels of performance than at beginning levels. That is to say, the learner is more externally controlled (visual cues, instructor's comments) at first and these become more internally controlled (kinesthetic feedback).
4. Kinesthesis may very well be related to rate of learning. It has been found that fast learners in bowling score higher on kinesthetic tests than do slow learners, and elementary school children who learn many tasks quickly do significantly better on tests of kinesthesis than their slower-learning counterparts.
5. Practice can improve kinesthetic perception as well as the acuity of

all the senses. For instance, when an individual is blindfolded and practices blindfolded a skill such as the golf swing, he relies more on kinesthetic cues and may improve this sense.

6. Balance is an important aspect of kinesthesis. Balance ability is determined to a great extent by proprioceptive activity, and tests of balance are recommended to be included in any battery of kinesthetic tests.

Tests of kinesthesis vary in nature and bodily involvement. Batteries of tests have been devised by a number of physical educators interested in the kinesthetic sense, notably Scott, Young, and Wiebe. M. Gladys Scott (1955) developed a twenty-eight-test battery that she administered to women college sudents. She noted a specificity in the function of the tests. A twenty-one-test battery was administered to thirty college men by Vernon Wiebe (1954), who also found a low intercorrelation between the tests and deduced a lack of general kinesthetic sense. Some tests of kinesthesis are illustrated in Figure 7–12.

Many tests of kinesthesis have been static, involving positional sense. Ex-

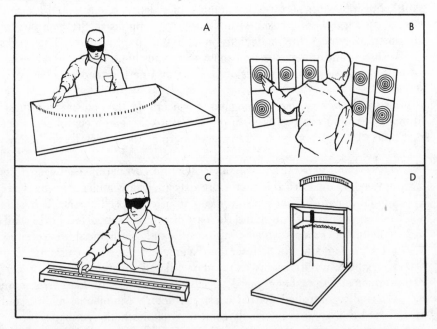

Figure 7–12.   Tests of kinesthesis which require kinesthetic discrimination. In these tests the blindfolded subject in A must reach a certain peg or in B mark a certain target, in response to verbal instructions. In tests C and D, he reproduces certain movements with a knob or a stick control. (From E. A. Fleishman, "An Analysis of Positioning Movements and Static Reactions," *Journal of Experimental Psychology,* 55:13–24, 1958.)

amples of some kinesthetic tests described by Louise Roloff (1953) are the Balance Stick, Arm Raising, and Weight Shifting tests.

- *Balance stick.* A stick, 1 inch by 12 inches, is taped to the floor. The subject has to close his eyes and balance on one foot on this stick as long as possible.
- *Arm raising.* The subject is tested on his ability to raise each arm to the horizontal position while blindfolded. Deviations in degrees are measured with a goniometer.
- *Weight shifting.* The subject has to straddle a scale and a block of wood. With the eyes open, he first practices getting the feel of running the scale up one-half his weight in pounds. Then, with eyes closed, he attempts to do the same, and deviations are determined to the nearest half pound.

Other investigators have expressed dissatisfaction with the design of these tests. Franklin Henry (1953) created a device that required continuing constant pressure exerted by the subject against a pad while the pressure continually changed under the influence of a cam. This dynamic test brought about an increase or decrease in muscular tension caused by the changing pressure of the cam. In two separate tasks, his twelve subjects were required to adjust to pressure changes or to perceive pressure changes. An objection to most kinesthetic tests was raised by A. T. Slater-Hammel (1957), who felt that the tests involved tactile stimulation as well as muscular force. He therefore suggested a task in which individuals had to reproduce a specific muscle contraction. With the use of muscle potentials, he measured the intensity of the muscle contraction after an initial prescribed contraction of 125 microvolts.

In summary, there are a variety of methods and means of measuring aspects of kinesthesis. In a general sense, kinesthesis is believed to underlie many discriminating functions of the body required for successful motor-skill performance: locomotion, perception of pressure changes, balance and body equilibrium, and overall body coordination. Its presence is thought to contribute to an individual's ability to learn as well as to perform motor skills. However, this presence must not be thought of as a general factor but rather specific to the skill or a group of skills that requires certain movements of the body.

Recent research has attempted to discover methods of improving proprioceptive activity in teaching for the transfer of skills. There is speculation as to the transfer effect from practicing with a lighter projectile to a heavier one, and vice versa. Whether a lighter projectile sharpens the proprioceptors' sensitivity and provides the performer with a greater *feel* for the heavier projectile is being currently investigated. This is another example of the interrelatedness of psychology of learning and neurophysiology showing why content matter associated with both disciplines must be studied together in order to obtain more answers to questions raised about aspects of the learning process.

Speed of Movement

The track sprinter awaits the starting gunshot. Bam! He's off. Did the time he took to respond to the sound constitute reaction time or reflex time? Is there any difference between these terms? What is movement time? All these terms are often used interchangeably, although, in fact, they are not synonymous. Actually these particular times can be isolated and recorded in experimental situations.

Reaction time (RT) involves an integration of the higher centers of the nervous system: perception of the stimulus (a noise, light, or the like) and the initiation of the appropriate movement. It is the elapsed interval of time from the presentation of a stimulus to the initiation of a response. A *reflex* is usually nonvolitional, involving the lower centers of the nervous system. It is an automatic response, predictable, and does not require perceptibility. *Movement time* (MT) may include reflex or reaction time, or, as it is usually viewed in research literature, the time a particular act takes to be completed after it has been initiated. *Response time* is the time it takes to complete the entire movement and includes the other times mentioned here (see Figure 7–13).

Returning to the track situation, the time elapsed from the pistol shot to the sprinter's response is referred to as his reaction time. From that point to the completion of the race, the time recorded is actually his movement time. Obviously, under normal conditions a typical time for the track man includes both his reaction and movement time. However, the initial reaction to the stimulus is as important as running speed, especially in the short

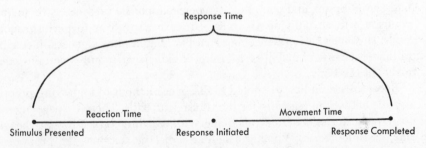

Figure 7–13. The relationship of reaction time, movement time, and response time.

sprints, and the time it takes to react to a stimulus may provide information concerning potential success or failure in the event.

If the track man was standing on a shock source at the starting line, the time elapsed from the stimulation to the initiation of movement would be recorded as a *reflex time*. Because a reflex requires neither willed movements nor judgment, it may be expected that an individual's reflex time will be faster than his reaction time.

Time factors, then, interest researchers. Under laboratory conditions, the usage of stimulus-response displays has provided much knowledge about reaction, movement, and reflex times. According to some investigators, the first reaction-time experiment was initiated in the 1860's by Donders, a Dutch physiologist. Contrarily, others claim that the first reaction-time experiment is associated with the efforts of Helmholtz in 1850. Since then, the technique for measuring reaction time has not been varied much except in the use of more elaborate equipment. The reaction time and the movement time of an individual have been compared to determine relationships between these factors; in other words, to see whether a person with a fast movement time also has a fast reaction time. Studies have also compared the reaction and the movement times of select groups, such as athletes versus nonathletes. Some examples of devices and methods utilized in obtaining these data are shown in Figure 7–14.

The simplest method of deducing reaction time is to have a subject place his finger on a button, with instructions to remove his finger when he views a light signal just above the button. The chronoscope starts with the presentation of a stimulus and stops when the button is no longer depressed. In the choice reaction-time method, the subject may be faced with a number of visual cues and is expected to react to one specific cue. If reflex time is desired, the button may be wired for shock, and the response is a result of withdrawal from a noxious stimulus.

Physiologists and experimental psychologists have investigated and suggested theories about the internal mechanism activated during a response. For example, Botwinick and Thompson (1966) proposed that reaction time be thought of as involving premotor and motor time. Premotor time includes the time elapsed from the stimulus presentation to the muscle firing, and motor time describes the point when the muscle fires to the actual response, which, in the study, was a finger lift. Interesting results of this study indicated that premotor and reaction time were highly related while no direct relationship could be discerned between motor and reaction time.

Franklin Henry (1961), one of the foremost physical education researchers in the reaction- and movement-time area, has provided similar psychological reasoning as to why reaction time should be considered a separate factor from movement time. Some individuals suggest a common factor—speed—as underlying RT and MT. Henry postulates that separate mechanisms are involved in movement speed and in reaction time. Muscular forces cause speed of the limb movement whereas reaction latency, a pre-

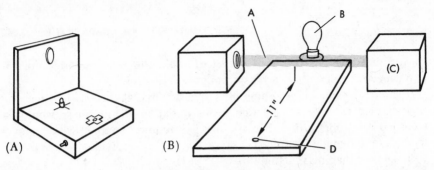

(A) (B) (C) D

Figure 7–14. Tests of reaction time and movement time. (A) Simple Reaction time. The subject must press the button as quickly as possible when the light comes on. (From E. A. Fleishman, "A Dimensional Analysis of Motor Abilities," *Journal of Experimental Psychology,* 48:437–454, 1954); (B) Reaction and Movement Time Apparatus. At the signal of the light stimulus (B) the subject releases the reaction key (D) and attempts to move his hand quickly through the light beam (A) generated from the photoelectronic eye (C) at a target just behind the light beam. Reaction time is recorded by one chronoscope which is activated on the presentation of the stimulus and broken upon the release of the key. A second chronoscope measures movement time, and it is activated upon the release of the reaction key and stopped when the hand passes through the light beam. (From L. Youngen, "A Comparison of Reaction and Movement Times of Women Athletes and Non-Athletes," *Research Quarterly,* 30:349–355, 1959.)

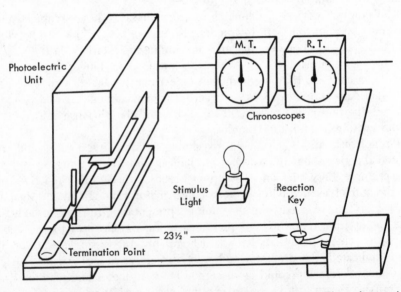

Figure 7–14 (continued). (C) Reaction and Movement Time Apparatus. The reaction chronoscope starts with the presentation of the light stimulus and stops with the release of the reaction key. The speed-of-movement chronoscope is then activated and upon contact with the terminating rod, is deactivated. (From Jean Hodgkins, "Reaction Time and Speed of Movement in Males and Females at Various Ages," *Research Quarterly,* 34:335–343, 1963.)

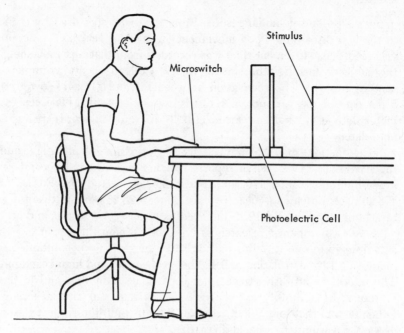

Figure 7–14 (continued). (D) Position of subjects in reaction and movement time experiment. A chronoscope is activated simultaneously with a neon stimulus lamp, a microswitch stops the chronoscope and activates another when the subject initiates the response, and his movement interrupts a photoelectric beam and stops the second chronoscope. (From William R. Pierson and Philip I. Rasch, "Isometric Strength as a Factor in Functional Muscle Testing," *American Journal of Physical Medicine,* 42:205–207, 1963.)

movement operation of the central nervous system, determines reaction time. Henry and his co-researchers have consistently obtained near-zero correlations between RT and MT, and in the present study, noted an r of 0.02 between these two factors.

Most sports require fast responses to changing stimuli. Therefore it is natural for physical education researchers to analyze the relationship of reaction time to athletic success. The abundance of evidence in the literature indicates that athletes do have faster reaction times than nonathletes. For instance, Olson (1956) compared athletes, nonathletes, and an intermediate group consisting of intramural and junior varsity players as well as participants in a recreation program. The athletes had the fastest reaction times. Other studies have produced similar results.

Furthermore, whereas most of the reaction-time and movement-time data collected in laboratory-controlled circumstances have revealed an independence of the factors, Groves's (1973) study with the racing start in swimming has produced similar results. From the pistol shot fired by the starter to the first discernible body movement (using film analysis), reaction time was recorded. Movement time was recorded from that first movement until the subject's feet left the starting block. College varsity swimmers were used as subjects. The correlation between RT and MT was low, and only 5 per cent of the variance of RT was association with MT. Even in gross motor skills as in laboratory artificial skills, RT and MT scores are apparently not related.

Reaction time may be induced by the presentation of light, sound, or touch stimuli. (One source reports reaction times in milliseconds as follows: light 180, sound 140, and touch 140.) In a study by Forbes (1945) 178 subjects provided a mean reaction time of 28.26 hundredths of a second to a light stimulus and 19.19 hundredths of a second to a sound stimulus. Although a number of researchers hold the opinion that a person who reacts quickly to one stimulus will do so to another, Forbes obtained only a modest positive correlation of 0.428 between sound and light reaction times. The intensity and distinctiveness of a particular stimulus, and in the case of sound, its audibility as well, are factors that can alter reaction time. Other factors that may affect reaction time include the subject's attention, age, prior warning, fatigue, and practice.

Reaction time does not seem to be an inherent constant response to a stimulus. Rather, it varies with the existence of certain conditions:

1. Reaction time varies according to type of stimulus (visual, auditory, tactile, olfactory, gustatory, and pain).
2. Sometimes the strength and/or duration of the stimulus influences the reaction time.
3. Another factor influencing reaction time is readiness for response; whether the subject is warned before the response and the length of time before warning the actual stimulus presentation.
4. A very important factor is practice, as reaction time usually improves with increased practice.
5. Reaction time also seems to improve to a point with age in the younger years and then worsens during old age.
6. Finally, reaction time varies as to the physiological and psychological state of the subject. If the subject is fatigued, sick, worried, and so on, his reaction time will probably be influenced.

In addition to quick reactions, speed of body or limb movement in a given space is required very often for success in various physical activities. In laboratory tests designed to measure quickness of body and limb movement, athletic performers have tended to realize more favorable results than their nonathletic counterparts. An interesting and logical deduction from the information presented thus far is that an individual who displays a low reaction time may not be expected to do likewise in his movement time. In the bulk of the research to date, reaction time and movement time, even when involving the same limb, have been shown to be measures independent of each other. Earlier in this chapter it was shown how, on the basis of reaction-time versus movement-time studies, the trend of thinking has followed the concept that the motor abilities represented in any given act are more specific than once thought for that act rather than generalizing factors.

PHYSICAL CHARACTERISTICS

Body Build

The idea of classifying man according to his physical structure is by no means new. From the days of Hippocrates body types as *phthisic habitus* (long and thin) and *apoplectic habitus* (short and thick), to the early 1920's and Kretschmer's *pyknic* (squat and compact), *asthenic* (thin, anemic in appearance), and *athletic* (muscular) types, and finally including Sheldon's (1940) concept of *somatotyping,* various methods of body typing have been employed. Sheldon's method and the suggested modifications initiated by various researchers, e.g., Cureton, have become widely recognized as the most promising and accurate means of body classification.

In order to classify individuals, Sheldon designated three components: *endomorph* (round and soft body), *mesomorph* (muscular and masculine looking), and *ectomorph* (tall and thin, linearly constructed). Individuals are photographed, and then are rated by judges on a 1 to 7 scale for each component according to the degree of component dominance. The somatotypes are described by three numerals, each of which contains a number ranging from 1 to 7, with 7 indicating the highest prevalence. The descriptive sequence of numbers refers to the components in the following order: endomorph, mesomorph, and ectomorph. Thus a rating of 1–7–1 indicates extreme mesomorphy, 7–1–1 extreme endomorphy, and 1–1–7 extreme ectomorphy. In actuality an individual will have certain amounts of each component and is thus not specifically one type. In all, eighty-eight different somatotypes have been recognized.

Of particular interest to recent researchers is the question of whether certain body types are associated with specific activities. For instance, Olympic athletes have been analyzed and categorized according to body structure. During the 1960 Olympics, Tanner (1964) compiled data on 137 track and field athletes; they were somatotyped and classified by event. His results indicate distinct somatotypes for the different events. For example, a somatotype of 3–6–2 was designated to the discus, shot, and hammer throwers; 2–5–3 for the sprinters; 2½–4–4 for the middle- and long-distance runners; and 2–6–2 to 2–3–6 for the high jumpers.

Present methods indicate a refinement of original somatotyping techniques, and the usage of somatotypes is widespread. There have been attempts to determine the body types of successful athletes in various sports so as best to predict the achievement one might expect in a given sport. Although there are exceptions to rules, research has shown the relationship of body type to given sports.

It is of interest to note the observation of Hirata (1966) at the Olympic Games in Tokyo, who made physical evaluations of the entries to the Games and classified them by event. Among the relations between particular sports and the morphology of the participants were the following:

Sport	Morphology
Basketball	Tall and lean
Canoeing	Large and stout
Cycling	
Long races	Short and lean
Short races	Short and stout
Fencing	Lean
Gymnastics	Small and stout
Hockey	Small and a little stout
Rowing	Tall
Soccer	Small and a little stout
Swimming	
Divers	Small
Free-stylers, Back strokers	Large and lean
Breast strokers, Butterfly swimmers	Stout
Track and Field	
Hurdles	Large and lean
Short dashes	Small
Middle distances	Larger
Long distance, Marathon runners	Small and lean
High jumpers	Large and lean
Long jumpers	Lean and not so large
Pole vaulters	Average
Throwers	Large and stout
Volleyball	
Forward players	Tall and lean
Back players	Small and stout
Water polo	Large and stout
Weight lifting	Stout
Wrestling	Stout

In some sports, it is important to have momentary muscular strength, and a muscular and stout build promotes successful performance for such events as weight lifting, wrestling, short-distance cycling, and throwing events. Longer-distance track events require more endurance than strength, and the combination of an efficient cardiorespiratory system with a lighter weight results in better performance times. In general, the evidence in this study appears to justify the idea that physique and constitution have an important effect on athletic performance, at least when the athletes have trained to top-level physical condition. Hirata expresses the opinion that the individual with the most adequate physique will win an event when the participants in that event have all trained hard and achieved maximal physical condition. Certainly the cultural, socioeconomic, and peer influences should not be overlooked as important determiners of activity interests and successes.

Morgan Worthy and Allan Markle (1970) suggest that blacks and whites may be expected to perform differently in self-paced and externally paced tasks. Using professional baseball and basketball data as well as college basketball data, these researchers concluded that black athletes outperformed white athletes in externally paced sports activities. Speculations offered to explain the findings included the possibilities that blacks prefer more risky and physical contact activities and lack some tolerance for a delay in gratification, which is associated with playing alone in a noncompetitive situation. Because very recent published basketball and baseball data (Jones and Hochner, 1973) refute these findings in some instances, the Worthy and Markle study is offered only as a departure point for further discussion. Perhaps a host of sociological and cultural factors and personal attitudes determine athletic performance.

In the Jones and Hochner study, blacks did outperform whites in baseball hitting, considered to be an externally paced event, and free-throw shooting in basketball, considered to be a self-paced activity. However, black pitchers were superior to white pitchers in this self-paced event, contrary to the findings of Worthy and Markle. No differences in field-goal shooting in basketball were noted between the groups. Worthy and Markle suggest that variations in athletic performance go beyond the simple placement of tasks into self-paced and externally paced categories. They propose consideration of three dominant motives—approval, achievement, and power—expressed in the following bipolar dimensions: team–individual, success–style, and competition–play.

There is much speculation over causative agents for differences in achievement of blacks and whites in sport. One possible advantage for the black in certain sports is the "type" of body build associated with him as contrasted with the white. For excellent reviews on the topic, the interested reader might want to examine articles by James Jordan (1969) and Martin Kane (1971).

Other investigations concerning body builds have noted a positive relationship between mesomorphy and athletic performance and a negative correlation between endomorphy and athletic performance; greater strength and general physical fitness with mesomorphy; and better balance and flexibility with ectomorphy. An important consideration is that *although a certain body type or build may contribute to success in specific activities, it is by no means necessary.* Skill attainment is the result of many complex factors, and a limiting body structure may very well be overcome by an emphasis on other variables.

Height and Weight

Researchers, especially in the 1920's and 1930's, attempted to classify physical education students by *age, height,* and *weight.* These factors appeared to be of some value in predicting general athletic performance. However, an increasing number of investigations has offered little encouragement to classify by age, height, and weight. Age is the best predictor of the three as to success in various physical activities, at least during preadolescence and adolescence. Although numerous studies may be located in the literature concerning height and weight and performance, a few studies representative of their general findings are described here. No relationship has been found between body height and weight of girls with fundamental skill achievement in a variety of sports. Little predictive value in height and weight to track and field performance of junior high school girls has been reported.

It would appear that only at extreme heights and weights will individuals benefit or suffer in certain physical activities. The volleyball player has an advantage in spiking if he is tall, but at the same time may be at a disadvantage in digging a ball that is low to the floor. The huge basketball player demonstrates success near the basket, but at a distance away from the goal, he may lack as good a shot as a smaller man. His size may cause him to lose the speed and agility, which generally characterize the smaller man. Therefore it may be generally stated that height and weight factors are not valid predictors of athletic success, at least, in physical education classes.

Strength

There is no doubt that in varying degrees, strength underlies all motor performance. In an isolated sense, *strength* may be thought of as the capacity of a muscle or group of muscles to exert maximum pressure against a given resistance in a limited period of time. A weakness in any area of the body may severely limit the coordination and effort needed for the performance of a skill. Thus, a minimum amount of strength is a necessity for motor-skill performance.

Strength has been measured in various ways: lifting of weights, grip strength by the hand dynamometer, the dynamometer for the back and leg, and a cable tensiometer for recording the tension supplied by various muscle groups responsible for thirty-eight joint movements.

Muscular Endurance

The capacity of a muscle or a group of muscles to contract repeatedly against a moderate resistance reflects *muscular endurance*. The individual must maintain a moderate energy output over an extended duration of time. Whether it be muscular or cardiovascular in nature, endurance permits the individual to prolong the performance of an act. Although the constant practice of a skill promotes improvement, a degree of muscular as well as mental endurance is needed in order for the performer to be able to concentrate at length on the skill itself. Many motor skills are arduous to learn and perform, and the development of such physical qualities as strength and endurance delay fatigue, thus permitting attention to be focused for a longer period of time on the skill to be learned.

Flexibility

Flexibility is determined by the range of movement of a joint. Mathews and others (1957) mention three factors that limit joint flexibility: the nature of the joint structure; the condition of the ligaments and fascia that surround the joint; and muscle extensibility. These investigators cite the need for a flexible range of motion among athletes, especially in track and swimming.

This premise has been verified by Thomas Cureton (1951), who found above-average flexibility in the champion athletes he measured from 1946 to 1948. In one study, he found the 1936 Japanese champion Olympic swimmers to have 31 per cent greater trunk flexion than the American swimmers. In comparing twenty-one Olympic swimmers with 100 college competitive swimmers, the Olympians proved to be superior in ankle flexion by 11 per cent and by 8 per cent in trunk flexion. Flexibility is a physical quality involved in many skilled motor patterns, and its inadequate development may well be regarded as another possible deterrent to achievement in certain sports.

THE SENSES

Whereas physical characteristics and motor abilities are always emphasized for successful motor-skill performance, the senses are often taken for granted. Those remarkable sense organs that have the ability to detect minor changes in stimuli are indispensably involved in many motor acts. Such senses as taste and smell rarely function as part of the typical performance of motor skills. Hearing, of course, plays an important role in iso-lated instances, such as responding to the starting gun. (There must have been many an occasion when visiting team players wished this sense could be turned off so that they would not be aware of crowd reactions in crucial situations.) The importance of *vision, equilibrium,* and *proprioception* to skilled performance is obvious. The range of sensory capacities among in-dividuals is great, another indication of differences in systems and poten-tiality and therefore in behavior.

Vision

There are many facets of vision. Following a moving projectile, and deter-mining peripheral activity, spatial relations, color, and brightness are ex-amples of the function of the visual system. The baseball batter must have eyes keen enough to follow pitches thrown at the rate of 90 mph, the in-fielder has to follow the ground ball visually and move his body and hands accordingly, and the outfielder is required to detect a little white sphere against a background of people, stands, and lights. Success is more probable for the performer with a visual handicap where the environment is stable and change is brought about by the individual himself, rather than in sports where external events are unpredictable. Respectable scores have been re-ported by blind golfers and bowlers.

During the initial photoelectronic process of visual activity, retinal poten-tials are formed. Messages, in the form of impulses, are sent by certain ganglion cells of the retina to the visual region of the occipital cortex. There is a perceptive interpretation of the information in this area. In most sports, this perceptive analysis must occur in a matter of moments if the performer is to react successfully to given stimuli often unpredictable in nature. The importance of early, normal visual experience for the development of visual capacities is stressed by Robert McCleary (1970). In order to determine accurately the spatial location of objects, one must first experience meaning-ful and integrated visual and motor experiences.

Many investigations in psychological literature yield results that stress the importance of vision, in addition to tactile and kinesthetic experience, in learning skills. Evidently, even for skills that require no perception of a changing external field, vision enhances performance. The body utilizes much of its sense information, and even though there may be considerable overlap and unnecessary information, the removal of one sense appears to be somewhat detrimental to performance. Yet the performer does not always attend to all available information, as R. B. Wilberg (1969) has shown with kinesthetic cues. However, individuals can be trained to make use of mini-mal visual information in given situations. In such tasks as balancing, re-stricted peripheral vision is apt to diminish performance. There are probably many occasions when learners need to be instructed as to how to gain more information from the presence of minimal visual cues.

A comparison of twins, one blind from birth and the other with full vision, was made by Williams and Blane (1969). Activities involving large amounts of space or powerful and fast movements of the body favored the sighted subject. Smaller space areas in which manipulation tasks occur favored the nonsighted subject. "Thus, where total body involvement was minimal and fine manipulative movements of the hands and fingers were stressed, lack of visual information seemed to have little effect. Frequently, blindness seemed to enhance the performance of such tasks, since the non-sighted individual was forced to rely upon other sources of sensory information as a basis for performing daily tasks" (p. 271). If the task permits compensation for sensory impairment, learning can occur effectively.

The relationship of visual attributes—e.g., depth perception, visual acuity —to skilled performance has been the topic of some investigations. The hypothesis tested is that the presence of high-quality visual sense apparatus is associated with greater proficiency in those tasks requiring visual scanning, spatial orientation, and target shooting. In a recent study, Beals, Mayyasi, Templeton, and Johnston (1971) tested the static and dynamic visual acuity of college varsity basketball players. Shooting records from the field and foul lines were kept for all home games. A relatively high correlation of 0.76 between field shooting accuracy and dynamic visual acuity and a moderate correlation of 0.57 between field shooting and static visual acuity was obtained. Characteristics of vision, according to these researchers, can be used reliably to predict basket shooting accuracy. Research findings are by no means in agreement. Consider, for instance, the lack of supportive evidence by Jacquelyn Shick (1971) for any relationship between foul shooting and depth perception with female college students.

Kinesthesis

Information concerning the kinesthetic sense seems more limited than that regarding the other senses. A leading reason for this circumstance is the great difficulty researchers have in isolating this sense for study. In spite of the difficulties in obtaining precision in experimentation those receptors responsible for informing the body of its conscious change in position as well as of the relationship of its parts in space have been demonstrated to be necessary for the smooth movements of the skilled act. Probably this sense is appreciated most by persons having visual limitations, for it is this sense they must rely on in order to perform motor skills adequately. Nevertheless, kinesthesis is a sense usually associated with the more gifted performers, and research appears to indicate its greater presence in those people demonstrating outstanding skill in motor activities.

A means of demonstrating the effects of kinesthetic impairment has been offered by Judith Laszlo (1966). By raising the systolic blood pressure 40 millimeters Hg higher than the subject's normal reading with the use of a sphygmomanometer cuff and having the subject continually tap on a Morse key as quickly as possible, Laszlo found an expected decrease in key-tapping efficiency with a loss of kinesthetic sensation. She also tested her subjects in other ways. Once again, with the cuff on the arm, and head turned away, each subject had his finger touched lightly with a cotton end stick. The finger was also manipulated up or down and the subject was asked to move it up or down. This was done regularly after the cuff was in place for ten minutes. On the average, the subjects lost their tactile sense after 19.2 minutes, their passive kinesthetic sense after 22 minutes, and their active kinesthetic sense after 22.4 minutes. The experimental methods employed in this investigation offer investigators ideas on how to study the function of kinesthesis when one learns and performs skilled movements. A complete description of the compression block technique is described by Laszlo and Bairstow (1971), which they feel is safe and useful in examining movement control in the absence of the kinesthesis. Further analysis of this technique suggests that it does not eliminate feedback in certain situations, and there is serious gamma impairment affecting fine motor control. Sensory restriction has provided a means for psychologists to determine sensory involvement in behavior, learning, and perception.

The confusion in the interchangeable use of the terms *proprioception* and *kinesthesis* has prompted Hopkins (1972) to address the issue. After a historical perspective of the problem, he offers four alternatives: (1) to accept the two terms as referring to the same thing; (2) to accept J. J. Gibson's interpretations—that proprioception is not a special sense but rather a function common to all systems, whereas kinesthesis is restricted to sensitivity of skeletal movement; (3) to use the terms *kinesthesis* when certain receptor mechanisms are activated and *proprioception* when additional mechanisms are activated; or (4) never to use the term *kinesthesis*. Hopkins favors the last proposed: to use *proprioception* exclusively.

Tactile Sense

Closely related to the kinesthetic sense is the tactile sense. The ability to detect changes of touch and pressure involves many of the same type of proprioceptors involved in informing the body of changes in its position. Senses that enable us to feel pain, temperature changes, touch, pressure, and the body's position in space are referred to as *somatic senses*. The receptors for pressure lie deeper in the skin and tissues than those for touch, although most of the same nerve endings serve both functions. Pressure is automatically considered a type of touch sensation.

Equilibrium

The nature of body balance and equilibrium has already been discussed from both physiological and psychological viewpoints. It should be sufficient merely to reiterate the role this sense plays as a basis for voluntary movement and control. Although posture and locomotion impulses can be distributed by the spinal cord alone, refinement of these impulses under changing body and environmental conditions is the responsibility of the higher nerve centers. Equilibrium must be extremely well developed in such performers as divers, trampolinists, and gymnasts, although it should be obvious that most skills require a certain degree of body equilibrium.

PERCEPTION

Limited knowledge of the structures involved in perception and in the nature of the perceptual process has proved to be a difficult obstacle in the past for psychologists to overcome in explaining the learning process. Perhaps this has been one of the reasons why traditional S–R (stimulus–response) theory, association theory, and reflex-arc models have been widely accepted in years gone by. After Gestalt theory, in opposition to S–R theory, made its mark in psychology in the 1920's and 1930's, its impact gradually weakened. In recent years, new research and theories have emerged from social psychologists, experimental psychologists, clinical psychologists, and physiological psychologists, once again emphasizing the role of perception as a factor in learning, adjustment, and personality.

This area of perception and perceptual learning is an exciting one, which psychologists are no longer avoiding, but rather meeting directly. Perception and the other cognitive processes are treated as an important facet of learning activity. Difficulties still arise in definition and clarification of terminology, as may be expected in an area where scientific knowledge is relatively recent.

Description and Definitions

There is no doubt that the senses underlie perception and that several senses probably interact simultaneously during the perceptive process. The old idea that perception is a passive process has met with disfavor, but it is now accepted that perception, as well as learning, is an active process. It is also evident that perception depends on psychological and physiological characteristics of the perceiver in addition to the stimulus itself.

The structure of the sense organs has much to do with what is perceived, a fact that perhaps leads to confusion in distinguishing sensation from perception. In a manner of speaking, sense receptors are analyzers, as they transmit specific messages to the higher centers of the nervous system. There are, however, no special lines to the central nervous system. Instead, the resulting perception of each sensation is initiated and determined by a complex interaction of many passageways.

The elementary process of sensation underlies the more complex perceptual process. The senses involved will depend on the object(s) to be perceived. Perception depends on differences between stimuli and perceptibility, or ease of discrimination, and is closely related to the magnitude of the difference between stimuli.

One's viewpoint of psychology might well determine his definition of perception as well as his definition of learning. However, it does appear that the older concept of perception being merely more complex than sensation is unacceptable today. Perception is dependent on learning and is influenced by such individual factors as personality, attitudes, emotional factors, experience, and expectations, in addition to environmental variables. It becomes more complex as learning becomes more complex. Adults may learn perceptions in a different manner from children.

Perception is usually distinguished from other processes involving thought, consciousness, and judgment. It is a form of discriminating behavior involving the overall activity of the person *immediately* following or accompanying stimulation of the sense organs. It may assume overt or introspective characteristics, e.g., viewing a painting is experiential, whereas reacting to a choice reaction-time apparatus produces observable motor activity. *Perception may be defined as knowledge through the senses of the existence and properties of matter and the external world.* It causes actions which in turn change it and is a continuous process. A clearer distinction between sensation and perception might help us to understand these terms better. A sensation involves the means for reception of stimuli. A perception, on the other hand, involves the means for the interpretation of stimuli.

Some scholars have found fault with the application of the same term, *perception,* to describe an act, an event, a process, and learning. Solley and Murphy (1960) in their book *Development of the Perceptual World* attempt to clarify the generalized application of perception. These authors would define an event experienced as a *percept. Perceptual learning* is "a change in the status of the logically-inferred perceptual state or process of an individual as a result of successive applications of the operations of a learning paradigm." The *perceptual act,* as they theorize it to be, involves five steps: expectancy, attending, reception and sensory reactions, trial and check, and conscious perception, or organization.

The critical student can thus observe that perception may be a process or a product. The process is stimulation structured and is referred to as perceiving. The product of the structural process is a percept. And finally, perception, along with such processes as memory, thinking, and imagination, composes the *cognitive process*. So far, perception has been discussed in a general and somewhat theoretical manner. Some specific references may help to clarify this area; therefore, the personal variables affecting perception are discussed at this point.

Personal Factors in Perception

How and what one perceives in a given situation have been shown to be affected by many personal factors. The ability to attend to, or to disregard extraneous and irrelevant information, contributes to perceptibility. Selectivity in perception reduces the number of stimuli surrounding the object, allowing it to be perceived more easily and quickly. *Selective attention* of stimuli is a process associated with highly skilled performance. The batter concentrates on the ball and disregards irrelevant cues. Similarly, the successful shooting of a foul shot requires attention to the feel of the ball and concentration on the rim of the basket. Possibly any awareness of the fans and their comments, of the other players, or any feelings of nervousness, will contribute to the player's ineffective performance. The athlete is faced with situation after situation where he must be able to discriminate, detect, and exclude stimuli, many times at the spur of the moment.

Actually, the amount of sensory information yielded in any situation is more than any one person can perceive. Because there are many sensory channels—auditory, visual, tactual, kinesthetic, and the like—much data is presented to the individual and duplicated at one time through the medium of the senses. The athlete must be *set*, to know what to look for. This factor of set, the ability to single out objects, is necessary in all motor activity. Skill is demonstrated when there is a minimal involvement of the senses; just those needed for the distinction of cues in order that the perceptual process will work quickly and accurately. There is no doubt that learning and performing motor skills certainly depend, to a great extent, on perceptual abilities.

Another factor that influences perception is *motivation*. A person must have the will to perceive if he is to attend to the necessary cues influencing discrimination. Need, drive, or other motivation prepares the individual; he develops a set or hypothesis as to what to expect. This anticipation, or expectancy, permits him to attend to the meaningful stimuli. In fact, sometimes we perceive what we wish to perceive with needs and wishes channeling the direction.

Previous experiences in the same situation with the same objects help in facilitating the perceptual process. These past experiences also promote a sense of expectancy, which in turn leads to better perception. Familiarity with stimuli in similar situations not only affects perceptual learning but learning in general, and it might be deduced at this stage of the discussion that many similarities exist between perceptual learning and motor learning.

Even as motor learning is altered favorably by motivated practice, so is perceptual learning. However, if there is no reinforcement or knowledge of results, there is little or no learning of motor skills. Knowledge of results cannot be withheld in perceptual learning, for the person always perceives something through his own efforts. This information reinforces the perceptual act even though it may not be accurate. Whereas in motor learning an outsider may provide the knowledge of results, for example, whether the tennis serve was executed in good form, an individual himself achieves the percept. But perhaps we can leave this issue to the theorists.

William Epstein (1967) concludes his analysis of research in the area of perceptual learning with five propositions (p. 290):

(1) Assumptions that are learned through everyday experience are important determinants of perception.
(2) Practice, in the form of prior exposure, controlled rehearsal, or differential reinforcement of selective perceiving, can modify perception.
(3) Extended exposure to conditions of conflict leads to a gradual modification of perception.
(4) When visual stimulation is transformed or distorted, the perceiver adapts to the distortion.
(5) A variety of perceptual functions exhibit developmental changes.

Theories of Perception

Gestalt theory, with the work of Wertheimer, Koffka, Kohler, and others, popularized the perceptual aspect of learning. Unfortunately, many of their principles were broadly stated, and these generalizations did not attract much research in this area. Because of the oversimplification of complex problems, it was difficult to analyze the theory experimentally. Basically, Gestaltists claimed that when dealing with things we acquire experiences with them, and this affects perception. The individual sees patterns or configurations in a particular field, which leads to the so-called *insight* he gains in problem solving. Gestaltists assumed that all people perceive the same way and that perception is influenced by the surrounding stimuli rather than by one's physiological and psychological structures.

In contemporary times, since the formal presentation of Gestalt theory, perceptual theories have taken different directions. Some psychologists, exemplified by Witkin (1954), emphasize the role of perception in personality development. Other theories stress that (1) the nature of what is perceived is determined by the environment and not influenced by the perceiver's needs, emotions, or other personality factors; or (2) the emphasis should be on the nature of the stimuli influencing perception and the sense organs involved; whereas Witkin (3) believes primarily that perception is

THE PERCEPTUAL ACT

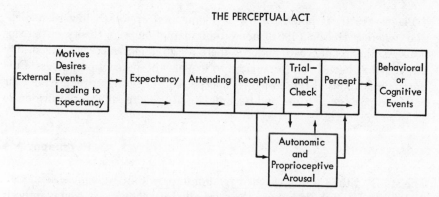

Figure 7–15.   Solley and Murphy schematization of the perceptual act. The arrows indicate the major transitions between expectancy, attending, reception, trial-and-check, autonomic and proprioceptive arousal, and the final structured percept. [From Charles M. Solley and G. Murphy, *Development of the Perceptual World* (New York: Basic Books, Inc., 1960).]

affected by personal factors. Perception is related to personality and contributes to adjustment. The perceptual capacities are part of the individual's resources in adjusting to life's problems and situations. Finally, we can examine perception by both the structure of the stimuli field and the personal characteristics of the perceiver.

The approach Solley and Murphy (1960) take is to compare perceptual learning to learning in general. A five-step description of perception (see Figure 7–15) is offered: (1) first stage—preparatory, whatever exists prior to stimulation affects perception; (2) second stage—moment before stimulation, attention to significant stimuli; (3) third stage—reception, neural mechanism action; (4) fourth stage—trial and check, inferences; and (5) fifth stage—meaning, consolidation of stimulus traces.

In their minds there is no doubt that, "Perceptual learning is dependent upon the level of maturation achieved by a child and, conversely, the full achievement of maturational potentials can be facilitated by the occurrence or nonoccurrence of specific learning experiences. Neither maturation nor learning can fully unfold independently." Richard Held (1965) describes a theory stressing the importance of movement and sensory feedback in perceptual adaptation. There is a close relationship between signals from the motor nervous system, producing active movement, and the consequent sensory feedback. He cites evidence to show that when one lives in isolation or monotony, performance of perceptual and motor tasks declines. Other research shows that the young of higher mammals do not develop normal behavior if they are deprived of sensory and motor experiences. Held believes that the motor–sensory feedback loop helps newborn babies to develop motor coordination and also accounts for the changed relation between sensory and motor signals resulting from growth.

Piaget (1950) is noted for his developmental approach toward perception, whereas Helson (1951) offered an adaptation level theory of perception. As the reader can deduce, there is an abundance of present-day theories that have been formulated to explain the perceptual process. Further modifications of these theories and perhaps closer agreement will occur with the passage of time and accumulation of more substantial evidence.

Psychophysics

The study of the sensations, their relationships within a given sense modality, and the stimuli that cause them is called *psychophysics*. Some authorities feel that the most precise knowledge of perceptions comes from the psycho-physical field. Certain aspects of the sensations have been studied more than others in their role in perception, notably, size, color, pitch, space, depth, and distance. Unfortunately, these as well as other information-offering processes are still not completely understood.

Certain laws concerning the sense modalities have been formulated through the years. One of the most famous is the Fechner and Weber law, describing a person's ability to distinguish between two stimuli. Weber's original law, written in 1834, stated that in order for a second stimulus to be discriminated from the first, there must be a noticeable difference. Increments must be in constant fractions of the original stimulus. For instance, perhaps we would have to add one gram weight to ten grams in order barely to observe the difference between two weights. If this is the case, a 20-gram weight would require two additional grams to the second stimulus in order for it to be perceived as different from the first. Consequently, a 40-gram weight necessitates the addition of 4 grams to the second stimulus; 80 grams would require 8, and so on. Fechner's law was a mathematical transposition of Weber's law. The Fechner–Weber law, which can be applied to the heavier of two weights, the longer of two lines, and the louder of two noises, has not always proved to be accurate but it is a generally accepted law.

The mathematical formulation for Weber's law is as follows:

$$\frac{\Delta I}{I} = k$$

where:
k = the constant fraction for the given type of physical energy
I = the intensity of the stimulus
ΔI = the differential threshold

The constant fraction must be determined for each type of stimulus. It describes the "just noticeable difference," that difference between two stimuli (two tones, two light intensities, and so on) of sufficient magnitude so that detection is possible. The differential threshold tends to approximate a constant fraction, as described by Weber's law. It has been ascertained from research findings, for example, that the ratio is $\frac{1}{53}$ for detecting lifted gram weight differences. The ratio is $\frac{1}{11}$ for distinguishing loudness in tones.

Johannes Müller developed a doctrine of specific nerve energies. According to this doctrine, the sensation is determined by the fibers stimulated. However, the interrelatedness of the sense modalities and the respective functions within them, such as the determination of brightness, color, space perception, as well as visual acuity in the sense of vision requires us to realize the complexity of any given act or process. Because sensations are the basic underlying factors in perception, the study of the sense organs and the receptors certainly aids in describing one phase of the perceptual process: the role of the senses.

Figural Aftereffects

A commonly occurring phenomenon in perception is the effect that an extended experience with a particular stimulus or situation has on the individual, once it has been discontinued. When a person continually observes curved lines and then straight ones, these straight lines appear to be curved in the opposite direction. Figure reversals can and have been demonstrated under a wide range of experimental conditions.

Every child has had the experience of turning in a circle a number of times, and then noticing, upon stopping, a feeling that the body is now turning in the opposite direction. The problem of maintaining balance after continued circular rotating confronts the ice skater attempting to master this skill. Other types of kinesthetic aftereffects are observed in sports situations. The baseball batter swings the weighted bat in the on-deck circle in order that his regular bat will appear lighter to him. Thus, he thinks he will be able to whip the bat around faster. The track man may practice with weighted boots in order to experience the feeling of lightness and speed once they are removed and his track shoes replaced during actual competition.

Figural aftereffects have been of particular interest to only a few scholars. Bryant J. Cratty and Robert Hutton (1964) define a figural effect as *"a perceptual distortion produced by prolonged . . . satiation of visual, auditory, tactual-kinesthetic stimuli, or some combination of these or of other stimuli. . . ."* The most pronounced effect is experienced immediately following the satiation. A kinesthetic aftereffect would be the effect of a movement experience, contrasted with, say, the visual inspection of a straight line after viewing curved lines. When Cratty and Duffy (1967) administered a number of movement-oriented tasks to their subjects, aftereffects of movement were found to be highly specific. Aftereffect observations from task to task are not consistent. Active tasks produced more aftereffects than passive tasks. These authors discuss their findings in the context of other research and theories as well as methodological considerations.

Although some investigations have obtained results favoring an overload prior to actual performance, such as throwing a heavier baseball before throwing a regulation baseball or warming up with a weighted bat, the bulk of the research indicates that little is to be gained by this practice. Interestingly enough, subjects invariably *feel* they perform better following an overload routine even though their performance does not improve more than the preoverload performance. Nelson has noted this phenomenon in a series of experiments. In one experiment (Nelson and Nofsinger, 1965) male students were tested for elbow-flexion speed prior to and following the application of selected levels of overload. The subjects all stated that they felt faster on the postoverload test, but in actuality, no significant differences were realized between pre- and postoverload tests. In other words, a kinesthetic illusion was created.

Perceived differences or distortions are generally temporary in nature, and the actual benefit to athletic performance has yet to be objectively substantiated through experimental research. However, the reported better feeling derived from practicing with weighted objects on subsequent speed and strength performances certainly necessitates a more thorough examination of this area.

Perceptual and Motor Learning

The role of perception and its importance in motor learning and performance should now be evident. Perceptual learning has been studied separately from learning in general, but there is no doubt that although one refers to the learning of athletic skills as motor learning, perceptual mechanisms operate in precluding any skilled motor act or subsequent to that act. A person's ability to receive and distinguish among available cues in a given situation enables him to perform more skillfully. The batter may have the smoothest, ideal practice swing. If he cannot concentrate and attend to the important cues when he is up at bat in a game, if he cannot follow the ball as it comes to the plate and perceive a fastball or curve, a ball or a strike, his performance will not be effective.

COGNITIVE PROCESSES

Cognition consists of such higher mental processes as concept formation, problem solving, imagination, perception, and intelligence. Cognitive processes are extremely difficult to study objectively, and much of our knowledge of them has been inferred from behavior. This was shown to be the case with perception. Although we rely on the senses for environmental information, the object ultimately perceived results from the complex involvement of many neural mechanisms and the state of the organism. Even learning, whether simple or more involved, must be measured through performance.

Most writings and research in the area of cognition have dealt with perception and intelligence. The other cognitive processes have usually been somewhat neglected, although there are certainly many questions, which, if answered, would be of interest to a number of people. Cognitive psychologists are interested in thinking, concept formation, and in general, the acquisition of knowledge. Similarities and differences between the viewpoints of cognitive psychologists and neobehaviorist psychologists have been presented by Anderson and Ausubel (1965). Neobehaviorists are concerned primarily with conditioning, rote verbal learning, and discrimination learning. Both groups of psychologists have attempted to explain all of learning and psychology through research completed in their respective areas. The behaviorists are interested in observed responses, and they manipulate environmental variables in order to determine cause-and-effect factors. The consciousness or *mentalistic* concept is pursued by the cognitive psychologists. They believe it is not only possible to study knowing, perceiving, meaning, and understanding (behaviorists say these processes cannot be objectively observed), but that they also provide the most important data.

The nature and development of cognitive abilities have been described in detail by Raymond Cattell (1971). The book offers a historical perspective as well as a contemporary way of looking at cognitive abilities: their structure and measurement.

Relationship of Intelligence to Motor Abilities and Physical Factors

Guilford factor-analyzed physical performance to arrive at underlying psychomotor abilities and has attempted to determine the component abilities comprising the intellect as well as their relationships (Guilford, 1959). Through the factor-analysis method, he examined data obtained from a series of intelligence tests and proposed the least common denominators, i.e., independent factors. From fifty intellectual factors, he derived five: cognitive abilities, memory, evaluative abilities, divergent thinking, and convergent thinking. He interpreted the process of cognition as including discovery and recognition abilities.

Evidently, interpretations and categorizations of the higher mental processes lack agreement among psychologists in many instances. Guilford's use of the word *intellect* might very well be used interchangeably with the term *cognition*, depending on one's viewpoint. However, this section of the chapter is particularly concerned with intelligence tests and what they measure, and the relationship of these scores to various physical characteristics, motor abilities, and athletic success. Much research has been completed that has attempted to determine the relationship of intellectual and physical factors.

Intelligence tests, which may measure various aspects of intelligence, depending on the nature of the tests, and academic achievement scores have been utilized as means of measuring intelligence. The most often used and respected intelligence tests are the Revised Stanford-Binet Scales and the Wechsler Intelligence Scale, both of which yield IQ's that correlate fairly well with academic achievement. These scales have been used in investigations in order to distinguish intellectual groups or relate intelligence to some other variable. The mentally retarded and the superior have been compared in physical performance, athlete and nonathlete differences in intelligence have been tested, and the relationship of motor-skill success to academic achievement has been investigated.

Intelligence and Physical Status

Some researchers have been concerned with the relation of intelligence to such physical factors as height and weight and performances on strength tests. In a sense, they have attempted partially to resolve the issue of whether a sound body usually coincides with a sound mind. The theory of organismic unity, that physical and intellectual factors are interrelated, has been questioned. There is considerable doubt upon the relationship of academic achievement and intelligence test scores with physical status. Early research evidence indicated that nothing more than low, positive relationships exist between physical status and mental status. Much of the present research permits the same conclusion. Exception to this has been demonstrated when mentally retarded children are compared to average and superior children in physical characteristics and motor abilities.

Intelligence and Ability to Learn Motor Skills

Some writers have argued for an MQ, a motor intelligence score depicting a child's ability to learn motor skills, in conjunction with his obtained IQ. Other writers feel there is a direct relationship between such variables because the organism reacts totally to all experiences. According to the latter group, if a student does well on intelligence tests, he should be expected to learn motor activities more quickly and proficiently than those students who obtain lower intelligence ratings.

In Ryan's (1963) investigation, eighty college students were required to learn how to balance on a stabilometer. Academic achievement did not distinguish the subjects in their ability to learn and perform the task. Start (1964) had forty-four college students mentally practice a novel skill for five minutes on each of six days. Performance on the skill, a single leg up-start on the Olympic high bar, was then rated by four judges. When the ratings were compared to IQ scores, a meaningless r of 0.08 was obtained.

Generally, it appears that the research, although by no means in agreement, indicates little relationship between cognitive abilities and the ability to learn motor tasks. The sheer frustration of resolving available research evidence with common beliefs is illustrated by Philip DuBois (1965, p. 64). He writes:

Up to the present time certain of the findings in the study of complex skills have been contradictory. Intelligence has been defined as the ability to learn, yet most of the correlations between measures of intelligence and changes resulting from training are reported to be essentially zero. One talks of the ability to learn, and yet gain in proficiency in one task is often reported to be unrelated to gains in other tasks. It is widely believed that new knowledge must be built on old, and yet many a study has come to the conclusion that those who know the most at the beginning of training profit least from instruction.

Using factor-analytic techniques, James Duncanson (1966) is more optimistic of being able to determine the relationship of measures of learning and measures of abilities in cognitive tasks. His conclusions, compromising between specificity and generality notions, were that

1. Learning is related to abilities.
2. There are learning factors independent of the abilities measured.
3. Learning in one situation is related to learning in other situations. (There is no general learning factor, but there are fewer learning factors than tasks.)

It might be emphasized that most experiments comparing intelligence to motor factors have utilized college or high school subjects where distinctions on intelligence tests and IQ's are slighter than when comparing an entire population. Research on preschool youngsters, elementary school children, and slightly older children tends to show greater interactions between physical, motor, and intellectual factors. Another concern is the nature of the tests employed. For instance, Ismail and others (1963) distinguished high academic achievers from low ones on tests of coordination and static balance. Tests of speed, accuracy, and strength did not differentiate the groups. The authors were able to conclude that for boys and girls between the ages of ten and twelve, coordination items were fairly good predictors of IQ and Stanford Standard Achievement scores.

Thus far it appears that research investigating intellectual and motor relationships has indicated higher relationships among young school-aged children than among college students. Child psychologists and others interested in growth and development have attempted to show the relationship of motor development to academic aptitude and achievement (e.g., Kephart, Delacato, and others). Their work and the research of others, as is summarized in the chapter dealing with developmental factors, is inconclusive as to prescribing motor patterns for children as a means of promoting intellectual growth.

Athlete Versus Nonathlete in Intelligence

For many years the popular conception of the big dumb athlete has plagued physical educators and the athletes themselves. It takes only a few examples to confirm a hypothesis, especially one that is quite entrenched in the mind of the believer. Fortunately, most of the literature dispels such thoughts.

Some isolated studies do show athletes to score lower on intelligence tests than nonathletes. However, the majority of investigations have found little difference between the two groups on intelligence tests and academic achievement tests. A number of studies have even produced results favoring the athletes. As far as grade-point averages are concerned, athletes do as well as, if not slightly better than, nonathletes.

Motor and Physical Characteristics of the Mentally Retarded

The "normal" population of children, from birth to college age, has been extensively investigated. For many years, the mentally retarded have been neglected. With federal encouragement and enthusiasm at the local level, much work has been recently undertaken by educators, physical educators, and psychologists in order to promote more effective learning situations for the mentally deficient child.

Evidence has been quite consistent with respect to certain points. It generally indicates a direct relationship between motor and physical factors and intellectual achievement. Thurstone (1959) undertook a comprehensive project concerned with educating the mentally handicapped. Her subjects, 559 boys and girls ranging in age from seven to fifteen years, had IQ's recorded from 50 to 79. One phase of the study had to do with the acquisition and performance of gross motor skills. All the subjects were tested on such skills as (1) volleyball or soccer ball punt for distance; (2) tennis ball or softball throw for distance; (3) grip strength; (4) 40-yard run; (5) standing broad jump; (6) tennis ball throw for accuracy; and (7) side stepping for fifteen seconds. The scores of the mentally retarded children were compared with those of the normal children at different ages. The scores of the normal children were consistently and significantly better on almost every test, at all age levels.

In another study Howe (1959) formed two groups of children from six and one half to twelve years of age, equated as to age, sex, and background. A number of physical skills were tested, including a jump test, grip strength, ball throw for distance, tapping speed, balancing ability, and others. The normal children were superior to the mentally deficient on these tests. An astonishing discovery made by the author was that forty-one of the forty-three retarded children *could not balance on one foot for one minute.* This information coincides with the data obtained by Ismail and others (1963) in their study already reported. They had found that motor coordination and balance tasks were highly related to the intellectual achievement of normal children.

The retarded child is usually two to four years behind the normal child on performance measures. In fact, motor performance appears to be more evenly equated when comparing the mental ages of children. The pattern of learning skills, that is, developmentally, is basically the same for both normal and subnormal boys and girls. However, at a given chronological age, the retarded perform with lesser degree of skill than normal children.

Can physical educators assist the retarded in improving their cognitive processes? A few studies have reported remarkable contributions of physical education programs to the total growth of subnormal children. Oliver (1958) matched two groups of mentally deficient boys. One group (the experimental group) had a ten-week course in conditioning; the other group (the control group) did not. For the experimental group, all academic subjects except arithmetic and English were replaced by physical education activities. The control group continued under their regular program. Both groups were given pre- and post-physical and mental tests. The experimental group improved significantly on both the physical and mental tests, and Oliver hypothesized that the change was because of the effect of achievement and success, improved adjustment, improved physical fitness, and the effect of feeling important. The experimental group improved significantly on many physical, motor, and intelligence measures, and their IQ significantly *improved 25 per cent!*

It might be concluded, then, that motor proficiency is directly related to intellectual ability, when groups of intellectually subnormal and normal children are compared. Children who range within the normal intelligence limits are not distinguished on motor-skill measures. This point has been well brought out in an experiment by Asmussen and Heebøll-Nielson (1956). Out of 204 boys, three groups were formed, two within the normal

IQ limits and one below them. They were tested on the vertical jump, strength of the leg extensors and finger flexors, and maximum expiration and inspiration force. These tests did not distinguish performers within the normal range, but did distinguish the low-IQ group from the other two. The investigators concluded that there is no difference in performance as long as the IQ is above 95. Below this (their low group had an IQ average of 83) performance is lower than in normal boys.

Although it might seem reasonable to expect the intellectually gifted to do exceptionally well in motor-skill performance because the retarded are below average efficiency, this is not the case. General findings indicate that a greater intellect and outstanding academic achievement are not related to physical performance.

PERSONALITY

An individual's personality, his characteristic way of behaving, is the result of learning and experiences in life. Heredity sets limits and predisposes the person to react in certain ways to environmental events. One's actions and feelings are the result of previous experiences; and the interaction of many traits, some more modifiable than others, determines his particular uniqueness. Personality may be viewed from two vantage points. One, the effect or impact an individual has on other people usually results in his evaluation on a social basis. For instance, is he pleasing and popular? Besides this so-called *external* personality, another type may represent the *real* him. Personality, according to most experts in this area, should be defined in terms of the way a person really is, not necessarily the way others see him. Other people may not see the real him. In determining an individual's personality, a difficult endeavor indeed, an indication of his behavioral patterns and actions is also uncovered. When we know an individual's personality, we understand him better. To know someone's personality, then, is to be able to predict his behavior.

Composition of Personality

This book does not undertake to delve into the many diverse interpretations of personality theories offered as to how personality develops and affects behavior. We are more concerned with a basic understanding of the term *personality*, in order to make it easier to discuss the interrelationships between personality and motor activity.

Let us accept Guilford's (1959) view that personality is composed of a unique pattern of traits. He groups these traits in classes called modalities,

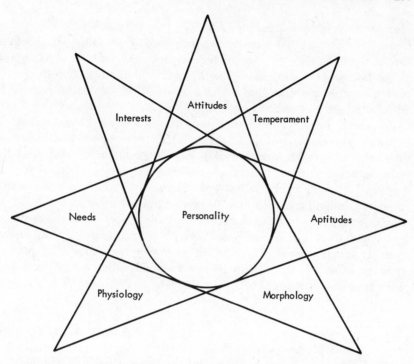

Figure 7-16.   Modalities of traits representing different aspects of personality. [From J. P. Guilford, *Personality* (New York: McGraw-Hill Book Co., Inc., 1959).]

and a diagram of the modalities of traits that interact to compose personality is found in Figure 7–16. He distinguishes modalities pertaining to the following features: soma, motivation, aptitude, and temperament.

The *somatic* modality includes physiological and morphological traits. The former concerns organic functions and the latter physical structure, such as height and weight. Three traits—needs, interests, and attitudes—are encompassed in the *motivational* modality. The *aptitude* modality includes one's abilities to perform at given tasks. Finally, the *temperament* modality refers to those traits that make up a person's disposition.

Rather than observing most traits, we observe acts that represent traits. These acts, indicating the nature of one's traits, serve to remind us that traits differ as to degree, not in kind, from person to person. The above traits (and perhaps many more) interact in such a way as to represent a distinct individual. Because most traits are modifiable, in varying degrees, personality can be looked upon as a general characteristic that also may be adapted. Perhaps this is one of the leading concepts guiding physical educators in believing that their organized programs will have beneficial effects on the participant's social, emotional, and personal behavior. The process of change, though, is slow and tedious. The true personality develops gradually. A quiet, sensitive person does not become an outgoing, devil-may-care individual overnight. An emotionally unstable person took many years to get that way; it will take a lengthy period of time for him to learn socially desirable qualities. Certain traits are relatively stable throughout life, whereas others are modified more easily with new experiences.

This discussion leads to another problem. How do we know what type of personality one has? How do we measure it? A reference to personality type infers the relative arrangement of a large segment of general behavioral characteristics. Without general classifications, it can be stated that everyone has a different personality type. Therefore it is quite convenient to categorize individuals according to predetermined criteria. Typically, personality-measuring techniques and devices are concerned with the motivational modality (needs, interests, and attitudes) and the temperament modality. There are many methods of measuring these aspects of personality, each of which contributes to our knowledge but not without being prone to severe criticism.

Measuring Personality

Because personality is viewed from diverse points of view, it is understandable that approaches for its measurement should also range in many directions. Personality is assessed from (1) interviews, (2) observation, (3) ratings, (4) projective tasks, and (5) psychological inventories. Defined personality types will be dependent on the evaluative tools used.

Interviews, observations, and ratings are quite subjective means of determining personality. Interview and observational techniques are self-explanatory; ratings are usually obtained from rating scales in which the rater develops a number of questions or statements for measuring certain attributes and proceeds to rate the subject on each phase, not discretely but to the degree that it pertains to the subject. Ratings may be on a 1 to 5 basis, with 1 indicating little relevance to the subject and 5 indicating extreme relevance. In any case a scale is formulated in order that the attributes may be measured in degrees rather than absolutes.

Projection-type tests are primarily used as clinical tools and they should be administered and evaluated by clinically trained psychologists. These tests contain unstructured stimulus objects, and as such, the subject is encouraged to respond freely to certain stimuli and thus reveal his true personality. Probably the two most popular and widely used instruments are the Rorschach ink-blot test and the Thematic Apperception Test (TAT). The Rorschach test consists of a series of cards, each containing a complex ink blot about which the subject is asked to interpret and orally express himself. Ambiguous situations concerning people are represented by the TAT pictures. The person is asked to relate a story concerning each picture orally. In all projection tests, it is hoped that the subject will project himself in his interpretations.

By far the most frequently used technique for obtaining information on a person's personality is through the personality inventory. This may be verified by merely glancing at the completed research on personality in psychology, education, and physical education. Inventories usually contain questions or statements concerning personal feelings, attitudes, and interests, and are designed to measure various aspects of one's personality. As such, they are easy to score (although validity measures may be questioned), permit group testing, and do not require an exceptional amount of administration time or clinical background on the part of the examiner.

They have been criticized on various fronts, namely: falsifications on the part of the respondent, willful or otherwise; the questions are interpreted differently by different people; the individual may not know himself well enough to respond accurately; and the test items are questionable in terms of what they are supposed to be measuring.

Here are some of the more popular instruments for making personality inventories.

1. *The Minnesota Multiphasic Personality Inventory (MMPI).* This is probably the most clinically oriented, and is used extensively in research. It was designed to diagnose pathological conditions, not for discriminating individuals from a normal population, yet it is amazing how often it is employed in the latter case in published research.

2. *The Cattell 16 Personality Factor Test.* This is another popular instrument. Through the factor-analysis method, Cattell obtained 16 independent scales representing aspects of the personality.

3. *The California Test of Personality (CPI).* This has been designed with four variations, for four different age groups from elementary school to college.

4. *The Edward's Personal Preference Schedule (EPPS).* This test is based on needs and is scored in such a way as to determine one's need to achieve, to be dominant, to affiliate, and the like. It is one of the few instruments that employs the forced-choice technique; that is, the interviewee is faced with paired descriptions (each unrelated) of himself for each question, and he must select the one that best represents him.

There are many other personality inventories currently in use, but those mentioned here probably are representative of those used. An easy-to-read paperback, prepared by Jozef Cohen (1969), provides a reasonable discussion and analysis of the various means of appraising personality.

By our definition of personality, everything we do will have an effect on us. By the same token, our behavior will be determined by unique personal characteristics. Personality relationships to motor activity is an important area of study in the psychology of sport. A number of studies have been completed on such topics as (1) differences in personalities between athletes and nonathletes, (2) differences in personalities between better and lesser athletes, (3) personality comparisons among various athletic groups, and (4) social status and athletic achievement. Personality variables, with the exception of anxiety and related emotional states, have rarely until recent years been the concern of motor-learning researchers. Yet it should be readily apparent that behavioral systems differ greatly in output because of personality distinctions among them. Attitudes toward the learning and performing of a task, the felt need to achieve, and interest in the activity are all aspects of personality contributing to performance yields.

Values and Attitudes

Our feelings toward something, our dispositions to evaluate and/or act in a certain way to certain stimuli are learned and develop with experience and maturity or even from tradition. These attitudes or ways of regarding something become more pronounced with age. They may be formed because of personal experience with the object or in the situation, rendering favorable or unfavorable attitudes. Complete lack of personal involvement will not hinder the formation of attitudes, for tradition, culture, subculture, and familial attitude formation encourage similar thought patterns in the member. For example, there are many people who have no valid reason for disliking blacks and Jews, yet do so because of traditional biases. In this case, an attitude is a predisposition to evaluate someone or something as good or bad, as desirable or undesirable.

The importance of the many types of experiences occurring with age in influencing attitudinal patterns has been demonstrated in experiments as well as through empirical observations. Extremely young children do not display the prejudices older children do, and adulthood brings fairly well-established attitudes. With age comes a greater awareness of social expectancies and pressures and a desire to conform to the value system of a culture or subculture.

The introduction of the word *value* in the previous sentence serves to place it in the context of our discussion and to point out its relationship to an attitude. The value system of a society establishes certain standards that provide direction to an attitude and account for its persistence. Attitudes are conditioned by values, they are not inseparable. Our attitude to make a choice from a number of alternatives is mediated by personal values. Some psychologists think of values as generalized attitudes, because attitudes supposedly have fairly specific objects. Regardless of semantics, both have a place in personality formation. The sequence of events leading to a value choice may be thought to occur in the following manner:

Expression of personality → attitudes and values → motivation → choice

Attitudes and values are primarily social in nature but also represent the individualized response. In other words, although social pressure will result in a great amount of conformity, each person perceives situations differently and varies in needs, desires, values, and other characteristics. Not only will individuals react dissimilarly in situations, but the same individuals may not be consistent in their values. The question of whether a person is dominated by a single unitary value system or demonstrates inconsistent values is a debatable issue. Once again, it appears as if people may fall into either category.

An interesting topic is the relationship of established attitudes to learning. If the matter to be learned contradicts these attitudes, possibly learning and retention will be hampered. One of the best examples of this occurrence has been reported by Levine and Murphy (1943) concerning the learning of controversial material. Learning as we have seen is not a simple conditioning process, and even our values and needs affect our perception and ultimately what we learn. This attitudinal effect on learning has been designated as *frame of reference*.

In the Levine and Murphy experiment two groups were formed, one strongly pro-communist and the other strongly anti-communist. All subjects first learned neutral prose material in order to determine their relative abilities at this task, and both groups were rated as being similar. Following this, both groups learned two passages, one pro-communist, the other anti-communist. They studied for four weeks and were tested for retention during a five-week period, and the data are illustrated in the form of curves in Figures 7–17 and 7–18.

Although the pro-Soviet selection did not distinguish the two groups significantly during the learning phase of the study, a significant difference in favor of the pro-communist group was observed during the retention period. A significant marked superiority of the anti-communist group over the pro-communist group on the anti-Soviet selection was found both during learning and retention test intervals. There is a tendency selectively to perceive and recall, to remember that which supports our social attitudes rather than that which conflicts with them.

An application of this knowledge may be made to the learning of motor skills. If the athlete or student does not respect the coach or teacher or agree with what is being taught, these negative attitudes will suppress learning effectiveness. Many times a person thinks he knows how a skill should be performed, and if he is set in his attitude, his unwillingness to accept a new learning approach will be evidenced in a lack of progress. Perhaps even more serious is the situation whereby the coach or instructor is not respected either as a person or for his seeming lack of knowledge and poor teaching ability. The barrier formed between learner and teacher will be difficult to overcome and certainly will not represent a favorable learning situation.

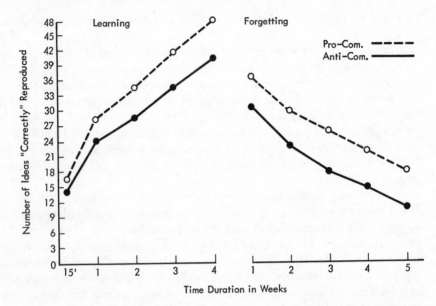

Figure 7–17.   Learning and forgetting curves for "correct" responses for pro-communist and anti-communist groups on the pro-Soviet selection. (From J. M. Levine and Gardner Murphy, "Learning and Forgetting of Controversial Material," *Journal of Abnormal and Social Psychology,* 38:507–517, 1943.)

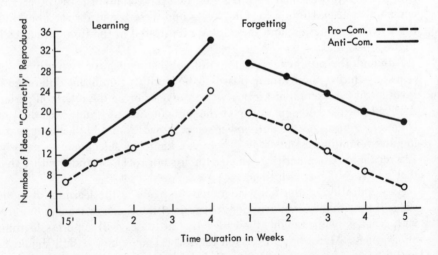

Figure 7–18.   Learning and forgetting curves for "correct" responses for pro-communist and anti-communist groups on the anti-Soviet selection. (From J. M. Levine and Gardner Murphy, "Learning and Forgetting of Controversial Material," *Journal of Abnormal and Social Psychology,* 38:507–517, 1943.)

Need to Achieve

Various types of activities service the needs and interests of people. Interests may be thought of as attitudes we have with respect to certain objectives. Usually attitudes refer to social or political opinions and feelings, interests to vocational or physical activity preferences. Needs are deeply rooted in biological drives and as such might be thought of as presupposing interests.

Needs determine behavior, for the body is in a state of disequilibrium when a need state is aroused. An individual's personality can be explained through needs. A person's actions are caused by an interaction of his personality needs and the surrounding environmental stimuli but are modified and restricted by social sanctions. In other words, the forces within an organism drive him to search for or react to various environmental objects.

It is commonly thought that needs can best be met through involvement in need-gratifying activities, and athletic participation helps to meet certain needs. Not only this, but the nature of the sport, e.g., team, individual, recreational, body-building, will dictate which needs are best met. The needs of athletes versus those of nonathletes have not been studied at any great depth. One investigation reported by Meyers and Ohnmacht (1963) found no difference in needs between participants in intramurals and interscholastics and nonparticipants. The subjects were junior high school pupils evaluated on a need instrument called the Self-Descriptive Form.

Successful undertakings are often dependent upon need to achieve. Of the many aspects of one's personality, though, need to achieve is probably not a sufficiently powerful trait to insure proficiency. There must be an ideal proportion and interaction of the many desirable traits. The relationship of a person's motivation or need achievement and his anxiety level on performance has been investigated by Atkinson and Litwin (1960). Evidently these two variables interact in such a way as to determine predictability of behavior.

These writers ascertained the need for achievement and test anxiety levels of their college subjects who were to perform in a ring toss game. The students were told to stand any distance up to 15 feet from the wooden peg and attempt to toss a ring over the peg. They thought they were being measured for score, but in actuality it was their chosen distance from the peg that was recorded. Subjects high in need for achievement but low in test anxiety preferred a distance of 9 to 11 feet away from the peg—of intermediate range. Those subjects who were low in need for achievement and high in anxiety level took the least number of attempts at the intermediate range; they performed primarily at the extreme distances. The other types of students selected distances somewhere between these two classified groups of subjects. In applying these findings to other types of testing situations, it would appear that a high need to achieve coupled with a low test-anxiety level results in realistically high levels of aspiration and superior performance. The inhibitive effects of high anxiety on complex test performance will be discussed shortly.

EMOTIONS

Rarely is a person not emotionally involved to some extent in any activity in which he performs. Emotions, like instincts and habits, are basically involuntary. They determine actions, and if strong enough, emotions will initiate activity before there is involvement of the higher nervous centers. Emotions or feelings represent a wide range of states in the human organism: joy and happiness, anxiety and fear, stress, and sorrow to name only a few. Even an individual who is motivated to do something would have his attitude changed, if he proceeds in a different emotional state. Not only are there many forms of emotion, but as many if not more varied causes. The athlete may be anxious before the event, fear his competition, dread the consequences, and/or react poorly in front of spectators. Although these emotions may be considered to have a negative effect, other emotional states, e.g., the optimal degrees of stress and motivation for the individual participant, will promote better performance. Emotions are a part of any activity, whether caused by the environment, the activity itself, or the mind of the performer.

Physiologically speaking, the parts of the brain involved in emotion appear to be the reticular activating system and the limbic system (parts of the thalamus, hypothalamus, and inner cortex). Pleasure and pain areas associated with the autonomic nervous system are located within the limbic system. During various emotions, such as stress, glands are stimulated and hormones are secreted in an attempt to recover body homeostasis (internal body equilibrium).

The word *emotion* means "agitation of the feelings" (from the French word *émouvoir*, "to stir up"). Emotion may be referred to in two ways: (1) as a conscious experience or feeling, or (2) by the physiological changes that take place within the body as a result of it. Emotions are psychological and physiological responses and reactions resulting from perceived situations. Some authorities feel that emotions are a special class of motives, whereas others disagree. There is no doubt, though, that emotions, much like motivation, may have an organizing or disorganizing effect on performance.

Although we are born with certain basic emotional instincts, other factors later influence them. Maturation brings about the development of various emotions, although many of them can be learned and even conditioned. Both maturation and learning increase emotions in number and complexity.

A person's emotion, his reaction to a particular stimulus, can be observed in his everyday behavior or in the research laboratory under controlled conditions. Under the latter condition, it is possible directly or indirectly to measure physiological changes taking place in the organism. Some methods employed in research efforts include:

1. *Measuring respirations,* their depth and rate. An increase is associated with an emotional state.
2. *Measuring body temperature.* It may rise or fall, depending on the nature of the stimulus and its particular effect on the organism.
3. *Determining amount of sweating.* It increases with the onset of stronger emotions.
4. *Analyzing electrical potentials of the brain (EEG or electroencephalogram).* They become irregular during emotional conditions.

Other specific physiological alterations are associated with particular types of emotions, such as stress and anxiety. It would be impossible to discuss here the impact all the various types of emotions have on the individual and his performance of motor skills. However, the general categories of tension, anxiety, and stress are familiar to most people, and research provides some interesting thoughts concerning them.

Tension

Tension may imply nervous reactions to situations, i.e., a mental feeling of anguish and overall bodily unrest, or the state of certain muscles of the body acting against a resistance. Physical educators are concerned with both conditions. In the first, hopefully, participation in physical activities would relieve the symptoms and suppress their tendency to occur. The second situation is most necessary for the successful performance of certain skills, for varying degrees of strength provide the basis for making participation possible.

Muscular tension and its relationship to motor-skill performance has been investigated by a few researchers who were interested in discovering the facilitating or detrimental effects of muscular tension on performance. Tension provides a state of arousal and a level of activation in the individual, and as such, is an aspect of emotion and motivation. The results of the research have been conflicting. For instance, Freeman (1938) tested his subjects on finger oscillation, mirror drawing, mental arithmetic, touch threshold, and the eyelid reflex during conditions of changing pressures on the body. It was concluded that body tension adversely affected the more complex tasks.

On the other hand, Eason and White (1961) found that tension led to better performance in rotary-tracking tasks where the tension was the result of effort at the same task. The authors reported these results from a series of five experiments with highly skilled subjects. It might be noted that tension in the study by Freeman was induced by a stimulus other than the task itself, whereas in the Eason and White experiment beneficial tension results were obtained from the effort displayed for the experimental task itself. When effort (tension) was associated with a second task, poorer performances occurred on the first one.

A third investigation, by Bell (1959) required tension to be induced by a weight, a 5- or 10-pound dumbbell held in the nonpreferred hand as the subjects were performing on the pursuit rotor. Other subjects were given motivational instructions as a means for inducing muscular tension. No significant differences in performance were noted when comparing the two methods of causing tension.

In these three studies, tension was induced by different means and the tasks varied. The results were not in agreement. Research is lacking on the direct effect of tension on the learning and performing of skills. Perhaps the nature of many motor skills is such as to provide enough tension in the performer without the necessity of additionally induced tension.

Anxiety

Anxiety can refer to a perfectly normal reaction to a given situation or to a type of neurosis. Anxiety states, which include symptoms of continuing unexplained fear, are the most common of personality disturbances. Anxiety and fear are terms used interchangeably in psychological research, as anxiety denotes a signal of danger to the organism leading to a protective defense.

Other theorists see anxiety not as a disrupter of effective action but rather as a main drive to action. Whether anxiety is to be considered as a neurosis or as a condition similar to stress, which might facilitate performance, depends on the context in which the term is used. Stress and anxiety have often been used as interchangeable terms and observable symptoms would tend to encourage this practice. Although there have been a number of attempts to distinguish these concepts, many present-day scholars feel that an anxiety state really is the same as the stress a person feels in a particular situation.

Most research in the area of anxiety has been concerned with comparing the performance of anxious versus nonanxious subjects on motor-skill tasks and written tests. Some researchers claim that anxiety disrupts and disorganizes behavior through a lowering of attention, concentration, and intellectual control. Supposedly there is a reduction in perceptual efficiency under anxiety. However, low levels of anxiety provide a general alerting mechanism whereby the organism can distinguish environmental stimuli better.

The Manifest Anxiety Scale [Taylor (1953)] and other written tests have been used to determine the anxiety level of a person.

The MAS is presented in Table 7–1. For many years it was the most popularly used test in research undertaken in the area of anxiety. At the present time, it is seriously being rivaled by Charles Spielberger's (1968) State-Trait Anxiety Inventory (STAI) for theoretical acceptance, in clinical usage, and as a research tool.

The MAS was developed from the drive-theory concepts of Hull and Spence. Taylor assumed that anxiety had drive properties, and that more anxious subjects could be conditioned in certain simple behavior more easily than less anxious subjects. Rainer Martens (1971), however, has found fault with the notion that drive theory can explain complex motor behavior satisfactorily. He favors the inverted-U hypothesis instead.

Theoretically, drive theory would support the notion that increased arousal, such as that caused by increased motivational level, results in improved performance. However, it is doubtful that this is true for all tasks. Those that require energy expenditure and effort would probably be best described by the predictable linear relationship between drive state and performance. There is another theory that is often described as a rival to drive theory. Termed the inverted-U hypothesis, it is usually discussed in terms of arousal, or activation theory. The hypothesis predicts a non-monotonic relationship between drive level and performance. More specifically, it is predicted that performance improves with increases in arousal, to a point. After that, increases in arousal result in increasingly poor performance. Figure 7–19 illustrates a comparison of these two models. Actually, both drive theory and the inverted-U hypothesis are plausible explainers of behavior. The hypothesis fits tasks requiring control, finesse, and complex skillful execution, whereas drive theory seems best to describe tasks that involve effort.

The STAI has been favored over the MAS because anxiety is viewed as two distinct anxiety concepts instead of one. State anxiety refers to how a person feels at a particular moment in response to a specific situation. Trait anxiety is the general disposition of individuals to respond to psychological stress. Whereas trait anxiety is relatively stable, state anxiety is considered to be a transitory emotional state. Some items from the STAI Inventory are presented in Table 7–2. When comparing anxious to nonanxious subjects on performance tasks, investigators have arrived at conflicting conclusions. This circumstance may be explained partly by the method of determining the personality nature of the subjects and partly by the varying test procedures employed by these experimenters. Such investigations have attempted to discover the effect of anxiety, hence drive, in learning and performance situations.

No major differences between high- and low-anxiety subjects are expected when tasks were not overly difficult. However, on more complex

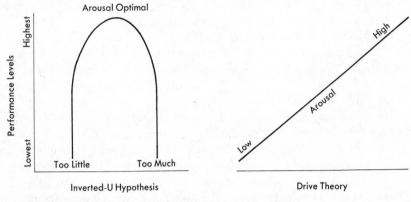

Figure 7–19. The inverted-U hypothesis, showing an optimal arousal level for best performance; drive theory indicating a linear relationship between performance and arousal levels.

TABLE 7–1.   THE TAYLOR MANIFEST ANXIETY SCALE *

Answer "Yes" or "No" after each question.

1. I do not tire quickly. ____
2. I am troubled by attacks of nausea. ____
3. I believe I am no more nervous than most others. ____
4. I have very few headaches. ____
5. I work under a great deal of tension. ____
6. I cannot keep my mind on one thing. ____
7. I worry over money and business. ____
8. I frequently notice my hand shakes when I try to do something. ____
9. I blush no more often than others. ____
10. I have diarrhea once a month or more. ____
11. I worry quite a bit over possible misfortunes. ____
12. I practically never blush. ____
13. I am often afraid that I am going to blush. ____
14. I have nightmares every few nights. ____
15. My hands and feet are usually warm enough. ____
16. I sweat very easily even on cool days. ____
17. Sometimes when embarrassed, I break out in a sweat which annoys me greatly. ____
18. I hardly ever notice my heart pounding and I am seldom short of breath. ____
19. I feel hungry almost all the time. ____
20. I am very seldom troubled by constipation. ____
21. I have a great deal of stomach trouble. ____
22. I have had periods in which I lost sleep over worry. ____
23. My sleep is fitful and disturbed. ____
24. I dream frequently about things that are best kept to myself. ____
25. I am easily embarrassed. ____
26. I am more sensitive than most other people. ____

TABLE 7–1—*Continued*

27. I frequently find myself worrying about something. ____
28. I wish I could be as happy as others seem to be. ____
29. I am usually calm and not easily upset. ____
30. I cry easily. ____
31. I feel anxiety about something or someone almost all the time. ____
32. I am happy most of the time. ____
33. It makes me nervous to have to wait. ____
34. I have periods of such great restlessness that I cannot sit long in a chair. ____
35. Sometimes I become so excited that I find it hard to get to sleep. ____
36. I have sometimes felt that difficulties were piling up so high that I could not overcome them. ____
37. I must admit that I have at times been worried beyond reason over something that really did not matter. ____
38. I have very few fears compared to my friends. ____
39. I have been afraid of things or people that I knew could not hurt me. ____
40. I certainly feel useless at times. ____
41. I find it hard to keep my mind on a task or job. ____
42. I am unusually self-conscious. ____
43. I am inclined to take things hard. ____
44. I am a high-strung person. ____
45. Life is a strain for me much of the time. ____
46. At times I think I am no good at all. ____
47. I am certainly lacking in self-confidence. ____
48. I sometimes feel that I am about to go to pieces. ____
49. I shrink from facing a crisis or difficulty. ____
50. I am entirely self-confident. ____

---

* From Janet A. Taylor, "A Personality Scale of Manifest Anxiety," *Journal of Abnormal and Social Psychology*, 48:285–290, 1953. Copyright 1953 by the American Psychological Association. Reprinted by permission.

tasks, studies generally show that high-anxiety people do worse than those low in anxiety. Also, those who score low on anxiety tests perform more effectively under stress (in complex tasks) than under normal conditions. This is not the case with high-anxiety individuals, who are less effective performers under stress. Even the ability to cope with stress early in learning is shown (Carron, 1968) to be a function of one's anxiety state. Using a stabilometer task and electric shocks, Carron concluded that stress was detrimental to the performance of highly anxious subjects in the early stages of practice. Low-anxiety subjects were hardly affected at all.

With regard to stress effects on the performance of a task at different levels of mastery, a number of researchers have found it convenient to use Clark Hull's drive theory. Apparently stress encourages dominant responses to occur. In any situation a number of alternate responses may be emitted. More complex situations and tasks create the possibility of the occurrence of alternative responses. During the early stages of learning, where incorrect response alternatives are usually dominant, stress would be predicted to be

TABLE 7-2A.   THE TRAIT ANXIETY TEST *

DIRECTIONS: A number of statements which people have used to describe themselves are given below. Read each statement and then circle the appropriate number to the right of the statement to indicate how you *generally* feel.

There are no right or wrong answers. Do not spend too much time on any one statement but give the answer which seems to describe how you generally feel.

	Almost never	Sometimes	Often
21. I feel pleasant	1	2	3
22. I tire quickly	1	2	3
23. I feel like crying	1	2	3
24. I wish I could be as happy as others seem to be	1	2	3

TABLE 7-2B.   THE STATE ANXIETY TEST *

DIRECTIONS: A number of statements which people have used to describe themselves are given below. Read each statement and then circle the appropriate number to the right of the statement to indicate how you feel right now, that is, *at this moment.*

There are no right or wrong answers. Do not spend too much time on any one statement but give the answer which seems to describe your present feelings best.

	Not at all	Somewhat	Moderately so	Very much so
1. I feel calm	1	2	3	4
2. I feel secure	1	2	3	4
3. I am tense	1	2	3	4
4. I am regretful	1	2	3	4

detrimental to performance. When higher levels of skill exist and correct responses are dominant, reasonable stress should benefit performance. The effects of stress will depend on the strength of the to-be-learned (correct) response relative to other competing (incorrect) responses. The impairment–facilitation effects of stress on performance have been discussed by Castaneda and Lipsitt (1959) within the theoretical framework described above.

A checklist instrument has been developed to measure perceived stress in situations, and Jacobs and Thornton (1970) defend its practical significance.

TABLE 7–3.   ITEM CONTENT, MEDIAN INTENSITY VALUES, SEMI-INTERQUARTILE RANGES (Q) AND FACTOR LOADINGS FOR THE PSI ITEMS *

Item no. and content	Median intensity value	Q	Factor loading I	II
6. Extremely terrified	10.72	.50	−.92*	.30
14. Scared stiff	10.04	.54	−.91*	.28
7. Fearful	9.38	.64	−.85*	.44
3. Threatened	8.74	.63	−.91*	.36
1. Distressed	8.24	.64	−.80*	.58
8. Uneasy	7.60	.65	−.75*	.60
5. Timid	7.21	.69	.95*	−.03
11. Not mattering	5.98	.32	.96*	.05
2. Unruffled	5.68	.68	.87*	−.37
10. Alright	5.12	.80	.85*	−.39
4. At ease	4.47	1.01	.75*	−.44
15. Keen	3.77	.70	.27	−.92*
13. Feeling good	2.99	.50	.38	−.91*
9. Marvelous	2.30	.64	.32	−.92*
12. Thrilled	1.97	.60	.18	−.98*

* From Paul D. Jacobs and David C. Munz. "An Index for Measuring Perceived Stress in a College Population," *The Journal of Psychology*, 70:9–15, 1968.

They found the self-report stress instrument, the Perceived Stress Index (PSI), to be sufficiently sensitive in distinguishing among groups of subjects administered different instructional sets as to forthcoming shock treatments. In an earlier publication, Jacobs and Murry (1968) present the final fifteen-item checklist with pleasant to unpleasant words and phrases ranging along a continuum (see Table 7–3).

Krahenbuhl (1971) was able to use level of catecholamine in the urine as a measure of stress reactivity. Six college tennis players were tested under basal, practice, competition anticipation, and competition circumstances. An elevation of catecholamines is related to physical exertion as well as to various emotional states. A significant difference in catecholamine levels between practice and actual competition situations appeared to show that the psychic variable more than physical activity influenced stress reactivity. No differences were noted between basal and practice conditions.

An obvious question and a real concern in training programs is whether procedures can be developed to prepare performers effectively for stressful conditions that might agree with real conditions. Assuming that stress of sufficient magnitude can be detrimental to performance, how can this circumstance be planned for and controlled in a reasonable way? If resistance to stress can be trained for, then it behooves the designer of training programs to build in appropriate mechanisms for this effect. In one of the few investigations on the topic, Prather, Berry, and Jones (1972) examined this problem along with other related concerns. These authors concluded that it was possible to train a resistance to aversive conditions. Implications are that training programs should include moderate stressful conditions that are related to the kind that will be present in real performance situations. Transfer of training would be quite positive and desirable. Always remember that proficiency in performance depends not only on the ability to coordinate appropriate responses to cues, but also on the demand characteristics of the situation.

This type of information is extremely pertinent to a better teacher-learner and coach-athlete situation. Understanding the personality nature of each of his students will enable the teacher to be more aware of possible problems. He may expect some students to learn certain tasks with ease and others to experience great difficulty with these same tasks.

Stress

Stress is another term which has meant different things to different people. However, through the earlier efforts of Cannon and other physiologists and recently, Hans Selye, the public has been greatly enlightened as to the nature of stress. Stress, which is unavoidable, results from psychological, physiological, and emotional origins.

Any situation or activity places the individual under stress, anything can cause it. Sometimes it is desirable, sometimes not; nevertheless, we are continually under stress. What may be stressful to one person may not be so to another, and one condition may promote or be detrimental to the performances of different people. A representative example of this paradox is the effect of spectators on athletic performance. Some athletes perform poorer in actual competition before an audience than in practice; thus, this circumstance is detrimentally stressful to them. Others perform about the same under both practice and game-like conditions and are relatively unaffected. Still other athletes put on a superior demonstration in front of spectators; it would appear that to them this stress is beneficial.

It is commonly observed that certain situations are stressful to some people. By the same token, some situations are generally stressful to everyone. Regardless of the cause, the general state of stress is apparently physiologically reacted to in a specific pattern of internal adjustments. Stress symptoms are nonspecifically caused but result in a specific physiologic state involving specific physiologic processes. It is a state that disrupts the homeostasis (internal body equilibrium) of the body.

Selye (1956) felt that the average reader encountered difficulty in understanding the preceding definition of stress, and he modified it to read ". . .

the rate of wear and tear on the body." Life is a process of adaptation, and Selye, through his numerous publications, has attempted to describe how the body specifically copes with stress. He postulates a *General Adaptation Syndrome* (*G.A.S.*) composed of three states:

1. *Alarm-reaction stage.* The body is prepared to defend and does; it is in a state of readiness.
2. *Stage of resistance.* The organism is able to do regular tasks as the body handles the stress.
3. *Stage of exhaustion.* The stress situation is too severe; death results.

Stress is most evident in the alarm-reaction stage and usually causes a total response of the body. It is minimized in the second stage as specific parts of the body are involved in handling a particular stress. Obviously, a typical stress does not go past this stage. The reaction of stress, then, affects the entire body first and specific body defenses later. Besides proposing the G.A.S., Selye also suggested the L.A.S., *the Local Adaptation Syndrome,* a local stress response, an example of which is inflammation.

Selye noted that all three types of stress caused certain physiological adjustments to occur. *The triad,* as he termed them, includes adrenal-cortex enlargement, shrinkage of the lymphatic structures, and the development of bleeding and ulcers in the stomach. During stress situations, the pituitary gland and adrenals react to return the body back to normal. Eosinophil (a type of white blood cell) count decreases considerably and respirations increase when a person is in a state of stress.

The prediction of performance under various stressful conditions is an important problem facing educators and trainers. Associated with this problem is the consideration of a general resistance factor to stress; more specifically, do individuals who react favorably to the effects of one stress do likewise to a second type of stress? To answer this question, Parsons, Phillips, and Lane (1954) had fifty-seven industrial workers perform on the Dunlap hand-steadiness apparatus. The task required the subjects to keep a stylus from touching the side of a hole one-eighth of an inch in diameter. Stress was introduced during performance either by distraction or by informing the subjects of failure through false results and comments. No significant relationship was obtained between the two stress performance scores, therefore not substantiating the concept of a general resistance factor to stress.

The physiological and psychological effects of stress have been tested. Michael (1957) reviewed the literature and concluded that adaptation to exercise (physical stress) provides a degree of protection against emotional stress. This statement would appear to indicate the transfer effects of stress resistance from one situation to another. Ulrich (1957) measured the physiological effects of psychological stress. She tested twenty-eight college women students (a) under normal conditions; (b) anticipating one of a number of events—such as a basketball game, a written test, and participation in the game—but then being deprived; and (c) after the stressor condition. Blood samples, particularly eosinophil counts, pulse rates, and respiration rates were determined under all three conditions. Ulrich found stress to be caused by anticipation as well as participation or denial after expectancy.

Research indicates that stress affects complex tasks in a different manner from simple tasks. Stress is usually more disruptive for the learning and performing of complex tasks, whereas simple task performance either is not affected or else is facilitated under stress. Other studies suggest that if a stress is introduced early in the learning of a skill, it will be more disruptive than if introduced later. Frequently, if the skill has been learned well enough, the effects of stress will be unnoticed. In some cases, stress will improve performance with increased learning.

There is great practical importance in understanding the effects of stress on the learning and performing of motor skills. Emotional disturbances, such as stress, may benefit, disrupt, or have no effect on a particular individual learning a specific skill. Emotional factors in general, then, are interwoven in every learning situation. Their effects will depend on the nature of the organism and the stimulus situation, which includes the to-be-learned skill and its relative difficulty, the stage of learning, and the surrounding conditions.

FORM

Just as an individual differs in the nature and extent of his abilities and characteristics, the manner in which he executes various motor patterns will probably be dissimilar to another's style. This method of expressing movement with a purpose, the way of doing something, is called *form*. The specific characteristics of one performer's act makes him different from others, sometimes worthy of emulation, other times best forgotten. Although form in executing skills is unique from person to person, generally accepted *good form* is usually associated with the outstanding athlete in a given sport. The desirability of molding a beginner in the style of the champion is open to question; certainly reasons may be provided for and against such a practice.

Differences

Differences in form exist between performers. Sometimes these differences may be extremely slight so as to be almost unnoticed by the untrained eye, or they are obvious to all. The following factors are associated with form dissimilarities: (1) skill of the performer in the particular act or sport; (2) his personality; (3) his age; (4) the nature of the act or sport, e.g., its complexity; and (5) the' physical characteristics of the performer.

Simple acts can be fulfilled in a similar manner from individual to individual. Form uniqueness becomes more observable when the act becomes more detailed, when there are a series of events that constitute a skill, or when gross motor movements are involved in the act. Most physical education skills are considered to be gross, as compared to the fine motor skills of tracing, typing, and tracking. Therefore participants in gross skills are more apt to display observable form differences.

The nature of the performer, physically, mentally, and emotionally, will decide the method he employs to perform. Some people are more flamboyant or introverted, and their personality may be reflected in their actions. Secondly, skill already attained in the to-be-performed act(s) distinguishes success and form. If we assume that the outstanding athlete generally displays good form, it is apparent that a beginner will not be able to duplicate it until he has had more experience. Thirdly, physical attributes determine performance potential as to relative skill attainment and the form in displaying it. Height, weight, body build, strength, flexibility, and other physical and motor factors usually moderate the manner in which one performs. In other words, the available means often contribute to the style of expression.

Maturation, from infancy to adolescence, often facilitates motor-skill performance. Children frequently have to approximate the way a skill should be ideally performed. Desired form in skill performance is assisted by mature minds and bodies, with knowing what to do and having the available resources with which to do it.

Relevance to Success in Skill Attainment

Successful performance may be displayed through a variety of forms and techniques, but it is rare when they violate established performance principles. In other words, for a given act or sequence of skills, there is a generally accepted good form, consistent with kinesiological, physical, and psychological evidence, with variations of the ideal form. This is not to deny the possibility of success in spite of form, but rather to emphasize the probability of success and form going together.

In actuality, in most sports, the outcome is more important than the means. Some sports, such as gymnastics and diving, are judged on skill and form. However, the baseball coach will not tamper with the batting style of a .300 hitter, even if he hits with his "foot in the bucket." The avid baseball spectator can readily picture the differences between the stances of Stan Musial and Ted Williams, yet both were great hitters. Evidently, at the point of ball contact with the bat both men had coordinated their body parts in a similar fashion, and both hit effectively for many years.

Some people have to adjust their style because of body build and other factors. Consistent conscientious practice can overcome many limitations. The displayed form may not be aesthetic, but effectiveness of the movement can be measured by the results. Perhaps one of the greatest problems the parent, physical educator, and coach is confronted with, is that of the youngster attempting to emulate a professional athlete, his particular idol. On the one hand, the practice is good, for the boy may gain great insight into the nature of the sport and the means of attaining success. However, progress may be impeded by differences in physical characteristics, age, and other factors.

It is usually poor practice, therefore, for a beginner or even an advanced learner to attempt to copy every phase of an act or activity from someone else. The physical educator and coach should explain the reasons for executing a movement in a certain style and then expect and allow for individual variations. Robots do not make the best performers. Form, to a certain extent, provides direction for the learner and facilitates the learning process, but probably not to the degree imagined in years past. If it is possible to designate a performer as displaying such a thing, reasonable form is to be expected for probable success in skill attainment. A thought to remember is that the ideal form for a given act is continually remodeled as new evidence is accumulated. Therefore open-mindedness and flexibility in style are necessary in order to take advantage of the research that points to more effective means of executing acts.

Aesthetic Appeal

One of the prime reasons for the demonstration of a certain form, other than that of scientific substantiation, is often merely to satisfy aesthetic appeal. Posture varies from person to person as does the concept of what good posture actually is, even so, form and ideal conceptual form for athletic performance also vary among individuals. Good posture implies either effective posture or pleasing-to-the-eye posture, or both, but these two conditions are not necessarily related. An individual can demonstrate physical efficiency with a scoliosis, lordosis, or kyphosis.

Good form can be likened to good posture. Is the reference to effectiveness, attractiveness, or both? Each type of good form can occur independently or in conjunction with the other. Whereas in the past the saying was, "Do it because it looks good," athletes now are more concerned with their own effectiveness in the performed skills, even if it means sacrificing aesthetic appeal.

For the same reasons that a pleasing posture impresses people and may promote an inner feeling of confidence, good form in skill execution can also be advocated. Professional and varsity athletes want to look good—aesthetically and skillfully—in front of spectators. A unique form, sometimes called showmanship when displayed at an extreme, helps to sell the player and sport to the fans. As long as skill is not worsened, this practice will serve its purpose. However, it is important for the individual to realize when he is performing primarily for aesthetic appeal and when he is performing for effectiveness. Ego involvement is the basis for one, whereas science is the foundation of the other.

LEVEL OF SKILL

In most situations learners possess a wide range of developed skills and potential abilities for achievement. The magnitude of the range will depend on whether the students are grouped at random or there is an attempt at homogeneity. It is often convenient to categorize students learning an activity as beginners, intermediates, or advanced. This classification is arbitrary, for individuals fall in a continuum on the range of skill development. Recognizing differences in achieved level of skill allows the educator or trainer to proceed in a more effective manner, for each level requires special learning considerations.

Considerations at Different Levels

At the onset, it should be emphasized that certain learning principles apply to the acquisition of motor skills, regardless of skill level. One of the major purposes of this book is to relate the general considerations for all learners. However, the status of the individual in skill achievement in a particular activity necessitates specific allowances and unique considerations. As might be expected, teaching techniques should be modified from the beginning to the advanced stages of an individual's motor-skill development.

The beginner, the person learning a specific skill for the first time, poses problems to the instructor unlike those he confronts with a highly skilled performer. Unfortunately, the beginner is often neglected, for it is much more rewarding to direct the progress of individuals who are highly skilled, coordinated, and motivated. Each novice requires individual attention, although in many cases this might be impractical. What general procedures, then, may be followed to promote learning in a group of beginners?

First, beginners must *understand the goal* that they will be attempting to achieve. If it is to swim the side-stroke the length of the pool, they should observe a demonstration of this stroke in its entirety. They will then become aware of what is to be expected, of how the parts of the body are coordinated for this skill, and generally, what lies ahead of them. The old adage of quickly immersing the learner into the activity for best results may be effective in elevating motivation or performing general movements but may not really be of most advantage in skill acquisition. Assuming the maturity of the organism, a clear picture of behavioral expectancies should be developed.

Second, beginners appear to *benefit most from activity*, thus verbal instruction should be kept to a minimum. Naturally, with increased age and maturity, there is less impatience and perhaps a greater mental capacity on the part of the students enabling them to benefit from verbal instruction. However, the generally accepted rule with beginners is to allow the actual physical activity to dominate the early lessons.

Third, this activity may be initiated by the performer or directed from *external sources*, such as the teacher manipulating a particular body area in order for the novice to get the feel of the desired movement. At the early stage of skill attainment, there is the unresolved question of introducing the mechanical and physiological principles related to the skill performance as well as the merit of using the problem-solving approach, of directing the students to attempt to determine the why's and the how's in their quest for skill mastery. Visual aids, in the form of movies, slides, and pictures are possible supplementary material. The methods and means of instruction to be utilized will depend on the background, nature, and ideas of the teacher. There is no one set method of instruction. The point here, though, is that *physical activity should be emphasized in the early stages of motor learning.* This is especially true with younger children.

The physical experience allows additional methods of instruction to be more meaningful. Attention to detail can then be provided in verbal instruction. Specifics can only be attended to when the general aspects of an activity have been mastered. One of the greatest mistakes a teacher can make with beginners is to spend too much time on details and talking too much.

The results of an investigation by Renshaw and Postle (1928) will serve to reinforce the concept of the importance of motor activity for beginners. These researchers formed three groups, all of whom learned a pursuit-rotor task. Group I received very brief demonstrations and instruction, Group II had additional instruction, and Group III observed a simple demonstration with detailed instructions. Groups I and II performed similarly on the task; Group III demonstrated the poorest performance. In this case, greater verbal instructions had the effect of impeding the acquisition of manipulatory skill. As Renshaw and Postle reason, progress in some motor skills may be inhibited where language (verbal habits) cannot substitute for direct sensory stimuli afforded by the task. The study is aptly and humorously concluded with the statement that the pursuit rotor is operated by the hands, not the voice box.

A learner will probably fare better in a skill new to him if the teacher attempts to build on skills familiar and already known to the learner. Resemblances of already-learned skills to those to be learned, if pointed out, promote faster learning. At least one leading tennis authority believes that it is quite difficult to teach anyone to hit the tennis serve if he cannot throw a ball overhand. Similarly, if students cannot swing their arms freely at the shoulder, parallel to the ground, learning of the forehand and backhand groundstrokes will be impeded.

Simple motor skills of throwing, catching, pivoting, and the like must be accomplished before reasonable tennis proficiency can be expected. The tennis stroke is then likened to some familiar skill, as exemplified by swinging a baseball bat. The acquisition of new skills would be more fun and a faster process as well if these rules were followed.

Consideration should be given to the length of the practice sessions. For most beginners, *frequent, short, spaced practice periods* are preferable to extended practice periods. Novice learners are more prone to a loss of interest and a lack of attention when they have to overcome the hurdles of learning something completely new. The acquisition of skill is usually a stubborn process.

The beginner demonstrates symptoms of tightness and wasted energy. As skill is acquired, efficiency in movement is observed. At first, it is as if the parts of the body are working independently, but later performance is characterized by minimal and only necessary coordinated movement patterns. Neurologically, control of unlearned or poorly learned skills is at the cerebral level, but this area has less of a role in the performance of advanced learners. The cerebellum is more active in the latter situation. It is as if the beginner has to attend to so many cues (many unnecessary) that his performance suffers. With experience and instruction, he learns what he should respond to, how to respond effectively, and how to direct his thought processes during motor performance.

New skills should be taught in such a way that the *learner performs in practice the way he is expected to in the actual situation.* Slow-motion practice or emphasis on one factor when several are equally important to the successful performance of an act only makes for additional learning and relearning problems. If speed and accuracy are required, both should be simultaneously practiced. One can learn to shoot a stationary jump shot in basketball, but in actual competition the player is usually on the move before shooting. Simulating gamelike skills in practice affords a better chance of success in the contest. An example of factor emphasis on the learning of a motor skill was demonstrated by Solley (1952). Three groups of subjects thrusted toward a target with their times and scores recorded. One group emphasized speed, the second accuracy, and the last group was directed to place equal emphasis on speed and accuracy. Among other conclusions, Solley found the following:

In skills in which speed is the predominate factor for successful performance, the most efficient results are attained by early emphasis of speed.

In skills in which both speed and accuracy are important to successful performance, emphasis on both speed and accuracy yields the most desirable results.

Many students have trouble learning motor skills because of a lack of experience with basic movement patterns in childhood. Ease in learning new skills will depend to a large extent on these many varied previous experiences. There are indications that even in later years familiarization with simple motor patterns facilitates the learning of more complex skills, e.g., those involved in sports. It is rare that new tasks require the learning of new motor skills. Basic, simple movements—those that are performed in childhood, including running, throwing, kicking, and jumping—underlie all sports. It is the means of organizing these patterns that differs from skill to skill and sport to sport. Therefore, learners who have not had the opportunity to play and develop the simple motor skills associated with childhood are handicapped in later, more complex undertakings.

Beginners should not be required to display the same ideal form for a specific skill. The important thing in the initial stages of learning is achievement and satisfaction, and casting a mold restricts the opportunity. Emphasis on particular desired styles can take place later as skill progresses.

The advanced learner, the one who displays a high level of achievement in a skill or group of skills, may be approached in a different manner from the beginner. More time can be spent with him on the critical details of his performance. Verbal instruction is more meaningful and, in general, the advanced are able to concentrate for a longer period of time on the task at hand. Practice sessions can be more intensive and extensive.

A highly skilled person usually achieves his status because of motivation, among other variables. Incentive will probably be less of a problem with this performer than the beginner, providing of course, his level of aspiration is high enough. As a standard rule, though, we all like to perform in activities in which we can demonstrate achievement. A beginner usually lacks confidence, the advanced learner typically does not.

All in all, teaching students who fall along the continuum of skill achievement presents general and special problems. Emphasis in instructional methods and considerations changes as skill progresses.

Early Versus Late Learners

Frequently early progress in skill attainment is misleading in predicting ultimate success. Some individuals demonstrate better performance than others in the early stages of learning, almost as if they gain quicker insight into the problem at hand. Various factors may be attributed to individual differences in early skill achievement, but one conclusion appears justified: early success does not indicate later achievement.

Marya Welch (1963) had her subjects perform a ladder-climb test (to go as high as possible before toppling). They were tested on six different days, with each test consisting of ten trials. Welch concluded that general skill-attainment prediction is poor unless an estimation of learning ability extends over at least half of the practice days. Fleishman and Hempel (1954) demonstrated that different factors are emphasized with increased practice and learning. Hence beginning success depends on certain factors and later achievement reflects the utilization of other factors. In other words, it would be quite difficult to predict end performance from beginning level of skill because variables vary in importance in each particular stage of learning.

Ella Trussell (1965) required forty college women students to learn a ball-juggling task. She found that the learning scores were not significantly related to initial scores and that the best predictability of final performance was obtained during the first 60 per cent of practice. Implications from the evidence are that people learn at varying rates of speed and that some might be handicapped if a particular unit or skill to be learned is covered too quickly. Everyone has his own optimal learning rate, and unfortunately, in mass learning situations such as those found in physical education classes, it is hard to consider individual differences. However, an awareness of this problem will at least allow the teacher to determine what is best for the group and where possible to adjust for extremes in fast and slow learners.

Further analysis of various parameters surrounding individual differences in learning is offered by Marya Welch and Franklin Henry (1971). Using a stabilometer task and sixty undergraduate college women, some conclusions were that final prediction from initial scores over several days is not effective unless nearly 95 per cent of the potential learning has been accomplished. In this particular study, which confirms the findings of the studies of Welch and Trussell, this point was reached after approximately 50 per cent of the total practice. In addition, rate of learning was not correlated with amount of learning. This finding has been well documented in the literature and is opposed to the popular belief in the high relationship of these factors.

THE STUDY OF
INDIVIDUAL DIFFERENCES

It has been argued for some time that behavior is studied from two vantage points: (1) from experimental data, with which groups of subjects are compared and inferences made about the "average" person from cause-and-effect relationships with appropriate statistics; and (2) from descriptive data, analyzed with correlations, factor analyses, and the like, to determine normative data on certain characteristics or the way individuals are likely to differ with regard to them. The study of individual differences, of human abilities and characteristics, has generally but not exclusively fallen into the latter category.

Interestingly enough, differences among individual subjects in the same group are a nuisance to experimenters attempting to determine significant treatment effects. The more limited the spread of scores around mean, the smaller the magnitude of individual differences, the smaller the "within-group error" score. Because this score is in the denominator of the fraction in which the treatment difference score is in the numerator, we can readily see that the larger the numerator is in proportion to the denominator, the better the probability of demonstrating statistically significant effects. Differential psychologists, on the other hand, are very much concerned with individual scores. Their research has been in measuring individual differences in abilities, interests, aptitudes, and personality. The relationship of factors with practice and the psychological processes that accompany learning are also in their province of study. The extensive work of E. A. Fleishman (e.g., 1972) has been alluded to in reference to psychomotor abilities, their measurement and contribution to task success. Factor analysis is the primary statistical tool he has employed.

Person and Task Models

Examining other learning factors, usually with correlational analysis, M. B. Jones has unearthed interesting patterns that seem to develop with more practice. One general observation is that, with more practice trials and higher mean scores, trial variances tend to increase as well, and vice versa. Individual scores surrounding the mean usually vary more as scores improve with practice.

Jones (1972) has identified the *superdiagonal form* when correlations among practice trials are examined. The correlations between any two trials are highest when the trials compared are closer together. The more removed the trials—say, the first and last of a number of trials—the lower the correlation. Figure 7–4 illustrates this point. For example, the correlation between trials 1 and 2 on the two-hand coordination test is 0.79. Between trials 1 and 5 it is 0.73 and between 1 and 8 it is 0.70. Note that the variances expressed in the form of standard deviations (SD) increase as do the mean scores with each trial. Furthermore, each succeeding pair of trials yields a higher correlation until the process of stabilization in scores sets in.

Jones recommends that the analysis of learning center on stabilization, which is the terminal process in learning. An average score on all terminal scores (as many trials as appropriate for score stabilization to be demon-

TABLE 7–4.   MEANS, STANDARD DEVIATIONS, AND INTERTRIAL COR-RELATIONS FOR THE TWO-HAND COORDINATION TEST *

Trial	1	2	3	4	5	6	7	8	X̄	SD
1	—	0.79	0.77	0.74	0.73	0.71	0.71	0.70	34.9	11.8
2		—	0.87	0.87	0.84	0.82	0.82	0.82	42.9	14.9
3			—	0.91	0.89	0.87	0.85	0.86	46.1	15.8
4				—	0.91	0.88	0.86	0.88	50.4	16.2
5					—	0.89	0.90	0.90	54.7	18.9
6						—	0.93	0.93	58.1	18.1
7							—	0.94	61.0	18.6
8								—	63.3	18.7

* M. B. Jones, "Practice as a Process of Simplification," *Psychological Review*, 69:274–294, 1962. Copyright 1962 by the American Psychological Association. Reprinted by permission.

strated through statistical analysis) would constitute the subject's learning score—his finished or accomplished skill. Bradley, as we saw in Chapter 4 when discussing learning curves, questioned whether a final asymptote is ever reached in performance. Although he makes some valid points, it is possible, as Jones and other writers have pointed out, to select what appears to be those trials in which reasonable score stabilization occurs to be used as the learning score.

Further implications from Jones's work parallel those that can be made from the work of Fleishman. Initial task performance is often related to general abilities, with differences in performance primarily the result of the presence of these abilities in desired amounts. As practice proceeds, differences among performer can be ascribed to task-specific requirements. The natural consequence of this relationship is the realization that prediction of terminal proficiency from initial performance is extremely tenuous with complex tasks in which an adequate amount of practice is provided. Jones and Fleishman, in attacking the prediction problem from different research strategies, generally agree that the relationship between usual task predictors and actual performance diminishes as a function of practice. Kenneth Alvares and Charles Hulin (1972) provide an excellent review of the two approaches and attempt to resolve theoretical differences.

The superdiagonal matrix shows adjacent trials to be highly related but more distant ones to be less so, and the study of abilities as task predictors reveals poorer predictability with increased time and/or practice. Alvares and Hulin suggest that apparently different and conflicting models (e.g., Jones vs. Fleishman) are really descriptions of the same underlying phenomena. In Jones's approach, fewer and fewer factors are posited to contribute to successful performance with practice. Fleishman believes that abilities contribute more or less to successful performance, depending on the status of the learner. The conflict, as Alvares and Hulin (1973) see it, is between belief in the "changing subject model" or the "changing task model." In the latter case, it is believed that the structure of the task undergoes change with practice and the acquisition of skill. The task is defined by the set of abilities necessary for performance. In the former case, it is believed that training changes the magnitude of the abilities. Alvares and Hulin suggest that the finding of decreasing correlations with more remote trials occurs because of changes in abilities rather than changes in the structure of the task.

Support for the notion of changing levels of abilities resulting from training is offered by Alvares and Hulin (1973), although in another article (1972) they do stress that both models can adequately offer *post hoc* explanations for the available data. Is it wiser to analyze the task according to ability requirements of a person with various ability dimensions that change with experience? In order to predict performance effectively, tests must be developed that will tap the ability requirements for termination-of-practice accomplishments, and cues and abilities most important at different stages of practice would be emphasized. Otherwise, equations must be established that predict changes in ability levels. This approach, associated with the changing subject model, is more dynamic and perhaps a potentially more fruitful area of investigation.

Intraindividual Factors

The study of intraindividual variability as related to experimental procedures and learning and performance variables provides additional insight into differential learning processes. The novice realizes that individuals will differ in performed scores at any time. However, the components of these scores deserve special consideration, for theoretical and practical purposes. Differences in scores do not necessarily reflect true score differences. Other factors that might influence performance include trial-to-trial fluctuations resulting from any one of a number of personal reasons as well as variable errors, in the form of limitations in apparatus or weaknesses in observation. As George Stelmach summarizes (1969, p. 201), "The total variability that is observed in a sample of performances consists of true score variance (individual differences), intra-individual variance, and error variance." Individual difference scores result from all these scores.

Franklin Henry and his many former students have investigated inter- and intraindividual variations in many contexts. Given that r_{ab} = the correlation between any pair of trials

S_a^2 and S_b^2 = the observed variance of subjects' scores for any two trials
$\quad S_t^2$ = true score (interindividual, individual difference variance)
$\quad S_i^2$ = intraindividual variance

interindividual and intraindividual variances are computed in the following way:

$$S_x^2 = \frac{S_a^2 + S_b^2}{2} = \text{average variance for a group of subjects for a pair of trials}$$

$$S_t^2 = r_{ab}\, S_x^2 \qquad = \text{individual difference variance}$$

Using these formulas, Welch and Henry (1971) found that stabilometer task practice of twelve trials per day for six days yielded interindividual and intraindividual variations that decreased exponentially as a function of the amount of practice. However, they point out that there was an increase in both factors with practice in ratio of variability to mean score. In this study, individuals tended to become more alike in performance as practice increased, a finding that is not typical with complex learning tasks.

Stelmach tested his subjects on a stabilometer for eight continuous minutes and recorded scores every thirty seconds. He found that true score variance (individual difference) slightly increased with practice. Intraindividual ability was relatively unaffected by continuous practice, but when performance improvement was canceled out by examining relative variability, both sources of variance increased. Intraindividual variability, repeated scores on the same subjects, interpreted as consistency in motor response, was found by Albert Carron (1970) to be moderately reliable but tended to be specific to particular response components.

It has been questioned whether response inconsistency is a random or a systematic variable, or a biological phenomenon. Many researchers favor the notion of systematic influences on performance inconsistencies. A number of studies indicate that the imposed practice conditions will differentially affect inter- and intraindividual variances. For instance, George Stelmach (1968) found the true score variance to decrease 49 per cent under distributed practice conditions on the stabilometer and to decrease 13 per cent under massed practice conditions. Intraindividual variance decreased 37 per cent with distributed practice and 11 per cent with massed practice. A review of all the recent literature on the topic of interindividual and intraindividual variance changes with practice indicates that individual differences become greater with practice or increases to a lesser degree than the individual difference variance.

The study of individual differences helps us to determine the nature of inter- and intraindividual variability of performance scores. With more literature, trends in the data will become more apparent in order that generalizations can be made. Actually, differential psychology, or the analysis of individual differences, is associated with research on personal abilities and characteristics. The establishment of normative behavior and ranges of deviation has provided a means of learning more about individuals and how they may be expected to perform in certain situations.

REFERENCES

ADAMS, JACK A., and CYLE R. CREAMER. "Proprioception Variables as Determiners of Anticipatory Timing Behavior," *Human Factors*, 4:217–222, 1963.

ALVARES, KENNETH M., and CHARLES L. HULIN. "An Experimental Evaluation of a Temporal Decay in the Prediction of Performance," *Organizational Behavior and Human Performance*, 9:169–185, 1973.

————. Two Explanations of Temporal Changes in Ability-Skill Relationships: A Literature Review and Theoretical Analysis," *Human Factors*, 14:295–308, 1972.

ANDERSON, RICHARD C., and DAVID P. AUSUBEL. *Readings in the Psychology of Cognition*. New York: Holt, Rinehart and Winston, Inc., 1965.

ANASTASI, ANNE. *Differential Psychology*. New York: Macmillan Publishing Co., Inc., 1958.

ASMUSSEN, ERLING, and K. HEEBØLL-NIELSEN. "Physical Performance and Growth in Children, Influence of Sex, Age and Intelligence," *Journal of Applied Physiology*, 8:371–380, 1956.

ATKINSON, JOHN W., and GEORGE H. LITWIN. "Achievement Motive and Test Anxiety Conceived as Motive to Approach Success and Motive to Avoid Failure," *Journal of Abnormal and Social Psychology*, 60:52–63, 1960.

BARROW, HAROLD M. "Test of Motor Ability for College Men, *Research Quarterly*, 25:253–260, 1954.

BEALS, R. P., A. M. MAYYASI, A. E. TEMPLETON, and W. L. JOHNSTON. "The Relationship Between Basketball Shooting Performance and Certain Visual Attributes," *American Journal of Optometry and Archives of American Academy of Optometry*, 48:585–590, 1971.

BECHTOLDT, HAROLD G. "Motor Abilities in Studies of Motor Learning," in Leon Smith (ed.), *Psychology of Motor Learning* (Proceedings of C.I.C., Symposium on Psychology of Motor Learning). Chicago: The Athletic Institute, 1970.

BELL, HOWARD A. "Effects of Experimentally-Induced Muscular Tension and Frequency of Motivational Instructions on Pursuit Rotor Performance," *Perceptual and Motor Skills*, 9:111–115, 1959.

BOTWINICK, J., and C. W. THOMPSON. "Premotor and Motor Components of Reaction Time," *Journal of Experimental Psychology*, 71:9–15, 1966.

BUXTON, C. E. and L. G. HUMPHREYS. "The Effect of Practice upon Intercorrelations of Motor Skills," *Science*, 81:441–442, 1935.

CARRON, ALBERT V. "Intra-Task Reliability and Specificity of Individual Consistency," *Perceptual and Motor Skills*, 30:583–587, 1970.

————. "Motor Performance Under Stress," *Research Quarterly*, 39:463–469, 1968.

CASTANEDA, ALFRED, and LEWIS P. LIPSITT. "Relation of Stress and Differential Position Habits to Performance in Motor Learning," *Journal of Experimental Psychology*, 57:25–30, 1959.

CATTELL, RAYMOND B. *Abilities: Their Structure, Growth, and Action.* Boston: Houghton Mifflin Company, 1971.

COHEN, JOZEF. *Personality Assessment.* Skokie, Ill.: Rand McNally & Co., 1969.

COZENS, F. W. *Achievement Scales in Physical Education Activities for College Men.* Philadelphia: Lea & Febiger, 1936.

CRATTY, BRYANT J., and KIRT E. DUFFY. "Studies of Movement Aftereffects," *Perceptual and Motor Skills*, 29:843–860, 1969.

————, and ROBERT S. HUTTON. "Figural Aftereffects Resulting from Gross Action Patterns," *Research Quarterly*, 35:116–125, 1964.

CRONBACH, LEE J. "How Can Instruction Be Adapted to Individual Differences?" in Robert M. Gagné (ed.), *Learning and Individual Differences.* Columbus, Ohio: Charles E. Merrill Publishers, 1967.

CUMBEE, FRANCES Z. "A Factor Analysis of Motor Co-ordination," *Research Quarterly*, 25:412–428, 1954.

CURETON, THOMAS K. *Physical Fitness of Champion Athletes.* Urbana: University of Illinois Press, 1951.

DuBois, PHILIP. "The Design of Correlational Studies in Training," in Robert Glaser (ed.), *Training Research and Education.* New York: John Wiley & Sons, Inc., 1965.

DUNCANSON, JAMES P. "Learning and Measured Abilities," *Journal of Educational Psychology*, 57:220–229, 1966.

EASON, ROBERT G., and CARROLL T. WHITE. "Muscular Tension, Effort, and Tracking Difficulty: Study of Parameters Which Affect Tension Level and Performance Efficiency," *Perceptual and Motor Skills*, 12:331–372, 1961.

EPSTEIN, WILLIAM. *Varieties of Perceptual Learning.* New York: McGraw-Hill Book Company, 1967.

FLEISHMAN, EDWIN A. "An Analysis of Positioning Movements and Static Reactions," *Journal of Experimental Psychology*, 55:13–24, 1958a.

————. "A Comparative Study of Aptitude Patterns in Unskilled and Skilled Psychomotor Performers," *Journal of Applied Psychology*, 41:263–272, 1957.

————. "Dimensional Analysis of Movement Reactions," *Journal of Experimental Psychology*, 55:438–453, 1958b.

————. "On the Relation Between Abilities, Learning, and Human Performance," *American Psychologist*, 27:1017–1032, 1972a.

————. *The Structure and Measurement of Physical Fitness*, Englewood Cliffs, N.J.: Prentice-Hall, Inc., 1964.

————. "Structure and Measurement of Psychomotor Abilities," in Robert N. Singer, (ed.), *The Psychomotor Domain: Movement Behavior.* Philadelphia: Lea & Febiger, 1972b.

————, and WALTER E. HEMPEL, JR. "Changes in Factor Structure of a

Complex Psychomotor Test as a Function of Practice," *Psychometrika*, 19:239–254, 1954.

―――――, and ROBERT W. STEPHENSON. *Development of a Taxonomy of Human Performance: A Review of the Third Year's Progress*. Washington, D.C.: American Institutes for Research, 1970.

FORBES, GILBERT. "The Effect of Certain Variables on Visual and Auditory Reaction Times," *Journal of Experimental Psychology*, 35:153–162, 1945.

FREEMAN, G. L. "The Optimal Muscular Tensions for Various Performances," *American Journal of Psychology*, 51:146–150, 1938.

GAGNÉ, ROBERT M. (ed.). *Learning and Individual Differences*. Columbus, Ohio: Charles E. Merrill Publishers, 1967.

GROVES, RICHARD. "Relationship of Reaction Time and Movement Time in a Gross Motor Skill," *Perceptual and Motor Skills*, 36:453–454, 1973.

GUILFORD, J. P. "Three Faces of Intellect," *American Psychologist*, 14:469–479, 1959.

―――――. *Personality*. New York: McGraw-Hill Book Company, 1959.

HELD, RICHARD. "Plasticity in Sensory-Motor Systems," *Scientific American*, 213:84–94, 1965.

HELSON, HARRY (ed.). *Theoretical Foundations of Psychology*. New York: Van Nostrand Reinhold Company, 1951.

HEMPEL, WALTER E., JR., and EDWIN A. FLEISHMAN. "A Factor Analysis of Physical Proficiency and Manipulative Skill," *Journal of Applied Psychology*, 39:12–16, 1955.

HENRY, FRANKLIN M. "Dynamic Kinesthetic Perception and Adjustment," *Research Quarterly*, 24:176–187, 1953.

―――――. "Reaction Time-Movement Time Correlations," *Perceptual and Motor Skills*, 12:63–66, 1961.

HETHERINGTON, M. ROSS, and THOMAS O. MAGUIRE. "Comparison of Generality and Specificity Factors Estimated with Squared Correlation and Analysis of Variance Techniques," *Research Quarterly*, 43:495–500, 1972.

HIGHMORE, G., and W. R. TAYLOR. "A Factorial Analysis of Athletic Ability," *The British Journal of Statistical Psychology*, 7:1–8, 1954.

HIRATA, KIN-ITSU. "Physique and Age of Tokyo Olympic Champions," *Journal of Sports Medicine and Physical Fitness*, 6:207–222, 1966.

HOPKINS, B. "Proprioception and/or Kinesthesis," *Perceptual and Motor Skills*, 34:431–435, 1972.

HOWE, CLIFFORD E. "A Comparison of Motor Skills of Mentally Retarded and Normal Children," *Exceptional Children*, 25:352–354, 1959.

ISMAIL, A., N. KEPHART, and C. C. COWELL. *Utilization of Motor Aptitude Tests in Predicting Academic Achievement, Technical Report No. 1*, Purdue University Research Foundation, P.U. 879–64–838, 1963.

JACOBS, PAUL D., and JERRY THORNTON. "Scale Sensitivity of the Perceived Stress Index," *Perceptual and Motor Skills*, 30:944, 1970.

―――――, and DAVID C. MUNZ. "An Index for Measuring Perceived Stress in a College Population, *The Journal of Psychology*, 70:9–15, 1968.

Jones, James M., and Adrian Ruth Hochner. "Racial Differences in Sports Activities. A look at the Self-paced Versus Reactive Hypothesis," *Journal of Personality and Social Psychology*, 27:86–95, 1973.

Jones, Marshall B. "Individual Differences," in Robert N. Singer, (ed.), *The Psychomotor Domain: Movement Behavior*. Philadelphia: Lea & Febiger, 1972.

Jones, M. B. "Practice as a Process of Simplification," *Psychological Review*, 69:274–294, 1962.

Jordan, James H. "Physiological and Anthropometrical Comparisons of Negroes and Whites," *Journal of Health, Physical Education, and Recreation*, 40:93–99, 1969.

Kane, Martin. "Black Is Best," *Sports Illustrated*, January 18, 1971, pp. 72–83.

Klausmeier, Herbert J., and Richard E. Ripple. *Learning and Human Abilities*. New York: Harper & Row, Publishers, Inc., 1971.

Krahenbuhl, Gary S. "Stress Reactivity in Tennis Players," *Research Quarterly*, 42:42–46, 1971.

Laszlo, Judith I. "The Performance of a Simple Motor Task with Kinesthetic Sense Loss," *Quarterly Journal of Experimental Psychology*, 18:1–8, 1966.

————, and P. J. Bairstow. "The Compression Block Technique: A Note on Procedure," *Journal of Motor Behavior*, 3:313–317, 1971.

Levine, J. M., and Gardner Murphy. "Learning and Forgetting of Controversial Material," *Journal of Abnormal Psychology*, 38:507–517, 1943.

Loockermen, William D., and Richard A. Berger. "Specificity and Generality Between Various Directions for Reaction and Movement Times Under Choice Stimulus Conditions," *Journal of Motor Behavior*, 4:31–35, 1972.

Lotter, Willard S. "Specificity or Generality of Speed of Systematically Related Movements," *Research Quarterly*, 32:55–62, 1961.

McCleary, Robert A. *Genetic and Experiential Factors in Perception*. Glenview, Ill.: Scott, Foresman and Company, 1970.

McCloy, C. H. "The Measurement of General Motor Capacity and General Motor Ability," *Research Quarterly Supplement*, 5:46–61, 1934.

Martens, Rainer. "Anxiety and Motor Behavior: A Review," *Journal of Motor Behavior*, 3:151–180, 1971.

Mathews, Donald K., Virginia Shaw, and Meria Bohnen. "Hip Flexibility of College Women as Related to Length of Body Segments," *Research Quarterly*, 28:352–356, 1957.

Meyers, Carlton R., and Fred W. Ohnmacht. "Needs of Pupils in Relation to Athletic Competition at the Junior High School Level," *Research Quarterly*, 34:521–524, 1963.

Michael, Ernest D. "Stress Adaptation Through Exercise," *Research Quarterly*, 28:50–54, 1957.

Nelson, Richard C., and Michael R. Nofsinger. "Effect of Overload on

Speed of Elbow Flexion and the Associated Aftereffects," *Research Quarterly*, 36:174–182, 1965.

OLIVER, JAMES N. "The Effect of Physical Conditioning Exercises and Activities on the Mental Characteristics of Educationally Sub-normal Boys," *British Journal of Educational Psychology*, 28:155–165, 1958.

OLSON, EINAR A. "Relationship Between Psychological Capacities and Success in College Athletics," *Research Quarterly*, 27:79–89, 1956.

PARSONS, OSCAR A., LESLIE PHILLIPS, and JOHN E. LANE. "Performance on the Same Psychomotor Task Under Different Stressful Conditions," *Journal of Psychology*, 38:457–466, 1954.

PIAGET, JEAN. *The Psychology of Intelligence*. New York: Harcourt Brace Jovanovich, Inc., 1950.

PRATHER, DIRK C., GENE A. BERRY, and GERALD L. JONES. "The Training of a Perceptual Skill by Either Rewarding or Aversive Feedback Compared on Efficiency, Transfer, and Stress," *Journal of Applied Psychology*, 56:514–516, 1972.

RENSHAW, S. and D. K. POSTLE. "Pursuit Learning Under Three Types of Instruction," *Journal of General Psychology*, 1:360–367, 1928.

ROBERTS, DENNIS M. "Abilities and Learning: A Brief Review and Discussion of Empirical Studies," *Journal of School Psychology*, 7:12–21, 1968–69.

ROLOFF, LOUISE L. "Kinesthesis in Relation to the Learning of Selected Motor Skills," *Research Quarterly*, 24:210–217, 1953.

ROSE, JERZY E., and VERNON B. MOUNTCASTLE. "Touch and Kinesthesis," in John Field (ed.), *Handbook of Physiology: Neurophysiology*, Vol. 1. Washington, D.C.: American Physiological Society, 1959.

RYAN, E. DEAN. "Relative Academic Achievement and Stabilometer Performance," *Research Quarterly*, 34:184–190, 1963.

SANFORD, NEVITT. "Higher Education as a Field of Study," in Nevitt Sanford (ed.), *The American College*. New York: John Wiley & Sons, Inc., 1962.

SCOTT, M. GLADYS. "Assessment of Motor Ability of College Women Through Objective Tests," *Research Quarterly*, 10:63–83, 1939.

————. "Measurement of Kinesthesis," *Research Quarterly*, 26:324–341, 1955.

SELYE, HANS. *The Stress of Life*. New York: McGraw-Hill Book Company, 1956.

SHELDON, W. H., S. S. STEVENS, and W. R. TUCKER. *The Varieties of Human Physique*. New York: Harper & Row, Publishers, Inc., 1940.

SHICK, JACQUELYN. "Relationship Between Depth Perception and Hand–Eye Dominance and Free-throw Shooting in College Women," *Perceptual and Motor Skills*, 33:539–542, 1971.

SINGER, ROBERT N. "Balance Skill as Related to Athletics, Sex, Height, and Weight," in Gerald S. Kenyon (ed.), *Contemporary Psychology of Sport: Proceedings of the Second International Congress of Sport Psychology*. Chicago: Athletic Institute, 1970, pp. 645–656.

————. "Comparison of Inter-limb Skill Achievement in Performing a Motor Skill," *Research Quarterly*, 27:406–410, 1966.

SLATER-HAMMEL, A. T. "Measurement of Kinesthetic Perception of Muscular Force with Muscle Potential Changes," *Research Quarterly*, 28:153–159, 1957.

SLOAN, W. "The Lincoln-Oseretsky Motor Development Scale," *Genetic Psychological Monographs*, 51:183–252, 1955.

SMITH, LEON E. "Influence of Neuromotor Program Alteration on the Speed of a Standard Arm Movement," *Perceptual and Motor Skills*, 15:327–330, 1962.

SOLLEY, CHARLES M., and GARDNER MURPHY. *Development of the Perceptual World*. New York: Basic Books, Inc., 1960.

SOLLEY, WILLIAM H. "The Effects of Verbal Instruction of Speed and Accuracy Upon the Learning of a Motor Skill," *Research Quarterly*, 23:231–240, 1952.

SPIELBERGER, CHARLES D. *The State-Trait Anxiety Inventory*. Palo Alto, Calif.: Consulting Psychologists Press, 1970.

START, K. B. "Intelligence and the Improvement in a Gross Motor Skill After Mental Practice," *British Journal of Educational Psychology*, 34:85, 1964.

STELMACH, GEORGE E. "Distribution of Practice in Individual Differences and Intra-variability," *Perceptual and Motor Skills*, 26:727–730, 1968.

STIMPSON, W. G. *The Art of Golf*, cited by Mrs. Stewart Hanley in "The Sense of Feel in Golf," *Journal of Health, Physical Education & Recreation*, 8:366, 1937.

TANNER, J. M. "Physique, Body Composition and Growth," in E. Jokl and E. Simon (eds.), *International Research in Sport and Physical Education*. Springfield, Ill.: Charles C Thomas, Publishers, 1964.

TAYLOR, JANET A. "A Personality Scale of Manifest Anxiety," *Journal of Abnormal and Social Psychology*, 48:285–290, 1953.

THURSTONE, THELMA GWINN. *An Evaluation of Educating Mentally Handicapped Children in Special Classes and in Regular Classes*, Cooperative Research Project Contract Number OE-SAE-6452 of the U.S. Office of Education, The School of Education, University of North Carolina, 1959.

TRAVIS, ROLAND C. "An Experimental Analysis of Dynamic and Static Equilibrium," *Journal of Experimental Psychology*, 35:216–234, 1945.

TRUSSELL, ELLA. "Prediction of Success in a Motor Skill on the Basis of Early Learning Achievement," *Research Quarterly*, 39:342–347, 1965.

TYLER, LEONA E. *The Psychology of Human Differences*. New York: Appleton-Century-Crofts, Inc., 1965.

ULRICH, CELESTE. "Measurement of Stress Evidenced by College Women in Situations Involving Competition," *Research Quarterly*, 28:160–172, 1957.

WELCH, MARYA. "Prediction of Motor Skill Attainment from Early Learning," *Perceptual and Motor Skills*, 17:263–266, 1963.

WELCH, MARYA, and FRANKLIN HENRY. "Individual Differences in Various Parameters," *Journal of Motor Behavior*, 31:78–96, 1971.

WHIPPLE, GUY M. *Manual of Mental and Physical Tests.* Baltimore: Warwick and York, Inc., 1914.

WIEBE, VERNON R. "A Study of Tests of Kinesthesis," *Research Quarterly,* 25:222–230, 1954.

WILBERG, R. B. "Response Accuracy Based upon Recall from Visual and Kinesthetic Short-Term Memory," *Research Quarterly,* 40:407–414, 1969.

WILLIAMS, HARRIET G., and VIRGINIA L. BLANE. "A Comparison of Selected Behavior of Indentical Twins, One Blind from Birth," *Journal of Motor Behavior,* 1:259–274, 1969.

WITKIN, H. A., H. B. LEWIS, M. HERTZMAN, K. MACHOVER, P. MEISSNER, and S. WAPNER. *Personality Through Perception.* New York: Harper & Row, Publishers, Inc., 1954.

WORTHY, MORGAN, and ALLAN MARKLE. "Racial Differences in Reactive Versus Self-paced Sports Activities," *Journal of Personality and Social Psychology,* 16:439–443, 1970.

8

DEVELOPMENTAL
FACTORS AND
INFLUENCE
ON BEHAVIOR

In an experimental sense, learning is usually measured independently of maturation. Practically speaking, though, maturation is related to behavior, and the two are inextricably interwoven. Maturation determines human potential and sets the upper limits of learning and performance.

As the youngster grows, develops, and matures certain patterns of behavior unfold, mostly learned, but in some cases occurring in spite of a lack of experience. Researchers can measure the effects of maturation on learning and behavior when practice in or experience with certain skills are held to a minimum. Those interested in distinguishing learned acts from the natural instinctive behavior of a species have used this method. Some simple reflexes and simple acts of human babies have been identified as being independent of learning. However, it is generally conceded that the attainment of complex skills and most behavioral patterns as defined by adult standards are the result of maturation and experience.

Certain behavior is primarily influenced by learning whereas other behavior is affected most by maturation. Educators by necessity should expect unique behavior and abilities relevant to an individual's age and maturational level. They should also understand how to teach, when to teach, and what to teach children at each level. Often a mistake is made in assuming that body size represents development and readiness to learn. *Growth* implies an increase in stature, *development* denotes increasing complexity of structure and function, and *maturation* indicates that the organism is approaching a somewhat stable structure. Behavior is more purposeful when development and maturation take place. Age is another factor that is misconstrued as representing maturity. This is why we should distinguish the chronological age from the maturational age of a child.

Throughout life from birth to that inevitable day, experiences accumulate and the body grows and changes, and individual differences in abilities and achievements will be observable. Age differences, sex differences, innate abilities, personality factors, environmental experiences—all and more interact to determine human attainment.

When should children be taught certain basic skills or introduced to particular sports? When is this age of readiness? What is the relationship between the ability to perform simple motor patterns and intellectual potential? Does sports participation really change behavior for the better and modify personalities? What exactly is the role of sports participation in personality development? At what ages do individuals reach their peak in skill performance? Up until what age is it possible to demonstrate a reasonable amount of skill in a given activity? How much of a factor in skill attainment is sex—why do boys usually demonstrate a greater proficiency in motor skills than girls during adolescence and later? How different are they in childhood?

These are but a few questions that may be associated with developmental factors and motor development. This chapter attempts to provide some information on the developmental factors related to motor learning but probably succeeds more in raising questions than in answering them. Insufficient research in this area is responsible for this situation. However, this fact should be an even greater stimulation to analyze those persistent problems that require satisfactory explanations.

CHRONOLOGICAL VERSUS MATURATIONAL AGE

Chronological age often misrepresents readiness skills and expectant behavior. All children go through the same sequence of developmental stages, but vary in their rate of progress. To post norms based on age is often a matter of convenience and practicality, and deviations should be weighed accordingly. It would be better to understand the child and his stage of maturational development, because early and late maturers do not display similar characteristics at the same chronological age.

Mental age, as represented by the IQ test, is, in a sense, independent of chronological age. The intelligence quotient is a ratio of the child's mental age as determined by an intelligence test over his chronological age. It is possible, indeed probable, that students in a given class composed of children of the same chronological age will be widely distributed according to mental age. By the same token, children making the transition from childhood to adulthood demonstrate physical development according to their rate of maturation rather than age. Such a factor as strength is an important determiner of potential success in many motor activities, and obviously early maturers may be expected to perform more ably in sports because their physical development has accelerated.

Caution in grouping children by chronological age without concern for maturation rate is pleaded by Robert Malina (1972). A child's growth status at any one time is dependent upon (1) final adult size and (2) the rate at which the size is being attained. Any two persons may reach the same ultimate size at different speeds. In this case, the factors are independent, for at different developing ages these two persons will show dissimilar growth profiles. The factors are related, however, in that one's size at a particular age is related to his maturation rate. Early maturers are larger than slower maturers of the same chronological age. Great variations among developing individuals, even those who will eventually attain similar size characteristics, is a warning to teachers in group-activity learning situations.

Numerous investigations have been completed relating motor achievements to chronological age. Reservations should be present in any application of norms to one person's scores, but there is value in comparing age and motor-performance variables. This information is somewhat helpful at the first level of understanding in order that generalizations can be made about behavior and age. Major deviations in behavioral expectations can then be examined on an individual basis, at which time other variables might be considered. A maturational average or advanced youngster at a given chronological age who is performing substandardly might be lacking in motivation, interest, and enthusiasm to learn and perform certain activities.

CRITICAL LEARNING PERIODS

One of the most fascinating concepts in psychology is that a certain period during a lifetime is optimal for affecting behavior and promoting learning. This phenomenon has been observed in a number of species, although it is more apparent in infrahumans. In fact, most research has been accumulated on animals and birds and indicates specific periods crucial for the development of certain behavior. Types of experiences and the periods in which they are experienced by the organism may have critical bearing on future behavior. *Critical periods*, as applied to human learning, *refer to the optimal periods for attempting to acquire fundamental and complex skills*. The *critical period* for any specific sort of learning is that time when the *maxi-*

mum sensory, motor, motivational, and psychological capacities are present.

A critical period for the learning of certain tasks or development of behavioral patterns may be determined by sense or experience deprivation, by introduction to the experience, or by environmental enrichment at a given time in life. Humans and animals have been subjected to all three conditions by researchers intent on discovering these periods. In order to discover the best time for learning, it is necessary first to examine the normal learning progress from birth to later childhood. In his earliest stage of development, the baby cannot walk, reach for objects, or perform relatively simple motor acts. These responses as well as more complicated ones are demonstrated with increased development of the nervous system. Earliest activity is primarily reflex in nature. Doctors can usually detect unusual neurological activity and disturbances if the baby exhibits certain involuntary movements or lacks others. Through examination of numerous babies doctors have come to expect the presence of specific types of activity with progressing age. After approximately six months of life many of the innate reflexes are replaced by purposeful responses.

Anna Espenschade has undertaken much research in children's motor development, and in 1960 she presented an excellent summary of the research in this area. She pointed out that early behavior patterns are generally consistent from infant to infant, but developmental rates differ widely. This may be because of heredity and/or environmental deprivation or enrichment.

A baby should receive much opportunity to explore and practice—to reach for toys, to walk, to roll over, to pull himself up. Throughout life more complex skills will be built upon a foundation of simple movements. With experience and maturity, the child will learn how to perform gross motor patterns and eventually finer motor skills. Genetic factors will influence performance potential. Within limitations, preadolescent children are able to perform in a wide range of sports, especially those based on running, throwing, and jumping skills. These skills are developed to an adequate degree in most children by reason of frequent opportunities for participation in activities requiring these movements. It should be emphasized that movement mastery, the ability to coordinate motor patterns into a highly skilled act, *is learned*. Skilled movements do not occur as a result of the maturation process.

The natural questions that follow are (1) Will intensive and extensive training at a relatively early age result in superior athletic prowess later in life? (2) What is this critical age and is it unique for each sport? (3) Will deprivation of certain motor experiences never be compensated for and thus result in producing subpar performers?

The impact of early experiences on later behavior and development has been explained through the recently popularized and accepted *stage* approach. The traditional concept embraced periods of expectant transition that occurred because of increments in age. At present, many psychologists

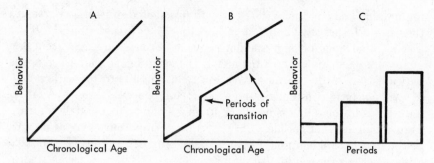

Figure 8-1.   Illustrations A and B represent the traditional concept of behavior expectancies according to chronological age. Illustration C discounts the importance of age and emphasizes the stage approach: children progress from one stage of behavior to another, irrespective of age.

believe that children do not go through the same experiences according to their chronological age but, rather, according to critical periods or stages. When one stage has been achieved, the child progresses to the next stage. Figure 8-1 illustrates the dissimilarity between the chronological age approach and the stage approach.

The works of a few outstanding psychologists have helped ,to substantiate the stage approach in child development. Sigmund Freud made child psychology an appealing area of study and emphasized the impact of early sequential experiences on later behavior. He attempted to explain adult neuroses through inadequate resolutions of certain sensitive periods in childhood. D. O. Hebb depicted stage evolvement through a neuropsychological approach to learning and behavior (see Chapter 3). One of the most influential men on child development is Jean Piaget, and he writes extensively on formal or specific stages that all children experience in a predictable manner. Finally, J. P. Scott has completed a considerable amount of work on critical learning periods in animals.

Freud, reports Lucy Freeman (1965), felt that specific types of drives become prevalent to the human during progressive stages in life. If the needs of these drives are not met during the specific periods then the individual will show some type of distress as an adult. Apparently these drives appear only at certain maturational stages and the satisfaction of such drives cannot be met before this time. Thus the relationship here seems to be not between the earliness of experience and attainment, but rather between timeliness of experience and attainment, which in Freud's case results in a well-adjusted individual. If this type of process plays a role in mental and psychological development, then it seems quite possible an identical process functions in the attainment of physical skills.

Piaget (1952) has presented a stage approach to child learning in which the child undergoes sequential stages during which specific types of learning unfold. The child may start out with unsolicited gross motor responses, then begin to perceive and respond to stimuli, and so on, until he reaches a conceptual stage of understanding abstract terms. The stages seem based on maturational and experiential factors. The learning accomplished appears dependent upon the learning stage for a child in one of the earlier stages. He will not be able to understand abstract and conceptual terms even when introduced to them unless he is maturationally and experientially prepared. Thus timeliness, not earliness of instruction, is important here, as may well be the case in skill learning. Piaget actually proposes a series of hierarchical critical periods for the human infant.

Supposedly, if an animal or human is exposed to a given experience at a particular critical period or stage, it has a greater effect on adult behavior than if the experience occurs at an earlier or a later period. Unfortunately because of the complexity of the problem, research on humans is lacking, thus permitting very few generalizations. However, as is the case in so many experimental areas, animal research has paved the way for implications in human behavior as well as for procedures that may be used in human research. John King (1958) discusses seven variables that should be considered in critical-period research. Although meant for animal investigations, they certainly may be applied to human study. These factors are (1) the age of the subject during the experience, (2) the age when tested, which is usually at maturity, (3) the type of experience, (4) the duration of the early experience, (5) the type of performance task, (6) the persistency of the test effects, and (7) genetic background of the subject.

Infrahuman research points to the fact that behavior development not only is dependent on heredity, maturation, and practice, but also is related to perceptual learning experiences in infancy. Beach and Jaynes (1954) have summarized animal-research investigations that were concerned with early experiences upon later behavior. The areas of study touched upon were

1. *Sensory discrimination and perception.* A lack of early visual stimulation results in an inability to respond to visual cues later in life. However, with the higher species, usually these defective responses are not permanent and disappear with experience. There are more pronounced effects with rabbits, pigeons, and fish. [Research by Dember (1960) indicates that when human youngsters undergo restricted environmental experiences, they later are deficient in form perception. Extra experience provides better later perception.]

2. *Touch and proprioception.* Studies on chimpanzees, who had their feet and hands bandaged in childhood, have demonstrated that these animals show abnormal behavior when the restrictions are removed.

3. *Feeding behavior.* In studying the pecking behavior of chicks, those who were spoon-fed in the dark for two weeks never did learn how to peck later.

4. *Hoarding.* If deprived of food in infancy (first fifteen days), afterward there is a tendency for rats to hoard. Also, these deprived rats eat faster in adulthood.
5. *Social behavior.* Birds and chicks raised in isolation have shown antisocial behavior.

Many studies demonstrate the fact that after certain times in life, an organism cannot perform a particular behavior if it has not been subjected to specific stimuli or experiences. Beach and Jaynes refer to numerous experiments that lend support to the critical-period concept. Their article is an excellent one for both reference and evidence, as it summarizes the major works on early experience and later behavior.

Konrad Lorenz (1970) has demonstrated a phenomenon termed *imprinting. Imprinting* refers to that first stimulus that evokes an instinctive reaction and becomes the only stimulus that will cause this reaction. It takes place in a critical stage of life and is irreversible throughout life. In a sense, it is a primitive form of learning. Geese that have been exposed to humans in childhood but never to adult geese tend later to stay near humans rather than geese. Certain species, after being brought up with humans, never can react normally to their own kind. In imprinting, a duckling within the first two or three days of life becomes attached to almost any object or organism that is introduced at this time. This behavior continues throughout life with the bird following the imprinting object even in the presence of its conspecifics. Thus the bird does not recognize its own kind and will not respond normally to them. Lorenz's work has been widely duplicated with many other organisms, so it seems such periods could occur for skill obtainment in humans, although it has been demonstrated that higher organisms can more readily overcome early deprivations.

Social behavior, as explained through critical periods, has been of particular interest to investigators. Young rats that have been stimulated (handled) learn quicker, are less timorous, and more vigorous. When rats are brought up surrounded by many playthings as compared to a barren environment, their performance on learning tasks is better. Ravizza and Herschberger (1966) raised some rats in an inhibited environment and allowed another group of rats to climb. As adults, the rats allowed freedom of exploration were more active in exploration tasks, showed superior performance on an intelligence test, and were less emotional in a novel situation. Mice reared in groups have a tendency to fight more than mice raised in isolation.

The study of the development of social attachments in dogs as a function of critical learning periods has led to interesting speculations about human behaviors (see, for example, Scott, 1969). Furthermore, even the development of tendencies to persevere at tasks, to show ideal motivational levels, is dependent upon early learning experiences and successes and failures.

Motivation in tasks undertaken later in life will be increased if successful experiences are had early in life. John Scott reports that it is extremely hard to remotivate a puppy that has failed repeatedly.

The irreversible characteristics of poor or limited experiences on the undesirable later behaviors of subhumans is well documented. We have just examined some of the convincing evidence. The evidence with humans is far less supportive with regard to the notion that a child will not be able to remediate at a later date nonquality earlier experiences. For instance, when Hopi Indian infants were studied, who, as dictated by their culture practices, were bound to a cradleboard with little movement allowed or encouraged during the first year of life, they were found to be no slower in beginning to walk than those babies who were not restrained (Dennis, 1940). Many current popular concepts dealing with the development of intelligence and academic aptitudes suggest the wonderful characteristics of the human to be able to make up early deficiencies. Apparently, we are far more plastic than non-humans. We can compensate for shortcomings. Many critical behavioral periods, which exist for a very brief period in subhumans, apparently are quite lengthy in humans. Perhaps, as Mussen, Conger, and Kagan (1969) suggest, the whole of infancy is a critical period. These thoughts bring hope to situations where despair might otherwise be present. They should, however, not be construed as supportive of nonenriching and limited experiences for the child. It is more likely than not that the child who has encountered meaningful experiences appropriate for his maturational level will demonstrate more advanced behavior with more ease in later periods.

According to Scott, there are three kinds of critical-learning periods: (1) optimal periods for learning; (2) infantile stimulation; and (3) formation of basic social relationships. Infantile (human or otherwise) stimulation, in the form of large amounts of perceptual experience leads to better learners later on than if these organisms are deprived of such experience. As development occurs, learning capacities change. When dealing with young children, we are obviously not concerned with complex sport and skill learning. Rather, we are concerned with basic movements and patterns that are performed as if by habit. Habits formed early in life persist in adult life and are resistant to change. It is therefore necessary that these learned movements be desirable, for the acquisition of one habit may prevent the learning of others. What is learned at a particular time may interfere with later learning. In the words of Scott, "organization hampers reorganization."

There is need to be concerned not only with what the child does experience but also with what he does not. Warren Johnson (1964) indicates that Luria stated at the 1959 World Health Organization seminar in Milan, Italy, "Sometimes, if a single link of training is missed, if a certain stage in the development of the necessary operation is not properly worked up, the entire process of further development becomes retarded. . . ."

What motor skills, then, should be taught to children, and when? Myrtle

McGraw's (1935) famous twin study indicated that learning varies for each motor activity; each activity has its own optimum period for rapid and skillful learning. Jimmy was the control twin and was raised in typical fashion. Johnny was the experimental twin and received special training to increase his neuromuscular development and demonstrated an ability to acquire many skills at an early age. This study refuted the concept that an infant is unresponsive to practice because of an immature nervous system, a concept espoused by leading child psychologists such as Gesell.

McGraw attempted to discover the period when a child would profit by a particular experience or practice. Johnny was stimulated daily whereas Jimmy was provided with a few toys and experienced a routine environment. At about one year of age, Johnny was directed in various motor activities usually experienced by children later in life, e.g., riding a tricycle, swimming and diving, roller skating, jumping from heights, and sliding. Jimmy received intensive practice and instruction in the same activities for two and a half months when he was twenty-two months old. When Johnny was less than a year old, he could swim the length of a 7-foot tank while supported by a strap. He swam the distance without support at 411 days, performed a dive into the tank at 422 days, and when 467 days old, dove off a 5-foot board into a lake.

After Jimmy's training period, the two boys were compared in performance. In swimming and diving behavior, Johnny demonstrated superior talents and better attitudes, which were attributed to his extensive swimming experience. As to skating, Johnny had the advantage because of his earlier training. He was adjusted to falling, a problem that Jimmy had difficulty in overcoming. It would seem that the best time to learn skating occurs when the baby is learning to walk, for he is gaining control of equilibrium factors. Johnny also demonstrated a more coordinated jump from heights, having overcome fear at the early age at which he had had related experiences. These activities were learned better because of their earlier introduction. Some activities were not facilitated by earlier practice—for example, walking. Both boys demonstrated approximately similar patterns despite the extra practice Johnny received. Other activities appeared to be disrupted because unskillful habits were formed. McGraw suggests that not only was Johnny not benefited by his earlier experience with the tricycle, but, in fact, these experiences actually hindered him. Jimmy practiced less on this skill, and the delay in his exposure to the tricycle proved to be more economical to learning.

McGraw (1939) retested the boys at school age. The skills were demonstrated in varying patterns in their tendency to be retained or forgotten. For example, Johnny and Jimmy were about equal in tricycling and in roller skating. However, whereas both boys demonstrated no loss of skill in tricycling after the long layoff, it appeared as if skating skill underwent deterioration. Nevertheless, *Johnny generally displayed greater motor coordination and daring in physical performance.* The retention of specific

skills, according to McGraw, depends on whether performance was composed of well-integrated movements. Poorly developed skills are not retained to a high degree.

The McGraw investigation allows other general assumptions. There is no
one critical period, no one chronological age for all skills, as periods differ
for each behavior pattern. In fact, the critical period is not determined by
chronological age but, rather, is based on the maturational status of the
nervous system for a given activity and evidently may extend for quite a
long period for the acquisition of many skills. As long as the organism
grows, so do the powers of restoration and compensation. Unless there is an
unduly long deprivation period (a time when the child does not have any
experience with the skill in question), he can usually be brought to approximate the achievement level of another child who has begun practice earlier
than he did. (Jimmy did approximately match Johnny's skill level in the
various activities after the intensive training period, but it should be remembered that Johnny demonstrated better overall motor coordination.)
Finally, because the twins were normal and about equal in intelligence-test
scores, exercise in special motor activities did not appear to accelerate intellectual functions. The important role that perceptual-motor experiences
have in contributing to potential intellectual achievements is not to be denied, though. This particular study merely indicates that additional motor
activity will not improve upon the normal intelligence.

Empirical evidence indicates that young children can learn much more
than they are given credit for. Investigations on outstanding athletes show
that usually they began learning their specialties at early ages, and have
undergone continuous intensive training. In McGraw's study, Johnny could
swim 7 feet (with one breath) at one year of age. Children in general are
learning sports associated with adulthood such as golf, bowling, and tennis
earlier in their lifetimes than was the case with preceding generations. If,
as Jerome Bruner (1963) says, *any subject can be taught in a legitimate way
so as to be of value to the child at any stage of development,* the implications are great for physical educators. Although Bruner's thoughts in general
lie more in the cognitive domain with great issues, principles, and values of
society, his concept also may be applied to the learning of motor skills. Certainly, physical education offers experiences that most children are receptive
to, i.e., a child usually does not have to be forced into participating in games
and play. It is up to the creative teacher to present the material in a meaningful way, by understanding the development stages of childhood.

Motor skills can be taught in a modified way to the child once he has
reasonable control of his body. However, the desirability of encroaching on
the maturing process, of teaching particular activities to children who are
too young to comprehend and respond to them adequately, is questionable.
*Successful skill attainment at maturity is not dependent on the earliness of
instruction but rather on its timeliness.*

John Scott (1968) feels that one answer to the problem of how to enhance the maximum development of motor skills in young children is to permit a great amount of freedom of movement. Confinement does not permit the experience necessary for developing motor capacities. Capacities attained reflect maturational level and practice. It is often found that children raised in orphanages have poorer motor capacities than those raised by their parents, perhaps because of less enriching and more constricted environments. The same is true when comparisons are made between upper- and lower-class children. In lower-class homes, children are often less controlled and confined; they demonstrate high degrees of motor development. Scott (p. 123) says:

It is desirable to give a child contact with a variety of physical objects which can be manipulated or climbed. This encourages the development of general motor skills that can be applied later to the learning of more complicated tasks. The results at both ages are more satisfactory than those obtained by trying to teach complex physical skills directly at an early age. Most children are not able to perform activities requiring good coordination of the whole body much before the ages of 7 or 8, and introducing them too early in such activities only results in unskillful performance or failure.

Research on critical-learning periods permits only generalizations from animal research to human behavior. It does not, at this time, tell us the optimal time in life in which to learn, say, basketball, golf, or archery. It does call attention to the theoretical impact of the proposition that there are critical periods in life for the learning of everything. It remains for researchers to investigate this area further, to determine the stage of approximate age of readiness for specific motor-skill experience.

It does appear, however, that the concept of critical-learning periods is slightly different for humans and infrahumans. In infrahuman studies, critical-learning periods are considered as points in time when a behavior is learned or else it probably will never be learned. For humans, on the other hand, the phrase *critical-learning periods* seems to be more correctly substituted with *optimal-learning-abilities periods*. This is the time when the minimal abilities necessary to learn a skill are present in the learner. Before this period he is unable to learn it and after that time certain aging or interfering factors might impair the learning. As long as prerequisite abilities and skills are present, the learner should be able to master more complex activities. If they are not, he must first acquire them before proceeding further.

HEREDITY AND EXPERIENCE

When discussing athletic performance, arguments are often heated as to whether the outstanding athlete is born or made. It is the old problem of nature versus nurture. What are the relative effects of genetics and experience on performance? Such descriptive phrases as "what a natural athlete" or "a born hitter" are ways of commonly referring to particular performers. Does the physical educator or coach waste his time training individuals "who don't have it" and "never will have it" (whatever "it" may be)?

An examination of the problem should probably begin with the effects of heredity and environmental circumstances on intelligence, for it is the development of the cognitive processes that has been the primary concern of educators and psychologists during this century. The results of their research pave the way for understanding motor-skill accomplishment. No informed person would state that what we are is caused by purely genetic factors or solely environmental experiences, but rather that the end product is formulated by the interaction of both. The problem is in determining the relative contributions each makes to one's level of attainment in a particular endeavor.

Various methods have been employed in investigations concerned with the relative effects of heredity and environment on the organism. The usual laboratory techniques with lower forms of organisms have included (1) selective breeding and (2) analysis of behavioral characteristics shown by different but ideally pure strains. Obviously these techniques are not possible with human subjects. Families may be observed in order to find the characteristics that are prevalent among members, and correlations are computed so as to determine the degree of relationship among members, on a specific variable.

Twins have been the subject of much research. If the twins are identical and raised in the same home, then behavior differences between them would probably be due to genetics. Twins who are reared apart also offer data valuable for gaining insight into the problem. Finally, a comparison of monozygotic twins (MZ) with dizygotic twins (DZ) permits further analysis of the relative effects of heredity and environment. Monozygotic twins are identical twins, coming from a single zygote and provided with identical hereditary endowments. Dizygotic twins are fraternal twins, coming from two separate zygotes and who may or may not be alike. When the genetic constitutions (genotypes) of the subjects are controlled and are more similar, deductions on environmental effects are more easily formulated. The particular characteristic of interest, observed and measured, is referred to as a *phenotype*.

It is no easy matter to control the many influencing variables adequately in order to estimate environmental versus hereditary effects accurately. Therefore results of studies must be accepted with reservation. Such findings are more suggestive than conclusive, although certain general assumptions may now be made because of accumulating evidence, as we will see.

MZ twins raised apart yield the simplest comparison data for the estimation of the heritability of a particular characteristic (the percentage of impact inheritance has on the characteristic relative to effect of environmental experiences on it). As described by Jensen (1970) a person's characteristics can be explained in the following formula:

$$V_P = V_G + V_E + V_{GE} + V_1 + V_e$$

where:

V_P = total phenotypic variance
V_G = the genetic component
V_E = a nongenetic, or environmental (experiential) component
V_{GE} = a covariance of genotypes and environments component
V_1 = an interaction of genetic and environmental factors
V_e = a measurement error component

More broadly speaking, heritability is defined as

$$h^2 = \frac{V_G}{V_P}$$

Although there have been occasions where researchers in this area have squared the correlations between twins to obtain the percentage of variance that can be attributed to genetic factors, Jensen (1971) makes a logical argument against this procedure. Instead, the original correlations should be used, as they provide the proportion of common variance. For a more elaborate discussion on problems in research methodology and statistical treatments of data in genetic versus environmental influences on behavior, articles by C. J. Eaves (1970) and Cyril Burt (1971) are recommended.

Cognition

With intelligence as well as with any other factor, environmental variables operate within the limits offered by heredity. How influential is heredity in determining intelligence? Apparently it is quite influential. The IQ's of identical twins raised apart correlate higher than those of fraternal twins raised together. Environmental circumstances, to a much lesser degree than heredity, also affect intelligence, for it is noted that the IQ of one identical twin can be predicted from the IQ score of the other, the accuracy of which is dependent on their upbringing. When the IQ correlation of twins raised in the same house is analyzed, a predictability of 80 per cent has been obtained. It is reported to be 60 per cent for identical twins raised apart. In other words, twins living apart have a greater difference in IQ scores than those twins living together.

Burt (1958) studied identical twins reared together and those separated early in life. He summarized his findings by indicating the relatively little effect environment had on intellectual growth, with the figure approximating 12 per cent. Other investigators have found similar results; some results show that less than 10 per cent of the IQ variance is accounted for by the environmental component and as much as 96 per cent of the variance is contributed by the genetic background. Jensen (1970), in summarizing the literature, notes that a comparison of MZ twins raised apart is probably the easiest way of determining the heritability of certain factors. These twins do not differ by more than seven to ten IQ points on the average when reared apart; they differ by about two or three points when raised in the same home. Jensen writes that twenty-four points is the largest IQ difference ever reported for a pair of identical twins raised apart, but more than 17 per cent of children, fraternal or nontwin, raised together differ by more than twenty-four points. Jensen concludes that the genes outweigh the effects of environment by 2 to 1 for the average person's IQ score.

Using thirty-three pairs of MZ twins and twelve pairs of DZ twins, ages thirteen to eighteen, Osborne and Gregor (1966) administered a battery of cognitive tests described as visualization, perceptual speed, and spatial orientation. The range of the heritability coefficients was from 0.15 to 0.89, indicating that specific abilities are independently inherited. That is to say, the role of genetics on task performance is different for different tasks. As might be expected, MZ twins showed higher relationships in task performances (0.46 to 0.91) than DZ twins (0.08 to 0.72). This article presents an excellent review of literature and demonstrates the degree of compatability of various techniques for determining heritability coefficients.

The heredity-versus-environment issue reveals an interesting history whereby similar questions are raised, but at no time was it so volatile as in 1969, with the publication of an article by Arthur Jensen in the *Harvard Education Review*. In this article and in a number of other ones, Jensen has strongly supported his stance with his own research and the interpretation of other research that heredity is by far the major factor in IQ scores. Most controversial was his claim that there are probably genetic differences of intelligence among races and that blacks have average inherited intelligence below that of whites. Major debates on the point have occurred on many campuses and have been covered extensively by the media. Major psychology and educational research journals are still publishing articles that include data or thoughts on both sides of the issue. Because the issues cover political and racial grounds, it is not at all surprising that howls of outrage from civil rights people have been heard. Scientists also disagree as to the practical interpretations of the position that heredity largely affects IQ. Data can and are being interpreted in different ways as scholars attempt to formulate acceptable theories and determine what kinds of environmental situations and programs can produce desired behavioral changes within genetic limitations.

Although environmental factors may not have a dramatic effect on intellectual growth, they have a great influence on achievement. Extremes in environmental surroundings will have a dramatic effect on IQ scores and academic achievement in general. It should go without saying that enriched environments will promote achievement but impoverished conditions will result in progressively poorer returns. The implication here is that although genetic factors limit potential, there is quite a distance between the operational level of an individual and his theoretical limits. Much can be done through environmental manipulations to raise the intellectual achievement of an average or below-average youngster.

Motor Skills

Just as differences in intellectual performance may be caused by hereditary and environmental factors, these same factors operate for potential success in motor-skill performance. The extent of influence is not easy to ascertain, for most of the research has been completed on mental growth and is still inconclusive. However, it may be readily apparent that it does not necessarily follow that the same amount of practice on similar skills will benefit all individuals equally. Some people will perform more effectively after a few trials, some will show skill following many practice sessions, and others may never reach the level of performance that might be termed skilled. Obviously, dissimilar capacities for performing various tasks will be due to hereditary factors and/or previous experiences.

There exists some relationship between the body build of the outstanding athlete and his chosen sport. To the extent that heredity might contribute to success in particular activities via physical characteristics, studies have found correlations approximating 0.50 between family physical qualities, such as height and weight (McClearn, 1964). [A statistical correlation (r) of 1.00 demonstrates a perfect relationship between variables, whereas one of 0.00 indicates no relationship.] Even anxiety level has been shown to have a firm genetic basis, and certainly the effective usage of emotions in activity can affect outcomes.

The influence of parent size on the size of offspring has been documented by Malina, Harper, and Holman (1970). Also studied were sex differences, race differences, gross motor performance, and static strength. Parent size differential effects on the strength and motor performance of their children are more noticeable during the first few years of life than by school age. In general, however, an inconsistent trend was observed between parent size and motor performance.

Genetics will usually determine body types, and it is often witnessed that identical twins have similar body constitutions. Anatomically speaking, body structures may be greatly influenced by nonhereditary variables, such as health, nutrition, and exercise. A good example of an environmental factor exerting influence over genetic tendencies is the fact that first-generation Japanese immigrants exceed their former countrymen in height by 2 inches. Nutrition and diet evidently had much to do with this situation.

McNemar (1933) undertook an early study to analyze the inheritance of abilities involving certain motor skills. The tests involved the use of the pursuit rotor, the whipple steadiness tester, the Miles speed drill, the Brown spool packer, and a card sorter. Ninety-eight sets of twins of junior high school age provided the necessary data. Forty-eight pairs were diagnosed as fraternal whereas forty-seven were identical. The fraternals achieved higher scores than the identicals on all five tasks, but only in spools and cards did the difference achieve statistical significance. The identicals showed a higher degree of resemblance in their performance than the fraternals.

As to actual research on the born-versus-made athlete, one of the leading contributors to knowledge in this area is Gedda (1961), who investigated the families of outstanding athletes and made comparisons of the sports practiced by twins. In this study, Gedda received data on genotype twins and twins with dissimilar genotypes. Among his many observations he noted a difference between type of twin and sports participation and success. Little dissimilarity in sports participation and practice could be found between genotype twins. It was equivalent to a 6 per cent difference in the case of identical genotype twins but was 85 per cent in the case of twins with different genotypes. Evidently, twins with contrary genotypes (fraternal twins) had individual interests and differed widely in general sports practice.

Gedda believes his data indicate that there is a great similarity between identical genotypes and the sports in which they participate successfully; hence the relationship of heredity factors to activity interest and certain characteristics to athletic success. He hypothesizes that sports aptitude is attributed to an exogenous factor or environmental conditions, including training, experiences, socioeconomic level, and an endogenous factor or inherited phenotype, which refers to the transmitted characteristics necessary for skill attainment in a specific sport.

In another investigation, Gedda (1964) and his co-workers surveyed the athletes who participated in the 1960 Olympic Games in Rome. After accumulating data on each athlete's family, the writers formulated two indexes: an Index of Isosportivation (number of the athlete's family members participating in the same sport as he); and an Index of Allosportivation (number of family members practicing some other sport). Interpretation of the information allowed the following conclusions: (1) the athlete and his family practice similar activities and (2) specific physical and psychological qualities of the Olympians may be attributed to heredity. Family and environmental influences are not sufficient, for specific psychological and physical characteristics are needed for success in a particular sport. These occur repeatedly in the same family and are therefore attributed to heredity and environmental influences.

It appears therefore that the capacity to perform motor skills is primarily determined by heredity. However, although achievement in intellectual pursuits and athletic endeavors will ultimately be determined by genetics, environmental experiences will do much to influence the level of achievement. Even the most favorably endowed individual, unless his energies are guided in a constructive manner and his abilities developed through instruction and practice, will not be an outstanding performer. Certain people are born with particular potential general talents or abilities, and these permit them to excel more easily in a given area. Yet if all success were based on hereditary components, what would be the purpose in developing a psychology of learning, of developing learning techniques and theories? Why attempt to modify behavior? Obviously, much can be done with any individual if he is taught effectively, and his life's experiences will either facilitate or hinder his development and acquisition of motor skills.

EARLY MOTOR
DEVELOPMENT
AND LEARNING

In focusing on critical-learning periods, we have already spent some time on the relation of timely (often early) learning experiences to later-life behavior. Now it is important to discuss early motor development and the evolvement of learning processes irrespective of critical learning periods so as to broaden the picture a bit. Perhaps a logical starting point is Lewis Lipsitt's (1971) statement that the newborn, contrary to usual expectation, is not "inept, befuddled, bewildered, disorganized, or diffuse" (p. 18). Older concepts held that the infant was rather nonresponsive and could not be encouraged to learn faster than "normal" maturation would allow. Thus the true learning potential of the infant has been virtually untapped until recent years.

Lipsitt dramatically emphasizes that the human newborn is a responsive organism. He is not in a state of helplessness; enrichment environments can have a considerable influence on his development. The degree to which an infant responds effectively to stimuli is usually used as an indicant of his intelligence. Although there are obvious motor patterns forming that can be viewed from a motor-development point of view, such responses can be regarded in their cognitive aspects. After all, the baby's perceptual and discriminating abilities, among others, are determined from the outcome of motor responses. As the sense organs and the nervous system develop, more advanced motor patterns can be displayed. The combination of maturation and enriched experiences helps to give rise to more highly differentiated and yet integrated coordinated responses. From the general behaviors related to manipulation and locomotion will come a variety of movement-oriented skills.

During the early portions of this century, G. Stanley Hall and later, Arnold Gesell, conceptualized a maturational hypothesis, or what Robert Gagné (1968) calls the "growth-readiness model." It was thought that environmental factors were supportive of behavioral changes, but generally speaking, organisms acquire the same motor patterns in a preplanned (genetic) manner. Genetics predetermine the evolvement of behaviors, regardless of situational and learning factors. Even the Piaget approach, mentioned previously, places minimal influence on learning on a child's behavior and heavy reliance on maturational factors. The child passes through stages that are maturationally associated, although environment can facilitate or inhibit the phasing in or out of a stage. Another early description of the process of motor development was behavioristic. Behaviorism embraced concepts related to the learning of stimulus–response associations, as we saw in Chapter 3.

Whereas Piaget relies heavily on maturational factors to explain the child's behaviors, Gagné talks in terms of the learning of prerequisite skills and behaviors, which can be related to maturation but is not of major concern. Gagné suggests that the learning of associations do not encourage the child to pass from one point to another in development. Rather, it is learning of an ordered set of capabilities. These build up in hierarchical fashion through the processes of differentiation, recall, and transfer of learning. In a simple sense, the reference is to building blocks, cumulatively adding up to more complex learned capabilities. This notion, primarily expressed by Gagné as an explanation of a child's intellectual development, has an analogy in Jerome Bruner's (1970) explanation of skill development.

According to Bruner, as a skill is learned (being developed), so are "rules" that include appropriate flexible orders and exclude inappropriate ones. Skilled activity involves a strived-for objective. Bruner favors computer terminology (see Chapter 3 and the discussion of Adaptive Models), and talks in terms of a master program and organized subroutines. These subroutines are performed serially in an orderly fashion when necessary. There also can be changes within the serial-order subroutines when situations make such demands. The child learns substitution rules as well as *the* rule. He develops a repertoire of, in Gagné's terms, capabilities.

Skilled actions are developed from (1) the innate repertoire of movement patterns that interact with the environmental conditions, and (2) a differentiation process that shapes gross acts into components for further use in new tasks and in new sequences. Programs are formulated that will contribute to the mastery of skilled tasks as well as to problem-solving activities. Bruner makes the startling observation that "it is difficult to say whether the tasks [that a child learns] . . . are instances of 'skill' or 'problem-solving'" (p. 91). All too often, even with adults, we think of skill as symbolic of learned associations and finely tuned response mechanisms. The cognitive elements of skilled activity are either neglected or minimally acknowledged in typical analyses of skilled behavior. Recent thoughts on the child's learning of capabilities, rules, plans, and strategies as underpinnings of cognitive and motor skills, and in fact, the emphasis on learning instead of maturational factors alone, reflect what might have been considered revolutionary ideas ten years ago.

Young children are at a disadvantage in learning skills, as compared to more mature individuals, but a consideration of certain factors can lead to more fruitful learning outcomes with motor skills. A child is limited in information-processing capabilities. He is distracted easily and his attention span is poor. Gross movements precede fine movements. Need to achieve is apparent, and failure results in frustration, loss of motivation, and little desire to continue the experience.

Children's learning can be improved if learning activities involve more gross muscle movements, simplified actions, and minimal cues to which to respond. For instance, a two-year-old learning to catch a ball should experience a large ball before a small one. Soft throws to a predictable location allow the child to concentrate on fewer alternative cues. Verbal cues by an outsider should be simple and limited. One or two of the most relevant to the child's developmental level should be emphasized. Too many cues are confusing. Experiences should be enjoyable and successful. With success, increased difficulty in the activity is appropriate; with failures, reversal to more simplified activity is a necessity. Children learn rules in the activity and expectations when certain situations and stimuli are present. Anticipation improves as will skill.

The child's limited channel capacity to process information dictates a concern for the quantity and speed at which cues are presented. Although it is true that for certain behavior adults and children will perform equally poorly, the reasons may be to some extent similar and to some extent dissimilar. The development of skill undergoes similar processes for the child as well as the adult. Yet differences in neurological organization and maturation, previous experiences, and motivation suggest different operational factors.

Learning general and basic movements is not the same as learning skills. The latter involves far more complex processes. The structural components, dependent upon maturation, must be present in the child, as well as precise practice of responses to cues under the direction of plans and strategies. As we have noted, motor behavior proceeds from primarily reflexive and generalized movement patterns to more differentiated, specialized, and integrated movements (Breckenridge and Murphy, 1969). Visual and neuromotor components are integrated in eye–hand coordination tasks. Although maturation provides the ability to control one's body and a readiness to learn, complex skills need specific rather than general practice. Maturation is important for generalized responses, but specific experiences lead to highly specialized behaviors.

Concepts and skills are built up with use. The child must continually react to environmental stimulation. Because a number of significant human characteristics develop most quickly in the first five years of life and changes in development are more difficult with age and development (Bloom, 1964), the implications for quality preschool and early school years are great in developing learning patterns and general achievement.

There is abundant information that cognitive processes can be accelerated with effective stimulation in early childhood. With little research on motor skills learning but continuing with the same rationale, it would appear that a similar statement could be made about motor-development processes. Of question are the long-term effects. Do early cognitive enhancement experiences make a difference in later years? What about special motor-enrichment programs? Arguments can be made in defense or attack of special early childhood programs, but the position taken here that, within the structural and functional constraints of the organism, enriched early experiences *of all kinds* experienced in a satisfying atmosphere should increase the likelihood of beneficial long-term effects.

The potential for young children to learn complex motor skills has been shown by Ken Leithwood (1970–1971). He reports the terrific gains made by four-year-olds learning standard gymnastic activities. During a period of four months, the children met for three times a week for a maximum of thirty minutes each session. With most activities, the specially trained group made gains almost five times as great as those made by comparison groups. The experimental subjects were all able to combine tasks into their own created routines. Leithwood also scaled down gymnastic apparatus (parallel bar, horizontal bar, balance beam, trampoline), and specially trained children learned one-third more tasks. A strong possibility exists that simple activities are generally learned at the same rate for specially trained and nontrained children, in which case the maturational hypothesis would be supported. But children are ready and can effectively learn complex motor activities when involved in specific training for development.

We have already stated that learning occurs soon after birth. Many experiments with human babies and other young demonstrate that conditioning can occur under appropriate conditions and manipulations. But do the young learn as well as the mature organisms? At the present it appears that it is difficult to relate age and learning, for performance is determined by a host of interacting variables. Rate of acquisition and capacity affect performance but are not always found to be related to age. As to a comparison of the retention of early and adult learning of responses, the research indicates that the earlier the learning the greater the probability it will be forgotten. These surprising findings, primarily obtained with rats as subjects, imply that a deficiency in the memory process rather than in the original learning exists in infancy. With neurological maturity, memory processes become more effective.

In order for stimulation to be meaningful, it must not only be provided early but *continuously* as well. Intellectually gifted children have stereotypically been stimulated early, intensively, and extensively. The gains from early intervention programs disappear shortly after termination of the programs, which is further rationale for continuity in programming, suggests Thomas Ryan (1971). It becomes clear that the young child is capable of learning a great deal, if the opportunities for learning are properly presented.

LATER LEARNING
AND MOTOR PERFORMANCE

Motor behavior in infancy and early childhood has been discussed already and need not be treated here. School-age children display characteristics of skilled movements in their play and the nature of their play is such that, with increasing age, more complex skills and diverse sports are mastered and demonstrated. Two widely used methods for obtaining performance data relevant to age are the *longitudinal* and *cross-sectional* approaches. Subjects at each age are sampled under the *cross-sectional* approach, whereas the same individuals are followed for a length of time with the longitudinal method. Both research methods contribute to our knowledge of growth and development, although the longitudinal technique usually is more time-consuming and contains more administrative problems than the cross-sectional method. However, the longitudinal study more accurately describes the changes that take place within individuals in succeeding years. Famous early longitudinal studies include Lewis Terman's follow-up of genius youngsters to adulthood and Harold Jones's observations at Berkeley of strength changes during the adolescent period. The longitudinal study permits an analysis of the growth process and does not conceal unusual occurrences, such as growth spurts.

The relative contributions of maturation and experience in development are not easy to ascertain. In order to determine the separate influences of specific transfer factors, nonspecific transfer factors, and maturation on performance, L. R. Goulet (1970) recommends two methods: the E/C method and the LTL method. *E/C* refers to "experimental/control" and *LTL* to "learning to learn." The best example of the E/C method is a 2×2 design (two age groups and an experimental and control group for each age). The control group does not experience any treatment, whereas the experimental group is administered one or two tasks. The typical case would be that all subjects in both age groups would be administered two tasks. Task 1 is the same for experimental and control groups. Task 2 would differ for these groups. Degree of specific transfer as related to developmental changes and age can be specified.

The LTL method suggests the comparison of at least two age groups across a series of tasks designed to provide LTL experience. There is no control here for differences among groups in pre-experimental specific transfer, as is the case with the E/C method. However the LTL method is more versatile. Age-related characteristics of LTL transfer can be determined with either cross-sectional or longitudinal studies. With more learning tasks, performance improves because of more experiences. Is this true at all ages? In the same predictable manner? Such models as these can be used to test the hypotheses and models of human development theorists.

When the child advances in age, on the average to five years, he demonstrates increasing control over actual movements, thought, and mediation processes. Highly skilled performance is related to the individual's ability to regulate it voluntarily. Apparently a child can transfer behavioral control from overt verbalization (guidance) to self-verbalization (thought) over task execution. Even infants two or younger can show some voluntary inhibition of performance. With age and appropriate experiences, skilled performances reflect the ability to use inhibitory control to regulate actions matching corresponding images and ideas. R. H. Wozniak (1972) recognizes the importance of the emerging abilities to self-regulate and control, and he writes:

> "Verbal regulation" or the transfer of the control of a child's behavior from stimuli external to the child (e.g., commands of an adult) to stimuli internal to the child (e.g., verbal planning) is a prerequisite for higher cognitive functioning. A child's success, therefore, in a wide variety of behaviors (e.g., control of attention, conscious recall, concept formation, problem solving, etc.) depends specifically upon the occurrence of this transfer.

Not only does the child learn to transfer control over his actions, but the repertoire of responses increases considerably, the ability to apply verbal labels to movements increases, and directions can be more detailed and lengthy because of the developing information-processing abilities. Attention, perception, imagery, and other abilities are developed corresponding to the increased maturity and quality experiences of the organism as he approaches adolescence. Such personal qualities are prerequisites for the skilled execution of complex motor skills (Singer, 1973).

Furthermore, as Singer indicates, positive transfer probably occurs more easily during youthful years rather than in advanced years. Previous learnings affect subsequent learnings to the degree they are related. This effect may be favorable or unfavorable. At older ages it becomes increasingly difficult to reorganize patterned behavioral responses. More established and practiced routines impede possibilities for modification and change. A child has less competing, and for that matter, well-learned responses that might interfere with new learnings.

When normative motor-skills-performance data are collected, without any present special learning or treatment conditions, one can expect performance to be directly related to age during the developmental period. As a general rule, performance increases with age throughout childhood. Running, throwing, jumping, balance, agility, stroking, and catching skills in primary-grade children have been found to be greater at each age level. Humphries and Shephard (1959) trained their subjects, from four to ten years of age, in a reversed task of the Toronto Complex Coordinator. These investigators noted that the level of performance was positively related to age and that all age levels constantly improved with training. Extending the

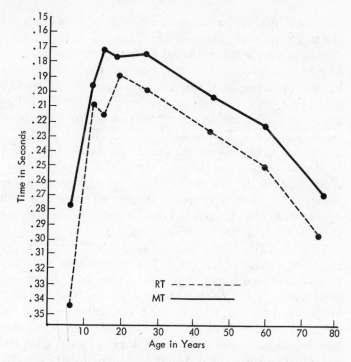

Figure 8–2.   Reaction time (RT) and movement time (MT) changes as a function of age. (From Jean Hodgkins, "Reaction Time and Speed of Movement in Males and Females at Various Ages," *Research Quarterly,* 34:335–343, 1963.)

analysis of age to performance in later ages, improvement increments are noticed to a certain time in life, depending on the skill. It should go without saying that individuals learn and improve in performance up to varying ages, and any evidence presented here is based on average performance.

The reaction times of children two-and-a-half and older decrease with age. Four hundred and eighty female subjects with ages ranging from six to eighty-four had their reaction times taken by Jean Hodgkins (1962). It was discovered that reactions improved from childhood to nineteen years, remained constant from nineteen to twenty-six, and decreased afterward. Similar results were obtained in another study by Hodgkins in which she tested both the reaction time and movement time of males and females. Figure 8–2 illustrates her findings.

Slowness of behavior is characteristic of older age and may be caused by many factors. Some evidence suggests the process of aging in the nervous system as being a leading cause. Some studies show a 10 to 20 per cent slowing of reaction times between twenty- and sixty-year-olds. However, the actual time difference may be as little as 0.02 of a second, which, practically speaking, is not much.

Some researchers have found conflicting results using different tasks to measure a similar variable. For instance, Cron and Pronko (1957) tested balance by having their subjects walk on a balance board, whereas Bachman (1961, 1966) used the stabilometer and vertical ladder climb. In the former study, 501 children were represented, spanning in age from four to fifteen. Balance ability improved with age, then leveled off, and declined in the twelve- to fifteen-year-old group. The girls were superior in the four- to eight-year bracket, but the boys exceeded the girls in the eight- to fifteen-year range. In the first study by Bachman, the subjects were from six to twenty-six years of age, and in the second investigation, they aged from twenty-six to fifty. In both tasks and in both studies, it was generally found that learning was not related to sex or age.

Talland (1962) tested three groups of men; members of group 1 were in their early twenties; of group 2, between forty and sixty-three; and of group 3, between seventy-seven and eighty-nine. There were eighteen subjects in each group. The tasks they performed were (1) continuous working of a manual counter, (2) moving beads with a tweezer, and (3) selecting beads of one hue from a mixed stock and moving them with a tweezer. Significant differences were found between each group in favor of each preceding younger group. The results suggest that even the simplest motor skill declines in speed with age, even though it involves little exertion or coordination of movement.

With regard to athletic skills, it appears that they are continually developed to a high degree of proficiency, especially in the first two decades of life. Individuals may continue to improve in skill attainment throughout a good portion of life, depending on the nature of the skill and the training habits and personality of the performer. Empirical evidence indicates the late twenties as the period before performance worsens. Many top athletes in baseball, football, and a host of other sports appear to reach their prime in their middle and late twenties.

A picture of Olympic champions raises serious questions as to whether we can indicate a given age for optimal athletic performance justifiably. Ernst Jokl (1964a) presents age and sport data from the 1952 Olympic Games in Helsinki. The swimming participants had the lowest mean age, twenty-one and a half. Boxers, cyclists, short-distance runners, hurdlers, and jumpers were on the average under twenty-five. As to the running events of over 1,500 meters, an average increase in age was noted as the distance increased. Those who participated in the decathalon, free-style wrestling, long-distance running events, and weight lifting were between twenty-five and thirty, on the average. The ages of the male Olympians were from thirteen to sixty-six, and a number of middle-aged men were observed to give excellent performances.

Data from the 1964 Olympics substantiated Jokl's earlier findings. Hirata (1966) categorized Olympic athletes by age and event. Much of his data indicates that those events in which a performer relies primarily on muscular strength are represented by more youthful athletes. Those events requiring more refined skill and technique are accomplished later in life. Swimming, for example, which does not demand so much technical ability, was represented by the youngest athletes. Male swimmers averaged approximately twenty years of age, whereas performers in such technical sports as gymnastics and wrestling were in the middle and late twenties. Some other mean ages, representing the male Olympians of various sports, were found to be as follows:

Sport	Age
Volleyball	26.2
Basketball	25.3
Foil Fencing	27.5
Track: 100-meter	24.5
Marathon	28.3
Cycling	24.0
Weight Lifting	27.2
Soccer	24.9

Although it would appear as if certain ages are more desirable for successful sports participation, there was a wide range of ages for the Olympic champions, as was the case in the 1952 Olympics. The male Olympians ranged from fifteen to fifty-four years in age, whereas the ages of the female Olympians went from thirteen to thirty-five years.

It is evident, then, that through ability and hard training, a person can demonstrate superior skills at earlier and later ages than ever before. Perhaps one of the reasons why drop-offs in performance are noted in early adulthood is because of incentive loss. Additional responsibilities, new values, and even boredom from practice repetition may contribute to a decline in performance with age. High levels of skill, once attained, are not easily forgotten. Most highly skilled activities demand a well-conditioned body, but once strength, endurance, and speed deteriorate, coordination also falls. Certain sports, with constant practice and the maintenance of good body condition, allow successful participation until a person is in the fifties and even sixties.

James Birren (1964) writes that industrial studies indicate that there is little change in worker performance up to the ages of sixty and sixty-five. Performance in typical industrial tasks should be little influenced by physiological changes except where time limitations are present, i.e., when a task must be performed in some time context. An older person may be limited in performing a number of tasks in a short period of time or over a long period where fatigue sets in. Older persons generally demonstrate poorer performance on complex and difficult tasks.

Athletic competition is usually more demanding. Reductions in such capacities as strength, sense acuity, and reaction time are more apparent in their relative effects. In those sports where the response is self-pacing—e.g., archery, bowling, and golf—high skill achievement can be more easily attained. Also, when the older person has a long time to anticipate or preview the stimulus conditions, there is a better chance for success. Certainly this is the case in noncompetitive sports. Finally, the quality and quantity of the cues present in the situation will determine task performance.

Summarizing the research literature, it has been shown that

1. Reaction time is longer in older people.
2. Older people need more time to finish complex tasks.
3. Older people process information more slowly.
4. Older people tend to pay attention to irrelevant information and on occasion, even warning signals do not measurably affect performance.
5. Strength decreases after the mid-twenties.

Learning is not only associated with growth, for it can continue throughout life. Changes with age in ability to learn are usually small up to sixty. Learning difficulty may be attributed to perception, motivation, set, attention, and the physiological state of the organism. Nevertheless, it is harder to teach an adult because of the complexity and maturity of the organism. A structured past and movements that have to be unlearned lead to learning difficulty. Motor abilities are more general in childhood, and with advancing age and varied experiences they become more specific. Differences in age and learning methods have been examined by Henry and Nelson (1956). Ten-year-olds were characterized by their ability to learn with less task specificity than fifteen-year-olds. The initial level of skill rather than ability to learn was important in the older group in ultimate task performance.

Thus it can be seen that age groups may be characterized by unique learning abilities, developed capacities, attitudes and interests, maturational levels, and physiological development. Specific sports and tasks differ in the optimal age a human should have for highest skill attainment. Even within a given activity, a wide range of age levels may be represented by successful performers. Increased sports knowledge, nutrition, health, training, and motivation interact to provide levels of skill attainable to young and old alike.

SPECIAL TRAINING
PROGRAMS

A child begins elementary school and displays poor readiness skills. It may appear that he had low intellectual potential, brain damage, or indications of mental retardation. Can anything be done to remedy the situation?

Obvious solutions include reading therapy, special training in intellectual skills, or allowing nature to take its course. A more practical approach would be to determine the cause of the child's problems and to proceed from there. Causes of problems associated with a low level of readiness for achievement in school may be genetic factors, brain injury, or inadequate environmental experiences. Barring extreme cases in the first two categories, research evidence indicates the possibilities and limitations in attempting to overcome intellectual difficulties through a corrective program. Basically this program includes introduction and practice in certain basic motor patterns.

Evidence for the low correlation between motor-skill achievement and intelligence in adults and older school-aged children is recognized. What of the relationship in infancy and early childhood? Statements by pioneer researchers, educators, and psychologists concur on the concept of a general maturational trend early in life. That is to say, "things seem to go together" at this time. Reasonably strong relationships exist among various maturational and behavioral characteristics of the young child. With increasing age, these associations lessen. Performance tasks that were general and gross become more specific and complex. Nonetheless, if a child goes through progressive development stages, the success in one may be dependent on the successes in the previous ones. We must pause and speculate about the ramifications of such a notion.

Crudely put, perhaps the stages are

1. Physical (reflexive, simple).
2. Motor (more purposeful).
3. Perceptual-motor (more complex).
4. Cognitive (various forms of intelligence).
5. Conceptual (abstract thinking).

Rationale would have it that a child with problems at the cognitive stage perhaps had difficulties in the perceptual-motor stage. He needs remedial activities that will prepare him better for the more advanced stage. With this kind of reasoning, a number of so-called perceptual-motor-training programs came into being in the 1960's. They often differ in emphasis and mode of operation but a commonality is in the general belief that cognitive learning disorders can be remediated through special programs that emphasize body awareness, multisensory stimulation, and a variety of movement experiences. A large number of these programs are in operation throughout the United States, in schools, but often as preschool experiences for the culturally and socioeconomically disadvantaged. Many have been supported by huge federal grants in the hope of preventing later learning problems or remediating existing ones.

Although special training programs are typically perceptual-motor or sensorimotor oriented with the hope of assisting the intellectual qualities of the child, it is of interest to note the lack of literature or programs whereby special programs are designed for youngsters to develop their movement patterns for later-in-life highly skilled movements. McGraw, as reported earlier, made a stab at this problem when she specially trained the twin Johnny at specific motor skills to determine effects in subsequent years on performance in these same skills. Perhaps a few reasons can be offered for the relative nonexistence of special skill training programs.

For one thing, our culture places a heavy emphasis on the mastery of intellectual tasks. Although we are noted as a country of great athletes and athletic teams and we support them well through attendance and finances, actual participation in and mastery of athletic and recreational skills—the effective use of the body in the attainment of skill and self-fulfillment through movement—is virtually underplayed in value relative to so-called intellectual attainments. The successful person is thought to be the wise one—the doctor, lawyer, or businessman. Children are encouraged to elevate their social prestige and their economic status by striving for such professional positions. Skill mastery has a lower prestige rating.

Also, a controversy exists as to the desirability of specially training young children in skills associated with athletics. Is the child ready to learn these skills and to compete? To what degree will his personality be enhanced or harmed through involvement in special programs? On top of this, to what degree should programs be structured for specific skill learnings versus spontaneous, open-structured, creative activities? We do know that children can learn skills to a much greater extent than usually believed. As to the long-term benefits and disadvantages of special skill training programs, we can only speculate.

Yet, as we mature and grow older, the effective use of our body in activities that require skilled motor patterns is a rewarding commodity. Mechanical skills, recreational activities, various occupational endeavors, and athletic events make perceptual-motor demands on the individual. What with more leisure time and interests in recreational pursuits, the ability to express oneself through skilled movement is quite an advantage. It is true that high degrees of proficiency result from prior general learning experiences that relate to the task at hand as well as task-specific practice. Precise spatially and temporally timed movements can only be acquired from extensive quality practice and experience. The general perceptual-motor abilities, developed in childhood, will contribute to later possible success in more complex activities. Throwing, jumping, and striking movements are similar in many skills. Many so-called new activities usually merely require a modification or restructuring in already existing routines or response patterns. Thus the argument can be made for programs of special instruction as well as unstructured programs that encourage general skill development in an enjoyable atmosphere, corresponding to the child's maturational level and readiness.

Development of the ability to move has long been the major concern of the coach and the physical educator. The relationship between this movement ability and later development of motor skills and physical fitness is justification enough for the inclusion of movement in the young child's learning experiences.

During the past few decades, this interest in movement has spread beyond the realms of physical education and into such fields as developmental psychology, neurology, educational psychology, remedial reading, and many others. With this diffusion of movement into other areas, recognition of the existence of a relationship between movement and cognitive development has occurred. The majority of the work that has been done in this area has generally been associated with attempts to overcome learning disabilities, particularly in the area of reading.

Although a paucity of research literature exists on special skill training programs, such is not the case with perceptual-motor training programs geared to enhance the general learning abilities of the child. Perceptual-motor programs have been approached from many different angles; thus there exists a variety of theories based on various aspects of perceptual-motor development. Carl Delacato joined with Glenn and Robert Doman to establish a theory based on neurological organization. Newell Kephart, also a prominent leader in the perceptual-motor area, bases his theory on the perceptual and integrative processes that result from a vast background of experience in the motor area. Other leaders in this field, G. Getman and Marianne Frostig, have worked in the direction of visual perceptual training. The program developed by Ray Barsch is referred to as a "movigenics" curriculum.

Perceptual-motor training programs are more individualized in nature than physical education programs, which tend to be group oriented. Typically an awareness of sensory skills is established and activities are geared to the developmental level of the child. James Fleming (1972, pp. 251–252) states that the common variables of all the perceptual-motor programs proposed appear to be

(a) the use of gross motor activities or physical exercises incorporating awareness of the necessary body movements.
(b) the use of structured activities organized in planned programmed procedures.

(c) training to improve basic sensory skills (visual, auditory, and tactile) as well as motor skills.

(d) the relative importance and emphasis that is placed on these programs in relation to academic learning and/or gains.

Differences within the various perceptual motor programs appear to stem from

(a) the theoretical models which [researchers] base their programs.

(b) the areas of major emphasis in remediation.

(c) the claims linked to the specific programs and procedures.

Let us examine some of the programs. In their book *Success Through Play*, along with subsequent books authored by Kephart, Radler and Kephart (1960) emphasize the importance of visual development in intellectual development, which in turn is dependent on simple motor skills. Poor motor coordination results in decelerated intellectual growth. According to Kephart, coordination is composed of (1) laterality—the sense of one's symmetry, of leftness and rightness; and (2) directionality—laterality projected into space, which is obtained through and experienced in motor skills. An inability to perform or realize laterality and directionality must be overcome if the child is to be successful in school. And indeed Kephart recommends various movement patterns that may be learned and practiced by youngsters needing a corrective program.

Kephart (1966) clarified his thoughts at the annual convention of the American Association for Health, Physical Education, and Recreation, held in Chicago. He offered the proposition that systematic motor exploration is the basis for all learning, because motor activity is information gathering. Ultimately, we may be teaching motor activity through physical education in order to promote reading. Kephart stated that 15 to 20 per cent of all children suffer from learning disorders; they have difficulty in learning. Children need generalized motor experiences; they need to explore, in order to have the background necessary for later success in school work. These motor generalizations include

1. *Balance and posture.* The child must know where gravity is as well as comprehend direction.

2. *Propulsion and receipt.* He should be able to move himself and objects away and toward something.

3. *Locomotion.* This refers to body movement through space, overcoming obstacles, and changing pace. Locomotive generalizations go on unconsciously so the child may explore.

4. *Contact and manipulation.* The child's relationship with objects is determined by such abilities as reaching, grasping, and releasing.

Because of the importance attached to motor generalizations in intellectual development, natural questions arise. Are professional athletes more highly intelligent individuals? Kephart states that this is not necessarily so, as they may have dropped out at one of the developmental levels above motor-skill accomplishment. Athletes have the potential for high intellectual attainment, but only if they have succesfully gone through all the development levels during childhood. He calls for more emphasis on the developmental aspects of sports and less on the competitive and social aspects. What about high degrees of skills in many motor performances? This is not necessary, but instead what is desired is a minimum ability in a wide range of activities. Overconcentration on one skill is not as effective as varied motor experiences in contributing to the cognitive processes.

Just as Godfrey and Kephart (1969) suggest that low achievers in school lack basic readiness (motor) skills that can be made up if they are taught, Delacato (1966) expresses similar thoughts. In a series of articles and books, culminating in *Neurological Organization and Reading*, Delacato favors a concept of neurological organization. It is used to explain deficits in readiness and to show how a child develops physically and neurologically in his early years and ultimately intellectually. Neurological Organization describes the process of activities control that begins at the level of the spinal cord and medulla at birth, then goes to the pons, to the midbrain, and finally to the cortex. This organization terminates when the child is approximately six to eight years of age. In other words, the neurological development process is complete at this time.

Delacato has tested children on various tasks to see whether they have progressed normally from one stage to the next stage. For example, cortical-level control is measured by the child's ability to perform cross-pattern walking and visual pursuit. A failure on a test at any control level indicates that the neurological organization is incomplete, with potential detrimental effects in reading ability. Reading problems are thus created before a child enters the school; the school merely points them out. The most important element for successful reading endeavors is cortical hemispheric dominance, or one-sidedness. Lack of complete and constant laterality results in reading and language problems. (Compare with Kephart's views.) From his observations, Delacato states that 60 to 80 per cent of the superior readers are completely one-sided. Preventive or corrective measures include mastering general motor patterns, such as homolateral crawling at the lowest stage, and creeping, walking, and walking in cross patterns at later stages.

A number of recent studies, on the other hand, have not found any difference in reading ability between established and nonestablished laterality groups. Capobianco (1967), for example, administered five tests of handedness and four tests of eyedness to subjects with special learning disabilities. These test scores were correlated with reading-ability measures. Results indicated that lateral dominance did not facilitate reading achievement; in fact, incomplete dominance, in certain cases, resulted in better reading performance.

Barsch (1967) also feels that movement efficiency is a fundamental principle underlining human development. His theory of movigenics is based upon the development of movement patterns and the relationship of these patterns to learning efficiency.

The child must learn to move within a space world. If he develops this movement efficiency completely, then learning will not be impaired. The development of this efficiency is dependent upon fifteen fundamental units that are placed under three separate headings. The first of these headings is Postural-Transport Orientation. Within this area of development of movement efficiency Barsch has placed: (1) muscular strength, (2) dynamic balance, (3) body awareness, (4) spatial awareness, and (5) temporal awareness.

The second heading, Percepto-Cognitive Modes, deals with reception and expression within the child and encompasses the information-getting gustatory, olfactory, tactual, kinesthetic, auditory, and visual modes.

The final heading, Degrees of Freedom, includes the qualities that allow the child to achieve range, amplitude, and broadness within his behavior. These qualities are bilaterality, rhythm, flexibility, and motor planning.

> All fifteen components are simultaneously active and developing from birth throughout life. The human performer is at all times a composite of relative efficiencies and inefficiencies of all components. Each component provides its own emphasis in contribution to the total in a hierarchial pattern from infancy. As they have been listed in order, we hold that order to be chronologic. The first to receive emphasis is muscular strength and the last to be emphasized is motor planning. Each provides a foundation for the emergence of the subsequent components and each subsequent one continues to enhance and enrich those that have gone before. All are interrelated and interdependent [p. 83].

Through this progress order of emphasis, Barsch looks at the physical phenomenon of each component, as well as the cognitive aspect of the development. Thus he views the individual as learning to move in space through the dual physical and cognitive aspects of these fifteen components of movement.

Marianne Frostig (1971) has developed a perceptual training program within the bounds of vision. Her theory deals with visual perception and remediation of visual perception and assimilation with some attention to certain motor responses.

Frostig has based her program upon the sensorimotor training of the child. This sensorimotor training includes four groups of sensorimotor skills that the child must develop. The first two groups are termed *awareness* and in these groups the infant becomes aware of his environment and the outside world as well as gaining awareness of himself. The third group of skills is comprised of the motor skills, in which the child learns to turn over, sit, stand, kneel, crawl, walk, and so on. The final group of skills includes those skills necessary to the child for the manipulation of objects. All of the skills within each group must be incorporated into a sensorimotor training program to insure total development of the child.

Based upon the idea of these four necessary groups of sensorimotor skills, Frostig evaluates the child to determine dysfunctions in these skills and then prescribes a movement education program that will enhance the development of these skills, thus improving movement function. She utilizes the Frostig Sensorimotor and Movement Skills Checklist in each evaluation and children who are admitted to the Marianne Frostig Center of Educational Therapy are prescribed remedial programs on the basis of their evaluation on this checklist. All programs are administered at the center under the supervision of qualified personnel.

Research that questions the Delacato theory was conducted by Melvin Robbins (1966). Delacato had made several claims concerning the educational benefits of his theory when used with children. Robbins questioned three of these assertions in his study of 126 children from three second-grade classes. Class I continued with its normal curriculum, Class II continued with its normal curriculum but was subjected to a program consistent with the Delacato theory in addition to its regular activities, and Class III was given a general program of activities not known to be correlated with reading achievement. A pre- and posttest was given in the areas of arithmetic, general intelligence, laterality, reading, and creeping. Robbins made the following conclusions:

1. The data did not support the relationships between neurological organization and reading achievement.
2. The addition of Delacato's program did not enhance the reading and lateral development of these children.

Based on these conclusions and literature that was reviewed by Robbins, he advises against acceptance of Delacato's work until more scientifically based research can be conducted concerning the validity of the theory.

A year later, Robbins joined with Gene Glass (1967) to examine the Delacato theory further. They present a brief overview of Delacato's theory of neurological organization and reading and review fifteen studies in an attempt to determine the validity of the theory. Each of the fifteen articles was critiqued and a great deal of inconsistency as well as lack of objectivity was reported in the Delacato studies and studies that support the Delacato theory. They concluded that research done by Delacato and his supporters "contained major faults in design and analysis" and if validity of the theory is to be found, studies must be designed without bias and be conducted in a scientific manner.

Research is still being conducted concerning the Delacato theory and there appears to be a trend of nonsupport in the majority of the newer literature.

Kephart's theory is of a more accurate nature and seems to be more "fact based" than the work by Delacato. His theory was endorsed by the Reading Research Foundation in 1970 and has achieved widespread support during more recent times, although there is research evidence to contradict the supposed benefits of the program.

In general, research that concretely supports any of the programs is sparse. It would almost appear that for every negative report, a positive report can also be found in regard to any of the proposed programs. The controversy continues to rage in the 1970's. Perhaps one of the more careful analyses of the research data and theory surrounding perceptual motor programs has been offered by Cratty (1970) in Chapter 10 of his book. He illustrates the frailties upon which these programs are based and, indeed, the weaknesses in the research and lack of research support for the various programs.

The theories of perception that exist now are being received enthusiastically as well as negatively. Responses range from total acceptance to complete rejection. Scientific research has found this to be a promising area but results are inconclusive at this point.

One idea that has evolved with the emergence of the perceptual motor training theories is the premise that the slow learner or underachiever need no longer be sent to the back of the room to color or play with blocks. Through perceptual training the underachiever has been brought into the limelight of education and an increasing amount of research, study, and work is being expended in order to help this child. Perceptual-motor training programs are far from being a panacea for educational difficulties, but they do afford the learner a new and different medium for learning and offer a break in the regular day-to-day curriculum.

There is evidence that perceptual-motor training can enhance achievement in the deficient and mentally retarded child. To what degree there is something inherent in these programs to cause beneficial results or to what degree these results are associated with psychosocial factors, such as parent, teacher, and learning enthusiasm in the possibility of curing deficiency, remains to be seen. Special attention and love may contribute much to achievement, although one might argue that the important concern is the outcome, not necessarily what causes it.

MOTOR DEVELOPMENT TESTS

Many of the perceptual-motor training programs suggest assessment techniques for determining the motoric development level of the child. Such tests can reveal where the learner stands in reference to normative data. They might also imply remedial work that needs to be accomplished.

For instance, the Purdue Perceptual Motor Survey surveys a number of behaviors that presumably undergird academic skills (Roach and Kephart, 1966). They are as follows:

1. Walking Board: Forward
2. Walking Board: Backward
3. Walking Board: Sidewise
4. Jumping
5. Identification of Body Parts
6. Imitation of Movements
7. Obstacle Course
8. Chalkboard: Circle
9. Chalkboard: Double Circle
10. Chalkboard: Lines, Lateral
11. Chalkboard: Lines, Vertical
12. Kraus-Weber (items 4 and 5)
13. Angels-in-the-Snow
14. Ocular Pursuits: Both Eyes, Lateral
15. Ocular Pursuits: Both Eyes, Vertical
16. Ocular Pursuits: Both Eyes, Diagonal
17. Ocular Pursuits: Both Eyes, Rotary
18. Ocular Pursuits: Right Eye, Lateral
19. Ocular Pursuits: Right Eye, Vertical
20. Ocular Pursuits: Right Eye, Diagonal
21. Ocular Pursuits: Right Eye, Rotary
22. Ocular Pursuits: Left Eye, Lateral
23. Ocular Pursuits: Left Eye, Vertical
24. Ocular Pursuits: Left Eye, Diagonal
25. Ocular Pursuits: Left Eye, Rotary
26. Developmental Drawing: Form
27. Developmental Drawing: Organization
28. Rhythmic Writing: Rhythm
29. Rhythmic Writing: Reproduction
30. Rhythmic Writing: Orientation

Roach and Kephart state that the survey is geared to detect errors in perceptual-motor development. Performance scores on the test can suggest areas for remediation. One admitted restriction in the survey is that it was developed with second-, third-, and fourth-graders in mind.

Recently Keith Kershner and Russell Dusewicz (1970) have attempted to modify the original Oseretsky Tests of Motor Development. Referred to as the K.D.K.–Oseretsky Test, they presumably measure

1. General static coordination.
2. General dynamic coordination.

3. Dyamic manual coordination.
4. Simultaneous voluntary movement.
5. Speed.

Time is shortened greatly in the administration of this abbreviated test, which can provide descriptive and normative information on motor development. Diagnostic purposes can be served as well. The Oseretsky test items are large muscle activities, often novel in nature.

From another perspective, Schulman, Buist, Kaspar, Child, and Fackler (1969) developed a battery of fine motor tasks that are to serve the purpose of assessing speed of fine motor functioning of children aged three to eight. Presumably the tests are most helpful in the study of brain-injured children. The tasks that comprise the test are

> *Pegs.*—The score is the length of time required to place the six pegs into the squarehole pegboard from the Cattell Infant Intelligence Scale. This is done for both the preferred and non-preferred hand.
> *Picks.*—This score is the number of seconds required to place 15 toothpicks into a styrofoam ball 2½ in. in diameter. This is done for both the preferred and non-preferred hands.
> *Beads.*—This score is the number of seconds required to string 10 beads ½ in. in diameter.
> *Taps.*—The number of seconds required for S to tap 60 times on a laboratory blood cell counter. This is also done for each hand. These tasks generate a total of seven measures.

From the data collected in the study, it was concluded that age and speed of performance are related in a negatively accelerated manner. Speed as an exponential function of age is plotted in Figure 8–3. Sex was not a factor in performance. Children with impaired intellectual functioning performed poorer on the motor tasks than the standardized population.

The literature is replete with tests that claim to measure general motor ability, specific motor abilities, developmental abilities, brain dysfunctioning, cognitive achievement predictable from motor test scores, and the like. An excellent survey of tests that are supposed to assess motor impairment, along with research findings, is presented by Morris and Whiting (1971). But in spite of the existence of so many tests with so many stated purposes, in reality their practical value, except in extreme cases, has yet to be determined. Conflict exists between theory and the stated functions of certain tests. Further confusion appears when generalization of the usefulness of some tests goes beyond the data presented. As developmental indexes of emerging perceptual-motor patterns, normative information, and potential clinical usage, a number of tests serve useful purposes. But care should be exercised in score interpretation and student evaluation. Diagnostic and remedial possibilities can only be realized when it is clearly understood what test scores really measure. And, without saying, the valid-

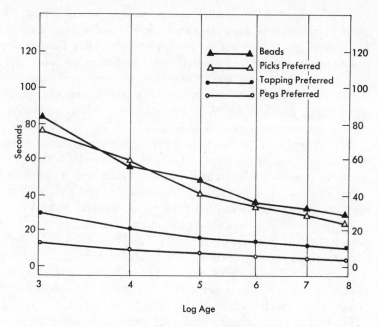

Figure 8–3. Speed with preferred hand × log age. (From J. L. Schulman, Charlotte Buist, J. C. Kasper, David Child, and Eleanor Fackler, "An Objective Test of Speed of Fine Motor Function," *Perceptual and Motor Skills,* 29:243–255, 1969.)

ity and reliability of any score, the care with which testing is administered, will influence performance outcomes and, in turn, evaluation.

SEX

Sex differences in motor performance become more apparent with increasing age. Young boys and girls can compete in similar activities with satisfaction until they approach adolescence. During this period, motor skills related to the dominant form of play of each sex distinguishes the two sexes. From adolescence to adulthood, boys continually advance in motor performance, girls improve very slightly or even worsen, and the gap in performance between the sexes widens. Why this occurs and indeed, if it actually should, is open to conjecture.

The female infant is distinguished from the male by her earlier maturation and more advanced motor development, which permits her to demonstrate a higher level of proficiency in movement-oriented behaviors.

Yet the males tend to participate in more vigorous activity. Because of greater strength and muscular development, the average male child, at the age of two and a half and beyond, performs better than the female in a great variety of gross motor activities. Throwing patterns are better for boys than girls at age five; at ages five to seven and nine to eleven, research shows that boys perform higher in tests of running, jumping, catching, striking, and kicking. Numerous studies in which normative data have been collected on boys and girls at school age indicate the superiority of boys to girls in gross motor activities. An excellent summary of sex differences in motor development and of motor tasks, abilities, and various cognitive processes is presented by J. E. Garai and A. Scheinfeld (1968).

An analysis of the research literature on sex differences in simple perceptual-motor tasks has led Broverman, Klaiber, Kobayashi, and Vogel (1968) to conclude that young girls and women exceed their male counterparts in tasks of fine manual dexterity. Furthermore, females perform better than males in the perceptual-motor behaviors associated with speech and reading, as well as in small-muscle, simple perceptual-motor activities that require speed, repetition, and skill. More specifically, Klaiber et al. indicate behaviors in which each sex is superior to the other.

The behaviors in which females are superior to males seem to have the following attributes (p. 28):

1. The behaviors appear to be based mainly upon past experience or learning, as opposed to problem solving of novel or difficult tasks. Thus color naming, talking, reading, etc., are based upon extensive previous experience.
2. As a result of extensive prior practice, the behaviors appear to involve minimal mediation by higher cognitive processes. Sensory thresholds represent an extreme of this attribute; but other more obviously learned behaviors such as typing, color naming, or conditioning are termed skilled or well-acquired as they move toward reflexive automatic responses.
3. The behaviors typically involve fine coordinations of small muscles with perceptual and attentional processes, such as in typing or reading, rather than coordination of large muscle movements as in athletics.
4. Finally, the behaviors are evaluated in terms of the speed and accuracy of repetitive responses, as in color naming, rather than in terms of production of new responses or "insight," as in maze solutions.

The behaviors in which males are superior to females seem to be characterized by the following (p. 28):

1. The behaviors involve an inhibition or delay of initial response tendencies to obvious stimulus attributes in favor of responses to less obvious stimulus attributes, as in the Embedded Figures Test.
2. The behaviors seem to involve extensive mediation of higher processes as opposed to automatic or reflexive stimulus response connections.
3. Finally, the behaviors are evaluated in terms of the production of solutions

to novel tasks or situations, such as assembling parts of a puzzle or object, as opposed to speed or accuracy of repetitive responses.

Klaiber et al. have determined an inverse relationship between the physiological processes associated in the simple perceptual-motor abilities and those involved in inhibitory restructuring tasks. Perceptual restructuring tasks often call for the identification of stimuli patterns from more complex patterns in which they are embedded. Another example is a widely used experimental task, the Rod and Frame Test, in which the subject while in a darkened room must adjust a luminescent rod from a tilted luminescent frame. Differences in performance in the two categories of tasks (simple perceptual-motor and restructuring), according to Klaiber et al., represent the balance between adrenergic and cholinergic neural processes. Androgens and estrogens influence activation and inhibition processes, thus helping to explain sex differences in the performances of the type of tasks examined in the Klaiber et al. article.

One of the more complete research projects having to do with the interaction of age and sex on performance was completed by Noble, Baker, and Jones (1964). A Discrimination Reaction Time apparatus was used (see Figure 8–4) that required the subject to snap one of four toggle switches in response to changing light-stimulus patterns. A total of 600 subjects took part in the study, ranging in age from eight to eighty-seven. Twenty males and twenty females were placed in each of fifteen experimental groups according to age. It can be observed in Figure 8–4 that the expected performance curves were obtained, i.e., peak performance for both groups was attained at approximately the late teens and early twenties and worsened with advancing age. These data coincide very nicely with those reported by Hodgkins (see Figure 8–2).

It is interesting to compare performance differences at the various ages. With the exception of the ten- to thirteen-year age bracket and the seventy-one- to eighty-seven-year age bracket, males displayed a general superiority over the females in response speed. Generally speaking, the two sexes perform similarly until the age of sixteen, when the females level off in performance and show decrements with increasing age. Males continue to improve until the early twenties, and then they too undergo declining performance.

The following measures were recorded by Singer (1969) for third- and sixth-grade children: height, grip strength of the dominant and nondominant hands, elbow flexion and elbow extension strength, hip flexion and hip extension strength, dynamic balance, ball-throwing accuracy, speed of hand–arm movement, eye–hand coordination, stimulus discrimination and hand speed, perceptual ability, academic achievement, and intelligence.

Static strength of the elbow and hip extensions and flexors was measured with the use of the Multiple Angle Testing Unit. Dynamic balance was

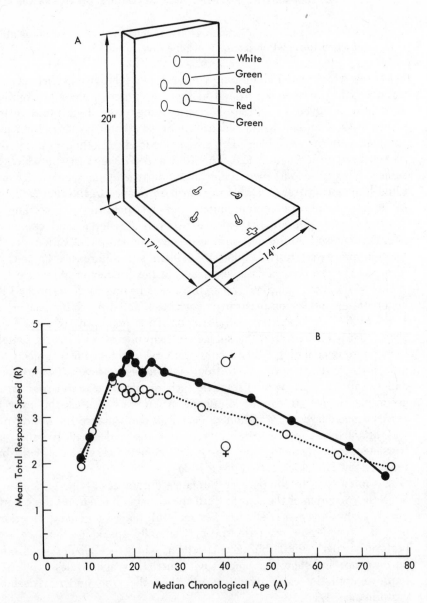

Figure 8-4. (A) Discrimination-reaction-time apparatus; (B) Mean total response speed (R) as a function of median chronological age (A) for the two sexes. Each point is based on the data for twenty subjects averaged over the entire practice period. (From Clyde E. Noble, Blaine L. Baker, and Thomas A. Jones, "Age and Sex Parameters in Psychomotor Learning," *Perceptual and Motor Skills,* 19:935–945, 1964.)

measured on a constructed stabilometer, illustrated in Chapter 4, Figure 4–3. The apparatus for the stimulus discrimination and hand-speed test involved a timer measuring to 0.001 second the speed of the subject's response to any one of the three lights or to a buzzer. Speed of hand–arm movement and manual dexterity was determined with a constructed version of the Minnesota Rate of Manipulation Test, the object being to place all the pegs in the holes as quickly as possible. Perceptual ability was measured with the Figure Reproduction Test, developed by Singer and Brunk. The subject had to reproduce geometrical patterns presented to them on paper to the board with the use of rubber bands (see Figure 8–5). Eye-hand coordinated performance was tested with the pursuit rotor, illustrated in Figure 4–1.

With regard to the Figure Reproduction Test and performance, Figure 8–6 shows the superiority of age but little difference between the sexes at each age. In balance (Figure 8–7), across all trials, once again the sixth-

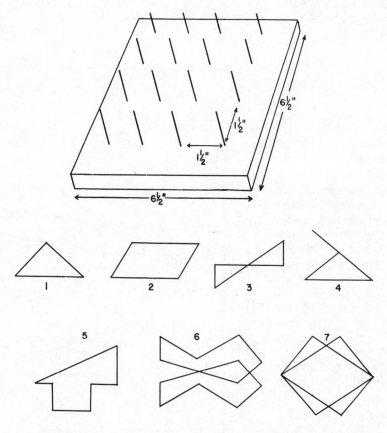

Figure 8–5. The board and patterns for the Figure Reproduction Test.

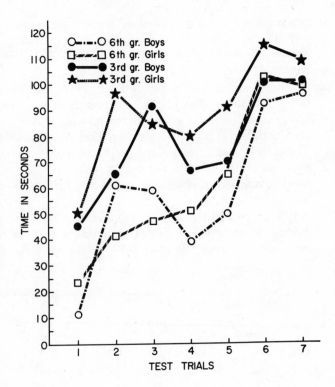

Figure 8–6. A comparison of four groups of children in perceptual-motor skill, as measured by their scores on the Figure Reproduction Test. Lower times indicate better performances. (From Robert N. Singer, "Physical Characteristics, Perceptual-Motor, and Intelligence Differences Between Third- and Sixth-Grade Children," *Research Quarterly,* 40:803–811, 1969.)

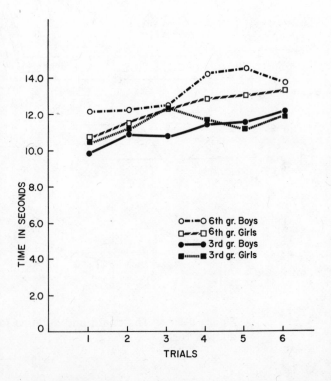

Figure 8–7. Comparison of four groups of children in balancing ability, measured by their performances on the stabilometer. (From Robert N. Singer, "Physical Characteristics, Perceptual-Motor, and Intelligence Differences Between Third- and Sixth-Grade Children," *Research Quarterly,* 40:803–811, 1969.)

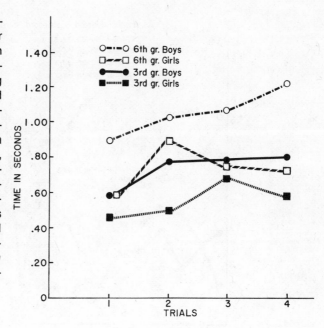

Figure 8–8. Comparison of four groups of children in eye-hand coordination, or tracking ability, as measured by their performances on the pursuit rotor. (From Robert N. Singer, "Physical Characteristics, Perceptual-Motor, and Intelligence Differences Between Third- and Sixth-Grade Children," *Research Quarterly,* 40:803–811, 1969.)

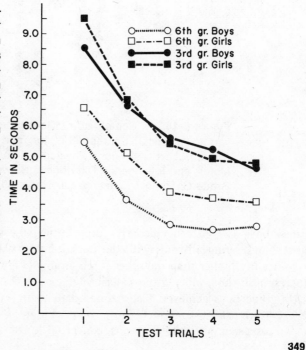

Figure 8–9. Comparison of four groups of children in response time as measured by the discrimination reaction time apparatus. Lower times indicate better performances. (From Robert N. Singer, "Physical Characteristics, Perceptual-Motor, and Intelligence Differences Between Third- and Sixth-Grade Children," *Research Quarterly,* 40:803–811, 1969.)

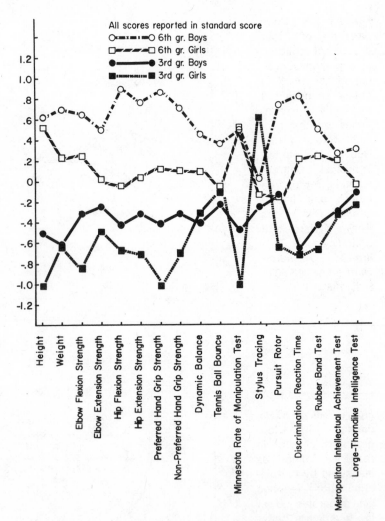

All scores reported in standard score
○—·—·○ 6th gr. Boys
□—·—·□ 6th gr. Girls
●——● 3rd gr. Boys
■—·—·■ 3rd gr. Girls

Figure 8-10.   Comparison of four groups of children on the various physical, perceptual-motor, and intellectual abilities. (From Robert N. Singer, "Physical Characteristics, Perceptual-Motor, and Intelligence Differences Between Third- and Sixth-Grade Children," *Research Quarterly,* 40:803–811, 1969.)

grade boys and girls significantly outperformed the third-grade boys and girls. Considering all trials with the pursuit rotor, sixth-grade boys scored significantly higher than the other three groups (Figure 8-8). With regard to response time, older groups performed better than younger ones, and sixth-grade boys achieved faster times than their female counterparts on every trial except trial 1 (Figure 8-9). Figure 8-10 includes all the measures taken on the four groups, converted to standard scores from raw

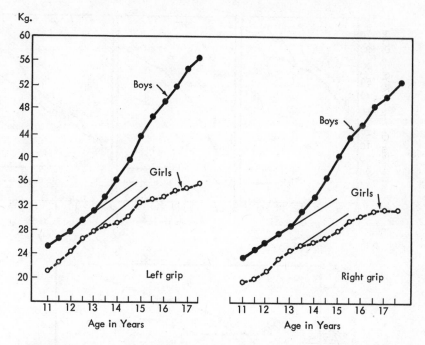

Figure 8–11.   Comparison of right and left hand grip strength of boys and girls from the ages of eleven through seventeen. (From H. E. Jones, "Motor Performance and Growth," *University of California Publications on Child Development,* 1949.)

scores. It can be concluded that sixth-grade boys had, in general, the most favorable recorded measures, followed by sixth-grade girls, third-grade boys, and third-grade girls.

In most gross physical and motor measures, both boys and girls compare favorably, with boys holding a slight edge until approximately the age of twelve or thirteen. Body size and strength has much to do with athletic accomplishments. During adolescence, boys generally grow larger and demonstrate a greater magnitude of strength, and as these differences between sexes become more apparent, so do motor performances. Jones followed the strength development of boys and girls over a period of time. Figure 8–11 presents a comparison between boys and girls, from age eleven through seventeen, in right and left hand-grip strengths. The girls begin trailing off at about fifteen years of age, whereas the boys are still increasing with great rapidity at the age of seventeen. Differences in strength, although in favor of the boys at eleven, become more noticeable at thirteen, and continue to widen at each succeeding age. The same trend is noticeable with most motor skills (see Figure 8–12).

In summary, generally it may be stated that boys typically increase in performance until the late teens, whereas girls decline in performance in

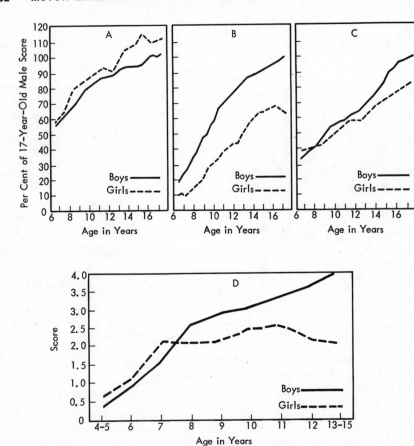

Figure 8–12.   (A) Aiming Test; (B) Baseball Throw for Distance; (C) Basketball Rapid Pass. [From *The Psychology of Development and Personal Adjustment* by John E. Anderson. Copyright, 1949, by Holt, Rinehart and Winston, Inc. Reprinted by permission of Holt, Rinehart and Winston, Inc.]; and (D) Balance Test. [Data from G. W. Cron and N. H. Pronko, "Development of a Sense of Balance in School Children," *Journal of Educational Research,* 51:33–37, 1957; illustrated in Luella Cole, *Psychology of Adolescence* (New York: Holt, Rinehart and Winston, Inc., 1965).]

the early teens. There are exceptions, of course. The relative performances of boys and girls at comparative ages may be attributed to many factors. One of the more prominent variables is the influence of social approval, which, of course, is culturally determined. For many years, whereas boys have been encouraged to develop their athletic prowess, girls have been told to act feminine, to avoid most sports and vigorous activities. With a lack of incentive, performance levels naturally decline.

Figure 8-13. The relationship of age, sex, and field of vision. (From Albert Burg, "Lateral Visual Field as Related to Age and Sex," *Journal of Applied Psychology,* 52:10–15, 1968.) Copyright 1968 by the American Psychological Association. Reprinted by permission.

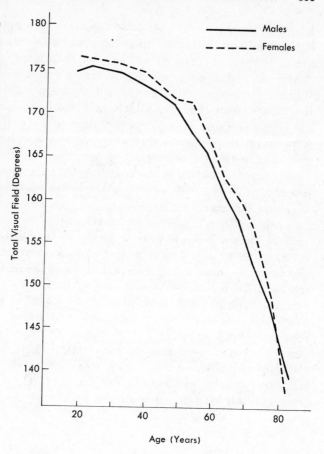

Age (Years)

Although much information on the nature of sex differences indicates the superiority of males over females in most gross motor activities, this does not necessarily mean any differences in learning abilities or rates between the sexes. Some possible reasons for performance dissimilarities have been offered. Physiological differences also provide the male with a more favorable apparatus (body build, strength, and so on) to exceed performances of females in a number of activities. A fair conclusion from the evidence is that males and females learn motor tasks in a similar way and at a similar rate. Differences in actual performances may be due to previous learnings and transfer possibilities, structural differences, motivational differences, and most obviously, sociocultural factors.

In fact, if a greater field of vision is related to more highly skilled performance in certain tasks, it is of interest to note that Albert Burg (1968) found that females consistently demonstrated slightly higher visual fields than men at just about all ages (see Figure 8–13). Eye fields peak at a later age for the females than for the males. As might be expected and being consistent with data on other personal abilities, visual field, after the early twenties, declines with age for both sexes.

More factual evidence offered by Hirata (1966) indicates the relationship of achievements in various athletic endeavors with sex and age. Using the 1964 Olympic champion athletes as subjects, he found the mean age of the male champions to be twenty-six years, whereas the female champions were twenty-three years in age on the average. Most of the male champions were in the twenty-to-thirty age group whereas the majority of female champions were located in the seventeen-to-twenty-five age bracket. Hirata concludes that the male's motor and physical development is completed later than the female's and is maintained for a longer time. However, other factors as well, perhaps social and psychological in nature, may account for some of the difference in peak-performance years between the sexes.

From a physiological point of view, various differences between sexes usually favor the male in athletic performance, but not to the extent once supposed. With social encouragement, girls and women are displaying remarkable skills in a wide range of activities. Jokl et al. (1964b) accumulated much data from the 1952 Olympics, and found that some women's records in track and field and swimming at these Olympic Games were better than men's records in the early 1900's. They also conclude that "the time-honored statement that women are invariably the weaker sex no longer holds true as an unqualified assertion (p. 691)." Constant hard drilling and training result in outstanding athletic performance, regardless of sex.

PERSONALITY DEVELOPMENT

Analysis of Personality

Everyday experiences and meetings with new individuals confirm our concept of individual differences in personality. Even as people display dissimilar physical, intellectual, and emotional characteristics their respective personalities are what sets them apart from others. A reference to one's personality usually indicates an identity, a uniqueness among many people.

Personality has been defined in many ways and the approach to the study of its development also varies. One of the more widely accepted definitions has been offered by Gordon Allport (1955, p. 48), who suggests that personality is the "dynamic organization within the individual of those psycho-physical systems that determine his unique adjustment to his environment." When the researcher studies personality, he actually is studying behavior. Personality develops as a result of a person's adjustment to many situations, and this personality is reflected by a tendency to react in a certain way in a given situation.

Personality, intelligence, and movement capacity all have the same problem: the determination of the relative influence of heredity and environmental experiences. As is the case with motor and intellectual variables, it would appear that personality is a product of both environmental and genetic factors. It is the result of inheritance, habits, intelligence, emotions, drives, and experiences—all blending together to promote a characteristic way of behaving. Innate qualities influence personality development, but environmental factors determine the sort of influence.

Does a person exhibit a particular personality because of heredity? Because of maturity and natural growth processes? Learning? To a certain extent, personality characteristics appear to be congenital. This is evident, for behavior differences in babies are noted almost immediately after birth, too soon for experience to be the reason. Also, personality traits at an early age generally characterize a person later in life. A child's personality structure is relatively consistent during the developmental period. With a certain degree of assurance one can predict later personality traits from those apparent at infancy.

Other psychologists insist that personality depends most on learning. Because personality represents a characteristic way of behaving and much of behavior is learned, the hypothesis is reasonable. Learning principles operate in the development of a personality, for adjustment in life is learned. Personality, intellect, and motor capacity levels are difficult to ascertain because of a number of factors, which creates a problem in determining the relative contributions of genetics and environment to each. There are weaknesses in insruments that presumably measure personality. Changes take place because of the maturation-learning process, thus the problem in identifying true levels. Regardless of research technique and instrument problems, inheritance and environment are acknowledged influences on personality development, the relative impact of each difficult to assess.

Personality and Sports

Those familiar with and interested in motor-skill development feel that an individual's personality might very well determine his choice of activity as well as his accomplishments. In reference to activity selection, psychological needs are better met through certain sports than others for particular individuals. An aggressive person might choose a sport such as wrestling for his personal outlet. Someone else who enjoys a social environment provided by a sport might participate in team sports. Others enjoy sewing, musical instruments, or craftwork.

Athletes representing chosen sports have been found by some researchers to contrast in personality profile with so-called nonathletes. From sport to sport there is the suggestion that participants will vary in personality. Finally, even within a given sport, perhaps outstanding champion performers may be distinguished from average athletes in personality profile. The drive to excel, to be best, often distinguishes the champion from the almost champion.

Another consideration in this area of personality and sports is the possible changes that occur within a person as a result of his experience in sport participation. Although an individual's personality is formed early in childhood, it can be and is modified by later experiences in life. To display desirable personality and character traits is admirable and therefore encouraged by the parent, teacher, and most peer groups. Of the possible methods of molding a more socially accepted personality, participation in organized physical activity has been acknowledged by many psychologists, sociologists, educators, and physical educators as one of the better means of transmitting this development. Then again, there are those who feel that this activity, especially in the more organized form of competitive athletics, might have undesirable social and emotional effects on the participant.

A problem arises as to whether people choose to participate in activities because of what they are or change because of what they participate in. Perhaps both factors operate in a typical situation. Longitudinal studies in this area are lacking, whereas cross-sectional studies having to do with the effect of programs of physical education and athletics on personal and social adjustment and emotional behavior of the participants are plentiful. Studies may also be found on the relationships between athletic abilities, physical development, and personality traits. Suffice it to say here that personality, although difficult to measure accurately, is affected and modified by experiences in life, with sports participation included in those experiences. The influence of personality on athletic achievement, choice of activity for participation in leisure, and changes that occur because of this participation has not been well researched. Heretofore, much of our knowledge has been based on subjective evaluations and empirical evidence. This previously neglected area of study shows much promise for future research.

BODY IMAGE

The child develops many characteristics in those early formative years that will be fairly well established, although possible to modify in subsequent years. Body image, the self-appearance of oneself, is one of those characteristics. Other terms often used along with *body image* are *self-image*, *self-concept*, and *body awareness*. They all refer to the impressions one has of his body, impressions that develop in the course of time, with perceptual sensitivity, experiences, and the like. In turn, an individual's self-image may very well be associated with activity involvement and possible success.

A review of the literature by P. R. Morris and H. T. A. Whiting (1971) reveals that body image or concept is associated with a variety of expressions, such as

1. The ability to make body movements appropriate to the demands of the environment.
2. Bodily sensations.
3. Imagination—mental imagery that is not purely representational.
4. Ego development.
5. Affective development.
6. Cognitive development.
7. Development of body boundaries.
8. Kinesthetic sensitivity.

Regardless of usage and interpretation, the development of an ideal body image is the result of a personal interpretation of one's actions and appearance as well as environmental feedback. It begins, according to perceptual theorists, with a child's differentiation of self and environment, of body and field. The awareness of the body's potential and limitations, in general and in relation to particular circumstances, is an expected process. Faulty development can lead to personality and learning disorders, according to many psychologists and special educators. Furthermore, fundamental to some perceptual-motor training programs to remediate learning disorders is the child's mastery of body awareness. Laterality (awareness of two sides of the body), sensory dominance (preferential use of one of the eyes, hands, or feet), and directionality (movement in space to a correct location) are aspects of body awareness thought to be important factors in the developing child.

In fact, Harriet Williams (1973) suggests three foundational components in the development of the image one has of himself: (1) a sensorimotor component, (2) a conceptual component, and (3) a feeling or opinion component. Body awareness first begins for the child through feedback received from his own activities. The senses provide input, which helps the child to learn more about his being. With development the child learns to verbalize and conceptualize about himself, his experiences, and his environment. At the same time, he develops attitudes about his body. A variety of experiences in which the child learns to perceive and accept reality helps him to formulate a more accurate body image. Personally rewarding experiences as an outgrowth of sensitive and quality child-rearing practices lead to a body image that is satisfying to the child.

The relationship between one's self-image, personality factors, activity interest and proficiency, body build, and other variables has not been clearly established. Positive but low associations have often been reported in the literature. Yet the effects of a sensorimotor training program on the body image of mentally retarded children were quite beneficial, report Maloney and Payne (1970). When compared to control subjects, the sensorimotor trained subjects showed better body image scores immediately after the two-month training session as well as eight months later. Assuming the value of a high body image, apparently special body awareness programs can produce desirable changes, at least in the mentally retarded.

REFERENCES

ALLPORT, G. W. *Becoming.* New Haven: Yale University Press, 1955.

BACHMAN, JOHN C. "Motor Learning and Performance as Related to Age and Sex in Two Measures of Balance Coordination," *Research Quarterly,* 32:123–137, 1961.

BARSCH, RAY H. *Achieving Perceptual-Motor Efficiency,* Special Child Publications, Vol. I. Seattle: Seattle Sequin School, Inc., 1967.

BEACH, FRANK A., and JULIAN JAYNES. "Effects of Early Experiences Upon the Behavior of Animals," *Psychological Bulletin,* 51:239–263, 1954.

BIRREN, JAMES E. *The Psychology of Aging.* Englewood Cliffs, N.J.: Prentice-Hall, Inc., 1964.

BLOOM, BENJAMIN S. *Stability and Change in Human Characteristics.* New York: John Wiley & Sons, Inc., 1964.

BRECKENRIDGE, MARIAN E., and MARGARET N. MURPHY. *Growth and Development of the Young Child.* Philadelphia: W. B. Saunders Company, 1969.

BROVERMAN, DONALD M., EDWARD L. KLAIBER, YUTAKA KOBAYASHI, and WILLIAM VOGEL. "Role of Activation and Inhibition in Sex Differences in Cognitive Abilities," *Psychological Review,* 75:23–50, 1968.

BRUNER, JEROME S. "The Growth and Structure of Skill," in K. J. Connolly (ed.), *Mechanisms of Motor Skill Development.* New York: Academic Press, Inc., 1970.

———. *The Process of Education.* Cambridge, Mass.: Harvard University Press, 1963.

BURG, ALBERT. "Lateral Visual Field as Related to Age and Sex," *Journal of Applied Psychology,* 52:10–15, 1968.

BURT, CYRIL. "The Inheritance of Mental Ability," *American Psychologist,* 13:1–15, 1958.

———. "Quantitative Genetics in Psychology," *The British Journal of Mathematical and Statistical Psychology,* 24:1–21, 1971.

CAPOBIANCO, R. J. "Ocular-Manual Laterality and Reading Achievement in Children with Special Learning Disabilities," *American Educational Research Journal,* 4:133–138, 1967.

COLE, LUELLA. *Psychology of Adolescence.* New York: Holt, Rinehart and Winston, Inc., 1965.

CRATTY, BRYANT J. *Perceptual and Motor Development in Infants and Children.* New York: Macmillan Publishing Co., Inc., 1970.

CRON, GERALD W., and N. H. PRONKO. "Development of the Sense of Balance in School Children," *Journal of Educational Research,* 51:458–464, 1957.

DELACATO, CARL H. *Neurological Organization and Reading.* Springfield, Ill.: Charles C Thomas, Publisher, 1966.

DEMBER, WILLIAM N. *The Psychology of Perception.* New York: Holt, Rinehart and Winston, Inc., 1960.

DENNIS, WAYNE. "The Effect of Cradling Practices upon the Onset of Walking in Hopi Children," *Journal of Genetic Psychology,* 56:77–86, 1940.

EAVES, L. J. "The Genetic Analysis of Continuous Variation: A Comparison of Experimental Designs Applicable to Human Data: II. Estimation of Heritability and Comparison of Environmental Components," *The British Journal of Mathematical and Statistical Psychology,* 23:189, 1970.

FLEMING, JAMES W. "Perceptual-Motor Programs," in Robert N. Singer (ed.), *The Psychomotor Domain: Movement Behavior.* Philadelphia: Lea & Febiger, 1972.

FREEMAN, LUCY. *Why People Act That Way.* New York: Thomas Y. Cromwell Company, 1965.

FROSTIG, MARIANNE. "Program for Sensory-Motor Development at the Marianne Frostig Center of Educational Therapy," *Foundations and Practices in Perceptual Motor Learning—A Quest for Understanding.* Washington, D.C.: American Association for Health, Physical Education, and Recreation, 1971.

GAGNÉ, ROBERT M. "Contributions of Learning to Human Development," *Psychological Review,* 75:177–191, 1968.

GARAI, J. E., and A. SCHEINFELD. "Sex Differences in Mental and Behavioral Traits," *Genetic Psychological Monographs,* 77: 169–299, 1968.

GEDDA, LUIGI. "Sports and Genetics, A Study on Twins (351 pairs)," in *Health and Fitness in the Modern World.* Chicago: The Athletic Institute, 1961.

————, M. MILANI-COMPARETTI, and G. BRENCI. "A Preliminary Report on Research Made During the Games of the XVIIth Olympiad, Rome, 1960," in E. Jokl and E. Simon (eds.), *International Research in Sport and Physical Education.* Springfield, Ill.: Charles C Thomas, Publisher, 1964.

GLASS, GENE V., and MELVIN P. ROBBINS. "A Critique of Experiments on the Role of Neurological Organization in Reading Performance," *Reading Research Quarterly,* 3:5–51, 1967.

GODFREY, BARBARA B., and NEWELL C. KEPHART. *Movement Patterns and Motor Education.* New York: Appleton-Century-Crofts, Inc., 1969.

GOULET, L. R. "Training, Transfer, and the Development of Complex Behavior," *Human Development,* 13:213–240, 1970.

HENRY, FRANKLIN M., and GAYLORD A. NELSON. "Age Differences and Inter-relationships Between Skill and Learning in Gross Motor Performance of Ten- and Fifteen-Year-Old Boys, *Research Quarterly*, 27:162–175, 1956.

HIRATA, KIN-ITSU. "Physique and Age of Tokyo Olympic Champions," *Journal of Sports Medicine and Physical Fitness*, 6:207–222, 1966.

HODGKINS, JEAN. "Influence of Age on the Speed of Reaction and Movement in Females," *Journal of Gerontology*, 17:385–389, 1962.

HUMPHRIES, MICHAEL, and ALFRED H. SHEPHARD. "Age and Training in the Development of a Perceptual-Motor Skill," *Perceptual Motor Skills*, 9:3–11, 1959.

JENSEN, ARTHUR R. "How Much Can We Boost IQ and Scholastic Achievement?" *Harvard Educational Review*, 39:1–123, 1969.

————. "IQ's of Identical Twins Reared Apart," *Behavior Genetics*, 1:133–146, 1970.

————. "Note on Why Genetic Correlations Are Not Squared," *Psychological Bulletin*, 75:223–224, 1971.

————. "The Heritability of Intelligence," *Engineering and Science*, 33:1–4, 1970.

JOHNSON, WARREN R. "Critical Periods, Body Image and Movement Competency in Childhood," *Symposium on Integrated Development*, Purdue University, 1964.

JOKL, ERNST. *Medical Sociology and Cultural Anthropology of Sport and Physical Education*. Springfield, Ill.: Charles C Thomas, Publisher, 1964a.

————, M. KARVONEN, J. KIHLBERG, A. KOEKELA, and L. NORO. "Olympic Survey (Helsinki 1952)," in Ernst Jokl and E. Simon (eds.), *International Research in Sport and Physical Education*. Springfield, Ill.: Charles C Thomas, Publisher, 1964b.

JONES, H. E. "Motor Performance and Growth," *University of California Publications on Child Development*, 1949.

KERSHNER, KEITH M., and A. RUSSELL DUSEWICZ. "K.D.K.-Oseretsky Tests of Motor Development," *Perceptual and Motor Skills*, 30:202, 1970.

KING, JOHN A. "Parameters Relevant to Determining the Effect of Early Experience upon the Adult Behavior of Animals," *Psychological Bulletin*, 55:46–58, 1958.

LEITHWOOD, KENNETH A. "Early Childhood Motor Learning," *Early Childhood Education*, 5:7–20 (Winter), 1970–71.

LIPSITT, LEWIS. "Infant Learning: The Blooming, Buzzing, Confusion Revisited," in Merle E. Meyer (ed.), *Early Learning, The Second Western Symposium on Learning*. Bellingham, Wash.: Western Washington State College, 1971.

LORENZ, KONRAD. *Studies in Animal and Human Behavior*, Vol. I, translated by Robert Martin. Cambridge, Mass.: Harvard University Press, 1970.

MALINA, ROBERT M. "Anthropology, Growth, and Physical Education," in Robert N. Singer, David R. Lamb, Robert M. Malina, and Seymour Kleinman, *Physical Education: An Interdisciplinary Approach.* New York: Macmillan Publishing Co., Inc., 1972.

————, ALBERT B. HARPER, and JOHN D. HOLMAN. "Growth Status and Performance Relative to Parental Size," *Research Quarterly*, 41:503–509, 1970.

MALONEY, MICHAEL P., and LAWRENCE E. PAYNE. "Note on the Stability of Changes in Body Image Due to Sensory-Motor Training," *American Journal of Mental Deficiency*, 74:708, 1970.

McCLEARN, GERALD E. "Genetics and Behavior Development," in Martin L. Hoffman and Lois W. Hoffman (eds.), *Review of Child Development Research.* New York: Russell Sage Foundation, 1964.

McGRAW, MYRTLE B. *Growth: A Study of Johnny and Jimmy.* New York: Appleton-Century-Crofts, Inc., 1935.

————. "Later Development of Children Specially Trained During Infancy: Johnny and Jimmy at School Age," *Child Development*, 10:1–19, 1939.

McNEMAR, QUINN. "Twin Resemblances in Motor Skills and the Effect of Practice Thereon," *Journal of Genetic Psychology*, 42:70–99, 1933.

MORRIS, P. R., and H. T. A. WHITING. *Motor Impairment and Compensatory Education.* Philadelphia: Lea & Febiger, 1971.

MUSSEN , H. P., J. J. CONGER, and J. KAGAN. *Child Development and Personality.* New York: Harper & Row, Publishers, Inc., 1969.

NOBLE, CLYDE E., BLAINE L. BAKER, and THOMAS A. JONES. "Age and Sex Parameters in Psychomotor Learning," *Perceptual and Motor Skills*, 19: 935–945, 1964.

OSBORNE, TRAVIS R., and JAMES A. GREGOR. "The Heritability of Visualization, Perceptual Speed and Spatial Orientation," *Perceptual and Motor Skills*, 23:379–390, 1966.

PIAGET, JEAN. *The Origins of Intelligence in Children,* translated by Margaret Cook. New York: International Universities Press, 1952.

RADLER, D. H., and NEWELL C. KEPHART. *Success Through Play.* New York: Harper & Row, Publishers, Inc., 1960.

RAVIZZA, R. J., and A. C. HERSCHBERGER. "The Effect of Prolonged Motor Restriction upon Later Behavior of the Rat," *The Psychological Record*, 16:73–80, 1966.

ROACH, EUGENE, and N. C. KEPHART. *The Purdue Perceptual-Motor Survey,* Columbus, Ohio: Charles E. Merrill Publishers, 1966.

ROBBINS, MELVIN P. "A Study of the Validity of Delacato's Theory of Neurological Organization," *Exceptional Children*, 32:517–523, 1966.

RYAN, THOMAS J. "Poverty and Early Education in Canada," *Interchange* (published by the Ontario Institute for Studies in Education), 2:1–11, 1971.

SCHULMAN, J. L., CHARLOTTE BUIST, J. C. KOOPER, DAVID CHILD, and ELEANOR FACKLER. "An Objective Test of Speed of Fine Motor Function," *Perceptual and Motor Skills*, 29:243–255, 1969.

SCOTT, JOHN P. "A Time to Learn," *Psychology Today*, 2:47–48, 66–67, 1969.
_____. *Early Experience and the Organization of Behavior*. Belmont, Calif.: Wadsworth Publishing Co., 1968.

SINGER, ROBERT N. "Motor Learning as a Function of Age and Sex," in Lawrence G. Rarick (ed.), *Physical Activity: Human Growth and Development*. New York: Academic Press, Inc., 1973.
_____. "Physical Characteristic, Perceptual-Motor, and Intelligence Differences Between Third- and Sixth-Grade Children," *Research Quarterly*, 40:803–811, 1969.
_____, and JASON W. BRUNK, "Relation of Perceptual-Motor Ability and Intellectual Ability in Elementary School Children," *Perceptual and Motor Skills*, 24:967–970, 1967.

TALLAND, GEORGE A. "The Effect of Age on Speed of Simple Manual Skills," *Journal of General Psychology*, 100:67–76, 1962.

WILLIAMS, HARRIET G. "Perceptual-Motor Development in Children," in Charles B. Corbin (ed.), *A Textbook of Motor Development*. Dubuque, Iowa: William C. Brown Company, Publishers, 1973.

WOZNIAK, R. H. "Verbal Regulation of Motor Behavior—Soviet Research and Non-Soviet Replications," *Human Development*, 15:13–57, 1972.

9

INSTRUCTIONAL
AND TRAINING
PROCEDURES

Individuals possess unique qualities and specific characteristics because of inheritance, enabling some people to have greater potential than others for success with a given motor skill. However, actual skill attainment does not depend only on genetic factors. Environmental experiences qualitatively and quantitatively will promote learning and ultimately determine performance levels.

Recognition of individual differences requires allowance for the fact that all people will not benefit in the same way from the same practice techniques and methods of instruction. This does not mean, though, that we proceed in a haphazard way in attempting to attain skill. Research has cleared the way for a better understanding of the learning process, with the result that certain generalized learning principles may be applied to practice. These principles indicate the most effective and efficient means of attaining skill for the majority of people. The learner can adhere to, and the instructor devise, practice routines that are most conducive to learning and the acquisition of skill.

This chapter is concerned with the possible ways of manipulating environmental and practice conditions in order to obtain favorable performance in motor skills. Consideration is given to the nature of practice itself, the importance of motivation, reinforcement, and feedback, the administration of practice sessions, transfer of training, and ultimate retention of that which has been practiced.

PRACTICE

Effect on Skill Acquisition

For the majority of motor skills and under certain conditions, learning progresses with an increased number of practice trials. It is foolish to expect skilled performance at the onset, although there is no doubt that some individuals learn faster and are endowed more favorably than others for the task at hand. However, practice, as a rule, is a necessary prequisitie for learning skills.

Unfortunately, there is more to learning than mere practice, for *practice alone does not make perfect*. Practice must be accompanied by such conditions as the performer being aware of his direction or goal, and his results, and, in general, by motivation or the desire to improve. Repetition of an act may result in no performance increments and even in an inferior performance. The first situation (no increments) can occur if the conditions mentioned earlier in this paragraph are not present. The latter (inferior performance) will be manifested under these conditions or when the participant practices incorrectly and with erroneous goals. Thus we can only assume the positive effect of practice on learning and performance when other desirable factors are operating in conjunction with practice, factors that are often taken for granted. (It might also be mentioned here that some learning theorists believe learning to take place in one trial and that further trials only enhance performance. However, this is a theoretical argument and does not concern us in this chapter.)

It is important to remember that drill may perpetuate error as well as eliminate error and improve skill. The advantage of practice lies in the attempts made to recognize and improve the human and environmental conditions surrounding the practice.

Attention

Practice is more meaningful and productive when the learner is attentive to particular cues. The learner, especially one who is a novice, typically experiences difficulty in isolating the most important elements in a given situation and concentrating on them. With practice and learning the individual becomes more selective in attending to stimuli—he even becomes conscious of less of them. The performer's attention is affected by the state of his organism as well as his knowledge of what to concentrate on. Improvement in motor performance during practice, then, is dependent on the attention the learner displays to the act in general and to certain cues in particular.

In psychological terms *attention refers to stimulus selection*. The following are some basic considerations of the selective process: (1) individuals differ as to what they will attend to when presented with identical situations; (2) stimulus selection will depend on the environment; and (3) stimulus selection will reflect the nature and state of the human organism. The problem of attention is not a simple one, for it encompasses many aspects of the learning situation. Inattentiveness or misdirected attention will severely limit the adequacy of the response in a particular situation.

Intent and Purpose

Practice is beneficial when it is purposeful. If the learner has the intention of improving and of attaining a goal, more than likely performance increments will be observed on succeeding trials. Thus both the instructor and student are obligated: the instructor to set the goals and provide motivation, the student to follow the lead. Of course, if the task to be learned is meaningful to the student, there is less of a problem in creating interest to promote learning.

Merely going routinely through an act is a pure waste of time. It is not untypical for students in programs or classes to demonstrate the same low levels of skill at the termination of a unit as at the beginning. Although many reasons may be cited for this unfortunate circumstance, certainly one is a lack of purpose and direction. Many physical limitations can be overcome if the individual desires to improve in performance through practice. The reasons for wanting to develop a motor skill are varied, ranging from pure enjoyment in skilled performance to building an ego, or for attention or for some material reward. Some reasons are better than others (who is to decide?) but the fact remains that any purpose is better than none at all, and performance will be contingent on intent to better oneself.

Amount of Practice

Of natural concern is the question of how much practice is necessary for a skill to be really learned. Where is that point of diminishing returns, that point when further practice will be wasted? Much depends on the criterion for skill attainment. Is the foul shot in basketball learned when the student can score one throw, five out of five, ten in a row, or twenty consecutive shots?

In psychological literature the criterion of success is usually one perfect trial or match. A trial may consist of learning ten nonsense syllables, tracing a maze, and the like. Any practice after the one-trial achievement, then, would be additional, and is termed *overlearning*. Researchers have investigated the effects of practice over and beyond the point when criterion learning has occurred and have invariably come to the same conclusion: overlearning results in better retention of the material learned than regular learning.

It is felt that continuous motor tasks are retained better than discrete ones. Speculations suggest that there are more opportunities to make gains in habit strength in continuous tasks. Absolute retention is increased with overlearning but relative retention is associated with a decrease with overlearning.

It is no secret that motor skills—e.g., bicycle riding, ball throwing, and typing—are retained for a much longer period of time than many of the so-called intellectual or verbal skills. When one is asked to recall from childhood the skills involved in bicycling or to remember the lines of a poem, he typically demonstrates much greater performance with the motor skill. One school of thought advanced to explain this situation is that usually motor skills are overpracticed. How much time is spent playing baseball and learning the swing as contrasted with learning prose material? For the average youngster the answer is obvious.

However, overlearning is beneficial to a point, after which there are diminishing returns. In laboratory studies, 50 per cent overlearning is advantageous, but practice beyond this does not afford a proportional gain for the extended effort. Although 100 per cent overlearning results in a better performance yield than 50 per cent overlearning, the gains are not very worthwhile in terms of economy of the practice time.

Overlearning is associated with drill. How much drill is necessary in learning motor skills? The lack of research on motor skills, especially practical ones, necessitates a cautious application of the overlearning principle. Perhaps too much drill occurs in typical situations: not only may this drill reach the point of diminishing returns, but it even may be detrimental because it (1) takes time away from learning other matter; (2) is boring to the learner; and (3) actually does not serve in improving skill retention significantly.

Enough practice to establish learning permanence is required for future success. But perhaps, instead of the number of repetitious trials providing greater motor-skill retention, the answer lies in the nature of the interpolated activity. From the time a skill is learned until it is to be demonstrated again, a few years later perhaps, a minimum number of competing responses has occurred. Most motor skills are somewhat unique. Not too many other learned skills will interfere with the originally learned skill. Therefore it may be reasoned that motor skills can be retained with less practice, proportionally, than is associated with verbal learning.

The reply, therefore, to the question of how much practice is necessary is a difficult answer that can be made only after deciding on one of two possibilities. What is the object of the practice: immediate success or later retention? For many skills, reasonable achievement comes after not too many practice sessions. If the goal is immediate successful performance and there is no concern for the future, then the time spent on learning can be more limited. Contrarily, if later performance is an important consideration, then evidently more practice, hence more overlearning, will be beneficial in determining the length of time the tasks are to be retained as well as the amount of skill that will be displayed at that time of recall.

No amount of practice is enough for the serious-minded athlete. Is it any wonder that even after many years of no practice have elapsed, former college athletes can still demonstrate a reasonably high degree of proficiency in their areas of specialty? Of course, the average individual does not desire and perhaps lacks the ability to attain such a high level of skill. Although his time and energy involvement will be considerably less than that of the varsity athlete, it should be remembered that more practice will increase the potential for later-in-life leisure-time skills to be available for use. Little early practice, which might result in immediate success, will certainly not produce beneficial long-range effects.

Meaningfulness

Tasks that are more meaningful to the learner elevate motivation and consequently are learned more effectively. Meaningfulness can be interpreted in two ways. For instance, some tasks are "logical"; they are not contrived or artificial. A nonsense syllable list is really meaningless; a poem contains meaningful contents.

Another way to analyze an activity is according to its meaningfulness to the learner. How does he perceive it as to the importance of demonstrating achievement? Will proficiency fulfill personal goals? Does it make any difference to the learner whatsoever if he succeeds with the task? In either case, whether task meaningfulness is analyzed according to acceptable interpretations in a society or on an individual and personal basis, a greater interest and perseverance will generally be noted in performance, as will longer-lasting learning affects. Instructional procedures encouraging favorable attitudes to the learning activity will help to make it more appealing, interesting, or challenging.

Often an activity may be conceived by the instructor as meaningful for the learner and he assumes that the learner holds the same values and perceptions. Unfortunately, such is not always the case. This possible discrepancy between learner and instructor could result in frustration and insufficient motivation for the occurrence of adequate skill acquisition.

Readiness

Effective training procedures must be sensitive to the learner's state of readiness. Readiness refers to the learner's (1) developmental stage and his maturational abilities to cope with the learning activities, or (2) predisposition at the time of instruction for favorable response to the instruction and the tasks. Both considerations of readiness need to be recognized if instruction is to proceed in a meaningful manner.

An entire chapter was devoted to developmental factors in which the importance of maturational readiness for skill learning was stressed. We need not go into this topic again. It is merely re-emphasized here. However, the learner's psychological state of preparedness to heed relevant cues, concentrate on task demands, and practice conscientiously is often taken for granted. Meaningful practice depends to a great extent on the learner's state of readiness. Although he may be in this condition because of personal reasons, there are many occasions on which the instructor must use methods to elevate learner readiness. In many ways readiness is related to motivational state. If the learner is optimally motivated, we may assume that he is optimally prepared to practice appropriately.

Abilities and Relative Importance

As we saw in Chapter 7, many abilities contribute to the successful execution of a task. These abilities change in relative importance to task proficiency. Some are associated with achievement at an earlier practice stage; others are associated with achievement at later stages.

The results of an investigation by Fleishman and Hempel (1954) would tend to support the idea of a change in factor pattern with practice. The Complex Coordination Test appeared to be more complex (in terms of the number of significantly important factors) in the initial phase of practice and less complex with the continuation of practice. Through the factor-analysis method, higher loadings on more factors were obtained at the beginning of practice. There were seven significant factors in the initial stages of practice but only three in the final stages. Beside this discovery, different abilities were found to be important during the various stages of practice.

To quote Fleishman and Hempel (on their results): "It is quite conceivable that the abilities contributing to individual differences in earlier stages of skill attainment. . . may be somewhat different than those contributing variance at more advanced and terminal levels of proficiency." This study lends further support for diffidence in predicting final achievement from early success, for those abilities needed for success are called upon in varying degrees, depending on the stage in practice. Also, teacher and learner should be aware of the desirability of emphasizing different factors as practice progresses. Figure 9–1 illustrates the data.

Fleishman offered further evidence in another investigation (1957). He studied the abilities involved in early and late stages of proficiency. His subjects were tested on six motor tasks, including the complex coordination

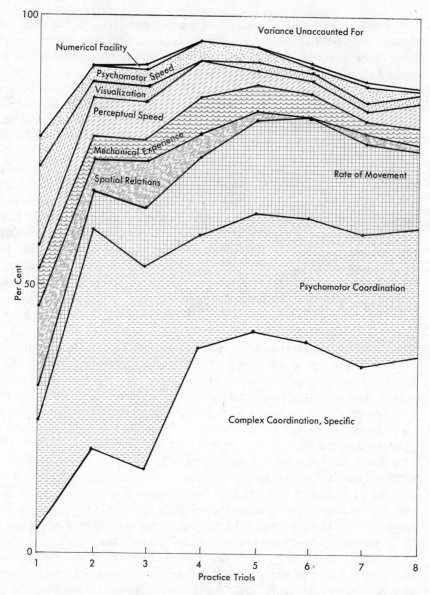

Figure 9–1. Percentage of variance (shaded area) represented by each factor at different stages of practice on the Complex Coordination Test. (From Edwin A. Fleishman and Walter E. Hempel, "Changes in Factor Structure of a Complex Psychomotor Test as a Function of Practice," *Psychometrika,* 19:239–252, 1954.)

test, pursuit rotor, and discrimination reaction-time test. As training continued he found a changing of abilities that contributed to proficiency on these tasks: the level of importance of some abilities increased, others decreased. For instance, the discrimination reaction-time task measures spatial orientation and response orientation early in practice, but speed of arm movement is important later. Fleishman attempted to isolate and predict factors necessary to high levels of skill on these complex motor tasks and found that the factors were not the same as those abilities emphasized early in training.

Although it seems reasonable to accept the hypothesis of different ability requirements at different stages of practice and to acknowledge the implications for practice settings, almost all studies citing such findings have been executed with laboratory apparatus tests as the criterion learning tasks. In one of the few investigations in which a real-life skill was analyzed, an exception was reported. J. Dickinson (1969) attempted to determine the relationship between kinesthetic sensitivity and distance perception with the task of aiming a shuttlecock with a badminton racket. Male and female subjects were novices to the sport of badminton. The aiming task consisted of striking the shuttlecock over the net into target areas, with each subject given five sets of twenty attempts.

Overall, kinesthetic sensitivity correlated 0.49 with aiming performance, whereas distance perception only correlated 0.20 against this criterion. Furthermore, a contradiction was indicated, as compared to other research data, in that kinesthetic sensitivity correlated at a constant level with both initial learning and postlearning performances. This would refute the concept of the change in relative importance of abilities at different stages of practice. Keeping these findings in mind, let us review data from Fleishman and Rich, which are indeed supportive of the hypotheses originally presented. Examine Table 9–1.

In general, and in spite of Dickinson's feelings, it would appear that visual cues are extremely important in the acquisition of skill in psychomotor tasks. Kinesthetic cues evidently are of secondary importance in these tasks, whereas in more complex motor skills, e.g., athletic skills, they seem to be more meaningful. Much depends on how and when abilities are measured during skill acquisition. It is possible that different cues are more important at various learning stages, for there is strong evidence that exteroceptive (visual) feedback and spatial orientation ability are related to early achievement in perceptual-motor tasks. Later, at higher skill levels, proprioceptive (kinesthetic) feedback and kinesthetic sensitivity ability are most important. Table 9–1 includes the data obtained by Fleishman and Rich (1963) and indicates the relationships between these two abilities in performance on a motor task.

Forty subjects received ten blocks of four trials each on the Two-Hand Coordination Test (THC). They were pretested on a kinesthetic sensitivity measure, the ability to judge the difference between lifted gram weights,

TABLE 9–1. PERFORMANCE DUR-
ING TEN TRIALS ON THE TWO-HAND
COORDINATION APPARATUS WITH
RESPECT TO OBTAINED CORRELA-
TIONS BETWEEN KINESTHETIC SEN-
SITIVITY AND THE CRITERION AND
SPATIAL-VISUAL ORIENTATION AND
THE CRITERION. [As practice con-
tinues, the correlations of Two-Hand
Coordination (THC) decrease with the
spatial ability measure and increase
with the kinesthetic sensitivity meas-
ure.]

THC Trial	Orientation Aerial	Kinesthetic Sensitivity
1	.36**	.03
2	.28*	.19
3	.22*	.15
4	.19	.15
5	.08	.10
6	.07	.09
7	.09	.23*
8	−.05	.28*
9	−.02	.38†
10	.01	.40†

From Edwin A. Fleishman and Simon Rich,
"Role of Kinesthetic and Spatial-Visual Abilities
in Perceptual-Motor Learning," *Journal of Experimental Psychology,* 66:6–11, 1963.
* $p < .05$, one-tailed.
† $p < .01$, one-tailed.

and a spatial–visual measure, through the United States Air Force Aerial
Orientation Test. An analysis of the data showed the spatial measure to be
significantly related to performance on the Two-Hand Coordination Test
only early in practice. The kinesthetic measure was significantly related to
THC performance only late in learning. It does appear that individual differences in sensitivity to kinesthetic cues may determine *higher* skill levels.
Other interesting results of this study point to the fact that both kinesthetic
sensitivity and spatial orientation are necessary to overall performance on
the task, as together they correlated 0.73 with the THC.

Assuming the validity of these suggestive findings and the possible uni-
versality of the generalizations, the implications are strong for instructional
guidelines. Task analysis and ability demands should be undertaken. Specific
cuing and practice on those abilities related to practice at a certain stage
of skill mastery would be most beneficial.

Prediction of Success

Owing to the specific nature of individuals and their previous experiences, performers will vary in their rate of skill acquisition. With any given task, some people appear to be faster learners than others. The value of practice, especially over an extended length of time, is obviously more beneficial to those learners who demonstrate initial difficulty with the problem at hand. The necessity of practice of long enough duration has been established from research findings pointing to the fact that one cannot usually predict ultimate achievement from initial progress. Researchers such as Welch (1963) and Trussell (1965) have demonstrated that sufficient data, collected over approximately one-half the intended duration of the practice days, are needed to reflect final levels of attainment adequately.

However, there are evidently at least some tasks in which later proficiency is directly related to early proficiency. The data from Jack Adams's study (1957) acquired from performance on a discrimination reaction-time test nicely illustrate this point (see Figure 9–2). Ten groups of subjects were

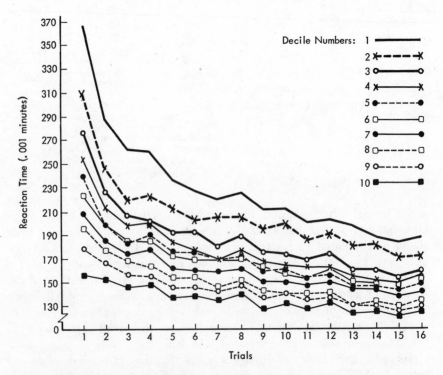

Figure 9–2.   Mean performance curves for ten ability groups. (From J. A. Adams, "The Relationship Between Certain Measures of Ability and the Acquisition of a Psychomotor Criterion Response," *Journal of General Psychology,* 56:121–134, 1957.)

stratified into deciles on the basis of their first trial scores. They were given 160 trials, and although some individuals shifted status with practice, the groups maintained their relative positions throughout the experiment. The reader can observe the unique asymptote for each group, and it does not appear as if the groups would converge toward a common level. All groups showed improvement with practice, and as might be expected, more improvement was noted with the low-ability subjects than the high-ability subjects.

There is good reason to believe, though, that the relationship between initial and final status is quite low on more complex tasks. Variations in the performance levels between learners throughout practice may be due to the relative ease of gaining insight into the problem; the transferability of related learned skills to the task at hand, which might be of special advantage in the early stages of practice; and various psychological, physiological, intellectual, and emotional adjustments that have to be made. Whatever the cause, initial individual differences will exist, as will later differences, but apparently they are not related in complex motor-skill learning. Hence practice will benefit individuals in dissimilar ways and they will show varying rates of progress.

To summarize, then, predictions of final accomplishments become more difficult if (1) the task is complex, (2) ample practice time for all is allotted, and (3) the group is relatively homogeneous to start with.

A final point should be made with regard to increasing the precision of predicting ultimate task proficiency. As J. R. Hinrichs (1970) emphasizes, on the basis of his data, prediction is enhanced when the reference or predictor tasks closely resemble the task itself. Also, predictor tasks are more successful when they attempt to be specifically related to later stages of performance than when they are measures of more generalizable abilities.

Warm-up

Athletes often prepare themselves for an athletic contest by engaging in certain pre-event rituals. Such activities are usually referred to as *warm-up*. They often take the form of exercises or specific practice in the skills that will be required in the contest. Presumably they prepare and prime the athlete for competition, enhancing his performance. We are all familiar with the concept of *warm-up* in this sense, for there are many practical examples of such activities.

A number of research articles have been published in this area and a review and analysis leads to surprising conclusions. The data by no means confirm the value of a variety of warm-up procedures in promoting more effective performance, nor, for that matter, is there a clear indication that athletic injuries are minimized by this practice, although common sense would suggest that this would occur. It does seem, though, that if warm-up activities are to be of benefit they should be directly related to the tasks that will ultimately be performed. Furthermore, they will probably be more beneficial for those skills that require a great deal of precision, timing, and coordination, and especially if there has been a long layoff from the last experience to the present event. It is extremely difficult to ascertain where the psychological aspects of these procedures outweigh the "real" benefits. In other words, if we *think* something will help our performance, performance output may be increased accordingly.

Warm-up has been of interest not only to those involved in practical situations, but to scholars as well who are concerned with psychological learning and retention theory. The term *warm-up decrement* (*WUD*) was coined many years ago to describe poorer performance after a layoff, even where it was as little as a few minutes. It might be thought of as a loss in retention as a function of time, and therefore *warm-up* practice trials may be thought of as having value in

1. Activating or elevating, or reducing or diminishing, the level of arousal necessary for task performance.
2. Reducing the performance decrement that occurs over time.
3. Increasing the set of the performer, which therefore reinstates the appropriate task adjustments and readiness to perform.
4. Promoting any combination of the above.

Warming up does not always increase the arousal state of the individual, for in some instances it decreases it and allows the performer to settle down to the task at hand. Furthermore, WUD is associated with a disappearing decrement in performance dependent upon the need to warm up for the task. It has been found to be different from the process of forgetting; the decrement is not simply due to a loss of habit strength. Interestingly enough, certain intervening or preliminary tasks do not always reduce WUD. Many of them increase WUD, in contrast to a rest period. The learning versus performance effects of WUD are confusing, but there is no evidence that it is a condition of practice that affects learning, only that it affects performance.

Richard Schmidt (1972) presents an excellent overview of the literature and theory related to WUD. The more interested reader will wish to examine his material and the relevant sources that bear on the different points of view offered to explain WUD.

INSTRUCTIONAL DESIGN

Systems approaches to instruction and training are prominent in contemporary literature. They suggest organized and systematic ways of scientifically creating learning environments that most efficiently and productively lead to favorable results. An example instructional or teaching model was presented in Figure 5–1. One of the first sources calling the attention of educators to this approach was published by Robert Gagné (1962). Many resources were developed in subsequent years.

The attempt has been to incorporate learning research and theory into models that are of practical value to the instructor. Learning need not proceed in a haphazard way. Although we are concerned here primarily with the identification of learning phenomena and summary of research findings, those readers who are interested in "putting it all together" in a systematic way for more meaningful instruction will want to familiarize themselves with systems approaches. Some directly applicable to skill learning were presented in Chapter 3. However, many recently published books, primarily in the area of educational psychology, provide a good background for those who wish to utilize systems models in their instruction.

A variety of instructional and training strategies exist. A preference might be dictated by situational constraints and individual differences. In the latter case, it is thought that students with dissimilar attributes, interests, and capabilities might benefit from alternative strategies. Entry characteristics of the students would be matched to the task demands and expected learning outcomes, thereby suggesting appropriate instructional procedures.

The point is that learning research might suggest the most favorable conditions for the average student. Yet a systematic and sensitive analysis of any situation where a number of students are involved leads to a realization of individual differences and ways of coping with them. The book by Singer and Dick (1974) contains content expressly for physical educators and promotes the use of systems approaches to enhancing instruction for all students.

Regardless of his area of interest, each teacher searches for methods of improving his teaching effectiveness. An understanding of learners and their individual characteristics, the knowing of oneself, including teaching strengths and weaknesses, and an awareness of varied teaching techniques will all contribute to the elusive objective: a more effective teacher.

There is no one way to teach. Some instructional methods are better than others, and a method's effectiveness may very well depend on the teacher and the task as well as the learner. To limit and direct all teachers to one procedure would be erroneous; certainly we do not attempt to require every baseball batter to stand and swing in exactly the same way! General principles should not be violated, but there is leeway for individual variation and initiative. A comparison of teaching techniques indicates that certain ones are more beneficial than others to a particular learner. Because of the complexity of the problem and the many operating and interacting variables, however, it should be apparent why conclusive evidence in favor of certain approaches is somewhat lacking.

In any given lesson or unit, the instructor is apt to face a series of challenges. Instructional techniques applicable to certain situations vary, and he should settle on those that are most appropriate and effective. Often these decisions are based on his own educational background, for there is much truth in the statement that we teach as we have been taught. The educator may select from a number of general teaching methodologies and many more instructional techniques, some of more proven merit than others.

All teachers must make certain judgments before class begins. These judgments involve various dimensions of the class situation, and, in a sense, reflect an individual's teaching style. Muska Mosston (1966) categorizes pre-class decisions in the following order:

1. Selection and apportionment of subject matter, e.g., time allotted for practice.
2. Quantity of an activity, e.g., consideration for individual differences.
3. Quality of performance, e.g., measurement standards.
4. Teacher involvement, e.g., to what extent and how.
5. Student involvement, e.g., to what extent and how.

Although Mosston is concerned with these variables primarily as they relate to teaching styles, there are other questions. In what manner should new material be presented to students? How should the student be guided during the practice of skills? How does a class, or social situation, assist or hamper individual progress? These questions are a few that may be raised as instructional materials and procedures are developed.

Management of Practice Sessions

Anyone interested in the most efficient means of skill learning must invariably consider the length of the practice sessions, their frequency in a given period of time, and the work–rest ratio within a practice period. The effective use of time, as defined by maximum productivity or skill development in minimum practice time, can be determined theoretically from the results of countless investigations found in psychological literature. From a practical point of view, though, there is the problem of generalizing in a particular task from data collected under a wide range of experimental materials and methods.

Of course, many factors other than time allotment and distribution are involved in the eventual acquisition of a skill. Some factors are obvious and observable, e.g., the relative complexity of the skill, the amount and quality of instruction offered, facilities and equipment, the motor abilities of the learner, his past experiences in relevant skills, and his maturity. Other factors are not so apparent and might include motivation and determination, emotional status, and mental and physical readiness. All these factors operating in various combinations in turn affect the outcome of the administration of practice sessions.

Many of these variables are difficult to isolate and control. One aspect of the learning situation that can be directed by the instructor is the amount and distribution of time to be designated for the acquisition of a skill or a group of skills. Any teacher or coach is interested not only in providing a period of long enough duration for skill attainment, but also in proportioning the time so that it might bring the most desired immediate and future results. Attempts to improve learning efficiency in any field of activity must consider the problem of optimal spacing of training sessions and the practice session itself.

Length and Spacing

What is the ideal length of practice periods and rest intervals? Although it would be satisfying to be able to provide the teacher and coach with a set answer, the problem is not so simple. Obviously, if the activity is a physically demanding one, attention to cues will diminish and learning in general will suffer as fatigue increases. In this case the length of the session should be relatively short if maximum learning potential is to be realized.

The skill level of the performer is another consideration. Beginners normally have shorter spans of attention than advanced performers and their motivation is extremely more variable. Hence, as a general rule, practice periods may be increased in length (to a point) as skill is attained. Children usually sustain interest in a specific activity for briefer time periods than adults, and instructional periods should be weighed accordingly. These are but two of the common-sense approaches toward practice scheduling.

In one of the more novel experiments on practice schedules, Knapp and Dixon (1950) had two groups of college students learn how to juggle. One group juggled three balls for five minutes each day and the other group practiced fifteen minutes every second day until the criterion of successful juggling was met: 100 consecutive catches. An analysis of the data indicated that the first group learned the task much faster, with one minute of practice in Group I equal to one minute and eighty seconds of practice in Group II. The investigators concluded from these results that learning a task such as juggling was enhanced by shorter practice and shorter rest periods. This one and other studies support the belief in shorter practice and rest periods and, in general, practice extended over a longer duration of time.

From a practical standpoint, many educators wonder whether the semester or trimester college plan is best for the assimilation of knowledge. Similarly, physical educators are concerned with the relative effects of each plan on skill acquisition. Waglow (1966) observed the effects of a seventeen-week semester and a fourteen-week trimester on skill achievement in tennis, golf, and handball. Actually, 1,800 minutes of class time were devoted to each activity under the semester plan and 1,820 minutes were likewise appropriated under the trimester plan. Even so, Waglow found a significant difference in favor of the semester plan for tennis and golf, but not for handball.

It would generally appear, then, that gross motor skills can be learned more efficiently with shorter but more numerous sessions spaced over a longer time period. Although the writer has made a deliberate attempt to review studies concerned only with the learning of athletic skills here, many other studies can be found employing such tasks to be learned as prose, nonsense syllables, inverted alphabet writing, digits, mazes, concepts, symbols, aerial gunnery, typing, piano playing, and pursuit rotors. Summarizing all this research, it is apparent that the optimal rest period necessary for the acquisition of verbal, written, or motor skills varies with the material used. Of twenty-four studies reviewed under the topic of optimal rest intervals between practice periods, thirteen showed superior performance with a greater distribution of practice, eight studies indicated a preference for a rest interval somewhere in the middle of those used, and three investigations did not find any difference in performance with the various intervals employed.

However, these results are somewhat misleading, as what may have been a minimum rest between trials for one study may have been the maximum rest interval used in another study. It is difficult to reach a conclusion, except perhaps that somewhere between too little rest and too much layoff is the desired condition for practice. Also, gross motor skills can be learned with more of a rest interval between practices than can other types of learning material, e.g., nonsense syllables and pursuit rotors.

In motor learning as in weight training there seems to be a point of diminishing returns. Present evidence does not support the contention that five days a week of weight lifting is more effective in increasing strength than three days a week of lifting. Similarly, Massey (1959) found very little difference in the manner in which three groups performed on a stabilimeter (hand–tracing) task as a result of their prescribed practices. One group practiced three days a week for five weeks, a second group practiced five days a week for five weeks, and a third group had only nine days of practice. On this particular task, nine days of practice were sufficient for skill acquisition, which means that actually sixteen of the twenty-five practice days that the second group had seemingly were wasted.

The work of Harmon and Oxendine (1961) is in apparent agreement with these findings. Three groups of junior high school boys learned a mirror tracing task, with all the subjects practicing two days per week for five weeks. The groups differed in the number of practice trials that were allowed each testing day. Although a greater number of practice trials resulted in better performance at first, the groups improved at the same rate throughout the remainder of the experiment.

Often thought is given to manipulating the practice schedule. Oxendine's (1965) groups of subjects learned a mirror-tracing task based on the following practice schedules: increased succeeding practice periods, decreased succeeding practice periods, and constant units of practice. The three groups completed the same amount of practice time. The constant-unit practice group did best on the task and the decreasing-practice group was found to do the poorest.

There are many ways in which practice and rest schedules can be altered. Most of the studies discussed here and even research not mentioned in this section have been interested primarily in immediate performance rather than in ultimate retention of that which has been learned. The next section, which deals with massed and distributed practice, also will include a number of investigations primarily concerned with the immediate effects of the varied practice schedules. The reader should wait until he examines the material on retention later in this chapter before he forms any conclusions on the relative effectiveness of various training procedures.

Massed Versus Distributed Practice

The distribution of time allotted for the learning of a specific skill has posed a serious problem to physical educators and coaches, especially because there are usually many skills to be learned in a limited period of time. Ultimately, the instructor may utilize one of the following methods of practice. On the one hand, he could have his students consistently and continuously practice the skill to be learned without any intermittent pauses. This method is termed *massed practice*. On the other hand, the students might learn the skill in shorter but more frequent practice sessions. These practice periods would be divided by rest intervals or intervals of alternate skill learning, a condition known as *distributed practice*. Is the continuous practice period more effective in skill acquisition and retention than one broken by spaced rest periods? Is it better to practice a task with very little interruption for rest or is rest beneficial to learning and performance? If pauses are desired, what are the optimal intervals between practice trials?

Attempts to improve learning efficiency in any field of activity must consider the problem of optimal spacing of training sessions. Some instructors are in favor of teaching a skill in one session and having the students practice this skill repetitiously in the one period. Other instructors believe in requiring the students to practice different skills for a short duration at each meeting. The actual length of time devoted to the learning of a skill under massed and distributed conditions might be the same. However, under massed conditions the practice of the skill occurs continuously in one session whereas the practice of this same skill under distributed conditions would be limited each session but practiced in a number of sessions.

The relative effectiveness of concentrating all practice or study into one sitting as compared with dividing it into smaller units sampled at varying intervals of time is an important problem in the study of the learning process. The problem exists throughout a wide range of activities from academic preparation to athletics. Numerous studies have been completed in psychology on the distribution of practice effects on learning, with the first demonstrated in 1885 by Ebbinghaus. Unfortunately, very little work may be found in the experimental literature relating to the effects of distribution of practice on the learning and retaining of gross motor skills, or more specifically, athletic skills. Nevertheless, leading physical educators are in general agreement in their opinion that short, frequent performances are more favorable and profitable to learning than long sessions crowded into a brief span of time.

An astounding number of studies dealing with massed and spaced practice have been undertaken. Two of them will be briefly reviewed here. In a laboratory setting, Ammons (1951) had two groups of ten subjects perform thirty-six practice trials on the pursuit rotor. The massed practice group was not allowed any rest between trials whereas the distributed practice group paused five minutes between trials. Distributed practice was favored under the various performance achievement criteria used by the experimenter.

In an athletic situation, Coleman Griffith 1932) noticed similar results. He had one group of basketball players continuously shoot a basketball for an hour, whereas another group shot three minutes and relaxed two minutes for an hour. The next day the procedures were reversed. Both groups shot about an equal amount of time; but when shooting with frequent rest periods, the men averaged 15 per cent more baskets than when shooting steadily.

These are but a sample of the investigations in this area of learning. Figure 9–3 typifies the relationship of massed and distributed practice effects.

In spite of the general findings indicating the preferability of some form of distributed practice over massed practice, leading theoreticians have had reservations in advocating this procedure. The reason for this is that in a number of recent studies in which measures of retention were employed, invariably no differences in performance are noted between massed- and continuous-practice groups. Although there is a distinct hazard in applying inferences from one experimental area to another one, there is little reason to doubt the *superiority of distributed practice over massed practice for immediate performance* in a variety of tasks. It appears that performance is greater under distributed practice, for superior task scores to those found under massed practice are invariably reported in the research literature. Yet this impression may be deceptive.

Skill retention is not favored so clearly under one practice condition. After a rest interval, tests of retention usually indicate a lessened dissimilarity in performance between groups trained under massed- and spaced-practice

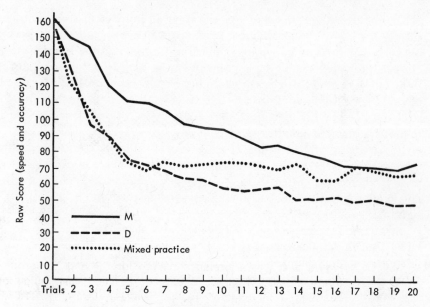

Figure 9–3.   Performance comparisons of massed practice (M), distributed practice (D), and mixed practice on a stabilimeter task. The massed-practice group had twenty consecutive trials, the distributed practice group was allowed a one-minute rest period between trials, and the mixed practice group had five trials of distributed practice and the remaining fifteen of massed practice. Notice how the mixed-practice learning curve assumes the characteristics of each practice method at the different points of the experiment. The distributed practice method is clearly more effective throughout the practice trials. (From I. Lorge, "Influence of Regularly Interpolated Time Intervals upon Subsequent Learning," *Teachers College Contributions to Education,* No. 438, 1930.)

conditions. In other words, it would appear that varied practice conditions, because of the temporary aspect of their influence, affect performance more than they do learning. Massed and distributed practice, when administered within reason, are equally effective in promoting learning. If distributed practice primarily affected learning, the wide differences at the end of practice in favor of distributed practice would remain the same on later performance tests.

Practice performance differences and retention comparisons may be observed in Figure 9–4, the data for which were collected by Jim Whitely (1970). A novel fine motor task involving foot tracking was administered to both groups of subjects. It is readily apparent that the differences and similarities between a massed-practice (MP) group and a distributed-practice (DP) group were in the expected direction.

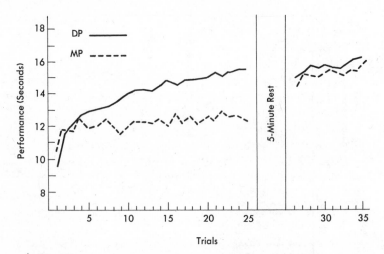

Figure 9–4.   Performance curves for DP and MP groups. (From Jim D. Whitley, "Effects of Practice Distribution on Learning a Fine Motor Task," *Research Quarterly,* 41:576–583, 1970.)

Whole Versus Part Learning

Most skills can be taught in their entirety or broken down into parts. For example, the side stroke in swimming contains a coordinated leg pattern, a coordinated arm pattern, a breathing phase, and a relaxation stage. All these aspects of the stroke may be learned separately before the completed stroke is attempted, or the stroke may be practiced in its totality at the initial stages of learning.

The basketball lay-up is an example of another skill that can be learned by the whole method or in parts (the approach and dribble, the aim, the release, and the follow through). Many times it is not so easy to distinguish whole from part learning. *Whole* could refer to the sport itself, a skill in that sport, or even a part of that skill. In the latter case, when the arm stroke in the side stroke is taught so that each arm is practiced independently, that is an example of part learning. But if the arms are practiced as they coordinate with each other, it could be argued that whole learning is now exemplified. It could also be argued that this is still part learning, because the complete side stroke is not being practiced. Therefore it is possible to confuse the terms and what they label; and one should view these terms as relative to each other and to the material learned. Broadly speaking, the problem concerns separate practice on each of several components compared to practice on the whole task.

Some researchers have attempted to combine the features of both whole and part methods, creating whole-part and progressive-part methods. Whereas the part method implies equal practice or equal time devoted to the units, it is possible to practice the sequential parts with additional repetitions on weak units. The latter procedure allows the student to move from unit to unit only after he has mastered each one. The whole-part method, according to some researchers, may describe the situation wherein the learner views the desired end product and then practices each part until the skill is finalized. The progressive-part, repetitive-part, or continuous-part procedure requires the individual to practice preceding learned units with each newly introduced unit. In other words, the subject practices one subtask, then the second subtask with the first, the third with the first two, until all subtasks are learned and performed together.

Psychologists would generally agree that if a skill is relatively simple, the advisable procedure is to employ the whole method. More complex skills require some sort of breakdown. Although Briggs and Brogden (1954) found a superiority of whole over part practice on a complex coordination test, an analysis of their data suggests that the "superiority of whole practice may disappear at high levels of task complexity." It is believed that if the learner knows his goal, is aware of how the final act should be executed, he will gain quicker insight into the problem. The parts will be more meaningful and will be more easily coordinated into the desired ultimate skill.

Researchers such as James Naylor and George Briggs (1963) have distinguished two aspects of the task that might be considered before designating the learning to proceed under part or whole conditions. *Task complexity* refers to the demands made on a person's memory and is a function of information processing. *Task organization* indicates the nature of the interrelationships of several task dimensions or components. A task has a low organization when there are only a few independent components comprising the task. The studies of these and other researchers suggest that part practice is more favorable for tasks of high complexity and low organization. When the organization is high, i.e., there is an increase of the component interaction, the whole method is preferable (see Figure 9–5).

Complexity in terms of task demands may be understood better by the following questions. How difficult does the learner perceive the task? How many things does he have to think about, to remember from previous related experiences? To what extent is it possible to forget the task over time and therefore pose a challenge to the learner to remember it?

Figure 9–5.   Part or whole practice as suggested against the criteria of task organization and task complexity.

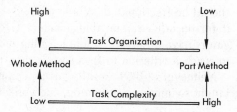

Because a highly organized task is one that contains a high degree of interrelationship among its components, it is necessary to be able to understand what interrelationship means. One criterion might be the sequence of movements involved. Another is the consideration for what the corresponding or opposing limbs (the entire body) are required to do at any one point in the execution of the task. Are many parts of the body involved or only a few? Are the arms working together or in different directions simultaneously? If the legs and arms are moving in similar patterns (e.g., the elementary backstroke), the task should be reasonably highly organized. With different patterns and other factors to consider (e.g., the crawl), the task becomes lowly organized. Thus it can be seen that task organization, or interrelatedness of parts, is a function of (1) the sequence of movements involved and (2) the type, extent, and demands of the movements made at any one point in the task execution.

The use of the task organization–task complexity model for motor skills as shown in Figure 9–5 is highly speculative at the present time. There is difficulty with this paradigm when we start to think about sports skills (the tennis serve or golf swing) and realize that no skill will fit snuggly at one end of the continuum for either criteria.

Because it is sometimes difficult to establish where a skill would fall on the continuum, the same holds true for suggesting the application of whole or part instructional methods. Other times there could be strong agreement on where a task may be placed in the paradigm. One of the cases where the most discrepancy lies is the golf swing. Where in the paradigm would you place it? The practical applications of the Naylor–Briggs model to physical education activities is described by Marion Johnson (1970). Furthermore, an attempt is made to define and discriminate among activity wholes and parts.

This problem of whole versus part learning is more complex for motor skills than for verbal materials. The fractionation of a task requires isolating components equal in difficulty and length, which is not easily done with typical motor skills. A survey of the research on physical education activities indicates little preference for one method over the other. Wickstrom (1958) compared learning of basic gymnastics and tumbling stunts by the whole method to the whole-direct repetitive method (similar to the progressive-part procedure, for the subjects practiced a part of a stunt and then moved on to the second part, combining both). He found little difference in the performances of the groups. In the teaching of sport skills, perhaps common sense might dictate which skills can be taught as wholes and which should be fractionated. Whole methods are to be advocated where possible if for no other reason than efficiency, for as Wickstrom and other investigators have observed, whole learning methods generally permit the student to reach a criterion in fewer trials than part methods.

Neimeyer's (1959) results further complicate the matter. His subjects were taught swimming, badminton, and volleyball under whole and part methods.

The data indicate the favorability of the part method for teaching volleyball, the whole method for swimming, and either technique for the teaching of badminton. These results serve as a further reminder not to generalize from task to task in favor of one particular method. Rather, it is more important to analyze what is to be learned. Perhaps the concepts of task complexity and task organization should be applied to the numerous physical education motor activities for a more accurate indication of those skills that might be favored under whole or part learning conditions.

As a final thought, there is some opinion that more intelligent subjects are likelier to fare better under the whole method. At least one investigation would tend to support this hypothesis. McGuigan and MacCaslin (1955) collected data on rifle marksmanship for four days of firing at different yard markers. Groups were taught either under the whole method, which consisted of watching a demonstration and being instructed and practicing on all the subtasks together; or with the repetitive-part method, learning one subtask for firing, then the second at the same time with the first, and so on. Although the whole method yielded superior performance for all levels of intelligence in slowfire, a more challenging task, sustained fire, was learned more effectively under the whole method for only the subjects with above-average intelligence.

Overt and Covert Rehearsal

For many years physical educators thought of their instruction as pertaining to learning through physical means. One aspect of this education includes the learning of motor skills, and there certainly is enough evidence to justify the impression that this learning will occur in organized programs of physical education in which students actively participate. Active participation has traditional connotations, for we think of it as primarily emphasizing physical movement; and although no act is purely physical or solely cognitive, we will refer to such terms in their usual context for the sake of convenience. Just how much activity is necessary, or to put it another way, to what extent the active participation can be exchanged with other forms of involvement, is not clearly understood.

Time spent in overt physical activity may be replaced with verbal instructions and directions, films, viewing another's performance, reading material, and mental imagery or practice. The effectiveness of these techniques alone and in conjunction with actual physical involvement are of great interest to educators who are concerned with the best combination teaching method.

Numerous experiments support the contention that learning motor skills occurs with active overt practice and specific instruction. Evidence on ideal ratios of overt practice to other means of learning is conspicuous by its absence. There are many people who feel the only way to learn a motor skill is through active physical participation. The results of studies on covert (mental) practice serve to question this belief; and certainly the value of lecture, films, reading material, and the like cannot be denied. How much time should be devoted to any of these techniques as a replacement for activity?

Empirical evidence suggests that beginners profit more from overt involvement in the activity. One investigation that provides contrary data is worth reporting here. John Jones (1965) found that overt practice was not necessary for his subjects to learn a gymnastic skill, the hock-swing upstart. Covert practice was a sufficient condition for learning, and interestingly enough, undirected covert practice was found to be more effective than directed covert practice. Verbal and written instructions appear to be more beneficial and meaningful as an individual's skill level increases. This would be especially true with complex skills. Although there is no total substitution for participation, as the learner progresses he may obtain greater skill when the activity is supplemented with various teaching aids, such as detailed verbal and written directions.

Worthy of our attention is the current interest in mental practice, which is a form of passive learning in the sense that overt practice does not take place. In order not to offend those who would claim that the individual actively responds even during mental practice, it must be restated that this concept is indeed true. However, relatively speaking, the learner *appears* to be passive. *Mental* or *image practice* or *conceptualization* refer to task rehearsal in which there are no observable movements. Researchers have compared the effectiveness of learning tasks through actual physical practice with mental practice or a combination of physical–mental practice.

As far back as 1899, the question was raised as to whether gymnastic movements could be learned through covert practice even if they were not practiced overtly. The relationship of skill learning and muscle activity to conceptualization has been demonstrated in various ways in a number of experiments since that time. One of the earlier studies was completed by Perry (1939) in which he administered five tasks to his subjects, tasks which ranged from simple motor tasks to those demanding ideational and symbolic activities. The tasks were a three-hole tapping test, a peg-board test, a card-sorting test, a symbolic digit-substitution test, and a mirror-tracing test. Perry compared the effects of actual to mental practice on the performance of each task.

Mental rehearsal was found to yield significantly better performances on four of the five tasks than no practice at all. Physical practice was superior to conceptualization on three tasks; however, the mental practice group was favored on the peg board task. Other studies have, in general, obtained similar results. Typically, physical practice is better than mental practice, which in turn is better than no practice at all. Clark's (1960) results are of interest because they were derived from practice on a physical education skill. His subjects learned the Pacific Coast one-hand foul shot under conditions of

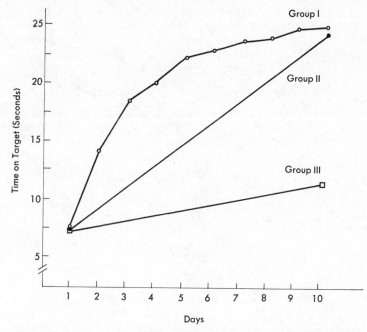

Figure 9–6.   Mean total time on target for Days 1–10 for Group 1 (physical practice), Group 2 (mental rehearsal), and Group 3 (control). (From Edna Rawlings, Irving L. Rawlings, Stuart S. Chem, and Mary D. Yilk, "The Facilitating Effects of Mental Rehearsal in the Acquisition of Rotary Pursuit Tracking," *Psychomonic Science,* 26:71–73, 1972.)

physical and mental practice and he found mental practice to be nearly as effective as physical practice.

In fact, Rawlings et al. (1972) report the equally beneficial effects of mental and overt rehearsal on the learning of a pursuit rotor task. Three groups of female subjects participated in the study for ten days. The mentally rehearsed subjects pictured the apparatus (not in view) and imagined themselves performing the task without actually making the movements. In the first experiment, the overt and covert practice groups performed similarly after the ten days of practice and better than the no-practice group (see Figure 9–6). In the second phase of the study, with male subjects, the rest interval between trials was examined. As can be seen in Figure 9–7 the rate of learning was fastest for Group I. This group mentally rehearsed the task following each overt practice session whereas the second group was engaged in a color memory task following each overt practice session.

Other researchers, although noticing the significant beneficial effects of mental rehearsal, have not obtained such effective results from this form of

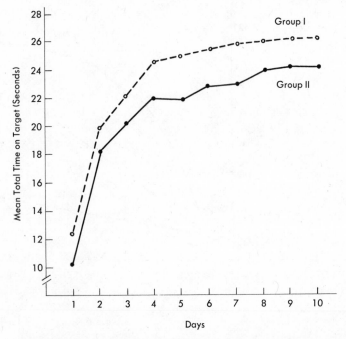

Figure 9–7. Mean total time on target for Days 1–10 for Group 1 (motor practice + mental rehearsal during rest period) and Group 2 (motor practice + color naming during rest period). (From Edna Rawlings, Irving L. Rawlings, Stuart S. Chem, and Mary D. Yilk, "The Facilitating Effects of Mental Rehearsal in the Acquisition of Rotary Pursuit Tracking," *Psychomonic Science,* 26:71–73, 1972.)

practice. More in line with the general research findings in this area is a study by Twining (1949) in which ring tossing was the skill to be learned. Three groups were involved, one that threw 210 rings on the first day and the twenty-second day; a second group that threw 210 rings on the first day and seventy rings each day from the second through the twenty-first day and 210 rings on the twenty-second day; and a third group that threw 210 rings on the first day, mentally rehearsed the skill for fifteen minutes daily from the second through the twenty-first day and threw 210 rings on the twenty-second day. The subjects without practice showed no significant learning. The subjects receiving physical practice improved 137 per cent. The subjects who had mental practice improved 36 per cent.

In investigations comparing a third group, one which is physically and mentally practiced, usual results indicate this method to be as effective as physical practice or slightly inferior to it. A combination of physical–mental practice is probably better than mental practice alone.

Present-day investigators have attempted to come to grips with the many variables that possibly might affect learning by mental practice. Some of these include the skill level of the learner on the skill to be learned, the novelty of the task, intelligence, kinesthetic sense, and ratios of physical to mental practice. Intelligence, for example, has a low correlation with various estimates of overt performance. Excellent summaries of the research on all topics related to mental rehearsal are presented by Alan Richardson (1967a,b).

Although it might be true that covert practice is only effective with tasks primarily experienced by the learners, the question arises as to how it might formally be introduced effectively into a practice regimen that includes overt practice of a motor skill. In response, Singer and Witker (1970) designed an experiment to determine the point of introduction, in relation to overt practice, that covert practice might best facilitate learning (see Table 9–2). Four groups practiced mentally at various designated points during the overt practice context; the fifth group practiced without any mental rehearsal. The data were analyzed in various statistical ways, but no significant performance differences were found among the groups. As we can see in Figure 9–8, however, there appears to be a trend indicating some value of early introduction of mental rehearsal within the context of overt practice.

Perhaps previous overt practice on the task at hand facilitates the ease with which conceptualization takes place. It is quite difficult to envision the intricacies of an act unless one has had actual experience performing it, a hint that mental practice has more value with the highly skilled individual. A number of studies indicate that the novice gains faster with covert practice than with overt practice alone.

Another consideration is the ability level of the individual in a given task; that is, the person must have the necessary skill to perform the actions if instructions of any kind are to be valuable. Organized actions must correspond to verbal concepts. Words and concepts are only valuable in the motor-learning situation to the extent that they can be translated into coordinated movements.

The learner must always have the correct task image in mind. For performance to improve, the individual probably has to have some match available—a match of his performance with an image of what the correct model is like. And he continually tries to better his performance until the image matches the model perfectly. The primary interest in the research reported here is how and to what extent deliberate mental rehearsal of a movement-oriented task affects the rate of learning and performance on it.

Aside from experimental data, empirical evidence indicates that almost all athletes subject themselves to some form of mental rehearsal before, during, and even after competition. They constantly review, analyze, and

TABLE 9–2.   PRACTICE SCHEDULES

Week	I		II		III		IV		V
Session	1	2	3	4	5	6	7	8	9
Group									
I	M	M	P	P	P	P	P	P	Posttest
II	P	P	M	M	P	P	P	P	Posttest
III	P	P	P	P	M	M	P	P	Posttest
IV	P	P	P	P	P	P	M	M	Posttest
V	P	P	P	P	P	P	P	P	Posttest

M = Mental Rehearsal
P = Physical Practice
(From Robert N. Singer and Janet Witker, "Mental Rehearsal and Point of Introduction Within the Context of Overt Practice," *Perceptual and Motor Skills,* 31:169–170, 1970.)

conceptualize their performances, although in a less structured manner than has been employed in formalized experimentation. Nevertheless, at least one high school tennis coach has turned to planned mental practice periods that precede and complement the actual play of the athletes. Following one of these conceptualizing sessions, a player was overheard to comment, "Hope I do in practice as well as I think!"

Mental rehearsal, under many but not all conditions, has been shown to be beneficial as a method of learning and improving motor performance. Exactly how this information may be applied practically to the learning situation faced by the physical educator and others concerned with motor skills has not been worked out as yet. It seems reasonable to expect, though, that in the future there will be a greater recognition of the cognitive processes in the learning of motor skills. The ratio of time allocated for covert and overt practice will be designated, as will designs of covert practice provided for different skills that are taught.

Skill Versus Accuracy

When a motor skill is newly introduced to the learner, the instructor might have to decide whether it is best to practice this skill as fast as possible, as precise as possible, or both. The right methodology can affect short-term as well as long-term success.

Many times the question is raised as to whether one should emphasize speed or accuracy in the early stages of learning. The tennis player might initially attempt to master accuracy in stroking by standing relatively still and concentrating on the stroke and the direction of the ball. On the other

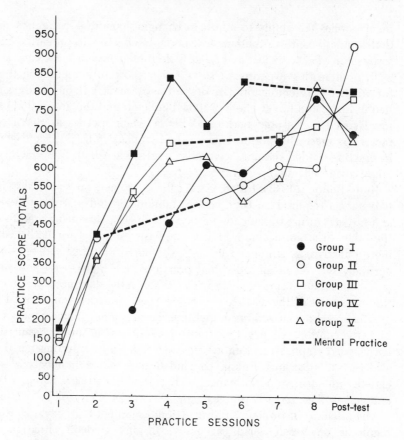

Figure 9–8.   Practice schedules of mental rehearsal and physical practice combinations for different groups. (From Robert N. Singer and Janet Witker, "Mental Rehearsal and Point of Introduction Within the Context of Overt Practice," *Perceptual and Motor Skills,* 31:169–170, 1970.)

hand, he could practice under gamelike conditions, striking the ball when constantly on the move, in and away from the net. The fencer might learn how to lunge by practicing slow, carefully calculated movements that emphasize form and accuracy. Or, he could practice making the swift and agile movements associated with actual competition.

When learning motor skills, accuracy has usually been emphasized first. However, there is evidence enough to justify that practice should resemble game situations, that a skill should be rehearsed as it would be performed in the contest. Many basketball players shoot well by themselves or even under lessened pressures of practice sessions. However, defensive hands in their faces, shooting on the move, game pressures, boisterous spectators, and other variables contribute to the downfall of these same players. Skill attainment implies the ability to adjust to changing conditions. Practice sessions that simulate contest situations will be more effective in preparing the performer for what to expect and what is desired of him in these contests.

Two interesting experiments serve the purpose of emphasizing the need for practice to resemble ultimate desired performance. In one study, subjects had to lunge at a target (Solley, 1952). Solley found the group that emphasized speed in learning performed better when speed was the necessary factor for successful performance. Equal emphasis on speed and accuracy in practice yielded the most favorable results when both these factors were important to effective performance.

Ruth Fulton (1945) tested sixty college women on two tasks, tracing movements required on the Snoddy stabilimeter and a striking movement at a target. During training, one group of subjects was encouraged to speed, the other to attain accuracy. Early emphasis on speed for both tasks was more effective, as stronger transfer was noted of the speed set than the accuracy set. When an individual practices at a high speed and then attempts to attain accuracy along with the speed, he does not have to change the movement of the act. However, low-speed practice transformed to the greater speed demanded in competition requires a new movement, a change in body control. No negative transfer effects on accuracy resulted from early speed emphasis in Fulton's investigation. In interpreting her data for athletic skill learning, Fulton concluded that where momentum is associated with effective performance, such as in tennis strokes, hammer throws, and golf strokes, an early practice emphasis on accuracy will be detrimental.

The dilemma of tradeoffs in instruction occurs not only when considering emphasis on speed versus accuracy. In any tradeoff situation where there are at least two alternative approaches, the instructor should weigh possible benefits against detriments. An extreme emphasis on speed negatively affects accuracy, and vice versa. In some respects, if practice proceeds to reflect real condition performance expectations, no tradeoffs have occurred. Learners should practice in conditions as realistic as possible. It is probably true that it is better in the long run for tennis beginners to practice the full stroke instead of a modified, slowed-down response. Situations should be created that will make adjustments easier from the learning conditions to the real performance conditions.

There are exceptions to this general proposal. First of all, certain students may be demonstrating performance problems and hampered progress. It may be necessary to make a tradeoff whereby the learner isolates particular task components and practices with slower movements. Learner difficulties may be remediated with an altered instructional approach. Secondly, it is not always practical or safe immediately to experience tasks under real conditions. Flying a plane, operating complex machinery, and other activities in which safety factors and costly equipment are involved suggest the initial use of simulated experiences.

We may also deduce from material presented in Chapter 7 on abilities that different abilities are related to stages of practice. In the Hinrichs study, accuracy was found to be more related to early achievement on the pursuit rotor task, whereas speed was more important at the latter stages. Thus it would seem that the ability to perform accurate movements quickly will ultimately differentiate the highly from the lowly skilled. This notion is borne out in a practical sense from the data compiled by John Woods (1967) with beginning tennis players. Three different instructional programs led to the following conclusion (p. 141):

> For a tennis skill which is deemed to require both ball velocity and ball-placement accuracy simultaneously, the most desirable results were obtained by equal and simultaneous emphasis on both the velocity and accuracy variables. The second most desirable results were obtained by beginning with velocity and terminating with accuracy. The least desirable results were obtained by initial emphasis on accuracy followed by velocity.

For practical research (using a ball-throwing skill) on the topic of speed versus accuracy, the apparatus described by Robert Malina and G. Lawrence Rarick (1968) is recommended. Speed and accuracy measurements of a ball throw can be effectively assessed. Theoretical directions on the relationship between speed and accuracy of movement have primarily come from the efforts of Paul Fitts. C. I. Howarth, W. D. A. Beggs, and J. M. Bowden (1971) have compared his formula to describe this relationship

$$T = a + b \log_2 \frac{2A}{W}$$

where:
T = duration of movement
A = amplitude of movement
W = width of the target

$\log_2 \dfrac{2A}{W}$ = a measure of information required to select the tolerance range from the total range of movements

with their own. Differences in equations are discussed, as is theory to describe the decrease in accuracy at high speeds of performance, and vice versa.

Sequential Order of Events

In any sport there are a series of skills that must be mastered before total satisfaction can be enjoyed when participating in that sport. Typically, more complex skills are taught after simpler ones have been learned. This practice is not always advisable or necessary in all circumstances. For now, though, let us be concerned with skills of approximately equal difficulty that comprise a particular sport.

Physical educators often touch upon the various skills of a sport at different class meetings. Traditionally they begin with one skill and usually progress according to a well-accepted, predesigned plan. Volleyball is an example of a sport composed of at least four distinct, unique skills: spiking, serving, digging, and setting. Volleyball instructors often teach the set first, the spike last, and serving and digging in interchangeable order. The concern here is for the acquisition of one part of a sport facilitating the learning of other phases, of placing the skills in such an order so as best to promote ultimate game performance.

If, in a series of things to be learned, some are more important than others, where should they be placed in the learning order? Psychologists have been able to control extraneous variables to a great extent by studying the learning of lists of nonsense syllables, prose, and poetry. The learning of sequential materials, a particular order of parts comprising a whole, has been termed *serial learning*. When nonsense syllables are presented at random arrangement and subjects are allowed to recall them in any order they desire, studies have usually found the words at the end of the list to be most frequently recalled (see, for example, Deese and Kaufman, 1957). However, when nonsense syllables are presented serially or organized material such as prose is learned, that which has been learned first is retained best, the last material is mastered second best, and the middle is last to be recalled.

Returning to the volleyball example, it seems only natural to ask if one skill is deemed most important and useful for satisfactory participation in a sport, will it be most effectively learned and retained if it is taught first, last, or in the middle of all the skills to be learned for that sport? Because the set is considered by many volleyball experts as the one skill most often used in a game, what should the position of this skill be in relation to others that will be taught?

Although the order in which skills are learned might affect later performance, it is surprising to discover how little research work has been done on this topic. In an attempt to gain some insight into the problem, Singer (1968) obtained data from college volleyball classes on the learning and retention effects of volleyball skills taught in an ordered sequence. Each of four classes learned four skills in a different order. Immediate and later retention tests indicated that the order in which the skills were learned had little bearing on test scores. Isolated significant differences demonstrated a lack of noteworthy patterns in between and within group differences.

Although one might have speculated from other research and theory that those skills learned first and last would be best retained, Singer's study does not substantiate the premise. Possibly, because of the nature of gross motor learning, one should not expect much difference in retention in a short period of time as a result of the sequence in which skills are taught.

That the learning of certain matter might promote the learning of other matter is a concept much relied on in educational thought and practice. A logical sequence of material presentation is the desired structure of the unit outline. There is still much debate as to what constitutes a "logical sequence," and an obvious consideration is the arrangement of tasks by their apparent difficulty. Transferring elements must be contemplated, and the topic of transfer is covered in detail later in the chapter.

Drill Versus the Problem-Solving Approach

Different educational teaching philosophies have been emphasized at various periods in this century. The revolt against the traditional method of learning (concerned with course content) inspired learning not by mere repetition but through questioning and probing. Deweyism brought about consideration for individual differences in interests, rates of learning, and, in general, a problem-solving approach to learning. Lately, many experts on educational curricula have spoken out against so-called student-oriented courses in favor of teacher-oriented courses. The plea is for a return to traditional teaching methods, i.e., "the command performance." Whether material can be learned more effectively through drill and memorization or problem solving and probing is the current argument. Perhaps different material can be learned better under either condition, and the goals of the instructor and the favored learning strategies of the student should be considered in any situation. Drill and problem-solving differences in approaches may be noted in Figure 9–9.

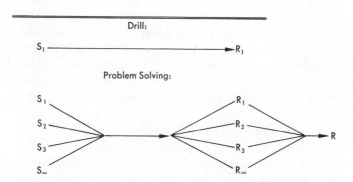

Figure 9–9. A comparison, in behavioristic terms, of drill and problem-solving methods. A specific response (R_1) is practiced to a particular stimulus (S_1) in the drill approach. In problem solving, a number of stimulus cues ($S_1 - S_x$) are present in the learning situation and there may be a variety of acceptable responses ($R_1 - R_x$) from which one (R) is selected by the learner.

What about a comparison of the application of these methodologies to motor-skill learning? Drill has always been the basic means of teaching motor skills, primarily because it does provide results and possibly because it does not require much creativeness and ingenuity on the part of the instructor. Arranging a situation that encourages the students to think, reason, and then act toward a goal is a methodology rarely practiced by instructors and coaches; hence its merits are difficult to ascertain. However, it should be of interest to speculate on the effectiveness of drill versus problem-solving approaches with motor learners.

The current state of problem-solving theory, with specific application to the human as an information-processing system (see Chapter 3 in the text for a discussion on models), is presented in an interesting manner by Herbert Simon and Allen Newell, writing in the *American Psychologist* (1971). Information processing related to environmental tasks is shown to be related to problem-solving problems and problem spaces. The authors believe current contemporary problem-solving theory adequately describes the information and problems possessed by the skilled performer.

There has been considerable attention given lately to exploration skills, especially by physical educators interested in educating elementary school-children. Instead of perpetuating traditional teaching methods, these people have attempted to guide youngsters to a greater awareness of factors associated with any activity, namely time, force, and space. The approach is such as to initiate individual creativity in mastering basic movement skills, those that underlie simple and complex sport activities in varying degrees. This rationale appears to be justifiable and the approach is refreshing. How effective the immediate and long-term results are in comparison with those of traditional teaching methods is a question unanswerable at the present time.

As to the athletic skills of older children, the drill method has the advantage of facilitating the execution of an act until it is habitlike. This method is fine for the high jumper, broad jumper, and diver, to name a few, who basically demonstrate a skill under the same static environmental conditions with each performance. Comparing this situation to the one faced by the tennis player, basketball player, and soccer player, we can observe that in the former case the environment is relatively stable; fixed responses not only are allowable, they are encouraged.

In the latter circumstance, environmental conditions are dynamic. Unpredictable stimuli require the performer to have a flexible repertoire of responses. If the player (say, the basketball player) becomes routinized in his movements, an alert opponent will take advantage of him. The player who can drive to the right side and invariably stops short to take a jump shot is easier to defend against than the player who is a threat to move in any direction and who varies his shots. A team which is overcoached may reflect this practice in the following manner. The offensive pattern calls for the guard to dribble the ball toward the side-line and pass it to the forward

Figure 9–10. The relationship of instructional approaches to type of task. The scheme is not to suggest that only one approach can be used for the learning of a task. Many times both approaches contribute to skill mastery. However, drill is usually favored for tasks that are oriented toward self-pacing and problem-solving for externally paced tasks.

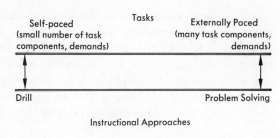

and then cut through the middle on the opposite side. From there perhaps a few team patterns may be executed. A smart defensive team expects the guard's initial pass to the forward and intercepts one or two passes. The guard has been so trained to perform the same routine that he does not adjust properly and perhaps his and the team's play may disintegrate totally.

Players who have been exposed to diverse game circumstances, who are not overdrilled, will react more favorably to the unexpected. Drill has its function. It encourages a consistency in performance and a skillfully executed act. Obviously, certain skills must be developed before complex movement patterns may be elicited. But if coaches or physical educators merely *train* instead of *educate,* if they make robots of their pupils, they have done them a great disservice. Active youngsters must be able to reason quickly in challenging situations and have the abilities to express their thoughts. Therefore both drill and problem-solving approaches serve in meeting teaching and student goals.

Even in sports that demand a skill to be performed in a relatively predictable environment, the problem-solving method might promote the learning of more complex skills. When the student is introspective and does not only repeat an act continually without understanding what he is really doing, he probably will gain quicker insight into other relevant skills. Perhaps overall swimming objectives are taught more effectively when the student, with teacher guidance and supervision, is encouraged to think of means of propulsion through the water on the side, back, and front, and then to react in a supervised trial-and-error method. The drilled individual learns the skill but maybe nothing more; the individual who has to reason and learn in a loosely structured situation may learn the skill as well as water principles, confidence, safety, and ways of transferring elements to other strokes and water conditions. Figure 9–10 contains the schematic relationship of task classification and instructional approach.

Traditional and innovated methods of teaching physical education skills are in existence throughout the world. Supporters of the teacher-completely-dominating drill approach, however, appear to be diminishing. Perhaps because the value of drills has been questioned, Ralph Wickstrom (1967) has seen fit to present a strong argument on behalf of the utilization of this teaching methodology. His emphasis is on skill development, however, and the importance of strengthening S–R bonds for the play that will follow later. Drills, like other teaching techniques, must be administered in an effective manner if their true value is to be realized. Wickstrom offers the following suggestions for successful results from the usage of drills:

1. Concentrate on drills until basically correct form starts to become automatic and thereby habitual. Drills need not be the only form of skill practice employed but they should be emphasized.

2. Encourage students to concentrate on the correct execution of the skill or skills used in the drills. Drills which are performed sloppily are useless and probably far more harmful than beneficial. If students do not improve in performance the situation must be analyzed to determine the cause.

3. Constantly make corrections during drills to keep attention on the proper techniques of performance. Early corrections of a general nature made with enthusiasm and to the entire group are stimulating and effective. Along with the corrections, general comments on the correct fundamentals are positive in nature and of particular value. The students should be kept aware of the purpose and objectives of the drill while they are doing it. It should be remembered that the drill is an opportunity to concentrate on certain aspects of correct performance and devleop a consistency in the performance.

4. Make drills game-like as often as possible. Drills of this sort are more interesting and challenging because they are a movement in the direction of regular play.

5. Advance to the use of multiple-skill drills to emphasize the proper use of combined skills. The transition from drills to the game is easier if drills have been devised to reflect the choices and problems possible in the actual game.

6. Make extensive use of modified games to create the much desired competitive atmosphere. Most games can be modified to emphasize one or two skills and still offer controlled practice. The modified game is one of the easiest ways to maintain a high level of interest and still retain the essential spirit of the drill.

7. Keep drills moving at a brisk pace and involve as many participants as possible. This procedure will increase the amount of individual participation and practice. Since motor learning involves the factor of trial-and-error, the student needs many opportunities to participate, evaluate and change. One or two chances per individual in a drill would not have much impact on learning.

Other educators are looking beyond the teaching approach that treats all individuals alike and in which the teacher dominates the activity. Mosston (1966) offers creative ways of teaching physical education students. After discussing the weaknesses of the traditional teaching method, which he calls the "command style," he delves into more desirable techniques, culminating in the *guided discovery style*, of which the problem-solving approach is an extension.

The individualized learning process, according to Mosston, brings the learner to a high level of development in four dimensions: the physical, the social, the emotional, and the intellectual. The teacher induces discoveries to problems in all activities, the solutions of which are not predetermined. That is to say, there are a number of ways of approaching a situation, and each student may cope with the problem in his own individualized manner. After all, there are many means by which one can express himself whether they be oral or physical. Examine the following example found in Mosston's book (p. 213) of a problem to solve in movements on the parallel bars:

The first area of problem design is the initial relationship between the body and the parallel bars. How do we get on? In relating the body to the given equipment (Level 1 in the structure of subject matter), one can observe that several possibilities exist in terms of *where* to mount the parallel bars. Thus, there is a need to develop problems, the solution of which will establish the possible relationships between the position of the body, the movement, and the position on the equipment.

Mounts onto the parallel bars are possible at the following locations:

1. At the end of both bars, outside the bars.
2. At the end of both bars inside the bars.
3. In the middle of both bars, inside the bars.
4. At *any* point of both bars, inside the bars.
5. At the above proposals, entry can be performed above, below, and between the bars.
6. 1–4 can be done from under or over the bars.
7. Some of the above can be done using only *one* bar. Which ones?
8. Some of the above can be done alternating one and two bars. Which ones?
9. Are there other locations?
10. Are there other possible bar conbinations (excluding for a moment various slope arrangements)?

Let us examine some problems to solve in mounting *at the end of both bars* (*from the outside*), *facing the bars:*

1. Design two mounts from a standing position which will land you in support position.
2. Using each one of the solutions of the previous problems, *end* in three different support positions.
3. Design four different mounts from four starting positions *other than* standing, ending in each of the suggested supporting positions of 2.
4. Are there still other alternative starting positions from which you can

execute four discovered mounts? How many? Are they all good? How do you determine that?

5. Using the new alternative starting positions, can you still find another mount to a support position?
6. Is it possible to end the previously discovered mounts in positions other than the front support position?
7. Can you end *any* of the previously discovered mounts with a turn? What kind of a turn?
8. Can you end any of the mounts on top of both bars?
9. Can you find three different end-mount positions on top of both bars?
10. On top of one bar?
11. Could you end the mount on no bars? Would this constitute a mount?

Although there are more steps on the parallel bars offered by Mosston, the quoted material should be adequate to reflect some possible procedures to follow in the problem-solving approach. The approach could be utilized with all sports, and Mosston does present some sports examples, such as soccer, tumbling, and football. However, the approach need not be consistent from teacher to teacher, and there is plenty of room for individual creativity in the formulation of problems.

There is no firm evidence to support a stand for the drill or problem-solving approach to all types of motor-skill learning. One may assume the prerogative of conjecture, as the writer has just done, to determine the values of each method. From an educational point of view, a problem-solving approach certainly is consistent with the philosophy of leading educators. From a skill-learning point of view, arguments can be justified for either method. Perhaps, as was mentioned previously, to be considered at the onset is the nature of the skill, its relation to other material to be taught, and the objectives of the teacher.

Peggy Whilden (1956), although not comparing the drill to the problem-solving approach, did investigate the effects of pupil-dominated and teacher-dominated groups. Two classes of junior high school girls learned beginning basketball skills. At the end of the unit, the teacher-dominated group (traditional instructional methods) was judged to display better basic skills, but the pupil-dominated group demonstrated a greater knowledge of the rules, a better attempt at improving the social status of near-isolated girls, and played together better as a team. Each learning method had unique value, and certainly an approach other than the conventional one apparently can more nearly fulfill particular objectives.

A master's thesis by Carol Berendsen (1967) concludes in favor of the structured problem-solving method rather than a structured practice drill method for beginning female college tennis students. Although no differences in attitude scores or in performance were noted on final attained proficiency levels in basic tennis skills, the problem-solving students scored higher on the written test and on the combined written and skill tests.

Programmed Learning

Our society is so besieged with technological advancement and innovations, it is not surprising that some enterprising educators rebel against the traditional classroom learning situation. Because manmade machines have substituted for human productivity and have been demonstrated to be more efficient in industry in certain cases, these educators suggest that machines can serve a similar purpose in education.

Actually, the concept of a teaching machine is by no means new. L. S. Pressey is credited for creation of a teaching machine in the 1920's and B. F. Skinner for streamlining it in later years. Skinner applied his laboratory research on reinforcement in learning to the device's design and is acknowledged as the leader in convincing the public of the machine's value as well as influencing its widespread popularity. In its simplest form the machine is constructed for individual usage, with the content of a course or course area presented to the learner in simple to more difficult sequence form. The learner has to respond correctly to the questions and is informed by the machine as to the correctness of his answer. Proper responses permit him to advance through the material; complex and more difficult material is learned only after simpler material has been mastered.

Courses have to be programmed in a logical way. The material is presented in detail step by step, ensuring progressive knowledge acquisition. The Skinner method encourages only correct responses whereas the Crowder technique permits errors, operating under the philosophy that a learner may profit from his mistakes. For an interesting discussion on programming and teaching machines, the reader is encouraged to read Travers's book, *Essentials of Learning* (1964).

Wilbur Schramm (1964) has listed the essential characteristics of programmed learning:

1. An ordered sequence of stimulus items.
2. A response by the learner to each of the stimuli.
3. Reinforcement of the response by immediate knowledge of results.
4. Progression in small steps.
5. Practice consisting of mostly correct responses and few errors.
6. Learning proceeding in successively closer approximations to the desired objectives.

Presently there are many types of teaching machines and programmed texts on the market. Some are relatively inexpensive but others, such as computer-assisted machines, can be quite costly. Basically, though, all these machines are geared to operate under certain accepted learning principles. One of these is the imparting of immediate knowledge of results, of reinforcing correct responses. Reinforcement, especially when directly following

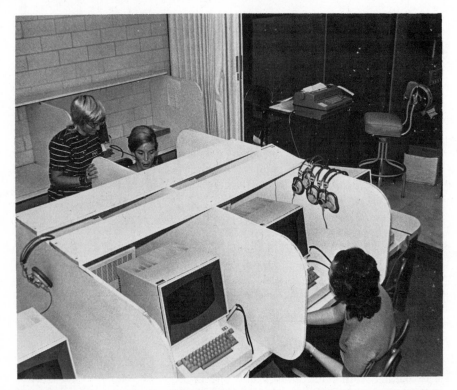

Figure 9–11. Students learning through a computer-managed course where the material is programmed.

a response, is essential for learning. Obviously, a teacher faced with a number of pupils in his class cannot provide individual attention. Hence, another strong feature of the machine; it permits students to work at their own pace and within their own abilities. Whereas the teacher must gear his lesson to the average learning speed of the class, programmed individualized units meet specific needs and abilities. There are other merits to teaching machines, but they need not be analyzed here. The use of computers and other media in education is increasing, and Figures 9–11, 9–12, and 9–13 illustrate some applicable situations.

Of most concern with these machines or programmed texts is their effectiveness in educating students. Although research is not yet ample enough nor experimental designs sufficiently sophisticated to warrant any conclusive statements, results are most promising. A number of investigations, if not finding programmed material to be better learned than material taught by traditional teaching methods, have noted greater efficiency in the form of time-saving benefits of the programmed method. As an example, Rawls, Perry, and Timmons (1966) found psychology course material to be learned at a substantial time saving with a programmed group as compared to a

Figure 9–12. In-
struction is being pro-
vided to a student in
the use of a computer
terminal for the learn-
ing of course mate-
rial.

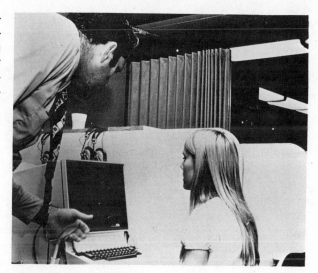

lectured-to group. Although no significant difference was noted between
the groups on a knowledge test administered at the end of the unit, a retention test given six weeks later favored the programmed group.

The advantages associated with these various devices have been derived
when the material to be acquired was *not* in the motor-skill area. This is
understandable, for motor skills have yet to be programmed in a satisfactory
manner. Programmed texts and teaching machines can be used, if desired,
for the learning of information related to athletic skills. With regard to a
particular sport, programs can be developed containing such matter as
relevant physiological and mechanical principles, rules, strategy, and history.
What about programming movement skills? Is it possible?

Figure 9–13. A re-
source center with
appropriate media
permits students to
learn at their own
preferred rates.

Milt Neuman and Robert Singer (1968) attempted to program beginning tennis skills in the form of booklet material. A programmed group of subjects was compared to a traditionally taught group at the end of the unit on various tennis measures. The data indicated the general skill level of the groups, as measured by the Hewitt Revised Dyer Backboard Tennis test and a single elimination tournament, was similar. The traditionally taught group improved significantly in general skills, whereas the programmed group did not. The programmed group received better subjective scores on form than did the traditionally taught group. Because only fourteen periods of instruction elapsed, it is interesting to speculate on the effects of a longer duration of time. The early mastery of form, such as that produced by the programmed method, might facilitate the attainment of better skill and playing ability in the long run more than the traditional method.

In Leonard's (1970) study, with beginning synchronized swimming stunts, a self-instructional group was compared to a teacher-directed group in achievements at the end of eight lessons. Performances were similar between the groups. With golf, however, Adler (1967) found greater improvement for the group using programmed lessons as contrasted with the group that received conventional lecture, demonstration, and practice instruction.

Possibly the future will bring more sophisticated attempts at programmed instruction of motor patterns. These efforts would certainly coincide with those in industry and education. Although some people would replace teachers altogether with machines, most educators favoring programmed instruction view the teacher as playing an important role in individual guidance along with the programmed material. The teacher is not to be replaced, but freed to devote more of his time to individual instruction and assistance.

Error-Free Versus Error-Full Learning

A logical next step in our discussion following "programmed learning" is to raise the question: Is it better to learn motor tasks with errors discouraged or encouraged? Can and should we learn from mistakes? Is it better to minimize the possibility of erroneous responses? A programmed learning approach encompasses the viewpoint that indeed errors (wrong responses) should not be experienced. The learner is supposed to experience success continually. Errors merely lead to frustration, a lack of reinforcement, and building up of undesirable responses. It is thought that when we learn errors, they will be repeated.

Yet when we think of motor skills, common sense suggests that by experiencing alternate and nondesirable responses, the learner learns how to adjust accordingly in future related situations. Adaptive behavior is extremely important in the successful execution of many complex skills, especially those that involve a long sequence of movements to unpredictable stimuli. The major dilemma here is that although the learner may benefit from his mistakes in the future, practice must be guided effectively enough so that errors are not continually practiced and conditioned. It is much easier to learn new responses than to have to unlearn old ones before making the appropriate responses.

Interestingly enough, the value of permitting or even encouraging errors in the learning of motor skills is difficult to assess because of the paucity of research on the topic. Fortunately a few recent studies provide some insights into the problem. Apparatus have been designed in some cases to create error-free learning situations in perceptual and motor tasks by providing prompts, cues, guidance, and feedback. The programmed learning technique, especially used for verbal materials, is an excellent example of an approach to instruction and training geared to minimize errors. Dennis Holding (1970) attempted to determine whether subjects tend to reject the same errors in the course of learning and if the repetition of errors depends upon a commitment to the learning of wrong responses in the early and formative stages.

A discrimination reaction timer with one of four pairings of red and green lights to be responded to by one of four keys was used with three groups of subjects. Some support for the idea that errors may be learned was reported. Furthermore, even errors that are not well learned may have long-term negative effects. The beneficial effect of errors on ultimate performance will probably occur in only one or two special cases, speculates Holding, although his experiment was not designed, in terms of the task employed, to support the following statements.

> The idea of learning by one's errors may have some validity in the case where the structure of a task tends strongly to elicit specific erroneous responses; executing the incorrect responses will then offer an opportunity for extinction and amendment. Alternatively, learning by making errors may occur in circumstances where gaining extra information about the task depends upon executing a wide range of responses. In this case, making or being offered to make only the correct responses may deny the subject "knowledge of alternatives," with detrimental effects upon the acquisition of skill. [p. 733.]

Error-full learning is typical in most motor-learning situations. That is to say, the trial-and-error learning method typically begins by making a variety of responses available in a given situation. The learner gradually acquires the appropriate responses to specified cues, if he is fortunate. As Dirk Prather (1971) indicates, a summary of the limited literature reveals that the errorless learning of simple tasks should be beneficial, especially if training is not restricted to a few trials. Consequently, he designed a study in which a complex task involved in flying was to be learned under error-free and error-filled methods. He did not find either method more superior in training on the task. The theoretical position that incorrect responses interfere with the learning of the correct response was not substantiated in his experiment. However, when teaching for transfer, error-full, or trial-and-error learning was superior to errorless training. Prather observed that the trial-and-error group seemed to be more actively involved in the learning situation whereas the errorless group was more passive. Because most real-life situations require transfer abilities in complex tasks, it appears that the trial-and-error method should be advocated, especially in learning to fly a plane.

A previous study by Prather and Berry (1970) supports this contention. A trial-and-error group outperformed a highly prompted group when the criterion was the transfer of the learned skill to a new skill. Achievement in the initial learning task was not favored under either method. Once again, the learning situation involved flight training.

The present state of the literature, although quite favorable in verbal learning situations to prompting and feedback devices (e.g., programmed instruction), indicates a tendency to support a learning-from-errors procedure with complex motor tasks, especially if positive transfer effects to other tasks are desirable. Where many alternative responses are possible, it is indeed possible, as Holding indicated, that the experiencing of errors may benefit the learning process in the long run, assuming that errors are not uniformly conditioned.

Learning Strategies and Rules

The typical motor-skills training and instructional program is conceived of as learning specific responses to designated cues. A heavy emphasis is on repetition of movements. If only the practiced task is of concern, this procedure is quite acceptable. Yet it does appear that the long-term expectations of many programs is to enhance the probability of the learner being able to apply knowledge and skills to new and related situational demands. It is hoped that positive transfer will occur.

Cognitive involvement, in the form of learning how to formulate rules and strategies for achieving presently introduced tasks, will no doubt enhance the probability of successfully meeting future-related activities. The learner should realize how to analyze tasks. Prerequisite and component tasks build up to complex task mastery. Identifying subtasks, learning how to do them, and eventually putting them all together constitutes a strong portion of ultimate achievement. Identifying errors, or debugging the system, is equally important. Remedial adjustments appropriately follow error identification.

New learnings must continually be tied back to old learnings. Establishing task relationships instead of learnings in sequential isolation will probably be an effective training medium for long-range goals, especially when it appears that the learner is expected to confront a variety of situations, not merely the situational tasks practiced in formalized programs. Time limitations in training programs often do not permit experiences in the variety of tasks and situations related to the overall activity. Therefore the importance of selecting the most appropriate learning tasks, seeing the relationships of tasks to each other, applying correct strategies and rules to newly introduced ones, and rectifying errors through problem solving is apparent.

One objective of any program should be the development of self-learning techniques. Extra cue and instructor dependency must be minimized. The availability of an external source of instruction and assistance becomes limited once training programs are terminated. The individual may be "on his own" or will receive limited guidance. The learner who can analyze tasks and self-prescribe procedures that will enable him to accomplish them is obviously at an advantage. The role of cognition, e.g., analysis, judgment, and problem solving, should never be underestimated in the learning of motor tasks. Beyond mere recognition of this fact, practice sessions should reflect and encourage the cognitive aspects of motor performance.

MOTIVATION

In any situation, at any time, and with any individual, performance is likely to fluctuate. Even outstanding athletes who have attained a high proficiency in certain skills do not perform consistently at a particular skill level, although they are more likely to than beginners or intermediates. Variability in response can be caused by external factors. For the basketball player, the basketball, the court, the basket, the gymnasium, the spectators, all of which may vary from location to location, are sources of potential alternations in performance to which adjustments must be made.

Apart from environmental sources, internal variables such as physiological and psychological drives and needs contribute to levels of performance. The study of motivation underlies the answer to the question: Why does a person behave as he does? The urge to push toward a specific goal has been termed *motivation*. Actually, motivation is a concept invented to describe the psychological state of the organism as it is affected by various influences. It is caused by specific motives (particular needs or drives), and attainment of the goal removes a particular need. A person is motivated when he desires some goal, a goal that will meet his needs or satisfy his interests. Best progress is achieved when the goal is of some personal value.

Perhaps all behavior is motivated (by something), although it is extremely difficult to isolate specific motivational variables. Much research has been initiated having to do with motivation, although for many years animals have been the primary subject of the investigations. Currently, strong disagreement exists among theorists as to the nature and scope of motivation, and in general, the area may be considered fertile for extensive experimentation. The basic conflict is between the clinical psychologist's subjective evaluation and the experimental psychologist's restricted and contrived means of measuring motivation. Recent years have brought forth a more thorough examination of the motivational process as it pertains to the learning of motor skills. In general, motivation influences (1) the selection of behavior, (2) the perseverance at behavior, (3) the magnitude or intensity of behavior, and (4) the suitability of a behavior.

Terminology and concepts related to motivation are often confusing because of the interpretations and interests of the particular investigator. It will not be the purpose of this book to present an extended treatment of such a complex field of study as motivation, but rather to interpret the basic research so as to satisfy the practical interests of the reader. Before delving into this research, further discussion is offered to clarify some basic terms.

There are at least four variables that will affect action or goal-directed behavior. A person's behavioral tendency to and in activities will be determined, according to David Birch and Joseph Veroff (1966, p. 6), by

(1) *availability:* situational and historical factors, ability to become familiarized with the situation
(2) *expectancy:* past associations and immediate perceptions
(3) *incentives:* extrinsic consequences of actions (positive or negative, degree and magnitude)
(4) *motives:* intrinsic cause of action (strength depends on experience with general class of incentives representing a particular consequence

The type, quality, and orientation of action will depend upon (1) the characteristics of the person and (2) the characteristics of the immediate situation.

Motivation in a practical sense encompasses wishes and acts. *Motives* and *incentives* are terms often used interchangeably and, in fact, they have much in common. An incentive is an object or condition that satisfies a motive and removes it, but a person can be motivated without an incentive. Also, incentives may be present but appeal to no particular motive.

Incentives can be used effectively to guide the learner to specified goals. Because they are distinguished and interpreted differently, depending on age, sex, socioeconomic class, abilities, and the like, care is necessary if they are to be of benefit.

Motivation has been acknowledged to be of utmost importance during practice. Many motives are themselves the product of learning. Although there is controversy over whether motivation affects learning or performance, it appears that rewards in the form of praise, grades, candy, and the like operate on performance rather than learning. Because unmotivated people do not practice or will not practice well, they do not learn. The following formula represents the role of motivation from a behaviorist point of view:

$$\text{Performance} = \text{Learning} + \text{Motivation}$$

(behavior in a   (past
situation)   experience)

Other psychologists are interested in the individual and his unique personality and find fault with experimental psychologists who would emphasize environmental manipulations to the neglect of individual considerations. It appears evident that a satisfactory explanation of motivation must resolve the interaction of the basic process (environmental influences on behavior) and individual personalities.

Recently, Martin Maehr (1973) has suggested new directions for the study of motivation. He would place behavioral patterns, which prompt motivational inferences, in a taxonomy. The three categories of behavioral patterns are change in direction (choice), persistence (in spite of or under failure), and performance level variations. When viewed in this manner, motivation can mean several different things. The theory of achievement motivation, formulated by D. C. McClelland, is modified by Maehr to consider differences in cultures and resultant effects on personal needs to achieve.

Any of the three categories of behaviors may be examined in the following way: Behavioral manifestations of motivation can occur when the social learning experiences in a given culture influence the personality (predisposition to react in a predictable way) of an individual. Motivational patterns can also be developed as a result of experiences in situations that affect such behavior, regardless of individual personalities. A third possibility is that, depending on the situation, motivational behavior will be affected by personality predispositions, which in turn are influenced by social learning.

A basic argument of Maehr's work is that the concept of need to achieve, or nAch, as expressed by McClelland, is not a generalized trait within a person. A ghetto youngster may score low on the nAch test and still reveal extremely motivated behaviors in athletic endeavors. Thus achievement tests often reflect the behaviors associated with a particular culture to those of another culture. The previous situations experienced by a person will strongly influence present motivational behaviors (persistence, choice, and performance patterns). The parameters of these situations assume many forms. The individual is probably influenced by

1. Social guidelines (social systems, norm comparisons).
2. Social expectancies (fulfilling prophecies).
3. Social values (adhering to guidelines).

4. Locus of control (individual control versus external control in situations).
5. Interpersonal variables (quality feedback from a significant other—social feedback, social competition versus self competition).
6. Task dimensions (difficulty, appeal, relevance).

Motivation is dynamically portrayed by Maehr as influenced by societal, experiential, and personal factors. Although it is often convenient to isolate individuals and incentives or environmental intrusions to examine effects on behavior, thereby deducing information about motivation, such an approach is limited in its ability truly to describe effects on and properties of motivation. The person, as a system, is influenced by his immediate situation (or system confines) as well as the present social and cultural system.

Measurement

Many techniques have been employed to measure the effect of various motives. David McClelland (1958) has done exceptional work in discussing these devices as well as general research problems related to the measurement of motivation. The different methods of measuring the presence or absence of a motive should reflect changes in motive strength in some way. Experimental research studies typically have investigated motivation in the following ways:

1. Providing special instructions or commentary.
2. Depriving the subjects (usually animals) of food or water.
3. Applying a strong persistent stimulus, such as an electric shock.
4. Varying the motivation by presenting objects of different magnitudes and attractiveness (rewards).
5. Measuring muscle-tension levels.

McClelland warns that the measure of a motive should be represented by variations in only the motive of interest. The problem of isolating a specific motive in a situation in order to determine its effect on behavior is indeed perplexing and difficult. In addition, the effect of a particular motive, when determined, should be consistent when the same conditions are present. In other words, reliability is necessary before confidence can be given to the suggested effect of a given motive.

In measuring human motivation, three general methods have been employed. Firstly, self-ratings or reports have been provided by the subjects regarding their feelings toward or feelings following a particular event. Secondly, an outside observer may rate the subject's state of motivation, such as in a clinical assessment. Finally, motivation may be determined from a person's behavior in an experimental motivationally induced situation. The ineffectiveness of these methods can be assessed from McClelland's general findings—that these three methods yield uncorrelated results.

A rather novel attempt at measuring motivation in motor-skill performance was made by Eysenck (1963). Using the pursuit rotor, he demonstrated how S–R learning theory can explain and predict motivational effects. He suggested the consideration of reminiscence, an extended period of no practice between the end of practice and its resumption. Reminiscence scores (the difference between end of practice scores and resumption scores) measure drive. Eysenck was able to determine the effect of high-versus-low drive on the learning and performing of the motor skill, among other findings.

However, there are standard laboratory methods used as motivational techniques for many years. Surwillo (1958) lists nine of them and suggests a tenth. They are

1. *Intrinsic interest.* The task is so interesting and challenging that S, the subject, on his own volition, applies himself to it.
2. *Social incentive.* Social incentives, in their simplest form, are E's (experimenter) requests of S, "Do well." "Try hard." "Try harder."
3. *Reporting scores and encouraging improvement.* E reports S's score at the end of each trial, indicates improvements or decrements, and and at times offers verbal encouragement. Cues pertaining to performance may also be given during a trial (e.g., a light may be flashed or an auditory signal given whenever S is off target, as in a tracking task). This motivational technique has been referred to in recent literature as *directive feedback*.
4. *Monetary incentive.* E offers S a sum of money for participating in the experiment.
5. *Importance.* S is told that the scores he achieves are important and may be used in the determination of norms.
6. *Socio-competitive incentive.* The task may be arranged that Ss engage in competition with each other or with some norm or previously recorded high score. In some studies, the false-norm technique is used.
7. *Reward incentive.* Bonuses are given for improved performance.
8. *Threats of punishment.* Some form of electric shock is widely used. To add to realism, electrodes may be attached and a mild shock administered with the threat that a stronger shock will be given if S does not meet some criterion.
9. *Administration of punishment.* Usually an electric shock is administered at the end of a trial for failure to reach a particular criterion.

10. *Heat-pain stimulation.* This is to be used in a lengthy experiment, where attention levels have a tendency to fall.

Another method for changing behaviors in the desired direction is with the use of placebos. A placebo, in medicine, is any inert substance that really does not have any value but is administered in such a manner as to convince the recipient that it possesses positive qualities. Placebos used as drugs have been shown to be as powerful as the true drugs themselves in relieving a patient's pain. Extended in interpretation, a placebo can be considered as any contrived situation, environment, or object that is valueless and yet might presumably positively affect behavior because of the psychological disposition of the person. In other words, if a person thinks he should do better, this reason alone might suffice to explain improved performance. The *placebo effect* has been demonstrated in a variety of situations. It may be considered as another form of motivation.

Task and Individual Considerations

Motivational effects depend not only on environmental manipulations and the individual's personality, but on the nature of the task itself. If motivational level can be held constant, it is observed that the relative simplicity or complexity of the skill to be learned will determine the ease with which it is learned. For instance, it is generally assumed that high or low motivation has the same effect on simple acts or skills.

However, the level of motivation will affect the performance of a complex skill. Evidence indicates that more difficult tasks require lower motivation, for high motivation has been found to impede skill acquisition in these tasks. Highest performance is attained by subjects with intermediate motivation (drive) and as tasks increase in complexity, subjects with less

Figure 9–14. The optimal level of motivation for the learner must be considered in relation to the task and personality variables. Performance is maintained or improved when optimal motivation is present. It falls when inappropriate levels of motivation are manifested.

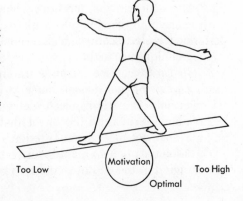

Too Low   Motivation   Too High
Optimal

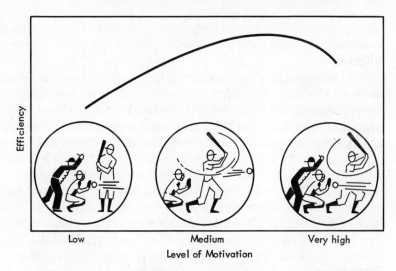

Figure 9–15.   A schematic representation of the relationship between level of motivation and efficiency of behavior. At low and high levels of motivation the result is the same, a strike-out, but the behavior of the batter is quite different. (From *Psychology,* revised edition, by Delos D. Wickens and Donald R. Meyer. Copyright © 1955, 1961 by Holt, Rinehart and Winston, Inc. Reprinted by permission of Holt, Rinehart and Winston, Inc.)

drive do better. The *Yerkes-Dodson Law* describes this phenomenon: there is an *optimal level of motivation for the level of task difficulty.* Although somewhat exaggerated, Figures 9–14 and 9–15 illustrate some possible effects of varying degrees of motivation.

With regard to task structure and the ideal degree of motivation, we have touched upon the contrasting effects of motivation on simple and difficult tasks. In sport we may contrast, for convenience, activities that are vigorous and that involve explosive power, strength, and endurance, with those that require control, precision, timing, and high degrees of coordination. The first category of activities would probably benefit from the presence of the highest levels of motivation. In these cases the act can be performed mechanically and subconsciously, and effort, as reflected by motivation, may determine final performance. The second category of activities suggests the controlled use of motivation. A reasonable degree needs to be present for arousal and cue attention, discrimination, and selection purposes. Response adequacy will also be reflected by this state. But too much motivation, either internally produced or externally imposed, will most likely hinder the control processes underlying skilled maneuvers.

The essentials of Clark Hull's drive theory describe the relation of the task to the performer in the following way. If the correct response is dominant over incorrect responses (typical in a simple task), increased motivation or anxiety should facilitate performance. In a complex learning situation there are usually a number of competing incorrect responses that are more dominant than the sole correct response. Performance is predicted as poorer in this case in highly motivated subjects. Figure 9–16 illustrates the data obtained in an investigation concerned with testing the theory. The subjects were children who were placed in extreme groups as a result of their scores on the Taylor scale of manifest anxiety (described in Chapter 7), which is a measure of motivation. Their task was to learn a light-button motor task that requires trial-and-error learning in attempting to find the correct button that turns off each light. As can be viewed in Figure 9–16, the nonanxious subjects were superior to the anxious subjects, thus substantiating evidence accumulated on adult subjects and further supporting Hull's theory. The more highly anxious person will learn and perform better if less motivated and the less anxious individual will do better if motivated to a higher degree. If an induced motivational level is too emotionally stressful, learning and performance will be inhibited.

For any learning task, motivation must be sufficient so that the learner will tackle it, especially if it is difficult. Attitudes toward the task before actual practice begins need to be oriented toward the goal of mastery and proficient performance. A state of arousal to respond to the situational

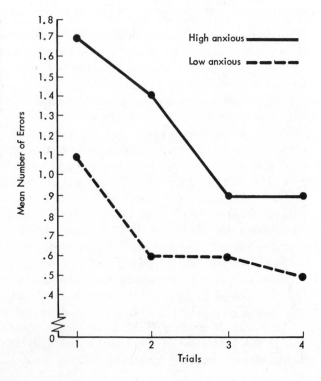

Figure 9–16. Error curves for anxious and nonanxious subjects. (From David S. Palermo, Alfred Castaneda, and Boyd R. McCandless, "The Relationship of Anxiety in Children to Performance in a Complex Learning Task," *Child Development,* 27:333–337, 1956.)

High anxious

Low anxious

Mean Number of Errors

Trials

demands is a prerequisite to good performances. Both the *preparatory state* of the individual and his desire to *sustain* practice should be considered. The presence of optimal motivational conditions encourages the learner to continue at practice and to train toward specific task goals. Many environmental factors can be varied in order to promote optimal motivation and thus facilitate performance. Responses are generally learned as a function of their consequences (Thorndike's Law of Effect). Hence rewards will encourage better performance, depending on the amount, frequency, and delay. Success and failure, reward and punishment, praise and criticism all will affect the organism in some way. Information provided in the form of knowledge of results can be beneficial, and methods and effects are discussed later. Other motivational factors include competition and rivalry and the presence or absence of witnesses or spectators.

The work of many psychologists is acknowledged in promoting interest in and discovering knowledge of the basic needs and drives of animals. There is much research on animals and artificial means of motivating humans, but these are not reviewed here because of their lack of practical application.

Extrinsic and Intrinsic Motivation

Motivation may stem from two basic sources: internal or external. When the origin of the drive is from within a person, that is to say, he does something for its own sake, he is said to be *intrinsically motivated*. He performs a skill or participates in a sport for personal reasons, namely joy, satisfaction, or skill development. Intrinsic motivation implies self-actualization and ego involvement. An *extrinsically motivated* person persists at an activity for the material gain he can receive from it. He studies hard in a class not so much to acquire knowledge as to attain a high grade. He may participate in a sport for the possible recognition and glory instead of for comradeship, inner satisfaction, and achievement. Extrinsic motivation is need-deficiency motivation.

From an educational and ideal point of view, intrinsic motivation is more desirable than extrinsic motivation. Unfortunately, because of cultural practices, we are frequently rewarded materially from childhood throughout life for demonstrating correct responses and acceptable behavior. We expect and become conditioned to rewards. Inner drive, though, is usually a more sustained and effective form of motivation. It should be acknowledged that in many situations both extrinsic and intrinsic factors operate, but with varying degrees of impact. If motivation from within is the primary source of the athlete's endeavors, he will be more likely to continue participating after the days of fanfare, hero worship, and excitement are over. Friedlander's (1966) study only partly supports the strength of intrinsic motivation. He used three measures of motivation and attempted to discover their relationship to two criteria of the job performance of white- and blue-collar workers. High performers reflected intrinsic motivation as most important to them, recognition second, and social environment as last in importance. Low performers were rated highest on social environment importance. However, within the blue-collar group, there were no significant motivation–performance relationships.

A number of examples exist where negative intrinsic motivation may be overcome by powerful extrinsic motivation. A person may not be intrinsically motivated to master a task, but may overcome this indifference if he becomes extrinsically motivated, such as seeking a high grade in a class. Studies with industrial workers indicate that motivation to achieve is increased when there is a chance of attaining an extrinsic reward (money, approval of others, and so on) in the future.

Nevertheless, there is research and theoretical support for the belief that an individual who has a strong belief that he can control his own destiny is likely to improve his situation and place greater value on skill and achievement. Intrinsic motivation, in this respect, is an extremely powerful influence on behavior. If an individual perceives he can control his own situation and reinforcement is dependent upon his own behavior, he demonstrates "internal control," according to J. B. Rotter (1966). "External control" describes a situation in which it is thought that one's behavior is dependent upon luck or chance. Expectations of reinforcement as a consequence of behavior and the locus of control construct of Rotter are necessary to consider in any attempts to explain behavior. Individuals differ in their attitude toward a situation, depending on its control by external or internal factors and develop expectancies accordingly. When individuals perceive a situation involves luck or fate, they have less expectancy for a reward. Performance is likely to deteriorate under this condition.

What of the concept of the presence of a generalized intrinsic motivation in certain individuals? Is it true that some people do try harder and use their potential more effectively in a variety of situations? Is there a generalized need to achieve and succeed or to avoid failure regardless of the task or the person's capabilities? Although such may be the case in some instances, research evidence by Bernard Fine (1972) does not bear these premises out. The relationship of predictor tests—including hand immersion in cold (5°C) water, the Cattell 120-A test and 16 Personality Factor test, the Maudsley Personality Inventory, and a biographical inventory—to criterion tests, anagrams, the digit symbol substitution test, screw sorting, and hand dynamometer performance was determined with various statistical analyses. Fine did not find any general motivational factor as an acceptable predictor of performance. A particular aspect of motivation may be related to any task and situation.

The relationship of task level of difficulty to intrinsic and extrinsic forms

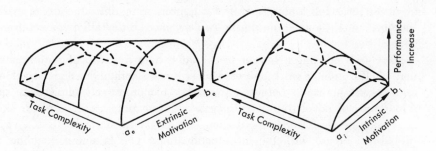

Figure 9–17.   Relation of performance-increase to task-complexity and intrinsic and extrinsic motivation. (From Margaret Clifford, "Competition as a Motivational Technique in the Classroom," *American Educational Research Journal,* 9:123–137, 1972.)

of motivation has been conceptualized by Margaret Clifford (1972). It can be observed in Figure 9–17 that as task complexity increases, intrinsic motivation plays a more important role. She writes (p. 135):

> The relationship between task-complexity and the effectiveness of intrinsic and extrinsic motivation suggests that while only a limited amount of intrinsic motivation is associated with a simple task, a noticeable performance-increase can be generated through extrinsic motivation. On the other hand, a significant performance-increase can be generated through extrinsic motivation. On the other hand, a significant performance-increase on a highly complex task will be dependent upon intrinsic motivation.

> In view of the typical problem-solving tasks students encounter, the model indicates that emphasis must be placed on intrinsic motivation. Educational researchers must attempt to systematically examine the effects of such intrinsic motives. This will involve the identification, measurement, and assessment of such factors as relevance of subject matter as perceived by the learner, need-achievement of the student, tolerance for ambiguity, and optimum learning rates for individuals. The extent to which intrinsic motives can be developed, controlled, and manipulated is debatable. However, two points of concern appear evident: (1) learning of complex tasks is heavily dependent upon intrinsic motivation, and (2) too little applied educational research has been conducted to preclude the possibility of effectively manipulating factors related to intrinsic motives.

Rewards

Most investigations have not been concerned with the subject's interpretation of a specific reward, but instead with the general effect of the reward on performance. Considering the possible variety of methods in motivating a person and the range of gross motor skills, it certainly is surprising to see the limited amount of work in this area. Here are some of the motivational techniques investigated: threats; praise; punishment; immediate knowledge of results; varying amounts of reward; prompting; introduction of bells, buzzers, sounds, and music during performance; cooperative ventures; and competition.

Merely introducing a buzzer or bell at certain intervals of performance may elicit a greater work output. Data from the military tasks of tracking and pursuit in which boredom from task monotony sets in indicate the importance of novel stimuli interspersed during practice. If a motor skill is repeatedly performed, motivation, which might normally lessen, will probably increase with the introduction of various stimuli throughout a practice session.

Sometimes experimenters do not find that various induced motivational factors influence performance. This may be because of the fact that the subjects are already operating at a high level of drive on the task. Therefore additional inducements will be ineffective. Many motor skills are by their very nature interesting and challenging to the learners. In such cases additional incentives are unnecessary. In fact, extra imposed motivational techniques may impede performance in certain activities.

Employment of verbal instructions or inducements is one of the most widely used motivational techniques. Research evidence does indicate this method helps in the learning of written materials and there is some evidence to support the idea that it is also beneficial to motor performance. Fleishman (1958) provides interesting data on the relation between ability levels and motivation. Four hundred subjects were trained on the Complex Coordination Test, on which a subject must make appropriate stick and rudder control adjustments in response to successively presented patterns of visual signals.

All of Fleishman's subjects were given five one-minute trials and then divided into two groups, one of which received continual verbal encouragement during certain rest periods between the remaining fifteen trials. In analyzing the data, high- and low-ability groups, based on scores made on the initial trials, were determined and compared under motivating and nonmotivating conditions. It was found that each group improved at about the same rate and in the same fashion. However, in the high-ability subjects, there was a significant difference in favor of the motivated group over the unmotivated group. The performance curves are presented in Figure 9–18. Environmental factors usually do not affect the performance of skills too much that are well learned. There is a general stability in performance unchanged despite different situations. However, personal observation and empirical evidence would point to the fact that it is possible for performance levels of the skilled to rise or fall when certain factors are present.

It is more likely, though, that during the acquisition-of-skill stage the effect of varying motivational conditions will be more noticeable. Before routines become well established and responses somewhat conditioned, en-

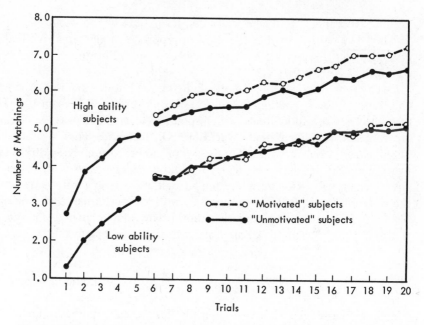

Figure 9–18.   Acquisition curves for subjects of different ability and motivation levels. (From Edwin A. Fleishman, "A Relationship Between Incentive Motivation and Ability Level in Psychomotor Performance," *Journal of Experimental Psychology,* 56:78–81, 1958.)

vironmental variations act as temporary depressants or facilitators to performance.

Varying the amount of reward appears to produce a change of performance in favor of the reward with the greatest magnitude. Studies on verbal materials have repeatedly demonstrated this occurrence. The same results appear in measuring short-term retention, for Weiner and Walker (1966) found that a greater strength of motivation during learning led to less forgetting. Four different incentives were used: 1-cent reward, 5-cent reward, shock for no recall, and withheld motivation. This investigation concerned the selecting of consonants for various colored slides, but it is inviting to speculate on the effect of similar incentives on motor performance. Assuming little or no inner drive of the learner, the instructor would have to turn to the most extreme motivating conditions in order to hasten skill acquisition. Once again, it is necessary to realize that individuals are not all motivated in the same manner by a particular form of motivation. Some respond better when they are yelled at and incited; others need inspiration as provided through different approaches. A grade, a position in the class or on the team, punishment, a note to the parents—these and many other techniques are specifically appropriate for a certain kind of person. Most ideal would be an in-depth analysis of the performer's personality and nature, so that the most appropriate motivational method, if needed, could be applied without subjecting an entire group to the same condition.

Coaches are often guilty of approaching all their athletes in the same way. One type of coach continually yells at the players to "fire them up." Unfortunately, some individuals will respond in a negative way when they are constantly under dramatic vocal fire. On the other hand, a mild-mannered coach who offers only praise when deserved and sympathy where warranted may be guilty of neglecting those athletes who need to be inspired vigorously. Anyone interested in motor learning must be aware of the desirability of instilling an inner drive in the performer, understanding his personality, and applying the appropriate motivational technique at the right time, one that is compatible with the task demands.

Level of Aspiration

Before performing a skill, we typically formulate hypotheses about our chance for success. Success itself is relative and depends on what a person will accept for himself as achievement. Some people would consider themselves successful if they shot golf in the 90's; other people attain this feeling when they score in the 70's. The setting of a goal is termed *the level of aspiration*. Past experiences in similar situations, resulting in successes or failures, affect the aspiration level. In turn, the immediate aspiration level for a given task may very well determine its outcome, as will be noted a little later in this section of the chapter.

An individual's level of aspiration for a given task reflects an optimism or lack of it when faced with the challenge. It denotes an attitude toward the task. It also indicates a level of reality—whether the goal is consistent with prior success, actual present achievement, and ability. Finally, it can be used to improve performance. If the level of aspiration is set high enough, it acts as an incentive, something for which to strive. For each person there may be different levels of aspiration, depending on interpretation of the term. It may mean a level hoped for, expected, or minimally accepted. In other words, a level of aspiration can indicate the discrepancy between previous performance and expected performance; between wished for and previous performance; or personally acceptable and previous performance.

It is unrealistic for a person to have a large discrepancy between estimated performance and actual performance. When the performance level is far below the aspiration level, the result is consistent personal failure. When the situation is reversed, there is a better chance of success. Therefore it can be seen that success and failure may be determined in relation to the level of aspiration. An unhealthy situation occurs when too many successes or failures are experienced by an individual; hence it is desirable to have an approximate relationship between hoped-for and actual performance.

For example, Leonard Worell (1959) found that students whose aspirations were related to previous performances and who did not wish to achieve much more than they had already, received the highest college grades. They were considered to be realistic. There is not universal acceptance as to what the intended level of attainment should be. Atkinson (1957) found that the maximum level of performance was obtained when the probability of success was moderate (0.5), and he predicted that it would be uniformly lower as the probability advanced in either direction.

Persons try harder in a competitive situation the greater the degree of uncertainty concerning goal attainment. With regard to achievement motivation, Atkinson feels that individuals in whom the achievement motive is relatively strong should and will prefer intermediate-risk tasks, whereas those in whom the motive is to avoid failure is relatively strong should and will avoid intermediate-risk tasks. These findings have been contradicted by Locke's recent study. Locke (1966) observed a linear relationship between intentions and actual level of performance. The higher level of intended achievement resulted in high levels of performance.

Locke and Bryan (1966) verified these findings. These experimenters utilized the Complex Coordination Apparatus, where red and green lights are arranged to form an *H* on the display. The subject has to move controls (foot pedals and hand stick) to match lights with those illuminated. When the match is right, a new stimulus pattern occurs, and this continues until all thirteen patterns have been presented in sequence. It was found that performance goals influence the level of performance. The subjects with specific but high goals did better on the task than those who were told just to do their best (see Figure 9–19). Implications from these results may be applied to teaching methods. Having the students set precise high but attainable goals may be more effective as a learning technique than haphazard methods of motivation.

Certain statements concerning level of aspiration appear to be warranted. Research findings by Irvin Child and John Whiting (1949) and other investigators are in agreement:

1. Success lends to a raising of the aspirational level whereas failure encourages a lowering of this level.
2. The greater the success, the greater the probability of a rise in the level.
3. The level of performance is influenced more by success than failure and the effect of success is more predictably stable (more upward shifts are noted after success than downward shift after failure).

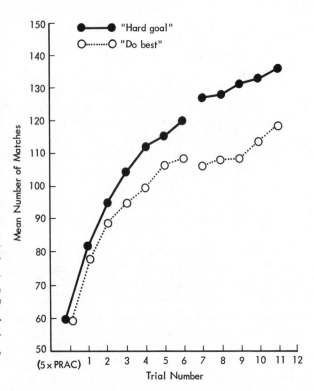

Figure 9–19. A comparison of two groups in performance on a complex motor task. One group had high standards and a difficult goal, the other group was merely told, "Do your best." The Hard-Goal group was significantly better than the Do-Best group. (From Edwin A. Locke and Judith F. Bryan. "Cognitive Aspects of Psychomotor Performance: The Effects of Performance Goals on Level of Performance," *Journal of Applied Psychology,* 50:286–291, 1966.)

Edwin Locke (1968) has summarized the literature on consciously set goals and intentions and task performance. It can be observed in Figure 9–20 that the harder the goal, the higher the level of performance; these data reflect the combined results of twelve investigations on the topic. It is true that subjects with very hard goals reached them less often than subjects with very easy goals. Yet the hard-goal subjects consistently outperformed the easy-goal subjects.

In theorizing about events that lead from a particular situation to action, Locke proposes the following schema (1968, p. 184):

    Environmental   Goal-setting
    Event → Cognition → Evaluation → Intention → Performance
    (e.g., incentive)

Goals and intentions can be manipulated by others. Instructions are commonly deployed, and will be especially valuable if the performer accepts them and indeed he possesses the capabilities demanded of him for the task. Providing evaluations (e.g., knowledge of the results of performance) or competition may suggest specific standards to the performer. The benefit of these conditions is contingent upon the desire of the person to use performance knowledge to compete against his own score or those of

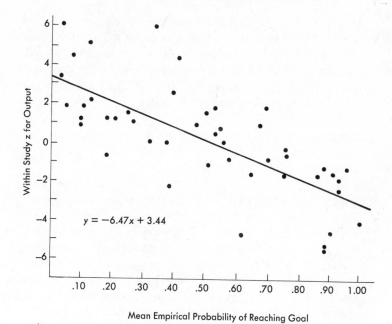

Figure 9–20.   Goal difficulty is a function of the number of trials in which subjects attempting to achieve a particular goal actually perform higher than it. Performance level is expressed in terms of the Within Study z-score (converted raw score to a standard score) for performance for a particular goal. Each point represents a particular group (a particular goal) in a particular study; it indicates the probability of the subjects in that group reaching their mean output in relation to the other goal groups in that study. (From Edwin A. Locke. "Toward a Theory of Task Motivation and Incentives," *Organizational Behavior and Human Performance,* 3:157–189, 1968.)

others. Various rewards and incentives (money, praise, and so on) may motivate the person generally to perform better, but much depends on the value of such rewards to him.

The importance of success to level of aspiration and ultimate achievement is thus established. It would appear, then, that physical educators and coaches should place students in situations in which they can attain a reasonable amount of satisfaction. Unfortunately, this may not be the case in many athletic situations. Smith (1949) in his study discovered that college freshman football players usually demonstrated a large discrepancy between level of aspiration and actual performance. A considerable number of these football players experienced repeated failure. They had high aspiration levels of playing, but rarely played the amount of time they thought they would.

To conclude, aspiration levels continually change with repeated experience on a task and may be dissimilar from task to task. The skill level of the learner as well as his desire to improve, as demonstrated by high but attainable goals, describe but another aspect of the learning process. The psychological impact of a person's level of aspiration should be viewed as an important part of motor-skill learning.

REINFORCEMENT

The term *reinforcement* refers to the occurrence of any event that increases the probability or maintains the strength of a particular act or behavior. For all intents and purposes, a reinforcer is a form of reward, and perhaps *reward* is a more general term than *reinforcement*. However, *reinforcement* has attained specific meanings with regard to the classical and instrumental learning experiments designed by psychologists. In unique animal experiments, men like Pavlov and Skinner have demonstrated the effect of a reinforcer on conditioning an act or directing behavior.

With reference to motor-skill learning, any statement that could be said about reward holds true for reinforcement. If the student is learning a motor skill, the encouragement, praise, grade, or money awarded to him after he performs correctly serves as a reinforcer. These rewards reinforce the act; they tell the individual that he is doing what is desired and that possibly further good performances will be rewarded in the same way. It has been found that more immediate reinforcement is more effective than any delay in reinforcement. Association of a correct response with a given stimulus becomes strengthened with immediate reinforcement, for during any delay other activity occurs and the individual is apt to confuse which response is being rewarded.

Operant conditioning theory, as developed by Skinner and his followers and described briefly in Chapter 3, is based on the effect of reinforcement contingencies on the acquisition of desired behaviors. Programmed learning techniques, referred to earlier in this chapter, also depend heavily upon the use of immediate reinforcement. Social approval or disapproval greatly influence the behaviors we express, whether we realize it or not.

Another aspect of reinforcement to consider is its ideal frequency. Although continual reinforcement is nice, it rarely occurs in real-life situations. There are many instances in which a series of attempts at performing an act according to standards end up in failure. They have not been reinforced. A number of nonreinforced behaviors may occur before one finally is, and this number may vary from occasion to occasion. Because continuous reinforcement is relatively nonexistent in the learning of tasks, some form of intermittent reinforcement, either by design or naturally, is available instead.

Experimentally, four types of schedules of reinforcement have been identified: ratio, interval, variable, and fixed. Because the type of reinforcement schedule may have a profound influence on behaviors, their formulation and potential effect are of great interest. Each schedule may be briefly described in the following manner:

1. Ratio schedule: a set or fixed proportion of nonreinforced responses to reinforced responses; e.g., twenty to one.
2. Interval schedule: a predetermined amount of time before reinforcement occurs.
3. Variable schedule: irregular reinforcements after a number of responses or an amount of time (applied to ratio or interval schedules).
4. Fixed schedule: reinforcements regularly given after a constant period of time or number of responses (applied to ratio or interval schedules).

Actually, typical situations do contain a large amount of uncertainty in reward. The baseball batter does not get a hit every time at bat, but certainly one hit in three attempts (unpredictable in occurrence) is sufficient to act as a reinforcer. He never knows when or what kind of hit he will make, but by achieving an adequate number of them, he is continually motivated whenever he goes to bat. This example of a variable-ratio schedule could be followed by many others, most notably the play in a slot machine, where one never knows when the payoff will be.

Variable-ratio reinforcements produces high and stable rates of responding while variable interval schedules usually yield lesser values in lower forms of organisms. A variable reinforcement schedule, with its inherent uncertainty, is quite effective in shaping, maintaining, and elevating behaviors, as long as reinforcements come after a reasonable number of responses. This is not always the case, however, as evidenced by the unbelievable persistence a person may show with a slot machine without a payoff reinforcement.

Success and Failure

In any given endeavor, the outcome will be viewed as relative success or failure, depending on the criteria for success. It may be recalled that personal success or failure depend on the level of aspiration, which in turn serves as a motivational force. The traditional concept of encouraging successes and avoiding failures in order to elevate motivation and at the same time improve performance is perhaps too simply stated. Recent evidence has shown that the relative effects of success and failure on motivation are much more complex than once believed.

John Atkinson (1957) offers research and theory to describe the probability of motivation increasing or decreasing as a result of experienced success or failure. For example, the expectant probability of success with a task of intermediate difficulty is 0.5. For a difficult task, one of say a 0.2 probability of success, motivation steadily increases with repeated success until the probability of success is 0.5. Motivation after that point *decreases* as the probability increases to certainty (1.00). The probability of success is so high that there is no interest or incentive. Atkinson concludes that one should always look for new and more challenging tasks.

Atkinson (1964) considers another aspect of the problem when he writes on the results of repeated failure in an easy task (*p*, or expectant probability = 0.8). Motivation should *increase* with failure until the expectant probability has been lowered to 0.5, and after that, the motivation should weaken. The motivation should lessen with the first failure on a difficult task. Success with simpler tasks increases motivation on subsequent more difficult tasks; the level of aspiration rises with success.

The old assumption that success automatically increases motivation and failure automatically decreases it is not always true, as has been shown theoretically. On the other hand, not all research substantiates all of Atkinson's concepts on motivation. Nevertheless, there appears to be justification for a number of these concepts. The difficulty of the task as it appears to the performer and his initial success with its undertaking contribute to his motivational level. Another consideration for probabilities and motivation is the anxiety level of the individual. An anxious individual confronts a new challenge with a probability of success different from less anxious people. Fear of failure results in quickened loss of motivation.

Finally, the number of successful acts before failure occurs may affect performance in various ways. Bayton and Conley (1957) divided seventy-five college students into three groups and administered the Minnesota Rate of Manipulation Test to them. One group received five trials of success before experiencing failure; for the second group failure came after the tenth trial; and the third group experienced failure after the fifteenth trial. Results indicate that early failure has an inhibitory effect upon that experience. As success increases through time, subsequent failures increase motivation. After ten and fifteen successful trials, a shift to failure increased the level of performance, whereas this was not so after five trials. Evidently, an application of these results to the learning of any motor skills would call for the learners to experience as much success as possible in the early stages before failure.

Reward and Punishment, Praise and Criticism

Although there have been many methods developed to influence the motivational process, perhaps the most widely used in everyday situations fall into reward and punishment categories. Examples of rewarding good behavior and correct responses and punishing the undesired are so familiar to everyone that there is no need to list them here. However, the relative effectiveness of each, as demonstrated by practical experience and research evidence, deserves examination.

Thorndike influenced ideas on punishment through a good part of this century. At first, on the basis of experiments with animals, he concluded that reward and punishment had equal effects on behavior. He later modified this position as evidence indicated reward to be a more stable and a stronger influence for desirable behavior than punishment. Skinner, working with rats, noted the more temporary and unpredictable effect of punishment. Punishment inhibits behavior, but wears off. Hence it has a temporary effect unless it is administered continually. A punishment is supposed to decrease the probability of particular behavior occurring again in the future.

At the present time, psychologists and educators agree that of the two, it is better to take a positive approach to the learning situation. Praise, because it is specific to the act and informative, tells the person when he does the correct thing. Punishment tells the person what not to do instead of what to do. After punishment, the desired response still has to be discovered. In our society, even the threat of the most dire consequences for antisocial behavior does not totally inhibit these acts. The implementation of threats, criticism, or pain, no matter how severe, does not always work. The effects of punishment are not consistent from individual to individual or situation to situation.

The ineffectiveness of punishment can be explained also by the usual delay between the time an act takes place and the administering of the punishment. Reward is almost always immediate; that is, the type obtained by the individual for himself. The youngster may take a cookie without permission from the jar—thus he is rewarded. When mother discovers what has happened, perhaps hours later, he is punished. The situation results in a conflict for the child. In a specific motor-learning situation, praise or criticism can occur immediately or else be delayed, with immediacy the more desirable.

Yelling and screaming at a child or striking him for performing a skill incorrectly may help in improving his skill level, but it also may cause confusion, anguish, and resistant behavior. On the other hand, positive reinforcement for ideal or near ideal performances by praise and encouragement will probably be more effective in attaining hoped-for goals. The work of Skinner has demonstrated the heights one can reach in controlling and hence predicting behavior through constant reinforcements.

A study by Hurlock (1925), although using addition problems as the task to be learned, serves to demonstrate the relative effects of various incentives. Children in four groups were tested under four different conditions: praise, reproof, no comment, and ignored (but heard praise and reproof given to others). The praised group did best, the reproved group was second best, the ignored group third, and the no-comment group finished last.

Yet it is possible that we truly do not know much about the properties of punishment and how it can be used effectively to shape behavior. James Johnston (1972) has surveyed the research literature dealing with punishment and has uncovered many myths and inaccuracies concerning its use. He pleads for a better understanding of the relative merits of positive reinforcement and punishment and that decisions be based on scientific evidence rather than on moral convictions. Recent evidence has shown punishment procedures to be quite effective in certain learning situations. For instance, Witte and Grossman (1971) administered a tactile form discrimination task to kindergarten children under three reinforcement conditions: reward only, punishment only, or reward and punishment. In terms of correct responses, the latter two conditions were equally effective, both being more superior in results than the first condition. Apparently, punishment in this study resulted in a greater attentiveness on the part of the subjects. Orientation to the task was at a higher level. The motivational properties of punishment in this type of setting were ruled out in favor of an attentional hypothesis.

Extrinsic reinforcers have been demonstrated by Brent Rushall and John Pettinger (1969) to be highly effective in influencing the work output and training efficiency of members of an age-group swimming club, ages nine to fifteen. The subjects performed laps under different conditions: (1) no designated reinforcement, (2) coach's discouragement and comments, (3) candy reinforcement for each lap completed, and (4) money (1-cent) reinforcement for each lap completed. The latter two conditions were equally effective and superior to the first two conditions in producing a greater distance of swimming attained by the subjects. Thus the importance of reinforcement contingencies was established, at least for this age group and level of skill. Rushall has developed a model for using reinforcement for affecting and directing behaviors. The stages suggested are

1. Define and list desirable and undesirable behaviors, noting their frequency of occurrence.
2. Structure the stimulus situation for teaching and controlling desirable behaviors.
3. Determine significant reinforcers and punishers.
4. Apply operant paradigms for behavior control.
5. Evaluate the effects of attempted control.

Rushall and Daryl Siedentop (1972) have gone so far as to produce a book based on operant conditioning and reinforcement geared for physical educators and coaches. Theoretical discussion and practical implications are contained throughout the text. It is an excellent and unique reference for both types of materials.

FEEDBACK (KNOWLEDGE
OF RESULTS)

An early experiment contributing to the concept that practice does not always make perfect was one in which the subjects had to draw a line of so many inches when blindfolded. Because they were never informed as to how they were doing, the subjects did not improve in their performances. Many studies since then, analyzing a wide range of methods and materials, have tended to demonstrate the importance of knowledge of results.

Knowledge of results (KR) is a form of reinforcement, for the individual is informed as to the correctness or incorrectness of his responses. This information may come from an external source, e.g., the teacher, or from the person's own performance on a skill in which he knows right from wrong. Although *KR* is a term widely used in the literature, present-day terminology, engrossed in man–machine dynamics, has popularized another term, *feedback*, which basically refers to the same state of affairs as knowledge of results. Feedback can best be understood when viewed in relation to the three major mechanisms needed for information processing.

As can be seen in Figure 9–21 the receptors stimulate the Perceptual Mechanism (P) to perceive and identify the information (stimuli). Then the Translation Mechanism (T) is activated to decide on a choice of action. The Central Effector (E) coordinates and phases the action, innervating specific effectors. Feedback, in this case proprioceptive information, comes from the Central Effector and influences the future information which might have to be monitored by the perceptual–translator process. Feedback is error information, for it informs the individual the extent to which performance matches the goal. The difference between the goal and the actual performance indicates error in the system. This information is helpful in reducing error.

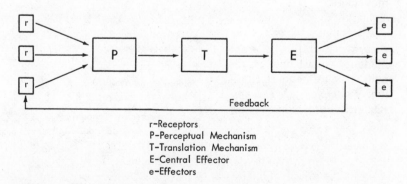

r–Receptors
P–Perceptual Mechanism
T–Translation Mechanism
E–Central Effector
e–Effectors

Figure 9–21.   Feedback with relation to the other major mechanisms in the information-processing concept.

Although feedback and KR have been used interchangeably in the research literature and in daily dialogue, they might be differentiated in the following way. Feedback is typically associated with self-regulated stimulation through movement, and the closed-loop control model is illustrated in Figure 9–21. Sensory feedback control over behavior is therefore an internalized process. Knowledge of results is more associated with external sources of information that the learner can use in his next attempt at a task. Ina McD. Bilodeau (1969) presents an excellent review of the research and acknowledges the confusion in the use of feedback and KR terminology. She favors the term *information feedback* to denote a stimulus presented by an external source during or after a learner's response. Such a term would be quite analogous to the way KR is referred to. Perhaps, as Holding (1965) suggests, internal feedback and external feedback should be distinguished, with the latter applied to the term *knowledge of results.* There is so much confusion in the interpretation of these terms that we will assume that they have similar connotations and will refer to them interchangeably for discussion purposes here.

We typically receive feedback, or KR, when we perform most athletic skills. In performing a swimming stroke, if it does not feel right, we try to adapt and correct our movements. The quarterback who continually attempts to pass into a particular zone only to find it well covered by defenders adjusts his offense. The archer can see if he is missing the target and compensates accordingly in his next responses. From merely making a basket, serving in the proper court, or making a putt, we are informed if our response is correct.

There are other cases when it is necessary for an outsider to provide relevant information. Sometimes we are not aware of what we do wrong to cause an inappropriate response. A violation of a mechanical principle, bad form resulting in inefficient performance, or other errors can be relayed to the performer by an instructor. Knowledge of results is useful to the individual whether provided by external sources or through one's own movement.

Figure 9–22. Different kinds of knowledge of results. [From Dennis H. Holding, *Principles of Training* (Oxford: Pergamon, 1965).]

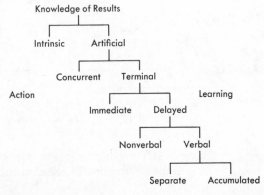

In practice or actual competition, knowledge of results serves a definite purpose. If the fencer is not rewarded by a point when he legally touches an opponent, he may make unnecessary adjustments. Enjoyment and learning are hampered. The same holds true for fouls not called in a basketball game. The foul call informs the player that the referee knows he violated a rule, and no call permits the player greater freedom and perhaps more violations of other rules. Without a knowledge of results, improvement cannot occur. Violations not called in practice severely limit the performance in a game, especially if the player is not aware he is committing illegal acts.

Types of Feedback (KR)

The variety of forms that knowledge of results can assume is best expressed by Dennis Holding (1965). When artificial (extrinsic, supplementary) KR is to be provided, considerations must be made for the type as well as timing. Figure 9–22 illustrates these considerations. Certain tasks will dictate the kinds of KR possible to provide to the learner. Other tasks provide more options. Channels and sources should also be considered. For instance, the typical sensory modalities (channels) associated with feedback are the visual, proprioceptive, and auditory. Sources may be internal (information through one's own activity and efforts) or external (information from another source, e.g., a person). The best situation for the learner is to receive the optimal degree of information, so that he can profit from it in any situation. Too little will be of minor assistance and too much will flood the information channel capacity of the system. Redundancy in feedback can assist on some occasions as reinforcing cues for each other for the benefit of the learner. On other occasions, it is useless and a waste of energies. Thus the whole question of augmenting feedback comes into question.

Considering the learner's abilities, skill level, and the task, when is there enough information present in the task and situation for the learner to use without any need for outside intervention and assistance? If additional information is to be supplied, what is the desired form, geared for which sensory channels, of what magnitude and duration, and how timed in relation to the task?

Evidence conflicts with regard to the advisability of employing *supplementary,* or *augmented,* feedback. Equivocal findings indicate the nonutility of attempting to generalize too far, across all kinds of tasks, learners, and forms of feedback. A more fruitful attempt would be to analyze situations more specifically, for obviously there are occasions when supplementary feedback is not only helpful but a necessity for effective performance. The desirability of kinds of feedback has been investigated under controlled conditions in which feedback sources are withheld from or added to learning situations.

The possible use of augmented feedback should be considered in relation to

1. The substantiality and value of the feedback intrinsic to the task.
2. The skill level of the learner (need and ability to use kinds of feedback).
3. Redundancy of cues and individual's information-processing abilities.

Theoretical interpretations of how feedback operates in motor behavior were alluded to in Chapter 3, especially in regard to the work of Jack Adams and his proposed closed-loop theory. Does response-produced feedback merely affect momentary performance or a more permanent state of learning? In an attempt to answer this and related questions, Adams, Goetz, and Marshall (1972) practiced subjects under augmented or minimal feedback conditions with a self-paced positioning task. Visual, auditory, and proprioceptive feedback were examined in various contexts. Conclusions were that

1. The acquisition of skill was directly related to the amount of feedback present.
2. Augmented feedback led to more effective performance than minimal feedback.
3. Response-produced feedback had a great impact on both learning and performance and should be central in theories of learning dealing with motor behaviors.

How precise should augmented information feedback be in order really to assist the learner? Obviously, the instructor has a variety of alternatives as to the degree to which specific feedback is provided to the learner. Frank Smoll (1972) attempted to resolve this issue. Using a duckpin bowling ball task, three different forms of feedback were provided to the subjects after each delivery: (a) quantitative feedback to 0.01 second, (b) quantitative feedback to 0.1 second, and (c) qualitative feedback (comments such as the delivery was too fast, too slow, or correct). Smoll concluded that the two quantitative feedback conditions led to superior performances as compared to the qualitative method. The two quantitative methods did not differ in effect on performance. It does appear that there is an optimal precision level of feedback that yields most favorable performances, and it should be in the direction of greater precision.

A distinction might be made between guidance cues and feedback, although they may on occasion refer to the same situation. Norman Gordon (1968, p. 24) suggests that

> Guiding cues differ from feedback in that they are always present regardless of the subject's action, whereas feedback cues vary as a function of the subject's response, although they may be considered to constitute a form of intermittent guidance as well. On the other hand, the provision of adding guiding cues designed to augment input cues, can have the effect of altering feedback information if the nature of the guidance is such as to markedly affect responses.

Gordon's data led him to conclude that augmented feedback benefited the learners. It increased motivation and enhanced attention to the appropriate cues. One of the dangers of supplementary information is too much reliance on them. In order to be of value later in task performance or in transfer tasks such cues should be withdrawn at an appropriate stage of performance.

Research and Theoretical Concerns

Research on the topic of knowledge of results is too vast to be presented here. Among the theoretical and minor issues raised are two questions: (1) Is the intertrial interval more important than the knowledge-of-results delay? (2) Will a delay of KR have the same effect on all types of tasks? The postknowledge-of-results interval during the acquisition of skill is of theoretical as well as practical import. Three important factors should be identified:

1. The effects of varying time durations before KR is given in this interval.
2. The effects of various interpolated activities in this interval.
3. The relation of length of time as well as activity with motor tasks of varying complexity.

It makes sense that there should be an optimal period following the execution of an act that KR will be of value. However, much evidence indicates that the delay alone of KR does not effect the acquisition of motor skills. Further research has been initiated to determine the effects of interpolated activity during the KR-delay interval. Although it seems reasonable to hypothesize that interference would occur during this period with the administration of activities, such has not usually been proved to be the case. The learner seems to learn a simple motor task adequately, whether or not he participates in simple interpolated activity, either similar or dissimilar to the one being learned, between each response and the time KR is provided.

With regard to the post-KR interval, or the length of time that expires from the provision of KR to the next response, some studies have investigated delay periods of from one, two, five, ten, twenty, or thirty seconds. In general it appears that one second is not sufficient time for KR to be processed effectively. However, different studies have indicated different periods of time as being ideal or else of no effect on performance. Experimentally, the paradigm illustrating the relationships of responses, KR, and delay periods would be as drawn in Figure 9–23.

Interpolated activities have assumed a variety of forms and their effects on learning and performance do not lend easily to any generalizations. The post-KR interval has been filled with verbal tasks or unique motor tasks. Because most of the research evidence is based on rather simple motor tasks, the value of KR at a particular interval of time or the effects of interpolated activities is difficult to assess for complex tasks. Nevertheless, the post-KR interval is of importance to consider because of the fact that the learner processes the information or results he has received concerning his previous response and then makes a decision as to how to respond in his next response. Yet little is known about the relation of this interval to the processes involved in acquiring a motor skill. One of the more recent attempts at examining interpolated activity and time-delay factors in a KR experiment has been reported by Richard Magill (1973). Tracking, positioning, reaction time, and complex tasks and the role of feedback have been discussed by John Annett (1969) in one of the chapters of his book.

Sensory feedback is obviously involved in the regulation of skilled performance in continuous tasks. Anthony Greenwald (1970) has analyzed four interpretations of this involvement, and pleads for the concept of an ideomotor mechanism that operates in tasks demanding extremely rapid movements where the performer cannot immediately use error correction information. The anticipatory image of feedback from some activity encourages selection and initiation of that activity. In serial chaining and closed-loop behavior, feedback produced by movements initiates proper responses. The ideomotor mechanism, in contrast, is conceived as a central

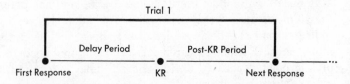

Figure 9–23.   Relationship of a response, delay period for the provision of knowledge of results, and the delay period from KR to the second response.

mechanism (see Keele's theory in Chapter 3) for action initiation in rapidly performed tasks. The serial chaining mechanism operates in tasks requiring coordinated performances within routinized response sequences. The closed-loop mechanism (see Adams's theory in Chapter 3) functions similarly except with tasks performed under nonconstant environmental conditions and unpredictable situations. Once again we are reminded that different feedback mechanisms may be appropriate to describe the way an individual functions in different categories of tasks.

Robert Ammons (1956) has summarized the research on knowledge of results and states eleven empirical generalizations from the research.

1. The performer usually has hypotheses about what he is to do and how he is to do it, and these interact with knowledge of performance.
2. For all practical purposes, there is always some knowledge of his performance available to the human performer.
3. Knowledge of performance affects rate of learning and level reached by learning.
4. Knowledge of performance affects motivation.
5. The more specific the knowledge of performance, the more rapid the improvement and the higher the level of performance.
6. The longer the delay in giving knowledge of performance, the less effect the given information has.
7. In the case of discontinuous tasks where knowledge of performance is given, small intervals between trials are generally better for learning than are longer ones.
8. When knowledge of performance is decreased, performance drops.
9. When knowledge of performance is decreased, performance drops more rapidly if trials are relatively massed.
10. When subjects are not being given supplementary knowledge of performance by the experimenter any longer, the ones who maintain their performance level probably have developed some substitute knowledge of performance.
11. When direct (supplementary) knowledge of performance is removed, systematic "undershooting" or "overshooting" may appear in performance.

Reinforcement, Motivation, and Feedback

Knowledge of results or feedback can serve to motivate, regulate, direct, and/or reinforce behaviors. The informational properties of knowledge of results will, depending on the task and the learner's capabilities, guide or cue ongoing movements in the continuous task or influence the next repeated response in discrete tasks. As far as motivation is concerned, KR may encourage or discourage performance efforts. Learned responses may be activated and sustained, alternative responses may be developed, and in general, a more favorable performing and learning climate will exist. Perhaps it may be suggested that feedback be classified in three categories, depending on the main intent:

1. Information feedback—used for comparison purposes to correct errors.
2. Rewarding (reinforcing) feedback—little information present, helps shape behavior in certain directions.
3. Motivating feedback—influences attitude to continue practicing the task.

Figure 9–24. Coach and performer review the athlete's routine seconds after its completion. (From Ampex Corporation; 401 Broadway; Redwood City, California.)

Information feedback, if theoretically pure, would be necessary either to improve or to maintain performance levels. Many times supplementary feedback, although not really necessary for regulation in task performance, will possess reinforcing and/or motivating virtues, shaping and motivating behaviors. Activity is thereby attended to more seriously, conscientiously, and in a persevering manner. Merely saying to the learner that his performance was good or bad, although not very helpful for detailed analysis of behavior, can be an encouraging or discouraging form of feedback information.

A most unusual approach to the topic of reinforcement is provided by Joseph Nuttin (1968). He analyzes the relative effects of rewards and punishments from a series of personally directed studies to challenge directly Thorndike's law of effect. Of importance here is that Nuttin emphasizes that rewards and punishments provide error information in many motor tasks. Thus the informational value serves to cue the learner for specific stimuli and particular responses.

In all the discussion on feedback, however, it can readily be deduced that cues can possess a variety of psychological properties. The serious scholar can easily be exasperated in any attempt to isolate functions. The use of videotape in an instructional setting is a good practical example where a particular medium may possess reinforcement, motivational, and feedback properties (see Figures 9–24 through 9–27 for examples in physical education and sport).

In a series of studies in which Roger Black was involved (e.g., Slayton and Black, 1971), similar effects of knowledge of results and reinforcement have been noted in resistance to extinction. That is, subjects provided with such information tended to persist longer at their tasks than those subjects who were controlled. Rewards or KR tend to strengthen an instrumental response; withdrawal leads to extinction of that response. The apparatus used was the pursuit rotor. The data were interpreted as suggesting that "the role of schedule of KR in determining resistance to extinction on a pursuit-rotor task is completely analogous to the role of schedule of reinforcement in instrumental conditioning" (p. 112).

TRANSFER OF TRAINING

Thus far in this chapter, the reader may have realized that there have been many references to the transference of instructional and training methods and materials to skilled performance. This particular section contains direct reference to the concept of transfer, in theory and practice.

Almost all of learning is based on the concept of transfer. *Transfer* im-

Figure 9–25.   A young woman is being recorded on videotape as part of a gymnastics class. After going through her performance, she is able to see herself immediately afterward on the television receiver, which is part of the portable Videotrainer at left. With videotape recording, students are given a chance to analyze their performance and correct their errors. (From Ampex Corporation; 401 Broadway; Redwood City, California.)

plies the influence of a learned task on one to be learned or the utilization of formed responses in a new situation related to the one in which they were learned. School curricula and educational theory reflect the realization of and need for formal education that will carry over into life's experiences and chosen occupations. Is it not true that the purpose of a general education is to prepare an individual to live more effectively within himself and within society? If we believe in this meaning of education, then we must accept the fact that responses and general behavior patterns may be transferable from one situation to another. In many cases, these occurrences are desirable.

Figure 9–26. A member of a gymnastics team performs a routine on a sidehorse. His routine is picked up by a television camera and recorded on a videotape recorder as part of a meet with the University of Illinois. Each team competed on its own campus, with an impartial panel of judges viewing the video tapes of both teams to render its decision. It was the first such meet ever held. Illinois was the winner, 180.65 to 173.10. (From Ampex Corporation; 401 Broadway; Redwood City, California.)

Transfer training may be practiced not only for present use but also for future application. Hopefully, what is learned in one context will be able to be carried over to another context. In a sense, then, transfer training is learning for later situations. Exactly how transfer takes place and what is transferred has been the subject of many investigations and the inspiration for theoretical speculation. Conflicting experimental results and different interpretations of the research confuse the issue but certain principles of transfer are fairly well accepted today.

Figure 9–27.   Students view their fencing form and style immediately after performing with an assist from a Videotrainer system. (From Ampex Corporation; 401 Broadway; Redwood City, California.)

Measurement

Typically, experimental procedures employed in studies of transfer assume two forms. In the first case, an experimental group learns Task A, the control group rests, and both groups are tested on Task B. The difference in performance between the groups on Task B, if any, would be due to the effect of learning Task A.

	Task A	Task B
Experimental Group	Learns	Learns
Control Group	Rests	Learns

One of the weaknesses in the design in this table is the possibility that the groups were not evenly equated at the start of the experiment. This problem may be overcome by pretesting the groups on the eventual task to be learned. If too much testing practice is given at this time, there is the danger that the potential influence of one task or a second task will be concealed.

	Task B	Task A	Task B
Experimental Group	Tested	Learns	Learns
Control Group	Tested	Rests	Learns

Transfer from one task to another task or from one situation to another situation will be dependent on the relationship between their stimuli and responses demanded of the individuals. Such psychological terms as stimulus generalization and response generalization are appropriate to this discussion. *Stimulus generalization* explains the condition such that when a particular response is learned to a stimulus, similar stimuli will evoke the same response. In *response generalization,* once a response has been learned to a given stimulus, the stimulus will cause similar responses to be elicited. It stands to reason that we can learn to associate the same response to a given range of stimuli (stimulus generalization) as well as a range of responses to a particular stimulus (response generalization). These terms will be discussed intermittently within the context of the material in this section.

Osgood (1949) has attempted to show stimulus–response relationships and to predict task-to-task transfer effects. Figure 9–28 depicts the Osgood Transfer Surface, a theoretical transfer model. It illustrates that after a specific response is learned to a given stimulus, S_1–R_1, maximum interference, hence negative transfer, occurs when a completely new response has to be learned to that stimulus, S_1–R_2. As the stimulus gradually changes until it is completely different from the first one and the response likewise, S_2–R_2, there is zero transfer. A new stimulus that requires an already learned response, S_2–R_1, results in zero transfer, although any relationship at all between these stimuli will result in positive transfer in behavior.

Although the Transfer Surface does a good job explaining and predicting transfer relationships, it does not take into account some potential influencing variables. One of these is the amount of training on the first task, S_1–R_1. More practice yields better transfer effects, for it is observed that little training results in broad generalization transfer and more training in sharper generalization transfer.

The Surface recognizes the possibility of transfer of training effects as being zero, negative, or positive. *Positive transfer* occurs when prior learning promotes present learning, and *negative transfer* infers the inhibition

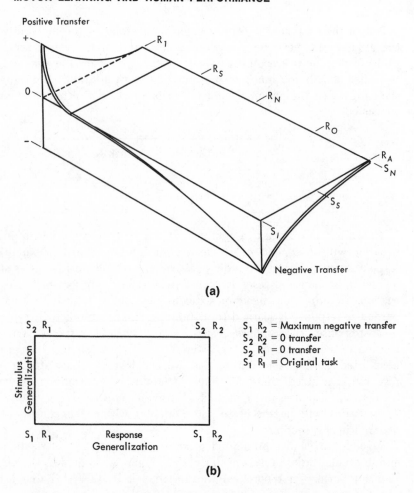

Figure 9–28. **(a)** The Osgood Transfer Surface. The medial planes represent effects of zero magnitude, response generalization is represented along the length, and stimulus generalization along its width. R_1 original or extremely similar response, S_1 original or extremely similar stimulus, R_S to R_A increasingly different responses, S_S to S_N increasingly different stimuli. The Surface may be used to find another task in relation to the original one to predict the extent of transfer as well as the presence of negative or positive transfer. (From Charles E. Osgood, "The Similarity Paradox in Human Learning: A Resolution," *Psychological Review,* 56:132–143, 1949.) **(b)** Osgood Surface modified. As the second response R_2 to the same stimulus S_1 becomes more unrelated to R_1, maximum interference occurs. As the stimulus is gradually changed at the same time the response is until the condition S_2–R_2 occurs, less interference is present. When the response remains the same but the stimulus gradually changes until S_2–R_1 is reached, positive transfer effects decrease until no transfer is present.

effect of prior learning on immediate learning. *Zero or no transfer* takes place when former learning has no effect on the learning of an immediate task. It would not be difficult for any of us to remember instances where all three conditions have occurred. There is an interesting relationship between amount of transfer, type of transfer, and amount of pretraining. It has already been stated that specific transfer is enhanced by more prior-task training; but, in addition, it is probable that negative transfer will occur with little practice whereas extensive practice will encourage more positive transfer.

Learning to hit a fast-pitched baseball might be considered as S_1–R_1. Assume that the ballplayer then will try to learn how to pull the ball (swing earlier), which is a variation of R_1. The stimulus remains the same but the response is slightly altered. We will probably expect some degree of positive transfer, perhaps some negative influence, with the ultimate transfer effect being either slightly positive or zero. Now suppose that the response to be mastered is a bunt. This response is quite different from the original one. If the batter has been conditioned to swing away at a pitched ball and now has to learn to bunt, interference between responses will probably occur (as predicted by the Osgood Surface).

Returning to the baseball scene, and S_1–R_1 as the original task, let us modify the stimulus. If a curve ball instead of a fast ball is thrown, and the same response as before is desired, positive transfer should occur. However, the more the stimulus is changed, the less positive the transfer. If an underhanded softball throw is the new stimulus, the batting behavior of the individual may little resemble that which was demonstrated with the pitched baseball, thereby revealing little if any in the way of positive transfer effects.

Whenever one performs in and reacts to a new situation, to a certain extent his responses will reflect previous experiences. Sometimes it is desirable to perform similarly as before, sometimes not. In experimental situations, the investigator can determine, through statistical analysis, any significant positive or negative transfer effects.

Conditions Affecting Transfer

There are numerous conditions associated with, and which may potentially affect, the transfer effects of one task to another task. Probably the most important of these is the *similarity* between the tasks. A greater resemblance between task elements, between their respective stimuli and responses, will result in the greatest amount of transfer. For instance, Ammons, Ammons, and Morgan (1958) trained their subjects on varying speeds of the pursuit rotor. Transfer effects were found to be proportional to the similarity between the speed rates of any two tasks. As in our discussion on this matter, especially the reference to the Osgood Transfer Surface, the probable negative and positive transfer effects are indicated when certain variables are present.

The *amount of practice* on the prior task has already been shown to be related to the amount and nature of transfer expected. More practice on a task that might positively influence performance on a second task will result in performance in the expected direction. Even experience with elements or components of a task can facilitate the learning of it (Vincent, 1968). Subjects practicing on specific perceptual components of motor skills showed the advantage of this experience when compared to control subjects. *Motivation* to transfer skill or knowledge from one situation to another situation is yet another consideration.

It is also possible that the *method of training* may have some bearing on the transfer effectiveness. In recent years, a few investigators have looked into the matter of whole-versus-part learning methods and their relative efficiency in facilitating transfer. In one experiment, Briggs and Waters (1958), using simulated aircraft control dynamics, found that it was important to practice the whole task if the highest transfer potential is to be realized. Part practice does not integrate component skills. For transfer purposes, the authors recommend that the whole task be simplified rather than fractionalized. Briggs and Naylor (1962) tested their subjects for transfer on a three-dimensional tracking task learned under different practice methods. The whole and progressive part methods were equal and significantly better than the pure-part and simplified whole methods for transfer effectiveness.

Intent of transfer is yet another factor of influence. If the instructor indicates the elements common to two tasks and provides the basis for insight and understanding, the learner will probably make greater use of what he has learned on the prior task when it comes time to perform a related second task. In other words, greater assistance is provided when skills are taught with the intention of transferring over to other skills. Although this is a generally accepted statement, an exception is reported by Nelson (1975b). His subjects were taught and tested on pairs of related skills: a badminton and a tennis volley against the wall; a volleyball and basketball tap for accuracy; and the track and football starting stances. Nelson concluded that deliberate teaching for transfer was ineffective, as many of the findings were not significant. However, he did note that initial tennis skill learning had some favorable effect on badminton skill as did basketball skill on volleyball skill.

One of the reasons for the lack of positive results in Nelson's study was possibly the simultaneous learning of the skills. He concludes his study by stating that skills and activities involving similar elements and patterns should not be learned at the same time. There is a great concern of physical educators over the effect of one activity on another activity, whether these activities are apparently related or not. Swimming is an activity that has usually been frowned upon during a particular varsity season. Supposedly, its nature is such as to have deleterious effects on other athletic endeavors. In another investigation by Nelson (1957a), one group of subjects learned certain gross motor skills and swam on alternate days while a second group did not swim. No difference was found between the groups in performance on the skills.

Referring back to skills with a certain degree of relationship, it is of interest to speculate if positive or negative effects will occur between such activities as tennis and badminton, baseball and golf, and basketball and volleyball. Let us use tennis and badminton as an example. They are both racket sports involving the striking of a projectile. Eye–hand coordination is extremely important in both sports, as is agility and quickness of movement. It might be hypothesized that outstanding ability in one of these sports should render the individual highly successful in the other sport. However, there are other considerations. Badminton strokes are made with a highly flexible wrist whereas a tennis ball is usually stroked with a firm wrist. A tennis ball has altogether different characteristics than does the badminton shuttlecock. It might, therefore, be argued that high skill in one activity would hinder the learning of the other activity.

Although task similarities encourage related movement patterns, this response generalization is not always desirable. Response generalization promotes initial skill acquisition but it is response distinction that is important at the highly skilled levels of performance. The precision and accuracy of a given task distinguishes it from that which is required in other tasks. So, in a sense, response generalization is the opposite of skill. Response generalization infers generalized movements common between two tasks whereas skill requires precision movements.

The attempted development of theoretical relationships between sports leaves much to be desired because of the complexity of these activities. When dealing with simple tasks, elements may be identified with much greater ease. Exactly how much transfer occurs from athletic skill to athletic skill is thus difficult to ascertain, especially if the entire context of their usage is considered.

Even the application of mechanical or learning principles to the learning task does not always afford expected transfer, as was explained earlier in this chapter. Because of the conflicting experimental results, it is felt that principles may, but need not, transfer. When they are taught specific to certain material, the probability is that transfer will be ineffective. If the situation in which principles are learned is similar to that in which they are to be applied, transfer effects most likely will be more beneficial.

Learning to Learn

Another aspect of the learning function, often neglected, is the transfer that occurs from merely learning materials similar in nature. When materials or tasks undertaken are alike, improvement results just from learning how to learn them. One has to learn how to take multiple-choice written tests, how to lift weights, or how to solve psychomotor tasks.

Learning how to learn involves learning the technique of attacking a problem of a particular kind. The individual acquires the appropriate *set*, he reduces general stimuli to specific cues. After repeated experience with the same type of tasks, after attentive adjustment is established, greater learning always occurs.

The psychologist most associated with calling this phenomenon to the attention of all those concerned with learning is Harry Harlow. Harlow (1949), working with monkeys, gave them different discrimination problems to solve. At first, the monkeys took a long time to learn the problems, but as they tackled more problems, there was a decrease in solution time. Therefore learning how to learn something is necessarily a partial explanation of how one task transfers over to another similar task.

Bilateral Transfer

There has been considerable evidence that indicates the transference of electrical activity and skilled movements from one part of the body to another. Physiologically, it has been demonstrated that mental activity causes electrical stimulation of the areas of the body being thought about. Mental practice, without any overt practice, can improve motor skill.

The contributions of Cook (1933a, 1933b) to that area of study he calls *cross-education* provided early evidence as to the transfer of a skill learned in one part of the body to another. Transfer was found to be greatest to the muscle group opposite and symmetrical; it was least to the muscle group opposite and unsymmetrical to the practiced limb. Even strength can be transferred from a trained to an untrained limb. Logan and Lockhart (1962) report contralateral transfer of strength from the knee extensors of the trained leg to the knee extensors of the untrained limb.

Thus in any act, there is a tendency for response generalization. Activity that is overt and apparently body specific has an overall effect on the individual. Internal activity is constantly going on during our periods of wakefulness and it appears as if the interwoven complexity of the nervous system permits motor patterns to be learned from practiced to unpracticed limbs.

Task Difficulty

If the ultimate objective is skill in a particular activity, the instructor may proceed in his class in one of three ways. He may guide his students from easy to more complex steps, thus providing the learners with initial success and satisfaction in the activity. He may teach the given skill(s) directly. Or, he may proceed in having the learners overcome the extreme difficulties of the task(s) before undertaking the precise task(s), thus operating under a complex-to-easy task procedure.

Theoretically, it makes good sense to build up to a particular objective, to master simple skills before learning more difficult ones and to gain the satisfaction which is supplied with successful attempts. Obviously, a person should be able to show the greatest achievement when attempting simple tasks. Contrarily, theoretical support could be mustered for the teaching of skills from the complex to the simple. When one confronts the more difficult task first, if it is not unreasonably complex, a progression to the easier tasks should bother the learner very little because the harder task contained all the elements of the simple ones. It appears as if there might be a conflict as to the desirability of introducing simple skills as opposed to complex ones when teaching for transfer. There is yet another alternative to the problem. If achievement on a particular skill is wanted, and perhaps it is of mediocre difficulty, should it be taught directly? Because of the specificity nature of skill learning, transfer from skill to skill, no matter how related they are, may not occur in the most efficient manner.

Skinner, as we have noted is one of the leading promoters of the teaching machine, and he has introduced the theory of shaping behavior. It is actually based on the concept of transfer of training from the simple to the more difficult. A sequence of events leads to the desired outcome, with the progressive transfer system increasing the probability of a correct response.

As to the actual research related to the problem of transfer and task difficulty, inconsistent results have been obtained among the investigations. Barch and Lewis (1954) trained 230 airmen on the Iowa Pursuit Apparatus. Four tasks were involved: the standard, first-learned task, two intermediate tasks, and one difficult task. The experimenters found a greater positive transfer from a simple to a difficult task than from a difficult task to a more difficult task or from tasks of equal difficulty.

Lordahl and Archer (1958), in two pursuit rotor experiments, varied task difficulty by manipulating target rotation speed or the radius of the target orbit. Direct practice was better than transfer practice. There was slightly more positive transfer when training from the simple to the complex than vice versa in one of the experiments, whereas there were no differential transfer effects from an easy or more complex task in the other experiment.

Baker, Wylie, and Gagné (1950) had subjects follow a signal on a target by turning a crank handle. Response rates were changed for each of four tasks. Training on a faster rate of speed produced more transfer to perform at the slower rate than vice versa. The investigators therefore concluded that a greater amount of transfer occurs when Task I is relatively difficult and Task II relatively easy. Gibbs (1951), utilizing a handle-winding task and a steering task, declared that the greatest transfer from a difficult to an easy task occurred when the same kind of ability was required in both tasks. However, he warns that an increase in task difficulty will not necessarily cause the most rapid rate of learning, as there is an optimum range of task difficulty.

In most cases direct practice on the task of concern leads to most favorable results. However, changes in task practice, whether from easy to hard or vice versa, may produce beneficial effects on performance. Richard May and Pam Duncan's (1973) data indicate that there may be an optimal amount of change in difficulty for best total performance. An intermediate degree of change led to most favorable results in a puzzle-block-skills task. Changes in task difficulty may promote attention to relevant aspects of the task, especially where identifying and isolating important stimuli is important. These authors wrote that, "It might be useful to consider a task continuum along which amount of cognitive vs. motor involvement is scaled. The greater the cognitive component the more changes in difficulty may facilitate performance. With maximal motor involvement, changes in the problem might disrupt or inhibit performance" (p. 128).

That extreme transfer practice subjects generally do poorer than central transfer practice subjects is a notion upheld by the data collected by Leonard, Karnes, Oxendine, and Hesson (1970) using a pursuit rotor. With the criterion task set at 45 rpms, those subjects who practiced at 40, 45, and 50 rpms performed better than those at 30 and 60 rpms.

It is possible to use the Naylor–Briggs task-complexity-task-organization paradigm alluded to earlier in this chapter in the section entitled "Part and Whole Practice." Table 9–3 suggests instructional procedures on the basis of task analysis.

As Day (1956) points out in summarizing the studies concerned with the effect of the difficulty of initial and final tasks on transfer training, there are inconsistencies from study to study in defining difficulty and discrepancies among experimental results. Difficulty of a task can be affected by manipulating stimulus or response variables. With regard to the response situation, Day concludes that there is a greater degree of transfer from a difficult to an easier condition than the reverse.

Singer (1966) designed an investigation using archery skill to study this problem with physical education activities. Three classes of students were practiced under different conditions: Class A learned and practiced archery at the 10-yard line; Class C began at the 40-yard line; and Class B started at the 25-yard line. The three groups were then tested on the 25-yard line. When testing for transfer, no significant difference was observed in the transfer effects from practice on an easier task (Class A) as compared to the transfer effects of a more difficult task (Class C) in comparison to precise distance practice (Class B). Ultimate success, as measured by the Columbia Junior Round, indicated no significant difference between the groups—task proficiency was not affected by the initial learning technique.

TABLE 9–3.   Hypothetical Model of Transfer of Training in Function of Motor Task Difficulty (Complexity and Organization)

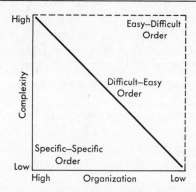

Within this model, assuming that we know the transferability of a component of a task to a whole task at a particular stage of learning, and its relative complexity and organization for an individual, we can decide which methods have the higher probability of positive transfer. It seems that this model within this context merits more research and has the potential to influence the teaching of motor or sports skills.

The matter of what level of skill to begin with is hard to resolve. Immediate reward and satisfaction are certainly important, but so is the time element. It appears as if many present-day writers are in favor of learning a more difficult skill directly rather than through lead-up activities. Many also favor progression from the more difficult to the simple rather than the opposite way. Perhaps the teaching method should reflect the instructor-student objectives. If what is desired is the development of a perfected act (in a stable stimulus environment), then possibly complex skills should be practiced first. If the technique is not as important as being aware of relevant cues and understanding the situation (in a changing environment), possibly, as Barbara Knapp (1964) suggests, the learning should progress from the simpler situation.

Adaptive Training

Support for the belief that practice should proceed from easier to more difficult task demands is found in the newly popularized concept of *adaptive training*. Thus far the interest has lodged in mastering equipment requiring the involvement of perceptual and motor behaviors. Equipment has been developed as training devices that provide the automatic adjustments according to problem difficulty and the person's level of performance. With improvement, the difficulty of the task is varied and increased. In the adaptive approach, the learner's errors are maintained at a constant level as task difficulty varies.

The contrasting approach is to set the task at a specified operational level and the performer's errors are free to vary. The roots of adaptive training rest in an individualized approach to skill mastery, with concepts apparently somewhat allied to programmed learning techniques. In the most informative article on the topic prepared so far, Charles R. Kelley (1969) indicates the limitations of traditional training programs:

1. Group instruction makes it extremely hard to be sensitive and to vary tasks according to each student's level of performance.
2. Automatic training devices contain preprogrammed tasks, and do not consider the person's level of performance and rate of progression.

According to Kelley, "machine-controlled adaptive training is merely the automation of a function performed by the skilled individual instructor" (p. 547). Figure 9–29 demonstrates the distinction between fixed and adaptive training. The feedback loop in the adaptive model serves to change the task demands as a consequence of the learner's level of performance. Fixed training is not as sensitive as adaptive training. It is a closed-loop approach. Machine-controlled adaptive training contains three unique elements:

(1) a means for measuring performance
(2) an adjustable feature of the task or problem which changes in difficulty (the adaptive variable)
(3) adaptive logic which automatically changes the adaptive variable as a function of performance measurement [Kelley, 1969, pp. 547–548].

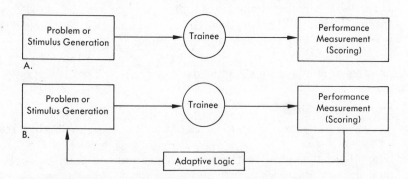

Figure 9–29.   Fixed versus adaptive training. A. Fixed (preprogrammed) training. B. Adaptive training. (From Charles R. Kelley, "What Is Adaptive Training?" *Human Factors*, 11:547–556, 1969.)

Training automatically becomes harder as skill progresses. Three training systems are illustrated in Figure 9–30. Graph A illustrates a fixed difficulty system that is not sensitive to learners' progress. In Graph B, one example of an adaptive model, the task becomes more complex with skill acquisition. The change is not as dramatic as in Graph C. In this case the performance measurement remains constant throughout training. One variable would ideally change systematically with adaptation, and therefore is the recommended procedure. System error is stated at the beginning of training which the learner must meet. The system adapts to the difficulty level of the performer and his control abilities.

Training devices and systems can be effective when carefully devised, when the difficulty level of the task is geared for the individual and not fixed. The magnitude of errors made is indicative of task load. The efficiency of the adaptive approach has been shown when compared to the success demonstrated in training on the criterion, or final, task itself, or when arbitrary levels of increasing fixed difficulty are used. Of course, in a group setting where individualized approaches to training are impossible, the mean level or constant level for a number of individuals during practice provides the best compromise training technique. But the adaptive approach provides the best indicant in the form of reliable measurements of learner progress.

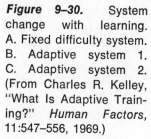

Figure 9–30. System change with learning. A. Fixed difficulty system. B. Adaptive system 1. C. Adaptive system 2. (From Charles R. Kelley, "What Is Adaptive Training?" *Human Factors,* 11:547–556, 1969.)

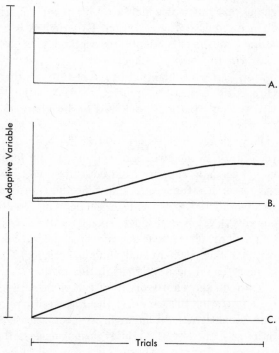

The adaptive variables that might be manipulated include modifications in the simulated environment, stress presence, augmented information, display changes, or task demands. The adaptive variable should systematically affect the difficulty of the task. A logical progression indicates which variable should be manipulated to move the task from simple to hard. The logic employed in the system is of paramount importance. This may depend on precise mathematical equations or common-sense adjustment rules. The concepts show much promise for the intelligent planning of individualized training programs.

Theories of Transfer

The transfer effect of learning certain skills or matter precludes the learning of anything new. Actually, nothing a person learns is truly completely new to him. Everything he undertakes he has seen and done before, only in different forms and shapes. What we learn and the speed of acquisition is dependent on positive and negative transfer situations and their interaction effects.

Examine, for instance, the situation in which a person learns the sport of tennis for the first time. He does not really start with a so-called carte blanche. His past experiences, such as in batting, catching, or throwing a ball, will transfer over to this activity. Previous experiences in racket games, examples of which are ping-pong, squash, and badminton, will influence tennis skill acquisition. Experiences in games requiring quick and sudden movements, depth perception, alert reactions, strategy, and the like, will also have an effect.

How can we explain and predict through theory the nature of transfer? How is the concept of transfer, as well as the abundant research evidence to date (only partially reviewed in this chapter), to be incorporated into a theory?

Perhaps the first theory of transfer, which was in existence for many years prior to the twentieth century, is the *formal-discipline theory*. It no longer has any support from educators who have even casually reviewed the research evidence. At one time the transferability of mental functions was considered to be wide in scope. The faculties of the mind were supposedly developed through specific courses, and these courses were not taught for their content but for their general mind-strengthening ability. It was felt that such mental functions as logic, concentration, reason, and memory could be developed in this manner.

Through the efforts of the great pioneer psychologist Thorndike in the earlier part of this century, the formal-discipline theory was discredited. One cannot train the mind in a general sense from particular courses or training. Course-work abilities do not necessarily transfer over to practical situations. Instead, Thorndike proposed the *identical-elements theory*, based on his belief in learning by association (S–R theory). To Thorndike, transfer between two tasks or situations was only as effective as the number of elements common to them. The definition of an element is a question continually raised. When the term *element* is narrowly interpreted, it leads to more rejection of the theory; and contrarily, more generalized interpretation results in greater acceptance.

Compare the theory to one termed *generalization theory*. In contrast to consideration for specific stimuli or specific information, generalization theory encompasses the transferability of principles and problem-solving situations. As we now know, evidence conflicts as to the validation of this theory. However, classroom teachings are often based on the premise that an individual can transfer matter learned in these ways to other situations. This theory is probably most consistent with educational philosophy. It, like the identical-elements theory, has its proponents and doubters.

Among the other theories proposed is the *transposition theory* by the Gestaltists, but this and others need not be presented here. Suffice to say that the numerous theories in existence to describe learning phenomena indicate at least some experimental support. Research findings may often be interpreted in various ways, thus resulting in the possible formulation of a number of theories from the same data.

RETENTION: FACTORS AND PROCESSES

Motor skills are often learned with the intention of successfully performing them at a later date. Although immediate performance is also a consideration, written or skill tests and athletic contests are examples of occasions when later recall or recognition of that which has been learned is demanded. Retention or long-term memory may be dependent on a number of factors, namely the nature of the task, its meaningfulness to the learner, the time lapse between the original learning and recall, interpolated activities, and the conditions under which the task was learned. Let us examine such factors as well as prominent theories describing this aspect of the learning process.

Retention and forgetting are terms used to describe the same process. Whereas *retention* refers to that which is remembered and can be determined by measuring the difference between the amount originally learned and the amount forgotten, the amount *forgotten* is equal to the amount learned minus the amount retained.

In the preceding section we discussed the nature of transfer of learning. Jack Adams (1969) has suggested a distinction between learning and retention. Presumably, of interest in transfer studies is the influence of

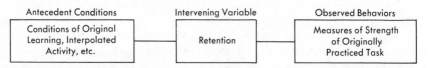

Figure 9–31.   The conceptual status of retention treated as an intervening variable. [From Jack Adams, "Retention: Nature, Measurement, and Fundamental Processes." Reprinted with permission of Macmillan Publishing Co., Inc., from *Learning: Processes,* Melvin H. Marx (ed.). Copyright © 1969, Melvin H. Marx.]

prior learning on a new task whereas retention studies are concerned with variables that govern the persistence of learned behaviors. This may not be a totally true picture. One of the factors that influences the retention of a particular once-learned task is the positive or negative transfer effects of the intervening experiences. Learning and retention will be the net result of a number of negative and positive effects of previous experiences. Transfer effects can indeed be prominent in the observation of retention, at least in the real world. Obviously, laboratory conditions can be developed to control for each factor. In any event, retention is inferred from behavior after a certain period of time has elapsed from previous practice, as depicted in Figure 9–31.

Normally we might expect to find a decrease in retention with the passage of time in which there is no practice, but research results indicate that this is not always the case. A number of studies have demonstrated that the retention curve does not always drop rapidly following the postrest learning period but instead continues to rise. This improvement instead of a decrement in the recall of a task after a period of rest has been termed *reminiscence*. It appears that certain practice conditions may be more advantageous for reminiscence than others.

For many years retention was examined in a fairly straightforward way. Recently, experimental and theoretical breakthroughs have led to a penetrating analysis of the processes underlying retention. As we will see shortly, the contemporary acceptance of at least two functional processes— short-term memory (STM) and long-term memory (LTM)—holds major implications for the understanding of the way one retains material and how long-term processes might be improved upon with appropriate training techniques.

Methodology of Retention Experiments

Three measures have generally been used in investigations concerned with retention. These include recognition, relearning, and recall. *Recognition* is the method so often used in written testing, an example of which is the multiple-choice test. A *recall* score is informative in that it indicates how much or how well something is remembered.

A *relearning* score is determined in the following way. The number of trials the subject needs to relearn a task—for example, 12 is subtracted from the number of trials it originally took him to learn it to a particular criterion—say, 15. The figure obtained, 3, is placed over the original learning trials, 15, and this results in a *savings score*. In this case, the savings score, otherwise known as the *retention score*, is 20 per cent. Conversely, the forgotten score would be 80 per cent. In terms of their retention effectiveness, recognition is best, whereas recall results in the poorest performances.

A comparison of research methodology typically employed in experiments dealing with recall or recognition methods of retention is presented by Harry Bahrick (1964). Implications for studies dealing with retention are made. Retention measures are compared with suggestions for experimental controls in order that artifacts are not produced.

When testing for retention, two methods have been employed. Older studies used repeated tests on the same subjects in order to measure retention at various intervals after the completion of practice. This procedure has been rightfully attacked, for each test influences the next test and becomes but another form of practice. This flaw in experimentation undermines the effectiveness or desirability of such a method. A designation of the subjects into subgroups after the practice periods are over to be tested at different times for retention adds precision to the experiment. This desired method requires the investigator to have an ample number of subjects at the beginning of his study.

The most pure measure of the retention of a once-learned skill would be a one-trial test at a later date. With more than one trial, relearning quickly occurs. Unfortunately, a one-trial test of retention may not be very reliable, for performance measures are prone to fluctuate from trial to trial and occasion to occasion. In addition, because retention scores usually represent the differences between scores at the termination of practice and at a later date, an accurate assessment of initial learning is necessary. The criterion of initial learning is about as difficult to agree upon as is an appropriate test of retention. Some aspects of this problem are addressed by Richard Rivenes and Martha Mawhinney (1968).

Short-Term and Long-Term Memory

To retrieve information accurately and repeat performances during some time period following an initial experience indicates the quality of the retention, or long-term memory, ability of the individual with regard to particular tasks. If behavior is considered to be reflected by an information-

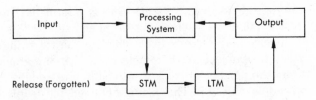

Figure 9–32.   After information is handled in the short-term memory (STM) storage, it will either be released from the system or transferred into long-term memory (LTM) storage for future usage. The flow of movement from STM to LTM is dependent upon adequate rehearsal time, coding techniques, and image formulation.

processing system, then the way we receive, discriminate and select, rehearse, and in general, hold on to material in storage for later usage is worthy of our understanding. And in Chapter 6, distinctions and relationships between two memory systems were described where man as a unitary system was analyzed according to the subsystems that contributed to motor performance and skill acquisition.

Information, if it is to be longlasting, must pass through the short-term memory system into the long-term memory system. And if it is not appropriately rehearsed and registered, this information will "float out" of the STM system. The alternative possibilities for the routing of information from STM storage is suggested in Figure 9–32.

Information-processing theorists inform us man has a limited channel capacity. Whether it has to do with distinguishing among various sensory inputs or deciding among choices of cues, there is just so much information that can be handled at one time. Overloading the channel capacity by attempting to rehearse too much material can result in information that will not be used and therefore wasted. Or, too much noise in the channel can distort and confuse the processing functions. The capacity of the STM system, or memory span, is probably larger than once was thought.

As to LTM storage, there is disagreement as to its capacity. But it would appear that it is rather limited, for our permanent storage capacities and retrieval abilities are rather ineffective too often, suggesting limitations of the system.

Besides the *appropriate amount* of input at any one time, *exposure time* will also affect STM and LTM processes. In order for information to proceed from STM to LTM, a reasonable exposure time for rehearsal, coding, and imagery is necessary. A number of verbal learning experiments point to twenty or thirty seconds as optimal, but there is little agreement with motor tasks. Adequate rehearsal time permits organization of materials and effective registration.

Also, *interpolated* activity has been thought to affect the short-term memory process. Interfering or rehearsal-preventing activities present immediately after exposure to some learning situation impedes STM. An excellent overview with a model of short-term and long-term memory is described by Richard Atkinson and Richard Schiffren (1971). The processes involved in STM are given prime importance because of their consequences. Control processes must be optimized for effective STM. These would include overt or covert repetition or rehearsal of material, coding, imaging (verbal input transcribed to visual images), decision rule formulation, and organizational schemes, retrieval strategies, and problem-solving techniques. They vary from person to person and task to task. But the subject has control over the processes selected in STM as contrasted to the permanent structural components of LTM.

Short-term memory is the transient process; long-term memory constitutes the permanent storage. Of course what is meant by permanency is debatable. There are arguments that favor the concept that permanent memories exist, but failure to reproduce behaviors lies in a poor retrieval system or inadequate set. On the other hand, there are those that believe that memory traces gradually fade out of storage. Data obtained by Richard Schiffren (1970) suggest that memory failure is due to an inadequate memory research during retrieval rather than a fading out of the memory trace.

There is also issue over what is actually stored, or remembered. More than likely an internalized model of rules or patterns of actions is available upon the appropriate signal. The right selection will depend upon previous experiences, the current situation, and retrieval capabilities.

Sometimes the terms *primary* (PM) and *secondary* (SM) *memory stores* have been used interchangeably with the terms *short-term* and *long-term memory storage systems*. As Norman (1969) indicates, information is rehearsed in the PM store, and may or may not be advanced to the SM store. Rehearsal is extremely important in increasing the likelihood of this passage. Figure 9–33 shows the interaction of three key systems: acquisition, memory, and decision. Once information goes into PM it is either forgotten after immediate usage or else enters SM. Actions (decisions) will reflect biases, situational impedence (noise, error), strategies, and the strength of the memory and ability to retrieve relevant items. Theory would suggest that much attention be paid to ways of transfering important information from the primary to the secondary store. As Steven Keele puts it (1973, p. 29), "Memory does not simply reflect whatever impinges on the senses. Stored material undergoes a series of transformations and abstractions. Storage [for STM] is quite brief, ranging approximately one second for visual and tactual inputs to perhaps twenty or so seconds for the kinesthetic system."

LTM is relatively immune to forgetting. To improve the functions of LTM, Keele suggests rehearsal, organization, and imagery. So far we have

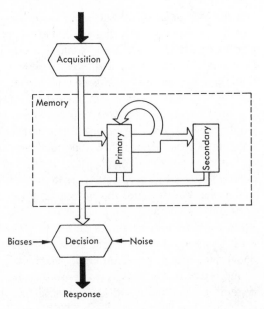

Figure 9–33.   Interactions among the three different processes affecting the subject's actions in a memory experiment. In the acquisition process, the sensory input is encoded for the memory process. Items in primary memory are rapidly forgotten, whereas items in secondary memory can be retained for long periods of time. In the decision process, the output of the memory is combined with the subject's biases to determine his response. Noise can be considered to enter the process at this point.

The loop labeled "rehearsal" indicates the effects of this operation: to renew the strength of material in primary memory and to help enter it in secondary memory. [From Donald A. Norman, *Memory and Attention* (New York: John Wiley & Sons, 1969).]

discussed a two-stage approach to memory: STM and LTM. From a biochemical framework, Ward Halstead and William Rucker (1968) feel that a two-stage model is too simple. They propose another phase of memory, an intermediate phase, which "holds information during the period while the dynamic trace is dissipating and the permanent or consolidated trace is still being constructed" (pp. 39–40). Furthermore, they suggest that neurons produce special proteins that help to record a memory trace. RNA (ribonucleic acid) is proposed as responsible for LTM, although evidence is unclear as to the specific role of RNA in memory consolidation. Writing from a neurological perspective, J. Anthony Deutsch (1968) suggests that certain memory disorders can be attributed to a lowered efficiency of impulse transmission across synapses. Special drugs may help to remediate this circumstance.

Neurophysiologically, Karl Pribram (1969) believes that there is substantial evidence to believe that memory occurs according to the principle of the *hologram.*

> In a hologram the information in a scene is recorded on a photographic plate in the form of a complex interference, or diffraction, pattern that appears meaningless. When the pattern is illuminated by coherent light, however, the original image is reconstructed. What makes the hologram unique as a storage device is that every element in the original image is distributed over the entire photographic plate. The hypothesis is attractive because remembering or recollecting literally implies a reconstructive process—the assembly of dismembered mnemonic events. [p. 73.]

Pribram believes that the organizer for complex events involves the association areas of the cerebral cortex. These areas exert control on inputs by way of other structures in the brain. However, they are responsible for providing a major part of the organizing process involved in memory. Perspectives from psychology, physiology, neurology, and biochemistry provide a more complete picture of the operation of memory as it affects behavior.

Practice Methods

Most investigators concerned with varying the practice–rest ratios have been interested primarily in the immediate acquisition of the tasks, whereas few have extended their investigations to observe retention effects of the practice conditions. This point was emphasized earlier in the chapter.

In line with the research evidence are the findings from an experiment, depicted in Figure 9–34. Although initial differences are small, there evidently is a critical point where massed practice inhibits and worsens performance, whereas distributed practice appears to be continually beneficial. A test one week after the termination of practice indicated little difference between the groups. A survey of research investigating retention effects after a period of at least twenty-four hours from the final moment of practice indicates little difference between groups as a result of their practice methods.

Reminiscence

Reminiscence is the opposite of forgetting, for it is the phenomenon in which performance increases after a rest interval and is therefore attributable to rest. It is also believed to occur only when the task has been partially learned. Reminiscence was not isolated as separate from the

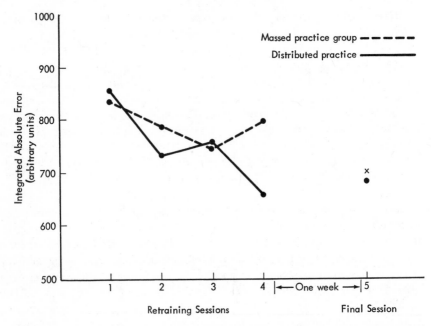

Figure 9–34.   Effect of different retraining programs during retraining and after a further one-week rest. The subjects were tested on a tracking task. (From E. A. Fleishman and James F. Parker, Jr., "Factors in the Retention and Relearning of Perceptual-Motor Skill," *Journal of Experimental Psychology,* 64:215–226, 1962.)

distribution effects of practice until the work of Ballard (1913). He read passages from "The Ancient Mariner" for fifteen minutes to elementary school children and then required them to write all that could be remembered. The students were then divided into smaller groups and were tested from one to seven days later. The reminiscence peak was found to be greatest after a two-day delay, as the students remembered more at that point than immediately after the reading.

Since the publication of this study, researchers have manipulated numerous variables in order to determine the effects on reminiscence. Reminiscence may be dependent upon a number of factors, such as the type of learning technique employed, type of subject matter, degree of mastery before rest, type of practice (degree of distribution), and length of the rest interval. Reminiscence in motor-learning studies has not received a great deal of attention, but it is interesting to speculate about its existence and the processes that contribute to it.

Gross motor skills have been of concern in some studies, but the nature of the designs and the tasks employed makes it difficult to make any definite statements about the way reminiscence works.

Fox and Young (1962) instructed two groups of students for six weeks and nine weeks in badminton skills. They were tested after six weeks and twelve weeks of no practice on a wall-volley test and short serve test. No reminiscence was noticed on the short service test. The group instructed for nine weeks did significantly better after six weeks than the group given six weeks of instruction, but there was no difference between the groups after twelve weeks. The former group regressed while the latter group improved and displayed the effects of reminiscence. Evidently, the additional three weeks of instruction did not contribute to long-term retention.

Purdy and Lockhart (1962) tested subjects one year after they had learned five novel skills, e.g., ball toss and foot volley. These investigators discovered that 89 per cent of the subjects displayed reminiscence in one or more of the skills, an incidence of reminiscence much higher than found in other studies. It is difficult to generalize how long after the termination of practice performance increases, and if indeed it will increase. The method most used in measuring reminiscence is a comparison of skill demonstrated after a specified interval of time with the amount displayed at the end of formal practice. Thus far, it appears that studies yield inconsistent results as to the optimal rest period following practice for reminiscence.

Research also indicates that the method of distributing practice might reflect greater or lesser degrees of reminiscence. It seems that relative massing of practice trials will afford the greatest amount of reminiscence, which in turn will result in a similar performance or in a performance slightly below that of a distributed practice group. A possible explanation is that at the immediate conclusion of practice the distributed practice usually yields a superior performance but after a rest period the distributed group performs less effectively, the massed group better, and therefore ultimately both are approximately equal.

The traditional explanation of reminiscence is associated with inhibition theory, where rest presumably allows the dissipation of reactive inhibition, a transient inhibitory potential that builds up within a person as a result of continuously responding in a task with little or no rest. Such suggestions were made by Clark Hull in the 1940's and still have appeal today, especially to classical behaviorists.

Another point of view has been expressed in recent years that has great appeal but insufficient research support at the present time. It is associated with activation theory. Possibly reduced performance following massed practice may be due to a diminished activation level and subsequent rest and the administration of additional task trials or a test resulting in reminiscence, or improved performance, is a consequence of the return to a more optimal arousal level. Some studies have shown the beneficial effects on reminiscence from interpolated activity situations geared to increase a subject's activation level. For instance, the data from David Hammond's (1972) two experiments were in accordance with the arousal theory explanation of reminiscence. A visual stimulus (a 1,000-watt light flash) or a cold temperature stimulus (hand immersion in water at 10°C) provided during rest after massed practice on a pursuit rotor led to a significant reminiscence effect. Reminiscence is also a function of ability level (Eysenck and Gray, 1971), as high-ability individuals demonstrate greater reminiscence effects.

Learning Tasks

As a general rule, it may be stated that gross motor skills are retained for many years at a higher skill level than any other learning materials, such as fine motor skills and prose. We may have last performed on a bicycle when twelve years of age, but even after an eight-year layoff, cycling ability would be extremely high. Compare this situation with a passage memorized from a poem or from history, learned years ago and not practiced for a long period of time. Would you expect to recall the passage with the same degree of accuracy that you demonstrated on the bicycle? Of course not.

The long-term retention permanence of motor skills was demonstrated in a series of experiments undertaken by Swift at the beginning of the twentieth century. Edgar Swift (1906), using himself as the subject, learned to type over a fifty-day period. Two years elapsed before he touched a typewriter again, and it took him only eleven days to reach the same proficiency he had attained after fifty days. Swift (1905) had two subjects practice keeping two balls going with one hand, one ball being caught and thrown while the other was in the air. After rest periods of over 600 days, retention tests indicated that the subjects in all but two instances performed better than they had at the close of regular practice. Employing the same skill (ball juggling), Swift (1910) practiced for forty-two days and then waited six years before attempting the skill again. It took him only eleven days to relearn the act and demonstrate a performance equivalent to that at the end of the original practice.

More specifically, within the motor-skill domain, continuous tasks are retained better than discrete tasks even after long periods of no practice. Riding a bicycle and swimming are examples of continuous tasks; a test of reaction time constitutes a discrete task. Apparently least interference from the experiencing of other activities occurs with continuous tasks. They are usually overlearned (overpracticed), contain kinesthetic cue characteristics that aid in immediately arousing memory traces, and errors can be corrected quickly. Discrete motor-learning tasks and verbal tasks may be less well remembered than continuous motor tasks because the factors primarily mentioned do not operate as favorably in this category of behavior.

An important consideration as to what is retained is the meaningfulness to the learner of that which is learned. Nonsense syllables are forgotten very quickly (compare the learning curves in Figure 9–35). Some prose is retained longer than other prose, depending on its meaningfulness, not only logically but also in importance to the person. Motor skills, especially to children, are held high in personal worth and efforts to achieve are intensive and extensive. There is a relative permanence to the meaningful material that we learn.

Although motor skills are generally retained better than other types of learned material, the more abstract they are the more the retention curve resembles that of verbal or written matter. For instance, Adams and Dijkstra (1966) had their subjects learn a motor task that required mastering the positioning of sliding elements on a bar. Retention was tested in intervals ranging from five to 120 seconds. The results fundamentally agreed with the findings of verbal research on short-term memory: that rapid forgetting occurs with the passage of time but the performance becomes more stable with reinforcement.

There is a danger in comparing the retention of verbal and motor tasks. Methods and measures differ in each situation. There is really no pure way of establishing and comparing the capacities of people to retain verbal and motor tasks. For instance, in many verbal tasks a person is asked to recall, without any prompts or cues. When asked to ride a bicycle, the person can recognize old cues, as is the case in swimming, where he is surrounded by a familiar situation. In other words, retention testing seems to be generally biased in favor of motor skills over verbal tasks.

Dean Ryan (1962) tested eighty men after three, five, seven, and twenty-one days had lapsed from practice on stabilometer and pursuit rotor

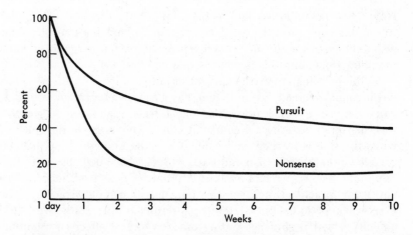

Figure 9–35.   Retention comparison of verbal material (nonsense syllables) and a motor skill (pursuit rotor). (From Harold J. Leavitt and H. Schlosberg, "The Retention of Verbal and of Motor Skills," *Journal of Experimental Psychology,* 34:404–417, 1944.)

skills. Little or no loss in performance was found on the retention days tested, and the pursuit rotor skill was retained better than that of the stabilometer. Ryan was interested in extending the retention periods to determine the lasting effects of a once-learned motor skill. In a second study (1965) Ryan gave eleven initial learning trials on the stabilometer to his subjects, who were divided later into three groups to be tested three months, six months, and one year after the termination of practice. There was no significant difference on the first retention trial for all three groups; all showed a loss in proficiency. A longer nonpractice period resulted in more trials needed to regain the earlier proficiency.

Once again, unusual motor tasks will not be retained as well as the familiar ones, for example, sports skills. Everyday experience and empirical evidence support the notion of the long-lasting effects of once-learned athletic skills. Explanations for this phenomenon may lie in one or all of the following suggestions. It may be due to the relative importance motor-skill achievement has to the individual. Perhaps it occurs because of the total body effort intellectually and physically needed to perform an athletic skill successfully. Athletic skill retention can also be explained by simply examining the number of hours devoted to its learning as compared to the time spent in learning a literary passage. Whereas a child may allocate a few hours for memorizing a poem, he plays softball incessantly. Is it any wonder, then, that the greater number of stimulus-response occurrences in the athletic situation results in superior retention?

Overlearning

How much should a task be practiced for it to be learned sufficiently? The rub in this question is the word *sufficiently*. Perhaps the question should be restated to read: How much practice is necessary for the greatest amount of retention (assuming this is what is desired)?

All things being equal, the amount of initial practice is directly related to the amount retained, as retention has been demonstrated to be higher when the task is well learned. Partially learned material is forgotten faster than mastered material. Of course, it would be extremely difficult to know when the skill is learned well enough and the individual has had enough practice. But, as Fleishman and Parker (1962) have demonstrated, the most important factor in retention is the initial level of proficiency. These investigators practiced their subjects on a highly complex tracking task over a six-week period. Other interesting results of the study were (1) the amount of verbal guidance during practice had no effect on retention; (2) massed and distributed practice effects did not differ on a retention test given one week after practice; and (3) retention on this motor task was quite high, even after a rest period of twenty-four months.

Retention will be even more enhanced if the skill is overlearned. *Over-*

learning, as defined earlier, refers to practice provided on a task after it has been learned according to some criterion. The criterion in many psychological studies dealing with the learning of written material is one perfect recitation. If precise experimental control is wanted, the number of trials it takes the subject to achieve the criterion measure is recorded. The researcher can then arbitrarily provide the subject with more practice trials on the task, and by dividing this figure by the original number of practices, the percentage of overlearning is derived. Invariably, studies concerned with overlearning find that greater practice beyond the learning criterion results in better retention performances.

Merrill Melnick (1971) conducted one of the few investigations in the overlearning area with a motor-learning task, balancing on a stabilometer. Subjects received 0, 50, 100, or 200 per cent overlearning. Retention tests were given one week or one month later. Absolute retention (immediate recall) was measured on the basis of the subjects' score on the first retention trial, whereas relative retention was arrived at with a per cent of saving score based on the ratio of trials taken for initial mastery and trials taken on the retention test to reach a criterion. The absolute retention measure showed retention intervals to be favored by overlearning, with the different overlearning percentages approximately equally as effective. Relative retention scores led to one major difference: 200 per cent overlearning was significantly better than 0 per cent in the one-month retention test.

There is some practical concern as to who are the best retainers, fast or slow learners. If a person acquires skill quickly, will he also retain it at a high level of proficiency? Early studies showed that fast learners were better retainers than slow learners. However, a weakness in testing procedure was that both types of learners had the same number of learning trials. The fast learners retained more because they learned more initially. Later studies have usually demonstrated that if all the subjects have to reach an initial learning criterion regardless of the number of practice trials, the slow learner will score higher on retention tests. This could be explained by the overlearning effect.

An exception to the notion that fast learners are at a disadvantage when compared to slow learners in retaining learned tasks is reported by Melnick, Lersten, and Lockhart (1972). Three groups of subjects were formed on the basis of speed with which (number of trials) they achieved a criterion score on a balance task. Retention scores were similar among the groups. The fast learners, those who took a relatively small number of trials to reach criterion, were not apparently handicapped in the one-week-later retention test. However, it should be pointed out that, between the initial learning trials and the retention test, all subjects were provided with 100 per cent overlearning practice. Coupled with a task ceiling effect, thirty seconds on any trial is maximum performance, it is possible that the additional practice allowed the "fast" learning group to have enough practice on this particular task to confound the retention test scores. Nevertheless, the problem is worthy of further study, for the implications are great for understanding retention theory and for practical implications in practice arrangements for learners who initially acquire skills at different rates of speed.

Proactive and Retroactive Inhibition

The things we typically learn are not isolated, but rather fall into sequential patterns of various learning materials. Because of this fact, the learning and retention of a particular response might very well be affected by what is learned, especially of a related nature, before and after training on this response. Going a step further and translating this to psychological terms, if a specific response is desired for a given stimulus ($S_1 - R_1$) and a second response is learned for this same stimulus ($S_1 - R_2$) either before or after $S_1 - R_1$ occurs, interference in retention of $S_1 - R_1$ will be observable.

Proactive inhibition refers to the negative effect one learned task has on the retention of a newer task. *Retroactive inhibition* describes the condition when a recently learned task impairs the retention performance of an older learned task. Generally, experimental designs to measure proaction or retroaction are as follows:

PROACTION

Groups	Prior Learning	Desired Learning	Recall
Experimental	Task B	Task A	Task A*
Control	None	Task A	Task A

RETROACTION

Groups	Original Learning	Interpolated Learning	Recall
Experimental	Task A	Task B	Task A*
Control	Task A	Rest	Task A

* Although Task A recall is desired, Task A and Task B responses will conflict.

Proactive inhibition has been investigated considerably less than retroactive inhibition and, at one time, was thought to be less of an influence on retention than retroactive inhibition. However, what is true of one condition is usually true of the other. It does not matter whether related tasks are learned before or after the desired learning task; inhibition of varying degrees will occur on retention tests. With retroaction, the desired response has been weakened by the second learned response; but in proaction, it is the first competing response that has been weakened by the learning of the desired response, the second one.

Forgetting is thought to occur because of a competition of responses, and certainly this is the case in proaction and retroaction. We live in a verbal world and learn many, many words in a lifetime. Retroaction and proaction are constantly building up, causing relatively much and rapid forgetting. Motor skills are not forgotten quickly, mainly because there are not that many to learn, many are unique, and they are practiced at great length. In learning to ride a bicycle, one has to adjust to such factors as balance and gravity. Bicycle riding will not be unlearned for there are no competing responses to this situation. It should be remembered, though, that negative transfer can occur in motor-skill learning, and any time S_1 is presented after R_1 and R_2 have become associated with it, there is the danger of conflict.

Theories of Retention and Forgetting

It is usually felt that forgetting is a decline in performance caused by the passage of time. However, experimental evidence points to the fact that ultimate retention will be more dependent on the intervening events than on time per se. Greater activity brings about the development of competing response tendencies, thus resulting in a higher degree of forgetting.

Experimentally, this idea is verified by holding the time period constant between the last original learning trial and the recall test but varying the amount of intervening activity. If time alone is responsible for forgetting, the recall scores should be the same, regardless of time spent in activity. But this is not the case. If four groups had learned certain material and were tested after twenty-four hours on a retention test, with Group A allowed only two hours of activity during this rest period, Group B four hours of activity, Group C twelve hours, and Group D actively responding for the entire twenty-four-hour period, performance on the recall test could be predicted. Whereas the least active group during the retention period would do best on the recall test the most active group would perform worst of all.

One can gather from this discussion that we should be able to retain more after sleep than following waking activities. Whether something, once learned, is ever truly forgotten is open to question. Freud's work as well as that of others interested in psychoanalysis indicates not only that early life experience and behavior are important in determining later life behavior, but also that many childhood experiences can be recalled under emotional recall situations. Things learned can be retained better under more favorable learning situations and more efficient learning techniques. Currently major advances are being made in the memorization of written and verbal material through coding techniques. However, the process of forgetting is still not well understood, from either psychological or physiological viewpoints.

How can we explain what is retained and the strength of this later performance? Theorists representing different schools of thought approach the matter in various ways. Walker (1958) believes that high arousal during the associative process (practice) results in greater permanent memory. Koffka (1935), a leader in Gestalt psychology, states that a greater organization of the stimulus trace results in less probability of its weakening over time. Broadbent (1958) writes that perceptual filters operate during attempted retention, and recall will occur if the correct channel is monitored and monitored at the right time. These concepts are still being explored today.

Interesting theories have been advanced to explain performance during and after massed and distributed practice. McGeoch (1961) has reviewed numerous theories and categorizes them as follows: work theories, perseveration theories, and differential forgetting theories.

Differential forgetting theories, according to McGeoch, generally handle massed and distributed practice effects by stating that during practice a subject learns incorrect and conflicting responses as well as correct ones. Because the conflicting associations are probably less well learned than the appropriate responses, the conflicting ones will dissipate with rest at a faster rate than during practice. Therefore, according to the theory, learning will take place faster during distributed practice because the incorrect responses will have had an opportunity to drop out more quickly than under massed practice conditions. However, there are theoretical limitations as to the desirable length of the rest interval.

Reminiscence would be explained in a similar manner: rest intervals provide an opportunity for the dropping out or forgetting of wrong associations that are less strongly favored than the right ones and hence are forgotten more rapidly. Under this theory, massed practice would probably be expected to yield a greater reminiscence effect than distributed practice.

Perseveration theories tend to hold that some activity persists in the individual after the termination of practice, therefore resulting in the learned response becoming more strongly fixated than it was previously. Neural processes presumably perseverate for a considerable time following learning. Distributed practice permits the setting-in process to proceed with minimal interference, whereas massed practice would not allow enough time to permit this activity to occur.

Work theories generally state that the act of repeating a response tends to build up either a loss of interest, boredom, physical fatigue, or mental fatigue. The interfering processes presumably disappear with rest and the more permanent learned responses would supposedly remain.

Clark Hull's (1943) theory, based on a theoretical construct called *reactive inhibition*, is most representative of the work theories and probably has encouraged more investigations in the area of massed versus distributed practice than any other theory. Hull postulates that two inhibitory processes occur when responses are made, reactive inhibition (I_R) and conditioned inhibition (S^IR). I_R is temporary by nature and dissipates with time whereas S^IR is relatively permanent. With increased practice the temporary work decrement increases and explains the poorer performance of subjects learning under massed practice conditions. By the same token, distributed practice permits I_R effects to disappear more easily; hence the superior performance of distributed-practice subjects. Also, reminiscence is described as occurring when the I_R effects have been rendered ineffective as a result of rest from repeating the desired responses.

However, Hull's work theory holds that over a long time interval reactive potential diminishes. Supposedly, reactive inhibition disappears after ten to twenty minutes of rest, resulting in increased performance at that time. Some writers are of the opinion that perhaps I_R lasts for a day or even a week. Even if it lasted for a month, there is no logical explanation as to why the disappearance of I_R should result in an eventual superior performance for massed-practice subjects than for distributed-practice subjects. Considering that all subjects had experienced the same number of practice trials, the associated strength for the habit should at best be equal under massed and distributed conditions.

Some investigators have applied Hull's basic concepts to motor-skill learning, more specifically, rotary-pursuit learning. Kimble (1949) calls his theory a "Two-Factor Theory of Inhibition." Proponents of this theory state that in many studies, especially those employing motor tasks, rest periods are too short to allow for the dissipation of the majority of the reactive inhibition. Figure 9–36 illustrates how pursuit-rotor performance would fit into this theory.

When a subject learns under relatively massed practice, an inhibition develops that hinders performance rather than learning. Therefore performance would be weaker under massed conditions than under distributed practice because the inhibition dissipates rapidly with rest. Precisely what the optimal rest period is for superior performance has been disputed as a result of the findings of various studies. Most likely, inhibition affects performance rather than what is learned.

Perhaps the amount of effort exerted by the subject in learning will have its effects on performance (Ellis, 1953). More effortful behavior might result in a greater amount of I_R present and therefore a greater need to cease activity. Effortfulness would depend on the physical energy required for the learning of the task and the length of time without rest while practicing.

The fact that greater overall bodily effort is required for the mastery of athletic skills as contrasted to learning nonsense syllables or rotary-pursuit tasks may be one of the reasons why reminiscence has been demonstrated after twelve or more weeks of no practice of athletic skills. Massed practice

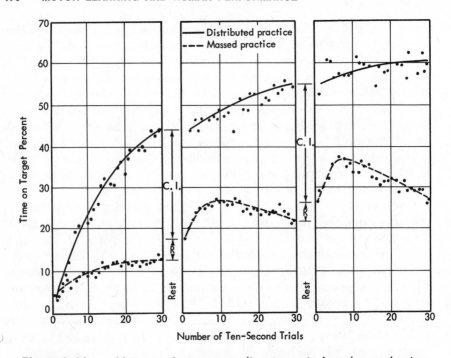

Figure 9–36. Motor performance as it represents learning and retention during and after massed and distributed practice conditions and according to Hullian Theory. Pursuit-rotor performance varies markedly with the spacing of the trial, or practice, periods. Each dot represents the average time-on-target during a 10-second period. The upper curve shows the performance of subjects who were allowed a 30-second rest pause between each 10-second trial. The lower curve shows the performance of subjects denied such a rest. Both groups were given two 10-minute rest periods. The improvement in performance shown by the massed-practice group immediately following the 10-minute break is called reminiscence (R), which is believed to be a measure of reactive inhibition accumulated during massed practice. The major depressant on scores of the massed-practice group, however, is conditioned inhibition (C.I.). (From H. J. Eysenck, "The Measurement of Motivation," *Scientific American,* 208:130–140, 1963.) Copyright © 1963 by Scientific American, Inc. All rights reserved.

would theoretically be less effective with the learning of gross motor skills than other learning materials because of the effort involved. On the same explanatory grounds, reminiscence should then be greater after practicing these gross motor skills.

Factors Contributing to Retention

At this point we can generalize from the material presented on retention as to those techniques or procedures favoring increasing probabilities of high retention.

1. Material should be well organized for the benefit of the learner, so there will be ease in internally organizing it for storage and retrieval purposes.
2. Material should be meaningful as perceived by the learner.
3. Material should be well learned (overpracticed).
4. Competing activities should be minimized, from time of practice to test of retention.
5. Time lag from practice to retention should not be too long, or else some related task experiences should occur in the interval.
6. Material should be presented in such a way as to be compatible with the information-processing abilities of the learner, considering transition from STM to LTM.
7. Retention tests should encourage the opportunity for the person to reorient.
8. The use of covert rehearsal or observation of others performing the task in the rest interval can be beneficial.

An excellent review of literature of factors involved in retention has been prepared by James Naylor and George Briggs (1961). The number of variables of conceivable influence is unbelievably large. A more recent and contemporary overview of the literature has been developed by George Stelmach (1974).

REFERENCES

ADAMS, JACK. "Retention: Nature, Measurement, and Fundamental Processes," in Melvin H. Marx, (ed.), *Learning: Processes*. New York: Macmillan Publishing Co., Inc., 1969.

―――. "The Relationship Between Certain Measures of Ability and the Acquisition of a Psychomotor Criterion Response," *Journal of General Psychology*, 56:121–134, 1957.

―――, and SANNE DIJKSTRA. "Short-Term Memory for Motor Responses," *Journal of Experimental Psychology*, 71:314–318, 1966.

―――, ERNEST T. GOETZ, and PHILLIP H. MARSHALL. "Response Feedback and Motor Learning," *Journal of Experimental Psychology*, 92:391–397, 1972.

ADLER, JACK DELBERT. *The Use of Programmed Lessons in Teaching a Complex Perceptual-Motor Skill,* unpublished doctoral dissertation, University of Oregon, 1967.

AMMONS, ROBERT B. "Effect of Distribution of Practice on Rotary Pursuit 'Hits,'" *Journal of Experimental Psychology,* 41:17–22, 1951.

_____. "Effects of Knowledge of Performance: A Survey and Tentative Theoretical Formulation," *Journal of General Psychology,* 54:279–299, 1956.

AMMONS, R. B., C. H. AMMONS, and R. L. MORGAN. "Transfer of Skill and Decremented Factors Along the Speed Dimension in Rotary Pursuit," *Perceptual and Motor Skills,* 11:43, 1958.

ANNETT, JOHN. *Feedback and Human Behavior.* Baltimore: Penguin Books, 1969.

ATKINSON, JOHN W. "Motivational Determinants of Risk-Taking Behavior," *Psychology Review,* 64:359–372, 1957.

ATKINSON, RICHARD C., and RICHARD M. SHIFFREN. "The Control of Short-Term Memory," *Scientific American,* 216:2–10, 1971.

BAHRICK, HARRY P. "Retention Curves: Facts or Artifacts?" *Psychological Bulletin,* 61:188–194, 1964.

BAKER, KATHERINE E., R. C. WYLIE, and R. M. GAGNÉ. "Transfer of Training to a Motor Skill as a Function of Variation in Rate of Response," *Journal of Experimental Psychology,* 40:721–732, 1950.

BALLARD, PHILIP B. "Obliviscence and Reminiscence," *British Journal of Psychology Monographs Supplements,* no. 2, 1913.

BARCH, A. M., and D. LEWIS. "The Effect of Task Difficulty and Amount of Practice on Proactive Transfer," *Journal of Experimental Psychology,* 48:134–142, 1954.

BAYTON, JAMES A., and HAROLD W. CONLEY. "Duration of Success Background and the Effect of Failure upon Performance," *Journal of General Psychology,* 56:179–185, 1957.

BERENDSEN, CAROL A. *The Relative Effectiveness of Descriptive Teaching and Structured Problem Solving in Learning Basic Tennis Skills,* unpublished master's thesis, University of Washington, 1967.

BILODEAU, INA McD. "Information Feedback," in Ina McD. Bilodeau (ed.), *Principles of Skill Acquisition.* New York: Academic Press, Inc., 1969.

BIRCH, DAVID, and JOSEPH VEROFF. *Motivation: A Study of Action.* Belmont, Calif.: Brooks/Cole Publishing Co., 1966.

BRIGGS, GEORGE E., and W. J. BROGDEN. "The Effect of Component Practice on Performance of a Lever-Positioning Skill," *Journal of Experimental Psychology,* 48:375–380, 1954.

_____, and LAWRENCE K. WATERS. "Training and Transfer as a Function of Component Interaction," *Journal of Experimental Psychology,* 56:492–500, 1958.

BROADBENT, D. E. *Perception and Communication.* London: Pergamon Press, 1958.

CHILD, IRWIN L., and JOHN W. WHITING. "Determinants of Level of Aspiration: Evidence from Everyday Life," *Journal of Abnormal Social Psychology*, 44:303–314, 1949.

CLARK, L. VERDELLE. "Effect of Mental Practice on the Development of a Certain Motor Skill," *Research Quarterly*, 31:560–569, 1960.

CLIFFORD, MARGARET M. "Competition as a Motivational Technique in the Classroom," *American Educational Research Journal*, 9:123–137, 1972.

COOK, THOMAS W. "Studies in Cross-Education: Mirror Tracing the Star-Shaped Maze," *Journal of Experimental Psychology*, 16:144–160, 1933a.

————. "Studies in Cross-Education: Further Experiments in Mirror Tracing the Star-Shaped Maze," *Journal of Experimental Psychology*, 16:679–700, 1933b.

DAY, R. H. "Relative Task Difficulty and Transfer of Training in Skilled Performance," *Psychological Bulletin*, 53:160–168, 1956.

DEUTSCH, J. ANTHONY. "Neural Basis of Memory," *Psychology Today*, 2:56–60, 1968.

DICKINSON, J. "The Role of Two Factors in a Gross Motor Aiming Task," *British Journal of Psychology*, 60:465–470, 1969.

ELLIS, DOUGLAS S. "Inhibition Theory and the Effort Variables," *Psychology Review*, 60:383–392, 1953.

EYSENCK, H. J. "The Measurement of Motivation," *Scientific American*, 208:130–140, 1963.

————, and J. E. GRAY. "Reminiscence and the Shape of the Learning Curve as a Function of Subjects' Ability Level on the Pursuit Rotor," *British Journal of Psychology*, 62:199–215, 1971.

FINE, BERNARD J. "Intrinsic Motivation, Intelligence and Personality as Related to Cognitive and Motor Performance," *Perceptual and Motor Skills*, 34:319–329, 1972.

FLEISHMAN, EDWIN A. "A Relationship Between Incentive Motivation and Ability Level in Psychomotor Performance," *Journal of Experimental Psychology*, 56:78–81, 1958.

————, and WALTER E. HEMPEL, JR. "Changes in Factor Structure of a Complex Psychomotor Test as a Function of Practice," *Psychometrika*, 19:239–252, 1954.

————, and JAMES F. PARKER. "Factors in the Retention and Relearning of Perceptual-Motor Skill," *Journal of Experimental Psychology*, 64:215–226, 1962.

————, and SIMON RICH. "Role of Kinesthetic and Spatial-Visual Abilities in Perceptual-Motor Learning," *Journal of Experimental Psychology*, 66:6–11, 1963.

FOX, MARGARET C., and VERA P. YOUNG. "Effect of Reminiscence on Learning Selected Badminton Skills," *Research Quarterly*, 73:386–394, 1962.

FRIEDLANDER, FRANK. "Motivations to Work and Organizational Performance," *Journal of Applied Psychology*, 50:143–152, 1966.

FULTON, RUTH E. "Speed and Accuracy in Learning Movements," *Archives of Psychology*, No. 300, 1945.

GAGNÉ, ROBERT M. *Psychological Principles in System Development*. New York: Holt, Rinehart and Winston, Inc., 1966.

GIBBS, C. B. "Transfer of Training and Skill Assumptions in Tracking Tasks," *Quarterly Journal of Experimental Psychology*, 3:99–110, 1951.

GORDON, NORMAN B. "Guidance Versus Augmented Feedback and Motor Skill," *Journal of Experimental Psychology*, 77:24–30, 1968.

GREENWALD, ANTHONY G. "Sensory Feedback Mechanisms in Performance Control: With Special Reference to the Ideo-Motor Mechanism," *Psychological Review*, 77:73–99, 1970.

GRIFFITH, COLEMAN R. *Psychology of Coaching*. New York: Charles Scribner's Sons, 1932.

HALSTEAD, WARD C., and WILLIAM B. RUCKER. "Memory: A Molecular Maze," *Psychology Today*, 2:38–41, 66–67, 1968.

HAMMOND, DAVID. "Effects of Visual and Thermal Stimulation upon Reminiscence in Rotary Pursuit Tracking," *The Irish Journal of Psychology*, 3:177–184, 1972.

HARLOW, HARRY F. "The Formation of Learning Sets," *Psychological Review*, 56:51–65, 1949.

HARMON, JOHN M., and JOSEPH B. OXENDINE. "Effect of Different Lengths of Practice Periods on the Learning of a Motor Skill," *Research Quarterly*, 32:34–41, 1961.

HINRICHS, J. R. "Ability Correlates in Learning a Psychomotor Task," *Journal of Applied Psychology*, 54:56–64, 1970.

HOLDING, D. H. "Repeated Errors in Motor Learning," *Ergonomics*, 13:727–734, 1970.

HOWARTH, C. I., W. D. A. BEGGS, and J. M. BOWDEN. "The Relationship Between Speed and Accuracy of Movement Aimed at a Target," *Acta Psychologica*, 35:207–218, 1971.

HULL, CLARK L. *Principles of Behavior*. New York: Appleton-Century-Crofts, Inc., 1943.

HURLOCK, E. B. "An Evaluation of Certain Incentives on School Work," *Journal of Educational Psychology*, 16:145–159, 1925.

JOHNSON, MARION C. "Gestalten Practice Pattern Selection: Methodology and Task Structure," *Quest*, 14:56–64, 1970.

JOHNSTON, JAMES M. "Punishment of Human Behavior," *American Psychologist*, 27:1033–1054, 1972.

JONES, JOHN GERALD. "Motor Learning Without Demonstration of Physical Practice under Two Conditions of Mental Practice," *Research Quarterly*, 36:270–276.

KEELE, STEVEN W. *Attention and Human Performance*. Pacific Palisades, Calif.: Goodyear Publishing Co., 1973.

KELLEY, CHARLES R. "What Is Adaptive Training?" *Human Factors*, 11:547–556, 1969.

KIMBLE, GREGORY A. "An Experimental Test of a Two-Factor Theory of Inhibition," *Journal of Experimental Psychology*, 39:15–23, 1949.

KNAPP, BARBARA. *Skill in Sports: The Attainment of Proficiency*. London: Routledge and Kegan Paul, 1964.

KNAPP, CLYDE G., and W. ROBERT DIXON. "Learning to Juggle: I. A Study to Determine the Effect of Two Different Distributions of Practice on Learning Efficiency," *Research Quarterly*, 21:331–336, 1950.

KOFFKA, K. *Principles of Gestalt Psychology*. New York: Harcourt Brace Jovanovich, Inc., 1935.

LEONARD, PEGGY L. *A Self-instructional Unit for Learning Beginning Synchronized Swimming Stunts*, unpublished master's thesis, Southern Illinois University, 1970.

LEONARD, S. DAVID, EDWARD W. KARNES, JOSEPH OXENDINE, and JOHN HESSON. "Effects of Task Difficulty on Transfer Performance on Rotary Pursuit," *Perceptual and Motor Skills*, 30:731–736, 1970.

LOCKE, EDWIN A. "The Relationship of Intentions to Level of Performance," *Journal of Applied Psychology*, 50:60–66, 1966.

————. "Toward a Theory of Task Motivation and Incentives," *Organizational Behavior and Human Performance*, 3:157–189, 1968.

————, and JUDITH F. BRYAN. "Cognitive Aspects of Psychomotor Performance: The Effects of Performance Goals on Level of Performance," *Journal of Applied Psychology*, 50:286–291, 1966.

LOGAN, GENE A., and AILEENE LOCKHART. "Contralateral Transfer of Specificity of Strength Training," *Journal of American Physical Therapy Association*, 42:658–660, 1962.

LORDAHL, D. S., and E. J. ARCHER. "Transfer Effects on a Rotary Pursuit Task as a Function of First-Task Difficulty," *Journal of Experimental Psychology*, 56:421–426, 1958.

MAEHR, MARTIN L. *Toward a Framework for the Cross-Cultural Study of Achievement Motivation*, paper presented at the Annual Conference of the North American Society for the Study of Sport Psychology and Physical Activity, Allerton Park, Illinois, May 15, 1973.

MAGILL, RICHARD. "The Post-KR Interval: Time and Activity Effects and the Relationship of Motor Short-Term Memory," *Journal of Motor Behavior*, 5:49–56, 1973.

MALINA, ROBERT M., and G. LAWRENCE RARICK. "A Device for Assessing the Role of Information Feedback in Speed and Accuracy of Throwing Performance," *Research Quarterly*, 39:120–123, 1968.

MASSEY, DOROTHY. "The Significance of Interpolated Time Intervals on Motor Learning," *Research Quarterly*, 30:189–201, 1959.

MAY, RICHARD B., and PAM DUNCAN. "Facilitation on a Response-Loaded Task by Changes in Task Difficulty," *Perceptual and Motor Skills*, 36:123–129, 1973.

McClelland, David C. "Methods of Measuring Human Motivation," in John W. Atkinson (ed.), *Motives in Fantasy, Action, and Society.* New York: Van Nostrand Reinhold Company, 1958.

McGeoch, John A. *The Psychology of Human Learning.* New York: David McKay Company, Inc., 1961.

McGuigan, F. J., and Eugene F. MacCaslin. "Whole and Part Methods of Learning a Perceptual Motor Skill," *American Journal of Psychology,* 68:658–661, 1955.

Melnick, Merrill J. "Effects of Overlearning on the Retention of a Gross Motor Skill," *Research Quarterly,* 42:60–69, 1971.

———, Kenneth C. Lernsten, and Aileene S. Lockhart. "Retention of Fast and Slow Learners Following Overlearning of a Gross Motor Skill," *Journal of Motor Behavior,* 4:187–193, 1972.

Mosston, Muska. *Teaching Physical Education.* Columbus, Ohio: Charles E. Merrill Books, Inc., 1966.

Naylor, James C., and George E. Briggs. "Long-Term Retention of Learned Skills: A Review of the Literature," ASD Technical Report 61–390, U.S. Department of Commerce, 1961.

Neimeyer, Roy. "Part Versus Whole Methods and Massed Versus Distributed Practice in the Learning of Selected Large Muscle Activities," *National College Physical Education Association for Men Proceedings,* 62:122–125, 1959.

Nelson, Dale O. "Effect of Swimming on the Learning of Selected Gross Motor Skills," *Research Quarterly,* 28:374–378, 1957a.

———. "Studies of Transfer of Learning in Gross Motor Skills," *Research Quarterly,* 28:364–373, 1957b.

Neuman, Milton C., and Robert N. Singer. "A Comparison of Traditional Versus Programmed Methods of Learning Tennis," *Research Quarterly,* 39:1044–1048, 1968.

Norman, Donald A. *Memory and Attention.* New York: John Wiley & Sons, Inc., 1969.

Nuttin, Joseph. *Reward and Punishment in Human Learning.* New York: Academic Press, Inc., 1968.

Osgood, C. E. "The Similarity Paradox in Human Learning: A Resolution," *Psychological Review,* 56:132–143, 1949.

Oxendine, Joseph B. "Effect of Progressively Changing Practice Schedules on the Learning of a Motor Skill," *Research Quarterly,* 36:307–315, 1965.

Perry, Horace M. "The Relative Efficiency of Actual and Imaginary Practice in Five Selected Tasks," *Archives of Psychology,* 243:1–76, 1939.

Prather, Dirk C. "Trial-and-Error Versus Errorless Learning: Training, Transfer and Stress," *American Journal of Psychology,* 84:377–385, 1971.

———, and Gene A. Berry. *Comparison of Trial-and-Error Versus Highly Prompted Learning of a Perceptual Skill,* paper presented at the 78th Annual Convention of the American Psychological Association, 1970.

PRIBRAM, KARL H. "The Neurophysiology of Remembering," *Scientific American*, 220:73–86, 1969.

PURDY, BONNIE J., and AILEENE LOCKHART. "Retention and Relearning of Gross Motor Skills After Long Periods of No Practice," *Research Quarterly*, 33:265–272, 1962.

RAWLINGS, EDNA I., IRVING L. RAWLINGS, STUART S. CHEN, and MARY DONIS YILK. "The Facilitating Effects of Mental Rehearsal in the Acquisition of Rotary Pursuit Tracking," *Psychonomic Science*, 26:71–73, 1972.

RAWLS, JAMES R., OLIVER PERRY, and EDWIN O. TIMMONS. "A Comparative Study of Conventional Instruction and Individual Programmed Instruction in the College Classroom," *Journal of Applied Psychology*, 50:388–391, 1966.

RICHARDSON, ALAN. "Mental Practice: A Review and Discussion," Part I, *Research Quarterly*, 38:95–107, 1967.

————. "Mental Practice: A Review and Discussion," Part II, *Research Quarterly*, 38:263, 1967.

RIVENES, RICHARD S., and MARTHA M. MAWHINNEY. "Retention of Perceptual Motor Skill: An Analysis of New Methods," *Research Quarterly*, 39:684–689, 1968.

ROTTER, JULIAN G. "Generalized Expectancies for Internal Versus External Control of Reinforcement," *Psychological Monographs*, 80(1), 1966.

RUSHALL, BRENT S., and JOHN PETTINGER. "An Evaluation of the Effects of Various Reinforcers Used as Motivation in Swimming," *The Research Quarterly*, 40:540–545, 1969.

————, and DARYL SIEDENTOP. *The Development and Control of Behavior in Sport and Physical Education.* Philadelphia: Lea & Febiger, 1972.

RYAN, E. DEAN. "Retention of Stabilometer and Pursuit Rotor Skills," *Research Quarterly*, 33:593–598, 1962.

————. "Retention of Stabilometer Performance over Extended Periods of Time," *Research Quarterly*, 36:46–51, 1965.

SCHMIDT, RICHARD A. "Experimental Psychology," in Robert N. Singer (ed.), *The Psychomotor Domain: Movement Behavior.* Philadelphia: Lea & Febiger, 1972.

SCHRAMM, WILBUR. "Programmed Instruction Today and Tomorrow," in Arthur Foshay et al. (ed.), *Programmed Instruction.* Washington, D.C.: U.S. Department of Health, Education, and Welfare, 1964.

SHIFFRIN, RICHARD M. "Forgetting: Trace Erosion or Retrieval Failure?" *Science*, 168:1601–1603, 1970.

SIMON, HERBERT A., and ALLEN NEWELL. "Human Problem Solving: The State of Theory in 1970," *American Psychologist*, 26:145–159, 1971.

SINGER, ROBERT N. "Transfer Effects and Ultimate Success in Archery Due to Degree of Difficulty of the Initial Learning," *Research Quarterly*, 37:532–539, 1966.

_____, and WALTER DICK. *Teaching Physical Education: A Systems Approach.* Boston: Houghton Mifflin Company, 1974.

_____, and JANET WITKER. "Mental Rehearsal and Point of Introduction Within the Context of Overt Practice," *Perceptual and Motor Skills,* 31:169–170, 1970.

SLAYTON, ARTHUR J., and ROGER W. BLACK. "Effects of Knowledge of Results and Amount of Stimulus Change on 'Resistance to Extinction' on a Perceptual Motor Task," *Psychonomic Science,* 22:111–112, 1971.

SMITH, CARNIE H. "The Influence of Athletic Success and Failure in the Level of Aspiration," *Research Quarterly,* 20:196–208, 1949.

SMOLL, FRANK L. "Effects of Precision of Information Feedback upon Acquisition of a Motor Skill," *Research Quarterly,* 43:489–493, 1972.

SOLLEY, WILLIAM H. "The Effects of Verbal Instruction of Speed and Accuracy upon the Learning of a Motor Skill," *Research Quarterly,* 23:231–240, 1952.

STELMACH, GEORGE E. "Retention of Motor Skills," in Jack Wilmore (ed.), *Review in Exercise and Sports Sciences,* Vol. II. New York: Academic Press, Inc., 1974.

SURWILLO, WALTER W. "A New Method of Motivating Human Behavior in Laboratory Investigations," *American Journal of Psychology,* 71:432–436, 1958.

SWIFT, EDGAR J. "Memory of a Complex Skillful Act," *American Journal of Psychology,* 16:131–133, 1905.

_____. "Memory of Skillful Movements," *Psychology Bulletin,* 3:185–187, 1906.

_____. "Relearning a Skillful Act: An Experimental Study in Neuromuscular Memory," *Psychology Bulletin,* 7:17–19, 1910.

TRAVERS, ROBERT M. *Essentials of Learning,* 2nd ed. New York: Macmillan Publishing Co., Inc., 1967.

TRUSSELL, ELLA. "Prediction of Success in a Motor Skill on the Basis of Early Learning Achievement," *Research Quarterly,* 39:342–347, 1965.

TWINING, WILBUR E. "Mental Practice and Physical Practice in Learning a Motor Skill," *Research Quarterly,* 20:432–435, 1949.

VINCENT, WILLIAM JOHN. "Transfer Effects Between Motor Skills Judged Similar in Perceptual Components," *Research Quarterly,* 39:380–388, 1968.

WAGLOW, I. F. "Effect of School Term Length on Skill Achievement in Tennis, Golf, and Handball," *Research Quarterly,* 37:157–159, 1966.

WALKER, E. L. "Action Decrement and Its Relation to Learning," *Psychological Review,* 65:129–142, 1958.

WEINER, BERNARD, and EDWARD L. WALKER. "Motivational Factors in Short-Term Retention," *Journal of Experimental Psychology,* 71:190–193, 1966.

WELCH, MARYA. "Prediction of Motor Skill Attainment from Early Learning," *Perceptual and Motor Skills,* 17:263–266, 1963.

WHILDEN, PEGGY P. "Comparison of Two Methods of Teaching Beginning Basketball," *Research Quarterly*, 27:235–242, 1956.

WHITLEY, JIM D. "Effects of Practice Distribution on Learning a Fine Motor Task," *Research Quarterly*, 48:576–583, 1970.

WICKSTROM, RALPH L. "Comparative Study of Methodologies for Teaching Gymnastics and Tumbling Stunts," *Research Quarterly*, 29:109–115, 1958.

————. "In Defense of Drills," *The Physical Educator*, 24:38–39, 1967.

WITTE, KENNETH L., and EUGENE E. GROSSMAN. "The Effects of Reward and Punishment Upon Children's Attention, Motivation, and Discrimination Learning," *Child Development*, 42:534–542, 1971.

WOODS, JOHN B. "The Effect of Varied Instructional Emphasis Upon the Development of a Motor Skill," *Research Quarterly*, 38:132–142, 1967.

WORELL, LEONARD. "Level of Aspiration and Academic Success," *Journal of Educational Psychology*, 50:47–54, 1959.

10

ENVIRONMENTAL
CONDITIONS AND
SOCIAL FACTORS

The human system obviously does not behave in a vacuum. We observed in the last chapter that practice settings could reflect a variety of learning considerations and in turn affect behaviors. In this chapter we will extend that discussion by examining the learning environment and performance in a broader context.

Intelligent modifications in the environment imposed by external sources can hasten insights into learning tasks, enrich the learning experience, and ultimately produce quality performance. But in some cases the environment is "given"; that is, the individual will have to cope with existing elements in the real performance situation. Thus we are interested here in the learner as he confronts his situation and attempts to master it. Three levels of interaction are indicated:

1. The individual and his task (isolation considerations).
2. The individual as he interacts with others (social considerations).
3. The individual as his attitudes and behaviors will be affected by sociocultural expectations and encouragement.

DISPLAYS

A currently popular notation for man–immediate situation interactions is display. A more limited interpretation of display is the characteristics of the task the individual confronts. For instance, reference is often made to the control panel of a plane as a display. The complex machinery that the industrial worker must operate is referred to as a display. Yet a display in which any type of motor activity is involved can go beyond these interpretations. We prefer to think of a display as the entire immediate performance environment and learning situation that involves the individual as he attempts to demonstrate skills to fulfill specified objectives.

Displays can be natural, untampered with by external sources. Or they can be modified for the convenience of the learner, considering the complexity of task, the skill level of the learner, and the apparent need to simplify the display to expedite the learning process.

Manipulations of displays can lead to more effective cueing devices, enriched and additional information, and augmented feedback. Modifications for such purposes can be introduced in timely ways but also must be removed gradually as performance improves and is to be demonstrated in the natural display setting. The design of a display compatible with task demands and learner capabilities is a real challenge. Displays can emphasize visual, tactile and proprioceptive, or auditory sensory modalities. Abilities related to these modalities may change in import as skill is acquired. The availability of aids and cues is another consideration. Any modification of displays should be made in accordance with scientific evidence and the unique dimensions of the learning tasks.

Most complex activities deserve special consideration, as more simple tasks can probably be handled without any modifications in the learning environment. Let us turn to possible ways in which a tampered-with display can be of benefit to the learner.

Communicative techniques between the instructor and learner that can impose situational modifications fall into three categories: the visual, verbal, and kinesthetic. The visual area encompasses modeling procedures whereby the student "gets the picture" of what is expected of him in performance standards. Direct observation of expert performances, films, illustrations, and television are some possibilities. The visual area also involves cuing or prompting techniques prior to or during performance, as well as feedback information (e.g., videotape) to be used as a performance regulatory mechanism. The verbal area includes words or sounds that might help the learner to understand task expectations, to cue, or to supplement feedback information about performance. The kinesthetic area includes physically guiding or manipulating the learner in difficult learning periods.

In engineering psychology, the concern is for man–machine, man–equipment interface. Inferior performances may be due to a poor interface, hence the need for designing effective ways for a human to integrate his behaviors with the capabilities of the equipment. A systems analysis suggests ways that this might occur. Display considerations, therefore, usually include man–equipment designs that lead to most productive results. Display aiding and cuing, and developing ways for people to master equipment and machinery, are factors that determine the functioning capabilities of the system.

Performance changes, for better or worse, may be due to training techniques or changes in equipment. It should be pointed out that when equipment is changed, training procedures should be modified accordingly. Aided displays and special training devices are used to simplify tasks, to encourage early and frequent correct responses, with the hope that such practice will effectively transfer to "real" tasks and "real" situations. So, in essence, whenever we refer to manipulated practice tasks and situations, *transfer of training* is at the heart of the matter.

Furthermore, display aiding and special training equipment hold implications for *mediated* instruction. In the traditional sense, the term *media* refers to the use of hardware and software equipment to aid the learning process. What with the current educational emphasis on technology and individualized instruction, a variety of media have been experimented with and implemented in instructional settings. Although certain contrived conditions may be expected to assist the average learner in skill acquisition, a respect for individual differences suggests a sensitivity to altering and adjusting instructional settings in particular cases.

Richard Burns (1971, p. 55) writes that "individualized instruction is a system which tailor-makes learning in terms of learner needs and characteristics." After learner diagnosis, a variety of instructional materials, aids, and experiences should be made available. Training should be as individualized as possible. Technological advancements, systems designs, and behavioral change principles help to facilitate the rate and quality of skill acquisition for groups and individuals.

Every instructor differs not only in respect to communication and planning, but also in methods of implementing and enriching particular experiences. Although some adhere to routinized training procedures, others look to supplemental materials and methods. Traditional procedures may be altered in many ways. Some of these approaches to motor learning are presented here, along with an evaluation of their worth as indicated by published research.

Verbal Aids

It is most uncommon to discover an organized instructional or training situation where verbal directions, comments, and cues are not issued by the instructor prior to, during, and following the practice of motor tasks. Words or sounds may (1) continually provide *instruction* and direction, (2) only be used as a *pretraining* technique for transfer value, (3) *prompt* the learner to respond to certain cues at specified moments, and (4) offer *correctional* advice following performance.

The latter two examples are found to some degree in many training programs, although the larger the ratio of learners to instructor the less likely they will be present. Without much in the way of research to refer to, circumstantial evidence would seem to encourage verbal cuing techniques in initial learning phases of a skill until internal timing capabilities can take over. Continuous tasks in which events occur requiring immediate responses could be verbally cued for a while. One particular act that contains a series of movements could be cued at various positioning points. As with any form of assistance, however, such cues should be removed from the learning situation as soon as possible before the person becomes too dependent on them.

With regard to the correctional values of verbal comments, once again there appears to be much inherent value in this procedure. Constructive suggestions help the individual to identify faulty and correct behaviors. Feedback of this type is especially useful when the task contains an insufficient amount of proprioceptive and visual information feedback. Feedback, or knowledge of results, can be received in a number of ways from a variety of sources, as we saw in the previous chapter. Verbal feedback, as is the case with any other kind, can be motivational, reinforcing, and directional.

Instructions for task learning can be presented orally or in written form. We cannot assume, however, that all types of instruction will be equally beneficial to all learners. Consideration must be given to

1. The ability of the learner to understand and relate verbal concepts to appropriate movement patterns. (Special problems exist with learners who are younger, are less intelligent, or have communication handicaps because of being raised in a different society, culture, or ethnic tradition.)
2. The meaningfulness of the directions (quality, length, and detail) as related to the particular task and learner.
3. The need for simplicity, explicitness, or detailed directions.

Some individuals respond better to certain modes of instruction than others. Drawing from this premise, certain people will learn faster than others from verbal comments on their motor activity. At the present time beginners as a group seem to benefit less than advanced learners from extensively detailed verbal directions. Younger children have less patience than mature learners and need to be immersed in activity. With respect to the nature of the task, a more complex one would probably require greater explanation and more teacher direction, but not necessarily at the beginning states of learning.

In fact, when verbal training is offered only at the beginning of a task, it is the simple task, not the complex one, that will be most positively affected. William Battig (1956) found verbal pretraining to facilitate performance on simpler motor tasks, but no benefit was shown from this pretraining on complex tasks. The subjects were tested on a finger-positioning apparatus. The degree of transfer from verbal pretraining decreased as a function of the complexity of the task. The more important actual performance is, as with difficult motor tasks, the less value verbal pretraining seems to have.

Verbal or written instructions can at best partially take the place of actual motor-skill practice, especially on skills containing a certain degree of challenge. Descriptions and ideas are one thing, experience another. The body must actively respond, and the kinesthetic receptors must be stimulated, if a high skill level is to be reached on complex motor tasks. Furthermore, verbal training that precedes motor training must be of sufficient quantity and quality in order to transfer favorably to motor-skill performance. This condition becomes evident in reviewing Baker and Wylie's (1950) experiment. Before practicing on a discrimination problem involving matching the correct switch to a light stimulus, their subjects received verbal training and memorized by the oral paired-associates method. The group that had eight verbal training trials did not show evidence of significant transfer to motor performance when time or the number of errors were used as measurements. However, the twenty-four verbal training trials brought about a significant transfer effect on both these measurements.

Actually, the things we usually learn are mediated by words. In the beginning stage of learning a task, the individual has to learn instructions to know how and what to perform. He must learn directions before he can obey. Not only are there words from external sources (instructors, teachers, and coaches) but words spoken to oneself during activity. This latter theoretical state has been termed *verbal mediation* and has also been referred to as conceptualization, ideation, or thought processing.

The ability, then, to succeed in motor performance may very well be related to a certain extent to being able to apply external and internal words to motor acts. Sometimes, however, the verbal mediation process may interfere with skilled performance. Consider, for example, the performer who thinks too much and gets confused, resulting in a delayed reaction to a given situation. This is especially detrimental in a game, where players have to respond immediately to unpredictable openings and occurrences.

Instruction can be informational, directional, and motivational. Its effectiveness therefore is dependent upon its timeliness, nature, and appropriateness for the learner. Instruction and cueing might occur more often where emphasis is on the demonstration of one correct behavior. Where the process of problem solving and discovery is desired, external verbal cues and aids should be minimal. Another consideration is the total time allotted to practice, more specifically, how much of it should be actual practice and how much should be devoted to instructions. Participants in most movement-oriented tasks are anxious to participate actively. They need sufficient direction, but not to the point where their channel capacity is overloaded and the information is dysfunctional. Nor to the extent that they become bored and frustrated. An optimal relationship between instruction and actual practice probably exists for any task.

Evidently an optimal amount of instruction was received in the study reported by Dorothy Davies (1945). Figure 10–1 illustrates the effects of tuition and a lack of it on learning archery skills. One group received regular and systematic instruction; the other had none. An interesting sidelight in this study was that brighter students, as measured by a mental ability test, tended to profit more from the instruction than the duller students. If the task to be learned is relatively easy, instructional material and cues will help the individual in the beginning to proceed on the right track. With practice on this type of task, further assistance from an outsider is usually unnecessary. Later in practice, the guidance will probably be remedial. Specific detail about the task and learner performance will lead to highest proficiency levels.

Further support for instruction in learning a motor task is offered by James Parker and Edwin Fleishman (1961). Detailed task analysis helped a group of college ROTC students to perform a tracking task better than two other groups (see Figure 10–2). Group I received no formal training

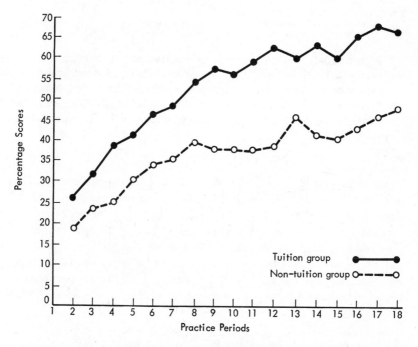

Figure 10–1.   Daily average percentage scores for two archery groups. (From Dorothy R. Davies, "The Effect of Tuition Upon the Process of Learning a Complex Skill," *Journal of Educational Psychology,* 36:352–365, 1945.)

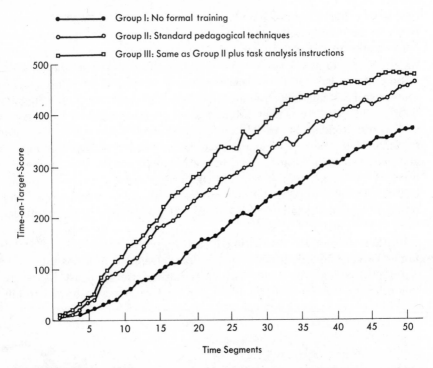

Figure 10–2.   The effects of instruction in the training process. (From J. F. Parker and E. A. Fleishman, "Use of Analytical Information Concerning Task Requirements to Increase the Effectiveness of Skill Training," *Journal of Applied Psychology,* 45:295–302, 1961. Copyright 1961 by the American Psychological Association. Reprinted by permission.)

other than a brief description of the task, performance expectations, and achievement score after each trial. Group II was administered in what Parker and Fleishman term a "common-sense" type of program, including explanation, guidance, assistance, and critiques of performance. Group III's training program was similar to that of Group II except that special ability demands of the task were used to develop special training procedures. Figure 10–2 illustrates that Group III's overall performance was superior to that of Group II, whose performance was higher than that of Group I.

Principles of Performance

From a theoretical point of view, it makes good sense to believe that if the individual understands what he is doing his performance should be facilitated. The ability to succeed in athletic and other skills depends many times on both intended and unintentional application of mechanical and kinesiological principles. Intentional usage of scientifically accepted movement patterns would seem to be a desirable objective. It is reasoned that the knowledge of mechanical principles will assist the learner in gaining quicker insight into and mastery of a given gross motor task.

Unfortunately, this "sound reasoning" of transfer has not been upheld consistently enough in experiments to gain acceptance. On the positive side, Dorothy Mohr and Mildred Barrett (1962) found that the learning of mechanical principles beyond actual physical activity was an effective teaching technique. In their study an experimental group of women learned mechanical principles associated with swim strokes; the other group did not. After fourteen weeks, the experimental group improved more than the control in all strokes except the elementary backstroke.

In an interesting study of principle transference to an assembly task, Johnson (1963) compared performance of experimental and control groups of normal and retarded children. With eighteen subjects in each of the four groups, the two experimental groups were instructed in a principle to facilitate performance on the motor task. Both experimental groups were superior to both control groups when they were timed on their rate of assembling ten items. The unusual finding was that the performance of the retarded experimental group was significantly better than that of the intellectually normal control group. One of the earliest studies on the problem of principle transference to task was reported by Judd (1908). The task involved was dart tossing at an underwater target, and one group of subjects received no theoretical training, they just practiced while the other group was given theoretical explanations and practice. Although no difference between groups was found with 12 inches of water, a change to 4 inches favored the experimental group. These subjects evidently applied the theory in this transfer situation.

Some sample experiments obtaining contrary results follow. Frances Colville (1957) attempted to determine the effect of knowledge of three mechanical principles on the learning of a number of motor skills. Two groups of college women were formed, one of which spent their time learning and practicing the skills, the other learning mechanical principles as well as having skill practice. The results indicated that (1) instruction in mechanical principles did not promote the initial learning of a motor skill any more than did an equal amount of time spent in skill practice; and (2) such knowledge did not facilitate subsequent learning as evidenced when similar or more complicated skills were learned, even though the same principles were applicable.

Reasons for contradictory evidence in this area may very well be partially explained by methodological differences in experiments. Consider the following major discrepancy in two groups of studies utilizing a specialized training consideration:

Alloted Time

	Group A	direct practice PL
Experiment I		
	Group B	direct practice

	Group A	direct practice PL
Experiment II		
	Group B	direct practice

The allotment of time to direct practice in relation to principle learning (PL) differs between groups in both hypothetical experiments. Both groups receive the same amount of direct practice on a task in Experiment I, with one group receiving additional time for the learning of performance principles. In Experiment II, PL is built into the direct practice time, and consequently that group will have less time in direct practice than the other group. All things being equal, we might expect the design in Experiment I to favor Group A and the design in Experiment II to favor Group B or neither group.

Wayne Sorenson (1966), an industrial researcher, was interested in the importance of a knowledge of mechanical principles for on-the-job success of mechanical repair men. He reports that "the better mechanics appeared to rely on mechanical intuition and experience rather than formally taught principles (e.g., physics, mechanics, electricity, etc.). . . . They seem to fit a picture of born mechanics rather than made mechanics."

Thus the question is raised once again of the importance of intellectual knowledge as contrasted to supposed "innate ability" on motor achievement. Perhaps the safest statement, in view of conflicting research results, is that some individuals will prosper more, some less, when time is devoted to learning mechanical principles, especially when this time is taken away from potential physical participation. On the more optimistic side, there is some evidence to suggest that the mastery of learning principles aids in the future discovery of new principles and in turn the solution of new problems.

The context in which the principles are learned and insight into how they are to be applied in given situations are conditions to be considered if such knowledge is to be beneficial to motor performance. Unfortunately, educators sometimes orate too much and expect the learner to know many things which do not interest him. To conclude, perhaps the following words of Hilgard and Marquis (in Kimble, 1961) demonstrate practical insight into the problem:

> There is a limit to the learner's curiosity in understanding something. The understanding which the learner wishes in a problematic situation is knowledge

of the essentials to economical goal-achievement, and nothing more can be counted on. The mistake is sometimes made in teaching students of assuming that they wish to understand what lies behind a process which for them is just a tool. They wish to know how to use the tool to reach immediate goals; the further curiosity is related to different goals, which may be goals for the teacher but not for them.

Visual Cues

Of all the ways to alter displays, visual cues and changes in structures that produce visual stimuli (hopefully helpful to the learner) are most often experimented with in training situations. Visually aided displays, it is often believed, can be especially beneficial to the learner at the earlier stages of learning. It is interesting to analyze just how visual stimuli facilitate or hamper the learning process. With a newly introduced skill, the learner typically attends to too many stimuli and he has to learn to be more selective, which will occur with experience and expert guidance. Too many visual stimuli can be distracting, and, in fact, perhaps none are necessary in the beginning stages of learning certain skills.

Let us examine the golf swing as an example. One of the greatest problems with the beginning golfer is to get him to concentrate on the swing and to feel the movement rather than worry about how far the ball has gone. A few instructors believe in blindfolding these beginners so that this kinesthetic sense may be developed further. Indeed, one study reported early in this century did show blindfolded golfers to demonstrate greater ultimate proficiency than golfers taught with full vision. Unfortunately, not enough carefully controlled investigations have been completed in this area for us to advocate one method over the other method. Other skills require the presence of a certain number of visual cues. Gymnastics, diving, and trampolining stunts necessitate vision for equilibrium, balance, and safety. And, of course, for many activities vision provides a knowledge of results (e.g., basketball shooting, archery, tennis, and the like), enabling the individual to know when to compensate for inaccurate responses.

Visual guidance can be provided for the learner by allowing him to view expert performance. This is a procedure usually advocated and practiced by many educators. It allows the beginner to visualize what the desired act looks like and supplies him with the ideal goal for which to strive. Merely watching others perform a task while not expecting to have to do it results in more effective learning.

Often certain visual cues are emphasized or artificial ones introduced in order to promote the learning of various skills. Examples of artificial visual cues are found in (1) basketball, where spots or marks on the backboard provide specific points at which to aim for backboard shots; (2) archery, where sometimes the point-of-aim method is employed (a marker placed before the target is sighted upon); and (3) bowling, where the spot method of aiming is often used (a spot placed on the alley is aimed at instead of the pins).

Artificial visual cues are used either as an initial learning technique, to be disregarded later, or as a continual performance aid. Although research is scattered and inconclusive on the value of these techniques, it does appear that many of them are of value in fulfilling certain objectives. Theoretically analyzing the problem, specific and precise visual cues are easier to attend to than general and vague ones. Furthermore, nearer cues should be easier to aim for than those more removed. However, not all learners will benefit equally from the identical cues in the same task.

The characteristics of a visual display can be altered to make the training task similar to or more difficult than the true task. The relative effectiveness of these approaches, as they transfer over to the task of concern, has been examined and compared with direct practice on the true task. A section in the previous chapter dealt with the wisdom of arranging task practice from simple to complex dimensions, or vice versa. An example of visual display modification can be found in basketball. Individuals could practice with the regulation rim, with a smaller rim, or with a larger rim. Logic might suggest that with beginners, especially young ones, larger rims (perhaps even placed lower than the standard 10-foot height) would be beneficial in that it would be easier to score. Thus motivation is increased, self-esteem is enhanced, and positive reinforcement operates in an influential manner. A smaller than standard rim might assist the better performer in refining techniques and developing pinpoint shooting accuracy. In most cases, however, direct practice with the standard rim should be most valuable as we adhere to the principle of practicing under conditions closely resembling true task conditions, assuming the task is not overly complex or risky.

Some devices are utilized to provide the individual with certain information needed to develop skill proficiency. Primarily, this would be the function of the instructor, but sometimes unfavorable teaching conditions do not permit the learner to receive all the assistance he needs. An example of such a device is the Golf-Lite, illustrated in Figure 10–3, patented by Donald Mathews and Joe McDaniel (1962). These investigators reported the value of having a small light attached to the shaft of a golf club and powered by a battery placed in the individual's trouser pocket. Supposedly, the light yields a bright spot on the ground during the swing which allows more effective use of the eyes. The learner receives information about his swing and is benefited by the after-image effect. In the study reported by these researchers, a skill test given to two groups indicated the group that learned to golf with the aid of the Golf-Lite improved more than the control group that received regular instructions and practice.

The necessity of visual cues for adequate motor performance can be analyzed in investigations in which reduced visual cues are presented to

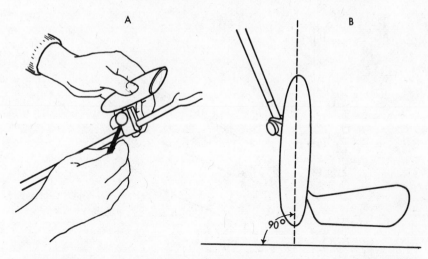

Figure 10–3.   **(A)** Affixing Golf-Lite to shaft of golf club. The universal joint permits easy adjustment in properly positioning the light. **(B)** Adjusting the Golf-Lite so that the light beam forms a perpendicular line to the ground as one addresses the ball. (From Donald K. Mathews and Joe McDaniel, "Effectiveness of Using Golf-Lite in Learning the Golf Swing," *Research Quarterly,* 33:488–491, 1962.)

subjects. In many continuous tasks, it is assumed that a complete visual tracking of objects is important for successful responses. "Keep your eye on the ball" is an often used expression associated with various sports activities. But is it really imperative that the ball (or some other object) be viewed until the moment of contact?

Some research evidence indicates that as visual cues diminish, so does performance. The ability to catch objects is directly related to the availability of light and visual cues; there is a need for sufficient time to preview the object prior to responding. Yet there are exceptions. A ball need not be watched all the time for effective catching if flight patterns can be accurately predicted. In other words, the length of time ball flight patterns need to be scanned depends upon the information available to the person in the situation and his skill level. Whiting, Gill, and Stephenson (1970) have shown a longer time period for scanning is necessary when the task is relatively unpredictable. With variable flight patterns and a dark room in which a ball to be caught was illuminated for 0.10, 0.15, 0.20, 0.25, 0.30, or 0.40 seconds from moment of release to the point of being caught, longer viewing time led to more successful catching (see Figure 10–4).

Whiting et al. discuss the possible existence of a perceptual moment, a critical time period for viewing an object in order that the central processing mechanism can function properly. A perceptual moment may be in the 0.05 to 0.20-second range. Once the visual stimulation is initiated

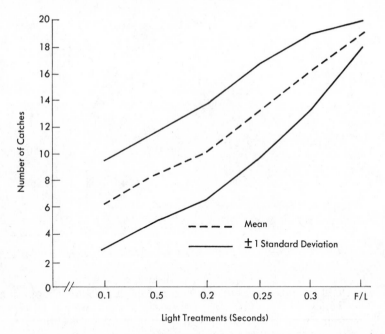

Figure 10–4.   Performance curve—combined means of all subjects. (From H. T. A. Whiting, E. B. Gill, and J. M. Stephenson, "Critical Time Intervals for Taking in Flight Information in a Ball-Catching Task," *Ergonomics,* 13:265–272, 1970.)

there must be an adjusted period of time to assimilate this conformation. The concept of a perceptual moment was not supported by the data in the Whiting et al. experiment, although subject variability and other rationales were offered for the lack of supportive data. It does seem that sufficient time for the registration of the stimulus and use of it for making acceptable responses is part of the process associated with skilled performance.

Norman Gordon (1969) has contrasted two types of events in terms of their functional properties when visual displays are altered. There are those, called input, that provide the subject with cues as to where and when to react. Others are derived from the subject's own activities and inappropriate responses and are termed feedback. Any cues added to a situation will hopefully assist the learner in making appropriate adjustments and adaptations. Gordon's research efforts have led him to question the advisability of aiding displays. Presumably such a circumstance facilitates early performance in a task but in the process encourages display dependency and discourages the learner from paying attention to feedback.

Early achievement in aided displays may occur because task demands are diminished and learner strategies are altered. The individual may learn less from such a situation, for less is demanded of him. Gordon has reported high performances in the early phase of practice in aided displays but poorer performance when attempting a transfer, or reference, task. We might speculate that if aided displays are constructed, be they visual, verbal, and tactual, their potential value must be considered in the context of (1) length of time in use, (2) the nature of the cues, (3) the type of task being learned, and (4) the ultimate (true) task to be mastered.

Aided displays will probably benefit tasks that are response oriented, such as self-paced tasks, in which fixed patterns of responses are desirable. Externally paced tasks make the kinds of demands on the performer that suggest the value of learning (1) from one's mistakes, (2) a variety of acceptable responses, and (3) effective copying strategies. To be of any value, supplementary situational cues should be temporary and deployed where task complexity suggests a need for learner guidance. An effective training procedure might be the gradual elimination of additional cues as the learner gains enough skill to cope with the true task. The usual practice reflects a dichotomy of procedures: from an aided display situation to an unaided situation. A gradual reduction in assistance and guidance could be preferable in those cases where cues are deemed appropriate in only the early learning stages.

Visual Aids

Visual aids, in various forms, have been experimentally investigated for their worth in promoting motor learning. They are represented by motion pictures, video tape recorders, force–time graphs, loopfilms, pictured representation of the task, slides, and the use of the tachistoscope. These aids serve such functions as demonstrating ideal performance (at regular or slow speeds), performance of the subject on the skill, or simple representative images or pictures of the task. The value of visual aids lies in their ability to allow the learner to view the task and critically analyze the task setting and bodily movements involved in skilled movements. This function is especially important if we stop to consider that the problem in executing most motor skills rests not with demands placed on the motor capacity of an individual, but rather in overcoming stimulus complexity in order to react with appropriate movements to particular environmental cues.

Whereas films are primarily used for modeling purposes, that is, providing an image of reference performance standards and helping to shape learner goals (see Figure 10–5), videotape possesses a feedback function. The individual can immediately see how he performed. This information can be valuable in modifying the next attempt. These aids have much intuitive appeal, but surprisingly, research evidence gives an only slightly favorable indication of their value in motor-learning situations. Many studies have indicated no differences in final skill proficiency between groups trained with or without these visual aids.

One may propose several reasons for the finding of no significant per-

Figure 10–5.   The super 8 projector can be used to display model performance, thereby helping the learner to understand the goals of the activity. (With permission from the Athletic Institute; 705 Merchandise Mart; Chicago, Illinois.)

formance differences among groups compared in a visual aid study. Films may be of poor quality. The learner may not be able to integrate the visual information into effective movement patterns. Criterion performance tests between groups may not be too reliable or valid. In other words, they may not be refined enough to distinguish among subjects. The duration of the film exposure or the training session itself might be of insufficient magnitude. In a few studies a problem may be associated with the use of inappropriate statistical techniques. Also, insufficient control of contaminating extraneous variables may lead to performance scores so variable that it is virtually impossible to detect performance differences between groups of subjects.

These and other attacks on the research methodology in which visual aids have been used allow us to suspect the data when the value of these aids is not demonstrated. Nevertheless, popular thinking and a reasonable rationale exist for the use of films as instructional aids.

The value of the videotape recorder (instant replay) is its capability to provide immediate visual feedback to the performer. Although research data are inconclusive in confirming its role in instruction, it is widely used in sports activities for performers of all skill levels. Especially in individual sports, like golf, skiing, bowling, tennis, and swimming, the videotape (VTR) is becoming more a part of instructional programs. We need not be reminded of often shown instant replays in football, basketball, baseball, and hockey matches shown on television. This viewing encourages a more penetrating analysis of strategy and performance. It also gives the television viewer who has missed the action (perhaps because of an urgent beer call and a step into the kitchen) another opportunity.

Typical of the studies not finding any benefits from the usage of videotape to develop sports skills are those reported by Kenneth Penman (1969) and I. Gasson (1967). Penman used beginning tumbling skills and Gasson dealt with badminton skills. In both studies two groups were formed. The experimental group received videotape exposure in the training procedures, and the control group did not experience any videotape. No differences in performance between the groups were noted on tests administered at the end of the duration of the studies.

Patricia Del Ray (1971) made an attempt to refine the experimental methodology with regard to performance criterion variables and task classification as related to training with or without VTR. A lunging task was made open or closed (see Chapter 1), and the dependent variables were latency, accuracy, and form. Performance in the open modification of the task as to form and latency was apparently aided with videotape. VTR with the closed version of the task led to higher accuracy scores. More detailed and sophisticated investigations like this one are needed in order to begin to answer questions regarding the value of VTR. Parameters need to be defined clearly, variables controlled, and performance measures made valid and appropriate for the circumstance.

The force-time graph is another means of supplying visual feedback to the learner. Max Howell (1956) used this device, a pen-drawn graph of force exerted as a function of time, to measure the pressure sprinters applied to the starting block at the start of their sprint. His experimental subjects viewed the graphs immediately following each start and heard them explained. The control subjects learned the sprint start by the conventional method. After ten meetings, the experimental group was rated as performing better than the control group. In skills such as this, where the speed of a complex act makes it difficult to analyze the movement, visual aids can apparently be of help.

Preliminary training on pictured representations of complex motor acts may help to provide greater insight into these acts. At least one experiment.

authored by Gagné and Foster (1949), found this to be the case. Subjects, before learning a discrimination reaction-time task, were presented with a paper-and-pencil representation of the task. This procedure was found to be effective in skill acquisition, and more premotor practice resulted in better motor performance.

Auditory Aids

Although music may serve as a stimulator, motivator, or relaxer, its exact role as an aid in motor-skill attainment and motor performance has not been determined. Melodies are piped into department stores and supermarkets in order to relax the customers and encourage purchases. Investigations are currently under way to determine the effects of music in general as well as different tempos and tones on sales. The dentist uses music to relax his patients and take their minds off the pending pain. Industrial workers have been observed to increase their output when motivated by music.

Because of the success tuneful and rhythmic melodies have had in these areas, it might be hypothesized that similar benefits would be derived in motor learning and performance. It is felt that lively tempos encourage more vigorous practice efforts; slow soft music relaxes individuals who are tense; and highly rhythmic music facilitates rhythmic and coordinated movements desired in the act. Some coaches and physical educators provide music as a background for the performance of skills with these objectives in mind. The difficulty in controlling experimental variables in determining the effects of auditory aids, hence the lack of research, permits little more than speculation. In one of the few studies done on this problem, Evelyn Dillon (1952) reported that her intermediate swimming students taught with music in the background achieved better form and speed than those swimmers taught without music.

Operating under the assumption that more repetitive, monotonous tasks would perhaps be more positively affected by the sound of music, Newman, Hunt, and Rhodes (1966) undertook a project to test this hypothesis. Workers in a skateboard factory heard four different types of music played on four different days; and no music was played on the fifth day. No difference in output was noted as a result of the type of music played or even the absence of music. It appears that in routine tasks, tasks in which the performers do not need a high degree of skill, music is not beneficial to performance.

However, other studies in vigilance situations have indicated that background music improved performance. Industrial productivity has been shown to improve with background music in a variety of settings (Fox, 1971). Although it is true that research is virtually nonexistent on the effects of music on learning, performance increments may be due to increased arousal and attention. Job performance and background music are currently being analyzed under the concepts of arousal theory.

There has been some thought on the relationship between rhythmic ability and the ability to perform movement patterns demanded in motor skills. Certain educators are of the opinion that by developing a sense of rhythm in children, they will promote the learning of skills that require the timing of responses. In this case, rhythmic ability is considered to be a more-or-less general factor. Implicit in the assumption is that positive transfer effects are highly probable. Although this concept has not been truly evaluated as yet, Marjorie Bond's results (1959) shed some light on the matter. Junior high school girls were given a test of rhythmic perception—where rhythmic patterns could be seen, heard, and felt—and five motor-performance tests. Her data yielded low insignificant correlations between the rhythmic test and five motor tests. Further analysis reveals some interesting findings: the correlation between IQ and motor performance was nearly zero whereas the correlations between IQ and rhythm abilities ranged from 0.24 to 0.36. These were low positive correlations but significant, nevertheless. Bond suggests that there is a need to analyze the rhythmical components of coordinated performance further if deficits are to be corrected.

Kinesthetic Aids

The role of the kinesthetic sense in skilled movement has been discussed throughout the book. A sensitivity to and awareness of body and limb position in movement is naturally an asset to performance. Can the kinesthetic sense be sharpened by means other than traditional practice?

An obvious method of attempting to accentuate this sense is to perform the desired act with the eyes closed (if it is a type of activity that can be practiced this way). Concentration is then on the movement rather than its outcome, such as projectile accuracy or distance. Environmental stimuli above and beyond response cues no longer serve as distractions. The eyes-closed or blindfold method of early skill learning has yet to be truly tested as a means of promoting learning. Therefore, at the present time, we must speculate on its effectiveness.

In order to encourage a greater awareness of the physical movement involved in certain acts, a *manual manipulation* technique is employed by teachers on occasion. The student relaxes as he is guided through a series of movement patterns. This practice serves to activate the receptors associated with the task and provides the learner with the desired movement experience. The manual guidance procedure is based on common sense and not on conclusive affirmative experimental findings; this is another area that needs more intensive research. However, Katherine Ludgate (1924) did find that manual assistance while learning a stylus maze helped subjects to learn faster.

A possible manner of activating and sensitizing more proprioceptors is through the use of heavier or lighter equipment. A measurement of transfer of skill would indicate the more desirable procedure. Projectiles of varying weights were thrown by the subjects in a study conducted by Egstrom, Logan, and Wallis (1960). Greater transfer was demonstrated from a light ball to a heavy ball than vice versa, and the writers reason that the lighter ball sharpened the sensitivity of the receptors and the feedback mechanism. Edward Wright's (1966) experiment neither supported nor rejected this conclusion. Young children were tested on physical fitness items and sports skills, and although his results were inconclusive, Wright's evidence suggests that if the children have limited strength, motor skills may be learned faster with lighter-weight equipment.

Does a player develop a greater sensitivity in basketball shooting if he practices with a larger ball? Weighted baseball bats for warm-up swings and weighted shoes for practice runs and jumps are intended to increase speed, power, and velocity during competition. In these cases and related areas, the research is much too scanty to analyze the effectiveness of such practice procedures. Franklin Lindeburg and Jack Hewitt (1965) practiced varsity and junior varsity basketball players with a regulation basketball and a larger basketball. On the tests administered, no difference between groups was observed on foul shots, dribbling ability, and lay-up speed skill. There was a significant difference on the passing test in favor of the group that had practiced with the smaller basketball. Unfortunately, the authors did not test the transference of accuracy from the larger to the regulation basketball.

In motor performance when too much kinesthetic information is withheld, the consequences can be severe. The relative importance of kinesthetic, verbal, visual, and auditory cues in the learning situation will be dependent on the skill in question and the skill level of the individual. All may provide necessary feedback messages, although in many cases they overlap, and duplication occurs between the senses and their information. The skilled performer is one who has learned to respond to specific cues and emphasize particular sensory modes at different stages of proficient movement patterns.

Comparison of Cues

There has been an attempt to compare the relative effects of emphasizing or restricting the various cues. Unfortunately, investigations have been based on isolated and unique laboratory tasks. Quite naturally, the results are not consistent from study to study. Purposes behind a number of these studies also vary.

One way of comparing cue effectiveness is in relation to the stage of practice of the learner. As indicated earlier in the book, we might expect a person to be more dependent on display characteristics (e.g., visual input) early in training. This is especially true with nonpredictable events. Later he might rely on proprioceptive (response-produced) cues. This rationale would be derived from the numerous studies in which Edwin Fleishman has been involved, demonstrating the differential relationship of visual and kinesthetic abilities to task achievement at different stages of practice. Furthermore, an individual might be expected to be more cue dependent at first and more selective at proficient levels of performance.

Assuming that cognition (understanding the nature of the task, learning strategies for task mastery, etc.) plays an important role early in practice (see the Fitts–Posner model in Chapter 3), an investigation by Trumbo, Ulrich, and Noble (1965) attempted to clarify the role of verbal and cognitive processes in skill acquisition. Examined were the three levels of effects of display cues and verbal pretraining on tracking performance. It was expected and found that display specific cues and verbal pretraining were more beneficial earlier rather than later in learning. However, this effect was not additive. Apparently the redundancy and irrelevancy of some cues suggest the careful planning of aiding displays. Because retention performance was not affected by display specificity or pretraining, it remains for other research to reveal the function of other cue combinations in retention in contrast to initial stages of practice.

Nevertheless, redundant information can facilitate performance in certain cases, such as with reaction times. Irving Biederman and Stephen Checkosky (1970) present data that demonstrate this fact. The value of redundant and relevant cues, according to these researchers, lies in a person's ability to process information in a parallel fashion rather than serially. If serial processing occurs, reaction time should be longer. If parallel processing occurs, it should be shorter. The latter occurrence with reaction data is explained theoretically in the framework of the parallel information-processing model.

Of course, in many situations, sensory information may be discrepant and therefore pose a conflict for the learner. If an information conflict exists between two sense modalities, how is it resolved? In an investigation by Pick, Warren, and Hay (1969) discrepancies between proprioception and audition, vision and audition, and vision and proprioception were analyzed. The dominance of one modality over another implies that they do not behave as an integrated system. The researchers feel that different processes are involved when conflicting information must be resolved. With regard to sense modality comparisons, it was reported that proprioceptive and auditory judgments were biased strongly by vision as were auditory judgments by proprioception. The dominance of vision over touch had been convincingly expressed earlier by Irvin Rock and Charles Harris (1967). They concluded that "the sense of touch does not educate vision; vision is totally dominant over touch" (p. 96). When conflicting information is present in a situation, visual information determines perception.

Further implications of the dominance of vision over proprioception are noted by Timothy Jordan (1972), who suggests that the demands of visual input for attention by the brain tend to result in longer response times. In his study, blindfolded practice on a fencing skill, the disengage and lunge, which was simulated with a blade deflection laboratory apparatus, resulted in faster response times than sighted practice. If, as Jordan states, "one is inclined to rely upon what one sees, rather than upon what one feels," he may also be correct in his observation that ". . . in skills where kinesthetic or proprioceptive cues are considered important, this can perhaps be a hindrance to the learning of an optimal response" (pp. 536–537). Jordan's study supports the notion that blindfold practice in the early stages of skill learning where *events are predictable* produces best results as far as speed in movement is concerned. When visual cues are restricted, attention is more easily focused on proprioceptive feedback, resulting in faster responses. Further evidence is suggested in favor of the idea that the visual and kinesthetic systems involve different information-processing mechanisms.

Cues may be presented during a performance (coincident) or terminal to it (noncoincident). Laurence Karlin and Rudolph Mortimer (1963) demonstrated the superiority of a noncoincident verbal cue over coincident visual and auditory cues during training and for a transfer task. Visual and auditory augmented information stressed the acceptable target area of the task. A score at the end of each trial provided to the subject was the verbal cue. It could be, as the researchers suggest, that augmenting cues affect transfer best when they function as incentives and in defining performance standards.

When cues are tampered with and removed in a systematic way, results are somewhat predictable. Standard practice is usually most effective, and the relative import of sensory cues can be deduced from the following example reports. In a comprehensive experiment, William Battig (1954) compared performances on the Complex Coordination Test when kinesthetic, verbal, and visual cues were eliminated or emphasized. Six groups of subjects were formed, with all subjects tested on the same task on the first and tenth trials but practiced under different conditions during the middle eight sessions. Standard practice afforded the best results. The sequence of cue importance, after standard practice, was determined to benefit skill acquisition as follows: visual, kinesthetic, and lastly, verbal.

Similar results were obtained in Dennis Holding's (1959) investigation. On a tracking task, normally trained and guided groups demonstrated little dissimilarity at the early stages of learning. The guidance group subjects gripped the control knobs, got the feel of the machine tracking itself, and finally had to track themselves. Also noted in the study was that full guidance was better than visual guidance; visual guidance was superior to kinesthetic guidance; and kinesthetic guidance did not yield a significant improvement in performance. The great success of the guidance group indicates the necessary occurrence of correct responses. Holding argues that knowledge of results is not necessary to learning, but the correct movements are, although KR is a means of correcting a response. Knowledge of results is synonymous with error feedback (to many psychologists), but there is no error to feed back if the performance is perfect.

For many tasks, conventional practice is not only sufficient but, from the evidence, often more beneficial than singling out and emphasizing either visual, verbal, or kinesthetic cues. As a final reminder, probably the best advice is to consider the nature of each task and to emphasize equally all sensory cues if the task so demands. Specific cue emphasis should be offered in such cases when one has to react to complex stimuli, execute a complex motor act, or compensate for a weakness in performance.

Training and Simulation Devices

For various reasons, industrialists, military personnel, and educators have turned to artificial equipment and devices for assistance in facilitating the learning of motor skills. The term *artificial* as used here simply implies that these devices are made especially for training purposes, to simulate to a certain extent the actual performance conditions or, perhaps, to prepare the individual for the actual task via audiovisual or tactile and kinesthetic cues. Technically speaking, we could distinguish these aids by categorizing them as trainers or simulators, although the dichotomy is not always obvious.

A *trainer* is some aid used to promote the learning of a task in the early stages. It could be a film, pictures, or a specially constructed piece of equipment. A *simulator,* on the other hand, is usually a device that more nearly approximates task conditions. It is realistic and provides the performer with concentrated practice when he is at that point of developing a high level of proficiency.

Certain tasks permit more favorable and, indeed, require more frequent usage of these devices if learning efficiency is the desired objective. Consider, for instance, industrial, military, and automobile tasks. The cost of training personnel as well as the inconvenience of activating complex machinery helped to inspire the development of simulators and trainers. Also, there is an element of danger in some tasks, such as piloting a plane. Finally, it is not practical to train a large number of people on tasks that require extreme proficiency on expensive equipment. Because of these factors, various types of aids are used instead of direct practice for the learning of complex motor skills.

Although fake cockpits and automobile controls have been devised for simulating practice flying a plane or driving a car, most athletic skills do not require the use of such costly and complex equipment. The best practice is afforded by on-the-job tasks or game situations. This is not always practical or possible, although it is certainly more reasonable to expect in educational situations than on military installations or in highly technical industrial work. But, even in education today, where teachers are faced with a greater ratio of students than ever before, training devices have certain advantages over traditional teaching procedures.

These aids allow students to practice skills which otherwise might be impossible to learn under equipment and facility limitations faced by many institutions. Thanks to the initiative of some physical educators, golf can be taught with a certain degree of effectiveness in the gymnasium with the use of plastic or taped balls. These balls do not travel far and are safer than regulation golf balls. The absence of a golf course does not inhibit the teaching of basic golf skills. Similar measures are currently being made so that such sports as water skiing and snow skiing can be simulated in the pool and gymnasium. Although these efforts are probably not as effective as learning the skills under actual conditions, they serve a definite purpose.

The aids also alleviate the situation where there are too many students for the instructor to provide individual instruction, attention, and direction. Devices that approximate real conditions provide each learner with an immediate knowledge of results, inform him of his performance status, and facilitate his progress. Ball-throwing machines in tennis and baseball are examples of pieces of apparatus that allow individuals to concentrate on hitting techniques. The machine for tennis tosses a ball at a preset speed and a server apparatus suspends a ball and releases it when contact is made. Both devices eliminate many of the complex factors involved in stroking and serving (see Figures 10–6 and 10–7). Solley and Borders (1965) were interested in determining the effectiveness of the Ball-Boy machine in promoting the learning of tennis skills. After comparing control and experimental groups, the investigators concluded that the machine was very effective. They recommended the procedure of using traditional teaching methods first, followed by the use of the Ball-Boy machine.

Another device that may have value in improving tennis skills is a rebounding net that permits the player to practice his stroking. The Ball-Boy Re-Bound-Net, pictured in Figure 10–8, overcomes a major problem associated with backboards, walls, or other hard surfaces, namely, the ball rebounding too quickly. With the net, a player can hit a ball without reducing stroking velocity because the rebound interval is lengthened. Continuous stroking is thus encouraged.

The Golf-O-Tron is an example of a type of equipment invented to facilitate golf learning. This highly technical instrument simulates a golf

Figure 10–6.   The automatic tennis ball machine in operation. (With permission from the Ball-Boy Company, Inc.; 26 Milburn St.; Bronxville, N.Y.)

course and playing conditions and allows the individual to play a round of golf without stepping on the course. Edward Chui (1965) taught two groups to use the 7 iron and then tested transfer skill to the 4 iron. One group was instructed in the conventional method and the other learned with the assistance of the Golf-O-Tron. Positive transfer effects were noted for both groups, with no significant differences between them.

Flotation devices are used in swimming to overcome fear of the water as well as to facilitate the learning of swimming skills. Although there has been very little experimental work scientifically to analyze their effectiveness as teaching devices, Richard Kaye (1965) reported that a group of college beginning swimmers using a waist-type flotation device was able to swim further at the end of his experiment than a group taught without it.

These examples indicate the type of training aids currently being introduced and evaluated in physical education and sport. Since audiovisual materials have already been discussed in this chapter, they have been omitted here. The value of viewing ideal performance or one's self performing should not be minimized, however. A final point to be considered with the use of trainers and simulators, and certainly not the least, is their value

Figure 10–7.   The Server. This apparatus holds a tennis ball at any height, and at contact, the ball is released for a completely normal flight. The Server minimizes some of the complexities of the serve by eliminating the toss. (With permission from the Ball-Boy Company, Inc.; 26 Milburn St.; Bronxville, N.Y.)

as motivators. Novel and different methods of instructing serve to elevate motivation. The anticipation, excitement, and challenge of learning under novel conditions can very well be reflected by increased performance scores.

Figure 10–8.   The Ball-Boy Re-Bound-Net. The net, which can be adjusted for the desired rebound, provides a "set-up ball" that allows the player continually to strike the ball. (With permission from the Ball-Boy Company, Inc.; 26 Milburn St.; Bronxville, N.Y.)

OTHER ENVIRONMENTAL VARIABLES

Work output is also related to the environment: temperature, noise, lighting, and the like. Many studies have been undertaken in industrial psychology to determine optimal working conditions. It would stand to reason that there is an optimal environment for learning and performing motor tasks. The literature is too extensive to report here, so one investigation is presented as an example.

Various heat stress environments were created and subjects' performance recorded on a tracking task and a reaction-time task, with a peripheral stimulus presented simultaneously. The temperatures under each condition were 84.9°, 89.8°, and 88.4°F. The subjects performed in one of these environments as well as in a comfortable environment. N. Z. Azer, P. E. McNall, and H. C. Leung (1972) found that the 89.8°F environment created a significant deterioration in tracking and increase in reaction time. Performances worsened with prolonged exposure to heat stress, as might be expected.

Although motor-learning researchers have generally not addressed such variables and their influence on learning and performance, they are of major concern in real-world learning environments. Hence they have attracted the attention of applied psychologists. Environmental factors, peripheral yet relevant to the performance activity, cannot be discounted in their potential influence on task learning, task persistence, and level of performance. The scientific study of work leads to a more effective design of appropriate environmental conditions.

Ergonomics is the name given the science of work. Attempts are made to reduce the burden on the person as he attempts to perform. Time and motion studies are geared toward this objective. Fatigue and impairment are net results of unsuitable working conditions, and factors that contribute to these constraints need to be identified and reorganized. O. G. Edholm's book (1967) provides a good overview of this area and of work output as related to various regulated and nonregulated environmental conditions.

SOME PSYCHOLOGICAL ERGOGENIC AIDS

Ergogenic aids have been defined by William Morgan (1972, p. xi) as "substances and phenomena which elevate performance above normal expectations." This interpretation is broad enough to include many things. A typical understanding of the term ergogenic aid is negative in a sense, that is, that work output is enhanced by the intake of illegitimate or immoral substances.

Certain aids, be they changes in environment or substances or strategies directly applied to the human system, may induce an appropriate intermix of physiological and psychological variables, resulting in elevated performance. Unfortunately, in most cases it is exceptionally hard to determine wherein such factors combine to produce beneficial results or the psychological component dominates the scene. For instance, many performers will do better *if they think they should*. A pre-event steak meal may lead to a greater than expected performance in a football game simply because the player thinks that steak is nutritious and will enhance his athletic capabilities in the contest. Yet there is little if any physiological justification for this.

Classic examples of intake ergogenic aids used in sport are pure oxygen, drugs, vitamins, hormones, special diets, and special beverages. Do these categories of substances benefit performance? There is some supporting evidence for this. For instance, oxygen can be an effective ergogenic aid when used in certain ways and for certain purposes. Oxygen inhalation is effective immediately before an event if the exertion is maximal and the duration is short. It is also effective during strenuous exercise to minimize fatigue effects, but to administer it during activity is usually not practical. Likewise, the stimulating effect of amphetamines (pep pills) on bodily activity has been documented with some qualifications (Cole, 1970).

Many of the food fads are overemphasized; their value, if any, must be more psychological than anything else because they are usually not supported by a sound nutritional base. Mineral and vitamin supplements, wheat germ oil, quick energy foods, high protein diets, and the like, have been discussed by Ellington Darden and Harold Schendel (1972). Conflicts in assumed values and scientific findings are shown. Yet it is indeed possible that a substance like wheat germ oil might produce greater work output simply because the athlete thinks that it should.

Other possible ergogenic aids include *placebos,* substances or situations that should not have a beneficial effect on performance but work because the person is convinced of their effectiveness. They will be discussed shortly. Hypnosis is an ergogenic procedural variable, operating on the human system, and it too will be reviewed subsequently. Either contrived or natural environments can yield ergogenic effects. The presence of an audience is a good example of this situation. This topic will likewise be dealt with later in this chapter. Warm-up has been discussed in a previous chapter, where psychological implications and a possible placebo effect were suggested as they relate to performance.

The problems involved in the use of a number of ergogenic aids (e.g., drugs, oxygen) become compounded when considered in a moral framework. Should they be recommended for usage even though segments of society oppose them? Should an ergogenic aid with no known "real" value but that operates through its placebo effect in elevating performance outcomes be introduced in training programs? Is this a violation of ethical conduct? These types of questions are beyond the scope of this section of the chapter but deserve the attention of interested and informed parties.

Placebos

Areas such as psychiatry, medicine, and psychology are replete with examples revealing the power of placebos, substances that have no pharmacological effect. The placebo effect refers to an individual's reaction in a particular situation to some nonindependent variable (e.g., medication) as a function of his expectations and beliefs interacting with procedures and someone else's expectations. When subjects are convinced of their value, placebos tend to elicit behaviors in an expected and often desirable direction.

Experimentation with drugs has shown that placebos can duplicate both positive and negative effects of active substances. For example, if a patient believes that a pill will reduce pain, he will report such effects, even though the pill was a placebo. The placebo is administered as if it is the real thing, but it really has no value. H. K. Beecher (1969) reports that saline solutions used as a pain killer in a battlefield situation when morphine was expected showed 90 per cent the effectiveness of morphine in reducing pain. In a hospital situation saline solution was 70 per cent as effective as morphine. Thus changes in feelings or behaviors must be attributed to the psychological properties of the substance.

The value of placebos in motor-behavior situations is by and large inferred from research in other fields. Their potential influence on the learning and performance of motor tasks is unclear. In one of the few articles dealing with physical performance and an administered placebo substance, David Pomeranz and Leonard Krasner (1969) reported findings in the expected direction. A placebo salve said to be of proved merit in relieving muscle fatigue was given to subjects who were sustaining a hand grip on a dynamometer. Less decrease in grip strength on a number of trials was found with the application of the salve.

But the placebo situation need not only be limited to substances taken into a person's system. If any treatment effect is potentially analogous to a placebo situation, then other factors can be included here. Warm-up could be the treatment. In certain cases it may very well operate like a placebo. As we mentioned earlier a person may perform better following warm-up, but is this change caused by body chemistry or primarily psychological factors? If it is thought that warm-up is an aid to performance, expectations may be fulfilled. The placebo effect arouses a person's expectancy level; it alters his attitude toward the particular circumstance.

Environmental modifications can produce a placebo effect. A popular term associated with this situation is the *Hawthorne effect*. This term evolved from a series of studies undertaken a number of years ago (Roethlisberger and Dickson, 1939) in an industrial situation in which the workers interpreted changes in their working conditions as favorable to their performance. Beginning in 1927 and continuing for twelve years, the effects of such manipulated factors as office illumination and temperature, wage rate, work-rest periods, and the like, on the productivity of six female subjects were examined. Even when usually perceived unfavorable conditions were present, production rate remained the same or increased. The workers may have interpreted such changes as a personal interest in them, thus inspiring greater work output.

Dale Hanson (1967) has shown the influence of the Hawthorne effect on the performance of selected physical activities. To summarize: (1) a group of subjects provided with a placebo after six weeks of no physical practice improved nineteen curls (a popular exercise) from the pretest to the posttest; and (2) a placebo group compared to a control demonstrated better performance in bench-stepping endurance.

Robert Rosenthal has repeatedly warned about the experimenter and teacher expectancy effect and its subtle influence on the direction of the outcome of an experiment or student performances in a classroom. Writing in a recent publication, Rosenthal (1970) summarizes 103 studies on the topic and concludes that in two thirds of the research, subjects as well as experimenters will give or obtain responses in the direction of the experimenter's expectancy. Of the studies reviewed, nine dealt with animal learning, ten with human abilities, six with laboratory interviews, and sixty-four with person perception.

In one of the few real-life motor-activity studies, John Burnham (1968) divided camper nonswimmers into a "chosen" group and a "non-chosen" group. Fifty per cent of each sex and age group was designated as chosen, that is, a test battery presumably predicted these children psychologically ready to learn to swim. The staff counselors were given the list of names. Based on the criterion of the number of Red Cross beginner swimmer tests passed, the experimenter's bias effect was shown. The chosen group performed significantly better than the controls.

Yet merely administering placebos or creating placebo environments does not always produce better performance scores. Performers have to be naive and susceptible. Perhaps present motivation needs to be low for the effect to operate. If not, incentives in addition to the normal practice and testing environment might tend to be ineffective. The beneficial psychological effects of a placebo are not ubiquitous across varied tasks and dissimilar situations (e.g., Singer, Llewellyn, and Darden, 1973). Placebo effects are evidently not universal in different tasks and situations. Motor-learning situations need to be investigated in more depth before more conclusive statements can be made. For many motor tasks, assuming they are nonrepetitive and reasonably challenging, sufficient performer motivation may be present.

Nonetheless, the placebo effect, the Hawthorne effect, and the experimenter and instructor expectation effect are intriguing areas of study. It is recognized that a person may perform as he perceives he is expected to do. Encouragement has a better probability of elevating performance, discouragement inhibiting it. The more a person wants to believe that his performance can be improved by some substance or environment, the more this feeling is apt to be realized.

Hypnosis

There is an increasingly accepted feeling that a hypnotic state can lead to more powerful feats. Some professional baseball players have credited hypnotists with their improved performances, and indeed, there are examples of hypnotists working with professional baseball teams. Yet, in summarizing an abundance of literature, William Morgan (1972, p. 193) concludes that "a review of the experimental literature does not justify the view that performance in the hypnotic or posthypnotic states will necessarily surpass performance in the motivated waking state."

One of the serious confounding factors in the experiments dealing with hypnosis and motor performance is suggestion and actual state. It is not easy to determine a person's hypnotic state following hypnotic treatment. Many procedural contaminants, some unfortunate and controllable, others resisting desirable control, make it difficult to undertake research on this topic. Likewise, interpretations of findings are equally distressing. Equivocal conclusions summarize the literature as we look for directions in the data.

Hypnosis has been studied in athletic events, with the learning of motor tasks, with work, strength, and endurance output, reaction time, and the like. It is beyond the scope of this book to treat the topic of hypnosis in detail, and it is recommended that the interested reader read Morgan's chapter for insight into the literature. But essentially, Morgan repeatedly concludes that there are contradictory findings as to the effects of hypnosis on performance.

SOCIAL INFLUENCE

A question often raised is whether performance is improved, worsened, or remains the same when it occurs in a social context. The situation may involve competition, working together cooperatively, or performing in front of people. These are examples of social situations in which the individual is not performing solely for his own satisfaction, but rather with the involvement of others. Actually, activity that involves social interaction is typical of many of our endeavors.

Competition

Competition is a strong motivating device. Two common forms are competing against one's own standards or against the performance of others. There is a strong feeling that learning does not occur without the presence of some type of competition. James Coleman (1961) defended the use of it in the schools on this basis, for he feels that children need a challenge. Without competition, or a substitute challenge, learning will not progress. He stresses that cooperation is not a substitute for competition as a means for bringing about motivation. A fundamental aspect of competition among children is their desire for respect and recognition from others. Competition can be associated with the following activities:

1. Performance against established group norm standards.
2. Performance against personal standards.
3. Performance alone against another person.
4. Performance within a group but against other members of the group.
5. Performance within a group against other groups.

Numerous investigations and empirical observations lend support for the contribution competition makes to performance. Typically, performance levels improve when the situation is a competitive one, especially if the task is not so complex as to cause the individual to falter under the stress. Well-learned skills should be performed with usual or higher-than-usual proficiency.

However, there is some concern as to the overall beneficial effects of subjecting children and young men and women to constant competitive situations. Although many circumstances in life foster competitiveness, many require cooperation. When working with or against people, performances are obviously subject to change. Many educators favor motor skills taught primarily in a cooperative situation rather than in a situation fostering extreme competitiveness. It would appear that the real issue surrounding competition is the extent to which it should be emphasized or de-emphasized.

Competition elevates the arousal level within the organism, and to the extent that it causes it to be optimal for the task at hand and the skill level of the person, it possesses merit. We might expect that competition might differentially affect higher and lower anxiety learners, to the advantage of those having lower anxiety. Logic and theory would support this notion. But Rainer Martens and Dan Landers (1969) did not find this to be true. A coincident timing task was administered to extreme scoring subjects on the Taylor Manifest Anxiety Scale. The study did not find that competition interacted with anxiety to affect performance differentially.

Although it is true that competition enhances arousal (e.g., physiological parameters such as heart rate, Evans, 1972), a corresponding improvement in motor performance may not be observed. Evans, as well as some other investigators, has not demonstrated expected relationships between physiological parameters of performance scores. The inverted U-shaped hypothesis (see Chapter 7) was not supported, in that the predicted relationship between arousal (obtained in heart rate) and incremental or decremental performance in a competitive situation was not found. Such evidence may imply weaknesses in the theory or in experimental methodology.

A person who is highly competitive in particular situations might be expected to perform better than others, assuming performance capabilities are present. This feeling is certainly prevalent in the sports world. By competitive spirit is meant the desire to win. Few data are available on the topic, perhaps because of the difficulty of measuring this trait. But Susanne Higgs (1972) has noted that good and average competitors differed in scores in a motor-ability test, in favor of the good competitors.

Cooperation

Invariably, experiments have indicated the superiority of competitive and cooperative ventures over a no-incentive situation. Because so many conditions contain both competitive and cooperative elements, it is not easy to decide which one is more effective in facilitating learning. In team sports and partner games, the performer has to learn how to play cooperatively as well as to express a desire for defeating the opponents. It would appear that pure competitive measures are more effective than cooperative ventures in motivating performance.

This is especially true with younger children. Competition is more of a basic or primitive instinct; cooperation involves greater degrees of maturation and intellectual involvement. Striving to "beat" someone is almost a natural urge. Joint ventures presuppose a sublimation of some personal drives and desires and, with children, require that certain understandings be transmitted to them. When comparing group versus individual performance, there is evidence that cooperative efforts may be more efficient. Weyner and Zeaman (1956) analyzed data obtained from groups of two and four subjects run as teams and individual efforts on pursuit rotor performance. It was found that by numerically increasing the team members, better performances were attained.

Group interaction can be a more powerful positive influence on performance than an individual effort. An implication is that working in small groups provides a pooling of learnings that benefits performance. Also, merely performing tasks in the presence of others serves as a social motivator. An example of the small-group approach lies in the teaching of swimming skills by pairing off students to mutually assist each other.

There are other advantages in working in groups. The subjects in William Johnston's (1966) experiment had to execute coordination skills demanded in a simulated radar-controlled aerial intercept task. No difference was found if the skills were individual or team taught, but the investigator suggests that the tasks in his study required much more teamwork than those used in other studies. Most physical education activities do not require such deeply involved participant interaction. In apparent agreement with the sentiments expressed throughout this book on the importance of practice conditions closely resembling game conditions is the conclusion to Johnston's report: "when transfer is characterized by team activity, it would appear desirable to train potential team members in a team context rather than individually in order that the necessary team skills may be developed."

The lack of transfer and predictability from skills performed alone to those performed in a group is further demonstrated in a series of studies published by Andrew Comrey (1953, 1954). Subjects were tested individually and in pairs on hand-manipulating tasks associated with the Purdue Pegboard Assembly Task. Less than half of the group performance variance could be predicted from individual performance on a similar kind of task. Evidently, individual skill alone is not enough to predict success in a group task, for there are variables to be considered. A warning from the results of these studies is that people should not always be paired up on the basis of individual abilities because group performance is not dependent on individual scores. It is probably best to learn under conditions similar to those in which the application will be made.

Social Facilitation Theory

The effects of others on the behavior of one was formulated into a testable hypothesis by Robert Zajonc (1965). His article entitled "Social Facilitation" is widely referred to in present-day literature dealing with social situations and behavioral effects. Actually, either facilitating or impeding effects on learning and performance may be noted when the subject is in the presence of another. And Zajonc's model predicts performance accordingly.

Remaining in the drive theory (Hull–Spence) tradition, Zajonc speculates that social presence increases the level of arousal (motivation) within a performer. In turn, response preferences are emitted. When the dominant responses in the repertoire of responses are correct ones, as is the case with the skilled performer, social presence should be of benefit to the individual. Conversely, if the dominant responses are incorrect ones (exemplified early in learning), the social presence effect should be detrimental. In other words, dominant responses tend to be activated under the stress of the social presence, thereby influencing the quality of the response. The learning process of difficult activities should be negatively affected under social presence conditions. Once high levels of proficiency are reached, performance should be facilitated. These thoughts are summarized in Table 10–1.

The typical test of the Zajonc hypothesis is through two types of social presence mediums: (1) coaction and (2) spectators. In the first situation, people are actively engaged in similar activities (cooperating, competing, observing each other, and so on). In the second situation, an audience views the behaviors of one or more performers. Presumably both forms of

TABLE 10–1.   SOCIAL FACILITATION THEORY *

Stage I Learning	*Stage II* Performance
Response Possibilities wrong right wrong wrong wrong wrong right wrong wrong	*Response Possibilities* right wrong right right right right wrong right right
Social Presence Effect Detrimental	Beneficial

* There is a greater probability of making a wrong response early in learning with social presence and making a right one at high skill levels.

social interaction should result in the same effects on an individual performing (although, as we shall see shortly, Bird's data do not support this contention).

Although data taking exception to aspects of Zajonc's theory have been published, by and large and a good deal of support exists. A practical interpretation of the theory would be as follows. Learn a complex motor task under solitary conditions, and when a reasonable level of achievement is obtained and the individual is prepared for the stress of social presence, he should not only bear it, but perform better as a result of it.

Coaction

Any discussion of the way individual behaviors are shaped by competition and cooperative training programs, or by being involved in an activity simultaneously with other individuals, refers to the effects of coaction. The presence of coactors implies that an individual is working in a social context. As we have seen, individual performance may very well be influenced by such a situation.

In a typical coaction experiment, subjects working together in a group are compared in their individual performances with those who work in isolated environments. Data generated with lower forms of organisms support the hypothesis that coaction situations generally stimulate greater activity than solitary conditions. Productivity with already learned behaviors is increased. The social facilitating effects of coaction environments are predictably more likely with familiar tasks than with less familiar and difficult ones. The negative effects of coaction, in the form of nondesirable stress, may operate to depress individual performance in initial learning stages of complex tasks.

Nevertheless, disregarding task peculiarities and learner characteristics for the moment, it does appear that social group settings can be quite favorable to learners. This is especially true when

1. Their knowledge and abilities are positively related to the topic.
2. They are a cohesive unit that can work and communicate together.
3. The size of the group is reasonable.
4. They are not passive but actively offer assistance, reinforcement, and feedback.
5. They compete against each other within the group (Singer, 1972).

Coaction settings often arouse individuals to greater performance levels. This may be due to the motivational aspects of the situation. The benefits of coaction, in this case individuals actively, independently, and simultaneously engaged in the same task, has been reported by Anne Bird (1973). The subjects in this investigation performed either a manual dexterity task or a hand-steadiness task. Of the three groups of subjects that were formed, one performed alone, a second performed in a coaction

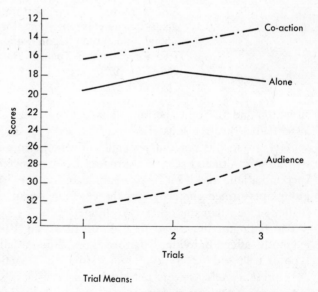

Trial Means:

Alone: 19.73, 17.63, 18.67

Audience: 32.47, 30.93, 27.63

Co-action: 16.27, 14.97, 13.00

Figure 10–9. Trial performance on the hand-steadiness task. (From Anne Marie Bird, "Effects of Social Facilitation Upon Female's Performance of Two Psychomotor Tasks," *Research Quarterly*, 44: 322–330, 1973.)

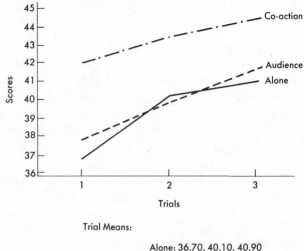

Trial Means:

Alone: 36.70, 40.10, 40.90
Audience: 37.74, 39.77, 41.60
Co-action: 41.97, 43.33, 44.37

Figure 10–10.   Trial performance on the manual dexterity task. (From Anne Marie Bird, "Effects of Social Facilitation Upon Female's Performance of Two Psychomotor Tasks," *Research Quarterly*, 44: 322–330, 1973.)

situation, and the third performed in the presence of a passive audience. Essentially, Bird's results were as follows: (1) in hand steadiness, the solitary group did not differ significantly in performance from the other two groups, although coaction produced better scores than did the audience situation; and (2) in manual dexterity, the solitary and audience groups performed similarly and the coaction group achieved significantly higher scores than the other two groups.

The data are illustrated in Figures 10–9 and 10–10. Social situations evidently affect individual performances differentially according to (1) type of task and (2) type of social situation. Coaction effects and audience presence effects were not similar in both tasks. But generally speaking, coacting subjects performed well in both activities. One limiting factor in interpreting Bird's data is the fact that the subjects were females, and the extent that we can generalize to males is argumentative. But then again, in most research projects, subjects of one sex (typically males) are used, and we can always raise the legitimate question of the generalizability of data to people of a different sex, age, cultural and geographical environment, and so on.

Contradictory results with different motor tasks within the same study have been reported by Clyde Noble and his co-workers (1958). Two motor

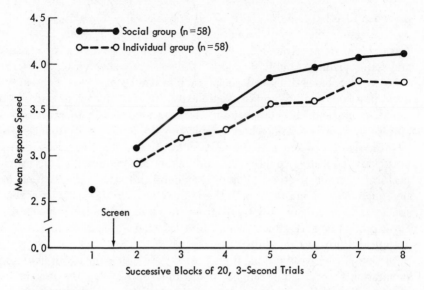

Figure 10–11. Acquisition curves of speed in discrimination reaction under individual (partitioned) versus social (nonpartitioned) conditions of practice. (From C. E. Noble, J. E. Fughs, D. P. Robel, and R. W. Chambers, "Individual vs. Social Performance on Two Perceptual-Motor Tasks," *Perceptual and Motor Skills*, 8:131–134, 1958.)

tasks were learned under isolated or social conditions. Pursuit rotor performance was not affected by the number of subjects in a group. However, the social competitive situation stimulated greater increments in performance than did isolated practice in a discrimination reaction time task. Figure 10–11 contains the learning curves derived from the data acquired in the discrimination reaction-time task. Perhaps unique task demands interact with various learning environments (e.g., social versus isolated) to produce task-specific results.

Audience Effect

It has been nearly everyone's experience to know individuals who can demonstrate a high degree of skill proficiency when performing alone or in the comfortable confines of a practice situation but who disintegrate during actual competition and in front of an audience. There are also people whose performance improves under this circumstance. Because of the complexity of the human organism and the degree to which a skill may have been learned, the presence or absence of spectators may seem to have unpredictable effects on different people.

Returning to social facilitation theory, there are indications that the presence of others might prove to be detrimental if the skill, especially a more complex one, is in the earlier stages of being learned. A skill well learned and demonstrated for viewers should be executed in a consistent and stable manner. Highly developed skills are less affected by distractions.

So far we have discussed social facilitation theory in a general way, excluding such factors as task complexity, individual anxiety and motivational levels, and the composition of the audience. There are many examples in the real world where people practice their art by themselves to perform later in front of others. Athletes, actors and actresses, dancers, musicians, educators, politicians, and others are required on occasion to perform in front of others. For experimental purposes, the situation must be much more controlled and therefore contrived in order to examine spectator effects. Having a small group of passive (neutral) spectators in close proximity to a subject watch him learning and performing a task is a typical study in the skills area.

In one such investigation, Rainer Martens's (1969) data upheld social facilitation theory. When subjects were initially learning the task in front of an audience, they performed more poorly than subjects learning alone. Once the task had been learned fairly well, subjects in front of spectators performed better than those performing in isolation. Furthermore, subjects performing in spectator presence were more consistent in their responses. Differences between the groups in performance can be observed in Figure 10–12.

A paradigm for subjecting social facilitation theory to scientific investigation can be arranged in the following way. Singer (1970) formed four groups of subjects, with each tested on two occasions under one of the following conditions: spectators–no spectators, spectators–spectators, no spectators–no spectators, no spectators–spectators:

Learning Trials	Performance Trials	
Spectators	Spectators	
	No Spectators	
No Spectators	Spectators	
	No Spectators	

Block I trials are considered learning trials. Block II are considered performance trials; that is, the skill level of the subjects is considered to be reasonably high at this point.

The performer's anxiety level may interact with audience presence or absence producing a number of possible outcomes. Evidence is reported in an investigation by Cox (1966). The effect of only the experimenter, mothers, teachers, peers, and strangers on primary grade children of varying anxiety levels performing a marble-dropping task was studied. Low-anxious boys showed better performances in general and high-anxious boys

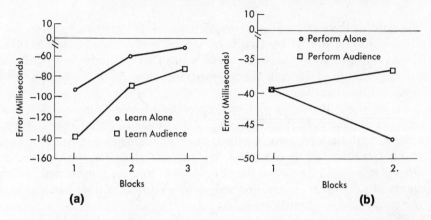

Figure 10–12.   **(a)** Learning phase: Conditions of Learning × Blocks interaction for arithmetic error. **(b)** Performance phase: Conditions of Performance × Blocks interaction for arithmetic error intravariance. (From Rainer Martens, "Effect of an Audience on Learning and Performance of a Complex Motor Skill," *Journal of Personality and Social Psychology,* 12:252–260, 1969. Copyright 1969 by the American Psychological Association. Reprinted by permission.)

poorer performances in the presence of people. Interestingly enough, when only the experimenter was present, low-anxious boys showed response decrements while the high-anxious group improved.

Because the presence of others provides some stress to the learner, the situation may be more disruptive to anxious persons. There are some contradictory data on this position, but other data and logic that would support it. Consideration for kinds of tasks (e.g., motor or verbal, simple or difficult), age level, sex, techniques for the measurement of anxiety, and other variables may help to explain discrepancies. In the meanwhile, it would appear that more anxious individuals will probably respond more sensitively and fully to stressful conditions, and that social facilitation theory can explain these behaviors.

The level of motivation affects the social facilitation of behaviors that have been well learned. A level-pulling task was administered by James Sorce and Gregory Fouts (1973) to subjects alone or with an audience present (the experimenter). Three motivational groups were formed according to changes in skin conductance between baseline and the first experimental condition. It was found that the high-motivation group performed more slowly than the low- or medium-motivated groups in the presence of a spectator. No differences in performance among the motivational groups occurred without an audience. Perhaps if someone is operating at a high motivational level, audience presence increases motivational level past the optimal point.

One of the outstanding attributes of the superior athlete is his ability to perform his specialty skills in a consistent, highly skilled manner apparently disregarding the tension-filled atmosphere associated with stadiums or gymnasiums full of spectators. Is this performance trait transferable to other situations? Are these individuals, after learning entirely new skills in privacy, able to perform in the same efficient manner, with the same success, before an audience?

In order to provide some insight into the problem, Singer (1965) attempted to determine the effect of spectator presence on athletes and nonathletes performing a novel motor task. A stabilometer, requiring balance ability, was the task practiced by the subjects alone on one day and in front of a group of spectators the next day. The athletes represented various sports at Ohio State University and were acknowledged as being among the better athletes at that university.

The nonathletes were observed to perform significantly better than the athletes in front of the audience. Apparently, there was no positive transfer effect for the athletes, who were used to displaying their motor abilities before spectators. Possibly, athletes are more sensitive to people watching them perform and feel uncomfortable demonstrating before a group a skill at which they are not extremely competent. Even when practicing alone, the athletes did not show superior balancing ability. In fact, although not significant, the nonathletes generally displayed superior performance to the athletes throughout the practice trials. The specificity with which we learn appears to be verified by the inability of the athletes to transfer the balance needed and developed for their particular sports to the task used in this study. Figure 10–13 contains the performance curves of the two groups, alone and before spectators. Thirty-second time trials were administered to the subjects and a decline in the curves indicates better performance.

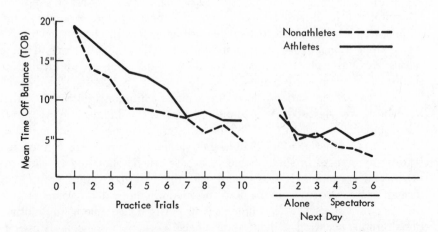

Figure 10–13.   Performance comparison between athletes and nonathletes before and during presence of spectators. (From Robert N. Singer, "Effect of Spectators on Athletes and Nonathletes Performing a Gross Motor Task," *Research Quarterly,* 36:473–482, 1965.)

The social influence on motor performance is certainly an area needing extensive research. Because of the many confounding variables acting on any situation involving the learning and performing of skills in a social context, many researchers have avoided attacking the various aspects of the problem. Because we usually do not learn or perform our skills in an isolated situation, any learning principles must be modified to consider the individual with his unique emotional qualities and dominant personality features as well as the environment surrounding the activity.

Social presence, considering a number of variables, probably works in the following way, according to Singer (1972). Simple tasks demanding physical energy, repetition, power, strength, or endurance are probably benefited by social presence. Social presence conditions stimulate behavior. For many of these events, the person has to be extremely motivated to mobilize his body's resources and to expand himself completely. However, motor skills requiring complex coordination, finely executed movements, and intense concentration may easily be impaired by the presence of others until they are well learned. The demonstration of any skill, once developed to a high degree of proficiency, should be favorably affected by an audience. Certainly, skilled behavior is not expected to be disrupted by the presence of others. Excellence in skilled movement implies control and self-directed use of emotions.

The more reactive audience adds to the possible effect on an individual's performance. Assuming its reinforcing and motivating properties, the audience should raise the drive level of the person. Dominant responses, right or wrong, probably tend to be emitted even more when an active audience, rather than a passive audience, is on the scene. Contrary to expectation, the best-skilled athletes in various sports are infrequently affected by crowd behavior. Their performances are relatively stable, consistent, and predictable. They have learned how to perform effectively under all kinds of favorable and nonfavorable conditions. That is why they are labeled "skilled."

For the average person, working in a motivated state is necessary for a reasonable performance yield. Every task requires that an ideal level of motivation be expressed by the learner. When the highest level of motivation is operating, audience presence can overstimulate and impair muscular coordination. The highly skilled athlete is able to control his emotions in front of spectators so that they work in a favorable way in his behavior. What of the athlete who does well in practice but cannot match his performance during the contest? If skill is defined as the ability to execute proper spatially and temporally timed responses to appropriate cues under varying environmental conditions, the "practice athlete" is obviously not highly skilled. He must learn to perform in front of spectators. Experience and emotional adjustments are the necessary remediation.

Social presence may be distracting as well as motivating but inevitably produces some effect on behavior. We must not forget that the performer places himself in a position of evaluation and appraisal when he demonstrates in front of spectators (Jones and Gerard, 1967). The attitudes and anxieties of the performer to being critically observed indicate sensitivity to the situation. Familiar and friendly audiences tend to make the average individual more comfortable, whereas unknown and even unseen audiences can have a deleterious effect on performance.

If the subject is self-conscious, he is more likely to suffer under social presence conditions. The gymnast who is concerned as to how he appears to the spectators viewing the contest is more likely to score more poorly than the gymnast who concentrates on his execution and form.

CULTURAL INFLUENCE

Preferences for and successes in various endeavors are strongly influenced by the family, peer groups, the community, and the society. The types of activities participated in by parents influence a child's selection. So does the reinforcement given by parents to a child's behaviors. Among other findings Eldon Snyder and Elmer Spreitzer (1973) state that their data indicate the role family influence plays in sports socialization. Family influence variables were predictive of sports involvement for both sexes.

The size of the family and even birth order are related to different family member characteristics and activity pursuits. The family exerts a powerful influence in shaping activity interests and individual drive for accomplishment. Social and economic class barriers are difficult to break down when individuals tend to enter occupational levels similar to those of their fathers. There are identifiable characteristic attitudes and values associated with certain social classes. Thus the social system tends to place constraints upon the human system, and these are manifested in a variety of behaviors.

Likewise, as part of the immediate system, one's friends will direct tendencies to like certain activities and dislike others. Need to achieve in them will be associated in part with perceived peer expectations or pressures. Mechanical skills, performing artistry, or athletic skills may be developed to some extent through family, peer, social class, and environmental influences.

Countries and their respective cultures may differ in representative values and supported activities. This point is quite apparent in sport and physical training. Popular sports vary from one country to another, or even from one community to another. Respect for physical fitness and discipline can also be shown to vary according to cultural influence. Members of a particular society tend to instill in other members an attitude to behave in a common way, in an accepted way. We are "shaped" by our culture in every way by the recognition of status symbols, reward systems, authority structure, child-rearing practice, and the like. The society and its structure encourage certain behaviors and discourage others. Although many of us like to think in terms of freedom of choice and independence, it is difficult to conceive of any individual whose behaviors have not been molded by social pressures, obvious or subtle.

REFERENCES

AZER, N. Z., P. E. McNALL, and H. C. LEUNG. "Effects of Heat Stress on Performance," *Ergonomics*, 15:681–691, 1972.

BAKER, KATHERINE E., and RUTH C. WYLIE. "Transfer of Verbal Training to a Motor Task," *Journal of Experimental Psychology*, 40:632–638, 1950.

BATTIG, WILLIAM F. "The Effect of Kinesthetic, Verbal, and Visual Cues on the Acquisition of a Lever-Positioning Skill," *Journal of Experimental Psychology*, 47:371–380, 1954.

———. "Transfer from Verbal Pretraining to Motor Performance as a Function of Motor Task Complexity," *Journal of Experimental Psychology*, 51:371–378, 1956.

BEECHER, H. K. "Measurement of Subjective Responses: Quantitative Effects of Drugs," in Robert Rosenthal and R. Rosnow (eds.), *Artifact in Behavior Research*. New York: Academic Press, Inc., 1969.

BIEDERMAN, IRVING, and STEPHEN F. CHECKOSKY. "Processing Redundant Information," *Journal of Experimental Psychology*, 83:486–490, 1970.

BIRD, ANNE M. "Effects of Social Facilitation Upon Females' Performance of Two Psychomotor Tasks," *Research Quarterly*, 44:322–330, 1973.

BOND, MARJORIE H. "Rhythmic Perception and Gross Motor Performance," *Research Quarterly*, 30:259–265, 1959.

BURNHAM, JOHN R. "Effect of Experimenter's Expectancies on Children's Ability to Learn to Swim," unpublished master's thesis, Purdue University, 1968.

BURNS, RICHARD. "Methods for Individualizing Instruction," *Educational Technology*, 11:55–56, 1971.

CHUI, EDWARD F. "A Study of Golf-O-Tron Utilization as a Teaching Aid in Relation to Improvement and Transfer," *Research Quarterly*, 36:147–152, 1965.

COLE, SHERWOOD O. "Experimental Effects of Amphetamine: Supplementary Report," *Perceptual and Motor Skills*, 31:223–332, 1970.

COLEMAN, JAMES B. *The Adolescent Society*. New York: The Free Press, 1961.

COLVILLE, FRANCES H. "The Learning of Motor Skills as Influenced by Knowledge of Mechanic Principles," *Journal of Educational Psychology*, 48:321–327, 1957.

COMREY, ANDREW L. "Group Performance in a Manual Dexterity Task," *Journal of Applied Psychology*, 37:207–210, 1953.

————, and GERALD DESKIN. "Group Manual Dexterity in Women," *Journal of Applied Psychology*, 38:178–180, 1954.

COX, F. N. "Some Effects of Test Anxiety and Presence or Absence of Other Persons on Boys' Performance on a Repetitive Motor Task," *Journal of Experimental Child Psychology*, 3:100–112, 1966.

DARDEN, ELLINGTON, and HAROLD E. SCHENDEL. "Food Fads in Athletic Training," *Clinical Medicine*, 79:31–34, 1972.

DAVIES, DOROTHY R. "The Effect of Tuition Upon the Process of Learning a Complex Skill," *Journal of Educational Psychology*, 36:352–365, 1945.

DEL REY, PATRICIA. "The Effects of Video-Tape Feedback on Form, Accuracy, and Latency in an Open and Closed Environment," *Journal of Motor Behavior*, 3:281–287, 1971.

DILLON, EVELYN K. "A Study of the Use of Music as an Aid in Teaching Swimming," *Research Quarterly*, 23:1–8, 1952.

EDHOLM, O. G. *The Biology of Work*. New York: McGraw-Hill Book Company, 1967.

EGSTROM, GLEN H., GENE A. LOGAN, and EARL L. WALLIS. "Acquisition of Throwing Skill Involving Projectiles of Varying Weights," *Research Quarterly*, 31:420–425, 1960.

EVANS, JAMES F. "Resting Heart Rate and the Effects of an Incentive," *Psychonomic Science*, 26:99–100, 1972.

FOX, J. G. "Background Music and Industrial Efficiency—A Review," *Applied Ergonomics*, 2:70–73, 1971.

GAGNÉ, ROBERT M., and HARRIET FOSTER. "Transfer to a Motor Skill from Practice on a Pictured Representation," *Journal of Experimental Psychology*, 39:342–354, 1949.

GASSON, I. S. H. "An Experiment to Determine the Possible Advantages of Utilizing Instant Television for University Instruction in Badminton Classes," unpublished master's thesis, University of Washington, 1967.

GERARD, HAROLD B. "Physiological Measurements in Social Psychological Research," in P. Herbert Leiderman and David Shapiro (eds.), *Psychological Approaches to Social Behavior*. Stanford: Stanford University Press, 1964.

GORDON, NORMAN B. "Varied Input Stimuli and Motor Learning," *Journal of Motor Behavior*, 1:149–161, 1969.

HANSON, DALE L. "Influence of the Hawthorne Effect upon Physical Education Research," *Research Quarterly*, 38:723–724, 1967.

HIGGS, SUSANNE L. "Personality Traits and Motor Ability Associated with Observed Competitiveness in Women Physical Education Majors," *Perceptual and Motor Skills*, 34:219–222, 1972.

HILGARD, E. R., and D. M. MARQUIS. *Conditioning and Learning*, edited by G. Kimble. New York: Appleton-Century-Crofts, Inc., 1961.

HOLDING, D. H. "Guidance in Pursuit Tracking," *Journal of Experimental Psychology*, 57:362–366, 1959.

HOWELL, MAXWELL L. "Use of Force-Time Graphs for Performance Analysis in Facilitating Motor Learning," *Research Quarterly*, 27:12–22, 1956.

JOHNSON, G. O. "Generalization (Transfer of a Principle) in Comparative Studies of Some Learning Characteristics in Mentally Retarded and Normal Children of the Same Mental Age" (Syracuse: Syracuse University Research Institute, 1958), as reported in Samuel A. Kirk and Bluma B. Weiner (eds.), *Behavioral Research on Exceptional Children*, N.E.A., The Council for Exceptional Children, 1963.

JOHNSTON, WILLIAM A. "Transfer of Team Skills as a Function of Type of Training," *Journal of Applied Psychology*, 50:102–108, 1966.

JONES, E. E., and H. B. GERARD. *Social Psychology.* New York: John Wiley & Sons, Inc., 1967.

JORDAN, TIMOTHY C. "Characteristics of Visual and Proprioceptive Response Times in the Learning of a Motor Skill," *Quarterly Journal of Experimental Psychology*, 24:536–543, 1972.

JUDD, C. H. "The Relations of Special Training to General Intelligence, *Educational Review*, 36:28–42, 1908.

KARLIN, LAWRENCE, and RUDOLPH G. MORTIMER. "Effect of Verbal, Visual, and Auditory Augmenting Cues on Learning a Complex Motor Skill," *Journal of Experimental Psychology*, 65:75–79, 1963.

KAYE, RICHARD A. "The Use of a Waist-Type Flotation Device as an Adjunct in Teaching Beginning Swimming Skills," *Research Quarterly*, 36:277–281, 1965.

LINDEBURG, FRANKLIN A., and JACK E. HEWITT. "Effect of an Oversized Basketball on Shooting Ability and Ball Handling," *Research Quarterly*, 36:164–167, 1965.

LUDGATE, KATHERINE E. "The Effects of Manual Guidance Upon Maze Learning," *Psychological Monographs*, 33:1–65, 1924.

MARTENS, RAINER. "Effect of an Audience on Learning and Performance of a Complex Motor Skill," *Journal of Personality and Social Psychology*, 12:252–259, 1969.

————, and DANIEL M. LANDERS. "Effect of Anxiety, Competition, and Failure on Performance of a Complex Motor Task," *Journal of Motor Behavior*, 1:1–10, 1969.

MATHEWS, DONALD K., and JOE McDANIEL. "Effectiveness of Using Golf-Lite in Learning the Golf Swing," *Research Quarterly*, 33:488–491, 1962.

MOHR, DOROTHY R., and MILDRED E. BARRETT. "Effect of Knowledge of Mechanical Principles in Learning to Perform Intermediate Swim Skills," *Research Quarterly*, 33:574–580, 1962.

MORGAN, WILLIAM P. (ed.). *Ergogenic Aids and Muscular Performance.* New York: Academic Press, Inc., 1972.

————."Hypnosis and Muscular Performance," in William P.

Morgan, (ed.), *Ergogenic Aids and Muscular Performance*. New York: Academic Press, Inc., 1972.

NEWMAN, RICHARD I., DONALD L., HUNT, and FEN RHODES. "Effects of Music on Employee Attitude and Productivity in a Skateboard Factory," *Journal of Applied Psychology*, 50:493–496, 1966.

NOBLE, CLYDE, JAMES E. FUCHS, DONALD P. ROBEL, and RIDGELY W. CHAMBERS. "Individual vs. Social Performance on Two Perceptual-Motor Tasks," *Perceptual and Motor Skills*, 8:131–134, 1958.

PARKER, JAMES F., JR., and EDWIN A. FLEISHMAN. "Use of Analytical Information Concerning Task Requirements to Increase the Effectiveness of Skill Training," *Journal of Applied Psychology*, 45:295–302, 1961.

PENMAN, KENNETH. "Relative Effectiveness of Teaching Tumbling with and Without an Instant Replay Videotape Recorder," *Perceptual and Motor Skills*, 29:45–46, 1969.

PICK, HERBERT L., JR., DAVID H. WARREN, and JOHN C. HAY. "Sensory Conflict in Judgments of Spatial Direction," *Perception and Psychophysics*, 6:203–205, 1969.

POMERANZ, DAVID M., and LEONARD KRASNER. "Effect of Placebo on a Simple Motor Response," *Perceptual and Motor Skills*, 28:15–18, 1969.

ROCK, IRVIN, and CHARLES S. HARRIS. "Vision and Touch," *Scientific American*, 216:96–104, 1967.

ROETHLISBERGER, F. J., and W. J. DICKSON. *Management and the Worker*. Cambridge, Mass: Harvard University Press, 1939.

ROSENTHAL, ROBERT. *Experimenter Effects in Behavioral Research*. New York: Appleton-Century-Crofts, Inc., 1966.

————. "Teacher Expectation and Pupil Learning," in Association for Supervision and Curriculum Development (ed.), *The Unstudied Curriculum: Its Impact on Children*. Washington, D.C.: N.E.A., 1970.

SINGER, ROBERT N. "Effect of an Audience on Performance of a Motor Task," *Journal of Motor Behavior*, 11:88–95, 1970.

————. "Effect of Spectators on Athletes and Non-athletes Performing a Gross Motor Task," *Research Quarterly*, 36:473–482, 1965.

————. "Methodological Controls for Social Psychological Problems in Experimentation," *Quest*, 20:32–38, 1973.

————. "Social Facilitation," in William P. Morgan (ed.), *Ergogenic Aids and Muscular Performance*. New York: Academic Press, Inc., 1972.

————, JACK LLEWELLYN, and ELLINGTON DARDEN. "Placebo and Competitive Placebo Effects on Motor Skill," *Research Quarterly*, 44:51–58, 1973.

SNYDER, ELDON E., and ELMER A. SPREITZER. "Family Influence and Involvement in Sports," *Research Quarterly*, 44:249–255, 1973.

SOLLEY, WILLIAM H., and SUSAN BORDERS. "Relative Effects of Two Methods of Teaching the Forehand Drive in Tennis," *Research Quarterly*, 36:120–122, 1965.

SORCE, JAMES, and GREGORY FOUTS. "Level of Motivation in Social Facilitation of a Simple Task," *Perceptual and Motor Skills,* 36:572–576, 1973.

SORENSON, WAYNE W. "Test of Mechanical Principles as a Suppressor Variable for the Prediction of Effectiveness on a Mechanical Repair Job," *Journal of Applied Psychology,* 50:348–352, 1966.

TRUMBO, DON, LYNN ULRICH, and MERRILL E. NOBLE. "Verbal Coding and Display Coding in the Acquisition and Retention of Tracking Skill," *Journal of Applied Psychology,* 49:368–375, 1965.

WEYNER, NORMA, and DAVID ZEAMAN. "Team and Individual Performance on a Motor Learning Task," *Journal of General Psychology,* 55:127–142, 1956.

WHITING, H. T. A., E. B. GILL, and J. M. STEPHENSON. "Critical Time Intervals for Taking in Flight Information in a Ball-Catching Task," *Ergonomics,* 13:265–272, 1970.

WRIGHT, EDWARD J. "Effects of Light and Heavy Equipment on the Acquisition of Sports-Type Skills by Young Children," paper presented at the annual American Association of Health, Physical Education, Recreation Convention, Chicago, Illinois, 1966.

ZAJONC, ROBERT B. "Social Facilitation," *Science,* 149:269–274, 1965.

Appendix

SELECTED AND ANNOTATED STUDENT REFERENCES

ADAMS, JACK A. *Human Memory.* New York: McGraw-Hill Book Company, 1967. Interestingly written on the basis of research, primarily the author's work in the motor learning area of experimental psychology.

ANNETT, JOHN. *Feedback and Human Behavior.* Baltimore: Penguin Books, 1969 (paperback). A convenient source which covers the parameters of feedback (knowledge of results).

BELL, VIRGINIA LEE. *Sensorimotor Learning.* Pacific Palisades, Calif.: Goodyear Publishing Co., Inc., 1970 (paperback). A simplified, general introduction and overview of research findings related to motor learning and applied to physical education.

BERELSON, BERNARD, and GARY A. STEINER. *Human Behavior: An Inventory of Scientific Findings.* New York: Harcourt Brace Jovanovich, Inc., 1964. (paperback or hardcover). Generalized findings pertaining to the behavioral sciences are condensed and organized from the vast supply of available literature.

BERLIN, PEARL (ed.). "A Symposium on Motor Learning," *Quest,* Monograph VI, 1966 (paperback). This edition is dedicated to attacking aspects of motor learning with contributions from leading physical educators.

BILODEAU, EDWARD A. (ed.). *Acquisition of Skill.* New York: Academic Press, Inc., 1966 (paperback, 1969). A highly sophisticated attempt by psychologists to interpret extensive research related to aspects of motor skill acquisition.

BORGER, RORERT, and A. E. SEABORNE. *The Psychology of Learning,* Baltimore: Penguin Books, 1966 (paperback). A paperback edition treating the area in a general manner.

BUGELSKI, B. R. *The Psychology of Learning.* New York: Holt, Rinehart and Winston, Inc., 1956. Traditional coverage of usual topics.

CARRON, ALBERT V. *Laboratory Experiments in Motor Learning*. Englewood Cliffs, N.J. Prentice-Hall, Inc., 1971 (paperback). Twenty-three experiments along with techniques in experimentation are presented.

CONNALLY, K. J. (ed.). *Mechanisms of Motor Skill Development*. New York: Academic Press, Inc., 1970. Scholarly multidisciplinary approach— probably the best source for materials on developmental factors and motor skills.

CRATTY, BRYANT J. *Psychology and Physical Activity*. Englewood Cliffs, N.J.: Prentice-Hall, Inc., 1968. Postulates are offered and what is known about learning is simplified.

————. *Movement Behavior and Motor Learning*. Philadelphia: Lea & Febiger, 1973. Provides excellent resource material related to human movement and learning.

————. *Teaching Motor Skills*, Englewood Cliffs, N.J.: Prentice-Hall, Inc., 1973 (paperback). A practical approach toward teaching motor skills, based on research and theory.

————. and ROBERT S. HUTTON. *Experiments in Movement Behavior and Motor Learning*. Philadelphia: Lea & Febiger, 1969 (paperback). Twenty-five experiments are presented, with an attempt to communicate simple experimntal designs, statistics, and information on motor learning.

DECECCO, JOHN P. *The Psychology of Learning and Instruction*. Englewood Cliffs, N.J.: Prentice-Hall, Inc., 1968. (See particularly Chapter 8, "The Teaching and Learning of Skills.") A practical approach to effective teaching, including models, a body of information, and guidelines.

DEESE, JAMES, and STEWARD H. HULSE. *The Psychology of Learning*. New York: McGraw-Hill Book Company, 1967. The core of the psychology of learning is presented, in classical form.

ELLIS, HENRY C. *The Transfer of Learning*. New York: Macmillan Publishing Co., Inc., 1965 (paperback). A general, easy-to-follow review of transfer considerations in the learning process.

FITTS, PAUL M., and MICHAEL I. POSNER. *Human Performance*. Belmont, Calif.: Brooks/Cole Publishing Co., 1967 (paperback). One's ability to perform tasks is treated in information processing form.

GAGNÉ, ROBERT M. *The Conditions of Learning*. New York: Holt, Rinehart and Winston, Inc., 1970. A classic in the field, this book shows the relationship of the process of learning to the design of better education.

———— (ed.). *Learning and Individual Differences*. Columbus, Ohio: Charles E. Merrill Books, Inc., 1967. Topics related to individual differences are discussed, many of them of particular interest to the physical educator.

————, and EDWIN A. FLEISHMAN. *Psychology and Human Performance*. New York: Holt, Rinehart and Winston, Inc., 1959. An introductory book in the area, dealing with the more practical aspects of human behavior and performance.

GLASER, ROBERT (ed.). *Training Research and Education.* New York: John Wiley & Sons, Inc., 1962. Papers contributed by many outstanding authors on all aspects of training and education.

GUROWITZ, EDWARD M. *The Molecular Basis of Memory.* Englewood Cliffs, N.J.: Prentice-Hall, Inc., 1969 (paperback). The nature of memory is handled from such areas as neurology, biochemistry, psychology, and so on.

HALL, JOHN F. *The Psychology of Learning.* Philadelphia: J. B. Lippincott Company, 1966. An extremely comprehensive coverage of numerous topics.

HARRIS, THEODORE L., and WILSON E. SCHWAHN (eds.). *Selected Readings on the Learning Process.* New York: Oxford University Press, 1961 (paperback). Primarily educational-psychology-oriented, with many experimental studies of the learning process.

HILGARD, ERNEST R. (ed.). *Theories of Learning and Instruction,* 63rd Yearbook of the National Society for the Study of Education, Part I. Chicago: University of Chicago Press, 1964. The work of America's leading behavioral scientists; varied approaches and topics.

———. *Theories of Learning.* New York: Appleton-Century-Crofts, Inc., 1956. Well-written, interesting presentation of the works of the leading learning theorists during this entire century.

HOLDING, D. H. *Principles of Training.* Oxford: Pergamon Press, 1965 (paperback). Although primarily written for industrial psychologists and workers, there is much material of relevance to physical education.

HYDEN, HOLGER, KONRAD LORENZ, H. W. MAGOUN, WILDER PENFIELD, and CARL H. PRIBRAM. *On the Biology of Learning.* New York: Harcourt Brace Inc., 1969 (paperback). A book of essays by acknowledged scholars on the neurophysiology and biochemistry of learning.

JONES, J. C. *Learning.* New York: Harcourt Brace Jovanovich, Inc., 1967 (paperback). A paperback written for teachers; the practical application of learning research.

KEELE, STEVEN W. *Attention and Human Performance.* Pacific Palisades, Calif.: Goodyear Publishing Co., 1973 (paperback). Fairly advanced book, although the author claims it is introductory, dealing with information processes associated with attention and memory.

KNAPP, BARBARA. *Skill in Sport: The Attainment of Proficiency.* London: Routledge & Kegan Paul, 1964. A book on motor learning written expressly for physical educators.

KENYON, GERALD S. (ed.). *Contemporary Psychology of Sport,* Proceedings of the 2nd International Congress of Sport Psychology. Chicago: The Athletic Institute, 1970 (paperback). Contains 101 papers from authors representing twenty-three countries on many varied topics.

LAWTHER, JOHN D. *The Learning of Physical Skills.* Englewood Cliffs, N.J.: Prentice-Hall, Inc., 1968 (paperback). Written by a physical educator, this paperback offers general material regarding learning and physical education.

LEGGE, DAVID (ed.). *Skills.* Baltimore: Penguin Books, 1970 (paperback). Includes many classic papers primarily from the English approach, with the emphasis on industrial problems, information processing, experimental psychology, and the like.

LOCKHART, AILEENE S., and JOANN M. JOHNSON. *Laboratory Experiments in Motor Learning.* Dubuque, Iowa: Wm. C. Brown Co., 1970 (paperback). Twenty experiments are suggested in simple experimental form.

LOGAN, FRANK A. *Learning and Motivation.* Dubuque, Iowa: Wm. C. Brown Co., 1970 (paperback). For the beginning student of learning, classical and standard areas of study and research are presented.

MAGGIO, ELIO. *Psychophysiology of Learning and Memory.* Springfield, Ill.: Charles C Thomas, Publisher, 1971. Interesting perspectives in the area.

MARX, MELVIN H. *Learning: Interactions.* New York: Macmillan Publishing Co., Inc., 1970. Shows the interrelationships between behavior changes (learning) and certain variables (motivation, perception, concept formation, and personality).

————. *Learning: Processes.* New York: Macmillan Publishing Co., Inc., 1969. A number of sections on aspects of learning by different authors, culminating in one on motor behavior.

————, and WILLIAM A. HILLIX. *Systems and Theories in Psychology.* New York: McGraw-Hill Book Company, 1963. Historical overview and in-depth discussion on theories developed through the years.

McGEOCH, JOHN A., and ARTHUR L. IRION. *The Psychology of Human Learning.* New York: David McKay Company, Inc., 1952. Although an early publication, it is a classic in the field.

MEDNICK, SARNOFF A. *Learning.* Englewood Cliffs, N.J.: Prentice-Hall, Inc., 1964 (paperback). Simply written, designed for the beginning students in learning.

MELTON, ARTHUR W. (ed.). *Categories of Human Learning.* New York: Academic Press, Inc., 1964. An attempt at formulating a new taxonomy of human learning, with discussions on the problems relevant to the seven categories representing the various types of research.

O'Connor, Kathleen. *Learning: An Introduction.* Glenview, Ill.: Scott, Foresman and Company, 1971 (paperback). Elementary coverage on the standard topics in the psychology of learning.

OXENDINE, JOSEPH B. *Psychology of Motor Learning.* New York: Appleton-Century-Crofts, Inc., 1968. Written by a physical educator as a text for a course in motor learning.

ROBB, MARGARET D. *The Dynamics of Motor-Skill Acquisition.* Englewood Cliffs, N.J.: Prentice-Hall, Inc., 1972 (paperback). A cybernetic approach to motor learning, easy to follow, with many practical examples.

RUSHALL, BRENT S., and DARYL SIEDENTOP. *The Development of Behavior in Sport and Physical Education*. Philadelphia: Lea & Febiger, 1972 (paperback). Intermix of theoretical bases of operant conditioning, reinforcement principles, and teaching and coaching situations in which behaviors can be effectively modified.

SAGE, GEORGE H. *Introduction to Motor Behavior: A Neuropsychological Approach*. Reading, Mass.: Addison-Wesley Publishing Co., Inc., 1971. Authored by a physical educator, one of the leading features of this book is the emphasis on the neuropsychology underlying motor behavior, although it encompasses many areas.

SAHAKIAN, WILLIAM S. (ed.). *Psychology of Learning: Systems, Models, and Theories*. Chicago: Markham Publishing Co., 1970. A compilation of papers of those who contributed greatly and distinguished themselves in the development of learning theory.

SHAFER, JAMES N. *Laboratory Exercises in Psychology*. New York: Holt, Rinehart and Winston, Inc., 1965 (paperback). Simplified laboratory procedures for the conducting of psychological experiments.

SIDOWSKI, JOSEPH B. (ed.). *Experimental Methods and Instrumentation in Psychology*. New York: McGraw-Hill Book Company, 1966. Designed for the advanced student of learning, this comprehensive book describes experimental methods and instrumentation used in the major areas of psychology.

SINGER, ROBERT N. (editor). *Readings in Motor Learning*. Philadelphia: Lea & Febiger, 1972. Major topical areas contain interesting and outstanding efforts by leading scholars.

_____. *The Psychomotor Domain: Movement Behavior*. Philadelphia: Lea & Febiger, 1972. Major disciplines and specialty areas are covered in the psychomotor domain, with each scholar demonstrating the kind of work currently going on and unique to each area.

_____, CONRAD MILNE, RICHARD MAGILL, LUCIEN VACHON, and FRANK M. POWELL. *Laboratory and Field Experiments in Motor Learning*. Springfield, Ill.: Charles C Thomas, 1975. Comprehensive coverage of contemporary topics, with a description of how to build or where to buy apparatus, many references, and explanations of learning curves, measurement, and statistics.

"Skill Learning and Performance," *Research Quarterly*, special issue, 43, October, 1972. Contains a number of interesting scholarly articles on the topic of skill learning.

SMITH, KARL U., and MARGARET E. SMITH. *Cybernetic Principles of Learning and Educational Design*. New York: Holt, Rinehart and Winston, Inc., 1966. Refreshing new approach to studying learning that should be

SMITH, WENDELL, I., and NICHOLAS L. ROHRMAN. *Human Learning*. New York: McGraw-Hill Book Company, 1970 (paperback). A simple version, largely self-instructional and semiprogrammed.

read for contrast with books containing traditional, classical approaches to learning.

STALLINGS, LORETTA M. *Motor Skills: Development and Learning*. Dubuque, Iowa: Wm. C. Brown Co., 1973 (paperback). Emphasis on current models and concepts in skill acquisition, with many implications for improving the teaching–learning situation.

STEVENS, S. S. (ed.). *Handbook of Experimental Psychology*. New York: John Wiley & Sons, Inc., 1951. Although not of recent vintage, this book still contains a wealth of knowledge on everything related to learning, with articles contributed by thirty-six psychologists.

TRAVERS, JOHN F. *Learning: Analysis and Application*. New York: David McKay Company, Inc., 1965 (paperback). Written for the teacher on the psychology of learning.

TRAVERS, ROBERT M. *Essentials of Learning*. New York: Macmillan Publishing Co., Inc., 1972. Analyzes the results of research on learning, with special implications for students in education.

WELFORD, A. T. *Fundamentals of Skill*. London: Methuen & Co., Ltd., 1968. A sophisticated reference, emphasizing psychophysics, information processing, and experimental psychology.

WHITING, H. T. A. *Acquiring Ball Skill: A Psychological Interpretation*. London: G. Bell & Sons, Ltd., 1969. Excellent source for semisophisticated treatment of psychological research applied to the learning of athletic skills.

WOODWORTH, ROBERT S., and HAROLD SCHLOSBERG. *Experimental Psychology*. New York: Holt, Rinehart and Winston, Inc., 1954. Truly a classic—presents fundamental materials on a wide range of topics.

WOOLDRIDGE, DEAN E. *The Machinery of the Brain*. New York: McGraw-Hill Book Company, 1963 (paperback). Beautiful analogy of brain and computer, with material interestingly presented for the beginner.

Name Index

Subject Index